T0394947

Policy Implications of Research in Education

Volume 10

Scope of the Series

In education, as in other fields, there are often significant gaps between research knowledge and current policy and practice. While there are many reasons for this gap, one that stands out is that policy-makers and practitioners may simply not know about important research findings because these findings are not published in forums aimed at them.

Policy Implications of Research in Education aims to clearly and comprehensively present the implications for education policy and practice drawn from important lines of current education research in a manner that is accessible and useful for policy-makers, educational authorities and practitioners.

More information about this series at http://www.springer.com/series/11212

Nic Spaull • Jonathan D. Jansen
Editors

South African Schooling: The Enigma of Inequality

A Study of the Present Situation and Future
Possibilities

 Springer

Editors
Nic Spaull
Department of Economics
Stellenbosch University
Cape Town, South Africa

Jonathan D. Jansen
Faculty of Education
Stellenbosch University
Cape Town, South Africa

Policy Implications of Research in Education
ISBN 978-3-030-18810-8   ISBN 978-3-030-18811-5   (eBook)
https://doi.org/10.1007/978-3-030-18811-5

This Springer imprint is published by the registered company Springer Nature Switzerland AG.
The registered company address is: Gewerbestrasse 11, 6330 Cham, Switzerland

Contents

1 **Equity: A Price Too High to Pay?** 1
Nic Spaull

2 **Educational Outcomes in Post-apartheid South Africa: Signs of Progress Despite Great Inequality** 25
Servaas van der Berg and Martin Gustafsson

3 **Pursuing Equity Through Policy in the Schooling Sector 2007–2017** 47
Martin Gustafsson

4 **Educational Funding and Equity in South African Schools** 67
Shireen Motala and David Carel

5 **Early Childhood Development in South Africa: Inequality and Opportunity** 87
Michaela Ashley-Cooper, Lauren-Jayne van Niekerk, and Eric Atmore

6 **Curriculum Reform and Learner Performance: An Obstinate Paradox in the Quest for Equality** 109
Johan Muller and Ursula Hoadley

7 **How Language Policy and Practice Sustains Inequality in Education** 127
Nompumelelo L. Mohohlwane

8 **Still Falling at the First Hurdle: Examining Early Grade Reading in South Africa** 147
Nic Spaull and Elizabeth Pretorius

9 **Mathematics Achievement and the Inequality Gap: TIMSS 1995 to 2015** 169
Vijay Reddy, Andrea Juan, Kathryn Isdale, and Samuel Fongwa

10 Teachers' Mathematical Knowledge, Teaching and the Problem of Inequality 189
Hamsa Venkat

11 Learner's Written Work: An Overview of Quality, Quantity and Focus in South African Primary Schools 205
Paul Hobden and Sally Hobden

12 Gender Inequalities in South African Schools: New Complexities 225
Tia Linda Zuze and Unathi Beku

13 Teacher Development and Inequality in Schools: Do We Now Have a Theory of Change? 243
Yael Shalem and Francine De Clercq

14 Inequalities in Teacher Knowledge in South Africa 263
Nick Taylor

15 Race, Class and Inequality in Education: Black Parents in White-Dominant Schools After Apartheid 283
Tshepiso Matentjie

16 School Leadership and Management: Identifying Linkages with Learning and Structural Inequalities 301
Gabrielle Wills

17 How Can Learning Inequalities be Reduced? Lessons Learnt from Experimental Research in South Africa 321
Stephen Taylor

18 Taking Change to Scale: Lessons from the Jika iMfundo Campaign for Overcoming Inequalities in Schools 337
Mary Metcalfe and Alistair Witten

19 Inequality in Education: What is to Be Done? 355
Jonathan D. Jansen

Index 373

List of Acronyms

ACE	Advanced Certificate in Education
ACER	Australian Council for Educational Research
ANA	Annual National Assessment
CAPS	Curriculum and Assessment Policy Statements
CHE	Council for Higher Education
CPD	Continuing Professional Development
CSI	Corporate Social Investment
DBE	Department of Basic Education
EMIS	Education Management Information Systems
ESF	Equitable Share Formula
FET	Further Education and Training
FFL	Foundations for Learning
GDP	Gross Domestic Product
GET	General Education Training
GHS	General Household Survey
GPLMS	Gauteng Primary Language and Mathematics Strategy
HSRC	Human Sciences Research Council
IEA	International Association for the Evaluation of Education
IQMS	Integrated Quality Management System
ITE	Initial Teacher Education
ITERP	Initial Teacher Education Research Project
LOLT	Language of Learning and Teaching
LTSM	Learning and Teaching Support Materials
NCS	National Curriculum Statement
NEEDU	National Education Evaluation and Development Unit
NIDS	National Income Dynamics Study
NQT	Newly Qualified Teachers
NSC	National Senior Certificate
NSES	National School Effectiveness Study
OBE	Outcome-Based Education
OTL	Opportunity to Learn

PCK	Pedagogical Content Knowledge
PILO	Program to Improve Learning Outcomes
PIRLS	Progress in International Reading Literacy Study
PISA	Program for International Student Assessment
RCT	Randomized Controlled Trial
REQV	Relative Education Qualification Value
RESEP	Research in Socio-Economic Policy
SACMEQ	Southern and Eastern Africa Consortium for Monitoring Educational Quality
SADTU	South African Democratic Teachers Union
SES	Socioeconomic Status
SGB	School Governing Body
SLM	School Leadership and Management
SMT	School Management Team
TD	Teacher Development
TIMSS	Trends in International Mathematics and Science Study

Chapter 1
Equity: A Price Too High to Pay?

Nic Spaull

1.1 Introduction

South Africa today is the most unequal country in the world. The richest 10% of South Africans lay claim to 65% of national income and 90% of national wealth; the largest 90–10 gap in the world (Alvaredo et al. 2018, p. 150; Orthofer 2016). Given the strong and deeply historical links between education and the labour-market these inequities are mirrored in the education system. Two decades after apartheid it is still the case that the life chances of the average South African child are determined not by their ability or the result of hard-work and determination, but instead by the colour of their skin, the province of their birth, and the wealth of their parents. These realities are so deterministic that before a child's seventh birthday one can predict with some precision whether they will inherit a life of chronic poverty and sustained unemployment or a dignified life and meaningful work. The sheer magnitude of these inequities is incredible. In 2018 the top 200 high schools in the country have more students achieving distinctions in Mathematics (80%+) than the remaining 6,600 combined.[1] Put differently 3% of South African high schools produce more Mathematics distinctions than the remaining 97% put together. Of

---

[1] This is based on my own calculations on the Matric 2018 National Senior Certificate data (i.e. it does not include IEB candidates, but does include Independent schools that write the NSC). 'Top' here is defined as the largest number of mathematics distinctions (80%+). In all of these schools there are at least six mathematics distinctions per school. Note that 19 of the 200 schools are independent schools writing the NSC exam. This analysis of Matric 2018 data is an extended analysis of a previous RESEP project analyzing this dataset for Tshikululu Social Investments for the "Maths Challenge" project.

N. Spaull (✉)
Department of Economics, Stellenbosch University, Cape Town, South Africa
e-mail: nicspaull@gmail.com

© Springer Nature Switzerland AG 2019   1
N. Spaull, J. D. Jansen (eds.), *South African Schooling: The Enigma of Inequality*, Policy Implications of Research in Education 10,
https://doi.org/10.1007/978-3-030-18811-5_1

those 200 schools, 175 charge significant fees. Although they are now deracialized, 41% of the learners in these schools were White. It is also worth noting that half of all White matrics (48%) were in one of these 200 schools. This is less surprising when one considers that in 2014/2015, White South Africans still make up two-thirds of the 'elite' in South Africa (the wealthiest 4% of society) (Schotte et al. 2018, p. 98).

In a few years' time when we look back on three decades of democracy in South Africa, it is this conundrum – the stubbornness of inequality and its patterns of persistence – that will stand out amongst the rest as the most demanding of explanation, justification and analysis. This is because inequality needs to be justified; you need to tell a story about why this level of inequality is acceptable or unacceptable. As South Africans what is the story that we tell ourselves about inequality and how far we have come since 1994? Have we accepted our current trajectory as the only path out of stubbornly high and problematically patterned inequality? Are there different and preferential equilibria we have not yet thought of or explored, and if so what are they? In practical terms, how does one get to a more equitable distribution of teachers, resources or learning outcomes? And what are the political, social and financial price-tags attached to doing so?

While decidedly local, the questions posed above and in the subsequent chapters of this book also have global relevance. Like few other countries in the world, South Africa presents an excellent case study of inequality and its discontents. As Fiske and Ladd (2004, p.x) comment in their seminal book 'Elusive Equity':

> South Africa's experience is compelling because of the magnitude and starkness of the initial disparities and of the changes required. Few, if any, new democratic governments have had to work with an education system as egregiously- and intentionally inequitable as the one that the apartheid regime bequeathed to the new black-run government in 1994. Moreover, few governments have ever assumed power with as strong a mandate to work for racial justice. Thus the South African experience offers an opportunity to examine in bold relief the possibilities and limitations of achieving a racially equitable education system in a context where such equity is a prime objective.

Inequality touches every aspect of South African schooling and policy-making, from how the curriculum is conceptualized and implemented to where teachers are trained and employed. Reviewing the South African landscape there are many seemingly progressive policies on topics such as school governance, curriculum and school finance. As the chapters in this volume will show, few of these have realized their full potential, and in some instances, have hurt the very students they intended to help (Curriculum 2005, for example). The ways that these policies have been formulated, implemented and subverted are instructive to a broader international audience, particularly Low- and Middle-Income Countries and those in the Middle East and Latin America. The visible extremes found in South Africa help to illustrate the ways that inequality manifests itself in a schooling system. In a sense, the country is a tragic petri dish illustrating how politics and policy interact with unequal starting conditions to perpetuate a system of poverty and privilege. Ultimately, we see a process unfolding where an unjustifiable and illegitimate racial education system (apartheid) morphs and evolves to one that is more justifiable and somewhat non-racial, all the while accommodating a small privileged class of South Africans who are not bound to the shared fate of their fellow citizens.

Based on their reading of the South African evidence, different authors paint a more, or less, pessimistic picture of South African education. Some authors focus on the considerable progress that has been made in both the level and distribution of educational outcomes since the transition, and particularly in recent periods (Van der Berg and Gustafsson 2019). Others document tangible interventions aimed at decreasing inequality by improving early grade reading outcomes in the poorest schools, principally through lesson plans, teacher-coaches and materials (Taylor S 2019). While generally supportive of these types of interventions a number of other authors caution that these gains are the low hanging fruits of an extremely underperforming system. Unless teachers have higher levels of content knowledge (Taylor N 2019), and meaningful learning opportunities to improve their pedagogical practices (Shalem and De Clercq 2019) any trajectory of improvement will soon reach a low ceiling. Moving beyond teachers' competencies, the book also foregrounds deficiencies in funding (Motala and Carel 2019), and the primacy of politics (Jansen 2019).

The aim of this introductory chapter is to provide an overview of the key dimensions of inequality in education and in South Africa more generally, showing that outcomes are still split along the traditional cleavages of racial and spatial apartheid, now also complemented by the divides of wealth and class. The argument presented here foregrounds the continuity of the pre- and post-apartheid periods and concludes that in the move from apartheid to democracy the primary feature of the story is a pivot from an exclusive focus on race to a two-pronged reality of race and class. This is true not only of the schooling system, but also of South African society more generally. Where rationed access to good schools was determined by race under apartheid, it is now determined by class and the ability to pay school fees, in addition to race. Rather than radically reform the former White-only school system – and incur the risk of breaking the only functional schools that the country had – the new government chose to allow them to continue largely unchanged with the noticeable exception that they were no longer allowed to discriminate on race and they were now allowed to charge fees. While there are thousands of students who succeed against the odds despite being in the dysfunctional part of the schooling system, these are the rare exception to the rule. The only reason why they emerge in sizable numbers nationally is because of the vast numbers of schools from which they hail. In absolute numbers no-fee schools produce a considerable number of high-achieving matrics, yet this is not surprising when they make up more than 75% of schools. In relative terms the probability of 'succeeding against the odds' when attending one of these schools is dismal (see Table 1.1 in the Appendix to this chapter).

After documenting some of the structural features of the South African education system, the chapter reviews some of the ways that poor children are excluded from fee-charging functional schools, provides a stylistic overview of how learning outcomes have changed in the post-apartheid period, before finally discussing the centrality of school-fees in the South African system. While there are many faces of educational inequality in South Africa, notably the racial composition of a school, its location, and legal status (public or private), the single most deterministic feature which subsumes all of these is whether the school charges fees or not, and if it does, how large those fees are.

It is not the aim of this chapter, or indeed of this book to dwell on definitions of equity, inequality, opportunity, adequacy and the like. While obviously important, these have been dealt with authoritatively elsewhere (Rawls 1971; Roemer 1998; Nussbaum 2011; Atkinson 2015; Sen 1973), and notably with specific reference to the South African context (Fiske and Ladd 2004). There is now widespread recognition that South Africa needs to move beyond mere 'sameness of treatment' (equality) towards a pro-poor, preferential treatment of those who were systematically disadvantaged under apartheid; the pursuit is equity not equality. What is missing is an authoritative, empirical, up-to-date account of inequality in South African schooling. That is the aim of our book and this framing chapter.

1.2 Setting the Scene: South Africa, a Country Divided

There is a strong case to be made that the most powerful meta-narrative available in South Africa at the moment is of a two-tiered or dualistic society. While all countries face educational inequalities, particularly that of low and middle-income countries, the levels and patterns of inequality in South Africa are extreme and still map onto the axes of apartheid oppression with uncanny regularity. The policy choices of the post-apartheid government, aided and abetted by the inertia of apartheid and the compromises of the negotiated settlement have resulted in two South Africa's co-existing within the same borders, poverty and privilege living side by side. The smaller group of about 20–25% are urban, multiracial, educated and employed, having access to quality schools and stable employment. By contrast, the second tier – who make up more than 75% of society – are subject to sustained unemployment and/or precarious work with few long-term benefits (Schotte et al. 2018).[2] This group is made up of largely Black and Coloured South Africans who own no assets and whose children are confined to low-quality no-fee schools (Van der Berg et al. 2011; Spaull 2015b).

---

[2]It is worth briefly situating the two school systems within a broader South African context. Recent scholarship points to five 'social strata' in South Africa with drastically different expenditure per-person-per-month (pppm) and probabilities of entering and leaving poverty (Schotte et al. 2018). On the one hand, one has the *Chronic Poor* (49% of society, R400 pppm), the *Transient Poor* (13% of society, R600 pppm), and the *Vulnerable* (14% of society, R2,000 pppm) who constitute the second tier of society (together about 70–75%). On the other hand one has the Middle Class (20% of society, R4,000 pppm), and the Elite (4% of society and R19,300 pppm) making up the upper tier of society. White South Africans still make up two-thirds (65%) of the Elite (Schotte et al. 2018, p.98).

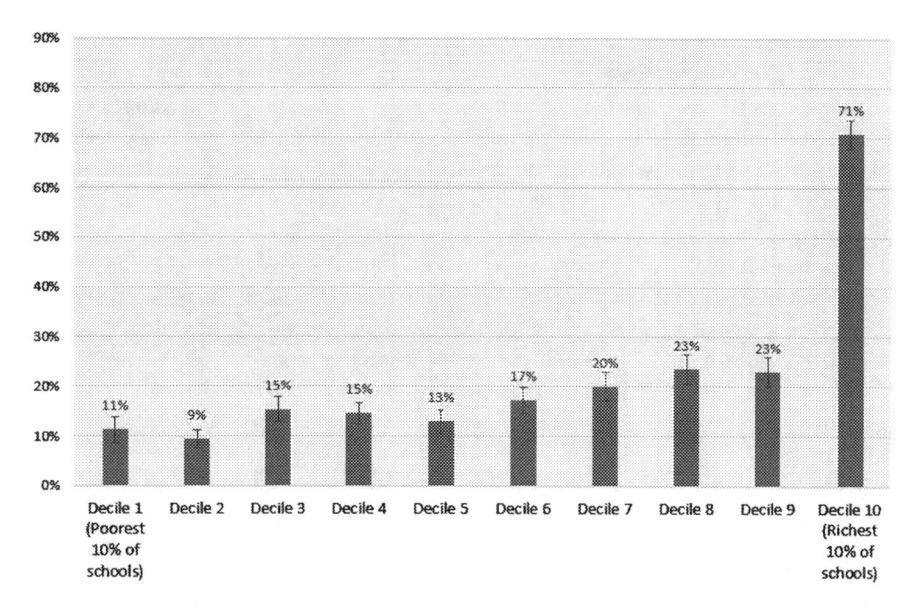

Fig. 1.1 The percentage of Grade 4 learners who can read at a basic level in any language (the PIRLS Low International Benchmark) by deciles of average school wealth. (Data: PIRLS Literacy 2016 with 95% confidence intervals, own calculations with schools weighted by learners)

Looking specifically at education, there is now a well-established literature pointing to two distinct schooling systems (Spaull 2013; Shepherd 2011; Taylor and Yu 2009; Van der Berg 2007; Fleisch 2008). This literature highlights the two-tiered nature of both the distribution of inputs and accountability-structures, but also of learning outcomes, as is evidenced by the stark contrasts in performance between the wealthiest schools and the rest (Figure 1 from Spaull and Pretorius 2019 in the current volume) (Fig. 1.1).

In trying to explain the existence of these two education systems, all researchers foreground the clear continuity between the pre- and post-apartheid periods, whether sociologists (Hoadley 2018; Badat and Sayed 2014), historians (Chisholm 2004); or economists (Fiske and Ladd 2004; Van der Berg 2007; Spaull 2013). While they use different data and methodological tools they come to the same conclusion. That is, that there exist two school systems in one, under apartheid this was by design, post-apartheid by compromise.

With the benefit of hindsight, one can debate whether or not the ANC government made the right choices during and after the democratic transition. Those who defend the historical policies and priorities of the country point to the myriad of social, political and financial constraints that seemed insurmountable at the time. They argue that the compromises made were not ideal but necessary, that they avoided a civil war, and that they have created a multi-racial middle-class. Opponents of this view argue that the ANC acquiesced too quickly on core socio-economic issues of land-redistribution, restitution and the payment of reparations, and furthermore that the status quo is simply the logical outcome of neoliberal policies. Yet both sides would agree that the current distribution of wealth and educational opportunity was never envisioned as one of the desirable scenarios three decades into democracy.

Whether intended or not, our particular journey into democracy has resulted in more income inequality, not less – driven primarily by increases in within-race inequality among Black South Africans (Leibbrandt et al. 2010). It has not cured or curbed extreme inequality. Instead, the ordering principles of the country have shifted from a racial hegemony to a market-oriented democracy (Seekings and Nattrass 2008). The de facto result of this was that the unequal two-tiered system of apartheid remained intact with the discriminating principle mutating from an exclusive focus on race to one that is now inclusive of class.

This is aptly encapsulated by Seekings and Nattrass (2008, p.6) who conclude that,

> The reason why extreme inequality has persisted after 1994 is, above all, that the distributional regime of the late apartheid period has been reformed (primarily through deracialization) rather than transformed or rejected in favour of a more egalitarian one.

The post-apartheid education system is an awkward fusion of apartheid systems serving post-apartheid societies. What the apartheid government used to perpetuate privilege and to act as a lever for rapid poor-white social mobility, post-apartheid society used as a lever for black middle-class mobility. Today Black and Coloured learners make up 60% of those attending former White-only fee-charging schools[3]). Thus, a small, separate and functional school system, created to privilege one section of the population and exclude others remained intact "but the composition of the privileged group and the basis of privilege has changed over time" (Seekings and Nattrass 2008, p.6; see also Southall 2016).

While the 'two-tiered education system' serves as helpful narrative short-hand, the empirical realities are slightly more nuanced than this and are important to understand. In large part the size of the two different groups is a function of how exclusive the metric of achievement is. It is illustrative to compare three levels of achievement in the school leaving exam known as matric: (1) *elite-performance* (80%+ in mathematics), (2) *high-performance* (60%+ in mathematics), and (3) *moderate-performance* (bachelor's pass[4]). As was mentioned in the opening paragraph to this chapter, at elite levels of performance the contrast is starkest; the top 3% of high schools achieve more mathematics distinctions than the other 97% combined. But looking at the high-performance category, Van der Berg and Gustafsson (2019) show that about half (45%) of all high-level mathematics passes

---

[3]This is based on the 156 former White-only schools (House of Assembly, HOA) included in the Verification ANA 2013 sample (Grades 3, 6 and 9).

[4]A 'bachelor pass' is the term used to describe the level of matric pass that allows a student to apply to university.

(60%+) in public schools actually come from no-fee (Q1-3[5]) or very low-fee (Q4) schools, with the other half (55%) coming from higher-fee schools (Q5). At moderate-performance (bachelor passes), no-fee and low-fee (Q1-4) schools produce twice as many bachelor passes as higher-fee (Q5) schools do. Part of the reason for this is that, in absolute numbers, 85% of high-school students are in Q1-4 schools and only 15% are in Q5 schools.

The reason why the two-tiered conceptual frame is still helpful is that for the average child it makes the world of difference if one is in the 20–25% or so of functional schools that charge fees or the 75% that do not. Yes, large parts of the emerging black middle-class may be from the large numbers of outlier students in the no-fee part of the system, but the probability of entering the middle class if one attends a no-fee school compared to a high-fee school are drastically different.

1.3 Retaining White Schools, Teachers and Students in the Public System

At the time of the transition (1990–1994) the government-in-waiting realized it would need to radically reprioritize education spending in order to address prior inequities. This necessarily meant that it would not be able to continue to fund former White-only schools at the same level as they had been under apartheid. This was problematic because there was a significant fear that declines in the quality of these privileged schools would lead to 'White flight' where White students and White teachers would move to the private sector en-masse, resulting in a low-quality Black public system and a higher-quality White private system. This was made explicit by Christopher Colclough, an influential finance specialist during the transition (see Jansen 2002, p.204) as well as Luis Crouch who referred to the same concept as the fear of the 'Latin-Americanization' of schools. The "notion that not having the middle classes vocally and publicly support public education as a matter of personal rather than abstract interest (because their own children were in private schools) would be deleterious to both accountability and budgetary support. This view was fairly commonly held in Latin America at the time" (Crouch 2018).

In order to allow these 10% or so of schools to maintain their resource levels *and* remain public schools, the South African Schools Act of 1996 made provision for public schools to charge fees as determined by the School Governing Body (Chapter 3, Section 29). This provision was 'balanced' by another somewhat contradictory proviso that "No learner may be refused admission to a public school on the grounds that his or her parent is unable to pay or has not paid the school fees determined by the governing body" (Chapter 2, Section 5.3.a). This second provision was, and still is, circumnavigated by almost all fee-charging schools in

---

[5] 'Q' here stands for 'Quintile'. All public schools in South Africa are classified from Quintile 1–5 with Quintile 1 being the poorest category and Quintile 5 being the wealthiest.

the country, as evidenced by the fact that only about 0,3% of students in the country receive fee exemptions.[6]

1.4   Strategic Ways of Excluding Children Who Cannot Pay Fees

This circumnavigation is made possible by some informal mechanisms of exclusion that are still not well understood (social networks, biased admissions interviews and policies, waiting lists etc.), but also by 'feeder zones' where schools have significant latitude to define the geographical areas from which they will accept learners – typically a few kilometres from their school (Department of Education 1998, p.5). Given the legacy of the Group Areas Act and the inertia of spatial apartheid, the consequences of feeder-zones are clear – former 'White' schools in 'White' neighbourhoods select learners from their immediate surrounds because they are in their 'natural' feeder zones. Incidentally, most of these learners *can* pay school fees. Even when these schools have desegregated, this is typically because Black middle-class parents (who can also afford fees) have moved into these neighbourhoods rather than due to more egalitarian or geographically-sensitive student selection policies.

Another form of exclusion – that is now better understood – is the use of a school's language of instruction as a tacit form of exclusion, particularly the use of Afrikaans. Most Black South African children do not speak Afrikaans and are therefore ineligible for admission at Afrikaans-medium schools. Given that School Governing Body (SGBs) can determine the language of instruction of a school, schools that are Afrikaans-medium and predominantly White can 'legally' exclude Black children on the grounds that they do not speak Afrikaans. Since the 2009 Ermelo judgement of the Constitutional Court,[7] this form of exclusion has been the subject of considerable scrutiny and litigation and seems to be on the decline.

In sum, under apartheid White schools received disproportionately more funding through inequitable race-based tax-funded subsidies. Post-apartheid the same

---

[6] As Gustafsson (2018a) notes, "An unpublished report from the 2009 Funding and Management Survey (FAMS) study provides figures indicating that around 20% of fees charged in the public system are not collected, with around half of the gap being due to formal fee exemptions, and the other half simple non-payment of fees due. According to the General Household Survey of 2016, only 0.3% of learners 'get a fee exemption', meaning they are in a fee-charging school but due to household circumstances are exempt from payment."

[7] Here the Constitutional Court judgement (Head of Department vs. Hoorskool Ermelo 2010, p.52) ruled that while children do have a right to receive a basic education in the language of their choice, this is only available when it is 'reasonably practicable' which depends on a variety of 'context-sensitive' factors including the "availability of and accessibility to public schools, their enrolment levels, the medium of instruction of the school... [and] the language choices the learners and their parents make". See Stein (2017) for a full discussion.

schools continued to receive disproportionately more funding but now this is channeled through class-based private contributions (fees) (see Motala and Carel in the present volume). The principals and SGBs managing these schools have proved adept at ensuring that their school communities are composed almost entirely of parents who can, and do, pay fees thus avoiding the legal provision to accept those who cannot pay fees. These principals and SGB members would argue that they do so to protect the quality of education in their schools – a quality they would not be able to maintain without these additional contributions.

Importantly, it is not only financial resources that remain concentrated in former White schools. Given that teachers and principals can choose which schools they want to work in, well-resourced schools can attract the highest quality principals (Wills 2019) and teachers (Motala and Carel 2019). Unsurprisingly, teachers and principals compete to work in these schools. This is for professional reasons; many teachers prefer to teach in schools with a rich educative environment that is conducive to learning – as well as materialistic reasons; they are in wealthier areas, have smaller classes, more learner and teacher support materials, better school administration and sometimes significant in-kind contributions such as subsidized housing and fee exemptions for the children of staff.

1.5 Problems of Capacity or Problems of Accountability?

Changing who has access to the functional (fee-charging) part of the schooling system, while important, will not fundamentally change overall inequality in the schooling system or society, purely because it is so small – at most 30% of learners in South Africa pay fees (DBE 2018, p.33). As some authors in this volume have argued (S. Taylor 2019), improving the learning outcomes of those in the large number of no-fee schools is the surest way of decreasing inequality overall and improving the life-chances of most children. How one does that is less clear. While there are a variety of different approaches, broadly speaking there are two schools of thought: those that focus on interventions to increase *accountability* (assessments, incentives, monitoring, etc.) and those that focus on improving *capacity* (training, resources, support, etc.).

The most recent and authoritative account of the accountability problems faced in the sector comes in the form of a 2016 report by the Ministerial Task Team headed by Professor John Volmink formed to investigate fraud and corruption in the sector, and specifically the sale of teacher and principal posts for cash and livestock (DBE 2016a). They found that the dominant teacher union – the South African Democratic Teachers Union (SADTU) was in "de facto control" (p.119) of the education departments in six of the nine provinces in the country. The investigators report that "all the Deputy Directors-General in the Department of Basic Education are SADTU members and attend meetings of that Union" and conclude that, "it is not improbable to say that schooling throughout South Africa is run by SADTU" (DBE 2016a, p. 93). One of the reasons why undue union influence is particularly acute in South Africa is that the national government, the African National Congress (ANC), is in a formal ruling alliance with the Confederation of South African Trade Unions (COSATU), of which SADTU is the largest member.

Despite wide-spread agreement that the majority teacher union (SADTU) plays a major role in influencing which policies are enacted and how they are implemented (or not), the specific mechanisms through which this is accomplished are not well-researched or well-understood. Martin Gustafsson's chapter in the current volume is a rare exception, documenting where and how key policies were supported or resisted by the teachers' unions over the 2007–2017 period (see also Patillo 2012).

The second main school of thought foregrounds problems of capacity – both state capacity and teacher capacity – as a key reason why there have not been more substantive improvements in learning outcomes in the poorest schools (Van der Berg et al. 2016). The most striking example of this is that 79% of Grade 6 mathematics teachers in the country cannot do Grade 6 or 7 level mathematics (Venkat and Spaull 2015). The chapter by N Taylor (2019) documents the full extent of this problem, while that of Shalem and De Clercq's (2019) illustrates why this has remained an unsolved problem.

Notwithstanding the importance of either of these constraints separately, it is likely that it is the joint lack of *both* capacity *and* accountability that is the major impediment to large improvements in learning outcomes in the majority of schools (Spaull 2015a), rather than due to just one factor. Without disagreeing with this, a number of scholars would still argue that one must begin focusing on improving capacity since capacity must precede accountability (Elmore 2004). One can only hold people accountable for things that they can actually do. We will return to this at the end of the chapter when discussing the way forward. Despite the lack of both accountability and capacity in the South African education system over the last two decades, there have in fact been some important gains in learning outcomes across the country. Since these new results have only been available for 2 or 3 years at most (since 2016) they are not yet well known or well understood and thus deserve some attention here.

1.6 Trends Post-apartheid

It is frequently the case that when scholars discuss the *distributions* of learning outcomes in a country that they lose sight of the levels of learning outcomes and how these are changing over time. While Van der Berg and Gustafsson (2019) in the present volume address this issue authoritatively and show that learning outcomes *have* improved in the post-apartheid period, irrespective of the data used or the grade assessed, for the general reader it is perhaps helpful to provide a stylistic overview of these trends in learning outcomes.

Like many middle-income countries South Africa participates in a number of international assessments every 3 or 4 years. By testing a nationally-representative sample of students from various grades and assessing a variety of subjects, these tests allow us to benchmark ourselves relative to other countries internationally and – importantly – to determine if learning outcomes are improving, stagnating or deteriorating over time. The three international assessments South Africa participates in are the Trends in International Mathematics and Science Study (TIMSS, Grade 9 Maths and Science conducted in 1995, 1999, 2003, 2011 and 2015), the Southern and Eastern African Consortium for Monitoring Educational Quality (SACMEQ, Grade 6 reading and mathematics conducted in 2000, 2007 and 2013), and the Progress in International Reading Literacy Study (PIRLS, Grade 4; conducted in 2006, 2011 and 2016). These are the only assessments that provide psychometrically valid[8] comparisons of learning outcomes over time.

Figure 1.2 below provides a stylistic overview of the trends in learning outcomes in the post-apartheid period. To do so it uses results from all waves of all three international assessments (TIMSS, SACMEQ and PIRLS) and averages the annual learning gains[9] across each cycle. What is immediately clear is that there *have* been some gains in learning outcomes in the post-apartheid period, notably between about 2003 and 2011. There is now a growing body of reliable and consistent findings documenting these gains (see Van der Berg and Gustafsson 2019 for a full discussion). As more corroborating evidence emerges, the position that learning outcomes have not improved in South Africa – or that "education is worse than it was under apartheid" (Ramphele 2012) – is increasingly becoming a fringe view that is not supported by the data or serious scholars. Broadly speaking one can see three periods which could loosely be referred to as (1) a '*stagnating*' phase (1995–2003) where learning outcomes did not improve at all (neither between TIMSS 1995, 1999 and 2003, nor between SACMEQ 2000 and 2007). (2) The '*improving*' phase (2003–2011) where learning outcomes improved relatively quickly, supported by data from TIMSS 2003–2011, SACMEQ 2007–2013 and PIRLS 2006–2011. (3) The '*stalling*' phase (2011–2016) where gains have flattened out as evidenced by the lower gains in TIMSS 2011–2015 and particularly the lack of any improvement between PIRLS 2011–2016.

While the international assessments are the most reliable indicators of progress in education, there are also other pieces of supporting evidence, including the fourfold increase in black university graduates between 1994 (11,339 black graduates) and 2014 (48,686 black graduates) (Van Broekhuizen 2016, p. 12), and the large increase

---

[8]For a discussion of comparability issues related to SACMEQ 2007 and 2013 results, and for a detailed discussion of the re-scaling procedures undertaken by PIRLS to make prePIRLS and PILRS Literacy scores comparable see Spaull and Pretorius (2019) in the current volume.

[9]To be specific it calculates the difference in test scores between the start and end of the period and expresses them as a percentage of the standard deviation of the earlier period. This is converted into 'years of learning' using 0,3 standard deviations being equivalent to 1 year of school (see Spaull and Kotze 2015, p. 20). The gray sections in the table below the graph indicate that there was no improvement in learning outcomes over that period. For SACMEQ 2007–2013 we use the classical test scores and standard deviation reported in Van der Berg and Gustafsson (2019) in the present volume rather than the Item Response Theory scores due to the psychometric concerns with the IRT scores discussed in Spaull and Pretorius (2019).

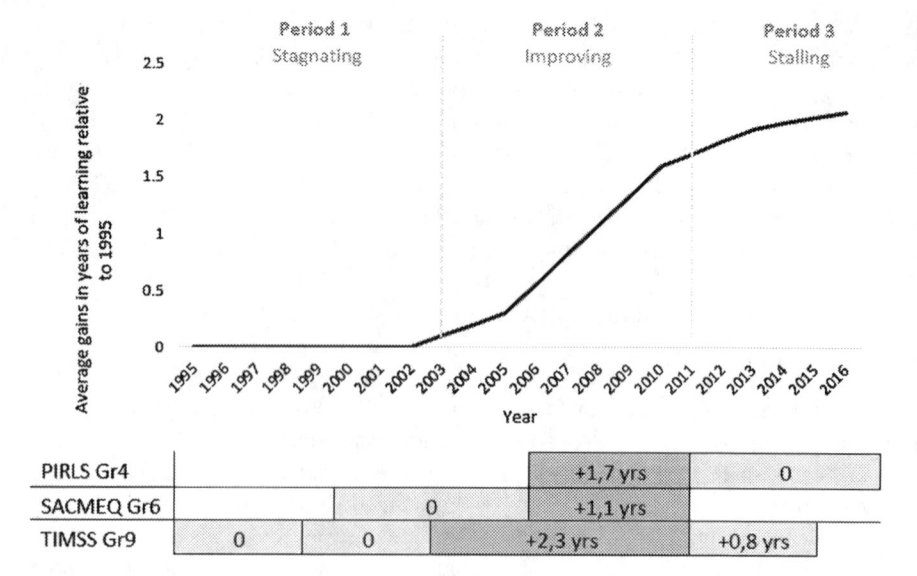

Note: This uses comparable scores for TIMSS 1995-1999, 1999-2003, 2003-2011, 2011-2015; SACMEQ 2000-2007; PIRLS 2006-2011, 2011-2016.

Fig. 1.2 Gains in learning outcomes in South Africa (1995–2016) expressed as average gains in years of learning relative to 1995

in the number of black matriculants receiving mathematics marks which make them eligible for engineering at university, increasing from 18,601 to 25,054 between 2002 and 2016 (Van der Berg and Gustafsson 2019).

1.7 The Correlates of Educational Inequality

Coming back to the distribution of these learning outcomes, Fig. 1.3 below provides an overview of inequalities in learning outcomes by race, fee-status, province and school quintile. Table 1.1 in the appendix provides the full information for this figure, together with corroborating evidence from five different data sources and six different grades illustrating that the trends are consistent and impervious to the subject under analysis, the dataset used, or the grade of assessment (Fig. 1.3).

Table 1.1 in the Appendix illustrates that while only 48% of Black Grade 3 learners pass mathematics, 85% of White learners do likewise. In Independent schools, 84% of Grade 5 learners can do basic mathematics in accordance with international norms (TIMSS), compared to 67% in fee-charging public schools and only 25% in no-fee public schools (Isdale et al. 2017). Similarly, large discrepancies can be seen between the two high performing provinces of Gauteng and the Western Cape and the weakest performing provinces of Limpopo and the Eastern Cape.

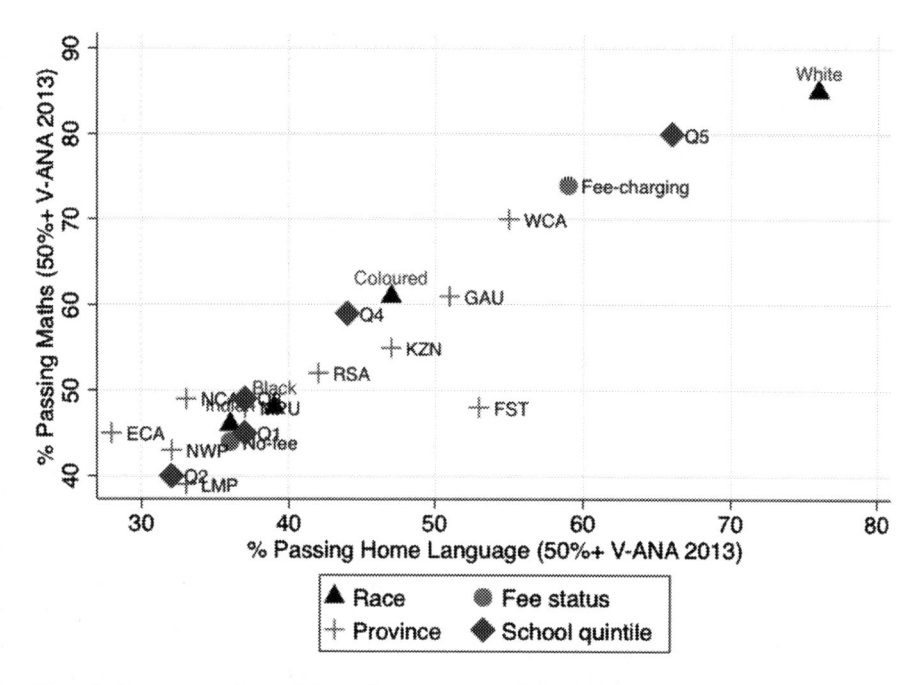

Fig. 1.3 Overlapping inequalities – the percentage of Grade 3 learners in Verification Annual National Assessment (ANA) 2013 passing mathematics and home language (50%+) (own calculations[12]). Note 'Race' is the race of the child not the former department of the school; Q1 is the poorest and Q5 the wealthiest of the school quintiles

The percentage of matrics receiving bachelor passes in the Western Cape and Gauteng is twice as high (40% and 39% respectively) as that of the Eastern Cape (22%) or Limpopo (19%). While 22% of White matrics achieve 60% or higher in Mathematics, only 3% of Black and Coloured matrics achieve at the same level. Similar patterns exist for learning outcomes in science and home-language across the grades (Table 1.1).

It is important to note that these five dimensions of inequality (race, fees, school-status, province and quintile) are simply different refractions of the same underlying inequalities. On average in South Africa, White students perform better than Black students, as do those attending Quintile 5, fee-charging or Independent schools, together with those living in either Gauteng or the Western Cape relative to their counter-part groups. In each case this is essentially repetition, the same tune in a different key. The common denominator across all dimensions is the fee-status of the school and the concomitant privileges and resources that come with

---

[12]This analysis of DBE's V-ANA 2013 data was part of a larger project undertaken by RESEP in 2014/2015 as part of the Programme to Support Pro-Poor Policy Development (PSPPD) commissioned by the South African Presidency.

that. A full 85% of White students attend fee-charging schools. Half of all fee-charging schools (47%) are found in the two wealthiest provinces; the Western Cape and Gauteng (V-ANA 2013, own calculations). Practically all Independent schools (99%) charge fees. In juxtaposition, 98% of students in no-fee schools are either Black or Coloured. The side of inequality that one happens to see depends on how one looks at the data. Yet they all come from the same underlying data-generating process; a dualistic interwoven system split on race, class and location. The school system bequeathed from apartheid has undergone a kind of transformation, and there are some fruits of that transformation, yet there are arguably more continuities than ruptures.

1.8   Where to from Here?

In light of the above, it should not come as a surprise that there is still room for the pro-poor allocation of resources as a route towards greater equity. This is not an especially popular argument in the South African literature. There is now a large body of work – primarily in economics – documenting how the allocation of additional resources to the poorest 60% of schools has not had the desired outcomes. As my colleagues Van der Berg and Moses (2012, p. 134) argue: "In education there is still no clear link between resource shifts to the poor and social outcomes, despite substantial improvements in access to and investment in public education in recent times." This view is echoed in earlier influential contributions by Crouch and Mabogoane (1998) who explain that "mere redistribution" of inputs without concomitant managerial expertise will not lead to meaningful redress. Similarly, Van der Berg (2006) states that "education spending is now quite well targeted to the poor, even in an international context" but that "equity of educational outcomes remains elusive" which "emphasizes the importance of improving efficiency in schools, particularly in poor schools." One interpretation of this body of research seems to suggest that the answer to educational equity lies somewhere other than additional resources, perhaps the efficiency and management of existing resources or issues to do with the political economy of education. However, it would seem that the extant literature has made almost no distinction between additional resources in the aggregate ('business-as-usual' resources) and additional resources for specific purposes (targeted resources).

1.8.1   Increased Targeted Resources

While it may well be true that decreasing class sizes from 45 to 41 by deploying regular teachers may not have a significant effect on learning outcomes, it remains to be seen what the effect would be of using the same funds but legally requiring that they be spent on new Funza Lushaka[13] graduates specializing in mathematics or literacy, or to eliminate extreme class sizes in the Foundation Phase – both examples of targeted resources. There is now also quite compelling evidence that new targeted interventions *can* raise learning outcomes in some high-poverty contexts in South Africa. The chapter by Stephen Taylor in the current volume reports on a local intervention (the Early Grade Reading Study) which has been rigorously evaluated and shown to have some impact for learners in the poorest urban schools (but not rural schools unfortunately). However, for targeted interventions such as these to be sustainable they require considerable ongoing investments. Implementing a coaching intervention where teachers receive monthly in-classroom support for 50% of South African primary schools might cost somewhere in the order of R1,3-billion[14] per year. The challenge here will be sourcing, recruiting and training a small army of highly competent teacher-coaches which do not currently exist. Such an intervention would require either additional resources from Treasury or a reprioritization of existing resources.

Benefit incidence analyses of public basic education spending in 1995 and 2000 (Van der Berg 2006) as well as in 2005 (Gustafsson and Patel 2006) both point to slight pro-rich allocations of personnel funds spent by government due to "differences in qualifications and experience, and hence salaries, between teachers in more and in less affluent schools" (Van der Berg 2006, p. 49). Essentially, more qualified (and therefore better paid) teachers are more likely to teach in wealthier schools. This is most acute for public expenditure on non-educators which is pro-rich. More recent analysis of the 2016 government payroll data (Persal) shows that personnel spending was only pro-poor in Limpopo and Mpumalanga, with the remaining provinces displaying a pro-rich allocation (Martin Gustafsson, 2018: personal communication). This is important because personnel spending makes up about 80% of overall expenditure on education in the country. Once one takes into account the pro-poor non-personnel public expenditure, and includes items such as expenditure on the school nutrition program, overall public expenditure on basic education is slightly pro-poor. As one might expect, including private contributions leads to a drastically pro-rich allocation of societal resources as Motala and Carel illustrate in the present volume.

When over 80% of the public education personnel budget in South Africa is pro-rich in seven provinces it is difficult to argue that there is no room for further pro-poor policies in the system. If funding formulas on personnel spending included even a modest ring-fenced pro-poor component, this could be used for a limited number of pre-approved evidence-based interventions. Although there have been

---

[13] The Funza Lushaka program is a bursary scheme offering funding to students studying to become teachers on condition that they study selected fields and work in selected government schools upon graduation.

[14] The cost for implementing the Early Grade Reading Study (EGRS) coaching intervention is approximately R3-million per year per grade for 50 schools (Stephen Taylor, 2018; personal communication), suggesting that for 7500 primary schools (50% of primary schools in South Africa) for three grades (Grade 1–3) this would be about R1,3-billion per year.

moves in this direction in the past – notably in a 2002 revision to the post-provisioning norms which allowed for up to 5% of school posts to be allocated in a pro-poor way (Government Notice 452 of 2002) – the uptake of this provision is patchy at best, monitoring is weak and reporting on it non-existent. The political will attached to these types of initiatives is clearly lacking.

If South Africa moved towards a pro-poor allocation of personnel resources (and not only non-personnel resources as is the case now), this would inevitably require a reduction in state funding to current public fee-charging schools. The fear is that this would lead to a growth in the private schooling system as middle-class learners and teachers leave fee-charging public schools due to a reduction in funding to these schools (cf. the Latin-Americanization discussion above). This is unlikely to be the case given how heavily subsidized fee-charging public schools currently are (primarily through government expenditures on personnel). Furthermore, there are tangible policies and laws that the government could implement relatively easily to ensure that private schools also contribute towards a more equitable schooling system. For example, one could legislate that all fee-charging private schools are required to accept (without state compensation) at least 20% of learners who are poor and cannot afford fees. A similar policy has been implemented in India, known as the Right to Education Act (see Skelton 2017, p. 41, for a full review also documenting some of the challenges with these types of policies). Given that there are many more fee-charging public schools than fee-charging private schools, one may wish to include some public fee-charging schools, for example those that charge more than R20,000 school fees per year. Given the small number of children in schools charging more than R20,000 per year (about 233,000 learners[15]), some may argue that this is just a drop in the ocean. However, if one considers that 46,800 predominantly Black children would access these high-functioning schools (as the 20% fee-exempt), this is not a trivial number. To put this in perspective, if one thinks that the average bachelor pass rate is about 80% in high-schools charging more than R20,000 fees per year,[16] this could potentially translate into a maximum of 40,000 students eligible for university coming from the poorest households over the next decade (i.e. as these learners reach and complete matric).

Seen in combination, these two policies (pro-poor personnel spending, and admissions quotas) lean on the privileged part of the school system (both public and private) in an attempt to offer improved educational opportunities to poorer learners. This is both through increased access to well-resourced public and private schools, as well as additional, targeted resources to improve learning outcomes in the no-fee schools which they currently find themselves in. While policies seeking to increase

---

[15]The DBE (2018, p. 33) report that according to the General Household Survey of 2016 about 1.8% of learners paid school fees of R20,000 or more. Given that there are 12,932,565 children in the schooling system (DBE 2016b, p. 1) this amounts to about 232,786 learners.

[16]This is based on Matric 2014 data for the Western Cape which has the most reliable fee data in the country (see Motala and Carel in the present volume). The exact statistic is that among schools charging more than R20,000 fees per year 81.8% of matrics receive bachelor passes compared to 31% among those charging less than R20,000 (including no-fee schools).

access to the fee-charging (and functional) part of the schooling system only affect a modest number of learners, these policies are of tremendous symbolic value and are disproportionately important given that the impact of higher education (and the subsequent labour-market prospects it provides) is arguably largest for the poorest communities.

1.8.2 Stopping the Decline in Per-Learner Funding

One of the underappreciated trends of the last 7 years is the declining per-learner public expenditure on basic education in real terms. It is difficult to think of any scenario where the South African education system becomes significantly *more* equitable with *fewer* resources than it has now. If anything, a decline in public funding is likely to exacerbate inequalities since it would increase the resource gap between fee-charging and no-fee schools. To be specific, between 2010 and 2017 there has been an 8% decline in per learner expenditure in purchasing power terms.[17] The reason this fact has gone largely unnoticed in South Africa is that they are hidden in aggregate figures and discounted using the wrong inflation rate. The *total* expenditure on basic education has *increased* by 7.5% per year between 2010 and 2017 to keep up with Consumer Price Index (CPI) inflation over the period. But CPI is the wrong index to deflate education expenditures since more than 80% of expenditures are on teacher salaries rather than a typical basket of goods. The salient question when discounting expenditures on education is thus, "What resources are required in 2017 to buy the same level of inputs used in 2010?" While inflation meant that the average basket of goods in 2017 was 45.7% more expensive than it was in 2010, teacher salaries over the same period increased by 64.7% due to above inflation wage agreements in the Education Labour Relations Council (ELRC). The second, and more important factor, is that the total number of learners across which the budget must be spread has been increasing significantly. Between 2003 and 2005 there was a large increase in births[18] of around 13% which led to a 13% rise in Grade 1 enrolments from 2009 to 2015 which has gone largely unnoticed by government officials (Gustafsson 2018b). Although births per year did come down somewhat in around 2008, the current levels are still higher than the pre-2003 levels. Seen together, these two factors explain why there has been an 8% decline in real per learner expenditure on basic education.

---

[17]This is based on my own calculations using Treasury's Estimates of Public Revenue and Expenditure (EPRE) data which is available on their website.

[18]This demographic phenomenon has been confirmed by Home Affairs birth registration data as well as age-specific data in the Department of Basic Education's Annual Survey of Schools (ASS) and the Learner Unit Record Information Tracking System (LURITS). The leading explanation is that the rise in births coincides with the roll out of Anti-retroviral (ARV) treatment. Thus larger cohorts of children have been moving through the schooling system, with the 'surge' reaching Grade 8 in 2018

Unpacking the education budget and discussing discount rates and demographic trends may seem an odd approach to framing equity and inequality in education. Yet it is difficult to think of a single factor other than the budget that has more impact on the lived reality of poor children in South Africa or on the equity of educational inputs and outcomes. The decline in state funding over the last 7 years is already starting to show up in international assessments. According to PIRLS the average class size in Grade 4 was 40 in 2011 which has now increased to 45 learners per class in 2016 (Howie et al. 2018, p.127). Yet this masks that the largest increases were found in the poorest schools. Among the poorest 60% of learners, class sizes experienced by the average learner increased from 41 to 48 learners per class between 2011 and 2016 (own calculations). For the richest 10% of learners, class sizes increased from 33 to 35 learners per class over the same period. This decline in funding is one of the leading explanations for the 'stalling' of educational improvement since 2011 described above. Moving towards a fairer distribution of teachers, resources or learning outcomes is not possible when the overall pie is shrinking, a shrinking that is felt most severely by the poorest learners.

One further point on overall funding that is worth mentioning is that South Africa spends a lower percentage of it's GDP on education than all of its neighbouring countries. This is counter to what many South African commentators believe. According to the latest year for which data is available on the UNESCO Institute for Statistics platform (http://data.uis.unesco.org/#) these are: South Africa (5.9%), Botswana (9.6%), Lesotho (11.4%), Mozambique (6.5%), Namibia (8.3%) and Zimbabwe (7.5%). Granted these regional figures are high by international standards.

1.9 Conclusion

In sum, there is no route to a more equitable South African education system that does not first chart the path of the development and distribution of teachers, and second who has access to the functional part of the schooling system. Neither of these are possible without significant buy-in from the majority teacher union, SADTU, which is itself not possible without the ruling party expending significant political capital ensuring productive labour-relations. Providing teachers with meaningful learning opportunities, being more selective about who is accepted to teacher training programs, incentivizing the best teachers to teach in the most challenging contexts, eradicating infrastructure backlogs, providing high quality early childhood education opportunities (and these are just some of the proposals put forward in this edited volume) are not possible without significant additional resources. Critiques of underspent budgets (Equal Education 2016), corruption, capacity constraints etc., while all valid, should not detract from the overall message that targeted interventions can and do improve the lives of the poorest South Africa learners and do not have to be prohibitively expensive. The National School Nutrition Programme (NSNP), the DBE Workbook initiative, and the Early Grade Reading Study (EGRS) are three good examples of large-scale government initiatives that have significant price tags and significant impact. Furthermore, the above-mentioned critiques should not stand as cover for the problematic decline in overall state spending on education per learner in purchasing power terms.

It cannot be denied that the level of inequity that exists in South African education today has been heavily influenced by apartheid. Access to power, resources and opportunities – both in school and out still follow the predictable fault lines of apartheid. Yet while these patterns are historically determined, it is also an ongoing choice to tolerate the extreme levels of inequity and injustice that are manifest in our schooling system. Because South Africa is still not willing to pay the price for greater equity, gross inequity is becoming the new norm. While there has been some tinkering around the edges of the political and economic possibilities available to us, we cannot point to a country-wide initiative that has made significant inroads into the gross inequity of the distribution of teachers, educational resources or learning outcomes in South African schools. Until such a time as equity in South Africa is seen by the public as an issue of historical justice that requires immediate action, and not merely an inconvenient allocation of resources and privilege, it is difficult to imagine the types of policies and budget reallocations necessary for a more just society.

Appendix

Table 1.1

Category	Sub-category	Grade 3 V-ANA 2013 % passing Maths (50%+)	Grade 3 V-ANA 2013 % passing HL (50%+)	Grade 4 PIRLS Lit. 2016 % Reaching Low Int. Reaching Bench-mark	Grade 5 TIMSS-N 2015 % Reaching Low Int. Math Bench-mark	Grade 6 V-ANA 2013 % passing Math (50%+)	Grade 6 V-ANA 2013 % passing HL (50%+)	Grade 9 TIMSS 2015 % Reaching Low Int. Math Bench-mark	Grade 12 Matric 2018 % Taking Maths	% Passing Maths (40%)	% Passing Maths (60%)	% Taking PhySci	% Passing PhySci (40%)	% Passing PhySci (60%)	% receiving Bach Pass rate
Race	Black	48%	39%			19%	70%		45%	12%	3%	32%	13%	4%	23%
	Coloured	61%	47%			31%	74%		22%	10%	3%	14%	7%	3%	32%
	Indian	46%	36%			55%	88%		59%	42%	22%	41%	34%	21%	60%
	White	85%	76%			74%	96%		48%	40%	21%	33%	28%	17%	78%
Fees	No-fee	44%	36%		25%	15%	55%		41%	11%	3%	32%	12%	3%	31%
	Fee-charging	74%	59%		67%	50%	85%		46%	18%	7%	30%	15%	6%	23%
Gender	Boys	49%	48%	16%	36%	21%	71%	33%	42%	16%	5%	30%	14%	6%	27%
	Girls	55%	35%	28%	42%	26%	81%	36%	45%	13%	4%	32%	13%	4%	28%
Indep Schools	Public				37%				43%	13%	4%	31%	13%	5%	27%
	Indep				84%				48%	25%	10%	34%	21%	10%	46%

		C1	C2	C3	C4	C5	C6	C7	C8	C9	C10	C11	C12	C13	C14
Province	Eastern Cape	45%	28%	15%	26%	8%	57%	24%	53%	12%	3%	35%	12%	4%	22%
	Free State	48%	53%	27%	37%	24%	82%	32%	37%	16%	5%	29%	15%	5%	32%
	Gauteng	61%	51%	31%	52%	37%	86%	49%	35%	17%	6%	27%	15%	7%	39%
	KwaZulu-Natal	55%	47%	18%	34%	31%	79%	34%	50%	13%	4%	31%	13%	5%	26%
	Limpopo	39%	33%	9%	25%	13%	88%	29%	47%	13%	4%	37%	14%	4%	19%
	Mpumalanga	48%	37%	17%	40%	18%	79%	31%	51%	14%	4%	41%	16%	5%	23%
	North West	43%	32%	22%	28%	20%	76%	25%	29%	11%	3%	24%	11%	3%	27%
	Northern Cape	49%	33%	19%	38%	17%	64%	28%	26%	9%	3%	21%	8%	3%	21%
	Western Cape	70%	55%	45%	69%	43%	78%	44%	29%	16%	7%	20%	12%	6%	40%
	National	52%	42%	22%	39%	24%	76%	34%	43%	14%	5%	31%	13%	5%	28%
Wealth	Quintile 1	45%	37%		20%	13%	55%		47%	10%	2%	34%	12%	3%	18%
	Quintile 2	40%	32%		26%	15%	54%		43%	10%	2%	31%	11%	3%	20%
	Quintile 3	49%	37%		31%	16%	59%		40%	10%	3%	28%	10%	3%	22%
	Quintile 4	59%	44%		57%	30%	73%		37%	13%	4%	27%	12%	5%	30%
	Quintile 5	80%	66%		79%	61%	91%		44%	28%	12%	29%	21%	11%	54%

Sources: Own calculations for verification ANA 2013 and matric 2014. For PIRLS Literacy 2016 see Howie et al. (2018), for TIMSS Numeracy 2015 see Isdale et al. (2017), and for TIMSS Grade 9 2015 see Zuze et al. (2017)

References

Alvaredo, F., Chancel, L., Piketty, T., Saez, E., & Zucman, G. (2018). *World inequality report 2018. Online.* Available: http://wir2018widworld/. Accessed: June 26, 2018.

Atkinson, A. B. (2015). *Inequality: What can be done?* Boston: Harvard University Press.

Badat, S., & Sayed, Y. (2014). Post-1994 South African education: The challenge of social justice. *The Annals of the American Academy of Political and Social Science, 652*(1), 127–148.

Chisholm, L. (2004). *Changing class: Education and social change in post-apartheid South Africa.* Cape Town: HSRC Press.

Crouch. (2018). Personal communication. January 17, 2018.

Crouch, L., & Mabogoane, T. (1998). When the residuals matter more than the coefficients: An educational perspective. *Journal for Studies in Economics and Econometrics, 22*, 1–14.

DBE. (2016a). *Report of the ministerial task team appointed by Minister Angie Motshekga to Investigate Allegations into the selling of posts of educators By Members of Teachers Unions and Departmental Officials in Provincial Education Departments.* Pretoria: Department of Basic Education.

DBE. (2016b). *School realities 2016.* Pretoria: Department of Basic Education.

DBE. (2018). *General household survey 2016: Focus on schooling.* Pretoria: Department of Basic Education.

Department of Education. (1998). *National education policy act, 1996 (Act No.27 of 1996) admission policy for Ordinary Public Schools.* Government Gazette 19377, Notice No 2432 of 1998 (Online). Available: https://www.education.gov.za/Portals/0/Admission%20Policy%20for%20ordinary%20public%20schools%20(Notice%202432%20of%201998).pdf?ver=2009-10-13-135307-413. Accessed June 24, 2018.

Elmore, R. (2004). *School reform from the inside out: Policy, practice, and performance.* Cambridge, MA: Harvard Education Press.

Equal Education. (2016). *Equal Education is disappointed at the underspending of ASIDI grant and condemns acceptance of failure by the DBE.* (Online). Available: https://equaleducation.org.za/2016/09/14/equal-education-ee-is-disappointed-at-the-underspending-of-the-accelerated-schools-infrastructure-delivery-initiative-asidi-grant-and-condemns-the-acceptance-of-failure-by-the-department-of-basic/. Accessed: June 26, 2018.

Fiske, E. B., & Ladd, H. F. (2004). *Elusive equity: Education reform in post-apartheid South Africa.* Washington, DC: Brookings Institution Press.

Fleisch, B. (2008). *Primary education in crisis: Why South African School children underachieve in reading and mathematics.* Juta and Company Ltd, Cape Town.

Gustafsson, M. (2018a). Personal communication. January 31, 2018.

Gustafsson, M. (2018b). *Understanding the sharp primary level enrolment increases beginning in 2011.* (Stellenbosch Economic Working Paper Series No WP08/2018 Stellenbosch).

Gustafsson, M., & Patel, F. (2006). Undoing the apartheid legacy: Pro-poor spending shifts in the South African public school system. *Perspectives in Education, 24*(2), 65–77.

Head of Department vs. Hoorskool Ermelo. (2010). Head of department: Mpumalanga Department of Education and another v hoerskool ermelo and another (cct40/09) [2009] zacc 32; 2010 (2) sa 415 (cc) ; 2010 (3) bclr 177 (cc) (October 14, 2009).

Hoadley, U. (2018). *Pedagogy in poverty: Lessons from twenty years of curriculum reform in South Africa.* London: Routledge.

Howie, S., Combrink, C., Roux, K., Tshele, M., Mokoena, G., & Palane, N. (2018). *Progress in international reading literacy study 2016: South African children's reading literacy achievement.* Pretoria, South Africa: Centre for Evaluation and Assessment, University of Pretoria.

Isdale, K., Reddy, V., Juan, A., & Arends, F. (2017). *TIMSS 2015 Grade 5 national report: Understanding mathematics achievement amongst Grade 5 learners in South Africa: Nurturing green shoots.* Cape Town: HSRC Press.

Jansen, J. D. (2002). Political symbolism as policy craft: Explaining non-reform in South African education after apartheid. *Journal of Education Policy, 17*(2), 199–215.

Jansen, J. (2019). Inequality in education: What is to be done? In N. Spaull & J. Jansen (Eds.), *South African schooling: The enigma of inequality*. New York: Springer Nature. https://doi.org/10.1007/978-3-030-18811-5_1.

Leibbrandt, M., Woolard, I., Finn, A., & Argent, J. (2010). *Trends in South African income distribution and poverty since the fall of apartheid* (OECD Social Employment and Migration Working Papers No 101 Paris).

Motala, S., & Carel, D. (2019). Educational funding and equity in South African schools. In N. Spaull & J. Jansen (Eds.), *South African schooling: The enigma of inequality*. New York: Springer Nature. https://doi.org/10.1007/978-3-030-18811-5_1.

Nussbaum, M. C. (2011). *Creating capabilities*. London: The Belknap Press of Harvard University Press.

Orthofer, A. (2016). *Wealth inequality in South Africa: Evidence from survey and tax data* (Research Project on Employment, Income Distribution & Inclusive Growth, pp. 1–50).

Patillo, K. (2012). *Quiet corruption: Teacher unions and leadership in South African Schools. BA Thesis*. Middletown (Connecticut): Wesleyan University.

Ramphele, M. (2012). *Education system worse than under apartheid: Ramphele*. Mail & Guardian 23 March 2012. (Online). Available: https://mg.co.za/article/2012-03-23-education-system-worse-than-under-apartheid-ramphele. Accessed: June 26, 2018.

Rawls, J. (1971). *A theory of justice*. Oxford: Oxford University Press.

Roemer, J. E. (1998). *Equality of opportunity*. Boston: Harvard University Press.

Schotte, S., Zizzamia, R., & Leibbrandt, M. (2018). A poverty dynamics approach to social stratification: The South African case. *World Development, 110*(2018), 88–103.

Seekings, J., & Nattrass, N. (2008). *Class, race, and inequality in South Africa*. New Haven: Yale University Press.

Sen, A. (1973). *On economic inequality*. Oxford: Clarendon Press.

Shalem, Y., & De Clercq, F. (2019). Teacher development and inequality in schools: Do we now have a theory of change? In N. Spaull & J. Jansen (Eds.), *South African schooling: The enigma of inequality*. New York: Springer Nature. https://doi.org/10.1007/978-3-030-18811-5_1.

Shepherd, D. L. (2011). *Constraints to school effectiveness: What prevents poor schools from delivering results*. Programme to support pro poor policy development programme Department of Economics, Stellenbosch University PSPPD Project–April.

Skelton, A. (2017). *Strategic litigation impacts: Equal access to quality education*. New York: Open Society Justice Initiative. Open Society Foundations.

Southall, R. (2016). *The new black middle class in South Africa*. Johannesburg/Woodbridge: Boydell & Brewer.

Spaull, N. (2013). Poverty & privilege: Primary school inequality in South Africa. *International Journal of Educational Development, 33*(5), 436–447.

Spaull, N. (2015a). Accountability and capacity in South African education. *Education as Change, 19*(3), 113–142.

Spaull, N. (2015b). Schooling in South Africa: How low-quality education becomes a poverty trap. *South African Child Gauge, 12*, 34–41.

Spaull, N., & Kotze, J. (2015). Starting behind and staying behind in South Africa: The case of insurmountable learning deficits in mathematics. *International Journal of Educational Development, 41*, 13–24.

Spaull, N., & Pretorius, E. (2019). Still falling at the first hurdle: Examining early grade reading in South Africa. In N. Spaull & J. Jansen (Eds.), *South African schooling: The enigma of inequality*. New York: Springer Nature. https://doi.org/10.1007/978-3-030-18811-5_1.

Stein, N. (2017). Language in schools (chapter 11). In F. Veriava, A. Thom, & T. Hodgson (Eds.), *Basic education rights handbook*. Johannesburg: Education Rights in South Africa.

Taylor, N. (2019). Inequalities in teacher knowledge in South Africa. In N. Spaull & J. Jansen (Eds.), *South African schooling: The enigma of inequality*. New York: Springer Nature. https://doi.org/10.1007/978-3-030-18811-5_1.

Taylor, S. (2019). How can learning inequalities be reduced? Lessons learnt from experimental research in South Africa. In N. Spaull & J. Jansen (Eds.), *South African schooling: The enigma of inequality*. New York: Springer Nature. https://doi.org/10.1007/978-3-030-18811-5_1.

Taylor, S., & Yu, D. (2009). The importance of socio-economic status in determining educational achievement in South Africa. Stellenbosch Economic Working Papers.

Van Broekhuizen, H. (2016). Graduate unemployment and higher education institutions in South Africa. *Stellenbosch Economics Document de Travails, 8*, 16.

Van der Berg, S. (2006). The targeting of public spending on school education, 1995 and 2000. *Perspectives in Education, 24*(2), 49–63.

Van der Berg, S. (2007). Apartheid's enduring legacy: Inequalities in education. *Journal of African Economies, 16*(5), 849–880.

Van der Berg, S., & Moses, E. (2012). How better targeting of social spending affects social delivery in South Africa. *Development Southern Africa, 29*(1), 127–139.

Van der Berg, S., Burger, C., Burger, R., de Vos, M., du Rand, G., Gustafsson, M., Moses, E., Shepherd, D. L., Spaull, N., & Taylor, S. (2011). *Low quality education as a poverty trap*. Stellenbosch: University of Stellenbosch, Department of Economics Research report for the PSPPD project for Presidency.

Van der Berg, S., Spaull, N., Wills, G., Gustafsson, M., & Kotzé, J. (2016). Identifying binding constraints in education. Stellenbosch: Research on Socio-economic Policy. Available from: http://resep.sun.ac.za. Accessed May 2016.

Van der Berg, S., & Gustafsson, M. (2019). Educational outcomes in post-apartheid South Africa: Signs of progress despite great inequality. In N. Spaull & J. Jansen (Eds.), *South African schooling: The enigma of inequality*. New York: Springer Nature. https://doi.org/10.1007/978-3-030-18811-5_1.

Venkat, H., & Spaull, N. (2015). What do we know about primary teachers' mathematical content knowledge in South Africa? An analysis of SACMEQ 2007. *International Journal of Educational Development, 41*, 121–130.

Wills, G. (2019). School leadership and management: Identifying linkages with learning and structural inequalities. In N. Spaull & J. Jansen (Eds.), *South African schooling: The enigma of inequality*. New York: Springer Nature. https://doi.org/10.1007/978-3-030-18811-5_1.

Zuze, L., Reddy, V., Visser, M., Winnaar, L., & Govender, A. (2017). *TIMSS 2015 Grade 9 national report: Understanding mathematics and science achievement amongst Grade 9 learners in South Africa*. Cape Town: HSRC Press.

Chapter 2
Educational Outcomes in Post-apartheid South Africa: Signs of Progress Despite Great Inequality

Servaas van der Berg and Martin Gustafsson

2.1 Introduction

It has become conventional wisdom that the South African education system is performing weakly and many commentators appear to believe that there is little sign of progress in the education system as a whole. In this chapter we investigate available evidence of system performance, drawing from data on educational attainment, performance in international tests and aspects of matric (Grade 12) performance. We conclude that there is indeed strong evidence of systematic improvement in the school system, both at the primary and high school level.

A central feature of the school system is the large performance differentials between the two main parts of the school system, the bulk of the system that historically served the black population and the historically advantaged former white schools. This system has been described as a bi-modal one (Van der Berg and Burger 2003; Fleisch 2008), implying that the two parts of the system perform very differently. These inequalities in performance have given rise to a common view that the South African educational system exhibits a large degree of inequality in outcomes. We will show that this inequality, though very high, is not surprisingly high for a country at South Africa's level of educational development, and that at least a handful of countries exhibit worse inequality in cognitive outcomes in international tests. What makes South African education inequality so disturbing is the fact that it largely follows the lines of race, thus the education system

S. van der Berg (✉)
Resep, University of Stellenbosch, Stellenbosch, South Africa
e-mail: svdb@sun.ac.za

M. Gustafsson
Department of Basic Education and Resep, University of Stellenbosch, Stellenbosch, South Africa
e-mail: mgustafsson@sun.ac.za

N. Spaull, J. D. Jansen (eds.), *South African Schooling: The Enigma of Inequality*, Policy Implications of Research in Education 10, https://doi.org/10.1007/978-3-030-18811-5_2

does not sufficiently contribute to reducing racial divisions in university outcomes, labour market prospects and even class formation. This relates to the very pertinent question of whether the educational system largely reinforces rather than overcomes economic, social and racial inequalities.

In presenting this information, we draw much from our previous work, in particular Van der Berg (2007), Kotzé and Van der Berg (2019), Gustafsson (2016), Van der Berg and Gustafsson (2017). This chapter provides the information in a relatively non-technical way. The reader who wishes to better understand the methodologies followed to arrive at the results presented here is referred to these earlier sources.

2.2 Progress in Educational Outcomes

2.2.1 Progress in Educational Attainment

Despite the ravages of apartheid, educational attainment expanded at unprecedented rates in the 1960s and 1970s. Simkins (2002) estimated that the completed school years of the population, what he refers to as "embedded human capital", grew by 4.5% per year between 1960 and 1996. Taylor and Mabogoane (2015) acknowledge the rapid growth in school education even during the apartheid period, but point out that, in addition to continued enrolment growth in the school system, the rapid growth of Grade R (a grade preceding Grade 1) and university enrolment was a new trend in the democratic era.

One measure of educational output is educational attainment, i.e. years of education completed, obtained from census and survey data. Figure 2.1 shows that even during apartheid, race gaps narrowed in terms of attainment levels of people still alive at the time of the 2011 census. While the gap between black and white was almost 9 years for those born in 1920, this gap is far smaller (about 2 years) for those born in 1990.[1]

Figure 2.2 considers the attainment levels of 21–25 year olds recorded in different censuses and the Community Survey of 2016. Most young adults of this age should have already completed their school education. As can be read from the graph, at the time of the 1970 census only 45% of this age group had completed at least Grade 7 (the end of primary school), but over successive censuses this proportion had risen to 95% in 2016, an increase of exactly 50 percentage points. For Grade

---

[1]The slight downward trend in attainment levels for the most recent cohorts towards the end of the period is because some members of the 1990 cohort were still engaged in education at the time of the 2011 census, mainly in universities (university education is included in years of education attained).

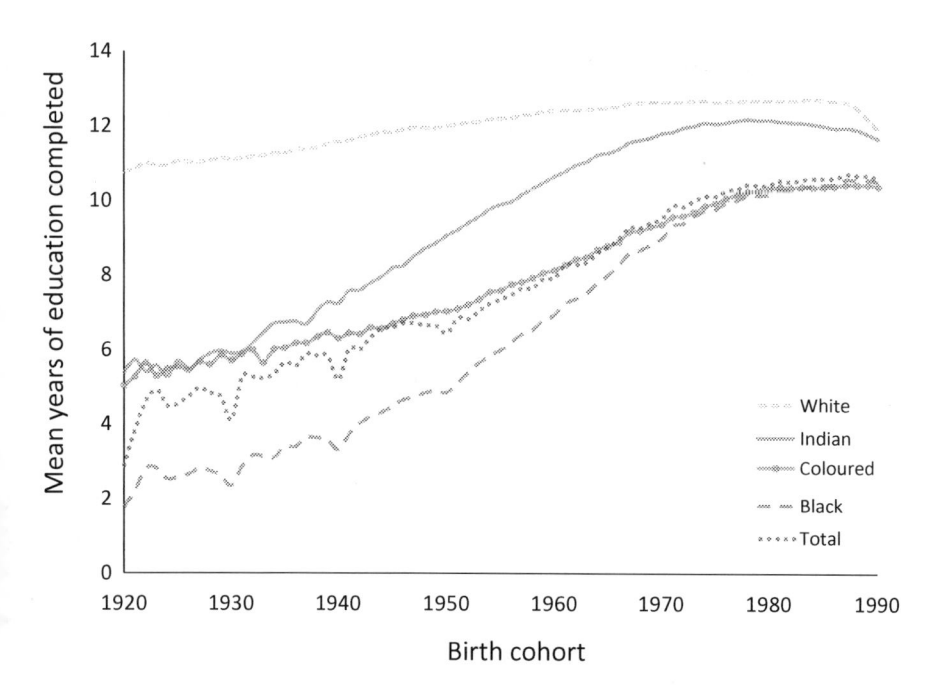

Fig. 2.1 Average years of education completed by race and birth year in census 2011. (Source: Own calculations from census 2011)

10 the proportion rose from 22% to 82% between 1970 and 2016, a 60 percentage point increase, and for matric from 10% to 53%, a 43 percentage point increase.[2]

Progress in attainment, while very important, cannot divulge much about the progress in learning outcomes. For that, we turn to international assessments.

2.2.2 *Progress in International Assessments*

South Africa participates in three international assessments that offer information for evaluating cognitive outcomes, viz. TIMSS (Trends in International Mathematics and Science Study), SACMEQ (Southern and Eastern Africa Consortium for Monitoring Educational Quality), and PIRLS (Progress in International Reading Literacy Study).

In TIMSS, mathematics and science in Grade 9 were tested in 2002, 2011 and 2015. The South Africa country averages point to a large improvement over this period, with average mathematics scores rising from 285 (2002) to 352 (2011) and 372 (2015) (Mullis et al. 2016, exhibit 1.6; Reddy et al. 2012, p.3). An alternative

---

[2]There is some exaggeration in the proportion responding that they have completed matric. Other surveys of StatsSA show that some people who indicate that the highest grade they have completed is matric admit in further questioning that they reached but did not pass matric.

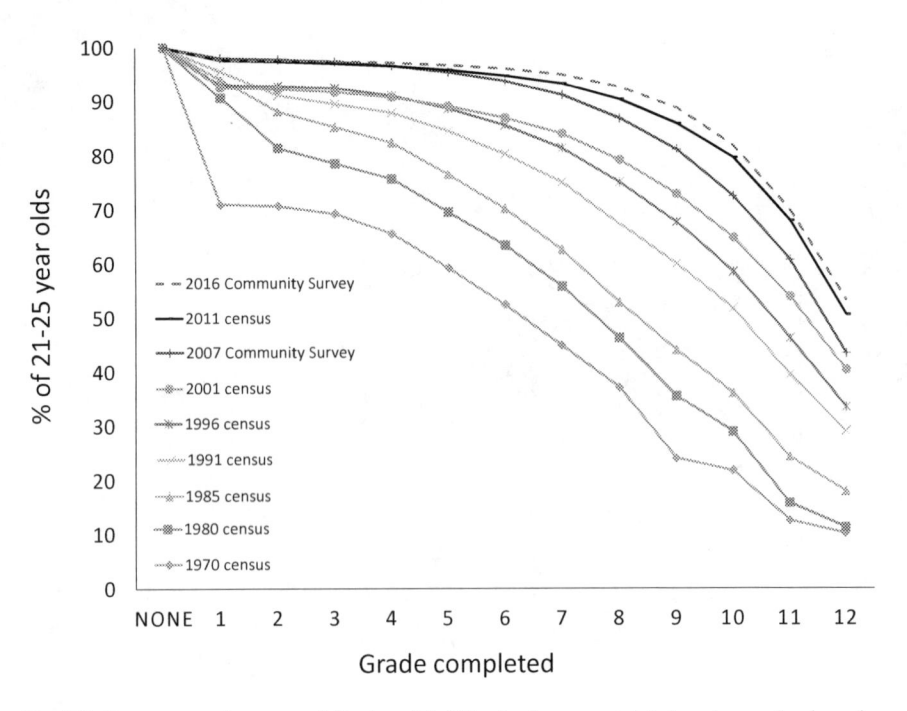

Fig. 2.2 Percentage of young adults (age 21–25) who have completed various school grades according to census and survey data from 1970 to 2016. (Source: Own calculations from various censuses and the 2007 and 2016 community survey)

method of reporting these gains is that they represent an improvement of around 0.95 of a standard deviation over the full period, or 0.07 of a standard deviation per year. This impressive 'improvement' is even slightly faster than the gains of 0.05 standard deviations a year over the 12-year period 2010–2012[3] achieved by Brazil, a particularly rapid improver in its PISA[4] mathematics scores. Bruns et al. (2012) regard the Brazilian improvement as very large and Hanushek and Woessmann (2007, p. 4) consider the rate achieved by Brazil as ambitious but obtainable for developing nations. South Africa performed well below neighbouring Botswana in 2002 and even 2011, but by 2015 had almost caught up to its neighbour. We may consider the 2002 score of 289[5] a 'base' or a 'floor' level after a long period of

---

[3]See Carnoy et al. (2015, p. 9). Note one PISA point is around 0.01 of a Brazilian standard deviation.

[4]Programme for International Student Assessment (PISA).

[5]Scores below 300 are often regarded as less reliable in TIMSS and PIRLS, inter alia because they may be strongly influenced by guesswork where there are multiple choice questions. This of course should cancel out to some extent across individuals. However, even if one accepts that this score is a 'floor' that cannot be exactly determined, the rise since then has been so large that there can be no question that there has been considerable improvement, although the magnitude of improvement is less clear.

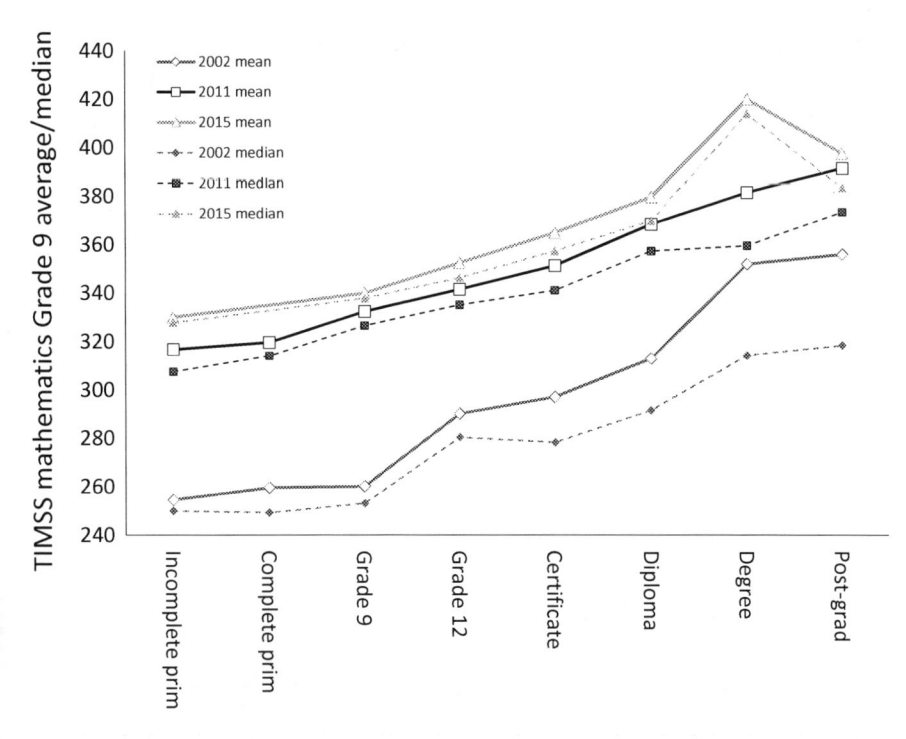

Fig. 2.3 TIMSS 2002–2015 mathematics performance by level of parental education. (Source: Calculated from the raw TIMSS data, as represented in Van der Berg and Gustafsson 2017. The 'Complete prim' point is missing from the 2015 curve as this category seems to have been merged with 'Incomplete prim' in the 2015 data)

stagnation, as South Africa's TIMSS performance across the years 1995 to 1999 to 2002 was virtually flat (Mullis et al. 2000, p. 36, 2004, p. 44). In these three years Grade 8 was tested, meaning that for 2002, both grades 8 and 9 were tested.

Figure 2.3 shows improvements for children of parents across levels of parental education (the highest level of education of either parent). It shows that children with less educated parents saw the largest gains and points to reduced inequality of educational performance.

Some of these inequalities are also reflected by school type and fee-status. Table 2.1 shows large differences in the proportion of Grade 9 children who reached the low international benchmark of 400 points in TIMSS 2015. In no fee (mainly quintile 1–3) schools, fewer than one in five students reached this level in either Maths or Science, in other public schools (largely quintile 4 and 5 schools) the proportions were about 60%, and in independent schools around 80%.

The cumulative distribution of performance for TIMSS illustrated in Fig. 2.4 shows that the major part of the improvement in mathematics performance occurred between 2002 and 2011, with progress slowing significantly between 2011 and 2015. Most progress in the earlier period occurred at the lower levels, even though

Table 2.1 Percentage of Grade 9 learners in various school types that performed above the low international benchmark of 400 in TIMSS 2015

	Public no-fee schools	Public fee-paying schools	Independent schools
Mathematics	19%	60%	81%
Science	16%	58%	81%

Source: Reddy et al. (2015, p. 8)

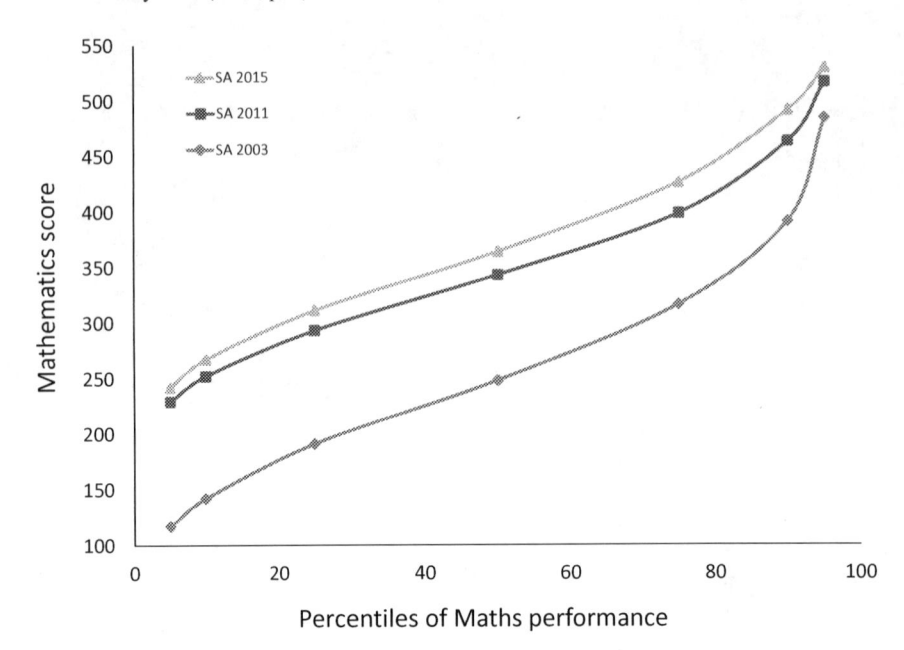

Fig. 2.4 Performance in Grade 9 TIMSS mathematics at the 5th, 10th, 25th 50th, 75th, 90th and 95th percentiles of the distribution in 2002, 2011 and 2015. (Source: Calculated from Mullis et al. (2016) and Reddy et al. (2012: 3))

progression to Grade 9 has also risen over this period, which would be expected to reduce performance gains at the lower end.

A second assessment in which South Africa participates is SACMEQ, which is a regional assessment of reading and mathematics at the Grade 6 level. South Africa's 2007 SACMEQ score of 495 in Grade 6 mathematics can probably also be considered a base, or a low-level point of departure. This was not statistically significantly different from the score of 486 obtained in 2000, indicating no progress over the 2000–2007 period (Makuwa 2010). Between 2007 and 2013, however, there was clearly a substantial improvement. The DBE's final report on SACMEQ 2013 points to an increase from 495 to 552 SACMEQ points, or around 0.57 of a standard deviation (0.10 standard deviations per year). This may overstate the true gains in reading outcomes over the period,[6] as a more reliable estimate derived by the DBE, comparing only 23 questions (items) that were common between 2007 and 2013, indicated an overall improvement of 0.34 standard deviations, or 0.06 a year. Though this is considerably lower than the gains obtained using the item response theory (IRT) scores calculated by SACMEQ, it nevertheless confirms that there were large improvements in South Africa's SACMEQ scores between 2007 and 2013. South Africa's Grade 4 reading scores did not improve between 2011 and 2016. Yet between 2006 and 2011, there was clearly considerable improvement. The 2011 Grade 4 learners performed around 0.15 standard deviations better than the 2006 Grade 5 learners. This means the 2011 Grade 4 learners would have performed better than the 2006 Grade 4 learners by a year's worth of learning, plus 0.15 standard deviations.

To reconcile trends from different grades, years and time intervals requires a more extensive investigation of the available data and an attempt, with some uncertainty, to draw all of this together. Here we offer our main conclusions from a thorough investigation of the data, with a brief insight into how we arrived at these conclusions. The methods used draw from an emerging body of literature dealing with comparisons of trends across different testing systems using standard deviations and gauging grade-on-grade learning gains. Improvements in learning outcomes in schools are sometimes expressed in years worth of learning, also referred to as equivalent years of schooling (EYOS) (Evans and Yuan 2017). Thus if learners in Grade 5 perform as well as the Grade 6 learners 10 years previously, one could say a gain equal to a year's worth of learning has occurred over 10 years.

For developed countries where national standardised tests allow comparison of the competencies of learners across grades, gains between grades in terms of standard deviations are larger in lower than in higher grades. The US estimates for mathematics range from a gain of 1.03 standard deviations between grades 1 and 2, to just 0.25 standard deviations between grades 9 and 10 (Hill et al. 2008, p. 173). For a small sample of developing countries, Evans and Yuan (2017, Table 5, p. 23) estimate the effect of a year of learning to be around 0.23 for Grade 3 and declining to 0.19 in Grade 12, yet there is considerable variation across their sample, with values for Grade 1 ranging between 0.14 in Vietnam to 0.26 in Ghana.

In South Africa, the Grade 5 PIRLS score for reading in 2006 was 0.36 of a standard deviation larger than the score of the Grade 4 learners who wrote the same test (Howie et al. 2008, p.19; Department of Education 2008, p.34). In the TIMSS mathematics tests in 2002 there was a difference of 21 TIMSS points (285 minus 264) between Grade 8 and Grade 9 performance (the test was administered in both grades in the same schools). This is roughly 0.21 of a South African standard deviation.

---

[6]In the absence of technical documentation about the SACMEQ equating of scores across the 2007 and 2013 surveys, the massive gains observed in SACMEQ 2013 cannot be verified.

Key National Statistics 2002–2016

Test year	Grade	Class of...	Series	Score	Std. Dev.	Comments (all calculations from microdata unless stated)
2007	6	2013	SACMEQ maths IRT	495	99	See Department of Basic Education (2017, p. 27)
2013	6	2019	SACMEQ maths IRT	552	101	See Department of Basic Education (2017: 27)
2007	6	2013	SACMEQ maths classical	39.3	17.9	Calculations by Department of Basic Education
2013	6	2019	SACMEQ maths classical	45.3	17.6	Calculations by Department of Basic Education
2002	9	2005	TIMSS maths	289	91	This is different from the score of 285 reported in Reddy et al. (2012, p. 3) as the score of 289 includes an estimate for the effect of including independent schools, which makes it comparable to other years of TIMSS
2011	9	2014	TIMSS maths	352	86	Mullis et al. (2012a, p. 488)
2015	9	2018	TIMSS maths	372	87	See Mullis et al (2016: Appendix G.4)
2016	4	2024	PIRLS reading	320	106	See Mullis et al. (2017, p. 321)
2011	4	2019	PIRLS reading	323	n/a	See Howie et al. (2017, p. 6). The 2011 Grade 4 results, using pre-PIRLS tests, were rescaled to the regular PIRLS scale, shortly prior to the release of this 2017 report. Hence the national pre-PIRLS average of 461 in Mullis et al. (2012b, p. 39) was converted to the 323 average here, which is comparable to the Grade 5 average of 302, implying that Grade 4 learners in 2011 scored 21 points better than Grade 5 learners in 2006, using a comparable scale

Let us now consider overall improvement as deduced from the international testing programmes compared to the 'Class of 2005', meaning the school cohort that should have reached matric in 2005, which appeared to have shown little improvement relative to previous cohorts. To do so requires a host of assumptions:

- Gains in reading in PIRLS tell the same story as gains in mathematics in SACMEQ and TIMSS, namely improvement in the education system's underlying performance.

- The more conservative SACMEQ classical score gains rather than optimistic IRT score gains[7] were used.
- The class of 2005 was taken to be the base year, as the discussion above suggests that there was little improvement before this cohort.
- Progress between any two observations was assumed to be distributed equally across intervening years.
- A grade-on-grade gain in terms of standard deviations for Grade 6 was chosen that lay between the gains suggested by PIRLS (for grades 4 and 5) and TIMSS (for Grade 9).
- It was assumed that year-on-year gains at Grade 1 were felt initially by the 'Class of 2014' (who would have been in Grade 1 in 2002), and that up to the 'Class of 2019' (in Grade 1 in 2007) Grade 1 performance improved by 1 year's worth of learning. This would imply slower improvement in Grade 1 than in grades 4 or 5, for which relatively good data are available through PIRLS. The 'Class of 2020' experienced no Grade 1 improvement, relative to the 'Class of 2019', in line with the flat trend seen in the newly released PIRLS Grade 4.
- The assumption was further made that there would be modest gains in grades 4 and above for the 'Class of 2025', which is still in school.

The three international assessments indicate that the major initial progress was in Grade 9 in TIMSS, with initially little progress at the primary level shown in SACMEQ and PIRLS. The 'Class of 2013' was tested by both PIRLS (in 2006 in Grade 5) and again in SACMEQ (in 2007 in Grade 6) but presented no improvement on earlier results. The 'Class of 2014' seems to be the first cohort to have benefited from primary-level improvements indicated by both the SACMEQ and PIRLS results.

Based on these assumptions, we get the estimates in terms of years of learning gains relative to the 'Class of 2005' as in Table 2.2.

Table 2.2 Estimates of cumulative learning gains attained relative to the matric co-hort of 2005, expressed in years worth of learning

	Gain in Grade 1	Gain in Grade 6	Gain in Grade 9
Class of 2005	0	0	0
Class of 2010	0	0	1.7
Class of 2015	0.3	0.4	3.2
Class of 2020	0.9	1.3	4.2
Class of 2025	1.0	1.8	4.8

Source: Own calculations based on data from TIMSS, SACMEQ and PILS and applying certain assumptions

---

[7]As discussed above, greater clarity is needed around the inconsistencies between the SACMEQ classical and IRT scores, clarity which should become possible when the technical documentation on the calculation of the IRT scores becomes available.

The improvement over the full period shown by the table is quite large, but should be considered in its context. Firstly, this was from a very low base. Secondly, the overall improvement is differently distributed across the school system: The gain in years of learning is only about 1 year for children in Grade 1, but rises to almost 5 years by Grade 9 for the cohort that would reach matric in 2025 relative to the 2005 matric cohort, i.e. a gain of 4.8 years in Grade 9 achieved over a period of 20 years. In addition, it needs to be emphasised that the gains considered to be a "year worth of learning" in the South African context are low, considering historically low rates of learning.

Given the many assumptions required to obtain these estimates, one should not over-interpret the magnitude of these gains. However, together the three international assessments provide a picture that suggests quite large improvements over an extended period of time, albeit from a low base. It also appears from the most recent TIMSS and PIRLS data that progress may recently have slowed. Nevertheless, taken together these international tests provide strong evidence of system improvement.

To provide another perspective on learning gains in the education system, we now turn to a discussion of matric performance, using Mathematics as the benchmark subject.

2.2.3 Progress in Matric Performance

One cannot take matric results at face value for measuring improvement over time, as they are affected by changes in the matric exams in 2008, varying difficulty levels of particular examination papers and changes in the learners writing the exam. Yet using relative performance can nevertheless yield important conclusions, as we have shown in two earlier reports (Gustafsson 2016; Van der Berg and Gustafsson 2017). To compare over time we set a threshold of performance derived from the performance of the top group of white matriculants (assuming that their performance would not have deteriorated over the period) to calibrate the performance of other students. Specifically, we set a threshold at the level of the 20th percentile of all white matriculation candidates in mathematics, with candidates not taking this subject considered to have a mark of zero; assuming that the performance of this top group of white matriculants would not have regressed – and we have no reason to believe they have –, this should approximate a constant or even rising performance threshold for mathematics, a threshold approximately similar to the mathematics entry requirements for engineering or related disciplines at universities. The total number of matriculants reaching the threshold then presents an indication of the (relative) quality of performance of the other groups. In 2002 there were 18,601 such students; by 2016 this total had risen to 25,054. Using this threshold, the number of black African learners attaining this high level mathematics performance has risen by 65% over the period 2002–2016. This expansion occurred across a rising number of schools, particularly schools largely serving poorer segments of the black African population. Whilst in 2002 less than half of high-level mathematics performers in the public examination system were black, indian or coloured, this proportion had grown to over two-thirds by 2016. Despite this remarkable improvement, white learners still stood a seven times better chance than black Africans of reaching this threshold level of mathematics performance in 2016.

Further analysis shows that gains were especially large over the period 2009–2016 (note, after the 2008 curriculum change). Mpumalanga and Limpopo accounted for a disproportionately large share of the gains in high-level performance in disadvantaged schools. Information on poverty quintile was available for 4,615 schools that could be linked across the period. The fastest improvement occurred in lower (poorer) quintiles (Table 2.3). Quintile 1 schools recorded a 160% improvement in the number of high-level maths achievers, and quintile 2 and 3 schools around 90%, while quintile 5 schools saw a deterioration that can probably be ascribed to the reduction in white student numbers due to demographic change and to some extent also perhaps migration to independent schools. However, independent schools did not show particularly large improvement.

Also encouraging is that the percentage of schools achieving at least some high-level mathematics passes increased for all quintiles, with as many as 41% of schools even in the poorest quintile now producing such performers.

The map (Fig. 2.5) shows that the growth of the percentage of Grade 12 learners becoming mathematics high-level achievers was the greatest in the historically most deprived districts in the east of the Eastern Cape and in some districts of Limpopo and Mpumalanga. This clearly indicates reduced spatial inequality in terms of the

Table 2.3 Mathematics achievement by school category

	Quintile 1	Quintile 2	Quintile 3	Quintile 4	Quintile 5	Independent
Number of high achievers in mathematics						
2002	465	687	1 403	1 476	10 107	948
2009	782	957	2 115	2 043	10 325	1 207
2016	1209	1 294	2 670	2 292	8 978	1 100
% increase 2002–2016	160%	88%	90%	55%	−11%	16%
% of schools with at least one high-level mathematics achiever						
2002	23%	28%	41%	56%	84%	51%
2009	34%	39%	52%	63%	86%	76%
2016	41%	48%	56%	67%	85%	73%

Note: A 'high-level achiever' is one who performs above the bottom of the range of the top 20% white Grade 12 learners. Roughly, this cut-off would permit a learner entry into a mathematically-oriented university programme. Only students attending schools that could be categorized by quintile or independent school and that could be tracked over the period concerned are covered in this table, which explains the differences between these totals and those mentioned in the text above

Source: Own calculations

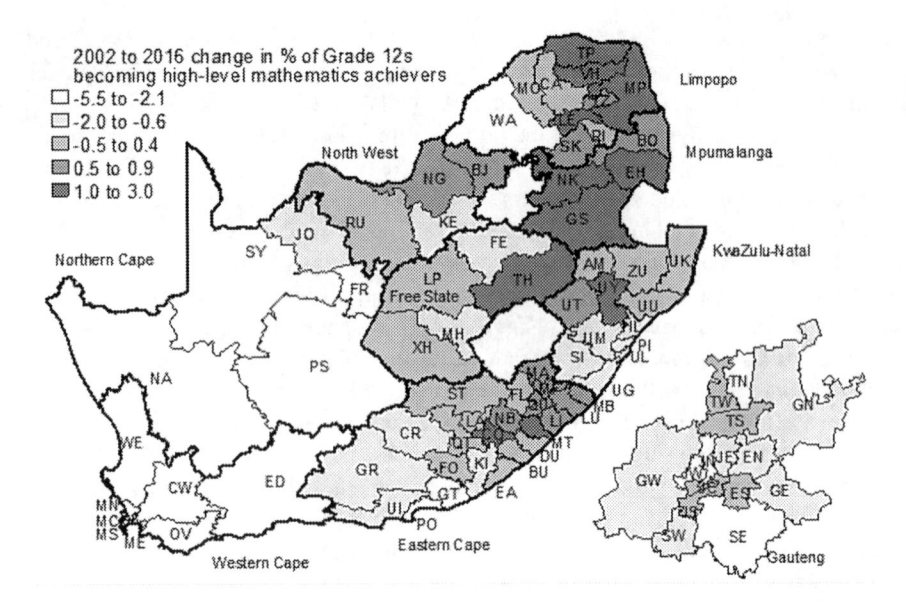

Fig. 2.5 2002–2016 mathematics trends by district. Note: The smallest geographical units shown in the map are the 86 education districts. Values refer to the percentage point change between 2002 and 2016 as seen in a trendline through the 3 years analysed (2002, 2009, 2016)

percentage of learners achieving these levels of performance. The negative values for districts in, for instance, Western Cape reflect mostly the fact that more socio-economically disadvantaged youths have gained access to Matric, resulting in a decline in the percentage of high-level mathematics achievers amongst Grade 12 learners, though on the whole the absolute numbers of such achievers would have grown.

2.3   Inequality in International Tests Results

Expanding access and rising attainment reduced inequality in educational attainment, but not necessarily in educational quality. The matric improvement was measured in terms of a measure of excellence (performing in Mathematics roughly at a level where it would allow entry into technical courses at university), but the fact that rising numbers of schools fed such performance is an indication of reduced inequality. The TIMSS improvement in 2003–2011 was especially strong at lower levels of performance, again pointing to improved inequality.

Yet schools still differ in their capacity to show improvement. In addition, levels at which most schools operate, even after the improvement, are still extremely low. At the same time, other social changes also influence educational outcomes. To illustrate, in 2003 only 41% of learners in schools had at least one household member with at least a Grade 12 qualification. By 2015, this figure had risen to 56% (calculated from StatsSA General Household Surveys). Better support in the household and urbanisation are both likely to have contributed towards test score improvements.

An aspect of inequality that has thus far received limited attention is South Africa's relative inequality in cognitive performance in international tests, as gauged by standard measures of inequality.

How unequal are learning outcomes in South Africa in an international context? This question is likely to receive more attention given the strong emphasis on inequality in the UN's Sustainable Development Goals.

Just as composite measures of income inequality, such as the Gini coefficient, can be calculated, so one can calculate such measures of test score inequality. This was done using the micro-data for 30 countries participating in the 2015 Grade 8 mathematics tests of TIMSS plus a further four participating in the same tests of 2011 but not in 2015. Here one should bear in mind that South Africa and Botswana tested Grade 9, and not Grade 8, in 2015 and 2011 and hence had test-takers with slightly higher ages. Eight well-known developed countries, plus all other countries, were selected for Fig. 2.6 below (being a high-income country and a member of the OECD was the definition we used for a developed country). Figure 2.6 illustrates both the average performance and the degree of inequality of each country.

The horizontal axis shows the TIMSS country averages whilst the vertical axis refers to the Theil T measure of inequality (the general entropy index with value 1.0).[8] The higher this value, the worse the inequality. The strong negative correlation between inequality and average quality is clearly visible: in countries with higher general quality of schooling there is usually less inequality. South Africa was the second-worst performer in TIMSS Grade 8 mathematics in 2015 (the worst was Saudia Arabia, though their Grade 8 students were tested, against South Africa's Grade 9 students). However, South Africa's level of inequality, whilst high, was normal for a country with a low average level of performance, at least if one uses the Theil T measure. Thus South Africa lies exactly on the trendline between TIMSS average performance and inequality. Several other developing countries, mostly from the Middle East and North Africa region, displayed similar or worse levels of inequality. This picture does not change if one uses a different measure of inequality, such as the Gini Coefficient or the ratio of the 90th percentile to the 10th percentile.

The 2007 SACMEQ Grade 6 mathematics performance does not depict a similar clear correlation between inequality and average quality. Where the Fig. 2.6 pattern produces a negative slope (the greater average quality, the less inequality), SACMEQ produces a weak 'positive' slope (R squared 0.24), perhaps due to the smaller variety of country types in SACMEQ. In SACMEQ mathematics, South Africa emerges as the second-most unequal country after Mauritius. A

---

[8]Theil T has been the preferred measure for gauging the inequality of test scores in a few analyses – see for instance Crouch and Gustafsson (2018) and Sahn and Younger (2007).

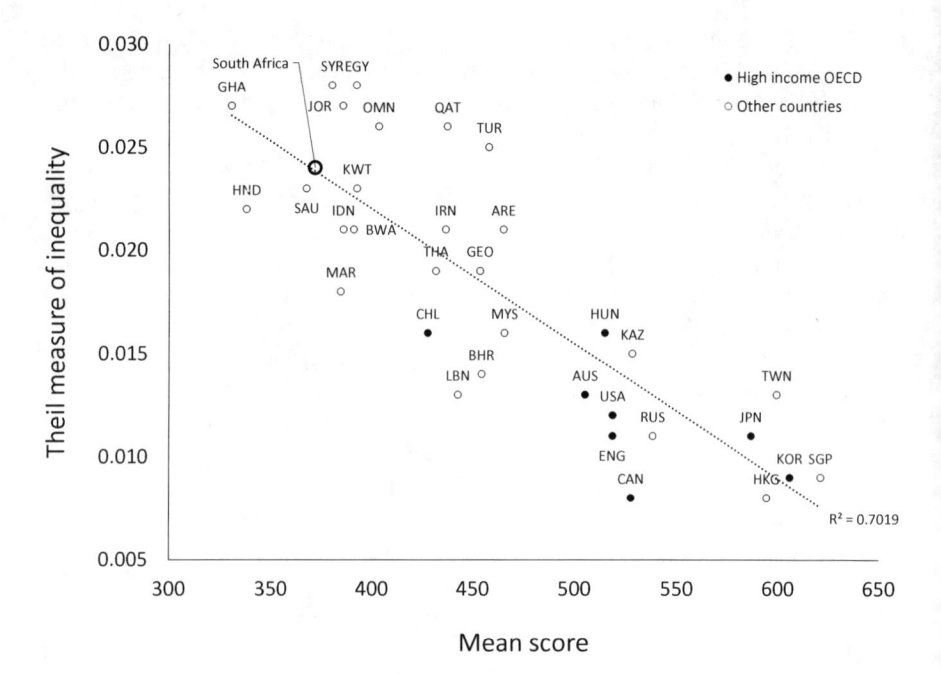

Fig. 2.6 TIMSS 2011 and 2015 mathematics Grade 8 means and inequality. (Source: Own calculations from the TIMSS microdata obtainable at https://timssandpirls.bc.edu To obtain country-level means and inequality measures each student's mean across the five plausible values was used. For the four countries appearing in the 2011 data and not in the 2015 data, the 2011 data were used: Ghana (GHA), Syria (SYR), Indonesia (IDN), and Honduras (HND). For all other countries, just 2015 data were used)

key difference between these two countries is that Mauritius produces a high mathematics average score – first of fifteen countries – whilst South Africa's performance is average – eighth of the fifteen. That South Africa should be an 'average performer' and amongst the most unequal in SACMEQ is concerning. Using the 2007 SACMEQ reading results yields an even worse picture: South Africa's average score was tenth amongst the fifteen, whilst the country's level of educational inequality, as measured by Theil T, was the highest of all countries.

Another way of assessing the difference in the nature of inequality between South Africa and Mauritius is to fit a regression line to the 2007 SACMEQ test data, with the only explanatory variables being the average socio-economic status of the school and also its squared value. In Mauritius, the wealth of the school statistically 'explains' only 6% of the variance in both the mathematics and the reading score. In contrast, in South Africa 41% of the variance in the mathematics score and 47% of that in the reading score are statistically 'explained' by the wealth of the school population.[9] Thus the school a student attends has an extremely strong influence on educational performance, with attendance of a school that mainly serves children from more wealthy backgrounds being strongly predictive of performance. Interestingly, after controlling for the wealth of the school, the socio-economic status of the child adds very little predictive power, indicating that attending a wealthy school is more important for performance than having wealthy parents.

Did South Africa's Theil T measure of inequality change between the 2011 and 2015 rounds of TIMSS? South Africa's Grade 9 mathematics mean improved considerably, by 20 TIMSS points, so in line with the general tendency for better average performance to be associated with less inequality, one might expect South Africa's inequality to decline. Yet the Theil T measure improved only marginally from 0.025 in 2011 to 0.024 in 2015.

Of course several different score distributions can produce the same single inequality measure. It is instructive to examine the shape of the distribution of educational performance in selected countries (see Fig. 2.7).

South Africa's distribution of student scores looks quite similar to that of Saudi Arabia and other developing countries. However, closer analysis reveals that educational inequality in South Africa is very different. This is illustrated in Fig. 2.8, which shows the "maximum score" in the school of each student. The aim was to see whether many students were in schools which were largely dysfunctional. One would expect that even in schools serving seriously disadvantaged communities and with very limited resources, a few 'bright stars' would emerge by chance, because gifted children are found everywhere. A complete absence of 'bright stars' could be a sign of general dysfunctionality of schools that is so severe as to obliterate the possibility of exceptional individual performances.

South Africa's curve in Fig. 2.8 stands out from those of other countries. In South Africa, in 47% of schools there was not a single learner who reached 475 points, the TIMSS Intermediate International Benchmark. In this respect South Africa did much worse than any other country. Second worst was Saudi Arabia, where 24% of schools were unable to produce even one student reaching this score. The comparison with Botswana is particularly important, because Botswana is within the same region but also because both Botswana and South Africa tested Grade 9. In the context of South Africa's skills shortfall and the need for more black professionals, it is particularly problematic that a large segment of the schooling system are in effect 'academic wastelands' which do not produce even a single learner performing at the intermediate international benchmark.

---

[9]The socio-economic status of schools was derived applying Multiple Correspondence Analysis on a set of 31 possessions of school children and their households, and can thus be considered an asset or wealth index. The proportion of the variance statistically "explained" was the coefficient of determination (R-squared) in determined in ordinary least square regressions, with population weights applied.

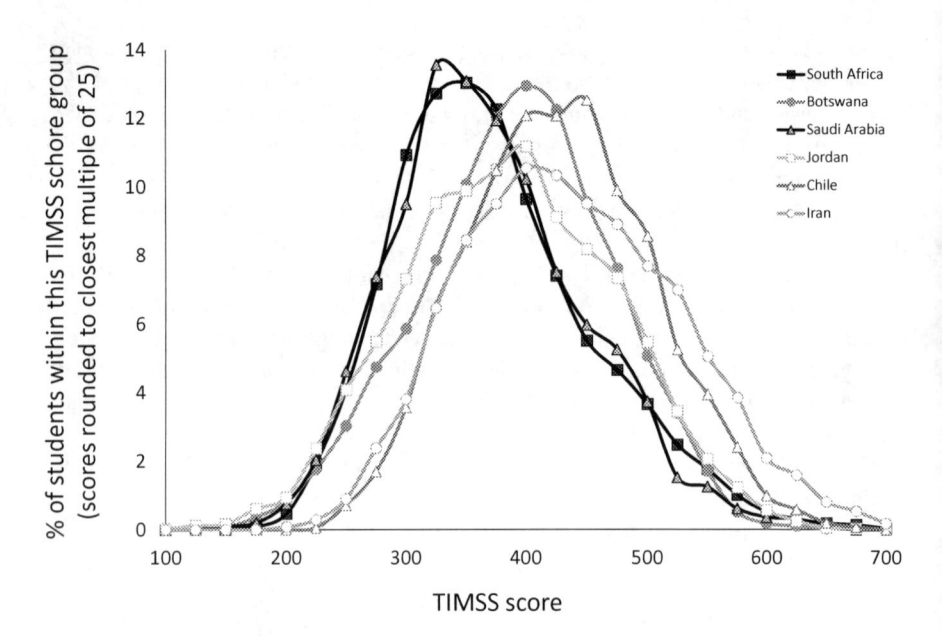

Fig. 2.7 TIMSS 2015 mathematics Grade 8 score distributions

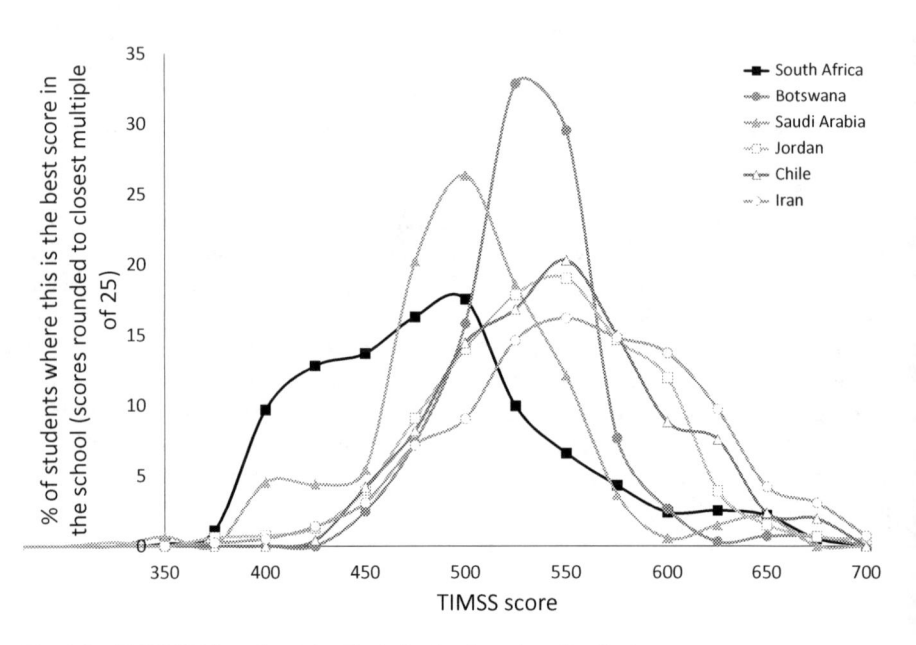

Fig. 2.8 TIMSS 2015 mathematics Grade 8 school maxima distributions

Often inequality in the South African schooling system is viewed in terms of inequalities between the very top 10–20%, and the rest of the system. This inequality is the most visible legacy of apartheid. However, there is also large inequality within the bottom 80% of the system, the historically disadvantaged part of the system. As discussed, for 47% of students opportunities appear severely limited due to school dysfunctionality. Such dysfunctionality is almost non-existent in Botswana. The next 33 percentiles of South Africa's students, from the 48th percentile to the 80th percentile, what we can refer to as the 'emergent middle', fare a lot better. Within this 'emergent middle', every school produces at least one student reaching the intermediate benchmark, though none has any student reaching the high international benchmark of 550 TIMSS points.

The SACMEQ 2007 data produce a similarly worrying pattern for South Africa. As seen in Fig. 2.9 below, which displays a selection of SACMEQ countries, South Africa and Namibia have a particularly high percentage of children in schools where no-one scored particularly well in mathematics in 2007. Officially, SACMEQ considers a score of 530 as reflecting 'beginning numeracy'. In South Africa, 14% of students were in schools in 2007 where no-one achieved this level of 530. Only three of the fifteen SACMEQ countries displayed a worse statistic: Uganda (15%), Namibia (17%) and Malawi (40%). The figure in Swaziland and Botswana was just 1%.

The following two graphs, which compare South Africa to Botswana, illustrate further the matter of under-performing schools. Because so much learning happens

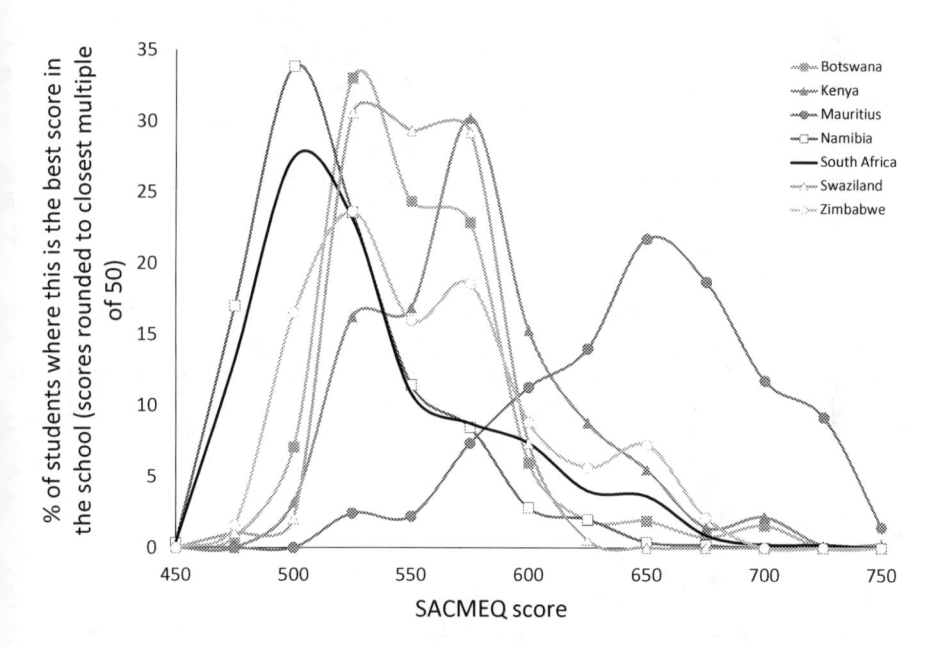

Fig. 2.9 SACMEQ 2007 mathematics Grade 6 school maxima distributions

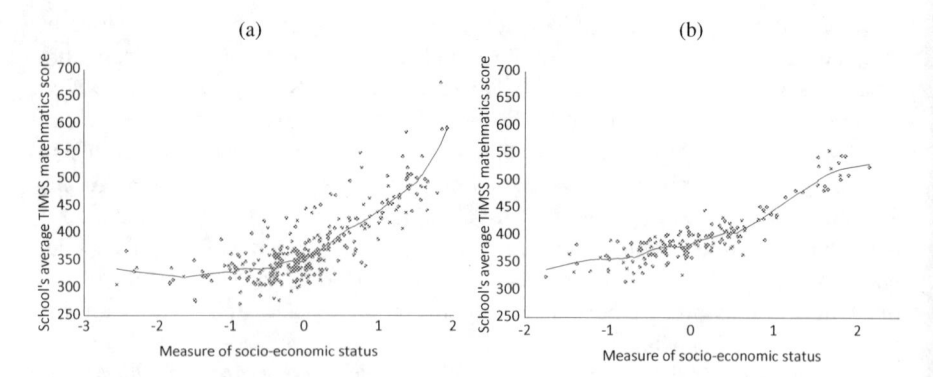

Fig. 2.10 Average TIMSS score and socio-economic status per school for South Africa (left) and Botswana (right). Note: The measure of socio-economic status is calculated using TIMSS student questionnaire data relating to the private ownership of certain items, or access to facilities: one's own computer, a desk, own bedroom, internet, own cellphone, a dictionary, electricity, water from a tap. The trendlines use Lowess estimation

in the home, on average students from more advantaged homes will perform better even in a well-functioning school system. This is why in both Fig. 2.10a, b above, the trend lines display an upward slope. Each point represents a school. If the vertical distance between the points is large, this means that different students with similar home backgrounds are achieving very different results, depending on which school they attend. This is symptomatic of inefficient or dysfunctional schools. The vertical distance between each point and the trendline is indeed higher in South Africa (on average 25 TIMSS points) than in Botswana (15 points).

Similar graphs as that in Fig. 2.10 can be drawn for individual performance of students against their socio-economic status (derived as an index of asset wealth). This relationship between cognitive performance and socio-economic status is known as a social gradient. The South African social gradient is steeper than in any other country that has participated in SACMEQ or even the Latin American SERCE testing programme (Ross and Zuze 2004; Kotzé 2017; Kotzé and Van der Berg 2019). This is the uniquely South African expression of educational inequality, where such inequality is strongly associated with other measures of privilege, leaving poor children with little chance to escape poverty in their lifetime through education and its association with life chances.

2.4   Conclusion

This chapter has shown strong evidence that cognitive performance is improving in the school system as a whole, despite the fact that levels of performance are still extremely low. The 2016 PIRLS results have shown that 78% of Grade 4 children cannot read for meaning in the language in which they were instructed in the first three grades, which for most children is their home language. This is very worrying and has to temper the encouraging findings in this chapter about systemic improvement. Moreover, international tests suggest that recent improvements in performance may have slowed.

The DBE's 'Action Plan to 2019' ascribed quality improvements to three important changes in schools. The first was better access to textbooks. In TIMSS 2002, only 30% of Grade 9 teachers reported using a textbook as their main classroom resource for teaching mathematics, but this had increased to 70% by 2011 (Department of Basic Education 2015, p.12). A second factor was better classroom practices brought about by more suitable curriculum documents and training. Evidence for this is still limited. The third and final factor mentioned was the Annual National Assessments (ANA) programme (since abandoned) that sent strong signals through the system that it was important to focus on the acquisition of basic mathematical and language skills.

Yet our analysis also showed that inequality in education is stark, despite the fact that South Africa is not as uniquely unequal in terms of cognitive performance as is often thought. The uniqueness of inequality in South Africa is rather how strongly it matches inequality of opportunity in the social and economic sphere, with the association between race and educational performance especially being extremely strong. This is well expressed in the slope of the social gradient that shows cognitive performance against socio-economic status.

Willms (2003) has expressed the challenge for countries with steep social gradients in education as being to both 'raise the bar' and also to 'tilt the bar', improving average performance but also reducing the steepness of the gradient and thereby the gap in performance between rich and poor. There is considerable room in South Africa to improve the average score and reduce inequality, by bringing up schools which perform below their full potential. Moreover, there is room to learn from schools which do well, relative to the socio-economic background of their students. This requires good information on both student performance and the socio-economic context of *all* schools, not just a sample of schools as in international tests. This emphasizes the need for measuring learning outcomes in primary schools, where our knowledge base is most deficient and where poor performance has devastating effects for higher levels of the education system.

References

Bruns, B., Evans, D., & Luque, J. (2012). *Achieving world-class education in Brazil: The next Agenda*. Washington, DC: The World Bank.

Carnoy, M., Khavenson, T., Fonseca, I., Costa, L., & Marotta, L. (2015). Is Brazilian education improving? Evidence from Pisa and Saeb. *Cadernos de Pesquisa, 45*(157), 450–485.

Crouch, L., & Gustafsson, M. (2018). *Worldwide inequality and poverty in cognitive results: Cross-sectional evidence and time-based trends* (RISE Working Paper 18/019, RISE Programme). https://www.riseprogramme.org/publications/rise-working-paper-18019-worldwide-inequality-and-poverty-cognitive-results-cross

Department of Basic Education. (2015). *Action Plan 2019 towards the realisation of schooling 2030: Taking Forward South Africa's National Development Plan 2030*. Pretoria: Department of Basic Education.

Department of Basic Education. (2017). *The SACMEQ IV project in South Africa: A study of the conditions of schooling and the quality of education*. Pretoria.

Department of Education. (2008). *Education for All: Country report: South Africa*. Pretoria.

Evans, D., & Yuan, F. (2017). *The economic returns to interventions that increase learning* (Background paper). Washington, DC: World Bank.

Fleisch, B. (2008). *Primary education in crisis: Why South African school children underachieve in reading and mathematics*. Cape Town: Juta.

Gustafsson, M. (2016). *Understanding trends in high-level achievement in Grade 12 mathematics and physical science*. Pretoria: Department of Basic Education.

Hanushek, E. A., & Woessmann, L. (2007). *The role of education quality for economic growth* (SSRN Scholarly Paper ID 960379). Rochester, NY: Social Science Research Network.

Hill, C. J., Bloom, H. S., Black, A. R., & Lipsey, M. W. (2008). Empirical benchmarks for interpreting effect sizes in research. *Child Development Perspectives, 2*(3), 172–177. https://doi.org/10.1111/j.1750-8606.2008.00061.x.

Howie, S., Venter, E., Van Staden, S., Zimmerman, L., Long, C., Scherman, V., & Archer, E. (2008). *Progress in international reading literacy study (PIRLS) 2006 summary report: South African children's reading literacy achievement*. University of Pretoria: Centre for Evaluation and Assessment.

Howie, S., Combrinck, C., Roux, K., Tshele, M., Mokoena, G., & Palane, N. M. (2017). *PIRLS literacy 2017: South African highlights report*. Pretoria: Centre for Evaluation and Assessment.

Kotzé, J. (2017). *Social gradients, early childhood education and schools performing above expectations: Empirical insights into educational issues*. Ph.D. thesis, University of Stellenbosch, Stellenbosch.

Kotzé, J., & Van der Berg, S. (2019). Mathematical performance amongst the poor: Comparative performance across developing countries. In A. Fritz, V. Haase, & P. Räsänen, (Eds.), *International handbook of mathematical learning difficulties: From the laboratory to the classroom* (Chapter 5, pp. 57–571). Hamburg: Springer.

Makuwa, D. (2010). The SACMEQ III project: Mixed results in achievement. *IIEP Newsletter, 28*(3), 2.

Mullis, I., Martin, M., Gonzalez, E., Gregory, K., Garden, R., & O'Connor, K. (2000). *TIMSS 1999 international mathematics report. Findings from the IEA's repeat of the third international mathematics study at the eight grade*. TIMSS & PIRLS International Study Center.

Mullis, I. V. S., Martin, M. O., Gonzalez, E. J., & Chrostowski, S. J. (2004). *TIMSS 2003 international mathematics report: Findings from IEA's trends in international mathematics and science study at the Fourth and eighth grades*. TIMSS & PIRLS International Study Center.

Mullis, I. V. S., Martin, M. O., Foy, P., & Arora, A. (2012a). *Timss 2011 international results in mathematics*. International Association for the Evaluation of Educational Achievement.

Mullis, I. V. S., Martin, M. O., Foy, P., & Drucker, K. T. (2012b). *PIRLS 2011 international results in reading*. Boston: TIMSS & PIRLS International Study Center.

Mullis, I. V. V., Martin, M. O., Foy, P., & Hooper, M. (2016). *TIMSS 2015 international results in mathematics*. Boston: Boston College.

Mullis, I. V. S., Martin, M. O., Foy, P., & Hooper, M. (2017). *PIRLS 2016: International results in reading*. International Association for the Evaluation of Educational Achievement.

Reddy, V., Prinsloo, C., Arends, F., & Visser, M. (2012). *Highlights from TIMSS 2011: The South African perspective*. Pretoria: HRSC Press. http://hdl.handle.net/20.500.11910/2877.

Reddy, V., Zuze, T. L., Visser, M., Winnaar, L., Juan, A., Prinsloo, C. H., Arends, F., & Rogers, S. (2015). *Beyond benchmarks: What twenty years of TIMSS data tell us about South African education*. HSRC Press. http://hdl.handle.net/20.500.11910/2004.

Ross, K., & Zuze, L. (2004). Traditional and alternative view of school system performance. *IIEP Newsletter*, 8–9.

Sahn, D. E., & Younger, S. D. (2007). *Decomposing world education inequality* (SSRN Scholarly Paper ID 779404). Rochester, NY: Social Science Research Network.

Simkins, C. (2002). *The Jagged Tear: Human capital, education and AIDS in South Africa, 2002–2010*. https://www.africaportal.org/publications/the-jagged-tear-human-capital-education-and-aids-in-south-africa-2002-2010/

Taylor, N., & Mabogoane, T. (2015). Policy research comes of age in South Africa. *South African Journal of Childhood Education, 5*(2), 16.

Van der Berg, S. (2007). Apartheid's enduring legacy: Inequalities in education. *Journal of African Economies, 16*(5), 849–880. https://doi.org/10.1093/jae/ejm017.

Van der Berg, S., & Burger, R. (2003). Education and socio-economic differentials: A study of school performance in the Western Cape. *South African Journal of Economics, 71*(3), 496–522.

Van der Berg, S., & Gustafsson, M. (2017). *Quality of basic education. A report to working group 1 of the high level panel on the assessment of key legislation*. Stellenbosch University.

Willms, J. D. (2003). Literacy proficiency of youth: Evidence of converging socioeconomic gradients. *International Journal of Educational Research, 39*(3), 247–252. https://doi.org/10.1016/j.ijer.2004.04.005.

Chapter 3
Pursuing Equity Through Policy in the Schooling Sector 2007–2017

Martin Gustafsson

3.1 Introduction

The decade following South Africa's first democratic elections in 1994 saw enormous policy shifts in the schooling sector, shifts which Luis Crouch has described as *the most profound education reforms attempted anywhere in the world* (Crouch 2005). The reforms were indeed far-reaching, shifting a highly unequal, and race-based, school financing model to one which has been described as amongst the most equal in the world (Sherman and Poirier 2007).

By 2007, however, the realisation had grown that equalising public funding was on its own not enough to reduce inequalities relating to what students learn. These inequalities, which remain stark, can be said to be rooted in two enduring factors: the home background disadvantage of most black students, and the racially segregated and unequal teacher training system of apartheid, a system which continues to influence the teaching practices of older teachers. Crucially, whilst financing reforms emphasised the equalisation of pupil-teacher ratios and salaries, there was virtually no emphasis on getting teachers in historically advantaged schools to teach in less advantaged ones. An additional contributor to inequality is the fact that around 70% of pupils, all of whom are black, must transition, in grade 4, from learning in an indigenous African language to learning in English.

M. Gustafsson (✉)
Department of Basic Education and ReSEP, University of Stellenbosch, Stellenbosch, South Africa
e-mail: mgustafsson@sun.ac.za

The decade 2007–2017 thus saw a different set of policy reforms, focused largely on reducing inequality through improving learning outcomes in historically black schools, in which around 90% of the country's students are enrolled.[1]

The chapter begins by describing, and critiquing, how educational inequality, and the best approaches to tackling this, were understood in around 2007 by stakeholders. The critique uses as a reference point the evolving evidence-based consensus on what brings about educational improvement in developing countries. The 2014 UNESCO Education for All Global Monitoring Report is, for the purposes of this chapter, considered a particularly useful gauge of what this consensus is.

The chapter then discusses key policy changes that occurred after 2007, but also changes which did not occur, the aim being to arrive at a high-level evaluation of how effective the schooling system has been at bringing about change, in particular through policy. In the chapter, the definition of 'policy' is fairly broad. Strategies and rules carrying legal force are considered to be the policy core, but official guidelines, and formal speeches of politicians are also considered 'policy' as these do influence the system. Whilst the chapter does not provide anything close to a detailed account of policy implementation, it must obviously take this matter into account when assessing whether policies have been successful or not.

The conclusion at the end weighs up priorities for the next decade of policy reform. The importance of inserting more rigour into the policy development process, across all policy areas, is emphasised. This requires capacity, inside government, but also among researchers and other actors outside government. Two complex policy areas rather urgently in need of innovation are underlined: rules governing teachers and school principal accountability. The second of these relies strongly on effective measures of the quality of learning in each school. Though curriculum has been a relatively successful policy area, one glaring gap stands out: proper guidance to teachers on how to teach reading in the initial grades.

3.2 How the Problem Was Understood in Around 2007

There was no single event in 2007 that signalled a policy shift towards learning inequalities, yet a shift was occurring at the start of the decade covered by this chapter. An important catalyst for the shift was the 2000 SACMEQ[2] tests, conducted in 14 African countries. The results of these, available initially in 2003, shocked many, though it took a few years for the reaction to the shock to take shape. SACMEQ revealed how much worse the reading and mathematics outcomes of South Africa's Grade 6 students were relative to that in countries spending much less per student, such as Kenya and Swaziland.

---

[1] This 90% can be broken down into 3% for historically Indian schools, 9% for historically 'coloured' schools and 78% for historically black African schools.

[2] Southern and Eastern Africa Consortium for Monitoring Educational Quality.

The resultant policy shift was away from viewing results in the Grade 12 examinations, the so-called 'Matric', in isolation from what was happening in the earlier grades. Little had been known previously about the quality of education at the primary level. SACMEQ confirmed that fixing inequalities at the Grade 12 level meant fixing inequalities lower down in the system.

There was also a policy shift away from thinking that more funding equity was a guarantee of more equal learning outcomes. The earlier financing reforms, whilst necessary, had clearly not brought about the latter. The shift was also away from viewing assessments of learning below Grade 12 managed by teachers, with minimal external quality controls, as a source of accurate information on absolute performance or inequalities between schools.

Before South Africa's policies are discussed, a general framework for the discussion is presented. This framework is informed by many sources, though UNESCO's 2014 report encapsulates them well. In many ways the framework is universal, yet it is somewhat tailored to meet the needs of a South African discussion.

We can think of two distinct levels in which policy works: the level of system-wide governance, and the level of the school. One could add a third level: pre-school. Policy on early childhood development is enormously important in determining children's chances of success in the schooling system. However, early childhood development is not within the scope of the current chapter (Ashley-Cooper et al. in the current volume).

3.2.1 System-Wide Governance

Given the societal nature of schooling, debates are highly influenced by popular perceptions, which are in turn influenced by knowledge and information generated by the government. In addition, government plays a crucial role in the development of the educational tools required for schooling, including textbooks, computer software and teacher training materials, tools which can carry high development costs. In South Africa, system-wide governance is the shared responsibility of one national and nine provincial education departments. How the national and provincial levels work together is critical for the success of policy. The use of all 11 official languages as mediums of instructions in grades 1–3, and pressure from some quarters to promote the use of indigenous African languages in grades 4–12, where mostly English but also Afrikaans are the mediums of instruction, make materials development particularly complex and costly in South Africa.

3.2.2 Policies Impacting on Schools Directly

Three broad policy areas can be identified as follows:

(a) *The right to offer schooling.*

Rules governing the very existence of schools, including those relating to the establishment of private schools and the rights of parents when it comes to school choice, are the foundations of any schooling system. Whilst South Africa facilitates private schooling, for instance through the public funding of less elite private schools, maintaining a large public system, even with considerable internal inequalities, is generally considered preferable to a situation, common in many developing countries, where much of the middle class makes use of private schools. In 2017, private schools catered for only 5% of all school students. Whilst public schools in some urban areas have somewhat rigid 'feeder zones', across most of the country parents are relatively free to choose between public schools.

(b) *Qualifications obtained through schools.*

How the certification of learning occurs, in particular through national examinations, shapes parental and student expectations, and the practices of schools, in many ways. Closely linked to national qualifications is of course the national curriculum. South Africa, unlike all her neighbouring countries, has no national qualification below the end of the secondary level. The Grade 12 Matric, obtained by just over half of youths in recent years, has a history of over a century and features prominently in the national debates. Though the system includes technical and vocational subjects, these are only offered by around 16% of the schools participating in the Matric, meaning that for most schools the Matric assumes a largely academic character.[3] The less academic subjects are disproportionately concentrated in schools that were historically reserved for whites.

(c) *Resourcing and accountability policies*

This is a large and complex policy area. Schools are given public resources, and through various systems they must account for the effective use of these resources. Policies can be centralist, for instance where the authorities decide on the exact resourcing package of each school, and control closely how resources are used. Alternatively, policies can be decentralist, involving the transfer of funding to schools, coupled to accountability systems focussing on learning outcomes, rather than processes. Advocates of the latter tend to emphasise the importance of accountability to parents as a means of promoting effective resource utilisation. South Africa, like many countries, features a complex mix of centralist and decentralist policies. While each school has considerable say in which teachers work there, the province is the official employer, and the national level negotiates national salary scales with the country's powerful teacher unions. The success of the entire human resourcing

---

[3] The 16% of schools examine at least one of the following Matric subjects: Engineering graphics and design, Civil technology, Electrical technology, Mechanical technology. These four subjects often define which schools are considered 'technical schools'. See National Senior Certificate Examinations data available through https://www.datafirst.uct.ac.za

system is dependent on policies governing the following issues: recruitment into the teaching profession; the quality of initial teacher training; the kind of in-service training that takes place; and the ability to retain teachers, in particular good ones. Pro-poor resourcing is widely recognised as necessary to offset, at least partly, home background disadvantage. Such resourcing should involve actions by the state to increase access to good teachers amongst students in poorer communities. Crucially, a rather equitable public funding system in South Africa co-exists with the right, enjoyed by the roughly one-third of schools serving better off communities, to charge fees. In exchange for this right, these schools must fully or partially exempt students from low income households.

So what was the thinking in South Africa, around 2007, on what aspects to change in the web of policies outlined above in order to reduce educational inequalities?

The annual budget speeches to Parliament in the years 2006–2008 of the national Minister of Education, Naledi Pandor, provide useful insights. They include an emphasis on stepping up existing initiatives, such as pedagogic support to teachers by district officials. But they also include commitments to school and teacher accountability, through programmes which would be new, and could require careful negotiation with unions. For instance, the 2006 speech refers to assessments of individual teachers which could lead to cash awards. The 2008 speech envisages student performance being taken into account within the teacher remuneration system. It also refers to the establishment of a new national 'inspectorate' of schools, a provocative term given the unpleasant memories of many black teachers of the school inspectors of the apartheid era, inspectors whose role was partly to maintain the political status quo.

Strong words against the mediocrity of many teachers and officials, and a statement that inadequate resources were no longer an excuse for poor schooling, all in the 2007 speech, are indicative of the policy shift that was under way away from a strong focus on school funding, towards a greater emphasis on efficiency.

Less controversial from a teacher union perspective would have been the Minister's commitment to a more consistent and generous set of policies governing teacher recruitment, professional development and promotions. The 2006 speech included a commitment to counteracting teacher shortages in remote areas through an incentive.

The 2007 speech emphasised the importance of strengthening the teaching of reading. A new programme referred to as the Early Grade Reading Assessment was announced. The 2006 speech implicitly admitted that measures of performance for all primary schools were a gap in the system, by declaring that geographical proximity to poorly performing secondary schools would be used to identify primary schools requiring an intervention.

Resolutions passed in 2008 by the South African Democratic Teachers Union (SADTU) suggest that, at least on paper, agreement between unions and government was strong. Though SADTU, accounting for 71% of all union membership amongst teachers, is officially an ally of the ruling African National Congress (ANC) party, of the various teacher unions it has also been the most vocal critic of the government. Yet the 2008 resolutions accept that poor quality schooling is a problem, and call for errant teachers to be disciplined. Key complaints directed at the government sound reasonable: curriculum change should be linked to a long-term strategy and programmes to evaluate teachers should be sensitive to the context in which teachers teach (South African Democratic Teachers Union 2008).

The 2008 policy on education of the official opposition, the Democratic Alliance (DA), did not differ greatly from the government's policy positions. One difference is that it proposed linking pay increases for teachers to subject knowledge tests that teachers would write. A key distinguishing feature of the DA's policy was a proposal to provide vouchers for 350,000 students from low income households to attend better schools (Democratic Alliance 2008).

A 2009 report on education by the Centre for Development and Enterprise, an influential policy think tank funded largely by business, echoes many of the concerns of government at the time and proposes no single 'magic bullet' to resolve the country's educational inequalities. What it does emphasise is the importance of practical policies, learning from the experiences of other countries, and paying attention to negotiating policies with, in particular, the teacher unions (Centre for Development and Enterprise 2009).

To conclude, there appeared to be a remarkable degree of policy consensus, or at least an absence of major disagreements, in the schooling sphere. Moreover, several of government's commitments seemed promising, such as streamlining policies on human resources, and strengthening reading acquisition in schools.

Yet on closer examination, the policy positions and consensus reveal important gaps and contradictions. In particular, the fact that at the time over half of youths emerging from the schooling system would not have acquired a national qualification probably warranted better attention. (Only around 2% of youths acquire a national qualification from an institution other than a school, without first obtaining the Matric (Department of Basic Education 2016c, p. 81). The Minister's 2008 speech emphasised getting all youths to complete Grade 12 successfully. However, given that completion of 12 years of education in South Africa was and remains at a level that is fairly typical for a middle income country, and given that progress against this indicator tends to be gradual, the obvious question is whether a second national school qualification, at an earlier grade, was needed to improve the chances that all students would receive at least some qualification. In fact, in the 1990s the ANC advocated a Grade 9 qualification in its policy documents (South Africa: Department of Education 1995).

A further contradiction relates to teacher incentives. The literature routinely warns about the complications of attempting performance incentives for individual teachers (UNESCO 2014). Such incentives tend not to recognise the fact that educational improvement in schools is the result of a team of teachers working together, meaning financial incentives directed at whole schools are more workable. One red flag in government's positions at the time, at least as represented by the Minister's speeches, seems to be insufficient sensitivity to the complexities of designing effective teacher incentives. This, in turn, suggests that lessons from other countries had not been internalised. A further concern would be insufficient consistency across the three ministerial speeches examined. For instance, the important matter of incentives for teachers in remote schools, referred to in the 2006 speech, is not followed through in the next two speeches. In fact, insufficient follow-through will be shown to be a considerable problem in South Africa's education policymaking processes.

3.3 Policy Changes in the 2007–2017 Period

Nine of many possible policy topics are discussed in this section. The nine, indicated by bold text, were selected on the basis of their strategic importance, but also for their ability to illustrate generic policymaking challenges, such as achieving consistency across and within policies, and allowing policies to be informed by empirical evidence and cost data. Most of the policy topics featured prominently in the news and debates, but a few did not. The latter were selected because they represent areas of policy where arguably there should have been more debate and perhaps even policy change.

The nine policy topics are as follows: (1) curriculum reform; (2) national workbooks; (3) Grade 9 qualification; (4) schools-based 'reception year'; (5) e-education; (6) rules governing teachers; (7) national assessments and school principal accountability; (8) charter schools; and (9) national planning systems. The common thread running through these topics is that they had at least the potential to bring about change, and specifically reductions in inequality.

The first policy area, **curriculum reform**, is one of three which are believed to explain to a large extent the fairly steep performance improvements South Africa displayed in the international testing programmes. Specifically, Grade 9 TIMSS[4] results in mathematics improved by one standard deviation between 2002 and 2015 (Reddy et al. 2016).[5] This was largely driven by improvements in schools serving more disadvantaged communities, meaning levels of inequality were reduced (Van der Berg and Gustafsson 2017, p. 7). PIRLS[6] Grade 4 reading results improved by around half a standard deviation between 2006 and 2011, or by more than a year's worth of learning, though between 2011 and 2016 no further improvement was found (Howie et al. 2008, p. 19, 2017).[7] In the Department of Basic Education's (DBE) list of likely factors contributing to this improvement, three stand out: curriculum reform, a new national assessment programme, and better access to

---

[4]Trends in International Mathematics and Science Study.

[5]Note that *TIMSS 2003* was in fact conducted in 2002 in South Africa, when both grades 8 and 9 were tested. In 2011, only Grade 9 was tested.

[6]Progress in International Reading Literacy Study.

[7]Note that the 2011 Grade 4 average national score appearing in the 2017 report is a rescaled average that is comparable to the earlier 2006 Grade 5 national average.

books in classrooms (Department of Basic Education 2015, pp. 10–11; Australian Council for Educational Research 2013, p. 12). Curriculum reform is discussed here, and the other two are dealt with further down.

Curriculum reform does in many ways stand out as one of the policy success stories of the 2007–2017 decade. In 2008, as part of the Foundations for Learning programme, the Department of Education[8] began producing guides aimed at grades 1–6 teachers in order to bring about greater clarity on what should be done in the classroom. This work evolved into a series of guides known as the Curriculum and Assessment Policy Statement, or CAPS, which were introduced between 2011 and 2014 for all grades. This effectively brought to an end a divisive and unpopular curriculum known as 'outcomes based education', or OBE, which was increasingly viewed as overly theoretical and impractical. OBE, in force since 1998, arguably exacerbated inequalities by expecting teachers to develop their own materials, which was only really feasible in historically advantaged schools. The rise and fall of OBE, or particular forms of it, across many countries, is a topic warranting a separate chapter.

Though generally welcomed by schools, the CAPS still appears to provide insufficient guidance on the crucial matter of teaching children to read. The DBE's 2017 annual plan envisages improving the teaching of reading through use of the Early Grade Reading Assessment (EGRA) tools and a set of reading norms. This sounds similar to priorities put forward a decade earlier, around 2007. Analysts have argued that insufficient follow-through and a lack of policy depth have hampered progress in this area (Van der Berg et al. 2016, p. 51). To illustrate, the DBE's plans are not clear on the fact that reading norms, meaning words per minute to be read by pupils in different grades, have not been developed for most of the languages, or on how this policy development work will proceed. Strategies on promoting reading, whilst well-intended, have mostly lacked solid monitoring plans, making it easier for initiatives to be forgotten, and then recycled. But there has been progress. The DBE's Early Grade Reading Study, involving a large range of local and international stakeholders, has clearly deepened the sector's understanding of what tools and practices in the classroom lead to better reading. A 2017 report details the findings of the study (Department of Basic Education 2017).

The next topic is **national workbooks**. An ambitious programme involving the distribution of high-quality and standard workbooks, meaning textbooks in which students would write, and which would complement traditional textbooks, was started in 2011 to further the goal of clarifying what teachers should do in the post-OBE classroom. The national workbooks, known formally as the Rainbow Workbooks, are believed to be a second likely factor contributing towards improvements in learning (the first being curriculum reform). As in the case of curriculum reform, better access to texts began earlier, with the Foundations for Learning programme, but the start of the full-scale national workbooks programme in 2011 took this intervention to a new level. The focus of the programme was

---

[8]In 2009 the Department of Education was split into the Department of Basic Education and the Department of Higher Education and Training.

initially grades 1–6, but this was expanded to R to 9. To provide a sense of the magnitude of the development work that underpinned the workbooks programme, in 2012 each Grade 6 student received two mathematics books with an overall total of 300 pages, each page consisting of colour illustrations and text, with some including space for the student's own writing. There were a further 300 such pages for home language, and a further 300 for first additional language (the two language levels had different materials). Versions in all 11 official languages were produced, making the programme one of the government's most important contributions to date with respect to the development and promotion of the nine indigenous African languages. The development work was done within the DBE, and electronic versions of the books are available online.

The workbooks programme was on the whole well received and prompted an uncharacteristic compliment by the leader of the official opposition party to the Minister of Basic Education (Zille 2013).[9] An external evaluation of the design and use of the workbooks by the Australian Council for Educational Research, ACER, was mostly positive. It was found that around 80% of schools used the workbooks – workbook use was not made mandatory by the national authorities, though some provinces and districts insisted strongly that they be used. Because students became the permanent owners of their books, over the years they would accumulate in households. The ACER evaluation found that this facilitated learning amongst other household members. One student's response that 'I do not understand the maths teacher but I understand the workbook', is telling (Australian Council for Educational Research 2013, p. 18). In some ways, the programme constituted a way of circumventing poor teacher quality. The programme was deemed sufficiently important to result in the inclusion, from 2013, of questions on access to the workbooks in Statistics South Africa's annual General Household Survey.

There were problems with the workbooks programme, relating mainly to the logistics of delivering, in the right language combinations, almost 40 million workbooks a year to schools. Though the workbooks were in themselves policy, in the sense that they constituted a standard recipe for getting something right, ACER suggested that actual policy on what the purpose of the workbooks was, and the communication of this policy to schools and parents, was needed.

What made this programme a success? Good leadership of the programme stands out. Moreover, the fact that just under half of the funding for the programme during the initial years came from the European Union could have strengthened accountability and quality control.

Other initiatives also contributed towards better access to books in schools. In particular, increases in the non-personnel financial allocations to schools allowed schools to purchase more textbooks (Wildeman and Hemmer-Vitti 2010, p. 6). Perhaps the most striking indicator of the impact of this is that in the TIMSS data, the percentage of lower secondary mathematics teachers reporting that they used a textbook as a basis for planning their teaching increased from 30% in 2002 to 71% in 2011.

---

[9]The programme also receives mention in (UNESCO 2014, p.285).

Apart from the revision of the Grade 12 examinations in 2008 to align them to the new post-apartheid curriculum, there were no major changes in the area of school qualifications. The new CAPS guides placed considerable emphasis on examinations in every grade from Grade 4, but did not require national examinations, or any new national qualification. A substantive 2014 report (Department of Basic Education 2014) by a ministerial committee looking into the Grade 12 qualification recommended that a **Grade 9 qualification** be introduced, but this appears not to have been given due attention by the DBE, or other stakeholders, such as the committee of Parliament dealing with basic education. The problem of weak follow-through, including insufficient engagement with recommendations emerging from official enquiries, appears to be a problem not just in the national and provincial departments, but also in the broader policymaking system, which includes Parliament and various forums that stakeholders, from unions to university academics to civil society activist groups, participate in.

Interest in a qualification below Grade 12 is weakened by a strong belief that 12 years of education for all youths is an ideal which can be realised relatively soon. This seems to reflect an inadequate understanding of educational development in other countries. Improving grade attainment tends to be a slow process, largely because it takes time to improve the quality of teaching, something which is necessary to advance student 'survival' in the system.

A **schools-based 'reception year'**, or Grade R, for children aged five at the start of the school year had been formally introduced in the national curriculum in 2002. Then, the percentage of the target population attending Grade R in a school was around 25%. This figure increased sharply to around 70% in 2014 (by which time if one also counted Grade R learners in centres outside schools, the figure stood at around 95%) (Department of Basic Education 2016c, pp. 11,58). Growth in Grade R was probably the most visible change occurring in primary schools over this period. This development was possible largely because of a tacit agreement between government and the unions that a low-cost model of employment would be used. Instead of using typical national salary scales, determined through a central bargaining process, schools would pay Grade R 'practitioners', essentially teachers, at rates decided between the school and the employee, using funds transferred to the school.[10] Over time, and in some provinces more than in others, unions succeeded in having province-wide minimum wages declared, but even these were around one-fifth of what a teacher in grades 1–12 was earning. This gap is huge, even if one considers the lower qualifications requirements for Grade R teachers. Grade R expansion could occur because there was sufficient trust between government and the unions, at least in this policy area. The trust rested strongly on the tacit assurance that the Grade R arrangement would not be replicated in other grades.

However, the Grade R policies lacked detail on how the quality of the expanded service would be assured and monitored. A 2014 report evaluating the impact of Grade R, produced by Presidency's Department of Planning, Monitoring and

---

[10]Government Notice 26 of 2008.

Evaluation (DPME), made use of innovative data techniques to conclude that between 2005 and 2011 the introduction of Grade R made no difference to test results in Grade 1 and above in the case of the poorest three quintiles of schools, and a small positive difference in more advantaged schools (South Africa: Department of Planning, Monitoring and Evaluation 2014). There is unfortunately no information on quality trends beyond 2011, a period that has seen a stronger focus on delivering Grade R materials to schools.

Progress with respect to policy on **e-education** has been disappointing. This policy topic is included here largely because in South Africa, as elsewhere, there is great public interest in increasing the use of modern information and communication technologies, ICTs, in schools. This has prompted many local initiatives. Data on ICTs in schools are scarce, but TIMSS data indicate that the percentage of Grade 9 students with access to computers in schools increased from 28% to 43% between 2002 and 2015. A problem with this trend is that the correlation between having ICTs and the school community's socio-economic status is high, meaning poorer communities have been left behind. South Africa's 2015 figure of 43% is in fact considerably lower than the comparable figures for other developing countries, including Ghana, Botswana and Indonesia (these three all display figures of over 70%). Improving access to ICTs amongst poorer communities, whilst at the same time dealing with the risk that weak strategies can result in no educational value being added by ICTs, requires very careful planning by the national government (UNESCO 2014, pp. 35,293). Reports on the e-education situation in South Africa emphasise the need for better national policy to guide both public and private investments (Meyer and Gent 2016). What is perhaps not made clear enough, in the area of e-education but also other education areas, is what is meant by an effective 'strategy'. Virtually all advisors on strategy will emphasise the need to have a vision and to think broadly. In this respect, South African e-education strategists have been relatively successful. However, strategy also requires a good diagnosis of the point of departure, an understanding of the resource constraints, and an ability to prioritise, which in some cases means making tough choices. It appears that these specific aspects of planning have not received enough attention.

The focus now moves from curriculum-related matters to the politically sensitive area of the **rules governing teachers**. In 2008, what appeared to be the most radical changes to these rules since the removal, in the 1990s, of the race-based salary scales, were promulgated. The Occupation Specific Dispensation[11] for educators involved paying larger annual increases to teachers classified in any year as 'good' or 'excellent' in the performance management system, known as the IQMS,[12] which had existed since 2003. Previously, one's IQMS classification had made virtually no difference to one's annual experience-linked increase. The additional costs of the new system were justified on the basis that this would improve learning outcomes, particularly in historically disadvantaged schools. However, there were serious gaps

---

[11] Education Labour Relations Council Resolution 1 of 2008.

[12] Integrated Quality Management System.

in the policy signed by the employer and unions, gaps which would be exploited by unions when they made an about-turn in 2009 and successfully cancelled the policy. How the financially lucrative IQMS classifications would be rationed across schools to prevent over-expenditure, or how one would deal with the increased need for anti-corruption controls, now that classifications were being attached to money, were not made clear. The latter policy challenge is particularly difficult to resolve, given inherent difficulties in individual performance-linked incentives for teachers.

In a dramatic turn of events, in 2009 SADTU ensured that the funding for the policy was retained, whilst removing the performance-linked differentiation across teachers, essentially meaning the money would be spread across all teachers. This was possible partly because the ruling party wanted to maximise votes from teachers in the upcoming 2009 elections. However, policy design weaknesses played a role too.

A general gap in the policy discourse around teacher pay is that the crucial trade-off between teacher pay and the pupil-teacher ratio barely features. This is a trade-off that teachers should have a direct interest in. In comparison to other middle income countries, South Africa's teacher pay is relatively high, whilst class sizes and pupil-teacher ratios are also high. To illustrate, in recent years a quarter of lower primary pupils in two large provinces, Eastern Cape and Limpopo, have experienced class sizes exceeding 50 pupils (Spaull 2016). The current imbalance suggests teacher pay should be carefully controlled to provide relief with regard to pupil-teacher ratios. Yet between 2007 and 2017, what are known as the cost-of-living adjustments for teachers have exceeded official inflation, and in real terms teacher pay improved by 27% over the period. This excludes experience-linked increments, at 1% a year for all teachers. These increases, in combination with weak economic growth, have made it virtually impossible to grow the size of the workforce with a view to reducing high pupil-teacher ratios. These dynamics ought to feature more prominently in the wage negotiations. There are important future opportunities, however. A large bulge of older teachers is nearing retirement. As these teachers are replaced by younger teachers entering lower salary notches, the average cost of a teacher should decline in real terms. With effective planning and good management of wage negotiations, these opportunities could translate into smaller classes.

Crafting better pay and incentive agreements is in part dependent on what happens in the larger public servant policy arena. Teacher pay increases have roughly been in line with those for other public servants. However, with 37% of all national and provincial personnel spending going towards the schooling sector, the sector is well-placed to influence the overall system.

The schooling sector could, for instance, lead the way in producing a holistic strategy on how incentives, financial *and non-financial*, encourage good service delivery. This would essentially be the 'align actors' leg of the three-pronged approach for schooling advocated by the 2018 *World Development Report* (the other two being 'assess learning' and 'act on evidence') (World Bank 2018). Gradually, better understandings of how incentives work in schooling are being reached. For instance, between the 2011 draft version of the National Development Plan and the final plan released in 2012 there was an important shift in emphasis from performance-linked increases paid to individual teachers, to financial incentives paid to schools as a whole in recognition of improvements. The latter, whilst also not easy to implement, has enjoyed some success in developing countries.

Perhaps the most important financial incentive for teachers, and one which has existed for decades, is promotion into a schools-based head of department (HoD) position. The ratio of ordinary teachers to HoDs is 6:1, being promoted to an HoD comes with, on average, a 20% pay increase, and 92% of teachers are in schools large enough for HoD positions to exist. Policy discussions of teacher incentives, such as those on the 2008 reforms, have tended to be silent on the matter of HoDs, which is surprising. A handbook by UNESCO's International Institute for Educational Planning warns that the 'need for system maintenance can be overlooked in the flood of enthusiasm that often accompanies innovation' (Inbar 1996, p. 42). Insufficient attention to entrenched aspects of the system can have serious consequences. A 2016 report, commissioned by the Minister following a number of alarming news reports, found that promotions into, for instance, HoD and principal positions were often corrupt and nepotistic, with a couple of tragic murders in KwaZulu-Natal having been a consequence of this (Department of Basic Education 2016b). Had ongoing monitoring of the promotions process been better, this could have been avoided. It is difficult to gauge from the report how widespread the corruption is, a matter which is important for designing a response. It seems the outcome of the report will be the transfer of some personnel hiring powers, across all schools, from parents to the provincial education department. This would understandably be opposed by schools running clean promotions processes.

Turning to other areas in the teacher policy space, two national frameworks for teacher development were published, one in 2006 and another in 2011 (South Africa: Department of Education 2006; Department of Basic Education 2011). The two prioritise similar things. Both seem lacking when it comes to considering benefits relative to the financial costs of various policy options, and in taking into account the incentives that drive (or demotivate) people. In this regard policymakers could have been more ambitious. It has been argued that they could have been less ambitious with regard to the development, begun in 2007, of a national database of each teacher's professional development activities. The viability of the plans for the database, a tool which few if any developing countries have attempted to build, was questioned in a 2012 report (South African Council for Educators 2012).

A policy that might have promoted greater equity by bringing outstanding teachers to disadvantaged students was a 2007 policy on financial incentives encouraging teachers to move to remote and 'difficult' schools.[13] UNESCO promotes this as a vital equity-enhancing strategy (UNESCO 2014, p. 249). In South Africa, policies that take disadvantaged students to good teachers have received much attention, the fee exemptions policy being one example, but the converse, taking good teachers to where disadvantaged students school, has received little attention. The 2007 policy

---

[13]Government Notice 25 of 2007.

led to hardly any change, however, perhaps because it lacked a convincing equity argument, and definitely because how it would be adequately financed was not made clear. Fixing this policy area is important in a context where the intake of younger teachers, who tend to be more mobile, is expected to grow.

The Funza Lushaka bursary scheme to address the under-supply of new teachers is an example of a policy relating to teachers which has made a positive difference (South Africa: Department of Planning, Monitoring and Evaluation 2016). The scheme, introduced in 2007, has worked relatively well because the problem being addressed, the under-supply of teachers, was understood and well researched, and because the various stakeholders, including the DBE, the Department of Higher Education and Training, and the National Student Financial Aid Scheme, worked well together. However, aspects of the scheme have not worked well. In particular, the aim of using the programme to oblige young teachers to work in disadvantaged schools has mostly not been realised, largely due to weak management and information systems. To a large degree, recipients of the bursary have themselves determined where they would work.

As politically sensitive as rules governing teachers, have been standardised national assessments, specifically the Annual National Assessments (ANA) programme, which ran from 2011 to 2014, reaching an unexpected and dramatic end, some would say pause, in 2015. This programme is discussed under the rubric **national assessments and school principal accountability**, given the inter-relatedness of these two issues. The DBE began encouraging the use of standardised tests in 2008, within the Foundations for Learning programme. From 2011, ANA was run across all schools offering grades 1–6 (and from 2012, also Grade 9). Tests were delivered in packages to schools, which were to be opened on national test days. Teachers at the school marked the tests, subject to limited external quality controls. Students' total scores, which were fed into a national database, were used to generate highly publicised reports containing aggregates at the national, provincial and district levels, but not the school level. ANA was supported by some for sending the right signals across the system about the centrality of basic competencies. It is these signals that are believed to have contributed to the improvements in the international tests, which also test basic competencies. But ANA was also heavily criticised, above all by SADTU. Unlike in 2009, when SADTU's opposition to performance-linked pay was not widely supported, in its opposition to ANA, SADTU was supported by many academics and, through an unprecedented statement, even the opposition Democratic Alliance.[14] As a result, the 2015 run of ANA was aborted in the last minute. In 2016 and 2017, the DBE has struggled to re-develop the national assessment programme in a manner than would be acceptable to SADTU.

Why did South Africa not succeed in sustaining an intervention which UNESCO and others have said is so central for advancing quality education for the disadvan-

---

[14] Article titled *SADTU is right: Annual National Assessments aren't working* at https://www.da. org.za/2014/10/sadtu-right-annual-national-assessments-arent-working (accessed January 2018).

taged? (UNESCO 2014, p. 90) Why did South Africa not succeed in replicating, say, Brazil's national assessment, which is said to have impacted positively on equalising learning outcomes (Bruns et al. 2012, p. 7)? A 2016 DBE report acknowledges that the absence of a policy explaining clearly the purpose of ANA led to confusion and that there were design flaws in the programme: too many grades were covered and the comparability of results across years was not given the attention it deserved (Department of Basic Education 2016a). The importance of policy clarity and the coherence of programme design in an area as contested as national assessments cannot be over-emphasised. It should have been made clear that ANA's main purpose was to provide a measure of each primary school's average learning outcomes, thus plugging an important gap in the South African schooling system. How these measures would be used, fairly and realistically, to hold, above all, school principals accountable should also have been explained. It should have been explained that holding individual teachers accountable was not a purpose of ANA.

A 2016 policy on the 'standards for school principals',[15] whilst more holistic than earlier policies in this area, lacked clarity on 'tough' issues such as definitions of persistent school under-performance, and the consequences of this for principals. It moreover skirts the related and crucial issue of whether South Africa's system of school poverty quintiles is an adequate basis for determining the socio-economic status of the school community, and fails to emphasise that judgements around a school principal's effectiveness need to be made relative to the type of school community served by the school.

Policies on the legal status of schools, or on the right to offer schooling, have not changed fundamentally since the South African Schools Act was promulgated in 1996. Nor did change in this area feature prominently in the policy debates. Yet the potential for change offered by this policy area according to stakeholders such as Centre for Development and Enterprise (CDE) seemed to make it important enough to include amongst the nine policy topics (Schirmer et al. 2013). Specifically, the CDE has promoted the creation of a new category of schools, akin to the **charter schools** of the United States, essentially semi-private schools contracted by the state to offer schooling in less advantaged communities.

Around 2008, the Department of Education was in fact considering the option of a new category of schools, as a means of creating more choice for parents in poorer communities (Historic Schools Restoration Project 2010). This did not lead to new national policy, but in 2016 the province of the Western Cape began piloting a few 'Collaboration Schools', public schools partly managed by external 'operating partners' paid to improve learning outcomes. Predictably, given the tendency of teacher unions worldwide to view these types of programmes with suspicion, the Western Cape authorities have faced stiff resistance. Given the sensitivities around such changes, realigning the incentives for schools and teachers within the existing framework should probably be the first priority. In public schools, many options

---

[15]Government Notice 323 of 2016.

remain largely unexplored (as seen in the foregoing discussions). Policies on private schools, or 'independent schools' as they are known in South Africa, could become more oriented towards quality schooling for poorer communities. These schools are increasingly catering for black children – by around 2013, just over 60% of students were black African whilst 20% were white (Van der Berg et al. 2017; Centre for Development and Enterprise 2015). At the secondary level, public subsidies for independent schools are conditional on the fulfilment of minimum academic outputs in the Grade 12 examinations. Were standardised tests to be re-introduced at the primary level, the same funding criteria could be introduced here.

Turning to **national planning systems**, the first term of the Zuma government, from 2009 to 2014, was in fact a period of remarkable innovation in this area. The benefits of these innovations are likely to be felt for a long time, and they undoubtedly facilitate better education policymaking. A National Planning Commission was established, in line with good practice in other countries, and South Africa's first long-term national development plan was released by the Commission in 2012. The new Department of Planning, Monitoring and Evaluation had by the end of 2017 published on its website five major evaluations relating to the basic education sector on the quality of textbooks, Grade R in schools, support for Grade 12 examination candidates, Funza Lushaka, and the national school nutrition programme.

In order to widen the pool of researchers with access to government microdata, the DBE began making school-level enrolment and examinations data accessible through the University of Cape Town's DataFirst facility in 2014. Strengthening data analysis skills, inside and outside government, to facilitate evidence-based policymaking, is clearly needed. More black education researchers are needed. The surnames of the authors of the most prominent education research published in the last decade confirm that black Africans, who constitute 81% of the population, are still grossly under-represented. This matters a lot in a country where policy debates are easily polarised along racial lines.

To conclude this section, one sometimes hears in South African education policy circles that national policies are essentially sound, and that tackling poor learning outcomes is largely a question of implementing existing policies properly, particularly in the provinces. Implementation and enforcement are indeed large and important challenges. However, this section has tried to demonstrate that there are significant gaps in the policy landscape. There is policy which ought to exist but does not. There are flaws in existing policies, and cases where such flaws hampered implementation, often because they raised the risk of conflict between government and the unions. More effective policy maintenance and innovation is necessary in South Africa. However, even the best imaginable policies are no guarantee that the schooling system will work well. To achieve this, good policies must be combined with sufficient public consensus around the policies, effective management, and well-functioning public accountability bodies, such as Parliament.

3.4   Conclusion and the Road Ahead

The last decade of education policy reform in South Africa has been more typical for a developing country, relative to her previous decade, where the focus had to fall strongly on undoing the unequal funding legacy of apartheid. South Africa and other developing countries, in particular those with strong teacher unions, stand to learn a lot from the 2007–2017 decade covered in this chapter.

The chapter has paid attention to what can be achieved when policymaking is rigorous in the sense that it is informed by the national and international evidence, when it focusses on the desired policy outcomes, and when it attempts as far as possible to achieve alignment across policies within the sector. But the risks inherent in fragmented policymaking, where fragmentation is often a manifestation of silo effects in the bureaucracy, are also illustrated, as are the risks associated with an over-enthusiasm to innovate, when adapting existing systems should perhaps have been the first priority. Moreover, the dangers of promulgating policies which fail to include information on their costs, and sources of funding, have been discussed.

Around 2007, a certain sense of despair had crept in as the realisation dawned that tackling the legacy of apartheid education inequalities required far more than simply dismantling the apartheid school funding model, and as it became clear how little South African children were learning, even relative to children in economically less developed African countries. But there were policymakers who set about refocussing the system so that it paid more attention to the effectiveness of classroom practices. These efforts paid off. Learning outcomes improved, according to the international testing programmes, and the improvements were large by international standards, though off a very low base.

How were the improvements achieved? In answering this question, it is important to bear in mind that not all educational change is the result of policy change. The fact that the education levels of adults in the households of students were increasing would have played a role (Van der Berg and Gustafsson 2017, p. 14). However, it is extremely likely that certain policy changes also played a role. The most impressive of these in terms of actual policy production must be the introduction of the CAPS curriculum guides, which brought to an end a period during which schools had struggled with the overly open-ended and largely impractical 'outcomes based education' curriculum. The CAPS guides, whose production clearly involved bringing together a large number of experts, attest to the ability of the national authorities to manage complex policymaking processes.

Two other interventions probably also contributed to the improvement. One was an ambitious programme aimed at providing every student in each year with a volu-minous set of full-colour national workbooks. It was not the only initiative aimed at improving access to books, but it was the most visible one. The other intervention was standardised testing aimed at providing a more objective picture of how well schools were performing. However, here good intentions, combined with much operational effort, proved not to be enough, and unions were able to halt the testing programme. This was in part due to a missing piece in the puzzle: a clear policy on the exact purpose of the new assessment system. This gap made the Annual National Assessments programme vulnerable, and created room for confusion.

There is now enough evidence to conclude that South Africa's educational improvement trajectory has slowed down in recent years. TIMSS Grade 9 improvements were around twice as steep between 2002 and 2011, as between 2011 and 2015. Whilst PIRLS pointed to improvements in reading at the primary level between 2006 and 2011, the 2011–2016 trend has been flat. The wider causes for this should be understood. The percentage of South Africans living in poverty, following a long decline up to 2011, has risen in recent years (Statistics South Africa 2017). This is a terrible context in which to be delivering education services, and one which makes further improvements especially difficult. One can only hope that these socio-economic setbacks are a temporary blip in the country's development.

In one important respect, the context for good education policymaking was better in 2017 than it was in 2007. In 2007 there was far less in terms of research, data and over-arching policies to turn to than 10 years later. In 2017, policymakers and education researchers had an imperfect yet substantive and well-focussed National Development Plan and, aligned to this, a long-term basic education sector plan, to frame their work. They had a sizeable volume of research and evaluation reports, and more publicly available data. A valuable 2017 addition to the stock of knowledge was a multi-sector report, funded by Parliament, evaluating existing legislation, specifically its ability to tackle inequality (South Africa: Parliament 2017). That report drew from several background reports, all available on the internet. If this leads to a more evidence-based policy discourse amongst legislators, that would be an important step forward.

So what should policymakers focus on in the next decade or so? What mistakes from the past should be avoided? Of the nine policy topics covered in the previous section, two stand out as both important and as requiring particularly complex policy work. One is policies governing teachers. The other is national assessments and school principal accountability (which has been considered one topic, given the inter-relatedness of the two matters).

Of the two, policy on teachers lags most behind, despite the fact that teachers account for the bulk of spending on schools. It seems South Africa is only beginning to understand the nature of teacher incentives, trade-offs between teacher pay and pupil-teacher ratios, and the need for a holistic policy framework for teachers. The 'one step forward two steps back' phenomenon, whereby apparently groundbreaking policy reforms, with an insufficient conceptual and analytical basis, are followed by a reversal and a breakdown of trust between the employer and unions, needs to be avoided. There is no substitute for careful policy analysis, most of which should be undertaken, by all parties, prior to and outside of the negotiations process. Perhaps an initial undertaking should be a good stocktaking of current conditions and incentives surrounding teachers. The current policy framework is a system which, for all its flaws, works in a basic sense.

Much more work has been done in the area of national assessments and principal accountability, though the link between these two components needs to become clearer. Parliament's review of existing legislation alludes to the technical complexities: in order to produce school-level measures of performance which are comparable over time, both a universal system of testing covering all schools is necessary, and a sample-based system using secure anchor items, essentially questions common across years which are not leaked to the public (South Africa: Parliament 2017, p. 45). Carefully designed overlaps between the universal and sample-based systems are needed, as well as the statistical adjustment of marks. These technicalities have become standard fare in many countries, including several developing countries such as Brazil and Chile. Parliament's review also emphasises the importance of what has been underlined above: a clear policy on the purpose of national assessments. By emphasising within such a policy that the focus is largely on the accountability of schools, and their principals, and not the accountability of individual teachers, union concerns can largely be put to rest.

In the area of curriculum, where much has been achieved over the last 10 years, one important gap remains: proper guidance to teachers on how to teach reading in the early grades. This is an area where the international evidence base, and the South Africa-specific one, are now relatively good. Moreover, this is an area where the risk of disagreements amongst stakeholders is low.

Acknowledgements Work on this chapter is funded by the National Research Foundation.

References

Australian Council for Educational Research. (2013). *Formative evaluation of textbooks and workbooks*. Pretoria: Department of Basic Education.

Bruns, B., Evans, D., & Luque, J. (2012). *Achieving world-class education in Brazil: The next Agenda*. Washington, DC: The World Bank.

Centre for Development and Enterprise. (2009). *International best practice in schooling reform: What can South Africa learn from other countries?* Johannesburg.

Centre for Development and Enterprise. (2015). *Low-fee private schools: International experience and international realities*. Johannesburg.

Crouch, L. (2005). South Africa equity and quality reforms: Possible lessons. *Journal of Education for International Development, 1*(1), 1–18.

Democratic Alliance. (2008). *The DA's policy on education – 'Preparing for Success'*. Cape Town.

Department of Basic Education. (2011). *Integrated strategic planning framework for teacher education and development in South Africa*. Pretoria.

Department of Basic Education. (2014). *The ministerial task team report on the national senior certificate*. Pretoria.

Department of Basic Education. (2015). *Action plan 2019 towards the realisation of schooling 2030: Taking forward South Africa's national development plan 2030*. Pretoria.

Department of Basic Education. (2016a). *Proposals on the re-design of the annual national assessments for 2016 and beyond*. Pretoria.

Department of Basic Education. (2016b). *Report of the ministerial task team appointed by Minister Angie Motshekga to investigate allegations into the selling of posts of educators by members of teachers Unions and Departmental Officials in Provincial Education Departments*. Pretoria.

Department of Basic Education. (2016c). *Report on progress in the schooling sector against key learner performance and attainment indicators*. Pretoria.

Department of Basic Education. (2017). *Summary report: Results of year 2 impact evaluation: The early grade reading study*. Pretoria.

Historic Schools Restoration Project. (2010). *Annual report 2009/2010*. Cape Town.

Howie, S., Venter, E., Van Staden, S., Zimmerman, L., Long, C., Scherman, V., & Archer, E. (2008). *Progress in international reading literacy study (PIRLS) 2006 summary report: South African children's reading literacy achievement*. Pretoria: University of Pretoria, Centre for Evaluation and Assessment.

Howie, S., Combrinck, C., Roux, K., Tshele, M., Mokoena, G., & Palane, N. M. (2017). *PIRLS literacy 2017: South African highlights report*. Pretoria: Centre for Evaluation and Assessment.

Inbar, D. (1996). *Planning for innovation in education*. Paris: UNESCO.

Meyer, I., & Gent, P. (2016). *The status of ICT in education in South Africa and the way forward*. Pretoria: NECT.

Reddy, V., Bhorat, H., Powell, M., Visser, M. M., & Arends, F. (2016). *Skills supply and demand in South Africa*. http://hdl.handle.net/20.500.11910/10186.

Schirmer, S., McCarthy, J., Oliphant, R., & Bernstein, A. (2013). *The missing sector: Contract schools*. Johannesburg.

Sherman, J. D., & Poirier, J. M. (2007). *Educational equity and public policy: Comparing results from 16 countries*. Citeseer.

South Africa: Department of Education. (1995). *White paper on education and training*. Pretoria.

South Africa: Department of Education. (2006). *The national policy framework for teacher education and development in South Africa*. Pretoria.

South Africa: Department of Planning, Monitoring and Evaluation. (2014). *The impact of the introduction of Grade R on learning outcomes*. Pretoria.

South Africa: Department of Planning, Monitoring and Evaluation. (2016). *Funza Lushaka Bursary programme implementation evaluation*.

South Africa: Parliament. (2017). *Report of the high level panel on the assessment of key legislation and the acceleration of fundamental change*. Cape Town: South Africa: Parliament.

South African Council for Educators. (2012). *The status of the CPTD management system: A report based on the pilot*. Pretoria: SACE.

South African Democratic Teachers Union. (2008). *SADTU national general council 22–25 October 2008 resolutions*. Kempton Park: SADTU.

Spaull, N. (2016). Excessive class sizes in the foundation phase. Policy Brief Research on Socioeconomic Policy (RESEP) (Online). Available: www.resep.sun.ac.za

Statistics South Africa. (2017). *Poverty trends in South Africa: An examination of absolute poverty between 2005 and 2015*. Pretoria.

UNESCO. (2014). *Education for all global monitoring report 2013/4: Teaching and learning: Achieving quality education for all*. Paris: United Nations Educational, Scientific and Cultural Organization.

Van der Berg, S., & Gustafsson, M. (2017). *Quality of basic education. A report to working group 1 of the high level panel on the assessment of key legislation*. Stellenbosch University.

Van der Berg, S., Spaull, N., Wills, G., Gustafsson, M., & Kotzé, J. (2016). *Identifying binding constraints in education* (SSRN Scholarly Paper ID 2906945). Rochester, NY: Social Science Research Network.

Van der Berg, S., Van Wyk, C., Burger, R., Kotzé J, Piek, M., & Rich, K. (2017). The performance of low fee independent schools in South Africa – What can available data tell?.

Wildeman, R., & Hemmer-Vitti, R. (2010). *Where to for provincial education?: Reviewing provincial education budgets 2006 to 2012*. African Books Collective.

World Bank. (2018). *World development report 2018: Learning to realize education's promise*. Washington, DC: World Bank.

Zille, H. (2013). *Well done, Angie Motshekga*. Available from: https://m.news24.com [Accessed January 2018].

Chapter 4
Educational Funding and Equity in South African Schools

Shireen Motala and David Carel

4.1 Introduction

This chapter addresses the questions of equity and inequality in the South African primary and secondary school system, with specific reference to the distribution of financial resources. The concepts of equity and inequality are of particular importance in South African policy discourse. While there has been progress towards equity, equality and redress in post-apartheid South Africa, the reality, noted by the National Planning Commission (2011), is that an estimated 48% of the population live on less than 2 US dollars a day, and that, at 0.67, the Gini coefficient is the highest in the world. The South African unemployment rate was 28% in 2017, the highest since 2004 (Statistics South Africa 2017).

The concepts of equity and equality are of particular concern in South African policy discourse, not least due to the slippage between these two concepts and that of discrimination (Motala and Pampallis 2001; Sayed 2002). Equality has to do with sameness or, in public policy terms, non-discrimination (Rawls 1972; Secada 1989), whereas the concept of equity that is utilized in this chapter is informed by Van der Berg's (2001) distinction between discrimination and inequality, Samoff's distinction between equity and inequality, Sayed's (2002) work on distributional justice, and Weber's (2002) view that equality helps us to define the specificity of equity. Drawing in particular on Rawls's (2001) later work, together with the work of Fraser (1997) and Gewirtz (1998), and seeking to differentiate between social justice and redistributive justice, and the conditions under which social and

S. Motala (✉)
Postgraduate School, University of Johannesburg, Johannesburg, South Africa
e-mail: smotala@uj.ac.za

D. Carel
Department of Economics, RESEP, Stellenbosch University, Stellenbosch, South Africa
e-mail: davidmcarel@gmail.com

© Springer Nature Switzerland AG 2019
N. Spaull, J. D. Jansen (eds.), *South African Schooling: The Enigma of Inequality*, Policy Implications of Research in Education 10,
https://doi.org/10.1007/978-3-030-18811-5_4

economic inequalities can be addressed, this chapter uses a definition of equality as sameness, and a definition of equity which encompasses social justice and advocates differential distribution to achieve its goals.

Examining equity and inequality in schooling in South Africa, and asking the simple question *How far have we come?*, we argue that while South Africa has made significant strides towards equalisation of resources in public schools and improved resource distribution in pursuing its pro-poor strategy, inequality and inequity persist. This is because of historical inequalities between provinces, the national finance redistribution model, the distribution of teacher qualifications in terms of the post-provisioning model, and private expenditure in public schooling, utilized to fund significant quality and efficiency differentials.

We begin with an overview of school finance history and policy in South Africa. We then present a detailed account of the current state of equity in school funding using new analysis of data from national and provincial Education Management Information Systems (EMIS), national and provincial treasuries, educator salary data (Persal), and the SNAP Survey of Ordinary Schools, and conclude with a set of proposals, including potential new financial models, about how to address inequality in the South African schooling system.

By providing an in-depth analysis of the extent and sources of inequalities in school funding we hope to provoke debate over the nature of the steps necessary to equalise funding in schools. We do not claim that changes in funding alone will be sufficient to equalise education outcomes, but more pro-poor funding will be necessary over succeeding decades if there is to be any chance of turning around the vast, failing and largely poverty-stricken schooling system. A quarter of a century into South Africa's transformation, we must urgently explore new ways of advancing equity – financial and otherwise – in the schooling system.

4.2   School Finance and Expenditure in South Africa: An Overview

Central to South Africa's efforts to transform its inequitable system of apartheid into a democratic society was the establishment of a good-quality, equitable and democratic education system. The right to an adequate basic education is enshrined in the South African Constitution, a right that is *immediately* realisable, not progressively realisable like most other positive constitutional rights (1996). South Africa has also ratified various international conventions entrenching the right to education, from the 1989 United Nations Convention on the Rights of the Child, through the African Charter on the Rights and Welfare of the Child, to the Millennium Development Goals, and more recently the Sustainable Development Goals. In terms of these commitments, government is obliged to provide free basic education to all children.

4.2.1 Resource Redistribution: Pro-poor Strategies and Inequality

In the immediate post-apartheid period, a major emphasis was placed on distributing resource inputs through policy and school finance legislation based on the principles of equity and redress. Yet by 1999 it was apparent that the education system continued to be characterized by *rampant inequality* (Education Minister Kader Asmal, in Modiba et al. 1999).

The South African Schools Act (SASA) of 1996 empowered School Governing Body (SGBs) to take *all reasonable measures within (their) means to supplement the resources supplied to the school in order to improve the quality of education provided for all learners at the school* (SASA, Sect. 21). In practice, this translated to the levying of school fees, justified by the limited state resources available for free education, as well as the desire to improve school-level accountability by increasing community control over school resources. User fees in public schooling were also intended as a means of preventing middle class flight from public schools by allowing wealthier, high budget schools within the public schooling system (Colclough 1995; Crouch 1995). It was questionable, however, whether the gap between richer and poorer public schools was closing, and it appeared, too, that the charging of school fees permitted what has been termed the privatisation of public schooling (Department of Education 2003; Fleisch and Woolman 2004; Sayed and Motala 2012).

Seeking to make education more accessible, government first introduced the exemption policy (SASA 1996) and later the *no fee* policy (2006). The latter, a refinement of the Norms and Standards for School Funding (NSSF), required that 60% of available non-personnel resources be distributed to the poorest 40% of learners. These funds, while significant, pale in comparison to personnel expenditure which constitutes over 80% of school spending. Studies have found that the *no fee* policy and the overall pro-poor approach to the financing of education in South Africa have had broadly positive redistributive effects, with the largest increases in allocations directed to poorer schools (Wildeman 2008).

No fee schools made significant revenue gains and were better off even when the loss of fee income was taken into account, while households were relieved of the burden of having to pay fees (Hall 2010; Mestry 2012). Non-personnel allocations through the latest NSSF are highly pro-poor in their structure. In contrast personnel spending, the vast majority of school expenditure across the provinces (explored in more detail below), is largely pro-rich. In addition, the state provides a range of additional provincial and national programmes that largely benefit poor learners, including the National School Nutrition Programme, scholar transport programmes, school infrastructure development, the Mathematics, Science and Technology Grant, the Dinaledi Schools Grant, and others.[1]

---

[1] In several of these programmes, underspending by provincial departments of education is an ongoing major challenge. For instance, see National Council of Provinces finance committee

In 2016/2017, education departments in South Africa spent about R310 billion on basic education (excluding private spending on schools), comprising around 7% of Gross Domestic Product (GDP) and just under 20% of consolidated government expenditure. Although education spending as a proportion of GDP is above the UNESCO benchmark of 6% for developing countries, some 80% of the budget is spent on personnel, suggesting that spending on other inputs is below international norms (UNICEF 2017). Such other inputs include government expenditure on school feeding schemes, school infrastructure, scholar transport, and other programmes primarily serving poor learners.

Despite these significant strides towards the equalisation of resources in public schools, inequality and inequity persist, due in part to differences in teacher qualifications, inadequate funding for non-personnel items, and differences between SGBs in terms of their capacity to efficiently govern their schools and manage their funds. Unequal performance outcomes continue to be the main differentiator between rich and poor schools and learners. SACMEQ (2010) focussed on education inequality, and noted that the poorest 20% of learners in South Africa perform far worse than their peers in other African countries. In the 15 countries in the region, the poorest learners in South Africa were at 12th place for reading, and 14th for numeracy (Spaull 2013).

Social equity and education equity need to be addressed simultaneously, so that the low quality of education offered in poor communities does not continue to perpetuate their exclusion. In line with Ball's (2003) view of interlocking inequalities, it is clear that the mobilisation of social resources is critical to the reproduction of advantage and disadvantage. Earlier research illustrates that school inputs are more evenly distributed than societal income (Gustafsson and Patel 2006). Simply put, equity in school funding has progressed at a faster pace than equity in our society. Willms (2001) describes this as the *hypothesis of double jeopardy*: people from poor backgrounds are educationally vulnerable, but poor people who live in poor communities are especially vulnerable.

Other research also shows the existence of a new set of class alignments, and new typologies of inequality, based on the ability or inability of parents to contribute financially to their children's education. While the anticipated middle class flight from public schools has not taken place, the emerging deracialised middle class has taken full advantage of better-resourced public schools. The poor continue to be the worst off in terms of combined public and private expenditure. At each end of the spectrum are learners who are vastly worse off (indicating greater internal differentiation within the poor), or much better off, than their peers (Motala 2013a,b).

Provincial departments of education inherited vast levels of inequality, reflected in the composition of their school systems. Table 4.1 below illustrates the variation in the socio-economic status of schools across provinces. Using quintile as a proxy

meeting Eastern Cape 2017/18 budget outcomes: Provincial Treasury briefing, https://pmg.org. za/committee-meeting/26375/, 15 May 2018.

Table 4.1 Percentage of
learners in each quintile by
province

	Quintile						
	1	2	3	4	5	Q1-3	Q4-5
EC	33.3	19.8	39.5	2.9	4.5	92.6	7.4
FS	31.4	24.2	26.2	7.7	10.5	81.8	18.2
GP	15.6	14.6	21.7	17.8	30.3	51.9	48.1
KZ	21.3	24.9	25.8	16.2	11.8	72.0	28.0
LP	35.0	39.6	21.9	0.8	2.7	96.5	3.5
MP	24.5	26.4	21.3	15.7	12.1	72.2	27.8
NC	25.8	18.0	22.3	13.9	20.1	66.0	34.0
NW	28.0	20.0	39.9	10.1	2.0	87.9	12.1
WC	9.4	13.2	16.6	26.6	34.2	39.2	60.8

Sources: EMIS National Ordinary Schools 2016 Quarter
4 (Department of Basic Education); 2015 SNAP Survey
of Ordinary Schools. Own analysis of the microdata

for fee-charging status, Limpopo and the Eastern Cape have 98% and 96% no
fee schools respectively. The Western Cape and Gauteng have 56% and 48%,
respectively, in fee charging schools. Looking at learner population, Limpopo has
just 2.7% of its learners in quintile 5 schools, whereas the figure in the Western Cape
is 34.2%. In terms of the wealth base of parents in schools, there is vast inequality
across the provinces.

4.3   Provincial Inequalities: The Intractable Legacy

4.3.1   How Equitable Is the Equitable Share Formula (ESF)?

The Equitable Share Formula (ESF) is calculated with the following weights:
education 48%; health 27%; basic component (derived from each province's share
of the national population) 16%; institutional (5%); and poverty (3%). Though the
formula has an education component, provinces decide how they allocate their total
allocation between spending priorities, including education (Table 4.2).

One ongoing critique of the ESF that is highly relevant to the school funding
debate, and also applies to the provision of other social services, is that the poverty
component of the formula is much too small, given the disproportionate poverty
burden that some provinces bear. An increase in the weight of the poverty allocation
of the formula would result in significantly more funds available to provinces that
inherited a much larger share of the nation's poverty in the transition. It would not
guarantee, but only provide the opportunity for this funding to increase education
spending in these provinces.

Second, the ESF does not sufficiently account for the increased real costs of the
provision of labour, goods and services in rural provinces. For instance, the large
costs of lower learner-educator ratios in small rural schools and the increased non-

Table 4.2 Equitable Share allocations by province to provincial education departments (2016/2017), in descending level of provincial poverty

Province	Actual ESF share allocation (R million)	% of equitable share allocated to education
Limpopo	48,709	50.6%
Eastern Cape	58,060	48.6%
North West	28,062	45.7%
Mpumalanga	33, 450	48.5%
Kwazulu-Natal	87,898	47.7%
Free State	22,995	46.5%
Northern Cape	10,863	43.9%
Gauteng	79,600	46.3%
Western Cape	41,062	42.5%

Source: McLaren (2016), Funding Basic Education (modified)

personnel costs of material resource provision to remote areas creates a significantly higher cost of education in rural provinces. In real terms, rural provinces have less discretionary funding left after such expenses are taken into account, both in education and other social service expenditure. As a result, on top of their elevated share of the country's poverty, rural provinces are allocated disproportionately less from the state to budget for the total basket of social services, with education being the largest component. This is not to say that all improvements to the ESF and its implementation would increase funding to poorer provinces. For instance, the rapid increase in population flows, e.g. into Gauteng, must also be accommodated. The accuracy of learner enrolment data by province, in particular the enrolment by age, must improve for the ESF to be calculated fairly.[2]

4.3.2 Inequalities in Personnel Expenditure

Personnel expenditure remains one of the least redistributive components of school funding, despite being overwhelmingly the largest. The Post Provisioning Norms do include a pro-poverty component, allowing Heads of Department to reserve 5% of total posts for redressing poverty,[3] and most of those posts are reserved for the poorest schools in each province. However, across most provinces personnel distribution and expenditure still remains pro-rich. As Table 4.3 indicates, in seven of the nine provinces the wealthiest schools spend more per learner on personnel than the poorest schools in the province. The Eastern Cape spends 15% more on

---

[2]Personal communication with Martin Gustafsson.

[3]Post Distribution Model formula, in Annexure 1 of the Employment of Educators Act, Amended by Regulation 1451.

Table 4.3 Personnel expenditure per learner using public funds by quintile and province in 2016

	Quintile					Non-fee Charging	Fee charging	
	1	2	3	4	5	Q1-3 average	Q4-5 average	% difference
EC	R 7 222	R 8 217	R 7 897	R 8 485	R 9 345	R 7 778	R 8 915	15%
FS	R 9 286	R 7 942	R 8 259	R 8 884	R 9 697	R 8 495	R 9 291	9%
GP	R 7 471	R 7 344	R 7 419	R 7 463	R 7 624	R 7 411	R 7 543	2%
KZ	R 8 338	R 8 263	R 8 225	R 8 329	R 8 941	R 8 275	R 8 635	4%
LP	R 8 445	R 8 362	R 8 223	R 8 453	R 8 099	R 8 343	R 8 276	-1%
MP	R 8 225	R 8 058	R 8 257	R 8 223	R 8 901	R 8 179	R 8 562	5%
NC	R 8 210	R 7 912	R 8 031	R 8 732	R 8 508	R 8 050	R 8 620	7%
NW	R 8 033	R 7 908	R 7 992	R 9 175	R 8 928	R 7 977	R 9 051	13%
WC	R 8 255	R 7 495	R 7 609	R 7 405	R 7 893	R 7 786	R 7 649	-2%

Sources: Persal 2016 (annual dataset), provided by the Department of Basic Education. (The authors are very grateful to the Department of Basic Education for providing access to the Persal dataset for analysis in this chapter, without which this detailed exploration of school funding would not be possible.) EMIS National Ordinary Schools 2016 Quarter 4. Own analysis of the microdata. Personnel expenditure is calculated as total cost to the departments of education, including benefits such as pension fund contributions. Employees in the Persal dataset whose school EMIS number did not match EMIS numbers in the EMIS National Ordinary Schools dataset were omitted from the analysis

educators in quintile 4–5 schools than those in quintile 1–3 schools. This spending pattern occurs for a number of reasons outlined below.

4.3.3 More Highly Qualified Educators in Wealthier Schools

In addition to SGBs in wealthier schools being able to hire more educators and support staff using private funding, wealthier schools consistently attract more highly qualified educators and other staff. Because salary is in part pegged to qualification level, this means that personnel expenditure in wealthier schools is much higher than in poorer schools. Moreover, Van der Berg (2012) observes that the main differences between the quintiles are the quality and efficiency differentials of educators, resulting in higher overall performance outcomes.

Table 4.4 and Fig. 4.1 reveal the extent to which schools in the top two quintiles consistently attract educators with higher levels of qualification. As a result, in all provinces, schools in the wealthiest areas consistently have more highly qualified staff than schools in poor areas. Gauteng has the least pro-rich gradient of teacher qualification: schools in quintiles 1–4 on average report the same levels of educator qualification; and the gap in Gauteng between average educator qualification in quintile 5 and non-fee charging schools is the lowest among the provinces.

Table 4.4 Average educator
relative qualification value
(REQV) level disaggregated
by province and quintile

	Quintile				
	1	2	3	4	5
EC	13.8	13.8	13.9	14.0	14.1
FS	13.5	13.8	13.9	13.9	14.1
GP	14.0	14.0	14.0	14.0	14.1
KZ	13.7	13.8	14.1	14.2	14.3
LP	13.9	13.9	14.0	14.1	14.1
MP	13.9	14.0	14.1	14.0	14.1
NC	13.4	13.5	13.7	13.8	13.8
NW	13.78	13.8	13.9	14.1	14.1
WC	13.7	13.9	13.9	13.8	14.0

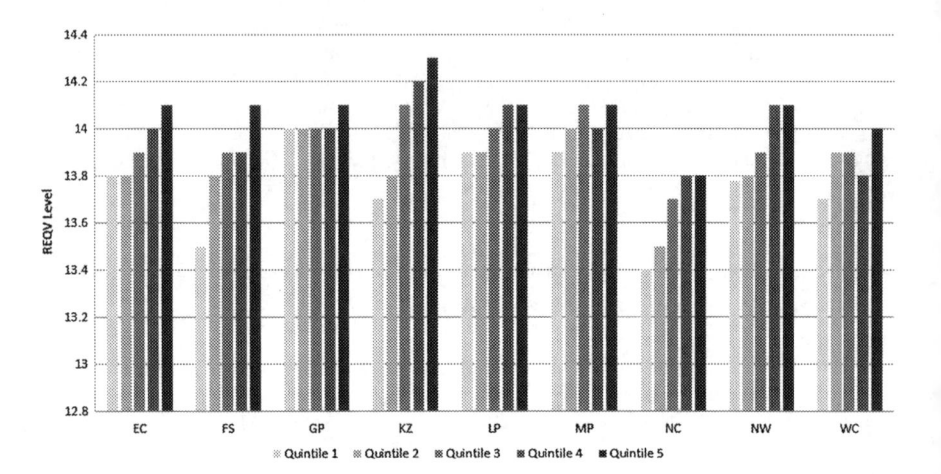

Fig. 4.1 Average educator relative qualification value (REQV) level disaggregated by province and quintile. (Sources: Persal 2016; EMIS National Ordinary Schools 2016 Quarter 4. Own analysis of the microdata)

The same patterns occur with school principals, as seen in Table 4.5 and Fig. 4.2. On average, fee-charging schools attract and hire more highly qualified teachers, as measured by REQV levels, roughly tracking the level of post-secondary education and training attained. For ease of reference REQVIS would be a bachelor's degree in education (B.Ed) with an honours degree, i.e matric plus 5 years hence REQVIS. The North West, Eastern Cape, and Western Cape see the largest gaps in principal qualification between quintiles 1 and 5. Mpumalanga and Gauteng have the smallest principal qualification gaps.

Table 4.5 Average principal relative qualification value (REQV) level disaggregated by province and quintile	Quintile				
	1	2	3	4	5
EC	14.1	14.1	14.4	14.7	14.7
FS	14.7	15.1	15.1	14.8	15.0
GP	15.1	15.2	15.1	15.0	15.2
KZ	14.7	14.8	15.0	15.0	15.2
LP	14.6	14.7	14.8	14.7	14.8
MP	15.0	15.1	15.1	15.1	15.1
NC	14.4	14.7	14.7	14.7	14.7
NW	14.5	14.7	14.8	14.9	15.3
WC	14.4	14.7	14.9	14.9	15.1

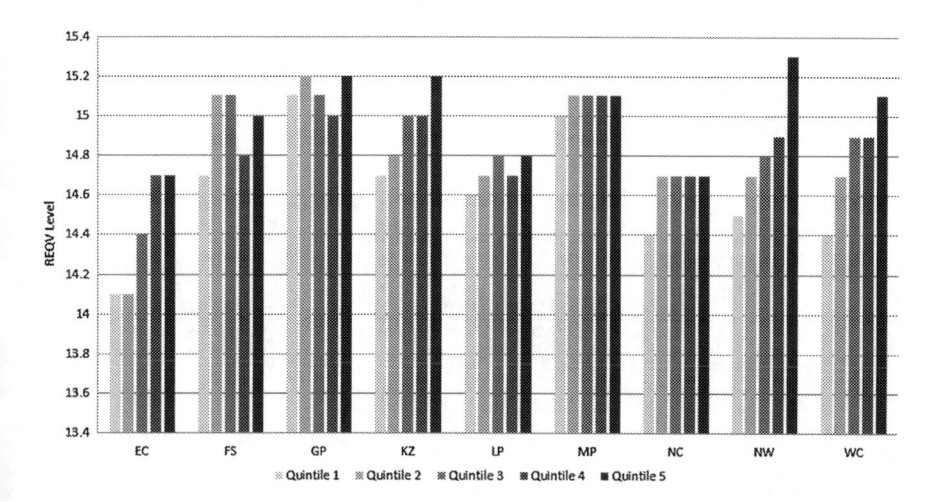

Fig. 4.2 Average principal relative qualification value (REQV) level disaggregated by province and quintile. (Sources: Persal 2016; EMIS National Ordinary Schools 2016 Quarter 4. Own analysis of the microdata)

4.4 Differential Weighting of Learners in Personnel Distribution

There are other potential sources of inequality in the distribution of educators that warrant further research and policy consideration. For instance, due to greater access to diagnosis, wealthy schools on average report learners with disabilities at higher rates than their peers. Inclusive education needs in schools are determined through the current post provisioning norms (PPN). Learners with disabilities are weighted three to six times more than other students in the model. The more diagnoses a school can make, which requires both financial and technical resources, the higher the per learner number of educators assigned to their school under the PPN.

A similar phenomenon occurs through the disproportionate weighting of certain subjects, such as higher personnel weights for drama and music. Wealthier public schools offer such subjects at significantly higher rates than poorer schools, resulting in further inequalities in educator placement and funding, despite the intended goals of redress in the post distribution model outlined above. This is not to say that learners with disabilities must not be receive the resources they need to thrive in school; quite the contrary, it affirms that all learners with disabilities, regardless of school resources, must receive the support they need. But in the current non-ideal scenario where wealthier schools are able to diagnose and report learners with disabilities at higher rates than their peers, additional research is needed to determine the most appropriate policy alternatives that uphold the rights of all learners without exacerbating resource inequalities.

4.4.1 User Fees: Contributors to Important Quality and Equity Differences

In South Africa, debates over the appropriate balance between the roles of government, other socio-political institutions and the market have been taken up in relation to issues of decentralisation and community participation (Grant Lewis and Motala 2004; Dyer and Rose 2005), particularly how and whether education equity targets can or have been met through state-led provision and private contributions.

Furthermore, what about those who cannot afford to pay fees at all, or only minimal fees? The market has responded to this in South Africa by creating a range of low cost private school options catering for families who cannot get their children into good public schools, but who can afford to pay fees. The proponents of low cost private schools (CDE 2016) argue in terms of promoting access and quality. There are risks attached to this approach, particularly how private forms of schooling affect the social functions of education, or the idea of the public good. To what extent does increasing private sector involvement imply that the state is relinquishing its responsibilities, particularly the social rights of all citizens? (Samoff 2017; Sayed 2016).

The effect of private forms of schooling on the public good is dependent on the nature of existing social and economic inequalities. Historical racial stratification of the education market has produced bifurcation and internal privatisation of wealthy public schools, with the logic of choice driving increased movement through quality levels in the system (Dieltiens and Motala 2008; Fataar 2015; Sayed 2016). In this context, privatisation results in further differentiation. The notion that enlightened self-interest best propels the public good can have only a limited effect in a context of systemic inequalities which push back against equity-driven interventions such as progressive funding policies. In this sense the individual choices made by parents have knock-on effects on the chances of others in the system (Grant Lewis and Motala 2004; Pedró et al. 2015).

Table 4.6 Annual school fees charged by decile

Decile	1–5	6	7	8	9	10
Fees charged	0	800	2475	8800	18,980	170,202

Research suggests that equality of educational opportunity has been significantly affected by the presence of school fees, in particular the levels of fees paid by those in quintile 4 and 5 schools (Fiske and Ladd 2004; Chutgar and Kanjee 2009). A survey of 2000 schools in Gauteng found that school fees supported important quality and efficiency differentials, lowering learner-educator ratios due to the employment of more educators (Motala 2006, 2009).

The quality of data on fees charged by schools nationally varies greatly by year and is widely regarded as incomplete and inaccurate. The Western Cape is not representative of all provinces due to its relative wealth and large number of fee-charging schools. It nonetheless offers the most accurate data on fees charged by public and independent schools. It serves below as a case study for understanding the contribution of private funding to the public system, as well as a testing ground for exploring potential policy alternatives to the current funding model.

4.5 Overview of School Fees in the Western Cape

In 2017, 45% of schools in the Western Cape reported charging fees, notably higher than most provinces. However, only a small portion of these schools charge much more than the state subsidy. Sixty percent of schools in the province charge R800 or less per annum. Only 10% of schools in the province charge R18 980 or more per annum (Table 4.6).

Total estimated fees raised by schools in the Western Cape is R4.4 Billion.[4] The total Western Cape Education Department (WCED) adjusted appropriation 2016/2017 was R19.53 billion. Private fees are equivalent to an estimated 19.9% of the provincial education budget (Table 4.7).

4.6 Personnel, Non-personnel and Private Fee Contributions

While state expenditure on public schooling has equalised to a large degree, and so thereby has racial equity, private contributions have offset this equalisation (Motala 2006). Figure 4.3 shows the disaggregated personnel, non-personnel and private fee allocations by quintile in the Western Cape.

---

[4]Calculated as total 2017 enrolment multiplied by fees charged per learner, minus an estimated 10% non-payment or exemption rate.

Table 4.7 Public funding source by quintile in the Western Cape (per learner)

Quintile	Non-personnel	Personnel	Fees	Total
1	1065	9443	989	11,497
2	1028	7938	1262	10,228
3	1023	7810	571	9404
4	817	7796	2201	10,814
5	282	8176	12039	20,498

Sources: Western Cape Provincial Treasury Gazette 116/2017; Persal 2016 provided by Department of Basic Education; Western Cape EMIS (wcedemis.pgwc.gov.za); EMIS National Ordinary Schools 2016 Quarter 4. Own analysis of the microdata

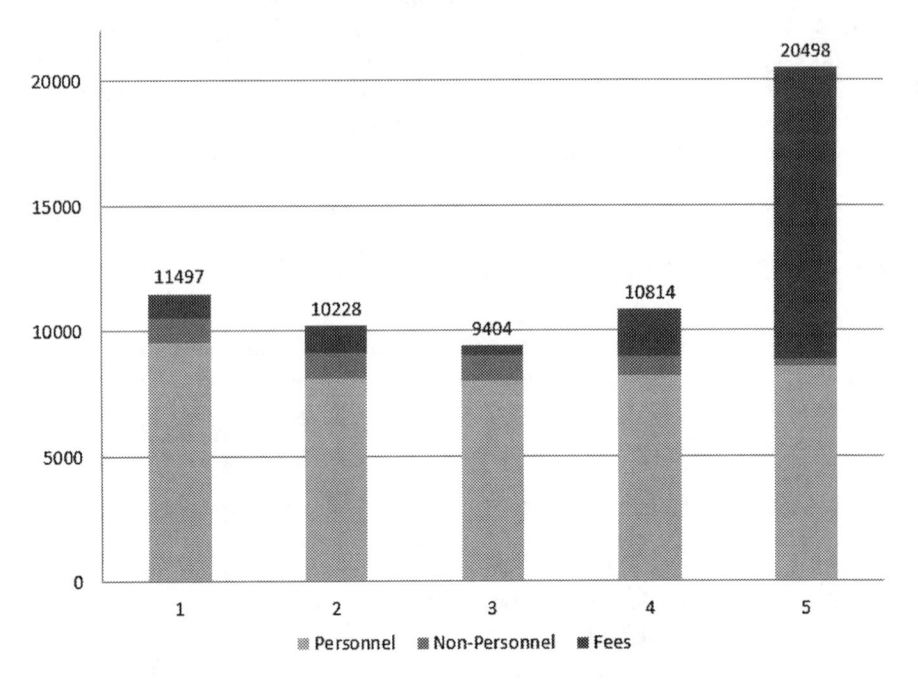

Fig. 4.3 Non-personnel expenditure, personnel expenditure, and private fees by quintile in the Western Cape (per learner). (Sources: Provincial Gazette; Persal 2016; Western Cape EMIS; EMIS National Ordinary Schools 2016 Quarter 4. Own analysis of the microdata)

Particularly in Gauteng and the Western Cape, parental contributions continue to be the main determinant of differentiation within the public schooling sector. Differences in personnel expenditure and non-personnel funding allocation by the state are dwarfed by the size of private contributions in the wealthiest schools. The role of school governing bodies, and the promise that decentralised and strengthened governance and self-managing schools would lead to greater equity, has not materialised (Motala and Pampallis 2005; Prew 2011).

4.7   Public School Expenditure Using Private Funds

The impact of private fees on education inputs is best illustrated through the data publicly available on SGB-paid staff in schools. We often speak in general terms about private fees outweighing the state redistribution of funds through the tiered quintile system, and how fees can supplement resources provided by the state. The SNAP Survey of Ordinary Schools, an annual study by the DBE of all schools in the system, hints at the extent to which schools are able to use school fees to increase the resources available in their schools, specifically human resources.

The hiring of additional staff by SGBs is used here as proxy for the magnitude of private contributions to schools. The salaries of staff members hired by SGBs are determined privately and are not reported to the DBE in the SNAP survey. As a result, the exact magnitude of the funding implications cannot be determined. Given that wealthier schools can, on average, afford to pay additional teachers higher salaries, it is likely that the figures below significantly underestimate the funding inequalities that are represented by differences in SGB-hired staff.

It is important to note that in the SNAP Survey data, we see many non-fee schools reporting SGB-paid educators and support staff. In 2015 quintile 5 schools reported 2.8 times as many SGB-paid educator posts in their schools per learner as quintile 3 schools, and 2.1 times as many as quintile 1 schools (Table 4.8).

There is a similar pattern with practitioners and administrative support staff (Table 4.9). Quintile 5 schools consistently use privately raised funds to hire additional support staff. In 2015, quintile 5 schools reported double the administrative staff per learner as quintile 3 schools and 2.2 times the number of SGB-paid practitioners per learner.

These data indicate that learner educator ratios are significantly more favourable in wealthier schools. If only state-paid employees are examined, the disparity in

Table 4.8 Average number of educators employed by School Governing Bodies disaggregated by province and quintile

	Quintile				
	1	2	3	4	5
EC	2.9	2.2	1.9	1.1	2.5
FS	1.1	0.0	0.1	1.0	1.5
GP	0.0	0.0	0.0	0.4	6.0
KZ	1.0	0.9	0.3	1.4	4.1
LP	1.0	0.7	0.4	0.3	1.0
MP	0.4	0.3	0.2	0.3	1.4
NC	0.1	0.1	0.2	0.3	0.5
NW	0.5	0.2	0.7	1.4	0.2
WC	2.0	1.4	1.2	3.0	13.3

Source: 2015 SNAP Survey of Ordinary Schools, accessed through University of Cape Town DataFirst. Own analysis of the microdata

Table 4.9 Administrative staff employed by school SGB disaggregated by province and quintile

	Quintile				
	1	2	3	4	5
EC	0.6	0.8	0.3	0.1	0.5
FS	0.0	0.0	0.0	0.1	0.2
GP	0.0	0.0	0.0	0.1	0.9
KZ	0.1	0.1	0.1	0.1	0.7
LP	0.4	0.6	0.2	0.1	0.3
MP	0.1	0.1	0.1	0.0	0.4
NC	0.1	0.0	0.0	0.0	0.1
NW	0.3	0.1	0.2	0.3	0.1
WC	2.2	0.5	0.3	0.6	2.4

Source: 2015 SNAP Survey of Ordinary Schools, accessed through University of Cape Town DataFirst. Own analysis of the microdata

Table 4.10 Learner-educator ratios by province (excluding SGB educators)

	Quintile				
	1	2	3	4	5
EC	31.5	28.0	33.8	34.3	33.5
FS	26.0	32.4	31.6	32.2	31.8
GP	38.8	39.0	38.5	38.3	39.3
KZ	30.1	31.3	33.9	34.2	33.4
LP	31.5	32.0	33.5	34.5	37.5
MP	31.3	32.7	32.9	33.3	33.9
NC	32.0	34.6	34.6	33.7	34.2
NW	33.3	34.0	34.8	32.0	34.1
WC	33.0	37.8	37.2	38.3	37.7

Source: 2015 SNAP Survey of Ordinary Schools. Own analysis of the microdata

learner-educator ratios is not particularly large and in most cases is quite pro-poor (Table 4.10). Once SGB-paid educators are considered, a pattern of much higher learner-educator ratios in poorer schools becomes apparent (Table 4.11).

Given the consistent findings in the literature about the significance of teachers in the classroom and adequate administration staff this particular form of inequality is likely to contribute to the inequalities in performance seen throughout the school system.

4.8 Exploring Alternative Policy Proposals

There remain many questions about whether the pro-poor and no fee policies are genuinely on track towards fundamental transformation or whether they are merely ameliorating, without overcoming, existing funding inequities. For example,

Table 4.11 Learner-educator ratios by province (including SGB educators)

	Quintile				
	1	2	3	4	5
EC	30.2	26.9	32.1	23.2	19.7
FS	24.7	30.9	30.3	24.8	21.3
GP	38.6	38.7	37.9	36.1	27.9
KZ	29.8	30.8	33.4	31.8	26.4
LP	30.9	31.6	33.0	26.7	23.8
MP	30.8	31.8	32.6	32.1	26.8
NC	32.0	33.4	33.7	30.9	29.7
NW	32.6	33.4	34.1	23.6	23.9
WC	30.4	35.4	35.4	34.5	23.8

Source: 2015 SNAP Survey of Ordinary Schools, accessed through University of Cape Town DataFirst. Own analysis of the microdata

in relation to the fee exemption policy, schools largely do not receive sufficient compensatory funding for exempted learners, creating a disincentive for schools to inform parents of this right (Hall 2010; Sayed 2016). Similarly, the no fee policy is unlikely to have a major impact on physical access to education, since South Africa already boasts a high net enrolment rate. For the policy's pro-poor effects to come fully into play, much more attention will have to be paid to improving the quality of education at all schools, no fee schools above all.

As in a number of other developing countries, massification of education has not led to an improvement in education quality. While fiscal resource inputs are not the only means to the desired educational outcomes, they do, however, have an effect on learner performance. Fiscal resources do not necessarily translate into scarce real resources (qualified teachers and school management) required to improve school performance, and even where resources are available, their effective utilization is not guaranteed.

The most significant challenge in school financing and equity in South Africa is the ability of government to deal with issues of adequacy rather than school fees (Amsterdam 2006; Fiske and Ladd 2004). This entails a strongly redistributive element, focusing on differential need rather than on available fiscal resources. Adequacy as a funding principle gives substance and content to the right of access to education.

In the South African context, a lack of clarity about how to calculate adequacy and the frequent focus only on non-personnel costs has meant that determinations of adequacy have been severely limited. Though continuous costing is being done by the Department of Basic Education, the Financial and Fiscal Commission, the National Treasury and the National Planning Commission, there is still no firm evidence that the current costing per learner is correctly estimated and that the national pro poor funding framework is sufficient.

A more robust framework worth considering would be a school allocation that favours individual poor learners, wherever and in whatever school they may be. An even more significant development would be a funding equity framework that targets not only the 20% non-personnel expenditure but the entire gamut of state education spending, nationally and provincially, including personnel expenditure in particular.

Using the Western Cape as a case study, given the unique availability of relatively accurate fees data, it is possible to model the implications of a new, much more pro-poor non-personnel fee allocation.

The WCED currently allocates R40.4 million in non-personnel funding to schools. If all non-personnel funding allocated for schools with fees greater than R8000 were reallocated to non-fee schools, it would result in an additional 8% increase in their non-personnel expenditure. A potential reduction in state subsidy for fee paying schools would of course require a commensurate compensation by fee paying parents. The plausibility of such a proposal depends on the size of this necessary contribution and the likelihood of parents and others paying fees withstanding such a shift. If these non-personnel funds were reallocated to no-fee schools, on average those paying fees would see an increase of only R123 per learner per year.

Alternatively, state funding – both personnel and non-personnel – could be made inversely related to private funds, or certain thresholds could be set to prevent state funds from reaching schools that raise more than a certain amount of money privately. For instance, if 5% of all public funding allocated for schools with fees greater than R20,000 were reallocated to non-fee charging primary schools, it would result in an additional R1,213 per learner. To put this in context, the Early Grade Reading Study, the most effective evidence based large scale reading intervention in the region, costs only R557 per learner, which will significantly decline as the intervention reaches scale (Taylor S, 2019; in this volume). This policy shift could pay for EGRS for every learner at non-fee charging schools in the province more than twice over.

These types of interventions would make current quintile 5 schools more *private* than they currently are, in a sense. The social and political implications of this must be explored in addition to the numerical consequences for school funding. Moreover, such policies would have more significant redistributive implications for wealthier provinces like Gauteng and the Western Cape given their relative proportion of high fee-charging schools. One could consider cross-subsidizing models to account for this, shifting portions of state funds allocated to extremely high fee-charging schools in wealthier provinces to non-fee charging schools in poorer provinces. Shifting funding to learners in need is not the only way to rethink equity in school resources; in a system where school quality is known to largely determine one's outcome in life, we must also consider moving less advantaged learners to higher resourced, more effective schools. To increase access by less privileged learners to higher quality education, the state should create more opportunities for schools to enrol children from different communities. The current soft zoning catchment policy, which prescribes that first preference be given to children in the immediate catchment area, results in schools being populated by the middle class with its great advantage in cultural capital. The recommended change of strategy would address poverty and disadvantage as well as accessibility and choice.

A revised policy could, for instance, require a minimum number of spaces to be allocated for the poorest learners at highly effective schools. There is global precedent for such policies: for instance, in a landmark 2011 judgement, the Supreme Court in India upheld a similar law that required nearly all the nation's private schools to reserve 25% of their intake for learners from disadvantaged backgrounds. These types of policies could apply in South Africa within the public system alone, or in both the public and private systems, though the latter would require more radical legislative action. The number of seats reserved for poor learners could be pegged at the fee level of the school. Each learner would represent a greater offset of state funds given the greater relative private contribution compared to state funding through personnel expenditure. Such schools have a much larger pool of wealth from which to draw, making the families more likely to be able to absorb the costs of additional poorer learners, similar to the way that fee exemptions are intended to work.

Colclough (1995) and Crouch (1995) recommended a policy along these lines in their influential recommendations to the Department of Education at the advent of democracy in South Africa: *each school could be asked to reserve a certain percentage [of poor learners] ... Exclusion [of poor learners] would then be due not to inability to pay but to the school's being too crowded* (Crouch 1995, p. 12). At the time, this element in their proposals was rejected (Fiske and Ladd 2004). However, given the urgent need to improve education outcomes for disadvantaged learners in the country, it is time to revisit this and similar policy recommendations.

There is an urgent need for better evidence to understand whether Crouch (1995) and Colclough's (1995) conclusion, that *wealth* flight would result in reduced support for state education, is likely to occur in South Africa today. If such a policy were to be introduced, we understand very little about what the likelihood, prevalence, or precise causes of wealth flight would be, nor have we sufficiently explored possible ways to mitigate it. There are several specific lines of research that could be prioritised to ensure we thoroughly explore such policy options.

4.9 Conclusion

A number of strategies have been put in place since the transition to address the many seemingly intractable problems in South African schooling, and to realise the goals of equitable and quality education. Above all, it is essential to affirm and embed the notion that education is a public good, and foreground the view that equity and justice must drive education reform. Redistributing school funding is assumed to neither be a panacea, nor a sufficient condition for improving education equity in the system. Rather, it marks a necessary step in exploring how the state could catalyse a transformation to a more just and equitable schooling system.

References

Amsterdam, C. (2006). Adequacy in the South African context: A concept analysis. *Perspectives in Education, 24*(2), 25–34.

Ball, S. J. (2003). *The more things change: Educational research, social class and'interlocking'Inequalities*. Institute of Education London.

CDE. (2016). *Low cost private schools*. Centre for Development Enterprise, Johannesburg.

Chutgar, A., & Kanjee, A. (2009). *School Money Funding Flaws, 7*(4), 18–19. http://hdl.handle.net/20.500.11910/4546

Colclough, C. (1995). *Report to the Department of Education*. Tech. rep., Department of Education, Pretoria.

Crouch, L. (1995). *School funding options and medium-term budgeting for education in South Africa*. Consultant's Report prepared for the DoE November.

Department of Education. (2003). *Review of the financing, resourcing and costs of the education in public schools*. Report to the Minister, Department of Education, Pretoria.

Dieltiens, V., & Motala, S. (2008). Beyond the ideological cross fire – Private schooling in South Africa. *Southern African Journal of Education, 14*(3), 22–33.

Dyer, C., & Rose, P. (2005). Decentralisation for educational development? An editorial introduction. *Compare: A Journal of Comparative and International Education, 35*(2), 105–113. https://doi.org/10.1080/03057920500129809

Fataar, A. (2015). *Engaging schooling subjectivities across post-apartheid urban spaces*. African SUN Media.

Fiske, E. B., & Ladd, H. F. (2004). *Elusive equity: Education reform in post-apartheid South Africa*. Washington, DC: Brookings Institution Press.

Fleisch, B., & Woolman, S. (2004). On the constitutionality of school fees: A reply to Roithmayr: Research article. *Perspectives in Education, 22*(1), 111–123.

Fraser, N. (1997). J*ustice interruptus: Critical reflections on the "Postsocialist" Condition*. New York: Routledge.

Gewirtz, S. (1998). Conceptualizing social justice in education: Mapping the territory. *Journal of Education Policy, 13*(4), 469–484.

Grant Lewis, S., & Motala, S. (2004). Educational de/centralisation and the quest for equity, democracy and quality. In L. Chisholm (Ed.), *Changing class: Education and social change in post-apartheid South Africa* (pp. 115–143). London/Cape Town: Zed and HSRC.

Gustafsson, M., & Patel, F. (2006). Undoing the apartheid legacy: Pro-poor spending shifts in the South African public school system. *Perspectives in Education, 24*(2), 65–77.

Hall, K. (2010). Children's access to basic services. In L. Jamieson, R. Bray, A. Viviers, L. Lake, S. Pendlebury, & C. Smith (Eds.), *South African Child Gauge 2010/2011* (p. 111). Cape Town: University of Cape Town/Children's Institute.

McLaren, D. (2016). Funding basic education. In: *Basic Education Rights Handbook* (p. Section 27: 49).

Mestry, R. (2012). *A critical analysis of the national norm and standards for school funding policy: Implication for social justice and equities*. Professorial Inauguration Address, University of Johannesburg, 12 June 2012.

Modiba, M., Motala, S., & Vally, S. (1999). "A Call to action": A review of Minister K. Asmal's Educational Priorities. *Quarterly Review of Education and Training in South Africa, 6*, 1–34.

Motala, E., & Pampallis, J. (2001). *Education and equity: The impact of state policies on South African Education*. Heinemann, Johannesburg.

Motala, S. (2006). Education resourcing in post-apartheid South Africa: The impact of finance equity reforms in public schooling: Research article. *Perspectives in Education, 24*(2), 79–93.

Motala, S. (2009). Privatising public schooling in post-apartheid South Africa – Equity considerations. *Compare: A Journal of Comparative and International Education, 39*(2), 185–202. https://doi.org/10.1080/03057920902750459

Motala, S. (2013a). Equity, quality and access in South African education: A work still very much in progress. In R. Southall & P. Naidoo (Eds.), *New South African review 3: The second phase-tragedy or farce* (pp. 221–235)? Johannesburg: Wits University Press.

Motala, S. (2013b). Making rights realities: Education reform in post-apartheid South Africa. In C. Harber (Ed.), *Education in Southern Africa* (pp. 47–67). London: Bloomsbury.

Motala, S., & Pampallis, J. (2005). *Governance and finance in the South African schooling system: the first decade of democracy*. Centre for Education Policy Development.

National Planning Commission. (2011). *Our future – Make it work. National Development Plan 2030. Executive Summary*. Pretoria: Government Printers.

Pedró, F., Leroux, G., & Watanabe, M. (2015). *The privatization of education in developing countries*. Evidence and policy implications, UNESCO Working Papers on Education Policy N 2, UNESCO.

Prew, M. (2011). Socialism and education: 'Peoples education for Peoples power': The rise and fall of an idea in Southern Africa. In T. Griffiths & Z. Miller (Eds.), *Logics of socialist education: Engaging with crisis, insecurity and uncertainty*. Jacana, (pp. 133–153).

Rawls, J. (1972). *A theory of justice*. New York: Oxford University Press.

Rawls, J. (2001). *Justice as fairness: a restatement*. Cumberland: Harvard University Press.

SACMEQ. (2010). *SACMEQ III Project Results: Pupil achievement levels in reading and mathematics. Southern and East African Consortium for Monitoring Educational Quality*. Tech. rep.

Samoff, J. (2017). Personal communication. Port Elizabeth.

Sayed, Y. (2002). Post-apartheid educational transformation: Policy concerns and approaches. In J. Jansen & Y. Sayed (Eds.), *Implementing education policies: The South African experience* (pp. 250–270). Cape Town: UCT Press.

Sayed, Y. (2016). The governance of public schooling in South Africa and the middle class: Social solidarity for the public good versus class interest. *Transformation: Critical Perspectives on Southern Africa, 91*(1), 84–105.

Sayed, Y., & Motala, S. (2012). Equity and 'no fee'schools in South Africa: Challenges and prospects. *Social Policy & Administration, 46*(6), 672–687.

Secada, W. G. (1989). *Equity in education*. London: Falmer Press.

Spaull, N. (2013). Poverty & privilege: Primary school inequality in South Africa. *International Journal of Educational Development, 33*(5), 436–447. https://doi.org/10.1016/j.ijedudev.2012.09.009

Statistics South Africa. (2017). *Quarterly Labour Force Survey (P0211): Quarter 1*. Tech. rep., Pretoria.

Taylor, S. (2019). How can learning inequalities be reduced? Lessons learnt from experimental research in South Africa. In N. Spaull & J. Jansen (Eds.), *South African schooling: The enigma of inequality*. New York: Springer Nature. https://doi.org/10.1007/978-3-030-18811-5_1.

UNICEF. (2017). Education. https://data.unicef.org/topic/education/overview/. Accessed October 2017.

Van der Berg, S. (2001). Resource shifts in South African schools after the political transition. *Development Southern Africa, 18*(4), 405–421.

Van der Berg, S. (2012). *Equity in Education Expenditure*. Stellenbosch Working paper series.

Weber, E. (2002). Shifting to the right: The evolution of equity in the South African government's developmental and education policies, 1990–1999. *Comparative Education Review, 46*(3), 261–290.

Wildeman, R. A. (2008). *Reviewing eight years of the implementation of the school funding norms, 2000 to 2008*. Institute for Democracy in South Africa, Cape Town.

Willms, J. D. (2001). Three hypotheses about community effects. In J. Helliwell (Ed.), *The contribution of investment in human and social capital to sustained economic growth and well-being*. Ottawa: Human Resources Development Canada.

Chapter 5
Early Childhood Development in South Africa: Inequality and Opportunity

Michaela Ashley-Cooper, Lauren-Jayne van Niekerk, and Eric Atmore

5.1 Introduction

In South Africa the majority of young children are adversely impacted by a range of social and economic inequalities. Apartheid, along with the resultant socio-economic inequalities, deprived most South African children of their fundamental socio-economic rights, including access to health care, education, social services and nutrition.

Available evidence indicates that access to quality early childhood development (ECD)[1] programmes play a critical role in offsetting inequalities by protecting children against the effects of poverty, poor nutrition, inadequate health care and lack of education (Van der Gaag and Putcha 2015). Early and appropriate provisioning and interventions make it possible for children to grow and develop to their full potential, resulting in increased primary school enrolment, enhanced school performance, lower repetition and drop-out rates, as well as reducing the need for costly remedial interventions to address developmental lag and social problems later in life (Atmore et al. 2012; Heckman et al. 2010; Department of

---

[1]For the purposes of this chapter, Early Childhood Development (ECD) refers to the physical, cognitive, and socio-emotional development of a child from conception up until the age of six.

M. Ashley-Cooper (✉)
Centre for Early Childhood Development, Claremont, Cape Town, South Africa
e-mail: mashleycooper@cecd.org.za

L.-J. van Niekerk · E. Atmore
Department of Social Development, University of Cape Town, Rondebosch, Cape Town, South Africa
e-mail: lauren.vanniekerk@uct.ac.za; eric.atmore@uct.ac.za

© Springer Nature Switzerland AG 2019
N. Spaull, J. D. Jansen (eds.), *South African Schooling: The Enigma of Inequality*, Policy Implications of Research in Education 10,
https://doi.org/10.1007/978-3-030-18811-5_5

Education 2001). The importance of early childhood development opportunities is thus profound.

More than one third (36%) of the 19.5 million children in South Africa are under the age of 6 (Hall et al. 2016). Of the children below 6 years old, approximately 4 million live in the poorest 40% of households, with the gap between rich and poor widening (Hall et al. 2016; Aubrey 2017). It is these children who live in the poorest conditions that have the least opportunities for growth and development. Poverty often limits a caregiver's ability to engage with their children, with the result that many children in poorer households receive less stimulation and parent-child interaction. These caregivers are also less likely to send their children to centre-based early childhood programmes (Hartinger et al. 2017). Income poverty is critically linked to reduced access to a range of services, compromising the child's right to education, nutrition, health care, and a safe environment.

5.2 Inequality in Early Childhood Development Opportunities

For young children in South Africa there is no equitable access to quality ECD provision and resources, and there is not equitable expenditure on ECD across geographic areas. The South African Early Childhood Review 2017 reveals stark inequalities that exist across the country, with children being exposed to considerable variation in the delivery of essential services based on the area in which they live (Hall et al. 2017). These services include healthcare, social security and education, the absence of which could lead to serious long-term consequences in the well-being, academic ability, and earning potential of South African children (Hall et al. 2017). Consequences of poor access to quality services results in poor maternal and child health (including maternal depression, stunting, and increased HIV rates), lack of nutritional support as well as social support, resulting in poor health and educational outcomes. This variation in service delivery is particularly prominent for children living in rural areas who are more severely marginalised than those living in urban areas.

Studies investigating early learning programmes in South Africa indicate that vulnerable communities most in need of high quality ECD programmes, have the most difficulty in accessing the resources required to realise this (Aubrey 2017). Remoteness of geographic location of many early learning programmes as well as affordability are key contributors to inequality. Striking inequality within the country is further illustrated in the finding that two-thirds of Black African[2] children

---

[2]In South Africa there are generally five racial categories by which people can classify themselves, the last of which is "Unspecified/Other". The other four categories comprise Black African; White; Coloured; Indian/Asian. Population estimates in 2016 showed that of the total South African population (55.9 million people), 80.7% were Black African, 8.8% were Coloured, 8.1% were White, and 2.5% were Indian/Asian (Statistics South Africa [StatsSA] 2015).

live below the poverty line, compared with only 2% of White children (Aubrey 2017).

5.3 Child Outcomes

International research has consistently illustrated the effects of various forms of ECD programming on child outcomes, including significant gains in cognition (Woldehanna and Gebremedhin 2002; Barnett 1995), language development and communication skills (Burchinal et al. 2000), numeracy, health (Barnett 2008), and socio-emotional development (Love et al. 2003). Children who receive a high quality ECD programme score higher across these domains compared to children who receive poor quality or no ECD programme interventions (Burchinal et al. 2016). South African research, although less prolific, shows comparable patterns of effect on child outcomes (Dawes et al. 2012; Gustafsson et al. 2010), including effects on literacy and numeracy (Southern and Eastern African Consortium for Monitoring Educational Quality [SACMEQ] 2011).

International research has also shown the effects of income level and socio-economic background on child outcomes (Rubio-Codina et al. 2015; Davis-Kean 2005; Aughinbaugh and Gittleman 2003). For example Rubio-Codina et al. (2015) found significant disparities in cognitive and language performance between children in the highest and lowest income quintiles[3] in their large scale study of young children, and found that these disparities became larger with age. In South Africa, most recently, researchers found similar effects of income levels on outcomes in young children. For example Dawes et al. (2016) found that performance on all domains, across all developmental areas, was poorest by children in the lowest quintiles and highest for children in the wealthiest quintile. These children from the poorest of backgrounds are thus set to enter formal schooling on significantly unequal footing when compared to their wealthier counterparts.

The interplay between income levels and quality ECD programming on child outcomes is key to understanding the current inequalities in South Africa, and understanding how to reduce these inequalities before the gap is widened in later years. The consequence of this inequality is that children enter the formal school system on an unequal footing with huge discrepancies in their development and school readiness levels. Following this, children go through a dysfunctional formal schooling system in South Africa, where differences in child outcomes in the early years are not remedied, but amplified, thus widening the inequality gap (for example, see Van der Berg et al. 2013; Spaull 2013).

---

[3]Income quintiles refer to the classification of household income according to five quintiles; with Quintile 1 being the poorest 20% of the country's population and Quintile 5 being the wealthiest 20% of the country's population.

Whilst access to ECD provision is crucial, it is generally agreed that "access must be coupled to quality if early childhood programs are to improve child outcomes, particularly in low-income settings." (Biersteker et al. 2016, p. 342). International and local researchers have shown that the quality of an ECD programme significantly affects child outcomes, including better performance on various developmental domains (such as cognitive, language, mathematics and socio-emotional development) and school readiness, with higher quality predicting better school outcomes (Biersteker et al. 2016). As such, it is important to explore those key features within ECD programmes specifically that produce positive child outcomes.

Research shows that, in terms of timing, a higher dosage of quality ECD services is "associated with greater cognitive gains, particularly for children from low-income communities." (Hall et al. 2017, p. 34). Moreover, for optimum child outcomes, a minimum of 15–30 h per week in ECD programmes is required; two years in an ECD programme is better than one year; and children benefit the most if they are enrolled in a quality programme before the age of 4 (Hall et al. 2017).

South African research has also identified which specific interventions are most effective at specific times in a child's development; providing the greatest probability of improving school readiness (Biersteker 2017). Specifically, it was found that non-centre, home-based programmes (including health, nutrition, welfare, protection and psychosocial support) for caregivers and children are effective from birth to 5 years of age. Quality ECD centre programmes are most effective from 18 months to 5 years of age; playgroup programmes with high-dose inputs aligned to school readiness are most effective from 3 to 5 years of age; and ECD practitioner and whole centre/school training and support are most effective for the beneficiary children from 3 to 9 years of age.

For ECD centre and Grade R programmes specifically, research has found that a quality programme should include: qualified and competent staff (a principal and/or supervisor, teachers, assistant teachers, and support staff); a functioning and effective governing body; oversight and support from relevant departments and/or facility managers; a safe and secure building of sufficient size; sufficient and age-appropriate education resources; and sufficient outdoor space for outdoor play. It is important to note that teacher qualification training is not enough to produce effective ECD practices; teachers require practical hands-on training, on-site support by external ECD experts in the field, and fair working conditions as well (Biersteker 2017). The classroom setting should include:

> a wide variety of age-appropriate activities to support development across domains: a focus on language; a balance of free choice and teacher-directed activities; warm teacher-child interaction that promotes learning...the acceptance of cultural diversity and the inclusion of local as well as global materials and content in the programme...and, as far as possible, mother tongue as the medium for learning and teaching. (Biersteker et al. 2016, p. 335)

More specifically, in terms of curriculum that best stimulates child outcomes, ECD learning programmes should utilise curricula that: promotes school readiness by focussing on specific school readiness skills (such as numeracy and literacy skills) as opposed to a more general approach; focuses on specific age-groups and ensures age appropriate content; and provides a balance of large group, small group and free choice activities (Biersteker 2017).

Quality elements of non-centre-based ECD programmes are specifically dependant on the aims and format of the programme itself.[4] Programmes such as playgroups, require similar features as ECD centre programmes. Family outreach home-visiting programmes, on the other hand, require their own set of specific quality elements. For these programmes the following is required: strict recruitment processes; intensive training (including pre-service, in-service training and on-going coaching and support); on-going programme monitoring and evaluation; administration and resource support (Fixsen et al. 2005); structured content and curricula; and fidelity to programme models and structure (Shonkoff et al. 2016). Programmes that work with caregivers directly should also specifically include: regular contact over an extended period of time (for at least a year in duration); a focus on transforming caregivers' attitudes and skills (as opposed to only transforming their knowledge on a specific topic); a focus on practical, hands-on exercises; working with both the caregiver and the child, independently and together; and a focus on building social support (with other caregivers and externally with local social support systems) (Richter and Naicker 2013; Zafar et al. 2014).

Across all ECD programmes, the most important feature in offering quality ECD programmes that produce the best child outcomes, is the quality of the interpersonal interactions between the child and the ECD practitioner, whether this is a teacher, family child care worker, or similar. For best results, practitioners need to engage children in a way that promotes a positive association with learning. This should include: tailoring interactions to fit the needs of each child; using responsive language; fostering independence; proactively preventing and redirecting challenging behaviour; and responding to a child's needs with warmth and respect. It is clear that ECD programmes that do not feature these aspects of quality in their programming do not, and cannot achieve the positive child outcomes promised by high quality ECD programmes.

---

[4]Due to low levels of access to ECD centres across South Africa, for vulnerable children, different types of ECD programmes have been designed to fill the gap. Non-centre-based programmes, as the name suggests, comprise "any ECD programme, service or intervention provided to children from birth until the year before they enter formal school, with the intention to promote the child's early emotional, cognitive, sensory, spiritual, moral, physical, social and communication development and early learning" (Republic of South Africa [RSA] 2015b, p. 13). These programmes include informal playgroups, toy libraries, as well as family outreach programmes that are specifically designed to support and guide parents and caregivers on early learning stimulation and development of their young children. These programmes are cost-effective in reaching the most marginalised children who cannot afford to access formal centre-based ECD interventions (van Niekerk et al. 2017).

5.4 ECD Programmes in South Africa: Enduring Inequalities

The current ECD landscape in South Africa is fraught with inequalities. Despite progress in expanding some ECD programmes and interventions, with children's access to ECD programmes in South Africa having increased over time (Hall et al. 2017; Statistics South Africa [StatsSA] 2017a), children in this country are still exposed to significant variation in the distribution of ECD programmes, including vastly different levels of access and exposure to ECD, different levels of quality in ECD programmes, and different levels of funding from government. These variations are clearly evident in terms of the age, race, gender, disability, socio-economic status, and home language of a child, as well as where a child lives, with stark differences across provinces in the country and across the urban/rural divide.

This section reviews data on the current inequalities in ECD in South Africa, in relation to age, race, gender, location, and income quintile (where applicable and available).[5] It explores data on three areas within ECD: early learning group programmes; Grade R provision; and ECD centre programmes; and examines current provision rates and explores differences in quality.

5.4.1   Early Learning Group Programmes

Table 5.1 presents the current available data on all early learning group programme provision rates for South Africa. These rates are inclusive of children in the 0–5 age cohort in any form of early learning programme outside of their homes. This includes children in all forms of out-of-home care including Grade R, ECD centres, and non-centre-based group learning programmes.

Whilst access to early learning programmes have increased in recent years, from 22% of children (in the 0–6 age cohort) in provision in 2002 (Statistics South Africa [StatsSA] 2003), and 29% of children (in the 0–4 age cohort) in provision in 2009 (Statistics South Africa [StatsSA] 2010) Table 5.1 shows that current enrolment in early learning programmes in South Africa varies according to the age of the child. It is clear that the older a child is, the more likely that child is attending a programme; with an estimated 17% of children 0–2 years old attending an early learning programme, and 63% of children in the 3–5 age cohort attending an early learning programme in the country.[6] This 63% includes children enrolled in Grade

---

[5]It is important to note here that figures reflecting averages can mask disparities within groups, but are presented here in order to assess the performance of the country and the inequalities that currently exist in the ECD field.

[6]In most countries across the globe, fewer than half of children in the 3–5 age cohort attend an early learning programme (United Nations Children's Fund [UNICEF] 2016), and as such, whilst 63% in not high enough, it is in the upper percentiles, globally.

Table 5.1 Enrolment in early learning group (ELG) programmes, by age group (2015)

Indicator	South Africa	Source
Number of children aged 0–2	3,151,000	Adapted from Hall et al. (2017, p. 38). Based on StatsSA 2015 GHS data
Percentage of children 0–2 attending an ELG programme	17%	
Number of children aged 3–5	3,083,000	
Percentage of children 3–5 attending an ELG programme	63%	
Percentage of children 0–5 attending an ELG programme	40%	
Percentage of children 0–4 attending an ELG programme	32%	Adapted from Statistics South Africa [StatsSA] (2015, 2016a) GHS data

R, and as such it is important to look at the 0–4 age cohort figures as well, which show an enrolment rate of 32% of children for early learning programming, in the country. Significantly, there are currently approximately 3,756,040 children under 6 in South Africa not in any form of early learning provisioning (Hall et al. 2017). It is also clear that, at a provincial level, children are exposed to significantly different levels of access to early learning programming across the country according to the area in which they live. For example, access for 0–2 year old children is at its lowest in KwaZulu-Natal, at 9%, and at its highest in Gauteng, at 28%.[7] For more on this provincial inequality, see Appendix.

Looking at access across income quintiles, it is clear that the wealthier a child's family is, the more likely that child is to attend an early learning programme. Figure 5.1 presents the General Household Survey data for early learning group programme attendance for 3–5 year old children by income quintile. As can be seen in Fig. 5.1, 58% of children (3–5 years old) in Quintile 1, the poorest quintile, attend an early learning programme, compared to 83% of children in Quintile 5, the wealthiest quintile (Hall et al. 2017). For four year olds specifically, this inequality is even starker; a four year old in Quintile 1 has a 50% chance of being enrolled in an early learning programme, whereas a four year old from Quintile 5 has a 90% chance (ibid). This data is broken down by age in Fig. 5.2. Figure 5.2 shows that attendance in early learning group programmes increases with age, and is consistently unequal across income groups in the early years of a child's life, from birth, with some interplay between the two variables. From birth to the age of 1, children in Quintile 4 are most likely to be in an early learning programme, with children in Quintile 1 least likely to be in a programme.[8] Starting from the age of 1, a significantly higher percentage of children in the wealthiest quintile access an early learning programme

---

[7] This finding is expected, as high service uptake is not generally expected in the 0–2 age cohort unless day care needs are high, such as in urban provinces, where caregivers are more likely to be working outside of the home.

[8] This could be due to various reasons including need for day-care, employment and affordability.

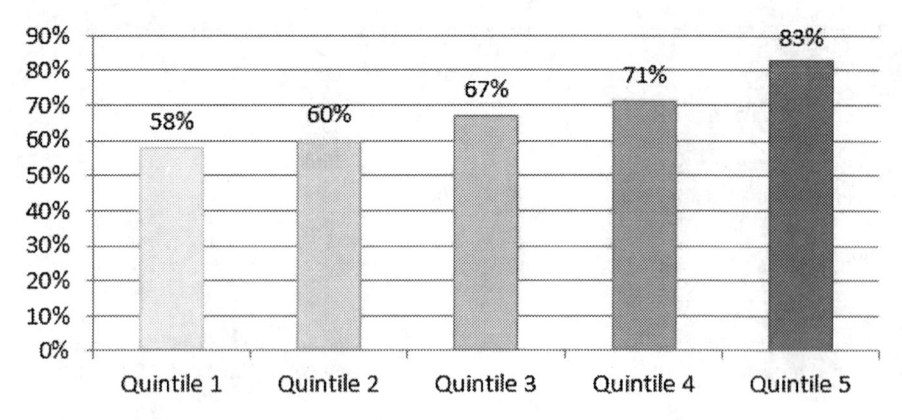

Fig. 5.1 Early Learning Group Programme Attendance for 3–5 year old Children, by Income Quintile. (Source: Hall et al. (2017, p. 36). Based on StatsSA 2015 GHS data. Reproduced with permission)

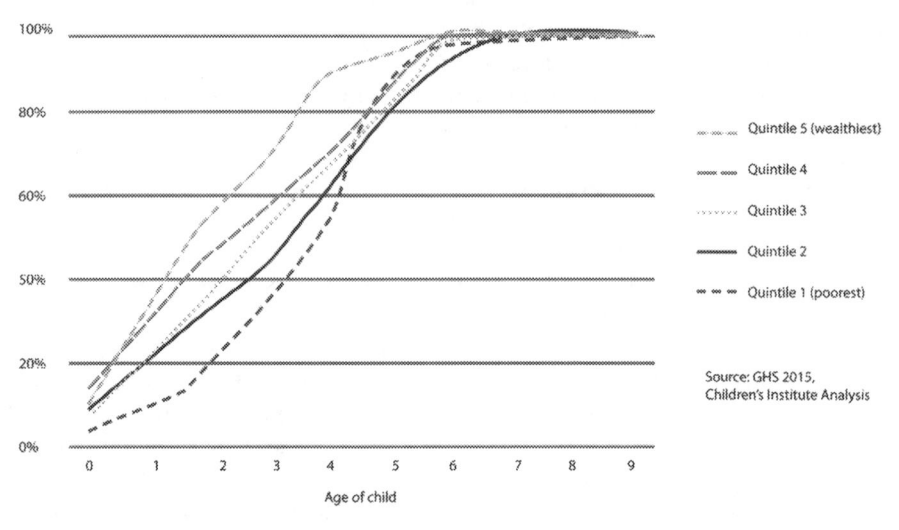

Fig. 5.2 Early Learning Group Programme Attendance, by Age and Income Quintile. (Source: Hall et al. (2017, p. 35). Based on StatsSA 2015 GHS data. Reproduced with permission)

compared to the children in all other quintiles. The inequality gap between Quintile 1 and Quintile 5 is particularly stark and concerning, with an average percentage point difference of over 20%. These findings show that those children most at risk and in need of intervention (those in the poorest quintiles), are currently the least likely to access an early learning programme, whereas those children who might require less intervention are currently receiving the highest level access (of greater quality); thereby widening the inequality gaps. It is clear that equality in terms of access between income groups is only achieved from about age 7; when children enter Grade 1; "the point where education becomes widely available, free, and

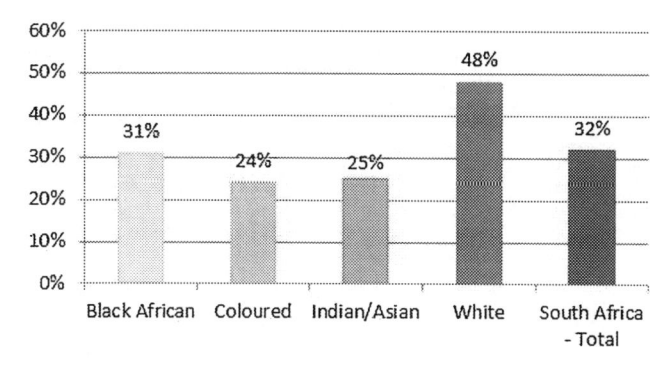

Fig. 5.3 Early Learning Group Programme Attendance for 0–4 year old Children, by Population Group. (Source: StatsSA 2016a, 2015 GHS data)

compulsory" (Hall et al. 2017, p. 35). These are important findings as this pattern depicts the inequality that is currently present during the early years. Access can also be viewed across population groups. Figure 5.3 presents this data for early learning programme attendance, for 0–4 year old children specifically. The data show that access to early learning programming varies greatly according to population group; with a much larger proportion of White children accessing an early learning programme compared to any other population group; with the percentage of White children in provision (at 48%) being double that of the percentage of Coloured children in provision (at 24%).

5.4.2 Grade R Provision

Grade R provision has increased substantially since its inception in 2001; arguably one of the South African schooling system's most significant developments since 1994 (Gustafsson 2017). Starting with 242,000 Grade R children in ordinary schools in its first year (2001), this had increased to approximately 813,000 Grade R children in ordinary schools in 2016 (Gustafsson 2017) of which 748,000 were first time Grade R learners (not grade repeaters). This figure is based on reliable enrolments rates calculated by the Department of Basic Education (DBE) and takes into account an 8% Grade R learner repetition rate (as estimated by DBE; Gustafsson (2017)). In addition to the 748,000, the number of children in Grade R classes at community ECD centres also needs to be added. There is currently no reliable information system that captures this data for Grade R classes at community based ECD centres, however there is reliable data on the number of children in registered Grade R classes at ECD centres. According to Van der Berg et al. (2013), utilising information gathered from DBE, in 2012 there were an estimated additional 55,000 children enrolled in registered Grade R classes in ECD centres in the country (Van der Berg et al. 2013). According to current information obtained directly from

Table 5.2 Grade R enrolment numbers

Year	2012	2015	2016
Learners in ordinary schools[a]	768,000	792,325	813,000
First time learners in ordinary schools	706,560[b]	728,939[b]	748,000
Learners in registered Grade R classes in ECD centres[a]	55,000	69,296	74,827[c]
First time learners in registered Grade R classes in ECD centres	50,600[b]	63,752[b]	68,841[b]
Total number of learners in Grade R in South Africa[a]	823,000	861,621	887,827
Total number of first time learners in Grade R in South Africa	757,160[b]	792,691[b]	816,841[b]
Source	Van der Berg et al. (2013)	DBE (2015) and sourced from DBE directly[d]	DBE (2016) and Gustafsson (2017)

[a]These figures include grade repeaters
[b]Figures in italics are estimated, accounting for an 8% repetition rate (as suggested by Gustafsson (2017)) and are not in the original source. As such these figures correspond to 92% of the original figure
[c]This figure is estimated using the 2015 figure and incorporating an 8% growth rate. It assumes the growth rate is currently constant
[d]Data supplied in November 2017 on special request by the Department of Basic Education from their Education Management Information System (EMIS)

DBE, this has since increased to 69,296 children, in 2015, showing an estimated growth of 8% per year.[9] If one applies the same 8% repetition rate (as suggested by Gustafsson (2017)) to the 2015 numbers, it can be estimated that roughly 63,752 first time registered Grade R learners were in an ECD centre in the country in 2015. This equates to an approximate 792,691 first time learners in registered Grade R provision across South Africa in 2015. These figures are presented in Table 5.2.

To determine the provision rate for Grade R, the 2015 mid-year population estimates by StatsSA can be used. These figures show that there were 5,537,225 children in the 5–9 age cohort in 2015 (Statistics South Africa [StatsSA] 2016b); equating to about 1.11 million children in the 5 year old age cohort. This would mean a provision rate of 71.6% of all 5 year olds accessing a registered Grade R programme in 2015. Alternatively one can use the 2016 Grade 1 enrolment figure as a marker, given that the Grade 1 provision rate is virtually 100% in South Africa. The Grade 1 enrolment rates for 2016 show that 1.21 million children entered Grade

---

[9]The data for 2016 and 2017 were not finalised at the time of writing, and as such were not available.

1 in 2016 (Department of Basic Education (DBE) 2016). DBE suggests that this figure includes a 15% Grade 1 learner repetition rate (Gustafsson 2017). Using a first-time learner Grade 1 figure of 1,027,643 then (85% of 1.21 million), this would equate to an approximate provision rate of 77% of all current Grade 1 children having been part of a registered Grade R programme in 2015.[10]

It is also clear that children are exposed to significantly different levels of access to Grade R across South Africa, according to where in the country the child lives.

Of most importance, when looking at Grade R programmes in South Africa according to income quintiles, Van der Berg et al. (2013) found virtually no measurable positive impact of Grade R for child outcomes for school children in Quintiles 1 to 3, on later school performance. This finding could be due to various reasons, including class size, limited resources, and a lack of qualified teachers in the sector.[11] Instead, researchers have only found "some impacts" for schools in the higher quintiles (Van der Berg et al. 2013, p. 2). As such "instead of reducing inequalities, Grade R further extends the advantage of more affluent schools." (ibid). This variation in child outcomes is likely due to the quality differences in Grade R programmes across the country, with the quality of a programme being correlated to the quintile level of the community in which it is based and the consequent access to resources and qualified teachers.

5.4.3 ECD Centre Programmes

The ECD sector and government currently have inadequate data with regard to ECD centres. With this in mind, Table 5.3 presents our estimates on ECD centre enrolment rates for South Africa based on the 2001 audit of ECD centres in South Africa, as this is the largest audit conducted in South Africa, achieving almost complete coverage of ECD centres in the country. These rates are inclusive of all children in the 0–6 age cohort, in both registered and not-registered ECD centres and includes children in Grade R programmes in ECD centres.

Table 5.3 shows that, assuming a modest annual growth rate of 2.5%, and an attrition rate of 0.5%, there should be an estimated 29,798 ECD centres in the country, with approximately 1,3 million children (0–6) in provision. This would equate to a provision rate of 21.8%.

It is evident that children's access to ECD centre programmes varies significantly across the country, according to the geographic area in which they live. For example, there are marked differences in enrolment rates across provinces in South Africa;

---

[10]It is important to note here that Grade R provision rates in South Africa are set to increase over the next few years, with the aim of reaching full provision by 2019; an admirable objective, but according to the data this is highly unlikely.

[11]Researchers have found that Grade R teachers are relatively un- and under-qualified, with only two-thirds of teachers in Grade R classes in ordinary schools having obtained a Grade 12 certificate, and only around 20% holding a degree; (Gustafsson 2017)

Table 5.3 Number of children in ECD centre provision in South Africa

Year	2000	2016
Number of ECD centres in South Africa	23,482	29,798[a]
Number of children enrolled in ECD centres in South Africa	1,030,473	1,307,655[b]
Number of children (0–6) in South Africa	5,600,000	6,012,000[c]
Provision rate	18.4%	21.8%
Source	DOE 2001	Estimates

[a]This figure is estimated utilising a 2.5% growth rate and a 0.5% attrition rate. The growth rate is based on the authors analysis of the General Household Survey from 2002 to 2016, showing a net growth rate of 0.9% for the total number of children (0–4) in provision from 2009 to 2016, and a net growth rate of 1.9% for the total number of children (0–6) in provision from 2002 to 2008, and adjusted to account for the growth in provision for older children
[b]Estimate based on 2001 Audit finding of number of children per ECD centre (43.9). This figure excludes children in Grade R in ordinary schools, but includes children in Grade R classes in ECD centres
[c]Estimate based on the General Household Survey 2016 (Statistics South Africa [StatsSA] 2017b)

with enrolment at its lowest in KwaZulu-Natal, for the 3–5 age cohort, at 12%, and highest in the Free State, for the 3–5 age cohort, at 41% (a 29% percentage point difference).[12]

Unfortunately, limited data exists exploring the quality of programmes according to indicators such as income quintiles or race categories. However, of the data that is available, a few examples of quality measures are provided here to illustrate the variation in quality of ECD centre-based programmes.

The *Tracking Public Expenditure and Assessing Service Quality in Early Childhood Development in South Africa* study by the DBE, the Department of Social Development (DSD), and UNICEF in 2011 (referred to as the PETS study) found a statistically significant difference in infrastructure quality of ECD centres between quintiles across South Africa; with children in the poorest quintiles attending ECD centres with unsafe infrastructure that do not meet the standards required by law to register as a Partial Care facility with the DSD (a requirement of all ECD centres operating in South Africa). They also found a statistically significant correlation between infrastructure quality and the quality of the ECD programme. The researchers note that this is a not necessarily a causal relationship, but rather that the underlying factors of income poverty levels and the quality of management at the ECD centre influences both the ECD programme and the quality of infrastructure (DBE, DSD and UNICEF 2011).

An unpublished study conducted by Biersteker and Hendricks in 2012, examined the educational resources at unregistered centres in one specific province in South

---

[12]This is based on data obtained from the 2014 Department of Social Development (DSD) and Economic Policy Research Institute (EPRI) 'Audit of Early Childhood Development (ECD) Centres' report, and as such reflects an underrepresentation of ECD centres in the country. As such, it is important to look at the differences in enrolment rate figures and not at the raw percentage data.

Africa; namely, the Western Cape. This study found significant discrepancies across socio-economic status (SES) levels, with more affluent areas significantly outperforming their lower SES counterparts in terms of resourcing (including blocks, books, concept toys and puzzles). Whilst this is not surprising, it speaks to the on-going perpetuation of inequality and the resulting poor child outcomes. The 2011 PETS study found that registered ECD centres more often had better levels of age-appropriate learning and teaching support materials (LTSM) compared to Grade R classes in public schools (DBE, DSD and UNICEF 2011). The study also found a statistically significant correlation between LTSM quality and ECD programme quality. Once again, this was not determined to be a causal relationship.

Unsurprisingly, the 2011 PETS study found huge variations in ECD centre fees across quintile groups (DBE, DSD and UNICEF 2011). Specifically, the report found that monthly centre fees for 2009 were an average of R143 per child per month, ranging from R58 per month per child in the Quintile 1 (the poorest quintile), to R531 per month per child in Quintile 5 (the wealthiest quintile). Biersteker et al. (2016) have shown that monthly fees strongly predicts ECD centre quality, acting as a "proxy for other factors that contribute to quality including the ability to employ and retain suitably effective staff, purchase materials, and provide facilities and infrastructure". As such, whilst this disparity in centre fees is not surprising, it is unfortunately contributing significantly to inequality in ECD in the country.

The 2014 DSD and EPRI 'Audit of Early Childhood Development (ECD) Centres' report provides extensive data on various indicators of quality of 17,846 ECD centres in their study. Key quality indicators included in the report were analysed to examine the inequalities that exist at provincial level. According to our own analysis on key areas of quality (including, for example, teacher qualifications, registration status, environment standards, and access to education resources), the ranked order of the provinces, from top performing province, to poorest performing province was: Western Cape, Free State, Gauteng, Northern Cape, KwaZulu-Natal, Limpopo, Eastern Cape, North West, and lastly, Mpumalanga. It is not surprising that the Western Cape and Gauteng were, overall, two of the top performing provinces, as these are largely urban provinces, with increased job opportunities for its inhabitants, and as such provide increased demand for access, with increased wealth for resources and quality ECD programming. Conversely, the three poorest performing provinces, Eastern Cape, North West, and Mpumalanga, are largely rural provinces.

5.5 Overcoming Inequality in ECD

Internationally, ECD is viewed as one of the most cost-efficient investments in human capital which leads to the sustainable development of a country (United Nations Children's Fund [UNICEF] 2014). Over recent years, the South African government has acknowledged the socio-economic potential of investing in ECD. Through the efforts of government and non-profit organisations, progress has been made in improving access to and the condition of early education for young children in their preschool years. These improvements have contributed to increased enrolment rates to ECD programmes, particularly in the provision of Grade R, however issues of inequality and access to ECD facilities in the most under-resourced areas continues to lag behind considerably (van Niekerk et al. 2017). In this regard, it is noteworthy that access to Grade R is highest in poorer areas across the country, however it lacks quality.

Moreover, since 2003 the number of children living in income poverty has decreased (Hall et al. 2017), which is largely attributed to the expansion of a government initiative during this time, namely the child support grant (CSG).

Despite progress in providing access to early childhood programmes, there remain too many children not able to access this form of early education, the majority of whom fall within the poorest quintiles. For those children that do have access, quality of these early learning programmes is evidently variable, and there are no reliable data sources that support national monitoring of quality (Hall et al. 2017).

In terms of policy initiatives, in December 2015, the South African Cabinet approved a new National Integrated Early Childhood Development Policy, which introduces a comprehensive and integrated package of ECD programmes that would be universally available so that all children enjoy an equal opportunity to access them (Republic of South Africa [RSA] 2015b). In this policy ECD is recognised as a universal right of children, a national priority and a public good to which all young children are equally entitled. The policy targets all children from conception until the age of 5 years and includes children with disabilities up to the age of 7 years (Hall et al. 2014). The prospects of this new policy are promising; however, ways in which it will be implemented are unclear. In fact, although the Department of Social Development has stated that it is in the process of finalising the 'National Integrated Plan for ECD', more than two years after approval of the policy by the Cabinet this implementation plan has not materialized.

While ECD has been taken more seriously by national government, South Africa has not managed to make a substantial dent in reducing inequality in the ECD sector for a number of policy and systemic reasons, including the following.

Firstly, there is a lack of government support for ECD policy implementation, with insufficient political will to make ECD a political priority and consequently insufficient government funding to achieve current policy objectives. (Currently South Africa's government prioritizes transforming the formal school system and higher education, with a mere 1.6% of the total education budget allocated towards ECD; Republic of South Africa [RSA] (2015a)).

Secondly, there are currently ineffectual government institutional arrangements in place for effective ECD programme implementation, with a lack of ECD policy and programme cohesion between different government departments responsible for ECD (namely, the Departments of Basic Education and Social Development).

Thirdly, there is currently a significant lack in ECD non-profit organisation capacity and resources to provide ECD programmes under the ECD policy and to impact on the numbers of children who are in need of comprehensive and integrated ECD programmes (Biersteker and Picken 2013).

For ECD policy to be effective it must be implemented comprehensively, in line with the policy vision and goals. If policy is not implemented the result is that young children do not receive the ECD programmes to which they are constitutionally entitled and the policy could be seen as 'symbolic'. Policy will not be implemented optimally without adequate financial resources to implement it.

The experience in South Africa is that despite the release of an excellent National Integrated ECD Policy in 2015, the political will and budget allocations did not support policy implementation which has been lacking. Jansen (2001, p. 275), following a study of policy-making and policy implementation in post-apartheid South Africa, sums it up as: "In most cases, however, implementation was never on the policy agenda at all."

To sum up these challenges and constraints, Jansen and Sayed (2001, p. 196) encapsulates this reflection when he writes: "... a consistent feature of educational policy is that symbolic commitments to overcome the legacy of apartheid inequities are not always realised in the crucible of practice."

5.6 Key Recommendations to Reduce ECD Inequality in South Africa

From the range of challenges facing the ECD sector, several recommendations are described here which would contribute to reducing ECD inequalities in South Africa. In order to achieve equity across the country, the following specific actions are required:

- Significant government political will and support of ECD policy is essential. For ECD policy to work it should be driven at the highest political level and should be part of the relevant government department's strategic focus. Government should take the lead in ECD policy-making through the relevant Cabinet minister who should lead policy-making as a 'political champion'. If there is no significant political will at the highest level, the policy is less likely to be a success. Supporting the political champion should be committed and competent government officials shaping ECD policy implementation.
- ECD should be positioned on the political agenda so that each child's right to quality ECD programmes, as set out in various ECD policies, is assured.
- International reporting commitments such as the Sustainable Development Goal 4.2 "By 2030, ensure that all girls and boys have access to quality early childhood development, care and pre-primary education so that they are ready for primary";

(United Nations [UN] 2015, p. 19) should be leveraged to drive the ECD agenda in the country.

- Government as the custodian of policy should create an enabling environment and conditions for policy to be made and implemented to achieve the goals set out in the policy.
- Government should lead the ECD policy implementation process given that it has the political mandate, institutional infrastructure and could acquire the necessary funding to achieve the policy goals. To this effect, the 'National Integrated Plan for ECD' should be finalised and released urgently.
- For an ECD policy to be implemented, sufficient financial and other resources must be provided by government to ensure that the ECD policy is implemented. In a country such as South Africa, equity can be an issue, and disparities in resource allocation are a problem. These resources should be provided equitably so that all children throughout the country benefit. Funding mechanisms to support the ECD policy and implementation should be put in place.
- Implementing ECD programmes requires government to enhance the skills and capacity of government officials to a level where they can effectively implement the National Integrated ECD Policy. National DSD should have dedicated ECD staffing in place.
- To realise ECD transformation and equity in the ECD sector in South Africa, the leadership skills and capacity of ECD non-profit staff needs to be developed and enhanced, to support communities to provide quality ECD programmes for young children.
- To maximise ECD impact and reduce inequalities, ECD non-profit organisations across South Africa should collaborate and partner with each other, with the private sector, and with government; sharing knowledge, skills and resources. By collaborating in a strategic way, working towards the implementation of the National Integrated ECD Policy, a holistic package of quality interventions and programmes can be implemented on a large scale, throughout the country. This collaboration is likely to result in cost savings, increased provision and improved quality.
- Data collection systems for the ECD sector are in the process of being developed, however progress is slow, and should be improved quickly. Being poorly informed on the needs of young children, the programmes they require and the current level of provision, limits our ability to ensure equitable distribution of services to children through population-based planning. This needs to be rectified if South Africa is to provide universal access to quality early learning programmes to its children. With better data collection systems and reporting in place, the ECD non-profit and civil society sectors should monitor ECD policy implementation to ensure that government meets the commitments made in the National Integrated ECD Policy.

If implemented, these actions will contribute towards reducing ECD inequalities in South Africa and towards meeting the early childhood development needs of young children and their families.

5.7 Conclusion

This chapter explores the current inequalities which exist in ECD in South Africa, the consequences of this inequality, why this inequality persists and offers recommendations for the future of ECD in the country. From what has been set out in this chapter, it is clear that young children are severely impacted by social and economic inequality. The reasons for these inequalities are many, including South Africa's Apartheid (segregated) history; resulting in gross infringements on the basic and constitutional rights of South Africa's children. Global evidence shows ECD interventions can protect children against the effects of poverty, poor nutrition, inadequate health care and a lack of early education; and that investment in quality ECD programmes for young children, particularly for vulnerable young children, has a significant effect on reducing poverty and inequality across society. This is a window of opportunity to support vulnerable young children to enter formal schooling school-ready, competent and confident. To bring about equity for children entering formal schooling, a number of government and national actions are recommended in this chapter. What is needed now, globally, is a prioritisation of ECD programming by governments, alongside sufficient financial investment. In a country with high levels of poverty and inequality, such as South Africa, prioritising ECD must be understood as a powerful social investment with a social and economic return, building human capital and enabling future participation in the labour market.

Appendix

Table 5.4 The status of children under 6 living in South Africa in 2015, by Province

	Indicator	South Africa	Eastern Cape	Free State	Gauteng	KwaZulu-Natal	Limpopo	Mpumalanga	North West	Northern Cape	Western Cape
Population	**Number of children under 6 years**	6,235,000	884,000	304,000	1,185,000	1,316,000	756,000	528,000	463,000	144,000	655,000
	Households with children under 6	4,785,000	582,000	288,000	1,142,000	874,000	561,000	422,000	354,000	112,000	449,000
		30%	34%	32%	24%	32%	37%	35%	29%	35%	25%
Area type	**Urban** Children <6 in urban areas (formal/informal)	3,528,000	350,000	258,000	1,152,000	515,000	127,000	186,000	224,000	97,000	620,000
		57%	40%	85%	97%	39%	17%	35%	48%	67%	95%
	Rural traditional Children <6 in rural former homeland areas	2,439,000	524,000	27,000	19,000	688,000	614,000	305,000	222,000	41,000	–
		39%	59%	9%	2%	52%	81%	58%	48%	28%	0%
	Rural farms Children <6 in commercial farming areas (old RSA)	267,000	11,000	18,000	14,000	114,000	15,000	36,000	17,000	7,000	35,000
		4%	1%	6%	1%	9%	2%	7%	4%	5%	5%

Service access	Inadequate water Children <6 without piped water on site	1,972,000	529,000	24,000	82,000	539,000	370,000	167,000	159,000	37,000	69,000
		32%	60%	8%	7%	41%	49%	32%	34%	25%	11%
	Poor sanitation Children <6 without a toilet or ventilated pit-latrine on site	1,504,000	151,000	65,000	97,000	375,000	372,000	196,000	141,000	32,000	75,000
		24%	17%	21%	8%	28%	49%	37%	30%	22%	11%
Poverty		3,875,000	701,000	195,000	456,000	984,000	581,000	335,000	298,000	83,000	242,000
	Child poverty Children <6 living in poor households (<R965 in 2015)	62%	79%	64%	38%	75%	77%	63%	64%	58%	37%
	Food poverty Children <6 living in food poor households (<R415 in 2015)	1,855,000	419,000	89,000	161,000	480,000	325,000	152,000	134,000	35,000	60,000
		30%	47%	29%	14%	37%	43%	29%	29%	24%	9%

Source: Statistics South Africa: General Household Survey 2015. Data analysed and compiled by Children's Institute, University of Cape Town as cited in the South African Early Childhood Review 2017 (Hall et al. 2017). Reproduced with permission

References

Atmore, E., van Niekerk, L., & Ashley-Cooper, M. (2012). Challenges facing the early childhood development sector in South Africa. *South African Journal of Childhood Education, 2*(1), 121.

Aubrey, C. (2017). Sources of inequality in South African early child development services. *South African Journal of Childhood Education, 7*(1), 1–9.

Aughinbaugh, A., & Gittleman, M. (2003). Does money matter? A comparison of the effect of income on child development in the United States and Great Britain. *Journal of Human Resources, 38*(2), 416–440.

Barnett, W. S. (1995). Long-term effects of early childhood programs on cognitive and school outcomes. *The Future of Children, 5*(3), 25–50.

Barnett, W. S. (2008). *Preschool education and its lasting effects: Research and policy implications.* Available via: Boulder and Tempe: Education and the Public Interest Center & Education Policy Research Unit http://epicpolicy.org/publication/preschooleducation. Accessed 11 Dec 2017.

Biersteker, L. (2017). *Quality ECD: What does it take to shift early learning outcomes?* Presentation at Education Fishtank workshop, Cape Town, South Africa, 3 Aug 2017.

Biersteker, L., Hendricks, S. (2012). *Audit of unregistered ECD sites in the Western Province 2011.* Report to the Western Cape Department of Social Development Western Cape (Unpublished).

Biersteker, L., & Picken, P. (2013). *Report on a survey of non-profit organisations providing training for ECD programmes and services (birth to four years).* Cape Town: Ilifa Labantwana.

Biersteker, L., Dawes, A., Hendricks, L., & Tredoux, C. (2016). Center-based early childhood care and education program quality: A South African study. *Early Childhood Research Quarterly, 36*, 334–344.

Burchinal, M., Zaslow, M., Tarullo, L., & Martinez-Beck, I. (2016). Quality thresholds, features, and dosage in early care and education: Secondary data analyses of child outcomes. *Monographs of the Society for Research in Child Development, 81*(2), serial No. 321.

Burchinal, M. R., Roberts, J. E., Riggins, R. Jr., Zeisel, S. A., Neebe, E., & Bryant, D. (2000). Relating quality of center-based child care to early cognitive and language development longitudinally. *Child Development, 71*(2), 339–357.

Davis-Kean, P. E. (2005). The influence of parent education and family income on child achievement: The indirect role of parental expectations and the home environment. *Journal of Family Psychology, 19*(2), 294–304. https://doi.org/10.1037/0893-3200.19.2.294

Dawes, A., Biersteker, L., & Hendricks, L. (2012). *Towards integrated early childhood development. An evaluation of the Sobambisana initiative.* Available via The DG Murray Trust http://www.educationinnovations.org/sites/default/files/Sobambisana%20Initiative%20-%20Evaluation.pdf. Accessed 11 December 2017.

Dawes, A., Biersteker, L., Girdwood, E., Snelling, M., & Tedoux, C. (2016). *Early learning outcomes measure. Technical manual.* Cape Town: The Innovation Edge.

DBE, DSD and UNICEF. (2011). *Tracking public expenditure and assessing service quality in early childhood development in South Africa.* Available via UNICEF https://www.unicef.org/southafrica/SAF_resources_pets.pdf. Accessed 22 Nov 2017.

Department of Basic Education (DBE). (2015). *School realities 2015, EMIS15/2/011.* Republic of South Africa, Pretoria.

Department of Basic Education (DBE). (2016). *School realities 2016, EMIS16/2/012.* Republic of South Africa, Pretoria.

Department of Education. (2001). *The national audit of ECD provisioning in South Africa.* Department of Education, Pretoria.

Fixsen, D. L., Naoom, S. F., Blase, K. A., & Friedman, R. M. (2005). *Implementation research: A synthesis of the literature.* University of South Florida, Louis de la Parte Florida Mental Health Institute, The National Implementation Research Network United States.

Gustafsson, M. (2017). *Enrolments, staffing, financing and the quality of service delivery in early childhood institutions.* South Africa (Unpublished).

Gustafsson, M., et al. (2010). *Policy note on pre-primary schooling: An empirical contribution to the 2009 medium term strategic framework*. Stellenbosch economic working papers 05/10 Department of Economics and Bureau for Economic Research, University of Stellenbosch, South Africa.

Hall, K., Sambu, W., & Berry, L. (2014). *Early childhood development: A statistical brief*. Children's Institute, University of Cape Town and Ilifa Labantwana, Cape Town.

Hall, K., Sambu, W., Berry, L., Giese, S., & Almeleh, C. (2016). *South African Early Childhood Review 2016*. Children's Institute, University of Cape Town and Ilifa Labantwana, Cape Town.

Hall, K., Sambu, W., Berry, L., Giese, S., & Almeleh, C. (2017). *South African Early Childhood Review 2017*. Children's Institute, University of Cape Town and Ilifa Labantwana, Cape Town.

Hartinger, S. M., Lanata, C. F., Hattendorf, J., Wolf, J., Gil, A. I., Obando, M. O., Noblega, M., Verastegui, H., & Mäusezahl, D. (2017). Impact of a child stimulation intervention on early child development in Rural Peru: A cluster randomised trial using a reciprocal control design. *Journal of Epidemiology and Community Health, 71*(3), 217–224.

Heckman, J. J., Moon, S. H., Pinto, R., Savelyev, P. A., & Yavitz, A. (2010). The rate of return to the HighScope Perry Preschool Program. *Journal of Public Economics, 94*(1–2), 114–128.

Jansen, J. (2001). Explaining non-change in education reform after apartheid: Political symbolism and the problem of policy implementation. In J. Jansen & Y. Sayed (Eds.), *Implementing Education Policies: The South African experience*. Cape Town: University of Cape Town Press.

Jansen, J. D., & Sayed, Y. (2001). *Implementing education policies: The South African experience*. Cape Town: University of Cape Town Press.

Love, J. M., Harrison, L., Sagi-Schwartz, A., Van IJzendoorn, M. H., Ross, C., Ungerer, J. A., Raikes, H., Brady-Smith, C., Boller, K., & Brooks-Gunn, J. (2003). Child care quality matters: How conclusions may vary with context. *Child Development, 74*(4), 1021–1033. https://doi.org/10.1111/1467-8624.00584

Republic of South Africa [RSA]. (2015a). *Intergovernmental fiscal reviews (IGFR) 2015: Provincial Budgets and expenditure review 2010/11–2016/17*.

Republic of South Africa [RSA]. (2015b). *National integrated early childhood development policy*.

Richter, L., & Naicker, S. (2013). *A review of published literature on supporting and strengthening child-caregiver relationships (parenting)*. Arlington, VA: USAID's AIDS Support and Technical Assistance Resources, AIDSTAR-One, Task Order 1.

Rubio-Codina, M., Attanasio, O., Meghir, C., Varela, N., & Grantham-McGregor, S. (2015). The socioeconomic gradient of child development: Cross-sectional evidence from children 6–42 months in Bogota. *Journal of Human Resources, 50*(2), 464–483.

Shonkoff, J., Levitt, P., Fox, N., Bunge, S., Cameron, J., Duncan, G., et al. (2016). *From best practices to breakthrough impacts: A science-based approach for building a more promising future for young children and families*. Cambridge, MA: Harvard University, Center on the Developing Child.

Southern and Eastern African Consortium for Monitoring Educational Quality [SACMEQ]. (2011). *Learner preschool exposure and achievement in South Africa*. Policy brief no 4 Ministry of Basic Education, Pretoria, South Africa.

Spaull, N. (2013). Poverty & privilege: Primary school inequality in South Africa. *International Journal of Educational Development, 33*(5), 436–447.

Statistics South Africa [StatsSA]. (2003). *General Household Survey 2002*. Statistics South Africa, Pretoria.

Statistics South Africa [StatsSA]. (2010). *General Household Survey 2009*. Statistics South Africa, Pretoria.

Statistics South Africa [StatsSA]. (2015). *General Household Survey 2014*. Statistics South Africa, Pretoria.

Statistics South Africa [StatsSA]. (2016a). *General Household Survey 2015*. Statistics South Africa, Pretoria.

Statistics South Africa [StatsSA]. (2016b). *Mid-year population estimates 2016*. Statistics South Africa, Pretoria.

Statistics South Africa [StatsSA]. (2017a). *Mid-year Population Estimates 2017*. Statistics South Africa, Pretoria.

Statistics South Africa [StatsSA]. (2017b). *General Household Survey 2016*. Statistics South Africa, Pretoria.

United Nations Children's Fund [UNICEF]. (2014). *Early Childhood Development: A statistical snapshot – Building better brains and sustainable outcomes for children* (p. 7). UNICEF, New York, Sept 2014.

United Nations Children's Fund [UNICEF]. (2016). *The State of the World's Children 2016*. Available via: UNICEF https://www.unicef.org/publications/files/UNICEF_SOWC_2016.pdf. Accessed 25 Nov 2017.

United Nations [UN]. (2015). *Transforming our world: The 2030 agenda for sustainable development (A/Res/70/1)*. UN General Assembly, New York Accessed from http://sustainabledevelopment.un.org.ezproxy.uct.ac.za. Accessed 28 Nov 2017.

Van der Berg, S., Girdwood, E., Shepherd, D., van Wyk, C., Kruger, J., & Viljoen, J. (2013). *The impact of the introduction of Grade R on learning outcomes*. Report to Department of Basic Education and Department of Performance Monitoring and Evaluation in the Presidency University of Stellenbosch, South Africa.

Van der Gaag, J., & Putcha, V. (2015). *Investing in early childhood development: What is being spent, and what does it cost?* Bookings Global Working Paper Series.

van Niekerk, L., Ashley-Cooper, M., & Atmore, E. (2017). *Effective early childhood development programme options meeting the needs of young South African children*. Centre for Early Childhood Development, Cape Town.

Woldehanna, T., & Gebremedhin, L. (2002). *The effects of pre-school attendance on the cognitive development of urban children aged 5 and 8 years: evidence from ethiopia*. Young Lives Working Paper 8 Oxford Department of International Development (ODID), University of Oxford, United Kingdom.

Zafar, S., Sikander, S., Haq, Z., Hill, Z., Lingam, R., Skordis-Worrall, J., Hafeez, A., Kirkwood, B., & Rahman, A. (2014). Integrating maternal psychosocial well-being into a child-development intervention: The five-pillars approach. *Annals of the New York Academy of Sciences, 1308*(1), 107–117.

Chapter 6
Curriculum Reform and Learner Performance: An Obstinate Paradox in the Quest for Equality

Johan Muller and Ursula Hoadley

6.1 The Context of Curriculum Reform

The very idea of curriculum seems fated to be trapped in a cyclical ideological antagonism between what is considered to be an outmoded '*traditional*' model – subject-based, content-driven, teacher led – and a '*progressive*' model – weakened subject boundaries, curriculum integration, low specification of content, learner independence. The words to describe them differ, but these are the most common labels, which we will consequently use until we introduce a more analytical classification below.

There are clearly discernible phases of enthusiasm for 'progressive' curricula, which, when they seem not to be working as envisaged, inevitably trigger a renewed enthusiasm for some or other 'back to basics' approach. In practice, these ideal prescripts have varied widely wherever they have been implemented. The reasons for this are many, and they include contextual conditions and the relative stability and level of development of the schooling system in question. A key reason little remarked in 'reform talk' lies with the embeddedness of existing social practices, which have the consequence that 'new' prescripts all too often become welded to, absorbed by, or simply re-interpreted in the light of the familiar way of doing things. We will discuss below how this has been consequential in South Africa's cycle of curriculum reform, but it is often interpreted by the opponents of the reform as 'proof' that the reform has not worked. In truth, there have been vanishingly few robust evaluations of curriculum models. This undoubtedly gives impetus to the next cyclical swing.

J. Muller (✉) · U. Hoadley
School of Education, University of Cape Town, Rondebosch, Cape Town, South Africa
e-mail: johan.muller@uct.ac.za; uk.hoadley@uct.ac.za

© Springer Nature Switzerland AG 2019
N. Spaull, J. D. Jansen (eds.), *South African Schooling: The Enigma of Inequality*, Policy Implications of Research in Education 10,
https://doi.org/10.1007/978-3-030-18811-5_6

The principal difference between curriculum reform in developed as against developing countries used to be more distinctive than it is now. Before, the Anglo-Saxon developed countries together with those of Europe and Asia had reasonably distinct national curriculum/pedagogical traditions – 'divergent intellectual worlds' as Shriewer (2000, p. 91) called them: the early specialising, streamed system in England as against the late specialising quasi-system in the USA, with autonomy for the different states to set their own criteria; the hermeneutically oriented *didaktik/bildung* wellspring of the Germanic and Nordic countries as against the scientific rationalism of the French system, at least until recently; the Confucian system in China and the East Asian countries to mention only a few distinct traditions. More latterly, the global ecumenism of TIMSS and the agencies driving a global agenda – like the IEA, UNESCO, OECD – have constructed a globalising marketplace for national comparisons which, despite a decades-long convergence of curricula (McEaneny and Meyer 2008), has given this convergence accelerated impetus. Convergences are now everywhere discernible. Nevertheless, the lineaments of the national traditions of the developed countries are still readily evident.

Many developing countries, particularly those emerging from colonial imposition, have schooling systems which bear the distinct imprint of their past colonial templates. Thus, South Africa's schooling system owes something to its English colonial roots and something to the Germanic roots from whence sprang apartheid ideology. This minor German legacy lingers in the once-Afrikaans speaking university departments of teacher training (Suransky-Dekker 1998; Hoadley and Muller 2018), but its main legacy lies in the late-established black schooling system, with most of the teachers still trained in an authoritarian form of *didaktik* stripped of its intellectual ambitions (ibid). This is the once-black schooling system, still today educating about 80% of the school-going population in the 'schools for the poor'. The once-white system, still modelled today on the English system (for the English schools) and a more elite form of *didaktik* for the (now diminishing number of) Afrikaans speaking schools, all now more or less non-racial, form part of the elite 20% of schools 'for the rich' (Hoadley 2018, p.12; Van der Berg and Louw 2007). The 80% resemble the schools in many developing countries. So, while the curriculum system lineaments come from the developed countries, problematically so, the resultant schooling looks much like that in the developing world. This is where the inequality in the system lies, and our focus in this chapter will consequently be on these schools. Most particularly, the question we will seek to answer is: why, despite successive waves of curriculum reform, have the schooling outcomes of the 'schools for the poor' remained so persistently low, despite some recent modest improvements? What could the curriculum or curriculum reform be doing, if anything, to mitigate this? What does an analysis of the South African case tell us about this?

6.1.1 Recent Curriculum Reform in the Developing World

'Traditional' curriculum and pedagogy in developing countries has had a depressing sameness about it: 'chalk and talk' teacher dominated lessons, with the learners positioned in a passive reactive role, a predominance of collective chanting, copywriting and drill, and most critically from a curriculum perspective, an extremely slow pacing leading to limited curriculum coverage.[1] When learners are then promoted to the next grade, there are inevitably knowledge gaps, which are especially disabling in concept-rich subjects like science and mathematics. The rapid rate in which knowledge deficits are generated in South Africa, by Grade 3, have been well documented (Van der Berg et al. 2016). The crunch comes in Grades 9 or 10, where learners either drop out or repeat in large numbers. There are two other significant features of this pedagogy worth mentioning. The first is that the encounter with knowledge is primarily an oral rather than a textual one. The second feature is that the unit of teaching is largely the class: the pedagogy is undifferentiated and undifferentiating, and there is little explicit marking out of individual performances. The most reliable evidence for the consequences of this is the persistent pattern of low performance outcomes (Glewwe and Muralidharan 2015; Pritchett and Beatty 2012). It is this pattern that curriculum reform has sought to reverse.

It is no surprise that the majority of proposals for reform were a variant of *progressive* curriculum and pedagogy, usually including educational process, an emphasis on outcomes with their concomitant low stipulation of content, an emphasis on relevance to both the worlds of the learners and the world of work, a thematic and integrated curriculum. This model was carried to the developing world in the 1980s first by the international lenders as part of structural adjustment packages, and later with more zeal by international aid organisations with the UNESCO 'Education for All' World Declaration a high-water mark for globalising progressivism (UNICEF 1990).

By the early 2000s the donor and international aid agencies were backing off from their prior advocacy of progressivism, and were transferring allegiance to a model of 'twenty-first century' generic skills and competencies said to be essential for the rapidly changing world of work in the twenty-first century. Superficially akin to progressivism – they both promoted interdisciplinarity and relevance, for example – as we will show further below, these superficial features mask a more fundamental shift in the social logic of the curriculum model, and marks a relative break with progressivism.

Notwithstanding this sea change in donor allegiances, the dominant ideology of curriculum reform in developing countries has remained progressivism of one form or another. The longevity of the popularity of progressivism has been variably assigned, but it is indisputable that a central feature has been the elision of education

---

[1] This section draws on Hoadley (2018).

and politics at its heart: political progressivism and educational progressivism have been assumed to march in tandem, such that to be politically progressive meant to be educationally progressive. To question the one was to question the other. In a country, newly liberated from colonial chains, as South Africa was in the late 1990s, to question progressivism was tantamount to political heresy as we will shortly show.

The impact of progressivism in the ex-colonies has been disappointing to say the least. The idea has been enthusiastically taken up and promoted, mainly by the education authorities, but the effects on student outcomes have been negligible, and traditional practices have persisted, more or less wherever progressivism has been tried – Hoadley (2018) cites studies in Africa and India, principally. In almost all cases, evaluations have noted the observance of the outward forms of progressivism but no substantive uptake of the deeper social logic of the model. What is evident in this recurrent pattern is the recruitment of the forms of progressive pedagogy, like group work, to the collectivising practices of a particular form of traditional pedagogy. Why that is, is commonly ascribed to traditional cultural practices within which the teachers remain embedded. What casts doubt upon this view, as Ensor (2015) points out, is the fact that the traditional culture appealed to differs widely across the cases in which this recalcitrant phenomenon has been observed.

An intriguing variant of this situation has been observed in Singapore, where the pedagogy has remained similarly immune to progressive uptake, despite government embrace of progressive policy prescripts from the OECD, a global patron of a variant of progressivism. What makes Singapore interesting is the fact that although the government has made concerted efforts to promote features of progressivism, through the introduction of programmes like 'Innovation and Enterprise' in 2004, and particularly 'Teach Less, Learn More' (2005), the schools have retained 'a strong focus on direct instruction and traditional pedagogic practices' (Deng and Gopinathan 2016, p. 460). They also continue to perform near the top of the ladder on the OECD's PISA test. Interesting too is the case of late-industrialising Finland, where one principal cause of their pre-eminence in PISA outcomes has been traced to 'a hierarchical and traditional schooling climate' (Sahlgren 2015, p. iii), and their more recent fall in performance to their belated shift to progressive pupil centred classroom methods.

It is fair to conclude that there is no unambiguously successful case of progressive curriculum reform in the developing world, and that a disabling caricature of traditional practice continues to hold sway. Indeed, where there have been demonstrable achievement effects in the developing world, as in Cuba (Carnoy and Marshall 2005) and Ecuador, and to a lesser degree in Peru and Chile (Schneider et al. 2017), these have coincided with curriculum reforms that look very like a stringent version of traditional pedagogy – with 'a strong focus on direct instruction and traditional pedagogic practices' (Carnoy and Marshall 2005, p. 460).

6.1.2 Recent Curriculum Reform in the Developed World: The Case of England and Elsewhere

Frustration about failures to address educational inequality are not particular to the developing world. In the course of a far-ranging analysis of educational policy in the UK, Fitz et al. (2006, p.83) ask rhetorically, 'How is it ... that over a sixty-year period, covering myriad policy initiates ... the gap between middle-class and working class students' attainment (in the UK) has changed so little?' The answer is not clear cut.

After a long passage of traditionalism with progressivism flourishing in isolated private schools only, English progressivism was advocated for the mainstream school system by the Plowden Report in 1967 (Plowden 1967). The swing back to a more traditional curriculum began with Thatcher in the 1980s, and a National Curriculum and standardised testing at 'key stages' was introduced by the Education Reform Act of 1998.This swing was continued by New Labour, but it was only with the appointment of Michael Gove in 2010 (until 2014) that a determined focus on traditionalism and the 'knowledge-based' (a content-directed) curriculum became firmly entrenched. By this time the National Curriculum had been reformed from an under-stipulated skills or outcomes based framework to one based directly on content, effective sequencing and the importance of disciplinary subjects, mirroring the swing back to traditionalism in the American Core Knowledge curriculum, and explicit standards-based framework. Both the English and American curricular frameworks were influenced by the writings of American literature professor E. D. Hirsch and his Core Knowledge Foundation (Simons and Porter 2015).

The latitude for autonomy in both the American and English systems had seen the emergence of a parallel phenomenon of new school types, which were basically publicly financed privately managed schools, starting with the American charter schools, which were the model for the English version of academies and free schools. We will not comment here on the structural features of these schools, which have attracted much adverse comment because of their 'privatised form'. The English schools in any case were introduced, first under New Labour, as an alternative for failing schools in disadvantaged neighbourhoods with the explicit aim to promote equity in attainment. Despite considerable divergence in the way these schools operate, quite a number of them have embraced a stringent form of traditionalism. In addition to content driven lessons, supervised homework, testing, and a discipline subject based curriculum, many if not most of these schools also have a strict disciplinary conduct policy; the curriculum is thus traditional in content and in the policing of conduct (Duoblys 2017). In some schools, it is called a 'zero tolerance' approach, and a particular brand of a chain of charter schools is called 'No Excuses'. 'No Excuses' schools, and another, the 'Knowledge is Power Programme' (KIPPS) schools, are direct imports to England from the US. 'Absolute Returns for Kids' (ARK) and SPARK schools are other analogous brands also operating in South Africa, albeit within the framework of the CAPS curriculum, as of 2017.

This model of schooling is now gaining ground, with some countries going in the opposite direction, like Finland cited above, and also France, with the promulgation of the 'loi Jospin'[2] reforms in 1989, for example. It now operates in Sweden, New Zealand, Venezuela, Columbia, Peru, Pakistan and Uganda in addition to the US, UK and SA. It will not be surprising that the achievements of these schools are variable. In the US, the 'No Excuses' and KIPPS schools show the greatest success at narrowing the equity gap (Epple et al. 2015). In the UK the gains are discernible but small (Hofmeyr 2018), and there is some doubt as to whether the increased cohort averages reflect gains for the whole class or mainly just for the top 20% of the distribution (Whitty 2016). The results from Sweden are similarly equivocal. As Whitty concludes, the rather disappointing success rates at narrowing the equity gap should not be taken to mean 'that schools cannot make a difference, or that they do not have a particularly important role in helping to narrow the attainment gap and thereby enhancing the life chances of disadvantaged children. It does mean that they cannot do it alone' (ibid, 72). To put that more plainly: test scores reflect the knowledge mastered from all sources, not only from the school. Advantaged students are constantly building up academic knowledge from both the school and the home, from class or absorbed by reading or self-study. Disadvantaged students gain proportionally most of their academic knowledge whilst at school – that is a core neglected meaning of 'educational disadvantage'. Advantaged students will thus always be gaining more than disadvantaged students even when the school and the teacher is doing a good job conveying academic knowledge. Test score disparities should thus be treated with caution when taken as the only indicator of educational inequity.

The purpose of this section of the chapter has been to outline the two curriculum models misleadingly called 'traditionalism' and 'progressivism', and to show how they oscillate in curriculum reform fashions. The next section will delve into the social logic of these models.

6.2 The Social Logic of Curriculum Models: Competence and Performance

The name 'traditional' is misleading in several senses. When related to curriculum, the term takes its first meaning, at least in Europe where schooling first began to massify, in the sixteenth century with Peter Ramus in Paris who was the first to codify a curriculum. Up until then, instruction was an oral art, and each teacher decided what to do as (invariably) he went along. There were no set subjects or topics, and pedagogical authority vested in the oral presentation of the teacher, but deriving in the last instance from Aristotle, hence also known as 'classical'. Ramus did not only produce the first written curriculum, but he also ordered the

---

[2]Loi d'orientation sur l'éducation.

curriculum topics, both horizontally – designing topic clusters into proto-disciplines he called 'arts'; and hierarchically, from particulars to universals. In this way was born the modern 'traditional' curriculum with its ordering into subjects which were internally ordered by curriculum sequencing and progression principles (Ong 1961; Hamilton 1990; Triche and McKnight 2004). This new pedagogical object could also for the first time be printed by Gutenberg's new invention, and the result went through 150 editions in 45 years. Also for the first time could the curriculum be disseminated for consideration at a distance, and knowledge progression could be topographically displayed.

German romanticism formed the philosophical basis for a revolt against this radical externalisation of knowledge, and the basis for proto-progressivist alternatives to what was by now the mainstream in schooling. These provided the template for nineteenth century alternatives such as Froebel, Hebart, Pestalozzi, Steiner and Montessori. Even Dewey's system derived from Hegel. The main point about these alternative systems was that, with the partial exception of Dewey, they all remained peripheral to the mainstream traditional curriculum. What they all had in common was a greater or lesser reaction to traditionalism's rationalism, an emphasis on the inner life of the learner, and the desire to release the inner nature of the learner through minimal direction and imposition. As Antonio Gramsci said of the progressive Gentile reforms in 1929,

> The new education created a kind of church that paralyzed pedagogical research. It produced curious aberrations like "spontaneity", which supposed that the child's brain is like a ball of string that the teacher should help unwind. In reality, each generation educates and forms each new generation. Education opposes the elemental biological instincts of nature[3]

These are, in brief, the antecedents to 'traditionalism' and 'progressivism'. But that tells us nothing about the particular purchase progressivism has exercised on mainstream educational thinking since the 1960s. The question we are more interested in is why and how did progressivism emerge from the alternative shadows and make a bid for the mainstream in the late 1960s. Bernstein traces this to a marked convergence in the social and psychological sciences around the concept of 'competence'.[4] A 'competence' is an inner or in-built potential for some or other specialised repertoire. It is something that must be activated and actualized, not something that is acquired from outside. Bernstein goes on to anatomise the 'social logic' of the concept of 'competence':

- One has a 'competence' – say, a competence for maths – by definition, just as one has for one's mother tongue. If one is not competent, it is not something that one lacks. Rather, the competence has just not been activated. Hence, as

---

[3]Quoted at http://www.nationalreview.com/article/445038/educational-reformer-hirsch-promotes-knowledge-against-its-enemies.

[4]In the vocational education literature, the term 'competence' takes a meaning opposite to the one ascribed to it here by Bernstein. There, it means an external skill or performance.

Bernstein (2000, p. 43) says, 'competence' prefigures a 'universal democracy of acquisition'.

- The learner is active and creative. External imposition of instructional content can thus hinder rather than enlighten the learner.
- This means in turn that the learner self-regulates; learning should be emancipatory, not regulatory.
- This leads naturally to a suspicion of pedagogical hierarchy, that between learners and between the learners and the teacher. The best teacher is thus a facilitator and midwife to the emergence of competence.
- The focus is on the present, not the past (the canonical curriculum and its content) neither on an anticipated future where the reality of work and its specialised cognitive requirements lies in wait; the active and emancipatory present is the space of creative enlightenment.

'Competence' is thus the emblem for the rejection of the externalised knowledge necessary for a common curriculum; 'acquisition', like 'transmission', points to educational activities of the outside and thus transgresses against the creative inner, the ideal wellspring of knowledge in the progressive classroom. Bernstein traces the new mainstream allure of this idea in education to various social movements of the 1960s – the rise of militant student protests, rock 'n roll, the emergence of the 'youth' as a sociological and political subject, and anti-authoritarianisms of various kinds. We might add, the emergence of popular democracy movements. It is small wonder that a younger cohort of educators and teachers would be drawn to the heady promise of emancipation, democracy and equality that progressivism embodied. In its giddier moments, progressivism seemed to promise something better than education. Who needs it? Not Willis' 'lads' who had their own counter-cultural competence, or the street urchins of Brazil and Mozambique, whose 'street mathematics' worked just fine for them, or Labov's non-standard speakers of English.

Above all, 'competence' presaged a genuine rupture with the staid and traditional model of schooling that had reproduced inequality so remorselessly, because of a special property. Competence did not so much embrace a route out of the power relations. Rather, as Bernstein put it, 'competences are beyond the reach and restraints of power relations and their differential unequal positionings' (ibid, 147). No wonder it was, and is, seen as radical. It is a self-legitimising notion, a 'means of bestowing ideological purity'(ibid, 148). To put it bluntly, the competence-progressive promise was to transcend the cruel strictures of class-determined educational destiny. Consider then it's attraction in a country like South Africa in 1994, newly liberated, in a new dawn of democracy. A progressive curriculum seemed not only a logical step but a political necessity, and any warnings against such a curriculum were seen as political heresy.

If the competence model locates its principle of dynamism as **internal** to the learner, the principle of dynamism of the alternative model, which Bernstein calls a performance model, is located **externally** in the intended curriculum and its design. A performance-based curriculum is driven by the amount of content to be covered, by the pace at which it is to be covered, and by the sequence in which it is set. What is evaluated in the competence model is the competence, or potential, of the learner as activated; in the performance model, in contrast, it is the learner's performance on the knowledge prescribed by the intended curriculum.

Two sub-forms of the performance model are relevant for present purposes. They are, first, the specialised sub-form developed during the slow growth of elite into mass schooling. This sub-form is sometimes conflated with elite schooling as a basis for its rejection. We will also refer to this sub-form as the autonomous performance form. The second is a form we shall call generic, where the external dynamism comes not so much from the knowledge base itself as from the presumed requirements of the marketplace, either those currently in place, increasingly those presumed to be in force in some or other future. These are skills such as 'working in a team', 'communication skills', sometimes referred to collectively as 'twenty first century skills'. Qualifications frameworks and outcomes-based curriculum systems are systems that stipulate the curriculum in such generic skills based terms, which if left unqualified, lead to an under-specified curriculum.

The generic performance sub-form is a confusing one because, as Bernstein says, it shares fundamental features in common with the competence model, in that it stipulates general attributes which all learners should, and the implication is could, attain. It shares thus some of the democratic aura of competence, and is consequently frequently seen as progressive. It is thus often seen, erroneously, as a component part of a competence model.[5] As Allais (2014) points out, however, the rationale for all generic skills is to be of instrumental service to the market. This makes generic skills integral to a neoliberal rather than a progressive emancipatory social project which would regard any attempt to bend the inner creative potential of learners to instrumental ends as a deformation of that creative spark.

6.3 South African Curriculum Reform

Post-apartheid, South Africa has gone through a number of curriculum reform processes that bear a striking resemblance to some of the reform processes described above. As in many newly democratizing and newly massifying systems, South Africa's initial reform effort was progressivist, centred on learner-centred reforms that sought to undo the politically tainted traditional curriculum of the past and herald a new curriculum for a new society. It also shifted the stipulatory template towards an outcomes-based curriculum design. This much is by now common knowledge. Less commonly remarked, there were also two parallel processes of reform: one for the General Education and Training (GET) band of schooling

---

[5]This confusion has been long remarked, see Jones and Moore (1993) and Bernstein (2000). As Muller (2000, p. 107) concludes, 'There is little doubt that this confusion is an integral part of the confusion of the policy field in South Africa'.

Fig. 6.1 Two parallel reform processes

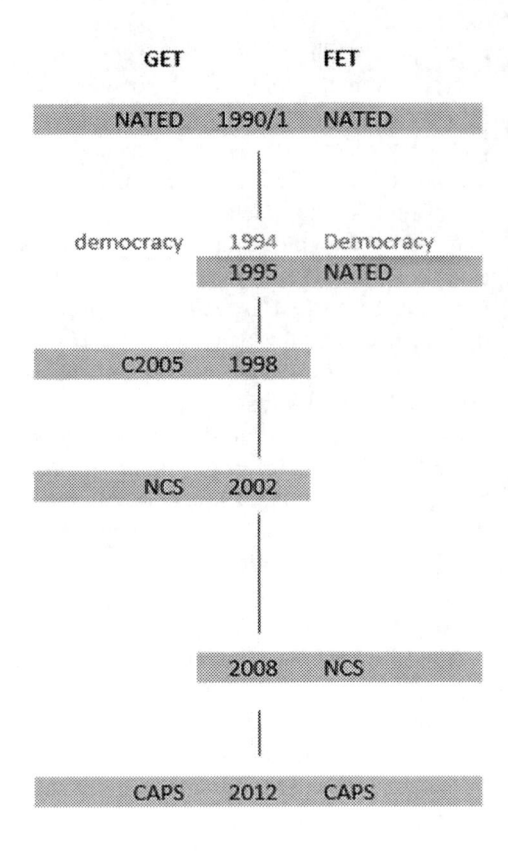

(Grades R to 9) and a different process for the Further Education and Training (FET) band, that consisted of the final three years of schooling, grades 10 to 12. The two processes are shown in Fig. 6.1 in the timeline above.

The first national curriculum initiative had been undertaken in 1995 by the National Education and Training Forum, but was restricted to an exercise of 'cleansing' offensive and outdated aspects of the last apartheid curriculum, the 'NATED', a specialized performance based curriculum which became the de facto curriculum for both the GET and the FET bands in the first years of the democratic regime. In 1998, a much-heralded new curriculum, Curriculum 2005 (C2005), was introduced, with the intention that it would be phased in, starting with the lower grades, until it was fully rolled out throughout the system in 2005. C2005 was a radical learner-centred, competence model set in an outcomes-based stipulatory framework. C2005 precluded the specification of formal subject knowledge. In this version of a learner-centred reform teachers and learners were expected to select their own content and devise programmes of learning. Given the schooling system from which most teachers had just emerged, the possibilities of teachers and learners co-constructing a curriculum with no guidance was extremely ambitious. It was rolled out in the lower GET grades in 1998.

C2005 was at root a hybrid model. On the one hand, it pulled in a progressive, competence-based direction in the emphasis placed on learner-centredness and an emphasis on the creative activity of the learners, in synchrony with shifts internationally. On the other hand, it pulled the curriculum in a generic performance direction. One reason for this latter leaning was the influence of the labour unions and of the business lobby in negotiations around the model to be adopted, with their demands for a skills-based curriculum linked to a National Qualification Framework (Jansen 1998). An outcomes-based framework was consequently adopted, focused on a discrete, generic, demonstrable performance required of the learner. This tension – between a competence-based progressive form and a performance model, compromised content stipulation. The competence arm decried explicit content stipulation on the grounds that this would infringe the rights of teachers and learners to together chart the learning course; and the outcomes based format required stipulation in skills based terms only. Together these produced a radical form of under-stipulated curriculum. And there was nothing to mind the gap between learners coming from this hybrid under-stipulated system and the last three years of the system that was still, during the early years of the reform roll out, operating with a specialized performance curriculum which placed entirely different pedagogic demands on learners.

The second post-apartheid reform, in 2002, resulted in the National Curriculum Statement (NCS). Here some gains were made in the specification of knowledge. However, the curriculum model produced in this reform effort was again hybrid, fuelled by strong political interests. Crucially, an outcomes-based framework was retained for this curriculum. OBE had become a highly-politicized symbol of change, and to reject OBE was still regarded as tantamount to being anti-transformation. The Minister of Education at the time, therefore, refused to abandon the framework despite its increasingly obvious pedagogical short-comings and the conceptual instability of the curriculum (Asmal 2000).

Finally, at the GET level in the third post-apartheid curriculum reform in 2012 – the Curriculum and Assessment Policy Statement (CAPS) – there was a decisive shift towards a specialised performance based curriculum. The curriculum provided high specification of subject content to be covered, as well as clear stipulations regarding the sequencing and pace of coverage. Summative assessment and textbooks, both quashed in the prior reforms, were reasserted as critical aspects of the learning process.

The FET, as Fig. 6.1 indicates, followed a somewhat different trajectory. Throughout its reform path it remained performance based. Clear knowledge specification was never abandoned at this level, most likely because content in these grades was anchored by the summative assessment requirements of the school leaving certificate exam (the 'matric'). When a revision of the NATED was finally undertaken in 2005, to try and align the FET with the GET phase of schooling, documents called the Subject Assessment Guidelines provided clear subject content specification, content that was blurred in the earlier statements based on outcomes. These Subject Assessment Guidelines documents effectively superseded the curriculum outcome statements in practice. In the third reform, the Curriculum and Assessment Policy Statement (CAPS), a similar process for GET and FET was followed. Numerous curriculum documents were rationalized into a single document that contained high specifications of subject content and expectations of sequencing and pacing of coverage. In the CAPS, both GET and FET were brought in line in a specialised performance-based curriculum.

At the GET level, we see a move internal to the curriculum towards greater design coherence and content specification, shifting the curriculum of C2005 from a competence/generic performance hybrid, to a non-generic performance-based curriculum. At the FET level content specification was retained throughout; C2005 was effectively halted by the Review Committee's report (2000); in the NCS process the FET curriculum was cosmetically brought into line with an outcomes-based framework while retaining high stipulation of subject content in the Subject Assessment Guidelines; in the CAPS process, external coherence between the GET and FET levels was achieved by placing both bands of schooling within the same framework.

At the end of the first cycle of curriculum reform in South Africa then, we can see that the first reform started out in a radical competence based direction. This thrust was first slowed down by the NCS, then halted in the CAPS. The FET curriculum was never reformed in a competence direction. Finally, coherence has finally been achieved between the GET and FET curricular models. Yet, the performance of South Africa's learners and the health of South Africa's schooling, while improving modestly when viewed over time (Van der Berg and Gustafsson 2017), is by most observers still regarded as being in crisis. In curricular terms then, where lies the worm in the bud? Is the bar set too high for our learners? Has the curriculum been over-stipulated (Shalem 2018)? A recent evaluation finds too much 'breadth of content' in some subjects, and too many assessment tasks (DPME/Department of Basic Education 2017). There is recognition from the Department of Education that there is a need to 'reduce content' in the CAPS and to concentrate on 'depth', possibly labelling some content 'optional' or 'for further study'. But we argue that the main problem does not lie with the CAPS but rather with what happens in the classroom.

6.4 The Problem of Pedagogy

In curriculum terms then, we see a shift towards greater coherence both internal to the curriculum at the GET level, and between the GET and FET levels. The curriculum is highly specified with respect to subject content, as well as its sequencing and pacing demands. It has become a stable signalling system for teachers, textbook writers, examiners and teacher training institutions. At the level of pedagogy and what was going on in classrooms, a different story remains to be told. At the GET level, the shifts from a non-functioning performance model (during apartheid) to a competence model (C2005) and then back to a performance model (CAPS) were accompanied by very little support for teachers. Under apartheid, a communalising pedagogy[6] predominated, where classes were treated as homogenous units and a rite of rote was established between teachers and learners with a heavy reliance on memorization and chorusing. In this pedagogy, the lack of individualized evaluation and the ritualized exchange creates a synchrony between teacher and students so that classroom activity is fundamentally communal. No distinctions or judgements are made of individual learners and their activity, and initiative and spontaneity on the part of students is foreclosed (Hoadley 2018). This form was sustained across the reforms, with teachers taking up features of the reform that were congruent with this pedagogic form. It is not surprising then, that 'group work' for many teachers defined C2005, and its implementation in classrooms became a marker for a changed pedagogy. Criterion referenced, summative assessment was eliminated in favour of peer assessment, group and continuous assessment which sustained a communalising pedagogic form.

Hoadley (2018) shows how this communalised form was sustained across the NCS and the CAPS reforms. In the absence of any effective in-service training (Council on Higher Education (CHE) 2010; De Clercq and Shalem 2014), and pre-service offerings with untested impact (NEEDU 2014), teachers were offered no opportunities to observe and acquire practices other than those they were schooled in themselves and that were reproduced in training colleges. In other words, there was no mimetic interrupter for teachers' practices and limited opportunity for their cognitive horizons (Craig 1989) to expand (Gueguen et al. 2009). In other words, there was literally no model of a different repertoire on offer to show the teachers what a different style of pedagogy would look like. All they had to fall back on was the old dysfunctional performance pedagogy of their own schooling and their teacher training. The shift to a performance mode in the CAPS entailed teachers taking on surface features of the new reform; the communal form was sustained in a rote, procedural approach to the stipulated content in the pedagogic enactment.

At the FET level, across the three reforms, the consistently performance-based curriculum model standardized pedagogy across time.[7] But this too was a form of dysfunctional traditionalism, often characterized as 'teacher-centred' with a heavy reliance on textbooks (Patel 1998). In mathematics Kazima et al. (2008) describes this pedagogic form as the teacher presenting a mathematical idea, followed by a worked example, followed by practice in the set textbook. Bertram (2009,

---

[6]A 'communalising pedagogy' is one where the teachers worked with the whole class as a homogeneous group, with little or no differentiation of tasks or differentiation of individual performances. In a communalising pedagogy, close scrutiny of what individual learners produce is not possible, and, consequently, the conditions for the successful production of the relevant pedagogic text are foreclosed.

[7]There is very little research at the FET classroom level. Prior to 1994, schools were hostile to the presence of researchers. After 1994, there was pressure to understand what was going on in classrooms, especially given anecdotal reporting of an on-going 'breakdown in the culture of teaching and learning'. However, given the implementation of C2005, the raft of studies of classrooms at the time focused on the GET level and the effects of the implementation of the 'new' (mainly C2005 and NCS) curriculum (see Hoadley 2012).

p.130) also identifies these 'traditional forms' in History, where 'the information transmitted was not open for discussion or debate, nor was there any sense that there may be other versions of it'. This is the antithesis of the autonomous or specialised performance pedagogy regime because by this time, communalisation as a core practice had become deeply engrained. As at the GET level, individuation of learners, a core tenet of the autonomous variant, was likewise absent from this traditional pedagogy at the FET level. In assessment practices, however, especially towards the end of the FET phase, a brutal form of individualisation took precedence, marking students out as passing or failing through stringent summative tests and the final school examination, the 'matric'. This must in part explain the fact that still only around 50% of the cohort starting grade 1 reach matric.

6.5 Conclusion: The Curriculum Paradox

Curriculum reform in South Africa in the post 1994 period has described a kind of arrested spiral. It properly began in 1998 with the roll out of C2005, a competence model with generic performance features in the form of outcomes. This model was partially halted by the Review in 2000 and only partly reformed with the NCS in 2002. The transition to a thorough-going performance model was completed with CAPS in 2012, concluding the curriculum re-design phase of school reform.

But what kind of performance model has this left us with? We have referred in this chapter to two kinds of performance model (the generic sub-form aside). The first we called an autonomous or specialised form; the second we called a 'dysfunctional' form. This calls for clarification. The autonomous performance model focuses on the specialisation of the learner's consciousness. Learners who come through successfully possess a specialised consciousness with attendant specialised knowledge and skills which in most cases serve as a preparation for tertiary study, or at least a semi-professional slot in the labour market. The problem with this model is that it does not specialise the consciousness of all learners to the same satisfactory degree, and so is sometime called an elite model since only a few do very well and many do not succeed at all. It is this model which has, for this reason, gained the opprobrium of progressives everywhere. Nevertheless, this is the most common form found in the 20% school system.

The performance form we have in South Africa in most of our classrooms for the poor, in common with much of the developing world, is the outward form of a performance pedagogy which, however, instills a common or communalised consciousness, based on shared values and practices, cemented by consensual classroom rituals that foreclose on individualisation. This is in comparison to the differentiating rituals that specialise consciousness, knowledge and skills in the autonomous performance classrooms.

Part of the paradox, then, is that within the same performance-modelled curriculum which is the CAPS, two pedagogic models can co-exist, one a communalising form, the other an individualising form, which both share some common external features – teacher led, strongly sequenced and paced – but which have quite different effects on the capacities and attributes of learners. We have called the communalised form 'dysfunctional' above, but that is not strictly accurate. It communalises not because the teachers are somehow inadequate. It communalises for two other key reasons. The first is because of embedded routines of communalisation which all schools with low social capital share. These routines, especially in the rural areas, are constantly reinforced by comparison with the routines in similar schools nearby. The second reason follows on: the teachers have no local role models to mimic or to learn from.

The intervention most commonly designed to interrupt these routines is a relatively low dosage teacher in-service course, which is simply too little too late to make up the shortfall in teacher knowledge (Taylor N in this volume) and in any case, can't deal with the problem of embeddedness. Of course, intensive treatments can show impact, but these are usually small scale, and when they do work, they interrupt not only the routines internal to the school but risk disrupting the pattern of community solidarity which the community communalising rituals were designed to foster under harsh conditions of poverty. This is the other arm of the paradox; communalisation is not simply a dysfunctional form of pedagogy, but is itself embedded in a larger set of community solidarity coping mechanisms rendered necessary by environments of endemic poverty. The problem is not in any straightforward way simply pedagogical. We must conclude that a sea change in these schools awaits a new cohort of teachers who have been more appropriately inducted into the knowledge they need to be effective teachers. It also awaits some form of betterment for the communities within which these schools are embedded.

It is not only knowledge that teachers require. We don't yet know what a successful pedagogy in the majority of South African schooling contexts looks like. The autonomous performance model cannot simply be inserted into any context, ignoring the established classroom routines that define classroom practice there. We need to shift teachers' 'cognitive horizons' (see Hoadley 2018) not just in relation to better subject knowledge, but in conceiving and demonstrating a successful pedagogy that engenders *learning in those specific contexts*. This may at times entail a careful calibration between a communal social form and an individualized knowledge orientation. What such a calibration might look like is not yet clear. But it is a worthy research and teacher development pursuit to find and install a role model that makes sense for teachers in especially poorer schools to mimic.

References

Allais, S. (2014). *Selling out education: National qualifications frameworks and the neglect of knowledge*. Rotterdam: Sense Publishers.

Asmal, K. (2000). *Outcomes-based teaching here to stay*. Business Day, 7 Aug 2000.

Bernstein, B. (2000). *Pedagogy, symbolic control, and identity: Theory, research, critique*. London: Rowman and Littlefield Publishers.

Bertram, C. (2009). Learning and teaching in grade 10 history classrooms at a time of curriculum reform. *Journal of Educational Studies, 8*(3), 111–134.

Carnoy, M., & Marshall, J. (2005). Cuba's academic performance in comparative perspective. *Comparative Education Review, 49*(2), 230–261.

Council on Higher Education (CHE). (2010). *Report on the national review of academic and professional programmes in education.* HE Monitor 11, CHE. Pretoria.

Craig, A. (1989). The conflict between the familiar and the unfamiliar. *South African Journal of Higher Education, 3*(1), 166–172.

De Clercq, F., & Shalem, Y. (2014) Teacher knowledge and employer-driven professional development: A critical analysis of the Gauteng Department of Education programmes. *Southern African Review of Education with Production, 20*(1), 129–147.

Deng, Z., & Gopinathan, S. (2016) PISA and high-performing education systems: Explaining Singapore's education success. *Comparative Education, 52*(4), 449–472.

DPME/Department of Basic Education. (2017). *Implementation evaluation of the National Curriculum Statement Grade R to 12 focusing on the Curriculum and Assessment Policy Statements (CAPS).* Pretoria: Department of Planning, Monitoring and Evaluation/Department of Basic Education.

Duoblys, G. (2017). One, two, three, eyes on me! George Duoblys on the new school discipline. *London Review of Books, 39*(19), 23–26.

Ensor, P. (2015). Regulative discourse, ritual and the recontextualising of education policy into practice. *Learning, Culture and Social Interaction, 6*, 67–76.

Epple, D., Romano, R., & Zimmer, R. (2015). Charter schools: A survey of research on their characteristics and effectiveness. In *Working Paper 21256 NBER*, Cambridge.

Fitz, J., Evans, J., & Davies, B. (2006). *Educational policy and social reproduction: Class inscription & symbolic control.* London: Routledge.

Glewwe, P., & Muralidharan, K. (2015). Improving school education outcomes in developing countries: Evidence, knowledge gaps, and policy implications. In Pritchett & Beatty and Eppel et al (Eds.), *RISE Working Paper 15/001.* Oxford: University of Oxford.

Gueguen, N., Jacob, C., & Martin, A. (2009). Mimicry in social interaction: Its effect on human judgment and behavior. *European Journal of Social Sciences, 8*(2), 253–259.

Hamilton, D. (1990). From curriculum to *Bildung* (Some Preliminary Considerations). In *Paper presented to the International Standing Conference for the History of Education*, Prague, 23–26 Aug 1990.

Hoadley, U. (2012). What do we know about teaching and learning in South African primary schools? *Education as Change, 16*(2), 187–202.

Hoadley, U. (2018). *Pedagogy in poverty: Lessons from twenty years of curriculum reform in South Africa.* London: Routledge.

Hoadley, U., & Muller, J. (2018). Pedagogic modality and structure in the recontextualising field of curriculum studies: The South African case. In: B. Barrett, U. Hoadley, & J. Morgan (Eds.), *Knowledge, curriculum and equity: Social realist perspectives* (pp. 80–101). London: Routledge.

Hofmeyr, J. (2018). Personal communication, 5 Mar 2018.

Jansen, J. D. (1998). Curriculum reform in South Africa: A critical analysis of outcomes-based education. *Cambridge Journal of Education, 28*(3), 321–331.

Jones, L., & Moore, R. (1993). Education, competence and the control of expertise. *British Journal of Sociology of Education, 14*(4), 385–397.

Kazima, M., Pillay, V., & Adler, J. (2008). Mathematics for teaching: Observations from two case studies. *South African Journal of Education, 28*(2), 283–299.

McEaneny, E. H., & Meyer, J. W. (2008). The content of the curriculum: An institutionalist perspective. In: J. Ballantine & J. Spade (Eds.), *Schools and society: A sociological approach to education* (3rd ed.). Thousand Oaks: Sage Publications.

Muller, J. (2000). *Reclaiming knowledge: Social theory, curriculum and education policy.* London: RoutledgeFalmer.

NEEDU. (2014). *National Report 2014: The quality of learning outcomes*. The National Educational Evaluation and Development Unit, Pretoria.

Ong, W. J. (1961). Ramist classroom procedure and the nature of reality. *Studies in English Literature, 1500–1900, 1*(1), 31–47.

Patel, B. V. (1998). *The teaching of South African history: Past and present*. Washington, DC: George Washington University School for International Training.

Plowden, B. (1967). *Central advisory council for education (England)(1967)*. Children and their primary schools: A report of the central advisory council for education (England) 1.

Pritchett, L., & Beatty, A. (2012). The negative consequences of overambitious curricula in developing countries. In *Centre for Global Development, CGD Working Paper 293*, Washington.

Sahlgren, G. H. (2015). *Real Finnish Lessons. The True Story of an Education Superpower*. London: Centre for Policy Studies.

Schneider, B., Estarellas, P., & Bruns, B. (2017, Unpublished paper). The politics of transforming education in ecuador: Confrontation and continuity, 2006–2017. Washington, DC: World Bank.

Shalem, Y. (2018). Scripted lesson plans: What is visible and invisible in visible pedagogy? In B. Barrett, U. Hoadley, & J. Morgan (Eds.), *Knowledge, curriculum and equity: Social realist perspectives* (pp. 183–199). London: Routledge.

Shriewer, J. (2000). Educational studies in Europe? In E. Swing, J. Schriewer, & S. Orivel (Eds.), *Problems and prospects in European education* (pp 72–96). Westport: Praeger Publishers.

Simons, J., & Porter, N. (2015). *Knowledge and the curriculum: A collection of essays to accompany E.D Hirsch's lecture at Policy Exchange*. London: Policy Exchange.

Suransky-Dekker, C. (1998). *'A liberating breeze of western civilisation'? A political history of fundamental pedagogics as an expression of Dutch-Afrikaner relationships*. Unpublished D Ed dissertation, University of Durban-Westville.

Triche, S., & McKnight, D. (2004). The quest for method: The legacy of Peter Ramus. *History of Education, 33*(1), 39–54.

UNICEF. (1990). World declaration on education for all and framework for action to meet basic learning needs. In *World Conference on Education for All*. Jomtien: UNESCO.

Van der Berg, S., & Gustafsson, M. (2017). *Quality of basic education: A report to working group 1 of the high level panel on the assessment of key legislation*. Cape Town: Parliament. Available from: https://www.parliament.gov.za/storage/app/media/Pages/2017/october/High_Level_Panel/Commissioned_reports_for_triple_challenges_of_poverty_unemployment_and_inequality/Diagnostic_Report_on_Quality_Education.pdf. Accessed Nov 2017.

Van der Berg, S., & Louw, M. (2007). *Lessons learnt from SACMEQII: South African student performance in regional context*. University of Stellenbosch, Department of Economics and Bureau for Economic Research Working Paper 16(07).

Van der Berg, S., Spaull, N., Wills, G., Gustafsson, M., & Kotzé, J. (2016). *Identifying binding constraints in education*. Stellenbosch: ReSEP.

Whitty, G. (2016). *Research and policy in education*. London: IOE Press.

Chapter 7
How Language Policy and Practice Sustains Inequality in Education

Nompumelelo L. Mohohlwane

7.1 Introduction

Approximately 81% of the 56.5 million people in South Africa are classified as African. Correspondingly 76% speak an indigenous South African language as their first language (Statistics South Africa 2017). Yet more than 80%[1] of Grade 4 learners tested in these languages could not make sense of explicitly stated information, actions or ideas in an internationally benchmarked reading assessment. The figure for those assessed in English or Afrikaans was 57% (Howie et al. 2017). There was a gap of 96 points between those that wrote in Sepedi or English; which is equivalent to more than two years of schooling.[2] This colossal difference is consistent across all the indigenous languages when they are compared to English. In summary; learners that are receiving their Foundation Phase education in indigenous South African languages are still performing far below their counterparts that are receiving this in English or Afrikaans. These are children born 10 years ago, in the foundational stages of their education today. The relationship between language and literacy continues to be one of the overlapping dimensions of inequality in education practice and outcomes.

---

[1]This is based on the performance of a nationally representative sample in the Progress in International Reading Literacy Study (PIRLS) 2016 assessment (Howie et al. 2017, p. 185).

[2]"In the PIRLS study, 40 score points are seen as a year of schooling (approximately half a Standard Deviation)" (Howie et al. 2017, p. 185).

N. L. Mohohlwane (✉)
Department of Basic Education, Pretoria, South Africa
e-mail: n.nyathin@gmail.com; Mohohlwane.N@dbe.gov.za

© Springer Nature Switzerland AG 2019
N. Spaull, J. D. Jansen (eds.), *South African Schooling: The Enigma of Inequality*, Policy Implications of Research in Education 10,
https://doi.org/10.1007/978-3-030-18811-5_7

The purpose of this chapter is to make an argument for how language in education policy and practice create and sustain inequality in post-Apartheid South Africa. This is done by synthesizing empirical data on the complex relationship and distinctions between language and literacy in indigenous South African languages (commonly referred to as African languages, this will be applied henceforth); followed by a discussion on the developments in curriculum and language in education policy and practice. The chapter then considers the theoretical discourse of language and power as a lens to interpret the status quo and then concludes with commentary on the gaps in language policy and practice with a focus on enabling improved implementation.

7.2 Why Language Matters

South Africa has a long history showcasing the overlap between power, identity and language. Language does not develop incidentally, it is the product of deliberate efforts. The development of Afrikaans as summarised in this section illustrates the concrete steps that were taken to develop the language. This section provides three such cases from different times in the country's history.

7.2.1 The Colonialization of South Africa

The first European language formally spoken by settlers in South Africa was Dutch. This followed the colonization of the Cape by European settlers who were mostly Dutch. Over time the local Dutch language evolved into Afrikaans[3] (Marjorie 1982; Silva 1997; Hans 2012). In 1795 the Dutch handed over power to the British following instructions from Holland. Although this transition was resisted, British rule persisted and in 1822 English was introduced as the language of learning, business and government in the Cape (Marjorie 1982; Silva 1997; Hans 2012). Further changes to the Dutch way of life were the abolition of slavery; and competition for land occupation and ownership. These changes are cited as the main reasons for the Afrikaner Great Trek in 1836. However, the Voortrekker meta-narrative emphasizes the loss of language autonomy amongst the reasons for the Afrikaners Great Trek. There is evidence that this careful reconstruction

---

[3]A Dutch company established a trading station in the Cape in 1652. The Cape had previously been used by the English and Portuguese as a trade stopover. These European settlers were mostly Dutch speaking but other European nationalities including the Portuguese, Germans and Huguenot French were present. They formed a new Cape Dutch community simply labelled "Dutch". This community later evolved into the Afrikaner nation with a new language known as Afrikaans (Marjorie 1982; Mesthrie 2002) The development of the language includes influences by the Khoi and San as well as Indian descent ethnic groups in the Cape in 1652.

emphasizing language was a fundamental part of Afrikaner patriotism and nation building efforts in the 1930s and 1940s (Grundlingh and Huigen 2011; Sparks 1990; Bond 2003).

7.2.2 The Union of South Africa

The initial development of literature was partly driven by a commitment to distinguish Dutch from English and subsequently Afrikaans; as well as political ambitions. The establishment of Naspers,[4] a publishing company in 1915 as an instrument to support Afrikaner nationalism provides compelling evidence of this. The publications by Naspers included an Afrikaans (initially Dutch) daily newspaper Die Burger published from 1915 and edited by DF Malan until 1924. Malan later became the Prime Minister in 1948 when the National Party came into power. The newspaper served as a mouthpiece of the National Party until 1990 (Pretorius 2014). The Genootskap van Regte Afrikaners (Society of True Afrikaners) is a further pivotal organisation that lobbied for the official status of Afrikaans as well as ensuring that the language was written and formalized (Roberge 2002; Mesthrie 2002). The explicit aim of this society was establishing Afrikaans as a language in its own right (Antonissen 2017). Through these and other efforts Afrikaans was recognized as an official language in addition to English in 1925 (Roberge 2002; Mesthrie 2002).

7.2.3 Apartheid

Afrikaans finally consolidated dominion from 1948 when the National Party came into power, conducting governance, business and administration almost exclusively in Afrikaans. The National Party segregated people by race and language, this was codified in policy including language in education policy. The 1961 Constitution provided that

> no court of law shall be competent to enquire into or pronounce upon the validity of any Act passed by Parliament, other than an Act which repeals or amends the provisions of section 128 or 113 ... [referring to English and Afrikaans as official languages] (Bond 2003, pp. 17–18).

Segregation was enforced at all levels of schooling and encompassed the development of universities offering education exclusively in Afrikaans to white students. To foster this development the government spent at least 10 times as much on white students as on black students (Bond 2003, p.16). This was complemented by increased resource allocation such as textbooks and intensive cultural promotion of

---

[4]Naspers was established under the name De Nationale Pers Beperkt (National Press Ltd).

Afrikaans (Silva 1997; Grundlingh and Huigen 2011). Afrikaner owned publishing houses became the principal providers of school textbooks. During 1990–1998 Afrikaans clearly dominated literary[5] publishing. The number of Afrikaans books published during this time is estimated at 2800; while only 970 were published in English and a total of 1200 were published across all 9 African languages (Galloway 2002, p. 221).

On June 16 1976 15,000 young people marched against the Apartheid government in opposition to the language policy as well as other educational inequalities (Marjorie 1982; Grundlingh and Huigen 2011). This was after the government's 1974[6] attempt to extend Afrikaans to additional subjects, as one of the languages of learning in Bantu schools (Oakes 1988; Ndlovu 2006). This language policy change was rejected by students, parents, teachers, school principals' and even homeland leaders. Evidence of this is demonstrated by the African Teachers' Association of South Africa's (ATASA) January 1976 submission of a memorandum to the Department of Bantu Education (Ndlovu 2006, pp. 330–331). This memorandum clearly articulated opposition to the language change but neither the Department nor Parliament recognized the seriousness of this. The opposition escalated, resulting in the June 16 protests by students, parents and communities. Placards at the march included slogans such as *Blacks are not dustbins – Afrikaans stinks*, *Away with Kaferkaans*, and *Afrikaans is a tribal language* (Marjorie 1982; Oakes 1988; Ndlovu 2006, p.335).

7.2.4   Democratic South Africa

More recently, between 2015 and 2017, the language in education debate gained particular focus in university provisioning. Universities have since made landmark changes by adapting their academic language policies. The Constitutional Court legitimized these developments by upholding the 2016 University of Free State Senate decision to have the single medium of English as the language of instruction (Constitutional Court of South Africa 2017; University of Free State 2016). The university historically provided teaching in Afrikaans then adopted dual-medium provisioning in English and Afrikaans from 1993 (Botha 2017). Similar changes have been made within the same timeframe by the University of Pretoria who now offer English as the single medium; and the University of Stellenbosch adopting a dual-medium language policy of English and Afrikaans (University of Pretoria 2016; University of Stellenbosch 2016). These changes largely occurred in response to criticism and student protest by learners excluded through the privileging of Afrikaans.

---

[5]Literary books are defined as poetry, drama and fiction books (Galloway 2002).
[6]The Bantu Education Act of 1953.

While all of these developments were clearly about political power and identity, it would be remiss to exclude the overlap of language and literacy as a common motif.

7.3   Language and Literacy

It is difficult to refer to literacy without discussing language, especially in South Africa where levels of literacy differ by language. There is however a distinction, language is not necessarily literacy. Understanding this distinction is helpful in determining whether inequality lies in language or literacy, or both. The purpose of schooling as articulated in the South African curriculum is *equipping learners... with the knowledge, skills and values necessary for self – fulfilment, and meaningful participation in society as citizens of a free country* (Department of Basic education 2011, p.4). Literacy skills and knowledge are central to realizing this goal. Literacy is defined by the curriculum as the ability to *collect, analyze, organize and critically evaluate information and communicate effectively using visual, symbolic and/or language skills in various modes* (Department of Basic education 2011, p.5). Literacy in this chapter should be understood based on this broad definition as well as the narrow definition of competence in reading and writing through proficiency in specific schooling languages. Language is embedded in the definition of literacy and serves as a tool providing access to knowledge and information. Formally, language is defined as a universal means of human communication for the purposes of receiving or transmitting information (UNESCO 2017). Table 7.1 below provides the figures for language speakers according to language group and province.

Studies contributing to understanding the effects of language on literacy using empirical data have been limited in South Africa. The difficulty in identify the causal impact of language is due to other confounding factors affecting overall learner performance including socio-economic status (SES), ineffective teaching and limited learning and teaching resources (Taylor et al. 2013). The National School Effectiveness Study (NSES) is amongst the first few large scale nationally representative studies examining the causal impact of language on Literacy and Numeracy. In 2007 the same test was administered to a national sample of Grade 3 learners through the Department of Basic Education's Systemic Evaluations (SE) and the NSES. The only difference was that the SE was administered in the school's Language of Learning and Teaching (LOLT)[7] and the NSES was in English. The tests were administered a month apart.

---

[7] The LOLT selected by schools mostly matches the language of the majority of learners and was an African language in the majority of schools. LOLT is often referred to as Home Language however this may not always be the case.

Table 7.1 Population by first language spoken and province

First language	WC	EC	NC	FS	KZN	NW	GP	MP	LP	SA
Afrikaans	2,820,643	683,410	606,225	340,490	161,876	309,867	1,502,940	289,446	140,185	6,855,082
English	1,149,049	362,502	37,842	78,782	1,337,606	120,041	1,603,464	124,646	78,692	4,892,624
IsiNdebele	15,238	14,854	6,023	10,008	111,675	43,988	380,494	403,678	104,283	1,090,241
IsiXhosa	1,403,233	5,092,152	60,187	201,145	340,832	190,601	796,841	48,993	20,275	8,154,259
IsiZulu	24,634	31,634	8,501	118,126	7,901,932	84,835	2,390,036	965,253	62,424	11,587,375
Sepedi	8,144	14,299	2,431	7,395	20,555	83,999	1,282,896	372,392	2,826,464	4,618,575
Sesotho	64,066	158,964	14,136	1,717,881	79,416	201,153	1,395,089	138,559	80,299	3,849,563
Setswana	24,534	12,607	373,086	140,228	52,229	2,191,230	1,094,599	71,713	107,021	4,067,247
Sign Lang.	22,172	42,235	3,933	32,910	48,575	14,924	52,744	8,932	8,230	234,655
Siswathi	3,208	2,020	648	2,246	8,347	12,091	136,550	1,106,588	25,346	1,297,044
Tshivenda	4,415	3,663	1,083	2,592	4,309	16,255	272,122	12,140	892,809	1,209,388
Xitsonga	9,152	3,092	1,201	8,039	8,936	127,146	796,511	416,746	906,325	2,277,148
Other	127,117	36,893	12,385	15,935	77,519	60,872	371,575	39,639	86,322	828,257
Total	5,675,605	6,458,325	1,127,681	2,675,777	10,153,807	3,457,002	12,075,861	3,998,725	5,338,675	50,961,458

Source: Statistics South Africa Census 2011

The average score on both tests was low at 23% in the NSES and 33% in the SE for Literacy; and 34% in the NSES and 37% in the SE for Numeracy. Learner performance for English LOLT learners was similar across both tests (approximately 50%) while performance was different for African LOLT learners. The African LOLT learners performed better when assessed in the African LOLT than in English, with a statistically significant difference of approximately 10 percentage points in the case of Sesotho. However, overall performance was low, below 30% on average, in both tests. Furthermore, there was little difference in achievement between the two tests for those at the lowest levels of performance (Vorster et al. 2013, pp. 135–156). The main conclusion from this empirical study was that South African learners receiving their education in African languages do not become literate in any language by the end of Grade 3. This applies even in the language they know best and have received schooling in for three years.

In a reanalysis of the NSES and SE data Spaull (2016) estimates that the size of the language effect is approximately one to two years' worth of learning for literacy and one year for numeracy. The largest effect however, comes from the factors affecting schooling such as SES, and school quality and this is estimated as four years' worth of learning. Spaull argues that the low performance in Home Language illustrates that language is not the most important factor determining learner achievement but that overall school quality has an even larger impact. This view is supported by qualitative research which identifies quality inhibitors as the loss of teaching time, lack of appropriate literacy and numeracy learning and teaching support (LTSM) such as graded readers in African languages, poor pre-service training of teachers to teach African languages or English to second or third language speakers (Murray 2002; Taylor et al. 2013; Department of Basic Education 2017b). In Hoadley (2012)'s review of classroom-based studies on teaching and learning in South African primary schools the pedagogical practices of teachers serving African learners prioritized an oral discourse of chorusing with little reading or writing in quality or quantity; slow curriculum pacing leading to a failure to sufficiently cover the curriculum; and little use of textbooks, extended texts and other LTSMs.

Notwithstanding the overall low performance discussed above, literature has shown the benefits of initial learning in the home language. The applicability of this in the South African context has been demonstrated in the work of Taylor and Von Fintel (2016). The authors used longitudinal administrative and assessment data from the population of primary schools. The sample was restricted to schools where at least 80% of children were black, and officially categorized as the bottom three poverty quintiles. When comparing learners receiving instruction in English to those receiving instruction in African languages, the authors found that learners with African language instruction in the Foundation Phase had significantly higher English scores, as measured in Grade 4, 5 and 6. In interpreting these findings it is important to note that English and Afrikaans Home Language speakers still far outperform learners receiving their education in African languages. However, when comparing the same type of African learners affected by the same poor schooling quality constraints and disadvantaged background, these learners perform better in

English after first receiving their Foundation Phase learning in their Home Language than in cases where these schools adopt English as the LOLT in the Foundation Phase. This does not negate the fundamental finding of poor literacy in any language but rather supports the theoretical arguments of Home Language instruction and asserts that the poor performance in literacy and language is not due to an incorrect language policy decision.

What is clear in the findings from the empirical data discussed above is that language is a factor that impacts on literacy. However, the quality of instruction in all languages, including African languages is inadequate. Furthermore, language is a secondary factor to the quality of schooling which includes factors such as teacher pedagogy and knowledge in teaching literacy and other subjects. The understanding of this distinction and overlap is crucial in addressing the persistent inequalities that manifest in language and literacy and in understanding the language in education policy. The small number of empirical studies on the language of instruction or African languages in general has hindered academic and policy cohesion. There are still largely unanswered questions on when the language transitions should take place in schooling, from which languages and how best this may be mediated. The discourse on language inequality in literacy amongst sociologist, educationists and policy makers has largely been ideological with little use of empirical data to inform objective contributions to this important area. Substantially more research has been completed on English and Afrikaans in South Africa than on African languages (Pretorius 2018). This is disproportionate to the demographics of South Africa.

7.4   Language in Education Policy and Practice

This section discusses the factors considered for policy in more detail. The language in education policy is intended to legislate education provisioning by specifying the official language to be utilized, the expected proficiency, and the grades and subjects which it applies to. It also serves to redress historical inequalities and future educational outcomes. The specific declarations on language in education in the Constitution are discussed below as well as the five key policies that respond to the Constitutional prescripts. These policies continue to form the basis for language in education to date.

The Constitution of South Africa recognizes 11 official languages and gives authority to provinces to use any of these languages for governance, with a minimum of two languages used. The national and provincial government are tasked with monitoring and regulating the use of languages. The Constitution then makes provision for the establishment of a Pan South African Language Board (PANSALB) with the purpose of promoting and creating conditions for the development and use of the official languages. In addition to the 11 official languages allowance is made for Khoi, Nama and San languages; and finally Sign Language. The promotion

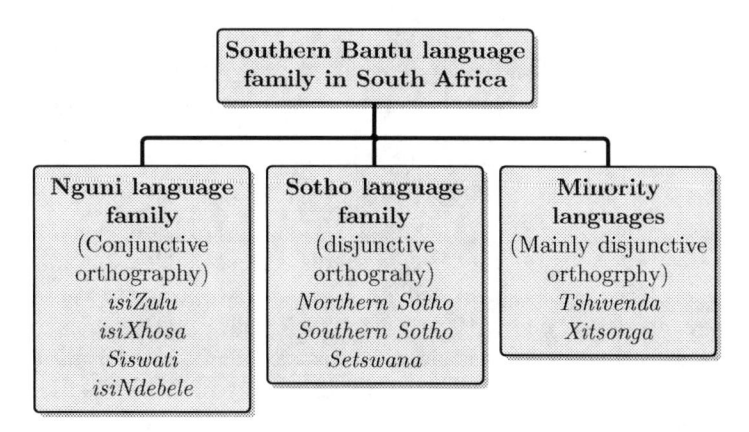

Fig. 7.1 The Southern Bantu language families in South Africa. (Source: Spaull N., Pretorius, EJ & N Mohohlwane (2018) based on approved national languages)

and respecting of other languages commonly used by communities in South Africa including Hindi and Greek is also mentioned. In the specific area of education, the Constitution enshrines the right for everyone to receive education in any of the official languages or that of their choice in public schools wherever this is reasonably practical. It further proposes that all implementation options should be considered including single medium education (Republic of South Africa 1996a). Figure 7.1 shows the African languages and their linguistic groupings, English and Afrikaans are not included in the table.

The National Education Policy Act (NEPA) of 1996 provides for the determination of national education policy by the Minister of Education after consultation with the Council of Education Ministers (CEM). The CEM members are the Minister, Deputy Minister and provincial political heads' of education. It specifies the function of the Minister as determining the language in education in addition to other functions; while provinces are mandated to co-ordinate administrative actions and implement national policy (Republic of South Africa 1996b). The South African Schools Act (SASA) of 1996 then mandates the Minister to determine norms and standards for language policy in public schools. The act delegates the responsibility to determine the language policy of the school to School Governing Body (SGBs) (Republic of South Africa 1996a).

The 1997 Norms and Standards for Language Policy in Public Schools is the third component of the language in education policies. It is based on the principle of the right to Home Language instruction while also providing learners with access to a global language such as English. Learners may study in their Home Language from Grade one to six (Republic of South Africa 1998). The policy design follows the additive multilingualism approach, where mastery of the Home Language arguably enables learning additional languages. The preamble points to the need for implementation of this policy to continue to be guidance by research. Further aims cited in the policy are the development of all 11 official languages; the development of programmes for the redress of previously disadvantaged languages; and redressing historically disadvantaged languages in school education (Department of Education 1997, pp. 3–4). The policy recognizes parent and learner choice in selecting the LOLT. They are given the discretion to select schools based on the LOLT. The role of the school as mandated in SASA is affirmed. In addition to determining the LOLT through the SGB, schools are required to stipulate how they will promote multilingualism through offering more than one language of learning and teaching.

A lesser known policy in this category is the Language Compensation policy in the National Senior Certificate (NSC). The NSC is a national school-leaving examination taken at the end of 12 years of schooling. The NSC examinations may only be taken in English or Afrikaans with the exception of the language subject which is taken in any of the 11 official languages or other additional languages. Since 1999 learners whose first language is not English or Afrikaans have received an additional five percentage points of their original mark on non-language subjects. This is intended to compensate for the language disadvantage experienced by the learners (Umalusi Council for Quality Assurance in General and Further Education and Training 2016). The policy was initially introduced as a short-term measure with the expectation that the English or Afrikaans proficiency of mostly African learners would improve. In 2016 the Umalusi Council[8] issued a statement that the language compensation would be retained at 3% from 2016 until 2022 (Umalusi Council for Quality Assurance in General and Further Education and Training 2016). Through the use of four statistical methods including the method used by Umalusi, Taylor (2014) provides empirical evidence of the presence of the language disadvantage. Using race as a proxy in one of the methods, black learners who score above 80% on non-language maths items scored lower than their white counter-parts on maths items which included language. This seems to point to a language disadvantage rather than poor content knowledge. Taylor concludes with asserting that if this language compensation policy is based on the existence of a language disadvantage then it should continue to be implemented.

As demonstrated in the discussion on why language matters, the pronouncement on official languages is a political decision in addition to it being a function of public policy. The pronouncement of the policies governing language in education was preceded by extensive debate and included considerations of the roles and responsibilities of government at the national and provincial level in addition to schools and parents. Although the policies are the most progressive language in education policies to date in South Africa there are gaps and omissions. Vorster et al. (2013) highlight the lack of definitions of bilingualism and multilingualism in the policies as a shortcoming. This could lead to misinterpretation resulting in differentiated implementation and a lack of standardization in measuring compli-

---

[8]Umalusi is the official education quality assurance council. It sets and monitors standards for general and further education and training in South Africa in accordance with the National Qualifications Framework Act No 67 of 2008 and the General and Further Education and Training Quality Assurance Act No 58 of 2001.

ance or competence. In recognition of the limitations of the 1998 policy in 2006 the then Minister of Education, proposed extending the provision of schooling in Home Language until Grade 6. Obstacles to implementing this proposal were identified as:

1. a lack of development of the African languages as academic languages;
2. a lack of curriculum statements in African languages;
3. insufficient quantities of teachers with proficiency in effective teaching of African languages;
4. societal lack of the valuing of African languages; and
5. the requirement to still transition to English and ensuring that adequate language development takes place in English to enable this (Vorster et al. 2013).

Murray (2002) argues that the landmark change is that schools may no longer refuse to accept learners due to their poor language proficiency as they did in the past. Schools may however continue to choose Afrikaans and English as LOLT as is the case in most high performing schools previously servicing white learners, and thus effectively exclude poorer African learners. The maintenance of the option to not offer any African languages also contributes to the low status of African languages. Finally, in relation to the role of parents and SGBs the assertion that parents and learners have the opportunity to fully exercise school choice based on language does not take into account the confounding factors already discussed that are mostly associated with underperforming schools offering African languages as the LOLT. The 2009 Mpumalanga Department of Education and Another v Hoërskool Ermelo and Another demonstrates the implementation challenges in delegating the LOLT decision to SGBs. The Constitutional Court ruled that legally the provincial Head of Department had the right to withdraw the function of determining the LOLT from the SGB if there are reasonable grounds; the applicability of this was also confirmed in this particular case. The case resulted from the school's refusal to admit 130 English speaking Grade 8 learners and amend the LOLT policy to the dual medium of English and Afrikaans. The Court found that the SGB failed to act within reason and had not sufficiently demonstrated that the LOLT reflected the community serviced by the school. Similar court cases have since taken place. The necessity of a Constitutional Court ruling prior to the acceptance of the language policies in universities discussed earlier are a further illustration that the 1994 patterns of language inequality persist with only symbolic changes initiated. There is still no single institution offering either primary or secondary or tertiary schooling in any African language although technically the policies make allowance for this. More specifically, the mandate to develop African languages academically for the purpose of schooling has hardly been realised almost 20 years after the policy was pronounced. All of the policy design and implementation gaps identified remain almost exactly as they were with the exception of developments in curriculum policy.

Curriculum policy is an integral tool in delivering the ideals informing the language of education policies. The curriculum has been reviewed and revised since the inception of schooling. A substantial body of work has been written on these changes, including reviews of curriculum design, policy and implementation. A detailed discussion of these is beyond the ambit of this chapter, however a discussion of the current curriculum policy in relation to language cannot be excluded. The current curriculum[9] is called the National Curriculum Statement Grades R-12 (NCS) and consists of three components, one of these being the National Curriculum and Assessment Policy Statements (CAPS). This curriculum is often referred to as CAPS. The NCS is based on four main principles:

1. Social transformation as a mechanism to create equal educational opportunities for the entire population;
2. Human rights, inclusivity, environmental and social justice;
3. Encouraging critical learning through engagement with the material as opposed to rote learning based on regurgitation instead of internalisation and reflection;
4. Clearly defined standards of knowledge and skills for each grade of education completed (Department of Basic education 2011, p.9).

In all of these curriculum developments, the same policy gaps discussed in relation to the language in education policy have not been sufficiently addressed. This is true even for the NCS curriculum. The shortcomings of the policy are discussed in a 2016 unpublished report by Class Act, one of the largest literacy NGOs in South Africa with extensive experience in implementing the literacy curriculum in the African languages. The report was developed as part of the DBE's research on reading in the Foundation Phase. The critique may be summarised as follows:

1. The curriculum documents specify that learners should use an expanding vocabulary but then does not specify how to do this. In the case of English First Additional Language a high-frequency word list is provided but this is not the case in any of the African languages.
2. There is insufficient progression across the years and grades in the listening and speaking curriculum subcomponent. It lacks specific objectives, and benchmarks and examples based on different types of stories and stages within stories.
3. There are suggestions on the kinds of phonics that should be taught each term but a comprehensive list is not provided and the guidelines are inconsistent across languages.
4. Phonemic awareness is mentioned but there is no consistency or a systematic progression in the teaching of this skill.
5. The curriculum emphasises reading but there is an insufficient supply of reading materials.

A Department of Basic Education (2017a) report on the Early Grade Reading Study in Setswana in the Foundation Phase also identified curriculum limitations as:

---

[9]The NCS was gazetted in 2011 and implementation was phased in across different grades. It was implemented in Foundation Phase and Grade 10 in 2012; the Intermediate phase and Grade 11 in 2013, and the Senior Phase and Grade 12 in 2014.

1. Insufficient allocation of time for group guided reading which results in substantial numbers of learners losing the opportunity to read individually;
2. Insufficient opportunities to read extended texts and;
3. Low cognitive demand in written work.

There has been substantial development in the curriculum provisioning and specification. However, the gaps in the broader policy, failure in micro policy at the classroom level and weak implementation continue to maintain the language inequality more than 20 years after democracy.There is still little research on how to effectively teach literacy or standards including the quantity of writing or reading required for effective education in African languages and English as an additional language. Neither the policies nor the curriculum has successfully specified reading benchmarks, minimum standards for reading materials, a growing body of academic vocabulary or proven programmes on language and literacy in the African languages.

7.5 Language and Power

There are several theoretical frameworks that are applied to language discourse in literature. The salient contributions amongst the classic international literature are those of Bourdieu. Locally, much has been written by Neville Alexander. Since this chapter grapples with the question of creating or sustaining language and literacy inequality, the discourse of language and power emerges as most pertinent. This lens is one way of interpreting why the language and literacy inequality persists. Two main points are discussed to explain the status quo and propose levers of change. The first is on the economic returns to language; and the second is on unification of languages in a multilingual context.

7.5.1 The Economic Domination of English

In colonial times language teaching and codifying African languages in South Africa were driven by economic advancements including an increasing need for improved quality of communication on the one hand and religious ambitions to share the Bible with indigenous speakers on the other hand. The establishment of formal schools was initially led through missionary efforts, culminating in the emergence of a small black middle-class that could read and write in English. In order to further enable the sharing of the gospel missionaries undertook the task of writing indigenous languages and then teaching a broader audience on the Bible. Over time this communication extended to non-religious areas such as administration and schooling. The generative nature of language and culture however meant this was not only an acquisition of language but of English culture

(Alexander 1989). This cultural change was both incidental and deliberative as the version of Christianity preached frowned upon several aspects of African practices promoting instead the adoption of Western culture. Over time then a small black middle class assimilated into 'black Englishmen'. In terms of the African languages used, the dialects that were codified became the standard version and gained prestige over other dialects within the same ethnic groups (Mesthrie 2002).

In current times role modeling by the middle class has maintained the high status of English and contributes to the notion that what is to be known is knowledgeable only in English and that South Africa is *Anglophone Africa* (Mesthrie 2002). Most African people are willing to maintain their first language in primary contexts of family but do not believe these languages have the capacity to develop into languages of power. This creates a dual economy where English proficiency seems to be the only bridge for transitioning from the informal to the formal. This is reinforced through the lack of economic returns for competency in African languages. English is used in the formal economy and the indigenous South African languages are used in the informal economy (Alexander 2005).

Internationally and in South Africa there are considerable economic returns to English. There is a direct relationship between English proficiency and earnings in South Africa. The earnings of African men reporting literate proficiency in reading and writing English was 55% higher than those who did not. These findings by Casale and Posel (2011) are based on an analysis of the National Income Dynamics Study (NIDS), the only nationally representative longitudinal study in South Africa. Participants that were proficient in English and had a post-schooling qualification signaling higher levels of literacy had an even higher advantage of an additional 97% in earnings. To further demonstrate the perceived upward mobility of English and inequality of languages, only 58% of Africans reported being able to read and write well in their Home Language, while this figure was 95% for Whites (Casale and Posel 2011). Being literate in English is therefore far more significant and meaningful for the majority of South African's than mastery of Home Language.

According to Bourdieu (1991) a language is only worth what its speakers are worth. When one language dominates the market, it becomes the norm against which the "prices" of other languages are determined and how competency is defined. Power and authority in economic and cultural relations correspond with social value as the social value of linguistic products is dependent on the market value. The economic value of English mastery is indisputable, and the valuing of English culture continues to define the South African middle class. The main question facing South Africa today is how to make multilingualism profitable such that the value is not only based on ideology and identity but that there is also material value. Alexander (1989) argues that the failure to create a market for multilingualism may reflect middle class passivity since the middle class possess the tools and opportunities to access English and are therefore not compelled to resolve the monolingual or dual-language dominance (the latter includes Afrikaans). The student led call for changes in the university language of teaching policies may be pointing to a growing understanding of the power and dominance of English amongst young people and a shift towards a demand for African languages. Over time this demand may propel the development and economic value of African languages.

7.5.2 Multilingual Policy Development

In the context of Africa and increasingly in the globalizing world, monolingualism is declining. What makes monolingualism problematic is the implicit exclusivity and the belief that if people cannot speak the same language they cannot form a nation. Alexander (1989) contests the notion of a nation being defined[10] as

> a people, or aggregation of men, existing in the form of an organized jural society, usually inhabiting a distinct portion of the earth, speaking the same language, using the same customs, possessing historic continuity, and distinguished from other like groups by their racial origin and characteristics, and generally, but not necessarily, living under the same government and sovereignty.

This definition could be dissected at length but for the purposes of this discussion the notion that a common language is a requirement to be a nation draws attention. This presents a Eurocentric nationalist movement perspective based on a historical experience where this was applicable. In the context of Africa and increasingly in the globalizing world, monolingualism is declining (Alexander 1989). The definition should rather address the function of language, namely an ability to communicate, rather than the mechanism of a single language. This point is not a mere ideological matter when considering nation building in multilingual South Africa and how this revised framing may foster inclusivity and social identity.

The similarities amongst distinct languages within the African languages also raises questions on whether the existing structures are not more heterogeneous than pre-colonial practices and identities. Mesthrie (2002) documents the formalization of African language in South Africa as a daunting task undertaken by missionaries and their assistants. Mesthrie comments that certain components such as prefixes, infixes and suffixes within subject nouns and verbs were only discovered and documented 30 years after the initial languages were documented. He also highlights the prestige and official status that the selected dialects enjoyed at the cost of other dialects or consensus within the language group. This continues to be a divisive factor amongst African language speakers. Heugh (2016) argues that the ethnic and language distinctions in much of Africa did not exist prior to colonization (before the nineteenth century), much the same as the geographical nation-state divisions. There is still dispute on this but the three plausible views on the orthographic development at the time are as follows. The first is that religious sectarianism resulted in competing flawed orthographies. Harries (1988) provides an example

---

[10]Black's Law Dictionary is the most widely used law dictionary in the United States. It is the reference of choice for terms in legal briefs and court opinions and has been cited as a secondary legal authority in many Supreme Court cases and is currently in its 8th edition.

of this in the broader African context: the division between Ronga and Gwamba[11] resulted from a rivalry between the Spelonken and Coastal branches of the Swiss Mission and their two linguistic representatives, Henry Berthoud and Henri Junod, representing two poles of contemporary linguistic classification. Part of the criteria used to determine these distinctions were territorial boundaries, and a deliberate effort to create smaller manageable societies (Alexander 1989; Errington 2001). A second view is that missionaries did not recognize the language similarities and applied classical Central European social theory from living amongst these groups (Heugh 2016). The third view is that the missionaries' own language influenced how they represented different vowels in African languages (Heugh 2016). This view supports that of Mesthrie. Each of these explanations find some credibility through examining history and the language structures; the point of departure however, is that the distinction and writing of the languages did not happen with fidelity or integrity. The chapter by Spaull and Pretorius in this volume provides specific information on the orthographies of African languages.

Alexander's (1989) conclusion on the question of how to dismantle this artificial language separation, is to firstly recognize the history and the significant role of language planning. He proposes a new discourse on language, moving from being the first component of forming identity and transcending into an important part of identity but within a broader communicative sphere. Based on this, Nhlapo (1944) and Alexander (1989) proposed the establishment of a single Nguni and Sotho language respectively. These new languages could then be standardized for academic purposes and adopted as national official languages while the remaining African languages could be adopted as regional languages, depending on the dominant language groups within the provinces. Once developed the first five to six years of schooling could focus on provisioning through one of these two African languages with English as a subject. Full transition to learning in the English medium could then take place in Grade five or six.

Firstly, the policy proposal by Nhlapo (1944) and Alexander (1989) indirectly ascribes power to the majority population in the country by consolidating on the similarities and recognizing that shared language, albeit not the criteria for a nation, has embedded power through consolidation. On the merits of dethroning English, or rather de-constructing and reconstructing the dominant language discourse, this proposal makes a considered argument.

Secondly, it proposes tangible ways of using language as an object of communication. The unification of languages between the Nguni and Sotho groups would dismantle the Colonial era classification and reimagine them based on a different criteria. To this end the development of Kiswahili and its growth as a regional language may provide valuable lessons and a relatively successful case study of a similar endeavour. The proposal is silent however, on how xiTsonga and Tshivenda would be accommodated. Thirdly, the proposal potentially creates an

---

[11] XiRonga also referred to as ShiRonga or GiRonga and Gwamba are South-Eastern Bantu language spoken in Maputo and Mozambique.

enabling environment for development by pooling resources. This in turn starts to undo the dialectical relationship between English and the indigenous languages by allowing prioritization.

The major critique however is that it presents diversity and multilingualism as a problem and does not celebrate this complexity which has come to define South Africa. This is particularly the case currently as ethnic identities, however flawed they are in their authenticity, have been established from 1955 (Heugh 2016). This exercise is even more infeasible now than then. The standardization process should be expected to be a near-impossible feat; as already discussed this has been problematic within a single language with varying dialects. It is difficult to imagine that the process within a language group would be any easier. More practical debates, should this be adopted as a policy option, would be how the final languages within these groups would be selected, whether the required expertise to merge them exist, and finally whether the South African society would be accepting of this.

7.6 Conclusion

This chapter has demonstrated the many overlaps between power, identity and language in South Africa. The recent legal cases cited confirm that this remains a current issue; and the proposals by Nhlapo (1944) and Alexander (1989) provide a theoretical lens to understand the continued undercurrent of this intersectionality.

There is a clear language disadvantage for learners receiving their education in African languages in the Foundation Phase. This does not however dismiss the educational benefit of Home Language education in African languages in the Foundation Phase but rather highlights the need for quality language and literacy teaching and learning in African languages. The inequality in both literacy and language and their interaction cannot be denied.

A further conclusion emerging from the chapter is the sparse availability of large-scale empirical data that may be used to estimate causality or the impact of language specifically in African languages or for African learners' English proficiency. The availability of such data and research would enable the debate to move beyond the broader language question to more detailed systematic question of how exactly the language in education policies should be enacted? What are the appropriate learner and teacher support materials? What is the optimal time allocation? What should the content of teaching in these languages be?

The chapter has also provided a summary of the language in education policies illustrating that changes in the official status and use of languages does not develop naturally but requires deliberate language planning. In critiquing the policies there are clear omissions and a lack of specificity in definitions, and incorrect underlying assumptions; for instance that SGBs would be adequately equipped to determine the appropriate language policy for the school, make concerted efforts to promote multilingualism and voluntarily opt for provisioning in African languages where

English and Afrikaans previously dominated. It is also clear that pronouncing on the development of African languages in policy has not yielded much beyond the basic implementation of the curriculum. It proves difficult to advocate for the reshaping of the 1998 language policy when its full implementation has not yet come to being and the existing critique on implementation is yet to be addressed thoroughly. Furthermore, there is silence in the academic and scholarly debate as to workable policy alternatives. A harsh interpretation of the scant existence of academic scholarly articles and substantive commentary may be that there is a disjuncture between the lived experiences of those excluded by language and the custodians of academic knowledge and literature or that this fundamental issue is seen as peripheral in academia. A more generous view may be that there is a limited understanding of the significance of language and literacy disadvantage. This along with limited human and financial resources may be key contributors to the limited body of work. Political will is still required to clarify the responsibility for the implied standards and guidelines from the policies; make provisioning possible through specific resourcing; and develop clear implementation details and respond to known and documented policy design and implementation shortcomings. This includes reviewing the functionality of PANSALB in relation to its mandate as well as a more systematic approach to language policies and development in universities. Without these not only will African languages continue to fail to progress; the state would inadvertently maintain the colonial and Apartheid status quo on inequality.

The discourse on language and power has permeated the overall discussion but the articulation by Nhlapo (1944) and Alexander (1989) offer a reminder to think broadly about the implications of the current inequalities. The call to commercialize multilingualism so that the majority of South Africans may earn returns on their language proficiency warrants some thought. It also points to the need to invest in language development beyond the Foundation Phase and perhaps model the development path followed for Afrikaans. The idea of a unified Nguni and Sotho language may be worth visiting although this would require a national paradigm shift on the role of language and the embedding of culture and identity in specific languages.

It is clear that language matters and why it matters historically, as well as in the current educational and societal experience of South Africa. The theoretical framework of language as power proves to be true in our reinterpretation of history and the prevailing discourse, yet seems to be uninterrupted and destined to be perpetuated. The only alternative reality requires the deliberate and careful development of indigenous South African languages foregrounded in education resourcing and prioritization.

References

Alexander, N. (1989). *Language policy and national unity in South Africa/Azania*. Cape Town: Buchu Books.

Alexander, N. (2005). *Language, class and power in post-apartheid South Africa*. Cape Town: Harold Wolpe Memorial Trust Open Dialogue Event.

Antonissen, C. (2017). Reshaping remembrance ~ English: Rozenberg quarterly.

Bond, P. (2003). The comparative apologetics of racially regressive laws in the confederate states of America and the South African Republic or how did they live with themselves. *Journal of Law and Social Change, 7*, 29.

Botha, C. (2017). Universities' language policies at a crossroads? The Interpretation of Administrative Action.

Bourdieu, P. (1991). *Language and symbolic power*. Cambridge: Harvard University Press.

Casale, D., & Posel, D. (2011). English language proficiency and earnings in a developing country: The case of South Africa. *The Journal of Socio-Economics, 40*(4), 385–393.

Constitutional Court of South Africa. (2017). AfriForum and Another v University of the Free State.

Department of Basic Education. (2011). *Curriculum and assessment policy statements: Mathematics grades* (pp. 7–9). Pretoria: Government Printers.

Department of Basic Education. (2017a). The early grade reading study (Egrs): *In-depth case studies of home language literacy practices in four grade 2 classrooms in treatment 1 and 2 schools*. Pretoria: Department of Basic Education.

Department of Basic Education. (2017b). *Report on implementation evaluation of CAPS. Summary Report*. Technical report, Department of Basic Education, Pretoria.

Department of Education. (1997). Norms and standards for language policy in public schools. In Government Gazette 18546, Government Notice 1701, Pretoria.

Errington, J. (2001). Colonial linguistics. *Annual Review of Anthropology, 30*(1), 19–39. https://doi.org/10.1146/annurev.anthro.30.1.19

Galloway, F. (2002). Statistical trends in South African book publishing during the 1990s1. *Alternation, 9*(1), 204–225.

Grundlingh, A., & Huigen, S. (Eds.). (2011). *Reshaping remembrance* (Critical essays on Afrikaans places of memory, SAVUSA series, Vol. 3). Amsterdam: Rozenberg Publishers.

Hans, N. (2012). *Comparative education: A study of educational factors and traditions*. Routledge. https://doi.org/10.4324/9780203816493

Harries, P. (1988). The roots of ethnicity: Discourse and the politics of language construction in South-East Africa. *African Affairs, 87*(346), 25–52.

Heugh, K. (2016). Harmonisation and South African languages: Twentieth century debates of homogeneity and heterogeneity. *Language Policy, 15*(3), 235–255. https://doi.org/10.1007/s10993-015-9372-0

Hoadley, U. (2012). What do we know about teaching and learning in South African primary schools? *Education as Change, 16*(2), 187–202. https://doi.org/10.1080/16823206.2012.745725

Howie, S., Combrinck, C., Roux, K., Tshele, M., Mokoena, G., & Palane, N. M. (2017). *Progress in international reading literacy study 2016: South African children's reading literacy achievement*. Technical report, Centre for Evaluation and Assessment, University of Pretoria, Pretoria.

Marjorie, L. (1982). Language policy and oppression in South Africa. *Cultural Survival Quarterly Issue, 6*(1).

Mesthrie, R. (2002). South Africa: A sociolinguistic overview. In R. Mesthrie (Ed.), *Language in South Africa* (pp. 11–26). Cambridge: Cambridge University Press.

Murray, S. (2002). Language issues in South African education: An overview. In R. Mesthrie (Ed.), *Language in South Africa* (pp. 434–448). Cambridge: Cambridge University Press.

Ndlovu, S. M. (2006). The soweto uprising. *The Road to Democracy in South Africa, 2*, 1970–1980.

Nhlapo, J. M. (1944). *Bantu Babel. Will the Bantu languages live?* Cape Town: The African Bookman.

Oakes, D. (1988). *Reader's digest illustrated history of South Africa: The real story*. Cape Town: Reader's Digest Association.

Pretorius, F. (Ed.). (2014). *History of South Africa-from the distant past to the present day*. Pretoria: Protea Book House.

Pretorius, E. (2018). Reading in the African languages, an annotated bibliography 2004–2017. PrimTed Project.

Republic of South Africa. (1996a). National Education Policy Act No. 27 of 1996. Government Gazette, Government Printers, Pretoria.

Republic of South Africa. (1996b). South African Schools Act No. 84 of 1996. Government Gazette, Government Printers, Pretoria.

Republic of South Africa. (1998). Norms and standards for language policy in public schools. Government Gazette 18546 Government Notice 1701.

Roberge, P. (2002). Afrikaans: Considering origins. In R. Mesthrie (Ed.), *Language in South Africa* (pp. 79–103). Cambridge: Cambridge University Press.

Silva, P. (1997). South African English: Oppressor or liberator. *The Major Varieties of English Papers from MAVEN, 97*, 20–22.

Sparks, A. (1990). *The mind of South Africa: The story of the rise and fall of apartheid*. London: Heinemann.

Spaull, N. (2016). Disentangling the language effect in South African schools: Measuring the impact of 'language of assessment'in grade 3 literacy and numeracy. *South African Journal of Childhood Education, 6*(1), 1–20.

Statistics South Africa. (2017). Statistical release P0302. Mid-year Population Estimates. Technical report, Statistics South Africa, Pretoria.

Taylor, N. (2014). *NEEDU national report 2013: Teaching and learning in rural primary schools*. Pretoria: Government Printer.

Taylor, S., & Von Fintel, M. (2016). Estimating the impact of language of instruction in South African primary schools: A fixed effects approach. *Economics of Education Review, 50*, 75–89. https://doi.org/10.1016/j.econedurev.2016.01.003

Taylor, N., Van der Berg, S., & Mabogoane, T. (2013). Context, theory, design. In N. Taylor, S. Van der Berg, & T. Mabogoane (Eds.), *Creating effective schools: Report of South Africa's national schools effectiveness study*. Cape Town: Pearson.

Umalusi Council for Quality Assurance in General and Further Education and Training. (2016). Umalusi retains language compensation for matric learners. Media Statement released 06 Dec 2016.

UNESCO. (2017). *Languages in danger*. Book of Knowledge. Technical report.

University of Free State. (2016). *Language Policy*. Technical report.

University of Pretoria. (2016). *Language Policy*. Technical report, University Of Pretoria Registrar.

University of Stellenbosch. (2016). Language Policy. Technical report, Stellenbosch University Council.

Vorster, C., Mayet, A., & Taylor, S. (2013). Learner performance in the NSES. In N. Taylor, S. Van der Berg, & T. Mabogoane, (Eds.), *Creating effective schools* (pp 135–156). Cape Town: Pearson.

Chapter 8
Still Falling at the First Hurdle: Examining Early Grade Reading in South Africa

Nic Spaull and Elizabeth Pretorius

8.1 Introduction

There are not many topics that encapsulate all of the different dimensions of South African inequality quite like that of reading. One could discuss the unequal provision of material resources like storybooks, graded readers and libraries, or move to human resources like well-trained reading teachers and remedial specialists. Alternatively, one could look at the processes in reading like pedagogy, or the outcomes of reading like comprehension. All reflect the structural inequalities of racial and spatial apartheid. Yet all of this is also true for subjects such as mathematics and science. Why is reading different? Essentially it is because reading is the vehicle for learning in all other subjects, and therefore all other inequalities have at least some of their roots in reading inequalities.

The aim of this chapter is to document important inequalities in reading inputs, processes and outcomes. After discussing three guiding principles of reading development, the chapter provides a summary of what we know about reading outcomes in South Africa, as well as the sub-components leading to those outcomes, notably oral language proficiency and decoding. The chapter concludes by pointing

---

The title *Falling at the first hurdle* was that of a research report by Taylor (1989) on literacy in South African schools. That we face similar challenges with similar diagnoses 30 years on is reason enough to reproduce Taylor's incisive title, with a slight modification.

N. Spaull (✉)
Department of Economics, Stellenbosch University, Cape Town, South Africa
e-mail: nicspaull@gmail.com

E. Pretorius
Department of Linguistics and Modern Languages, Unisa, Pretoria
e-mail: pretoej@unisa.ac.za

© Springer Nature Switzerland AG 2019
N. Spaull, J. D. Jansen (eds.), *South African Schooling: The Enigma of Inequality*, Policy Implications of Research in Education 10,
https://doi.org/10.1007/978-3-030-18811-5_8

to six factors we believe contribute to the current impasse: (1) the paucity of reading research in African languages, (2) the inequality of policy attention – which is itself a resource, (3) the continued prioritization of matric over early grade reading, (4) the inadequate training provided to pre-service and in-service teachers on the specifics of how to teach reading, (5) a lack of quality print resources in schools, and lastly (6) the wholesale lack of a primary school assessment to monitor reading outcomes in the early years.

8.2   Learning to Read in South Africa

Access to knowledge and information in the twenty-first century is largely mediated through written language, either digitally or in print. Technological advances do not leapfrog over literacy. Similar reading skills that were required for print in the twentieth Century, are required for digital print in the twenty-first Century. The recent exponential growth of digital information means learners require sophisticated sifting mechanisms that enable them to read with a critical eye, to read beyond the literal level, to discern 'real' from 'fake' knowledge. Similarly, work in the twenty-first century presupposes familiarity with the production and manipulation of knowledge through text, i.e. it requires reading literacy.

Throughout this chapter we focus on reading literacy. The Progress in International Reading Literacy Study (PIRLS) defines reading literacy as "the ability to use and understand those written language forms required by society and/or valued by the individual" (Mullis et al. 2009, p. 19). The teaching of reading literacy should be the 'core business' of primary schools. By the end of their third year of schooling, children around the world are expected to read fluently and with understanding in at least one language. In languages with regular orthographies (such as Spanish and Finnish, for example) Grade 1s read faster and more accurately than English children with an opaque orthography (Aro and Wimmer 2003). The nine African languages in South Africa have regular orthographies, so early reading success is possible. To reach that goal functional education systems have a shared understanding of what the core business of reading entails; what it is, how it develops, how it is measured and how it is taught. In addition teachers and policy-makers must also grapple with questions of reading failure and understand where, when and why this happens, how best to fix it, and how long the fixing takes.

The South African evidence suggests that on most of these fronts there is no such shared understanding – of the problems, the causes or the solutions. Results from the most recent nationally-representative assessment of reading comprehension (PIRLS Literacy 2016) show that 78% of Grade 4 learners in the country cannot read for meaning in any South African language (all 11 were assessed) (Howie et al. 2017). It also revealed that South African learners had the lowest performance in reading comprehension across all 50 participating countries. There is nothing inevitable about these outcomes. The knowledge and instructional practices required to teach children to read – as well as the resources needed to do it – are known and well understood internationally, even in high-poverty contexts. Teaching reading is not a mystery. South Africa's GDP per capita is higher than that of Iran's, yet while 78% of South African Grade 4s cannot read, only 35% of Iranian Grade 4s are similarly handicapped (Mullis et al. 2017, p. 55).

The PIRLS results point to the need to pay more attention to comprehension in schools, but what are the PIRLS results not revealing? PIRLS only assesses the outcome of the reading process, namely reading *comprehension*, but not the necessary 'input' components of reading such as fluency, vocabulary, decoding, and oral language proficiency. If the components of reading are well-known and measurable then surely failure in reading comprehension outcomes can be traced to earlier failures in reading process inputs?

Before discussing reading comprehension outcomes and reading process inputs in South Africa, we first summarise three guiding principles of reading development and highlight the points that are relevant in the South African context. These are based on converging evidence in the broader field of reading research (Castles et al. 2018).

8.3 Three Guiding Principles Underpinning Reading Development

8.3.1 The Bidirectionality of Language and Literacy

Oral language proficiency and literacy development are inextricably linked through strong *bidirectional* or *reciprocal* ties. Although debates about the exact nature of the relationship between oral and written language are still ongoing, there is general consensus that (1) language proficiency is foundational to learning to read, and (2) the relationship is reciprocal, in that as learners become proficient in reading, reading influences language proficiency and provides a rich and powerful resource for new learning in general. This applies equally to reading in a home language (HL) or an Additional Language (AL).[1]

Research shows that various aspects of oral language skills that children bring with them when they start school affect how successfully they learn to read (Chall et al. 1990; Whitehurst and Lonigan 1998; Sénéchal et al. 2006). In turn, the ability to read confers a large cognitive advantage on individuals. Through reading, children learn more words, acquire more concepts, learn to use complex syntactic structures, and increase their general knowledge of the world (Cunningham and Stanovich 1997; Pikulski and Templeton 2004; Lee 2011).

[1] In keeping with official South African curriculum terminology, we use the terms Home Language and Additional Language. In the literature more broadly, these are synonymous with first language (L1) and second language (L2) learning.

The majority of children in South Africa come to school with some degree of oral language proficiency in their home language, and considerably less proficiency in either English or Afrikaans which are the languages of learning and teaching (LoLT) from Grade 4 onwards. The majority of children (70%+) first learn to read in one of the nine African languages in Grades 1–3 before switching to English in Grade 4 and continuing in that language until they leave school (Pretorius and Spaull 2016). Thus, these children must overcome two consecutive hurdles to succeed at school. Firstly, literacy in the home language and then literacy in an additional language, typically English. To do so they need to become both bilingual (able to orally communicate in two languages) *and* biliterate (reading and writing in two languages). There are likely to be complex bidirectional relations not only between oral language proficiency and literacy within each language, but also jointly between these two oral languages and literacies.

In a multilingual developing country context like South Africa the reading journey is further complicated by dialects and multilingual urban environments. Dialectal varieties can introduce differences between spoken varieties and the standard written forms of a language. As a result even though children may be learning to read in their home language, they may not be familiar with the standardised written version, adding a further hurdle to their journey. In South Africa there is little empirical research indicating how widespread the use of dialects in schools is, or how large a problem it is when learning to read (Gxilishe 1996; Mtsatse 2017).

Similarly, children who live in multilingual, usually urban, environments may be forced to learn to read in a language that is not their home language. Because most South African schools teach in English from Grade 4 (90%+), if there is no single dominant language among learners in urban areas, schools typically choose to go 'straight for English' from Grade 1, irrespective of the children's home languages. In most provinces in South Africa this is not a large problem because most children in a school share a single home language. However, in urban contexts this is often not the case. For example, PIRLS Literacy 2016 shows that nationally 75% of learners spoke the Foundation Phase LoLT at home either 'always' or 'almost always' (own calculations). However, in Gauteng – the most urban province – the figure is only 53%. A 2011 review of all South African schools provides large-scale corroborating evidence, showing that 72% of learners are in schools where most children (75%+) have the same home language as the one that is used in their school in the Foundation Phase (Table 8.1). However, in Gauteng this is only 30%. For many learners in Gauteng (and to a lesser extent also those in Mpumalanga) they must overcome an additional hurdle of learning to read in a language that is not their home language.

8.3.2   Language Is Acquired, Reading Is Taught

Reading is not part of our genetic makeup in the way that vision and oral language are. Writing systems (and concomitantly, reading) are only recent cultural artefacts

Table 8.1 Percentage of South African Grade 1–3 learners whose home language is the same as the largest home language in the school

% of Gr1–3 learners	EC	FS	GP	KN	MP	NC	NW	WC	SA
≥ 90%	85%	48%	17%	86%	41%	69%	63%	55%	61%
> 75%, < 90%	5%	24%	13%	7%	17%	14%	15%	14%	11%
≥ 50%, < 75%	8%	22%	29%	6%	24%	14%	14%	26%	16%
> 0%, < 50%	2%	6%	41%	1%	18%	3%	8%	5%	12%
Total	100%	100%	100%	100%	100%	100%	100%	100%	100%

Source: Martin Gustafasson's calculations on Annual Survey of Schools 2011 data (2014: personal communication)

in our human history (Wolf 2008). While children acquire oral language naturally, they only learn how to read if they are taught to do so. How well they learn to read depends on how well they are taught and how many opportunities they are given to read. The ability to understand the abstract symbolic representation of speech sounds – print – "is an optional accessory that must be painstakingly bolted on" in our brains (Pinker 1997; see also Dehaene 2009 and Seidenberg 2017). One does not simply 'pick up' reading as one does oral language. While some precocious children, especially from middle-class homes, will do so and enter school already able to read at a basic level, this is not true for most children and especially not those from high-poverty low-text homes (Adams 1990; Snow et al. 1998). While there have been many generic critiques of the 'whole language' approach to early reading (Adams 1990; Vellutino 1991), particularly in the last two decades (Stanovich 2000; Tunmer et al. 2013; Seidenberg 2017; Castles et al. 2018), the most pertinent for the South African context is that this method does not readily work for agglutinating languages, especially those with a conjunctive orthography resulting in long words (Pretorius 2019). Furthermore, it is unlikely to work outside of an extremely print-rich environment and intensive individual attention both of which are in scarce supply in high poverty contexts with large classes and limited resources, as in South Africa (van der Berg et al. 2011). Less than a third of Foundation Phase learners are in classes of 35 learners or less, and more than one in four are in classes with 46 or more learners (Spaull 2016a). In such an environment a systematic phonics or balanced approach (as advocated in the South African curriculum) is best (National Reading Panel 2000; Pressley 2006; Castles et al. 2018).

8.3.3 Environmental Input Matters

The kind of linguistic input and the nature of the input that children receive at home and in the classroom affect both language and literacy development. Although practically all children will acquire the basics of their home language through a process of natural acquisition, research has documented how socioeconomic factors impact on language ability, particularly the amount and quality of language exposure that children receive in their homes (Tunmer et al. 2006; Hart and Risley 2003; Farkas and Beron 2004; Vasilyeva and Waterfall 2011). For example, vocabulary development is heavily influenced by the home environment (Hart and Risley 1995; Corson 1997; Biemiller 2012), and also correlates with listening comprehension, reading comprehension, writing, general background knowledge, and academic performance in general (Alderson 2005; Helman and Burns 2008; Staehr 2008; Marchman and Fernald 2008; Stahl and Stahl 2012).

Disadvantaged children need more time at the beginning of their reading journeys than those who come to school with high language skills and vocabularies (Brown and Saks 1986). While schools cannot change the socioeconomic status of their learners' home backgrounds, they can change what happens in their schools and classrooms. Given that at least 75% of South African primary schools serve poor communities, making schools centres where children receive rich language and literacy input irrespective of their home background should be a priority. The status quo in South Africa is that children with the biggest backlogs attend schools with the least capacity (Spaull 2015; NEEDU 2013, see also Fig. 1). Thus the initial home disadvantage is compounded by a school literacy disadvantage.

8.4   What Do We Know About the End Point of Reading: Comprehension – In South Africa?

Reading is essentially about meaning. The main goal in primary school is to produce learners who are independent readers, that is, they can read fluently, with comprehension, on their own. Most of our knowledge about the reading comprehension ability of South African learners and how this has changed over time comes from periodic large-scale nationally representative assessments. The most prominent of these is PIRLS which assessed Grade 4 and 5 learners in all 11 official South African languages in 2006, 2011 and 2016. South Africa also participates in another international assessment – the Southern and Eastern African Consortium for Monitoring Educational Quality (SACMEQ) which assesses reading at the Grade 6 level in English and Afrikaans (in 2000, 2007 and 2013). Because there are a number of doubts[2] about the reliability of the most recent SACMEQ results (2013), when discussing time trends we choose to focus on PIRLS.

A number of other local assessments have contributed to the picture of reading comprehension in South Africa which include the Systemic Evaluations (2000,

---

[2]While SACMEQ has released its 2013 results and claimed they are comparable, they have not released any technical documentation or data as is standard practice in previous rounds of SACMEQ (Ross et al. 2005), and in other international assessments (see the 300+ page technical reports for TIMSS, PISA or PIRLS for example). Because there are open and unanswerable questions around their validity (Spaull 2016b), notably that the assessment instruments used and the analytical assumptions made changed between 2007 and 2013, we do not discuss the SACMEQ 2013 time trends in reading.

2004 and 2007), the Annual National Assessments (2011–2014), the National School Effectiveness Study (NSES) (2007–2009), and the National Education and Evaluation Development Unit (NEEDU) studies of 2012 and 2013. We choose not to dwell on these latter assessments because the vast majority of their findings on reading are subsumed in the PIRLS results and they are not as rigorous, authoritative, psychometrically comparable, or recent.

8.4.1 PIRLS 2006 to 2016: Stalling Progress and Stark Inequalities

The best evidence available in South Africa suggests that between 2006 and 2011 there was a significant improvement[3] in reading outcomes across the country (see also Van der Berg & Gustafsson in this volume). Table 8.2 shows that the Grade 4 PIRLS[4] scores increased from 253 (in 2006) to 323 (in 2011) and thereafter stagnated for four years with a statistically equivalent score of 320 (in 2016). To indicate how large these magnitudes are, one can consider 50 PIRLS points being equivalent to one year of learning in South Africa.[5] As such, reading outcomes improved[6] by about 1.4 years of learning (70 points) between 2006 and 2011 with

---

[3] A technical note of some importance is that older reports of the prePIRLS 2011 results (Howie et al. 2012; Mullis et al. 2012) use a different scale to the traditional PIRLS scale. This was because the prePIRLS assessments were not calibrated to be equated to PIRLS in 2011. This was rectified with the release of the 2016 PIRLS results where the International Association for the Evaluation of Education (IEA) retrospectively rescaled the prePIRLS scores to be comparable to the PIRLS scores. Thus while in 2011 one could not compare PIRLS-2006 and prePIRLS-2011, by 2016 one could compare PIRLS-2006, prePIRLS-2011 and PIRLS-Literacy-2016 all on the same PIRLS scale (as in Table 8.2 below). All three included nationally representative samples of Grade 4 learners who were assessed in whatever the language of learning and teaching was used in that school in Grades 1–3. (Note prePIRLS and PIRLS-Literacy are easier versions of PIRLS that use texts of approximately 400 words rather than the 800 word texts of PIRLS, although for equating purposes there are two PIRLS passages in PIRLS-Literacy and two PIRLS-Literacy passages in PIRLS (Mullis and Martin 2015, p. 28)).

[4] We do not report the Grade 5 results from PIRLS 2011 or PIRLS 2016 since these assessments were not administered to a nationally-representative sample of primary schools. They were only administered to English- and Afrikaans-LOLT schools in 2011 and English, Afrikaans and isiZulu-LOLT schools in 2016.

[5] The oft-cited 40-point figure for a year of learning is based on three Nordic countries which each assessed two consecutive grades in PIRLS; namely 3rd and 4th Grade in Sweden, and 4th and 5th Grade in Iceland and Norway. The overall differences were found to be 41 points in Sweden, 39 points in Iceland and 43 points in Norway (Rosén 2010, p. 7). The more correct 50-point figure comes from the South African PIRLS experience in 2006 where a nationally-representative sample of Grade 4 and Grade 5 learners from the same schools were assessed at the same time and on the same assessment yielding a 49-point difference (Howie et al. 2008, p. 19).

[6] As an aside, it is also worth noting that the improvement in performance between 2006 and 2011 is not undisputed. For example, the official PIRLS 2016 report indicates that the trend results for South Africa are only comparable between 2011 and 2016 and that between 2006 and 2011 the data

Table 8.2 A decade of PIRLS reading outcomes in South Africa (2006 to 2016)

Study	Year	Grade	Schools	Students	Mean	Std. Error	% reaching PIRLS low international benchmark	Std. Error
PIRLS	2006	Gr4	429	16 073	253	4,6	13%	0,5%
prePIRLS	2011	Gr4	341	15 744	323	4,3	24%	Unavail.
PIRLS literacy	2016	Gr4	293	12 810	320	4,4	22%	1,5%

Sources: PIRLS: Howie et al. 2008; p14, p19, p.26; prePIRLS: Mullis et al. 2017, p.58; PIRLS Literacy; Mullis et al. 2017; p.33, p.55; Howie et al. 2016: p.2

no improvement from 2011 to 2016. Because the concept of a 'year of learning' is relatively amorphous and difficult to conceptualize, Table 8.2 also includes the percentage of learners reaching the PIRLS Low International Benchmark of 400 points. A learner who reaches the PIRLS Low International Benchmark can "locate and retrieve explicitly stated information, actions or ideas; make straightforward inferences about events and reasons for actions; or begin to interpret story events and central ideas" (Mullis et al. 2017, p. 53). Essentially, they can read at a basic level. In 2006 only one in eight South African Grade 4 learners were at this level (13%), compared to about one in four or five in 2011 (24%) and 2016 (22%). However, to put these numbers in context, one finds considerably higher figures in countries like Egypt (31%), Morocco (36%), and Iran (65%), not to mention Chile (87%), the United States (96%) or England (97%) (Mullis et al. 2017, p. 55).

It is a sobering realization to see that even after the gains of the 2006 to 2011 period, three-quarters of South African Grade 4 children still could not read in any meaningful way, in any language. Perhaps of even greater concern is that reading outcomes now seem to be stagnating at this low post-improvement level of performance.

Moving beyond the national averages – which are always misleading in South Africa – stark inequalities emerge when the results are disaggregated by school

is "not comparable for measuring trends to 2016, primarily due to countries improving translations or increasing population coverage" (Mullis et al. 2017: 303). In the case of South Africa this is primarily because in the PIRLS 2006 assessment, the psychometric scales and instruments were not calibrated to measure performance accurately below 300 PIRLS points (Personal Communication, Dirk Heystedt (2017)). In 2006 South Africa's score was 253. This may be an underestimate due to motivation problems where learners become demotivated by encountering texts that are far too difficult to them. Notwithstanding the above, it is highly unlikely that the full improvement from 2006 to 2011 is accounted for by motivation problems alone rather than a real improvement in reading outcomes.

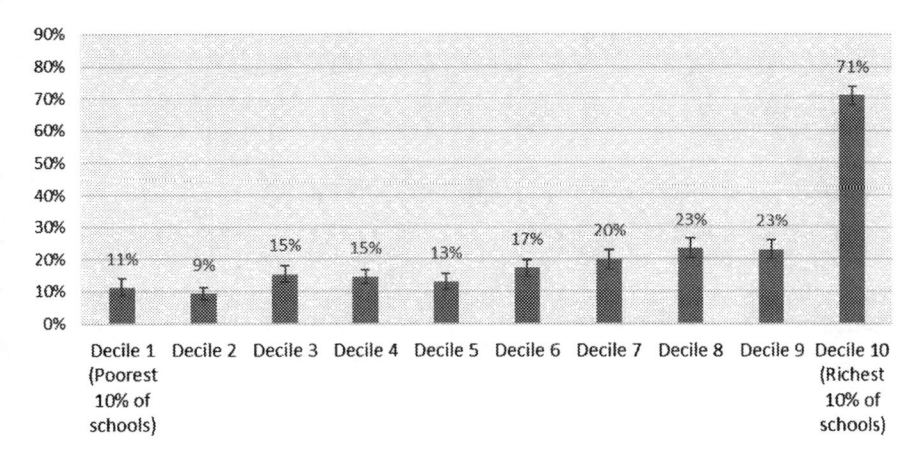

Fig. 8.1 The percentage of Grade 4 learners who can read at a basic level (the PIRLS Low International Benchmark) by deciles of average school wealth. (Data: PIRLS Literacy 2016 with 95% confidence intervals, own calculations)

wealth.[7] Figure 8.1 reports the percentage of PIRLS Grade 4 learners who can read at a basic level by deciles of school wealth in 2016. The graph shows the stark contrast between the wealthiest 10% of schools (all fee-charging) and the poorest 90% of schools (almost all no-fee schools, with a few low-fee schools). A child in the wealthiest 10% of schools in South Africa is five times more likely to learn to read at a basic level by Grade 4 than a child in the poorest 50% of schools.

The 'split' between the wealthiest 10% of schools and the poorest 90% of schools reported here might seem to be at odds with previous work on the two-tiered bimodal schooling system. For example, (Fleisch 2008, p. 21) suggests an 80%–20% split and Spaull (2013) argues for a 75%–25% split – both separated along school wealth with the smaller group being the wealthier one. However, these two studies use SACMEQ literacy data (2000 and 2007 respectively). It is plausible – and indeed probable – that the process determining the size of the respective systems is at least partly a function of the difficulty of the assessment. The more difficult the assessment the smaller the 'functional' part of the school system is and vice versa. The SACMEQ assessment, which was developed for an African context, is considerably easier than the PIRLS assessment which was developed for a predominantly high-income country context.

---

[7]School wealth here is calculated as the average of student asset wealth in the school. Student wealth is calculated using Multiple Correspondence Analysis (MCA) on the eight possession questions in PIRLS Literacy 2016 (PIRLS, 2018a: S1.1; 2018b: 2,7). While this is unlikely to create an accurate cardinal indicator of wealth, the purpose here is to create an ordinal ranking and this is arguably the best measure of student wealth available. Calculations on the PIRLS Low International Benchmark use the first plausible value.

While Fig. 8.1 provides a summary of the data, it does not reveal whether those who do learn to read in poorer schools are concentrated in a few exceptional schools (an 'outlier school' hypothesis) or whether in each school there are a few children who learn to read while the vast majority do not (an 'outlier child' hypothesis). Figure 8.2 suggests the latter. It shows the percentage of Grade 4s per class that learn to read at a basic level in each of the 293 PIRLS 2016 schools (y-axis), overlaid on average school wealth (x-axis). A clear deterministic relationship between the probability of learning to read and average school wealth is evident. In this PIRLS sample there were only 20 schools where more than 70% of children in the class had learned to read at a basic level by Grade 4. Every single one was from the wealthiest decile of schools and 14 of these were from the wealthiest 3% of schools. The fact that some Decile 10 schools report high percentages of children not learning to read suggests that even in the wealthiest 10% of schools reading acquisition is not universal (as it is in most high-income countries).

The steep gradient seen in Figs. 8.1 and 8.2 reflects a society where learning to read is largely a function of the average wealth of the school you attend. While it is true that some children in no-fee schools manage to succeed against the odds, it cannot be stressed enough that they are the exception to the rule. The average child in the poorest 75% of schools has a five times higher probability of not learning to read than of learning to read (85% compared to 15% respectively).

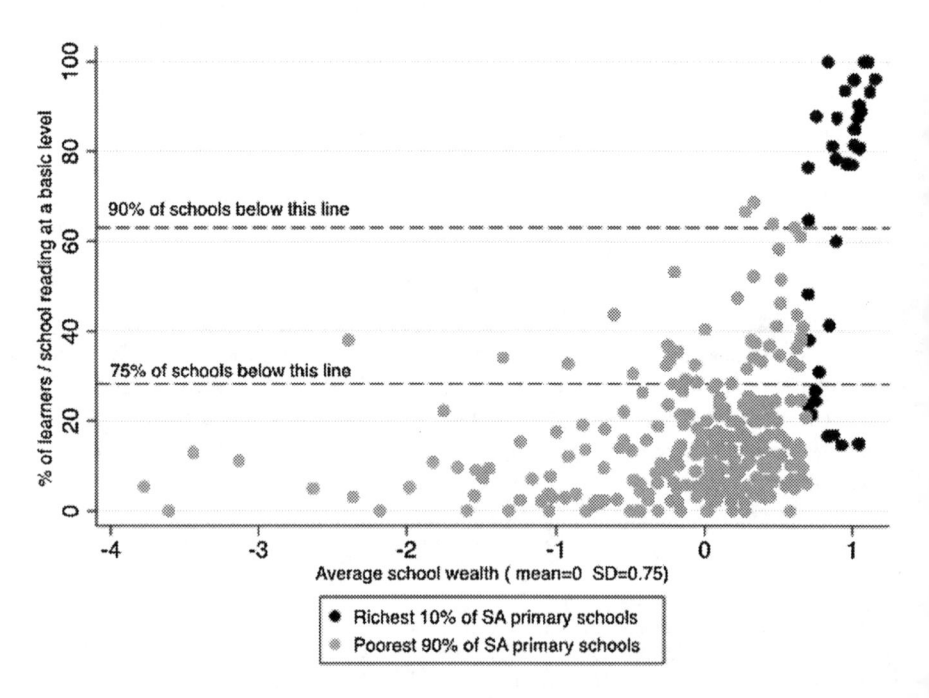

Fig. 8.2 Percentage of Grade 4 learners per school reaching the PIRLS Low International Benchmark by average school wealth (PIRLS Literacy 2016) (Note: the two y-axis reference lines are drawn at 28% and 63%)

8.4.2 Conflating Language of Instruction and Quality of Instruction

While the above results present the PIRLS Literacy 2016 data by wealth, similar patterns are seen by Language of Learning and Teaching (LoLT). More than 80% of learners attending an African language LoLT school could not reach the PIRLS low international benchmark, while for those attending English- or Afrikaans-LoLT schools the figure was 56–57% (Howie et al. 2017, p. 5). Given the strong correlations between wealth, socioeconomic status, school location and language (Spaull 2013), this finding is to be expected. To the familiar refrain that fee-charging schools offer higher-quality instruction (Spaull et al. 2018), one can now add the nuance of language of instruction. Almost all fee-charging schools (95%+),[8] public or independent, are either English- or Afrikaans-medium schools. It is therefore understandable that many parents in South Africa conflate language of instruction and quality of instruction, using the former as a proxy for the latter. Given many teachers' own lack of proficiency in English – which is usually their second-language – it is concerning that many parents are advocating for their schools to go 'straight for English'.

8.4.3 Moving from Outcomes to Processes and Inputs

Much of the South African discourse on reading, and indeed most of this chapter so far, has focused on the end point of the learning-to-read journey, namely, reading comprehension. Studies such as PIRLS, SACMEQ or the NSES reveal a wealth of information about who can read, by when, and at what level. What they do not reveal is *why* children cannot read. They tell us almost nothing about the initial and intermediate stages in the learning-to-read process. Which of the building blocks of reading are children stumbling on and when are they doing so? Elsewhere we have described this as the 'comprehension iceberg', arguing that we need to move beyond a repetitive focus on weak comprehension outcomes and instead look below the surface at the causes of reading failure (Spaull et al. 2018). It is telling that South Africa has assessed reading comprehension outcomes of a nationally-representative sample of Grade 3–6 learners at least 10 times in the last two decades, yet it has not once assessed a nationally representative sample of learners on the sub-components of reading (decoding, vocabulary, listening comprehension etc.).

---

[8] According to V-ANA (2013), 90% of fee-charging schools in the sample had English or Afrikaans as their language of assessment. In addition, given that virtually all independent schools are either English or Afrikaans medium and fee-charging, this adds a further 4–5% of learners to this group.

8.5 What Do We Know About the Subcomponents (Inputs) of Reading in South Africa?

While comprehension is the main goal of reading, it is underpinned by two sets of skills (1) oral *language comprehension* (the ability to use and understand spoken language), and (2) *decoding* (the ability to accurately read familiar words and decode unfamiliar words out of context) (Scarborough 2001; Hoover and Gough 1990). Without decoding, there can be no text comprehension; but skill in decoding does not automatically guarantee text comprehension. Both decoding and comprehension rely on oral language proficiency, which includes vocabulary knowledge, listening comprehension and morphosyntactic knowledge (knowledge of grammar).

The South African empirical research base on *language* comprehension among African-language primary school learners is almost non-existent. This would involve studies focusing on vocabulary knowledge, listening comprehension, morphosyntactic knowledge and verbal reasoning. Of these topics, when looking specifically at African languages in Grades 1–3 in relation to these topics, vocabulary and morphology have probably been the areas that have received the most attention, and there have only been four studies in total. The studies that included vocabulary looked at Grade 3 in two Setswana-medium schools in the North West (Malda et al. 2014) and Grade 1 in two Northern Sotho schools in Gauteng (Wilsenach 2015). The studies that looked at morphology included Grade 3 in two isiXhosa schools (Rees 2016) and Grades 3 and 4 in two Setswana and isiXhosa schools respectively (Probert 2016). One cannot base any national conclusions on language comprehension in the Foundation Phase in African languages on small scale studies of eight schools. The fact of the matter is that we simply do not know the levels of language comprehension for this group. There are no norms or reference criteria. There are no psychometrically-validated instruments in African languages to measure these constructs. In short, there is almost nothing one can draw on to make empirical conclusions about 70% of South African children's *language skills* (i.e. not their *reading* comprehension skills).

The second set of skills that underpin the development of reading comprehension are decoding skills. In languages with an alphabetic writing system, spoken language is represented in print by letters that stand for speech sounds. These letters form the code. Decoding, which is the ability to decipher the code, in turn relies on various sets of skills such as *phonemic awareness* (the ability to identify single sounds within spoken words), *letter-sound knowledge, word reading* and *reading fluency* (Adams 1990). Skilled reading involves the rapid processing and integration of all these components. Problems in any one – or several – of the subskills can affect processing problems elsewhere in the reading system, resulting in poor reading outcomes. In this way, differences in reading outcomes between children or groups of children can thus be traced back to differences in each of these components.

In the last five years there has been a proliferation of South African research measuring the various elements involved in skillful decoding. The Early Grade

Reading Assessment (EGRA) provides one 'standardized' tool to assess children's decoding ability. There have been five relatively large studies that have included decoding assessments. These have been administered in five African languages across six provinces. A discussion of each of these subcomponents is beyond the scope of this chapter, so only two are singled out for discussion, viz. letter-sound knowledge and oral reading fluency.

There is consensus in the reading literature that decoding subskills derive from a finite knowledge base that is highly generative: knowledge of letter-sounds enables children to blend letters together into words, and the rapid recognition of word patterns enables fast oral reading fluency. These skills enable children to decode words that have not been encountered before. Because these are finite skills they can, if taught systematically and explicitly, develop quickly and mastery should be attained by nearly all children at an early stage of reading, within a year in transparent orthographies. Speed matters in these subskills – they should be executed rapidly and accurately, so that working memory is freed up for comprehension. These skills are also more immune to the effects of socioeconomic factors than more complex aspects such as language proficiency, vocabulary development and reading comprehension. In addition, research indicates that additional language learners can perform as well as home language learners on letter-sound tasks (Muter and Diethelm 2001; Lipka and Siegel 2007).

Table 8.3 provides an overview of two components of decoding: (1) Letter-sounds (measured as letter-sounds read correctly per minute, LCPM) and (2) Oral Reading Fluency, measured as words read correctly per minute (WCPM). These results reflect decoding outcomes in 'business as usual' schools. For this reason, where the data come from a study involving an intervention (as in EGRS and Zenex) we have only included information on the control schools and not the intervention schools.

Two points from Table 8.3 have relevance here. Firstly, Grade 1–3 learners' letter-sound knowledge and oral reading fluency scores are generally low and slow. Benchmarks for letters sounded correctly per minute are given as 40 LCPM for Grade 1[9] (Kaminski and Good III 1996; Good et al. 2001); some of our learners are only approximating this at the end of Grade 3. With oral reading fluency, it is more difficult to assess levels because of the differences in average word length between languages with conjunctive orthographies (isiZulu and isiXhosa) and those with disjunctive orthographies (Northern Sotho and Setswana). For example, the sentence *Nobody had any food* (4 words) is *Abantu abengenakho ukudla* (3 words) in isiZulu, and *Go be go se na yo a bego a na le dijo* (12 words) in Northern Sotho. This makes any direct comparison of ORF scores across language groups problematic. Nevertheless, nascent benchmarks for the end of Grade 2/start of Grade 3 for both disjunctive and conjunctive orthographies (Spaull et al. 2018) suggest that the results in Table 8.3 illustrate severe problems with oral reading fluency. For

---

[9]Although this benchmark is derived from learning to read in English, all languages that use the Roman alphabet in their orthography should reflect fairly similar benchmarks.

Table 8.3 Letter-sounds and oral reading fluency

Study	Language	Total letters read correctly per minute			# Learners	# Schools	Reference and notes
		End Gr1	End Gr2	End Gr3			
EGRS 1	Setswana	22	39		1200	80	
EGRS 2 (DBE, forthcoming)	EFAL	18			1459	80	Q1-3 schools in Mpumalanga. Mostly remote rural.
Spaull et al. (2018)	Northern Sotho		31	43	113	9	End of Grade 2 is actually start of Grade 3 (Spaull et al. forthcoming)
	Xitsonga		35	47	89	10	
	isiZulu		27	36	414	42	
Mouton (2017)	isiZulu	6	11	16	60	4	Rural
	isiXhosa	24	41	47	60	4	Urban
E-LIT	isiXhosa	29			63	7	Q1-3 WC
		Oral Reading Fluency (wcpm)					
		End Gr1	End Gr2	End Gr3	# Learners	# Schools	
EGRS 1	Setswana	7	24		1200	80	
EGRS 2 (DBE, forthcoming)	EFAL	5			1459	80	Decodable words
	EFAL	5.3			1459	80	Sight words
	isiZulu	6.1			427	22	CVCV words
	Siswati	5.3			1032	58	CVCV words
Spaull et al. (2018)	Northern Sotho		39	55	113	9	End of Grade 2 is actually start of Grade 3
	Xitsonga		41	59	89	10	
	isiZulu		21	31	414	42	
Mouton (2017)	isiZulu	1	12	21	60	4	Rural
E-LIT	isiXhosa	7	16	21	60	4	Urban
	isiXhosa	12			63	7	Q1-3 WC

example, at the end of Grade 2 in a disjunctive Sotho-language orthography one would expect 66–84 WCPM to allow for comprehension (Spaull et al. 2018, p.18). Yet students in the EGRS control schools are reading at half this speed. The same can be said for the isiZulu schools using conjunctive orthographic norms (32–43 WCPM). Almost none of our learners in Table 8.3 are achieving these benchmarks at the end of Grade 2 and a small fraction are achieving a score within this range at the end of Grade 3.

These foundational subskills that should reflect 'finger-tip' execution of decoding processes are slow and onerous, making comprehension virtually unattainable. Provided teachers are well trained and have access to resources for reading practice, these are the "low hanging fruit" of reading instruction which could be realistically mastered by all learners.

8.6 Resources for Reading

The most critical resource for teaching reading is the teacher. If a teacher knows what the goal of reading is (comprehension), as well as how to develop the various components that lead to comprehension, she is well on her way to becoming an effective reading teacher. In addition, she needs practical knowledge of how to actually teach these components in the classroom and the resources to do so, — the reading activities, books, routines and assessments to take all her learners from novice to competent readers. Very few South African teachers are thus equipped. Consistent research findings in the South African literature reveal communalized rather than individualized instruction (NEEDU 2013), little formal teaching of vocabulary, spelling or phonics (Taylor and Vinjevold 1999), as well as insufficient time dedicated to the formal instruction of reading (Reeves et al. 2008). See Hoadley (2012) for a more comprehensive overview.

These are teachers who have never received what Shalem (2003) refers to as "meaningful learning opportunities" to acquire the theoretical and practical knowledge to teach reading. The situation for pre-service teachers is not much better. A recent curriculum review at one of South Africa's most prominent universities found that only 6% of the credits in the Foundation Phase Bachelor of Education program was allocated to literacy (personal communication, Taylor, 2018). The overall study to which this contributed – the Initial Teacher Education Research Project (ITERP) study – found that the curricula offered to Bachelor of Education students across 5 of the 23 universities in South Africa gave little attention to the explicit teaching of reading and writing and to teaching English as a FAL (ITERP 2014, see also Taylor N 2019 in this current volume. Many university education faculties favour particular theoretical approaches that may not always lead to effective early reading instruction. For example, social constructivism is a dominant theory of learning that prevails in many education faculties around the country and texts on Piaget and Vygotsky form common prescribed reading. While these worthy scholars dedicated their lives to the study of learning in educational contexts, none of them were reading specialists. Much of what we have learned about decoding has occurred in the past 40 years or so (Adams 1990; Stanovich 2000; National Reading Panel 2000; Castles et al. 2018), and advances in technology have brought about new insights into how the brain processes reading (Dehaene 2009; Seidenberg 2017).

8.6.1   Access to Books

It goes without saying that it is not possible to teach reading for meaning without books. Teachers need a basic supply of graded readers, 'Big books', storybooks and non-fiction books if they are to teach reading effectively. Furthermore, having enough books and the right kinds of books is a necessary but not sufficient condition for teaching reading. Teachers need to know how to use them in their daily reading lessons, how to determine which books are appropriate for which children and for what purpose, not to mention performing the administrative functions of managing and replenishing the books that they do have.

Table 8.4 reports the percentage of children in schools that have a school library, a mobile library, a classroom library or any library whatsoever (cumulative across all categories). The data are also split by primary and secondary schools and by the schools' apartheid classification. The inequalities in the provision of school libraries are particularly extreme. While 87% of children in former White primary schools have access to a school library, only 4% of children in the former Venda and Lebowa homelands are similarly resourced (there is clearly a Limpopo-specific library deficit that is currently unexplained). Although the percentage of schools with a school library may already seem low at 37%, this is likely to be an over-estimate since many libraries are not functional. The 2018 report of the National Education Infrastructure Management System (NEIMS) indicates that while 5,423 schools out of 23,471 have libraries (30%), only 3,304 were actually stocked (17%) (Department of Basic education 2018, p. 5). Little is known about the contents of these libraries or whether they are actually used. Perhaps of greater importance are the classroom books and classroom 'reading corners' that teachers use to teach reading. The qualitative literature on this points to a severe lack of good print materials in classrooms as well as limited opportunities to handle what books do actually exist (Reeves et al. 2008; Hoadley 2012).

8.6.2   Managing and Mediating Books

In the South African education system there have been a number of 'book-flood' interventions – both by the non-profit sector and the State over the past two decades. Because none of these have ever been evaluated properly it is difficult to say if they 'worked' or not, or which ones were more effective than others. The closest approximation to an evaluation is the 2015–2016 Early Grade Reading Study in the North West (see Taylor S 2019, in this volume). In this study reading materials were

Table 8.4 Availability of classroom and school libraries

	Historical category	All schools in sample	% of learners in schools		
			All	Primary	Secondary
Former department	White (HOA)	167	80%	87%	69%
	Indian (HOD)	38	81%	78%	91%
	Coloured (HOR)	189	51%	52%	47%
	Urban African (DET)	535	47%	36%	64%
Former homelands	Bophuthatswana	89	33%	28%	44%
	Ciskei	53	28%	20%	48%
	Gazankulu	32	10%	14%	0%
	KaNgwane	37	38%	37%	37%
	KwaZulu	216	19%	18%	19%
	Labowa	155	7%	4%	11%
	Ndebele	20	35%	34%	26%
	Transkei	202	11%	13%	12%
	Venda	43	2%	4%	0%
	Other	199	34%	35%	34%
	Total % with school library	1975	37%	35%	39%
			Alternative libraries		
All schools	Total % with classroom library		26%	31%	16%
	Total % with mobile library	1975	5%	6%	3%
	Total % with any libary		58%	60%	51%

Source: Department of Basic Education (2014, p. 20) report on the School Monitoring Survey 2011

provided to various Foundation Phase classrooms as part of a randomized control trial. One of the treatment groups received reading materials (in addition to lesson plans and centralized teacher training). However, after two years of the intervention there was no statistically significant difference in the reading outcomes of the children in this group compared to the control group who received no resources. (Note any effect that would have been found would be an upper-bound limit of materials provision because this was a more considerable intervention than simply providing reading materials). All of this is not to say that the State should not prioritize the provision of a basic set of reading materials for all Foundation Phase classrooms, it should. However, the provision of reading materials in the absence of training and support on how to use and manage them is unlikely to accomplish much.

8.7 Conclusion

Throughout this chapter we have made hierarchical arguments about how children learn to read and what material and human resources they need to do so. If children have not mastered the basics of decoding in their home language by the end of Grade 1, reading for meaning or pleasure is challenging. Without a basic set of books that are used and managed effectively, one cannot teach children to read beyond a superficial level. If teachers do not possess a basic knowledge of how children learn to read and how to teach this in the classroom it is naïve to expect their learners to acquire this all-important skill. In each case a one-sided focus on the tip of the iceberg is unhelpful. Knowing that 78% of Grade 4's cannot read for meaning in any language is important and sobering information, but probably not as helpful as knowing which components of reading children are struggling with and why teachers are struggling to teach them. Recognizing that in-service teachers do not currently teach reading well or that pre-service teachers are ill equipped is necessary information but it is more important to know why, and why this is so resistant to change. Perhaps unsurprisingly, given our hierarchical reading of the evidence, we have advocated for a focus on the basics – of how to teach, what to teach and when to teach it. If children and teachers are 'falling at the first hurdle' (Taylor 1989) does it make sense to focus on the seventh or eighth hurdle and ask why learners and teachers are not making it over?

There are various reasons why so little is known about what lies beneath the surface of the comprehension iceberg. The paucity of research on the components of reading in African languages in the Foundation Phase suggests a neglect of something that should be a national priority. Secondly, South African politicians, bureaucrats and the media continue to focus obsessively on the school-leaving matric exam. This inevitably leads to policy attention, resources and accountability pressures being channeled to high schools rather than primary schools. For example, teachers in Grades 10–12 are 36% more likely to have been visited by a curriculum advisor in the last year compared to those in Grades 1–3 (Wills 2016). While difficult to quantify, policy attention is itself a resource. In order to garner and sustain policy attention, an ongoing, reliable metric of performance is required, as is the case with the matric exam. In light of this one should note that South Africa is almost unique in the region – and certainly among middle-income countries – to not have a provincial or national primary school exam (the Western Cape is an exception here). With the abolishment of the Annual National Assessments in 2015 – largely due to teacher union objections – there is now no objective measure of which primary schools are successfully teaching their children to read and which ones need the most support.

Staying with the hierarchical lens, one can easily see the lasting effects of early reading failure. Grade 3 reading ability predicts how well children will perform later in their schooling careers and consequently in the labour market (Lesnick et al. 2010; Hernandez 2011). Those who do not master the code in their first three years of school face an almost insurmountable challenge as they continue their journey through school and into society. The majority of those who are left behind in Grade 4 stay behind for the rest of their lives, precluded from further learning and excluded from meaningful work.

Getting reading right is necessary not only for success at primary school but also for secondary and tertiary education, not to mention national economic prosperity. No country can succeed when half of its workforce are excluded because they have not mastered foundational numeracy and literacy skills. More importantly, it is difficult to think how one can live a truly dignified life in the twenty-first Century without being able to read for meaning. And those who cannot read for meaning will not read for pleasure.

The inequalities evident in the schooling system (Fig. 8.1) and subsequently in the labour market have their roots in unequal life chances doled out at birth and consolidated through differential reading trajectories. For the vast majority of children in South Africa their life chances are determined before their 10th birthdays. While there are many reasons for this, including inadequate nutrition and early childhood stimulation, a significant contributing factor is early reading failure. Those who do not learn to master the basics of reading remain in catch-up mode for the rest of their lives. There are many tangible and specific things that can be done to avoid this – some of which have been mentioned in this chapter and others in this volume. However, ultimately the solution to the South African reading crisis will depend entirely on whether the Department of Basic Education, and the government more generally, prioritizes the universal acquisition of basic literacy above all other policy priorities.

References

Adams, M. J. (1990). *Beginning to read: Learning and thinking about print.* Cambridge: MIT Press.

Alderson, J. C. (2005). *Diagnosing foreign language proficiency: The interface between learning and assessment.* London: Continuum.

Aro, M., & Wimmer, H. (2003). Learning to read: English in comparison to six more regular orthographies. *Applied Psycholinguistics, 24*(4), 621–635.

Biemiller, A. (2012). Teaching vocabulary in the primary grades: Vocabulary instruction needed. In E. Kame'enui & J. Baumann (Eds.), *Vocabulary instruction: Research to practice* (pp. 34–50). New York: The Guilford Press.

Brown, B. W., & Saks, D. H. (1986). Measuring the effects of instructional time on student learning: Evidence from the beginning teacher evaluation study. *American Journal of Education, 94*(4), 480–500. https://doi.org/10.1086/443863

Castles, A., Rastle, K., & Nation, K. (2018). Ending the reading wars: Reading acquisition from novice to expert. *Psychological Science in the Public Interest, 19*(1), 5–51.

Chall, J. S., Jacobs, V. A., & Baldwin, L. E. (1990). *The reading crisis: Why poor children fall behind.* Cambridge: Harvard University Press.

Corson, D. (1997). The learning and use of academic English words. *Language Learning, 47*(4), 671–718.

Cunningham, A. E., & Stanovich, K. E. (1997). Early reading acquisition and its relation to reading experience and ability 10 years later. *Developmental Psychology, 33*(6), 934.

Dehaene, S. (2009). *Reading in the brain: The new science of how we read.* London: Penguin.

Department of Basic Education. (2014). Second Detailed Indicator Report for Basic Education Sector. Pretoria.

Department of Basic Education. (2018). NEIMS Standard Reports January 2018. National Education Infrastructure Management System. Pretoria.

EGRS. (2018). *Early grade Reading study (EGRS I & II).* Pretoria: Department of Basic Education.

Farkas, G., & Beron, K. (2004). The detailed age trajectory of oral vocabulary knowledge: Differences by class and race. *Social Science Research 33*(3), 464–497. https://doi.org/10.1016/j.ssresearch.2003.08.001

Fleisch, B. (2008). *Primary education in crisis: Why South African school children underachieve in reading and mathematics*. Cape Town: Juta.

Good, R. H., Simmons, D. C., & Kame'enui, E. J. (2001). The importance and decision-making utility of a continuum of fluency-based indicators of foundational reading skills for third-grade high-stakes outcomes. *Scientific Studies of Reading, 5*(3), 257–288.

Gxilishe, D. (1996). The dilemma of dialect in the classroom: A case for Xhosa. *Per Linguam, 12*(1), 1–14.

Hart, B., & Risley, T. R. (1995). *Meaningful differences in the everyday experience of young American children*. Baltimore: Paul H Brookes Publishing.

Hart, B., & Risley, T. R. (2003). The early catastrophe: The 30 million word gap by age 3. *American Educator, 27*(1), 4–9.

Helman, L. A., & Burns, M. K. (2008). What does oral language have to do with it? Helping young english-language learners acquire a sight word vocabulary. *The Reading Teacher, 62*(1), 14–19.

Hernandez, D. J. (2011). *Double jeopardy: How third-grade reading skills and poverty influence high school graduation*. Baltimore: Annie E Casey Foundation. http://www.aecf.org.

Heystedt, D. (2017). Personal Communication. 1 December 2017.

Hoadley, U. (2012). What do we know about teaching and learning in South African primary schools? *Education as Change, 16*(2), 187–202. https://doi.org/10.1080/16823206.2012.745725

Hoover, W. A., & Gough, P. B. (1990). The simple view of reading. *Reading and Writing, 2*(2), 127–160.

Howie, S., Venter, E., Van Staden, S., Zimmerman, L., Long, C., Du Toit, C., Scherman, V., & Archer, E. (2008). Progress in International Reading Literacy Study 2006. University of Pretoria: Centre for Evaluation and Assessment.

Howie, S. J., Mokoena, G., Dowse, C., & Zimmerman, L. (2012). PIRLS 2011: Progress in international reading literacy study 2011: South African children's reading literacy achievement. Centre for Evaluation and Assessment (CEA), University of Pretoria.

Howie, S., Van Staden, S., Tshele, M., Dowse, C., & Zimmerman, L. (2017). *Progress in international reading literacy study 2016. South African children's reading literacy achievement*. Summary Report. Centre for Evaluation and Assessment, Pretoria.

ITERP. (2014). *An examination of aspects of initial teacher education curricula at five higher education institutions. Initial Teacher Education Research Project*. Johannesburg: JET Education Services.

Kaminski, R. A., & Good III, R. H. (1996). Toward a technology for assessing basic early literacy skills. *School Psychology Review, 25*(22), 215–227.

Lee, J. (2011). Size matters: Early vocabulary as a predictor of language and literacy competence. *Applied Psycholinguistics, 32*(1), 69–92.

Lesnick, J., Goerge, R., Smithgall, C., & Gwynne, J. (2010). *Reading on grade level in third grade: How is it related to high school performance and college enrollment* (Vol. 1, p. 12). Chicago: Chapin Hall at the University of Chicago.

Lipka, O., & Siegel, L. S. (2007). The development of reading skills in children with english as a second language. *Scientific Studies of Reading, 11*(2), 105–131. https://doi.org/10.1080/10888430709336555

Malda, M., Nel, C., & van de Vijver, F. J. (2014). The road to reading for South African learners: The role of orthographic depth. *Learning and Individual Differences, 30*, 34–45.

Marchman, V. A., & Fernald, A. (2008). Speed of word recognition and vocabulary knowledge in infancy predict cognitive and language outcomes in later childhood. *Developmental Science, 11*(3), F9–F16.

Mouton, J. (2017). *Evaluation of Zenex literacy project*. Commissioned by the Zenex Foundation.

Mtsatse, N. (2017). *Exploring differential item functioning on reading achievement between English and isiXhosa*. Unpublished MA dissertation, University of Pretoria, Pretoria.

Mullis, I. V., Martin, M. O., Kennedy, A. M., Trong, K. L., & Sainsbury, M. (2009). PIRLS 2011 assessment framework. International association for the evaluation of educational achievement. ERIC.

Mullis, I. V. S., & Martin, M. O. (2015). *PIRLS 2016 assessment framework international association for the evaluation of educational achievement* (2nd ed.). Boston: TIMSS & PIRLS International Study Center.

Mullis, I. V. S., Martin, M. O., Foy, P., & Drucker, K. T. (2012). *PIRLS 2011 international results in reading*. Boston: TIMSS & PIRLS International Study Center.

Mullis, I. V. S., Martin, M. O., Foy, P., & Hooper, M. (2017). *PIRLS 2016: International results in reading*. Amsterdam: International Association for the Evaluation of Educational Achievement.

Muter, V., & Diethelm, K. (2001). The contribution of phonological skills and letter knowledge to early reading development in a multilingual population. *Language Learning, 51*(2), 187–219.

National Reading Panel. (2000). *Teaching children to read: An evidence-based assessment of the scientific research literature on reading and its implications for reading instruction.* Washington, DC: US Government Printing Office.

NEEDU. (2013). NEEDU National Report 2012: The state of literacy teaching and learning in the foundation phase. National education and evaluation development unit. Department of Basic Education, Pretoria.

Pikulski, J. J., & Templeton, S. (2004). Teaching and developing vocabulary: Key to long-term reading success. In *Current research in reading/language arts* (pp. 1–12). Boston: Houghton Mifflin Co. http://www.eduplace.com.

Pinker, S. (1997). Forward. In D. McGuinness (Ed.), *Why our children can't read, and what we can do about it: A scientific revolution in reading.* New York: Simon and Schuster.

Pressley, M. (2006). *Reading instruction that works: The case for balanced teaching.* New York: Guilford Press.

Pretorius, E. (2019). Getting it right from the start: Some cautionary notes for early reading instruction in African languages. In N Spaull & JP Comings (Eds.), *Improving Early Literacy Outcomes: Curriculum, Teaching and Assessment* (pp.63–80). Leiden: IBE/BRIL. https://doi.org/10.1163/9789004402379_005

Pretorius, E. J., & Spaull, N. (2016). Exploring relationships between oral reading fluency and reading comprehension amongst English second language readers in South Africa. *Reading and Writing, 29*(7), 1449–1471.

Probert, T. (2016). *A comparative study of syllables and morphemes as literacy processing units in word recognition: IsiXhosa and Setswana.* Unpublished MA dissertation, Rhodes University, Grahamstown.

Rees, S. (2016). *Morphological awareness in readers of isiXhosa.* Unpublished MA dissertation, Rhodes University, Grahamstown.

Reeves, C., Heugh, K., Prinsloo, C. H., Macdonald, C., Netshitangani, T., Alidou H, Diedericks, G., & Herbst, D. (2008). *Evaluation of literacy teaching in primary schools of Limpopo province.* HSRC http://hdl.handle.net/20.500.11910/4984

Ross, K. N., Dolata, S., Ikeda, M., Zuze, L., & Murimba, S. (2005). *The conduct of the SACMEQ II project in Kenya.* Harare: Southern and Eastern African Consortium for Monitoring Education Quality.

Rosén, M. (2010). *On the degree of comparability in trend studies as a function of differences in age and schooling.* Paper presented at the IEA IRC, Sweden. Retrieved from http://www.iea.nl/sites/default/files/irc/IRC2010_Rosen_Strietholt

Scarborough, H. S. (2001). Connecting early language and literacy to later reading (dis) abilities: Evidence, theory, and practice. In S. Neuman, D. Dickinson (Eds.), *Handbook of early literacy research* (pp. 97–110). New York: Guilford Press.

Seidenberg, M. (2017). *Language at the speed of sight: How we read, why so many can't, and what can be done about it.* New York: Basic Books.

Sénéchal, M., Ouellette, G., & Rodney, D. (2006). The misunderstood giant: On the predictive role of early vocabulary to future reading. *Handbook of Early Literacy Research, 2,* 173–182.

Shalem, Y. (2003). Do we have a theory of change? Calling change models to account. *Perspectives in Education, 21*(1), 29–49.

Snow, C. E., Burns, M. S., & Griffin, P. (1998). *Preventing reading difficulties in young children.* Washington, DC: National Academy Press.

Spaull, N. (2013). Poverty & privilege: Primary school inequality in South Africa. *International Journal of Educational Development, 33*(5), 436–447. https://doi.org/10.1016/j.ijedudev.2012. 09.009

Spaull, N. (2015). Accountability and capacity in South African education. *Education as Change, 19*(3), 113–142. https://doi.org/10.1080/16823206.2015.1056199

Spaull, N. (2016a). *Excessive class sizes in the foundation phase*. Policy Brief Research on Socioeconomic Policy (RESEP)(Online) Available: www.resep.sun.ac.za

Spaull, N. (2016b). Shaky data skews literacy results. https://mg.co.za/article/2016-09-23-00-shaky-data-skews-literacy-results/

Spaull, N., Pretorius, E. J., & Mohohlwane, N. (2018). *Investigating the comprehension iceberg: Developing empirical benchmarks for early grade reading in agglutinating African languages.* Stellenbosch University. RESEP working paper (Series no. WP01/2018). Available: www. resep.sun.ac.za.

Staehr, L. S. (2008). Vocabulary size and the skills of listening, reading and writing. *Language Learning Journal, 36*(2), 139–152.

Stahl, K., & Stahl, S. (2012). Young word wizards! Fostering vocabulary development in preschool and primary education. In E. J. Kameenui & J. F. Baumann (Eds.), *Vocabulary instruction: Research to practice* (pp. 72–92). New York: Guilford Press.

Stanovich, K. E. (2000). *Progress in understanding reading: Scientific foundations and new frontiers*. London: Guilford Press.

Taylor, N. (1989). *Falling at the first hurdle: Initial encounters with the formal system of African education in South Africa*. University of the Witwatersrand, Education Policy Unit.

Taylor, N., & Vinjevold, P. (1999). *Getting learning right: Report of the president's education initiative research project*. Braamfontein: Joint Education Trust

Taylor, S. (2019). How can learning inequalities be reduced? Lessons learnt from experimental research in South Africa. In N. Spaull & J. Jansen (Eds.), *South African schooling: The enigma of inequality*. New York: Springer Nature. https://doi.org/10.1007/978-3-030-18811-5_1.

Taylor, N. (2019). Inequalities in teacher knowledge in South Africa. In N. Spaull & J. Jansen (Eds.), *South African schooling: The enigma of inequality*. New York: Springer Nature. https:// doi.org/10.1007/978-3-030-18811-5_1

Tunmer, W. E., Chapman, J. W., & Prochnow, J. E. (2006). Literate cultural capital at school entry predicts later reading. *New Zealand Journal of Educational Studies, 41*(2), 183.

Tunmer, W. E., Chapman, J. W., Greaney, K. T., Prochnow, J. E., & Arrow, A. W. (2013). Why the New Zealand national literacy strategy has failed and what can be done about it: Evidence from the progress in international reading literacy study (PIRLS) 2011 and reading recovery monitoring reports. *Australian Journal of Learning Difficulties, 18*(2), 139–180.

van der Berg, S., Burger, C., Burger, R., de Vos, M., du Rand, G., Gustafsson, M., Moses, E., Shepherd, D. L., Spaull, N., Taylor, S., van Broekhuizen, H., & von Fintel, D. (2011). *Low quality education as a poverty trap. Research Report for the PSPPD project for presidency.* ID 2973766, University of Stellenbosch, Department of Economics, Stellenbosch.

Vasilyeva, M., & Waterfall, H. (2011). Variability in language development: Relation to socioeconomic status and environmental input. *Handbook of Early Literacy Research, 3*, 36–48.

Vellutino, F. R. (1991). Introduction to three studies on reading acquisition: Convergent findings on theoretical foundations of code-oriented versus whole-language approaches to reading instruction. *Journal of Educational Psychology, 83*(4), 437.

Whitehurst, G. J., & Lonigan, C. J. (1998). Child development and emergent literacy. *Child Development, 69*(3), 848–872.

Wills, G. (2016). *An economic perspective on school leadership and teachers' unions in South Africa*. Thesis, Stellenbosch University.

Wilsenach, C. (2015). Receptive vocabulary and early literacy skills in emergent bilingual Northern Sotho-English children. *Reading & Writing-Journal of the Reading Association of South Africa, 6*(1), 1–11.

Wolf, M. (2008). *Proust and the squid: The story and science of the reading brain* (reprint edition ed.). New York: Harper Perennial.

Chapter 9
Mathematics Achievement and the Inequality Gap: TIMSS 1995 to 2015

Vijay Reddy, Andrea Juan, Kathryn Isdale, and Samuel Fongwa

9.1   Introduction

Numerical, mathematical[1] and analytical skills are key for participation as citizens in a modern society and as workers in the new knowledge economy.

> [Mathematics] is a human activity that involves observing, representing and investigating patterns and quantitative relationships in physical and social phenomena and between mathematical objects themselves. It helps to develop mental processes that enhance logical and critical thinking, accuracy and problem-solving that will contribute in decision-making (Department of Basic education 2011, p. 8).

Foundational reading and numerical skills are critical for any future learning and knowledge and skill acquisition in these domains cannot be leap-frogged.

Mathematics achievement is a signal of the ability of learners to participate in society as engaged citizens, to continue studying mathematics, science and other technical subjects, as well as an important indicator of the competencies available for the workplace. Learners with sound mathematical skills, can participate in

---

[1] We acknowledge the importance of reading and literacy skills. These are dealt with in the Chaps. 8 and 9.

V. Reddy (✉) · A. Juan
Education and Skills Development, Human Science Research Council, Durban, South Africa
e-mail: vreddy@hsrc.ac.za; ajuan@hsrc.ac.za

K. Isdale
QER Consulting, Cape Town, South Africa
e-mail: kate.isdale@gmail.com

S. Fongwa
Education and Skills Development, Human Science Research Council, Pretoria, South Africa
e-mail: sfongwa@hsrc.ac.za

© Springer Nature Switzerland AG 2019
N. Spaull, J. D. Jansen (eds.), *South African Schooling: The Enigma of Inequality*, Policy Implications of Research in Education 10,
https://doi.org/10.1007/978-3-030-18811-5_9

higher level cognitive reasoning and problem solving tasks and possess abilities that make them more easily trainable in a number of jobs, giving them higher labour market mobility and freedoms. Currently the jobs which are in highest demand and are best rewarded in South Africa, are those with mathematics and science foundations (Reddy et al. 2016a). South Africa has embarked on an inclusive economic development pathway dependent on science, technology and innovation for which mathematics and science competence are necessary for social and economic progress (National Planning Commission 2012).

However, results from national, regional and international achievement studies (Annual National Assessments, Southern African Consortium for Monitoring Educational Quality, Progress in International Reading Literacy Study, Trends in International Mathematics and Science Study) all point to poor performance in reading, mathematics and science for South African youth. This chapter aims to tease out some of the contextual factors linked to the current achievement trends observed from the studies. The chapter uses the lens of inequality to show how access to socioeconomic resources at the individual, home and school levels shapes the mathematics performance of learners. The first part of this chapter uses grade 9 data from the Trends in International Mathematics and Science Study (TIMSS)[2] to paint a textured picture of South African mathematics achievement patterns over the last 20 years. The second part of the chapter will examine the continuities and discontinuities in home and school conditions and their influence on achievement patterns using grade 5 TIMSS data.

9.2 Mathematics Achievement, Inequality and Quality

The journey towards improved educational outcomes (including achievement) is a long and arduous process for policy makers and researchers globally. This is further complicated in low income countries and households where achievement outcomes are both a determinant and consequence of the stage of development. Children from poor families are less likely to start, progress or complete schooling successfully due to contextual and personal challenges linked to their socioeconomic backgrounds. These challenges are exacerbated in the science related subjects where more individual and social resources are needed to support learners through the challenging curriculum and content. The reasons for these achievement patterns are complex and multi-dimensional, and go beyond simply household incomes.

We borrow the framework of inequality of opportunities (UNDP 2013) to enhance our understanding of achievement levels and gaps in unequal societies. Inequality of opportunity refers to actual opportunities that give people the freedom

---

[2]TIMSS is designed to assess the mathematics and science knowledge of learners. South Africa participated at Grade 5 and 9. See the TIMSS 2015 Grade 9 National Report (Zuze et al. 2017) and the TIMSS 2015 Grade 5 National Report (Isdale et al. 2017) for the TIMSS methodology.

to pursue a life of their own choosing. Lanzi (2007) expands that any evaluation of human training outcomes will be limited if it does not adequately account for the effects of social norms, inequalities and individual freedoms (or lack thereof), as well as power structures explicitly or implicitly responsible for the outcomes.

What then would constitute an equality of opportunity framework to explain achievement gaps? TIMSS uses the curriculum, broadly defined, as the organising concept in considering how educational opportunities are provided to learners (Mullis and Martin 2013). This framework is structured around four broad areas: home contexts, school contexts, classroom contexts and learner attitude towards learning. In this chapter we will focus on home and school contexts, as well as early learning environments and experiences.

9.2.1 Homes

Home resources refer to the tangible assets within a home and provide an indicator of home socioeconomic status, as well as the intangible assets like parental education, exposure to early literacy and numeracy activities, parental involvement in homework and pre-school education. A meta-analysis of 58 studies, found that socioeconomic status (measured by parental education, parental income, and parental occupation) is a moderate to strong predictor of academic achievement, with low socioeconomic status predicting low achievement (Sirin 2005). Learners with more educated mothers tend to exhibit higher academic achievement scores (Reynolds and Walberg 1991; Carneiro et al. 2013).

Other researchers, however, argue that it is actually what goes on in the home that is associated with learners' achievement, in combination with socioeconomic status. Variables such as parental support, encouragement and expectations for their child's schooling play an important role in academic achievement. Arguably learners from better social classes seem to have better parental support and learning expectations from parents compared to those from families of a lower social status. The early learning environment, experiences and nurturing of children are correlated with the extent of their cognitive development and school readiness (Melhuish et al. 2008). For children from different social and economic circumstances, disparities in cognitive and non-cognitive, as well as literacy and numeracy skills are already evident when they enter school and these abilities are predictive of subsequent academic performance (Shonkoff et al. 2000). Cunha et al. (2006) explain that *skill begets skill*, and that skill formation is a life cycle process. The attainment of skills at one stage of the life cycle consequently raises their ability to attain skills later on. Early childhood education is therefore an integral part of basic education as the skills formed during this period are necessary for the attainment of future skills (Cunha et al. 2006).

9.2.2 Schools

Children enter schools with different levels of readiness for learning. The role of the school is to start the learning process from where the child is, and to bridge the gap between the less prepared and better prepared learners through various forms of pedagogical support. However, in South Africa due to the historical imbalances in the provision of educational resources from the previous government, two types of schools have emerged: affluent, functional schools and poor, dysfunctional schools (Van der Berg 2008). These historical inequalities are again compounded by current managerial inefficiencies which continue to affect the historically disadvantaged schools. Only about one third of schools could be considered as functional (Van der Berg 2008).

Many teachers seem to underestimate the role that the school and classroom environments play in learner success. As with the home environment, the school environment cannot simply be characterised just by the availability of resources. Aspects such as classroom morale, teacher support, availability of classroom materials and a goal directed school and classroom enhance the learners' cognitive and overall development. Murugan and Rajoo (2013) posits that the quality of classroom learning and the instructional environment is a significant determinant for learners' mathematics achievement. The time that learners spend engaging in the learning experience, including engaging with the teacher, and the time spent on personal learning through doing homework and group work, affects their final achievement scores.

South African studies have established that the availability of key school resources influences educational outcomes, with higher levels of resources being linked to better educational outcomes (Fiske and Ladd 2004; Oosthuizen and Bhorat 2006; Van der Berg 2008). Socioeconomic inequalities at the school level play a role in the educational outcomes of South African learners, as learners in the richest quintile of schools outperform schools in the other four quintiles substantially (Van der Berg 2008). Zuze et al. (2017) showed that although schools with more resources and better facilities were at an advantage, the climate of learning played a unique and significant role that went beyond resources.

A noteworthy factor in performance among learners, is the disjuncture between the language of classroom teaching and learning, and the language of home communication. For the majority of learners in Grades 4 to 12 the language of teaching is different from the language spoken in the home (Howie et al. 2017; Reddy et al. 2015). Poor performance in both literacy and numeracy assessments across the foundation phase Grades 1 to 3 has been cited as one of the major factors linked to poor learning outcomes later in school (Bergbauer 2016; Van Staden 2016), with many children completing these early grades unable to read properly in their home language and with very little understanding of English, the main language of instruction used from Grade 4 (Spaull et al. 2016; Howie et al. 2017).

Given these inequalities of opportunity, Stewart's (2002) notion of horizontal inequality helps shape the analyses. She defines horizontal inequalities as those among a group which have emerged based largely on historical biases, often as a result of colonialism and which tend to persist over many generations because of manifold connections between dimensions of deprivation and privilege. She argues that horizontal inequality is not only unjust, but may lead to reduced resource allocation as well as lessening societal attainment of quality health and education, especially for the deprived group.

The next section provides a broad overview of South Africa's mathematics achievement. We show that while South Africa has made significant progress in mathematics performance, it continues to show low achievement levels when compared to countries at similar levels of development. Furthermore, using fee-paying and no-fee schools as two schooling groups experiencing horizontal inequality due to historical biases, we show how personal level inequalities and schooling level inequalities result in achievement gaps within the system.

9.3   South African Mathematics Achievement from 1995 to 2015: Improving but Overall Low Achievement

The TIMSS offers a dual opportunity to benchmark South African mathematics achievement against other participating countries, and to monitor that achievement over time. The TIMSS was first administered in South Africa in 1995, and subsequently in 1999 to Grade 8 learners. In 2003, TIMSS was administered to Grade 8 and 9 learners, and in 2011 and 2015 just to Grade 9 learners. This unique trend dataset offers an opportunity for the country to measure and analyse mathematics achievement patterns over 20 years.

In TIMSS 2015, South Africa, with a mathematics achievement score of 372[3] (SE,[4] 4.5), was one of the lower performers (again) of the 39 participating countries. The five highest ranked countries were from East Asia: Singapore (mathematics achievement score of 621), Republic of Korea (606), Chinese Taipei (599), Hong Kong SAR (594) and Japan (587). The five lowest ranked countries were from Africa and the Middle East: Botswana (391), Jordan (386), Morocco (384), South Africa (372) and Saudi Arabia (368).[5]

While South Africa's low ranked position of the participating countries is the focus of much of the public discourse, the more informative story is how South Africa's average mathematics achievement score changed from 1995 to 2015.

---

[3]The TIMSS CenterPoint is 500 and the standard deviation is 100.

[4]Standard Error (SE) is a measure of the statistical accuracy of an estimate.

[5]Of the five lowest achieving countries, the only country with a statistically different score to that of South Africa was Botswana

Mathematics	Average Scale score	Score distribution: At 5th & 95th percentile	Achievement distribution
Grade 9 2015	372 (4.5)	242-529=287	
Grade 9 2011	352 (2.5)	229-516=287	
Grade 9 2003	285 (4.2)	152-472=320	
Grade 8 2003	264 (5.5)	117-484=367	
Grade 8 1999	275 (6.8)	113-485=372	
Grade 8 1995	276 (6.7)	142-496=354	

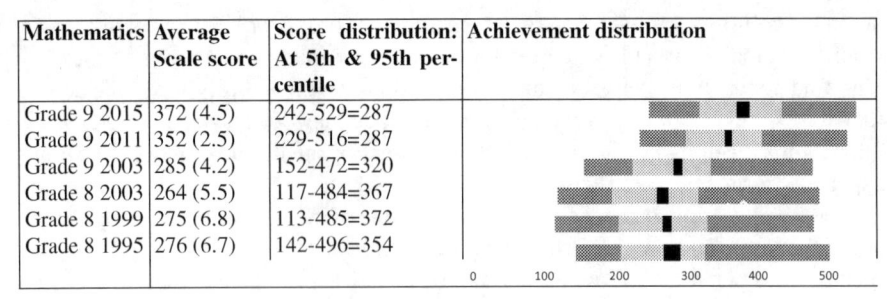

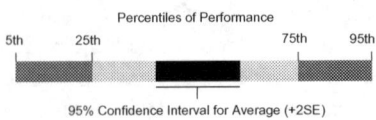

Fig. 9.1 Trends in mathematics achievement in TIMSS 1995, 1999, 2003, 2011 and 2015. (Sources: Reddy et al. 2016b; Zuze et al. 2017)

Figure 9.1 plots the South African mathematics achievement for TIMSS 1995, 1999, 2003, 2011 and 2015.[6]

The first piece of good news is that the South African average mathematics achievement increased from 1995 to 2015. The changes can be described in three phases: from 1995 to 2003 the average mathematics achievement was not statistically different, possibly because of the collateral damage due to the political and structural changes that took place with the change to a democratic country in 1994. In contrast, from 2003 to 2011 the average mathematics achievement improved by 67 points (Reddy et al. 2012), an improvement of an average of 7.4 TIMSS points per year. From 2011 to 2015 mathematics achievement improved by a further 20 points (Reddy et al. 2016b), an improvement of an average of 5 TIMSS points per year.

The achievement distribution between the 5th and 95th percentile provides a measure of the achievement gap. In 1995, this difference was just over 3.5 standard deviations. In 2015, the achievement gaps narrowed slightly, by 0.6 cf a standard deviation, to 287 points.

TIMSS further categorises learners who achieve above 400 points,[7] as having met the minimum competencies for that grade (Mullis et al. 2016). In 2003, 11% of Grade 9 learners achieved a mathematics score higher than 400 points, in 2011 this more than doubled to 25% and in 2015 increased further with one third of the learners achieving above this minimum competency benchmark. While

[6]The percentile graph plots the trend in mathematics achievement distribution between the bottom and upper ends at the 5th and 95th percentile at the Grade 8 level (1995, 1999, 2003) and at the Grade 9 level (2003, 2011,2015).

[7]Learners have some knowledge of whole numbers and basic graphs.

this improvement is laudable, the other side of the coin is that in 2015 two-thirds of Grade 9 learners were unable to achieve these minimum mathematical competencies. Likewise, the change in the overall average mathematics achievement from *very low* (1995 to 2003) to *low* (2011, 2015) is to be applauded, but the concern is that progress and gains in learning seem to be slowing down. If the progress continues at the current rate, in the TIMSS 2027 cycle, South Africa could be closer to the National Development Plan mathematics achievement target of 430 TIMSS points (National Planning Commission 2012). In addition, half the learners should achieve above the minimum competency level. TIMSS 2019 will provide a third data point to better extrapolate the achievement trajectory.

The second piece of good news is that although South Africa is one of the lower performing TIMSS countries, from 2003 to 2015, it showed the largest positive improvement of all participating countries in mathematics. South Africa started from a very low base and thus had greater potential to improve (Reddy et al. 2016b), but it is nevertheless encouraging to note that the highest achievement gains were at the lower end of the distribution spectrum, that is, the most disadvantaged groups. TIMSS scores at the 5th percentile, improved by almost one standard deviation[8] from 152 points in 2003 to 242 points in 2015. At the 95th percentile, mathematics scores increased by 0.6 of a standard deviation from 472 points in 2003 to 529 points in 2015. The achievement improvement at the 5th percentile is possibly due to the many social protection policies and interventions for the most disadvantaged households and schools (social grants, school feeding programme, no-fee policy for schools, free health care). These social protection policies, even though not implemented optimally, have made a difference in decreasing the levels of poverty, and would have had a knock on effect of improving living and learning conditions and learning outcomes (Woolard et al. 2011).

South Africa is characterised by high levels of unemployment, income poverty and inequality, so a single average achievement score does not tell the full story. For a more textured achievement story we would need to disaggregate the achievement score for different socioeconomic status groups. To provide economic relief to the low income households, government has removed the barrier of school fees for two thirds of school going learners, thus public schools are categorised as either fee-paying or no-fee schools. We use these school types, fee-paying and no-fee schools, as a proxy for school SES.[9] Figure 9.2 sets out the mathematics achievement (average scores and competence levels) for learners in no-fee and fee-paying schools.

The average mathematics achievement for learners in no-fee schools was 341 (SE 3.3) and 430 (SE 8.9) for learners in fee-paying schools, reflecting the achievement gap between learners from higher and lower SES households. The achievement gap between these two school SES types is approximately one standard

---

[8]The standard deviation (SD) measures the dispersion of a dataset relative to its mean.

[9]The TIMSS 2015 Grade 9 sample comprised of 65% learners who attended public no-fee schools and 35% who pay fees (31% in public fee-paying and 4% in independent schools).

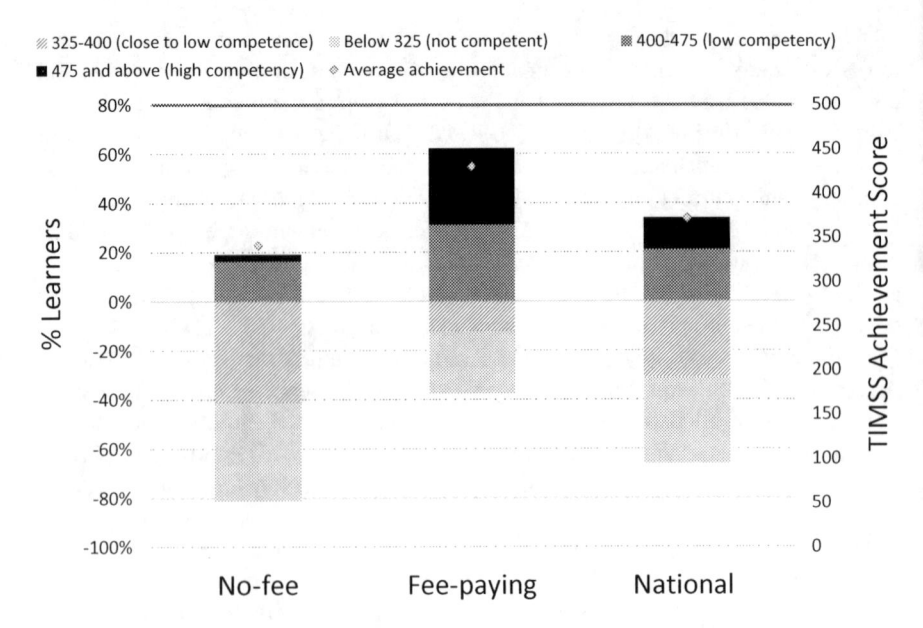

Fig. 9.2 Average TIMSS 2015 mathematics score and competence level by no-fee and fee-paying (public and independent) schools

deviation, meaning that performance levels are almost four grade levels apart.[10] This further demonstrates the extent of inequalities between school types. While low achievement levels in no-fee schools are well documented, the TIMSS results also showed that the average mathematics achievement score of learners in fee-paying schools fell well below the centerpoint and placed this group at a similar performance level as Chile, Thailand and Iran.

When the mathematics achievement scores are analysed for each of the school types, the patterns reveal the extent of the inequalities: only one in five (19%) learners in no-fee schools and three in five (62%) learners in fee-paying schools had accumulated knowledge and skills above the minimum competency level. This means that 81% of learners in no-fee schools and 38% of learners in fee-paying schools did not have the minimum knowledge and skills needed for that grade. We introduced an additional benchmark, at 325 points, to establish how close learners were to the minimum benchmark. It is promising to note that in no-fee schools, half the group below the score of 400 points were categorised at close to the minimum competence level and two thirds of learners in fee-paying schools were in this category. This group of *almost competent*, could, with the appropriate school-based interventions be supported to achieve mathematics scores over 400 points.

---

[10]The difference between Grade 8 and 9 scores in TIMSS 2003 was 21 points (see Reddy 2006). We estimate with the learning gains over time, the score difference between Grade 8 and 9 is around 25 TIMSS points.

Within the general national profile of low and unequal performance, 13% of learners scored above 475 points. These learners would have a higher probability of passing the Grade 12 examinations and gaining access to post-secondary education. It is encouraging to note that 3.2% of South African mathematics learners achieved mathematics scores at the *high level* of achievement (above 550 points), an achievement higher than other low performing countries.

In trying to understand the depth of inequalities responsible for the achievement gaps between fee-paying and no-fee schools, further analysis was conducted. Based on these analyses, three key factors emerged as important in understanding achievement gaps within the South African context. These relate to home conditions, the early education environment and school learning conditions.

9.4 Home to School: Continuities or Discontinuities?

The South African educational challenge, as in other middle income countries, is to raise the achievement levels of children in schools, decrease the inequalities between the affluent and the poor, and increase the rate of change of progress in achievement outcomes. There are many factors that shape individual learning. In this section we will demonstrate the influence of the continuities and discontinuities in home and school conditions on achievement patterns.

We use the TIMSS 2015 Grade 5 data, which included information about both home and school contexts and activities, to describe the conditions in which learners attending fee-paying and no-fee schools live and learn. Although interrelated, we structure our argument through the description of home resources, early learning environments and school resources and climate separately. Though important for a holistic understanding of learning experiences and outcomes, this analysis does not engage with teacher and classroom effects for which adequate data was not available.

9.4.1 Inequalities Begin in the Home

Learning starts at home and schools should build on the educational capital accumulated there. The learning process is shaped by home contexts and the interactions within them; key are the basic physical resources, family background characteristics, and the learning resources. For South Africa we found that three-quarters of learners' households received at least one government social grant to contribute to the household income. As would be expected, a higher proportion of households of learners attending no-fee schools are recipients of social grants.

Household resources were vastly unequal across learners attending fee-paying and no-fee schools as shown in Fig. 9.3 below: overall 83% of Grade 5 learners had access to electricity; but access to basic amenities is concerning as only 64%

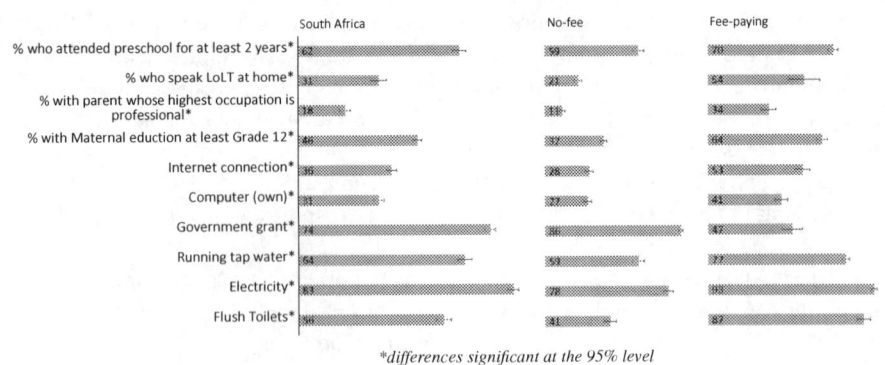

*differences significant at the 95% level

Source: Authors' own calculations based on TIMSS 2015 Grade 5 early learning and learner
questionnaire data

Fig. 9.3 Reported percentages of learners' household assets, by overall frequency and frequency by school type (with 95% confidence intervals). *differences significant at the 95% level. (Source: Authors' own calculations based on TIMSS 2015 Grade 5 early learning and learner questionnaire data)

had access to running tap water and 56% to flush toilets in their homes. There is a statistically significant difference for these resources in the homes of learners in fee-paying and no-fee schools: in fee-paying schools 87% of learners had access to flush toilets compared to 41% in no-fee schools. Furthermore, while 77% of learners in fee-paying schools had running tap water, only 59% in no-fee schools had this amenity. Another resource which is becoming increasingly important for learning is digital technologies. The overall access to digital technologies and the internet in South Africa is low at approximately one-third of households. It is also unequal; learners in fee-paying schools have double the access compared to those attending no-fee schools.

Maternal education and parental occupation are two indicators of human and social capital, and signal what parents are able to afford for their children. These factors have consistently been shown as key predictors of achievement. On average, 37% of learners from no-fee schools and 64% of fee-paying learners came from households where mothers had a post-grade 12 education. This home educational difference led to one in 10 learners in no-fee schools and one in three learners in fee-paying schools having at least one parent in a job categorised as a professional occupation. These differences between fee and no-fee schools were statistically significant and contributes to learners' subsequent mathematics achievement.

The equivalence between the home language and the language of instruction in schools was another factor considered. Ninety one percent of the TIMSS Grade 5 assessments were completed in English and 9% in Afrikaans, giving those who were more proficient in English (or Afrikaans) a distinct advantage. Only a third of learners (31%) taking the TIMSS 2015 assessments always spoke the language of learning and teaching (LOLT) in the home. These patterns are statistically different in the two school types, with 54% of learners in fee-paying schools and 21% from no-fee schools speaking the same language at home and at school.

The effects of these variables on mathematics achievement were estimated in a conditional correlational model, when all variables were considered jointly in a single regression. The analysis confirmed that higher levels of household education and occupations, speaking the language of the test at home, having an internet connection, and having more books in a home all positively influenced mathematics achievement (Isdale et al. 2017).

9.4.2 Varied Early Educational Environments

A growing body of global evidence demonstrates that learning is more than a formal process that begins on entering a Grade 1 classroom, but is a cumulative endeavour beginning at home with the understanding of basic cognitive, linguistic, perceptual and motor processes which provide the building blocks for subsequent learning (Isdale et al. 2017). Parents of the Grade 5 learners who participated in TIMSS 2015 reported on the early educational activities[11] of their children. Close to one third of parents reported regularly engaging in some type of educational activities with their children: 35% read books, 30% played with alphabets, 34% sang counting songs, 31% played with number toys, 36% played with shapes and 31% played with building blocks. Figure 9.4 shows that, as expected, parents participated in these activities more in the homes of learners attending fee-paying than no-fee schools.

It is a social policy success that attendance to pre-Grade 1 facilities has increased considerably over recent years (Statistics South Africa 2017). Almost nine out of ten of the 2015 TIMSS learners reported pre-school attendance prior to Grade 1. The length of pre-Grade 1 attendance varied, with 62% of learners having attended two or more years of pre-school (59% for no-fee schools and 70% for fee-paying schools, a statistically significant difference). The mathematics achievement for learners who attended a pre-school for two years or more is statistically higher than those who did not attend (389 vs 353 TIMSS points).

Parents' assessment of their children's levels of literacy school readiness revealed that half of all learners were able to recognise most letters of the alphabet, 35% were able to read some words and 43% could write letters. For numeracy, one in four learners were able to count numbers up to 100 and one in five were able to recognise and write numbers up to 100 (Fig. 9.5). Parents of learners in both school types reported similar levels of skill in readiness for reading words, writing letters and writing numbers. The statistically significant difference between learners in the two school types, with learners in fee-paying schools scoring higher, are in recognising

---

[11]Notwithstanding that this is self-reported data from six years ago and the reported extent of the activities cannot be triangulated, these educational activity patterns still provides useful insights into home educational activities.

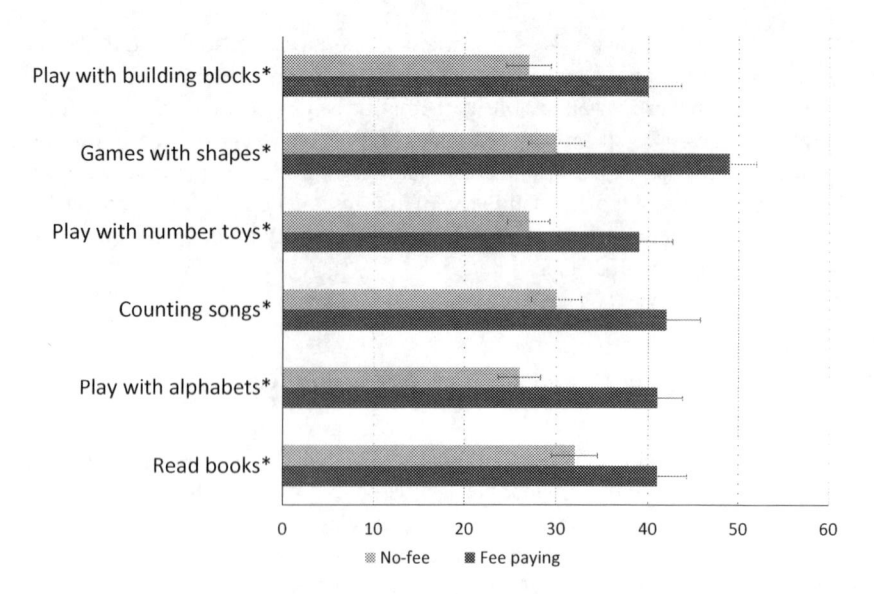

differences significant at the 95% level

Source: Authors' own calculations based on TIMSS 2015 Grade 5 early learning questionnaire

Fig. 9.4 Percentage of parents who reported 'often' engaging in early educational activities, by school type (with 95% confidence intervals). *differences significant at the 95% level. (Source: Authors' own calculations based on TIMSS 2015 Grade 5 early learning questionnaire)

letters of the alphabet (by 9 percentage points), counting on their own up to 100 (by 14 percentage points) and recognising written numbers up to 100 (by 8 percentage points).

There was an association between the reported early literacy and numeracy skills and Grade 5 mathematics achievement scores: learners who were rated as having high levels of readiness in literacy and numeracy skills achieved an average mathematics score of 422; while those rated *moderately* achieved an average score of 376, and those rated as *not well* only scored an average of 338 points. This is corroborated by the conditional correlation model that found that levels of literacy and numeracy skills at school entry positively influence later mathematics achievement, even when taking into account a host of other variables known to influence academic performance (Isdale et al. 2017). This continuity in cognitive performance from home to school is one of the most replicated findings in developmental studies and further highlights the importance of the early educational environment.

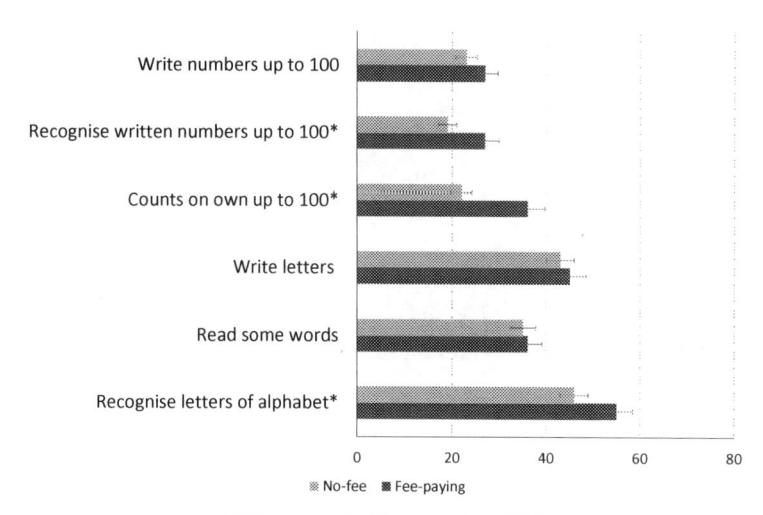

differences significant at the 95% level
Source: Authors' own calculations based on TIMSS 2015 Grade 5 early learning questionnaire
data

Fig. 9.5 Proportion of learners with strong literacy and numeracy skills prior to Grade 1 by school type (with 95% confidence interval). *differences significant at the 95% level. (Source: Authors' own calculations based on TIMSS 2015 Grade 5 early learning questionnaire data)

9.4.3   Inequalities Continue into Schools

With these unequal educational starting points for children entering Grade 1, the expectation is that the schools with high quality resources and environments supportive of learning, will offset the home disadvantage. Inequalities, however, seem not to be limited to the home environment, but continue to the school environment and compound the inequality levels between learners in fee-paying and no-fee schools. Government policy highlights the importance of social transformation (that imbalances of the past are redressed and equal educational opportunities are provided for all) and inclusivity as a central tenet for the organisation, planning and teaching at each school (Department of Basic education 2011). However, these policies are silent on the resources needed for implementation. In this section we will examine whether schools contribute to the social transformation and inclusivity goals for all learners by examining the school resources and learning climate in fee-paying and no-fee schools (Fig. 9.6).

School resources are important to establish for a conducive learning environment. One of the key interventions of the South African government to improve learning outcomes was to develop and supply workbooks to all learners. This intervention is a policy success, with 90% of all learners reporting having access to workbooks, and there is positive association between having a workbook and a higher mathematics achievement score (Isdale et al. 2017). However, increased access to other resources

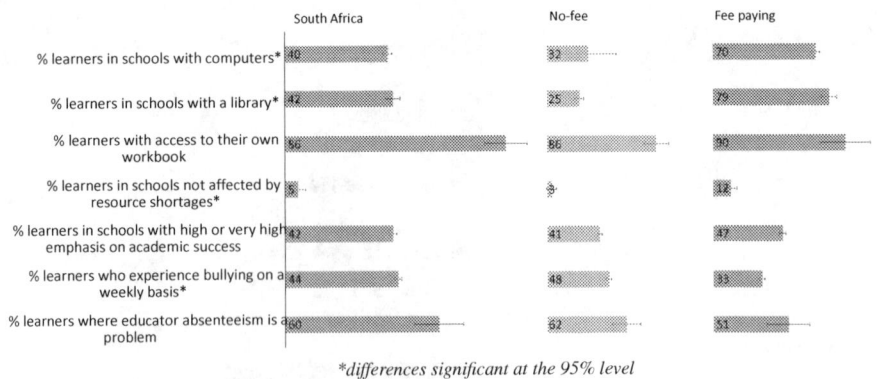

*differences significant at the 95% level

Source: Authors' own calculations based on TIMSS 2015 Grade 5 early learning questionnaire
data

Fig. 9.6 School resources and climate characteristics by school type (with 95% confidence intervals). *differences significant at the 95% level. (Source: Authors' own calculations based on TIMSS 2015 Grade 5 early learning questionnaire data)

has not been achieved. Only 40% of Grade 5 learners attended schools where they had access to computers or a library, and this access was statistically significantly higher for fee-paying than no-fee schools. Principals' assessed the levels of resource shortages in their schools and only 5% of learners (against the international average of 27%) were rated as being in an environment not affected by resource shortages.

One-third of South African learners came from households considered to have few resources in comparison with an overall international average of 9 percent.[12] While household resources are linked to individual achievement, this relationship is also context dependent. Table 9.1 shows the TIMSS *Home Resources for Learning Index* by school type, with the results illustrating the interaction between household and school-level resources. As would be expected, across school types, those with few resources fare poorly, and achievement scores in both fee-paying and no-fee schools increased for learners with more resources. Learners with similar levels of home resources perform at different levels, with those in fee-paying schools performing at a much higher level than those in no-fee schools. Notable is that in fee-paying schools, the level of resources is strongly related to mathematics achievement (387 for few resources vs 460 for some resources). This is less so in no-fee schools (339 for few resources vs 352 for some resources), suggesting that even though the achievement score differences are statistically significant, there are factors other than resources that influence achievement.

In addition to resources, school climate has been identified as an important indicator influencing teaching and learning in schools. There are multiple dimen-

---

[12] A Home Resources for Learning Index was constructed from the number of books in the home, number of home study supports and the highest level of education for either parent.

Table 9.1 Proportion of learners and average mathematics achievement scores by Home Resources for Learning Index

	Few resources		Some resources		Many resources	
	% learners	Ave. score	% learners	Ave. score	% learners	Ave. score
South Africa	34 (1.2)	348 (3.2)	65 (1.2)	391 (4.1)	2 (0.4)	599 (10.0)
Fee-paying	19 (1.8)	387 (7.1)	75 (1.8)	460 (6.2)	5 (1.1)	605 (9.2)
No-fee	40 (1.5)	339 (3.7)	60 (1.5)	352 (3.8)	0.1 (0.0)	Too few to estimate
International	9 (0.1)	427 (1.5)	74 (0.2)	501 (0.4)	17 (0.2)	569 (0.9)

South African figures based on authors' own calculations from TIMSS 2015 Grade 5 learner questionnaire and achievement datasets. International figures from Mullis et al. (2016)

sions of school climate, many of which contribute to enhanced learning. A critical aspect of school climate relates to school safety and discipline, and incidences of bullying. A high proportion (44%) of Grade 5 South African learners reported experiencing at least one form of bullying on a weekly basis: one in two learners in no-fee schools and one in three learners in fee-paying schools (the difference is statistically significant). Forty-two percent of learners were in schools which placed a high emphasis on academic success and surprisingly this pattern is similar for both school types. Another factor contributing to school climate is the extent of teacher absenteeism. 60% of learners are in schools where teacher absence is a problem, and these patterns are also similar in fee-paying and no-fee schools.

In addition to low and unequal resources and poor learning climates in schools, there is a high variation of learner achievement in any one classroom (Fig. 9.7). The mathematics achievement distribution between the 5th and 95th percentile in fee-paying schools was 289 TIMSS points and in no-fee schools it was 223 TIMSS points, signalling higher levels of learner variation in fee-paying than no-fee schools. TIMSS tests intact classes of learners. In Fig. 9.7 we plotted the average class mathematics achievement against the mathematics distribution in the class (at the 5th and 95th percentile). In no-fee schools, the class average mathematics achievement scores are lower than for fee-paying schools, and the achievement distribution for the majority of no-fee classrooms are between 100 to 200 TIMSS points. In the case of fee-paying schools, the achievement distribution within the classroom are between 150 and 260 TIMSS points. These high achievement distributions place a serious burden on classroom teachers in terms of responding to the diverse needs of *all* learners.

Many of these factors are related to mathematics achievement. The conditional joint regression correlational model, estimates that achievement scores were slightly correlated with the presence of computers and libraries in a school and that achievement scores are negatively related to higher incidences of teacher absenteeism, poor school discipline and higher incidences of bullying (Isdale et al. 2017).

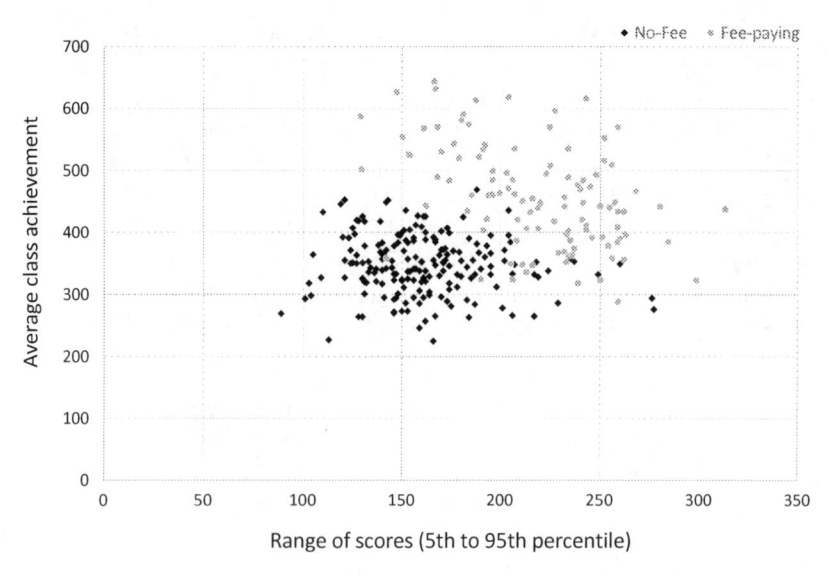

Source: Authors' own calculations based on TIMSS 2015 Grade 5 early learning questionnaire data

Fig. 9.7 Grade 5 intra-class achievement distribution. (Source: Authors' own calculations based on TIMSS 2015 Grade 5 early learning questionnaire data. Note: TIMSS tests intact classes)

9.5 Breaking Out of Low and Unequal Achievement

One cannot separate the discussion of educational inequalities (achievement gaps) from that of educational outcomes (achievement levels). In summary, South African mathematics achievement, though improving, is still low and unequal. Between 1995 and 2015, South African mathematics achievement improved by 0.9 of a standard deviation. The highest improvement was at the lower levels of the achievement spectrum, that is, for the most disadvantaged groups, probably as a result of social protection policies instituted by the state. The achievement distribution has decreased slightly (0.6SD) from 1995, but is still one of the wider distributions (2.9SD) of all TIMSS participating countries. The achievement gap for those attending fee-paying and no-fee schools is close to one standard deviation and only 19% of learners in no-fee schools and 62% in fee-paying schools, demonstrate mathematical competencies above the minimum threshold value. In addition, there are wide achievement distribution patterns within classrooms, and more so for classrooms in fee-paying schools.

There is a general continuity in conditions from home to school. On most of the indicators important for supporting educational outcomes: home and school physical and educational resources, the early educational activities that parents are involved in with the children, and the characteristics of school life, our findings show that they are not available to the majority of the population. Further, there are differences for learners attending fee-paying and no-fee schools, reflecting the inequality of opportunities. The learners in fee-paying schools are advantaged by both home and school conditions, leading to higher achievement scores. School climate characteristics, however, are similar in both school types. The story in general is that advantage begets advantage, and while a few of the disadvantaged learners have evaded their predicted pathway, for the majority of these learners the school environment reproduces the conditions at home leading to low achievement outcomes.

Improving educational outcomes is a complex and multi-dimensional exercise, especially in an educational system starting from a low achievement base with high achievements gaps. The state must continue with social protection policies and resources for the homes that poorer children live in and the schools they attend, in order to improve the material conditions. Further, the quality of the learning experience for all learners must be addressed, through improved teaching and learning practices and learning climates in schools and classrooms.

The long term strategy to improve the achievement outcomes is to target the early years of learning. *Skill begets skill* and therefore solid knowledge and skills foundations are essential to move towards further learning. Social policies must prioritise investments in the earlier years of formal learning. This means two years of pre-Grade 1 schooling must be compulsory. It is not enough for children only to attend these institutions, the institutions in turn must be staffed by competent and caring teachers who provide high quality learning experiences and support to learners. In addition parents must be supported in terms of how to engage with their children to stimulate cognitive development. The first 1000 days of a child's life are focused on interventions for a healthy being, the next 1000 days of schooling (Grade RR, R, 1,2,3) must create a solid learning foundation.

While there are policies in place to address inequalities in schools and classrooms, they have not been accompanied by resources (financial and human) and support mechanisms to effectively implement the policies. Disrupting inequalities will require political will, additional resources and support and the commitment from all members of society. The process to increase achievement levels is not linear or smooth. It will involve the interplay of home and school material conditions, accompanied by high quality classroom teaching and learning interactions. This process will take time and we must set realistic expectations for the changes.

References

Bergbauer, A. (2016). *The role of non-conventional inputs in South African education: An analysis of prePIRLS 2011*. Stellenbosch: University of Stellenbosch.

Carneiro, P., Meghir, C., & Parey, M. (2013). Maternal education, home environments, and the development of children and adolescents. *Journal of the European Economic Association, 11*(suppl_1), 123–160. https://doi.org/10.1111/j.1542-4774.2012.01096.x

Cunha, F., Heckman, J. J., Lochner, L., & Masterov, D. V. (2006). Chapter 12 interpreting the evidence on life cycle skill formation. In E. Hanushek & F. Welch (Eds.), *Handbook of the economics of education* (Vol. 1, pp. 697–812). Elsevier. https://doi.org/10.1016/S1574-0692(06)01012-9

Department of Basic education. (2011). *Curriculum and assessment policy statements: Mathematics grades* (pp. 7–9). Pretoria: Government Printers.

Fiske, E. B., & Ladd, H. F. (2004). *Elusive equity: Education reform in post-apartheid South Africa*. Washington, DC: Brookings Institution Press.

Howie, S., Van Staden, S., Tshele, M., Dowse, C., & Zimmerman, L. (2017). Progress in international reading literacy study 2016. South African Children's Reading Literacy Achievement. Summary Report. Centre for Evaluation and Assessment, Pretoria.

Isdale, K., Reddy, V., Juan, A., & Arends, F. (2017). TIMSS 2015 grade 5 national report: Understanding mathematics achievement amongst Grade 5 learners in South Africa. https://doi.org/20.500.11910/11847

Lanzi, D. (2007). Capabilities, human capital and education. *The Journal of Socio-Economics, 36*(3), 424–435. https://doi.org/10.1016/j.socec.2006.12.005

Melhuish, E. C., Phan, M. B., Sylva, K., Sammons, P., Siraj-Blatchford, I., & Taggart, B. (2008). Effects of the home learning environment and preschool center experience upon literacy and numeracy development in early primary school. *Journal of Social Issues, 64*(1), 95–114.

Mullis, I. V. S., & Martin, M. O. (Eds.). (2013). *TIMSS 2015 assessment frameworks*. TIMSS & PIRLS International Study Center, Boston College.

Mullis, I. V., Martin, M. O., Foy, P., & Hooper, M. (2016). *TIMSS 2015 international results in mathematics*. Boston: Boston College.

Murugan, A., & Rajoo, L. (2013). Students' perceptions of mathematics classroom environment and mathematics achievement: A study in Sipitang, Sabah, Malaysia. In *International Conference on Social Science Research*, Malaysia.

National Planning Commission. (2012). *National development plan 2030: Our future–make it work*. Pretoria: The Presidency.

Oosthuizen, M., & Bhorat, H. (2006). Educational outcomes in South Africa: A production function approach. In *Canada: Secretariat for Institutional Support for Economic Research in Africa Working Paper No. 2006/05*.

Reddy, V. (2006). *Mathematics and science achievement at South African schools in TIMSS 2003*. HSRC Press.

Reddy, V., Prinsloo, C., Arends, F., Visser M (2012) *Highlights from TIMSS 2011: The South African perspective*. Pretoria: HRSC Press https://doi.org/20.500.11910/2877

Reddy, V., Zuze, T. L., Visser, M., Winnaar, L., Juan, A., Prinsloo, C. H., Arends, F., & Rogers, S. (2015). *Beyond benchmarks: What twenty years of TIMSS data tell us about South African education*. HSRC Press. https://doi.org/20.500.11910/2004

Reddy, V., Bhorat, H., Powell, M., Visser, M. M., & Arends, F. (2016a). Skills supply and demand in South Africa. https://doi.org/20.500.11910/10186

Reddy, V., Visser, M., Winnaar, L., Arends, F., Juan, A. L., Prinsloo, C., & Isdale, K. (2016b). TIMSS 2015: Highlights of mathematics and science achievement of grade 9 South African learners. https://doi.org/20.500.11910/10673

Reynolds, A. J., & Walberg, H. J. (1991). A structural model of science achievement. *Journal of Educational Psychology, 83*(1), 97.

Shonkoff, J. P., Phillips, D. A., & National Research Council. (2000). The developing brain. In D. A. Phillips & J. P. Shonkoff (Eds.), *From neurons to neighborhoods: The science of early childhood development*. Washington, DC: National Academies Press.

Sirin, S. R. (2005). Socioeconomic status and academic achievement: A meta-analytic review of research, socioeconomic status and academic achievement: A meta-analytic review of research. *Review of Educational Research, 75*(3), 417–453. https://doi.org/10.3102/00346543075003417

Spaull, N., Vvan der Berg, S., Wills, G., Gustafsson, M., & Kotzé, J. (2016). *Laying firm foundations: Getting reading right*. SSRN Scholarly Paper ID 2973191. Rochester: Social Science Research Network.

Statistics South Africa. (2017). *Education series volume III: Educational enrolment and achievement, 2016*. Pretoria: Statistics South Africa.

Stewart, F. (2002). Horizontal inequalities as a source of conflict. In F. O. Hampson & D. Malone (Eds.), *From reaction to conflict prevention: Opportunities for the UN system* (pp. 105–136). Boulder: Lynne Rienner Publishers.

UNDP. (2013). *Humanity divided: Confronting inequality in developing countries*. New York: UNDP.

Van der Berg, S. (2008). How effective are poor schools? Poverty and educational outcomes in South Africa. *Studies in Educational Evaluation, 34*(3), 145–154. https://doi.org/10.1016/j.stueduc.2008.07.005

Van Staden, S. (2016). *Language and grade 4 reading literacy achievement in prePIRLS 2011*. Stellenbosch: University of Stellenbosch, ReSEP Working Paper Series 03/2016.

Woolard, I., Harttgen, K., & Klasen, S. (2011). The history and impact of social security in South Africa: Experiences and lessons. *Canadian Journal of Development Studies/Revue canadienne d'études du développement 32*(4), 357–380. https://doi.org/10.1080/02255189.2011.647654

Zuze, L., Reddy, V., Winnaar, L., & Govender, A. (2017). *TIMSS 2015 grade 9 national report*. HSRC Press: Cape Town.

Chapter 10
Teachers' Mathematical Knowledge, Teaching and the Problem of Inequality

Hamsa Venkat

10.1 Introduction

There is ample and ongoing evidence in South Africa of gaps in primary teachers' mathematical knowledge and competence with mathematics teaching. The evidence also points to these issues featuring prominently in the inequities in educational outcomes that have marked the national terrain. Teachers working in lower socio-economic status schools score at lower levels on content knowledge tests than their counterparts in higher status schools. In studies of pedagogic practice, slower pacing, and an absence of evaluation pointing to correct and incorrect answers have been noted as more prevalent in schools serving poorer children, with more limited input into how to go about producing correct answers.

This combination of issues suggests the urgent need for policy attention to improving primary teachers' content knowledge and classroom practices related to mathematics, as a key route to addressing issues of inequality. In this chapter, attention is given to the foci of 'resources' that have been put in place to address inequitable educational outcomes relating to primary mathematics teaching and learning in the national policy terrain. This analysis identifies a disjuncture between what the existing evidence related to teacher knowledge and practices suggests as gaps in terms of resources on the one hand, and what resources were provided via key national interventions on the other.

This disjuncture leads into a concluding argument: that primary teachers' mathematical knowledge and classroom practices are currently in the peripheries of policy goals. This peripheral location presents a problem for addressing inequality. Possible reasons for this gap are also addressed, with attention to contestations

H. Venkat (✉)
Wits School of Education, University of the Witwatersrand, Johannesburg, South Africa
e-mail: Hamsa.venkatakrishnan@wits.ac.za

© Springer Nature Switzerland AG 2019
N. Spaull, J. D. Jansen (eds.), *South African Schooling: The Enigma of Inequality*, Policy Implications of Research in Education 10,
https://doi.org/10.1007/978-3-030-18811-5_10

in the international research base that are echoed in South Africa, which present difficulties for policy suggestions and mandates backed by some consensus.

10.2 Adler's Theorization of Resources

Adler (2000) developed a focus on teachers' mathematical knowledge and classroom practices from the perspective of resources. In this work, Adler categorizes resources for school mathematics practice into three key domains: material, cultural and human resources. These categories include what she describes as some 'basic' resource elements, for example, teacher-pupil ratios and class sizes in the human resource category, and school buildings and access to electricity in the material resource category. These basic resources organizationally, are often beyond the teacher's ability to exert control over or impact upon. The basic resources are also, for the most part, generic, rather than mathematics specific in their orientation, and thus the focus in this chapter is on Adler's descriptions of the mathematics specific elements of resources in each of her three categories. Her descriptions of resources within each of these domains include the following aspects pertinent specifically to the practices associated with school mathematics:

10.2.1 Material Resources

Mathematical resources in Adler's formulation include the more obvious material elements of mathematical equipment such as rulers, compasses and calculators, but also materials that can mediate the curriculum in the form of textbooks and worksheets. Adler also incorporates what she describes as 'mathematical objects' within her notion of material resources, with the theorems, procedures and representations selected and worked with by teachers and in texts among this group.

10.2.2 Cultural Resources

Language and time form the two key elements in Adler's cultural resource category. Both elements are described in multi-dimensional ways. Language is noted as encompassing learners' home languages, learners' relation to the language of instruction in mathematics classrooms, as well as learners' verbalizations of mathematical ideas in class. Advocacy of the use of language as a resource for mathematics teaching and learning has international support, and – on paper at least – South African policy support for multilingualism in schools in the post-apartheid context appeared to support this position. However, as Setati (2008) points out, complexities related to English functioning as the language of access to power and social goods produces contradictions in practice, with the press for English language instruction taking priority over the need to understand what is being said.

The ways in which time for mathematics is allocated in schools, globally at the level of timetabling and length/number of periods a week, and locally in terms of different teachers' pacing and sequencing of content, feature within attention to time as a resource.

10.2.3 Human Resources

The teacher's mathematical knowledge base and orientations to mathematical knowledge are both described as key constituents of the human resource category, but Adler also includes knowledge of general educational theory and practice within her delineation. She notes too, the need for attention to: 'knowledge bases for teaching culturally and linguistically diverse learners' and 'for teaching across urban and rural, under-resourced schools' (p. 210).

In Jita's (1998) earlier writing on resources supporting science teaching that Adler draws upon, emotional and affective aspects related to teachers' commitment to their disciplinary work are also included in the human resources category.

Looking at mathematical knowledge and practice via the lens of resources is useful for a number of reasons. Firstly, the categories emphasize knowledge and practice as embedded in a broader system of resources that historically were, and currently continue to be, inequitably distributed. This point is critically important when considering research focused on primary teachers' knowledge and practices: that until access to high quality resources can be broadened, exhortations for high stakes teacher testing and evaluation are likely to be premature, unfair and doomed to failure (see Shalem & De Clercq in the present volume). Secondly, Adler (2000, p.207) notes that attention to how resources are taken up and used allows for a focus on resources as: 'an extension of the mathematics teacher in the teaching-learning process'. In this view, resources in the material and cultural senses can have impacts independent of the human resources of the teacher. More ideally of course, policy should work to cohere with, and capitalize upon material and cultural resource provision through human resources.

These categories are of particular interest in primary mathematics education where the ground differs from the secondary mathematics education context in focus in Adler's work. Drawing on existing evidence on primary mathematics education in relation to each of the three categories the chapter also notes where the research base points to gaps in one resource category having knock-on effects into others.

10.3   Resources and the Primary Mathematics Terrain

10.3.1   Evidence Relating to Material Resources

Inequitable provision of basic material resources continues to be a reality across the South African schooling system, situated within what an SAHRC and UNICEF (2014) report describes as a 'confluence of maladies': 'poorer health status, low and inferior educational attainment, social exclusion, and community environments that harm childhood development'(p.36).

In relation to mathematics, access and use of mathematical texts and textbooks have been noted as important contributors to providing access to mathematical learning. The key line of research relating to textbooks in South Africa has attended to issues of basic access to textbooks, with data drawn from comparative datasets like SACMEQ 2007. Indicators in this thread focus on aspects such as the number of textbooks available per 100 learners, with provision rising to two-thirds of learners having their own mathematics textbook in SACMEQ 2013. Inequitable provision of texts was highlighted in the 2011 School Monitoring Survey reporting that 28% of Quintile 1–3 Grade 6 learners were in classes where children could not show them a single mathematics textbook.

Internationally, where access to textbooks is more widespread, research has gone beyond basic attention on access to consider the selections of mathematical content, and coherence of sequencing of this content within particular textbooks (Schmidt and Prawat 2006). In South Africa, this strand was taken up in critiques of the orientations to mathematics in Curriculum 2005, in which integration of subject areas was promoted, with concerns voiced about the lack of mathematical coherence and progression within contextually-oriented curricular goals (Taylor 2000). These broader aspects of the mathematical content and sequencing in textbooks are returned to in the context of initiatives that have sought to improve provision of texts in South Africa.

Adler's consideration of material resources extends to the forms of mathematical objects presented in instruction. In South African research on primary mathematics teaching and learning, the use of concrete unit counting well beyond the number ranges in which this approach may be effective and efficient is a recurring leitmotif (Schollar 2008). Studies of Foundation Phase mathematics teaching suggest that these approaches used by learners reflect the strategies presented, sought or accepted by teachers, and again, well beyond the number ranges in which these strategies are appropriate (Ensor et al. 2009).

10.3.2   Evidence Relating to Cultural Resources

Language and time are the two key cultural resources referred to in Adler's descriptions. Both of these features have substantive salience in the South African research base relating to primary mathematics education. The principle of multilingualism was embraced at the policy level in South African education policy post-1994, but the sociopolitical press for access to English has been described as competing with, and sometimes dominating over, the need for epistemic access to mathematics (Setati 2008). This reality predictably led to some calls in the academy for a move away from the multilingual policy turn towards a focus on development of English language proficiency (Howie 2003). Smaller-scale South African evidence, aligned with the international literature base on multilingualism as a resource for teaching and learning, has pointed to more conceptual discourses featuring within home language segments of instruction in lessons than in English language segments (Setati 2005). However, larger-scale studies suggest more limited language-related effects on numeracy performance in comparison to school quality/home background effects at Grade 3 level (Spaull 2016). In this contestation, Hoadley (2012) has called for attention to language of instruction to be set within attention to the quality of instruction, rather than displacing the latter. The use of time in classrooms has been studied and raised as a concern extensively in South Africa. Echoing Jita's (1998) emphasis on subject-related commitment, some of these attendance or punctuality concerns are viewed at national policy level as underpinned by a lack of a more general commitment to teaching:

> Above all, it is the commitment of teachers that will ensure the success of the education system: to arrive at school on time, every school day; to be prepared for each day's lessons; and to be in their classes, teaching. If the system can ensure this, better basic education and effective expenditure will be within reach (National Treasury 2014, p. 49)

Similarly, the NEEDU (2013) Report's characterization of some of the poor uses of time among Foundation Phase teachers are related in some cases to a 'can't do' stance (underpinned by human and material resource constraints) but in some cases also to a 'won't do', reflecting a more emotional, and less researched, rejection of policy requirements for professional practice that can be linked to Adler's human resource category.

The slow pacing of content coverage has been noted in South Africa, with evidence from Foundation Phase (Ensor et al. 2009) and Intermediate Phase mathematics (Reeves and Muller 2005, p.126). In this latter study, the authors concluded by noting, in the context of the Revised National Curriculum Statement (the second wave of post-apartheid curricular reform in South Africa, in which a reversion to a separate subject and grade based specification of content was enacted) that:

> policy documents such as curriculum frameworks and guidelines in South Africa may need to provide schools and teachers with a concrete picture of the entire trajectory of each learning phase (across grade framing over pacing) and more in the way of guidance in relation to the pace they should maintain in order to cover the grade level expectations. Teachers appear to need greater signaling as to how much time learners should be given to work on topics or subtopic's.

Taken together, the evidence on cultural resources therefore pointed to the need for interventions to attend to quality of mathematics instruction across language contexts, and greater support for improving mathematical sequencing and pacing.

10.3.3   Evidence Relating to Human Resources

At the basic resources level, the 'generalist' view of mathematics teaching in the primary school means that much higher numbers of primary teachers are involved in mathematics teaching in primary schools than in secondary schools, although accurate data on the numbers of teachers in both phases is limited. At high school level, the 'specialized' nature of subject teaching results more often in only the teachers in mathematics departments being responsible for mathematics teaching. This feature has obvious consequences for the scale of initiatives focused on primary mathematics teacher development, and the likely costs and logistics involved in these enterprises – a point discussed later in the chapter.

In a mathematics-specific treatment of human resources, the notion of specialized knowledge relating to mathematics teaching forms a central element. In international research, Heather Hill and her colleagues have shown that this specialized knowledge base, based on ways of understanding mathematics that are particular to the work of teaching, is strongly correlated with learner performance in mathematics (Hill et al. 2005). In South Africa there are both concerns and contestations in relation to teachers' knowledge of mathematics and its teaching. On the concerns side, at Intermediate Phase, a number of national, regional and international studies have included a teacher testing component focused on mathematics. The Southern and East African Consortium for Monitoring Educational Quality (SACMEQ) 2007 analyses have pointed to substantial gaps relating to content at the level at which Grade 6 teachers are teaching and uneven distributions of knowledge resources across the school socio-economic status profile (Venkat and Spaull 2015):

> Teachers with relatively high levels of mathematical content knowledge are highly inequitably distributed and highly concentrated in the wealthiest 20% of schools (i.e. Quintile 5). (p.126)

In Taylor's (2011) National School Effectiveness Study (NSES), a test consisting of five Grade 6 level items was administered to their eight-province sample of Grade 4 and 5 teachers. Results showed that only 12% of this teacher sample was able to answer all five questions correctly, with the broader NSES analyses indicating a significant positive effect on mathematical performance for learners taught by the teachers getting all five items correct. Carnoy et al. (2012) echoed these findings, showing a relatively weak content and pedagogic content knowledge base (the mean percentage score attained on the test was 47%), with higher performance on routine procedural items, and lower performance on more non-routine and/or conceptual items, and pedagogic content knowledge items. They pointed further to curriculum coverage issues being underpinned by weak content knowledge – with teachers omitting content that they were unsure of, and avoiding higher-order thinking items.

In the Foundation Phase, the paucity of studies involving teachers' mathematical knowledge makes 'direct' claims on the nature of their mathematical knowledge impossible. Instead, what is available are a range of classroom based studies that have drawn inferences about teachers' mathematical knowledge and their orientations towards mathematics and its teaching. These studies of Foundation Phase mathematics teaching have added nuance to how mathematics is presented in teaching. Hoadley's (2007) study pointed to the phenomena of an absence of offering any evaluative criteria in Foundation Phase mathematics teaching – a situation in which learners were simply left unaware of whether their answers were correct or incorrect. A body of work has also drawn attention to problems with coherence and connection in the rationales and explanations presented in Foundation Phase mathematics teaching: not working from given information towards unknowns (Mathews 2014) which result in answers simply being 'presented' rather than derived, and allied disconnections in linking tasks with representations and explanations (Venkat and Adler 2012). There is also evidence of examples being worked with in highly disconnected ways, ways that have been described as 'ahistorical' in their disregard of previously established results (Venkat and Naidoo 2012), and producing the widely-reported reliance on lengthy and error-prone concrete counting strategies for solving number problems. At the heart of these findings, there is evidence of teacher explanations that make it difficult for learners to make sense of, replicate and adapt the problem-solving processes that are at the heart of more autonomous working with mathematics tasks.

Taken together, there is a strong case for attention within teacher education across pre- and in-service to primary teachers' mathematical knowledge, their mathematical working, and translating these understandings into coherent and connected classroom teaching. In earlier work (Venkat and Spaull 2015), we suggested that the evidence of gaps in primary teachers' mathematical content knowledge pointed to the need for primary mathematics teacher education to build what Liping Ma (1999) has called 'profound understanding of fundamental mathematics' – essentially a deep and coherent understanding of mathematics in the primary grades that incorporates a sense of the trajectory of topics over the span of primary school. We recommended that Intermediate Phase mathematical content should provide the initial base upon which this profound understanding could usefully be built. The evidence base also suggests that primary mathematics teacher education needs to emphasize ways of working with mathematics as making sense, and as 'reason-able', rather than as arbitrary and without basis.

But raising issues relating to teachers' mathematical knowledge and classroom mathematics teaching remains contentious, with disagreements on what counts as good teaching and critiques of 'deficit' discourses and their implications. The Initial Teacher Education Research Project that studied the nature of mathematics and language course content in five South African Intermediate Phase B.Ed programmes pointed to findings that reflected some of this contention: a variety of mathematical levels and orientations as well as a variety of time allocations to mathematics and mathematics teaching methodologies across the programmes in different institutions. In some courses, they noted that mathematical content from FET or even tertiary level mathematics was being covered with highly procedural orientations (Bowie and Reed 2016), in spite of the widespread evidence of weak foundational knowledge.

10.3.4 Concluding Comments on the Resource Terrain

Shalem and Hoadley (2009) describe the realities of work for 60–70% of South African teachers as mediated by conditions in which access to all of Adler's resource categories are compromised. In material resource terms, they note that mediation of the curriculum in ways that developmentally guide learning are often absent at the school level. More broadly, curriculum reform and textbooks have not been careful enough in their presentation and sequencing of mathematical content. In cultural resource terms, they note that dysfunctionality at school leadership levels results in poor management of teacher time dictated by more bureaucratic, rather than more instructional foci. At the human resource level, there is evidence of lower levels of teacher knowledge, all compounded by cognitive backlogs, limited home resources that can support learning, and poorer basic health. Shalem & Hoadley argue that in this cocktail of impeding resources, low morale and low job satisfaction are near-inevitable outcomes. This low morale, over time, thus becomes part of the human resource fabric that interventions have to contend with. This fabric, in turn, with 'maladies' relating to all the resource categories, was the ground that key policy interventions had to address. The extent of the reach of these interventions is in focus in the next section.

10.4 Large-Scale Interventions Seen Through the Lens of Resources

Key interventions emanating from the national policy terrain for primary mathematics in the last decade (2007–2017) with associated research writing, that are analysed through the lens of the resource categories described above are:

- The Foundations for Learning policy with its associated curriculum framework, with two central policy level documents (DoE 2008a,b), and the distribution of texts related to these documents.
- The introduction of the Curriculum and Assessment Policy Statements (CAPS) that constituted the third post-apartheid wave of curriculum reform.
- The rollout of national learner workbooks.

The central tenets of each of these interventions are overviewed, followed by an interpretation of these tenets in terms of the resource categories introduced above.

10.4.1 The Foundations for Learning Policy

Responding to the critiques about insufficient guidance for teachers on translating the curriculum specifications in the Revised National Curriculum Statement into well sequenced and paced teaching, the Foundations for Learning policy offered a package of materials intended to remedy this situation. Firstly, a repackaging of the curriculum into termly 'milestones' was offered, with the aim of assisting teachers to pace the content in line with curricular goals. Quarterly assessment rubrics, detailing the skills to be assessed were also included in the Assessment Framework document (DoE 2008a), with documentation supplied relating to the monitoring and recording of individual learner performance. The materials sent to schools included lesson plans associated with the milestones and assessments, and also included some sets of resources for supporting mathematics teaching and learning. The suggested 'recommended resources' included classroom apparatus such as number lines, 100 squares, and place value blocks. The Gazette document (DoE 2008b, p. 17) also detailed the minimum time per week to be dedicated to mathematics teaching across the primary grades, and outlined a lesson structure with activity types allocated for specified time segments across all lessons – among these whole class counting, oral mental mathematics and number sense problems, work with differentiated groups and individual working. A programme of meetings and workshops involving provincial and district personnel to support the translation of the documentary guidelines into classroom practice was also offered to schools (Meier 2011).

At the level of documentation, the policy texts provided a package with elements that worked across all of Adler's resource categories.

Primary in this package perhaps, was a desire to impact on teachers' existing cultural norms relating to time and pace of working, with improved teaching quality viewed as the outcome of this change:

> The teaching of Literacy and Numeracy (Languages and Mathematics) will be improved by ensuring that all teachers in Grades 1 - 3 actually teach reading and numeracy skills every day. We also expect that: [...] every teacher in the Foundation and Intermediate Phase will also teach Numeracy (Mathematics) for at least 1 hour every day. This will include 10 minutes of stimulating mental mathematics (arithmetic) exercises at the appropriate level in all grades. (DoE 2008b, p.6)

Changes in material resource provision were also seen in the distribution of apparatus sets to schools. These sets included a range of resources that can be seen as 'structured' in that they are inlaid with attention to mathematical relationships – for example, the base 10 relationship between tens and units that underlies the design of 100 squares and abaci. This provision allowed for the possibility of shifts in instruction away from the use of 'unstructured' concrete counting resources such as cubes or counters, towards resources that could be used to mediate moves towards more efficient calculating based on the use of the structure of number relationships. Some research suggested though that the provision of structured resources did not necessarily lead to instructional explanations that elaborated this structure –

Venkat and Askew's (2012) excerpts of teaching using abaci show unit counting approaches being presented with no reference to the base 10 structure inlaid into this manipulative. Here, human resources related to mathematical knowledge of mathematical progression disrupted the potential of improving material resources provision to support learning.

While workshops and meetings were offered as part of the FFL package of support, research findings suggested that the focus of these workshops was largely on compliance with the timelines of pacing and coverage in the frameworks, and use of the reporting formats for monitoring performance on assessments (Meier 2011).

The picture that emerges is one where the 'direct' measures offered in the policy attended to material and cultural resources as routes into changing the form of classroom practice. Teachers' understanding of mathematical ideas, and their awareness of ways of presenting, explaining, connecting and progressing these ideas were not the central focus of the raft of measures.

10.4.2 The Curriculum and Assessment Policy Statements (CAPS)

The implementation of CAPS in 2012 incorporated the FFL's increased specification of content sequencing and pacing into the curriculum across all grades, adding in detail on the suggested number of lessons to be allocated to topic areas within terms. It also combined curriculum, pedagogic advice, and assessment documents that had previously been presented separately into a single streamlined documentary form for each phase, following critique that the proliferation of documents was impractical for teachers (Umalusi 2014). Pedagogic advice on how to cover specified topics was also increased in CAPS with the offer of 'clarification notes' in the curriculum documents – for example, details on the kinds of tasks to be set, representations for use and learner approaches.

In the CAPS policy too then, a similar combination of resource categories to the FFL was attended to, with increased attention to human resources via additional details on the pedagogic content knowledge base related to topics in the curriculum documents. This specification of tasks, representations and common learner approaches suggests an attempt to address human resource gaps in relation to content/pedagogic content knowledge and classroom practices through the provision of material resources in the form of mathematical objects relevant to the teaching of the topic in focus. However, the research evidence suggests that the detail on teaching is haphazard in comparison to the literature base available. Roberts (2016, p.106), for example, drawing on the literature on additive relations situations, points to 'inconsistencies and errors' in the Foundation Phase CAPS document in the nature and range of examples presented and how they might be worked with. Similarly, the detailed considerations of connections and progression in the literature on whole number arithmetic, taking into account how tasks and representational sequences might need to be sequenced and orchestrated to support development (e.g. Van den Heuvel-Panhuizen 2008) is presented in piecemeal ways in CAPS: progressions and range in strategies are mentioned, as are a range of representations and tasks, but what constitutes a good remediation or extension task and representational context for a child presenting a particular strategy remains opaque. The teacher is expected to know this for herself.

Time as a cultural resource becomes more closely specified in terms of content coverage, sequencing and pacing. This standardization suggests a view that inequities in learning outcomes are underpinned by differences in content coverage – a position that has support in the evidence base outlined earlier. In specifying standardized timeframes for content coverage, there is also an 'over-ruling' of the teacher as the professional best placed to skillfully and responsively make decisions about content coverage, sequencing and pacing in ways that meet the learning needs of the children in their charge. While the evidence of gaps in teachers' content and pedagogic content knowledge suggests that this position is not without basis, the piecemeal detail on tasks, progressions and representations points instead to skillful teaching in sequencing of tasks and representations in classrooms. Thus, there are contradictory messages in the interplay between cultural and human resources.

The presentation of standardized time-frames also presents some tensions. Much of the evidence of inequitable learning outcomes in South Africa emphasizes a view of mathematics as vertically hierarchical in which learning at a particular level rests on a network of prerequisite understandings and competences. Following from this, learning mathematics is seen as cumulative, as emphasized in Spaull and Kotze's (2015) noting of accumulated learning deficits over time for children who start off behind in mathematics in the early grades. But this evidence of high differentials in learning suggests the need for responsively differentiated, rather than standardized, curricula. A child who cannot calculate 24×19 numbers because they have not yet mastered basic multiplication facts requires a different response to a child who is able to work this problem out mentally as 24×20, and then subtract 24. Responding constructively to both of these children requires a re-centering, rather than de-centering of skillful and responsive teaching, with attention to the underpinning human resources required for this. The lack of direct attention to human resources in the form of teachers' mathematical and pedagogical content knowledge bases thus represents a key absence in this regard.

10.4.3 Rollout of National Learner Workbooks

The rollout of national workbooks for Mathematics and Language across all primary grades began in 2011, as a key intervention aimed at addressing the widely-reported inequities in access to mathematical texts in South Africa. The mathematics workbooks were made available in all eleven official South African languages for Grades 1–3, and in English and Afrikaans for Grades 4–9. Hoadley & Galant reported in 2016 that workbooks by that point had been made available to 9 million learners in the country. The DBE's stated aim with workbook provision was to provide learners with resources that would allow them to: 'practise the language and numeracy skills they have been taught in class'. On the teaching side, the increased provision of material resources was stated as supporting the monitoring of learning, and the planning of teaching:

> They are also meant to help teachers track the progress of learners and provide extra support if needed. They are a simple way to structure learning activities for learners. (DBE 2017)

Hoadley and Galant's (2016) analysis of the Grade 3 Mathematics textbook indicated a high degree of alignment with the CAPS curriculum, with what they suggest as strong to moderate attention to progression across three of the broad topic areas. Given the evidence of problems with coherent and connected explanations in teacher talk that inhibits openings for learners to solve similar problems, Hoadley & Galant's attention to what they term 'conceptual signaling' within curriculum-related texts is of interest, as these offer the potential for the 'extension of the mathematics teacher' that Adler suggested as possible through resource provision. Hoadley and Galant's (2016, p.4) description of conceptual signalling is as follows:

> the extent to which a text makes the concepts being taught explicit, what is required of students, and what an appropriate production on the part of a learner might look like

While in their analysis of the workbooks, these authors suggest 'moderate' levels of conceptual signaling, they note that the explicitness of the content/concepts/skills/components being worked with often occurred at the level of headings, but that: 'instructions are not always clear and definitions and worked examples occur only occasionally' [p.9]. Hoadley & Galant's key finding is that the high degree of curriculum alignment suggests, as the aims associated with the workbooks suggest, a material resource that provides examples for practice. This practice though depends on instructional presentations that provide coherent explanations in the first instance for procedures that can then be practiced. Mathews et al.'s (2014) paper looking at empirical studies of teachers' use of workbooks, presents data pointing to limited responsive handling of incorrect learner offers, and sometimes in ways that sidelined the intended concept/skill. This suggests, once again, a missed opportunity to impact on the human resource teacher knowledge base relating to useful explanations and approaches to central ideas. Once again also though, the alignment with the timelines and sequencing and pacing of content in CAPS, points to efforts to provide material resources that were structured to support change in cultural norms relating to use of time, with the provision of home language texts also indicating intentions to promote and support the use of these languages as cultural resources for supporting epistemic access.

Of interest across this study of three recent national policy intervention strategies, is the common sidelining of direct attention to human resources relating to mathematical knowledge and mathematical teaching knowledge. Given the bulk of evidence suggesting these human resources as both critical to teaching, and as problematic on the ground, this sidelining is troubling. Essentially, the provision of material resources and cultural resources hit a low ceiling when teachers are unable to provide coherent and connected instructional expectations, or provide appropriately pitched responses to learner offers. And this issue is compounded by material resources that are less careful in their working with mathematical content than they could be. In the concluding section, a discussion of possible reasons for recent national policy interventions foregrounding material and cultural resources, and backgrounding human resources is offered.

10.5 Policy Sidelining Human Resources: A Discussion

The numbers of teachers involved in primary mathematics teaching is substantially larger than the numbers involved in secondary mathematics teaching. This immediately renders professional development initiatives focused on primary mathematics more expensive and more logistically difficult to rollout than secondary mathematics initiatives. However, earlier post-apartheid national policy initiatives had included the roll-out of university-based Advanced Certificate in Education (ACE) programmes, designed specifically to enhance in-service teachers' subject and/or phase specific knowledge and competence, so explaining the more recent sidelining of attention to human resources in terms of relatively higher costs was implausible. Looking at the reasons for the discontinuation of the ACE model provides more useful insights. The Council on Higher Education (2010) report noted significant variations between programmes, but expressed particular concern that the majority of programmes were failing on their central obligation:

> The absence of a sustained plan that addresses the continuum of learning that is required, and in particular that addresses poor subject specialisation knowledge, is perhaps the greatest weakness of the ACE programmes. (p.135)

When coupled with similar findings of substantial variations between programmes in the ITERP Study (Bowie and Reed 2016), the pointer here is to poor capacity issues for subject specialization within primary mathematics teacher education at the in-service and pre-service levels in universities. Such capacity issues in teacher education then feed into human resource capacity issues in teaching.

But this does not explain why supporting development of the primary mathematics teaching knowledge and practice base appears to be so difficult to achieve. To answer this question, international concerns with the content knowledge, pedagogical content knowledge and classroom practices of primary teachers of mathematics that have been raised in many countries are useful to look at, as these have also been linked back to concerns with initial teacher education. Tatto et al.'s (2012) findings from an international comparative study of primary and lower secondary mathematics initial teacher education across 17 countries provide some useful insights. Firstly, they found substantial differences between countries in location of initial primary teacher education, the orientations towards primary teachers as specialist or generalist subject teachers, the grade-span of preparation and the degree of specialization, and the nature and range of mathematical content dealt with in the programme. Policies for recruitment into initial teacher education and for subsequent employment also varied. Underneath this breadth, Tatto et al. (2012) note an underlying lack of consensus in the research base:

> Although experts may not be able to consensually define and measure all aspects of what it takes to teach well, all agree on the importance of subject-matter knowledge (Monk, 1994). But agreement ends there: marked differences exist among stakeholders on what knowledge is important for teachers to acquire, how teachers should acquire that knowledge, and how important that knowledge is to each teacher's success. (p.20)

It is this issue that perhaps constitutes the critical concern for capacity building in the teacher education sector. Where capacity is weak and needs to be built, a strong consensus around what is important mathematically, and how to develop teaching and learning for these foundations is important for policy-makers and practitioners. Such consensus is hard to come by in mathematics education, as the 'math wars' in the United States attest to. Teacher educators are therefore faced with an extensive, but frequently disparate and contested body of evidence, that they have to select from. Ideally, these selections would be made with strong rationales for choices made, and with awareness of the approaches that might be either backgrounded or rejected. These choices would be skillfully selected as mathematically and contextually appropriate. In this regard, the establishment of the recent Primary Teacher Education (PrimTEd) project by the DHET, aimed specifically at strengthening primary teacher education capacity for language and mathematics teaching through building collaboration between institutions represents a platform for building some national-level consensus on 'non-negotiables' in relation to fundamental mathematical content, pedagogic content and mathematical orientation selections in initial teacher education, as Taylor, in this volume, suggests. There is space here for institutions to collaborate to 'capture the middle ground for the majority' as Schoenfeld (2004, p.283) put it in the context of the math wars.

Contestation continues about whether raising concerns about teachers' mathematical knowledge and classroom practices is inherently 'deficit' in its orientation.The argument here is that insufficient attention to developing human resources represents a ceiling on the possibilities for impact of resources focused on the other resource categories. This limits the success of initiatives seeking to address inequality of access to quality primary mathematics education.

References

Adler, J. (2000). Conceptualising resources as a theme for teacher education. *Journal of Mathematics Teacher Education, 3*(3), 205–224.

Bowie, L., & Reed, Y. (2016). How much of what? An analysis of the espoused and enacted mathematics and english curricula for intermediate phase student teachers at five South African universities. *Perspectives in Education, 34*(1), 102–119.

Carnoy, M., Chisholm, L., & Chilisa, B. (2012). *The low achievement trap: Comparing schooling in Botswana and South Africa*. Pretoria: HSRC Press.

Council on Higher Education. (2010). Report on the national review of academic and professional programmes in education. he monitor no 11. Pretoria: CHE.

DBE. (2017). Workbooks home page. https://www.education.gov.za/Curriculum/LearningandTeachingSupportMaterials(LTSM)/Workbooks.aspx. Retrieved on 18th Jan 2017.

DoE. (2008a). *Foundations for learning: Assessment framework – foundation phase*. Pretoria: Department of Education.

DoE. (2008b). *Foundations for learning campaign. Government Gazette. Letter to foundation phase and intermediate phase teachers*. Pretoria: DoE.

Ensor, P., Hoadley, U., Jacklin, H., Kuhne, C., Schmitt, E., Lombard, A., & Van den Heuvel-Panhuizen, M. (2009). Specialising pedagogic text and time in foundation phase numeracy classrooms. *Journal of Education, 47*(2009), 5–30.

Hill, H. C., Rowan, B., & Ball, D. L. (2005). Effects of teachers' mathematical knowledge for teaching on student achievement. *American Educational Research Journal, 42*(2), 371–406.

Hoadley, U. (2007). The reproduction of social class inequalities through mathematics pedagogies in South African primary schools. *Journal of Curriculum Studies, 39*(6), 679–706.

Hoadley, U. (2012). What do we know about teaching and learning in South African primary schools? *Education as Change, 16*(2), 187–202.

Hoadley, U., & Galant, J. (2016). An analysis of the grade 3 department of basic education workbooks as curriculum tools. *South African Journal of Childhood Education, 6*(1), 1–12.

Howie, S. J. (2003). Language and other background factors affecting secondary pupils' performance in mathematics in South Africa. *African Journal of Research in Mathematics, Science and Technology Education, 7*(1), 1–20.

Jita, L. (1998). Resources for transforming science teaching in schools in Africa. In J. Hubert, A. Miller, & T. Moja (Eds.), *Education Africa forum* (2nd. ed., 5255). South Africa: Education Africa.

Ma, L. (1999). *Knowing and teaching elementary mathematics: Teacher's understanding of fundamental mathematics in China and the United States*. Mahwah: Lawrence Erlbaum Associates.

Mathews, C. (2014). Teaching division: The importance of coherence in what is made available to learn. In H. Venkat, M. Rollnick, J. Loughran, & M. Askew (Eds.), *Exploring mathematics and science teachers' knowledge: Windows into teacher thinking* (pp. 84–95). London: Routledge.

Mathews, C., Mdluli, M., & Ramsingh, V. (2014). The use of workbooks in South African grade 3 mathematics classrooms. *South African Journal of Childhood Education 4*(1), 80–94. Retrieved 18 Jan 2018, from http://www.scielo.org.za/scielo.php?script=sci_arttext&pid=S2223-76822014000100006&lng=en&tlng=en

Meier, C. (2011). The foundations for learning campaign: Helping hand or hurdle? *South African Journal of Education, 31*(4), 549–560.

Monk, D. H. (1994). Subject area preparation of secondary mathematics and science teachers and student achievement. *Economics of Education Review, 13*, 125–145.

National Treasury. (2014). Provisional budgets and expenditure review 2010/11-2016/17. Pretoria: National Treasury.

NEEDU. (2013). *National report 2012: The state of literacy teaching and learning in the foundation phase*. National Education Evaluation & Development Unit.

Reeves, C., & Muller, J. (2005). Picking up the pace: Variation in the structure and organization of learning school mathematics. *Journal of Education, 37*(1), 103–130.

Roberts, N. (2016). Additive relations word problems in the South African curriculum and assessment policy standard at foundation phase. *African Journal of Research in Mathematics, Science and Technology Education, 20*(2), 106–118.

SAHRC, UNICEF. (2014). *Poverty traps and social exclusion among children in South Africa 2014*. Pretoria: SAHRC & UNICEF.

Schmidt, W. H., & Prawat, R. S. (2006). Curriculum coherence and national control of education: Issue or non-issue? *Journal of Curriculum Studies, 38*(6), 641–658.

Schoenfeld, A. H. (2004). The math wars. *Educational Policy, 18*(1), 253–286.

Schollar, E. (2008). *Final report: The primary mathematics research project 2004–2007–towards evidence-based educational development in South Africa*. Johannesburg: Eric Schollar & Associates.

Setati, M. (2005). Teaching mathematics in a primary multilingual classroom. *Journal for Research in Mathematics Education, 36*, 447–466.

Setati, M. (2008). Access to mathematics versus access to the language of power: The struggle in multilingual mathematics classrooms. *South African Journal of Education, 28*(1), 103–116.

Shalem, Y., & Hoadley, U. (2009). The dual economy of schooling and teacher morale in South Africa. *International Studies in Sociology of Education, 19*(2), 119–134.

Spaull, N. (2016). Disentangling the language effect in South African schools: Measuring the impact of 'language of assessment' in grade 3 literacy and numeracy. *South African Journal of Childhood Education, 6*(1), 1–20. https://doi.org/10.4102/sajce.v6i1.475

Spaull, N., & Kotze, J. (2015). Starting behind and staying behind in South Africa: The case of insurmountable learning deficits in mathematics. *International Journal of Educational Development, 41*, 13–24.

Tatto, M. T., Peck, R., Schwille, J., Bankov, K., Senk, S. L., Rodriguez, M., Ingvarson, L., Reckase, M., & Rowley, G. (2012). *Policy, practice, and readiness to teach primary and secondary mathematics in 17 countries: Findings from the IEA teacher education and development study in mathematics (TEDS-M)*. Amsterdam: IEA.

Taylor, N. (2000). Mathematics in curriculum 2005: Submission to the ministerial review committee. *Pythagoras, 59*, 8–9.

Taylor, N. (2011). *The national school effectiveness study (NSES): Summary for the synthesis report*. Johannesburg: JET Education Services.

Umalusi. (2014). *What's in the CAPS package? A comparative study of the national curriculum statement (NCS) and the curriculum and assessment policy statement (CAPS) further education and training (FET) phase overview report*. Pretoria: Umalusi.

Van den Heuvel-Panhuizen, M. (2008). *Children learn mathematics: A learning-teaching trajectory with intermediate attainment targets for calculation with whole numbers in primary school*. Rotterdam: Sense Publishers.

Venkat, H., & Adler, J. (2012). Coherence and connections in teachers' mathematical discourses in instruction. *Pythagoras, 33*(3), 1–8.

Venkat, H., & Askew, M. (2012). Mediating early number learning: Specialising across teacher talk and tools. *Journal of Education, 56*, 67–90.

Venkat, H., & Naidoo, D. (2012). Analyzing coherence for conceptual learning in a grade 2 numeracy lesson. *Education as Change, 16*(1), 21–33.

Venkat, H., & Spaull, N. (2015). What do we know about primary teachers' mathematical content knowledge in South Africa? An analysis of SACMEQ 2007. *International Journal of Educational Development, 41*, 121–130.

Chapter 11
Learner's Written Work: An Overview of Quality, Quantity and Focus in South African Primary Schools

Paul Hobden and Sally Hobden

11.1 Introduction

Within the classroom learning environment, learners are provided with a number of different learning opportunities. These opportunities occur when they observe and listen to the teacher, when they read curriculum materials such as textbooks, when they interact with the teacher or peers through talk and discussion, or when they respond to a task set by the teacher, by writing their responses. Our focus in this chapter is on the opportunity to learn provided to learners through the various writing tasks assigned to them by the teacher. Situated between the teacher input and the many formal summative assessments on which progress is typically judged, individual written work provides important opportunities for constructing understanding, and for formative assessment and remediation. Given that the educational literature affirms the value of children's writing in the learning process (e.g. Dechaismartin 2013; Langer and Applebee 1987), we view evidence of appropriate written work as the primary visible indicator of curriculum engagement and opportunity to learn within the school learning environment.

Learner writing refers to the instances when learners are given a task which involves putting pen to paper, be it writing a paragraph, answering a comprehension, doing a worksheet of questions or multiple arithmetic exercises. The writing could be recorded in a workbook, notebook, or exercise book and makes learning visible. This writing provides evidence of learner involvement with the curriculum topics when they have tried to answer questions by engaging with their own ideas, expressing their thoughts, explaining and recording ideas. Further, Langer and Applebee (1987) contend that "written language not only makes ideas more

P. Hobden (✉) · S. Hobden
University of KwaZulu-Natal, Durban, South Africa
e-mail: hobden@ukzn.ac.za; hobdenpaul@gmail.com; hobdens@ukzn.ac.za

© Springer Nature Switzerland AG 2019
N. Spaull, J. D. Jansen (eds.), *South African Schooling: The Enigma of Inequality*, Policy Implications of Research in Education 10,
https://doi.org/10.1007/978-3-030-18811-5_11

widely and easily available, it changes the development and shape of the ideas themselves" (p. 3). Writing tasks would fall under the definition of a practice tool defined by Hoadley and Galant (2016) as a "text that provides opportunities for the rehearsal of concepts/concept/skills through tasks and activities. The practice tool may provide routine tasks, tasks that challenge and extend students or tasks that offer opportunities for remediation" (p. 3).

Tasks are central to students' learning, shaping not only their opportunity to learn but also their view of the subject matter. The cognitive demand of tasks can vary significantly. Not all types of writing task have the same value in learning. If the child is going to learn with understanding then the task must require the learner to make sense of the new material i.e. productive cognitive demand, as opposed to requiring minimal demands on their reasoning simply relying on memorisation to regurgitate information or following procedures to solve routine problem tasks without connecting them to the relevant concepts being learnt (Kilpatrick et al. 2001, p. 335) i.e. reproductive cognitive demand. Copying teacher summaries from the chalkboard is obviously different from a learner producing their own summary. In the same way, struggling over an unfamiliar word problem in science requires different cognitive processes to answering a number of routine problem tasks (Hobden 1998).

Several studies and reviews have been done on learner writing (especially workbooks). Some of the themes emanating from this literature indicate that; writing is an important component of the learning process; learners do less than the prescribed norm; learners do very few paragraphs or extended writing and; learners do very few tasks associated with higher cognitive demand. Most of the studies have limited their focus to mathematics and language and have been once off snapshot studies. In this chapter, we will extend this work based on the results of a number of evaluation studies we have carried out in primary township schools over the last ten years. In the most recent, we have analysed learner work in nine primary schools each year over a four year period providing interesting longitudinal data of changes within particular classes. Our analysis was based on all the writing of learners in workbooks, exercise books, notebooks and tests during a school year with a specific focus on the learning areas of Language, Mathematics, and Natural Science and Technology from Grades 1 to 7.

Our research question had as its focus the opportunities learners were given to actively learn through writing such as note taking and answering worksheet questions. In addition, we were trying to ascertain if these opportunities increased while the schools were involved in a whole school development project. Our analysis of individual learner written work indicates that providing these opportunities to learn through writing are a neglected area by teachers. It is our argument that this lack of meaningful learner engagement with the curriculum topics across the curriculum reduces learners' opportunities to learn resulting in unequal opportunities to learn. We will argue that many of the problems encountered with learner achievement can be traced to the primary years in which many foundational curriculum topics are disregarded, very little independent learner practice on tasks is done, constructive feedback from teachers is minimal, and monitoring of teachers by school management appears to be ineffective due to the lack of accountability. We will argue that the inequalities in opportunity are primarily a consequence of the didactical contracts constructed by all involved, rather than specific factors such as educational policies, curriculum demands, school resources, or teacher qualifications.

11.2 Interpretive Framework

Central to our understanding and analysis of learner writing are two main constructs, the didactical contract, and opportunity to learn, which taken together form the foundation of our interpretive framework.

11.2.1 Didactical Contract

In the school context, children learn how to respond in the learning environment based on many experiences with their teacher. Mutual expectations between the teacher and learner become established and enable the business of teaching and learning to proceed (Schubauer-Leoni and Grossen 1993). This is referred to as the didactical contract and accounts for and helps us understand the actions of the teacher and learners. A didactical contract is "an interpretation of the commitments, the expectations, the beliefs, the means, the results, and the penalties envisaged" by the participants within the learning environment (Brousseau et al. 2014, p. 1). The contract will for example, determine how many writing tasks are given to learners, how learners are expected to engage with the tasks, and what the teacher will do with the completed tasks once they have been attempted. It is related to the construct of 'instructional core' which is defined as the relationship between teacher, learner and content (City et al. 2009, p. 23). Doyle and Carter (1984) emphasize the instructional or academic task which lies at the centre of this instructional core. They describe it as the actual work students are asked to do in the process of instruction. It is our position that learner writing provides significant historical evidence of these academic tasks which lie at the centre of the instructional core.

11.2.2 Opportunity to Learn

Within the classroom, the teacher plans and organises a learning environment which, among other learning activities, will require learners to listen, observe, answer oral questions and to write answers to tasks. The situation that exists within the classroom (and to some extent outside the classroom) that allows learners to engage in learning tasks is labelled 'opportunity to learn' (OTL). Kilpatrick et al. (2001) states that learners OTL is widely considered the single most important predictor of

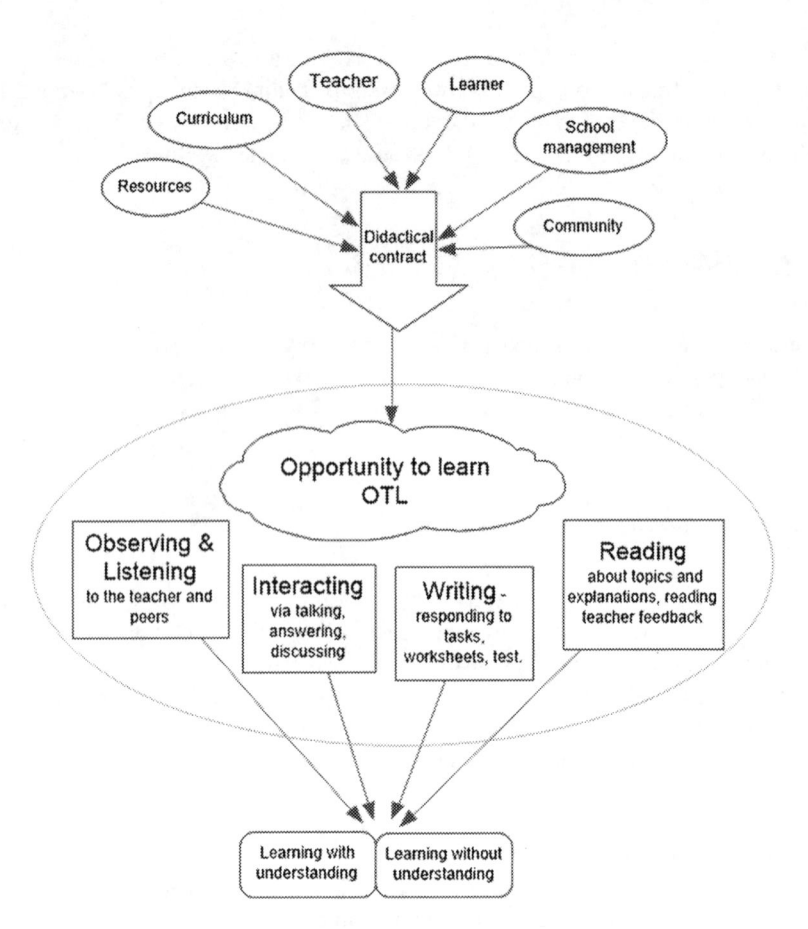

Fig. 11.1 Components of the teaching and learning environment

learner achievement (p. 343). The argument is given that in order for the learner to make meaning of new information and to develop proficiency in answering assessment questions they need to engage with the information in some way. What is known is that the teacher has control over curriculum and instructional decisions and thus plays a major role in shaping and creating these opportunities to learn (Stols 2013). In particular, and of relevance to this chapter, the teacher determines how much time and effort is allocated to learners writing tasks. However, this opportunity can be influenced by a number of factors, primarily the quality and effectiveness of the teacher (Gates 2010; Hanushek and Woessmann 2007) resulting in different school classrooms having very different opportunities to learn.

From the framework diagram in Fig. 11.1 it can be seen that the didactical contract is influenced by the interaction of a number of factors such as available resources and expectations of the community. This implicit unstated contract about expected behaviours of the participants leads to the teacher organising the learning environment to include a variety of learning activities and tasks. The selection of the classroom tasks and activities is influenced by the teacher's understanding of the didactical contract, the teacher's past experience and expertise with the curriculum topics. These planned tasks constitute the opportunity to learn which can lead to learners rejecting the opportunities or taking the opportunities resulting in learning with or without understanding depending on the nature of the task.

11.3   Measuring the Writing that was Done

The empirical data on which the views expressed in this chapter are based, have been derived from learner book analyses over the last ten years in functioning township primary schools involved in school improvement projects. Our basic assumption was that a key indicator of teacher effectiveness and learner progress was the quantity and quality of written work and teacher feedback evident in the learner books. This assumption is supported by researchers in the National School Effectiveness Study (NSES) study who contend that "an examination of children's writing at the end of a school year tells us a great deal about what has happened in the class over the year" (Taylor and Reddi 2012, p. 14). The NEEDU report Taylor (2014) and Hoadley and Galant (2016) both provide support for the contention that the *quantity* of work done (as counted in both workbooks and exercise books) is a measure of curriculum coverage but not necessarily of *quality* of work, opportunity to learn or of achieved learning. Nevertheless, they [the workbooks] "present a relatively simple and quick way to measure basic curriculum coverage at a very basic level" (Hoadley and Galant 2016, p. 11).

With this in mind, besides a focus on curriculum coverage and quantity of work done, data collection and analysis also focused on the level of work done, and on the teacher marking and feedback. When collecting the learner books from schools, in each case, the class teacher was asked to nominate the two 'best' learners in his/her class to provide workbooks, note books and exercise books for scrutiny – all of the books in which learners wrote in the key project subjects of English FAL and Mathematics, with Natural Science and Technology added in some projects. The schools from which learner books were obtained, were part of whole school development projects with a specific focus on mathematics, science and language. They were public government schools situated in townships or rural areas serving low socio-economic status communities. In all cases, the schools were selected because they were functioning schools with resources such as qualified teachers, the departmental workbooks and textbooks, and teaching and learning was taking place each day according to a timetable.

Different designs were followed in the learner book analysis. For example, in the one project the focus was on the last grade of each phase so only third and sixth grade books were collected for a period of three consecutive years (2009–2011) providing longitudinal data from successive cohorts with a focus on the grade teacher. More recently, we have analysed learner writing changes over a four year period (2013–2016) in nine primary schools who were also part of a school intervention project. The analysis was done in four consecutive years, each year selecting one Foundation Phase grade, one Intermediate Phase grade and Grade 7 from the Senior Phase. The analysis followed a cohort in successive grades through each of the Foundation and Intermediate phases, and then went back to the original grade in the fourth year. This design excludes year on year same grade comparisons but does allow for an initial project year and a final project year comparison and the total amount of writing done over a phase by a learner in the cohort being followed. We have also obtained other learner writing from two highly-resourced fee paying schools situated in high socioeconomic status communities, enabling us to do informal snapshot comparative case studies (Grades 1, 2, 3, and 6) by comparing the work done in the township schools with the work done in highly resourced multicultural schools.

11.4   What Analysis of Learner Writing Revealed

Several themes with implications for equality of opportunity to learn have emerged from this analysis of learners' written work. The sets of learner books were collected from the schools in late November after the examinations and returned once schools reopened in the following January giving the researchers ample time to do careful analysis of a complete year's work. The analysis was carried out by subject specialists (university teacher education lecturers) using the same data templates, and in most cases the same person in all four years. The instruments used for learner book analysis have been refined over time, and in accordance with changed curricula, and a need to obtain more nuanced data particularly regarding the quantity, curriculum coverage, and quality of teacher marking. The main unit of counting was an exercise. An exercise was considered a set of questions on the same topic normally completed during a lesson or for homework. For example, ten mathematics sums involving multiplication of two digit numbers, an English comprehension with a set of questions, and five questions naming the parts of a plant would all be considered as an "exercise". The data collected was somewhat different for each subject. In Mathematics the instruments called firstly for a count of individual sums done, and secondly for a count of exercises identified with each topic area. The English FAL instrument comprised a count of exercises under the headings of language structures and grammar, writing, comprehension, and other. The Natural Science and Technology (NS&Tech) instruments distinguish the types of writing done, for example counting pages of notes separately from practice exercises. Unfortunately, departmental sponsored workbooks were discontinued for NS&Tech in the last few years so analysis was restricted to writing found in learner notebooks, exercise books and test books.

11.4.1 *Quantity of Work*

The quantity of work done in the primary schools appears to be approaching the required norms particularly in subjects where departmental workbooks are provided.

In addition to the formal curriculum documents governing primary school work, the DBE has provided schools with an indication of the minimum quantity of work to be done in each grade and in each subject. So, for example, in Grade 3 learners are expected to complete five pieces of written Mathematics work in a week and in Grade 7 this increases to daily Mathematics exercises of at least five questions, and two Mathematics homework exercises per week. The project staff involved in the whole school development, encouraged the teachers to make good use of the workbooks and to comply with the minimum quantities of work expected.

The mandatory use of workbooks (Department of Basic Education 2014) added a clearly structured framework to the assessment of the quantity of work done, and of the coverage of curriculum topics. This is due to the close alignment of the workbooks to the CAPS curriculum, both in terms of content and the proportion devoted to each content area (Hoadley and Galant 2016). This level of prescription of the content and time allocation and curriculum aligned workbooks is a clear effort to achieve standardisation, and one might argue, equality in curriculum delivery and opportunity to learn across all South African schools. The evidence of increased quantity and coverage in recent years indicates that curriculum scripting through use of workbooks appears to encourage some levels of compliance.

The quantity of useful written work has in the past been inhibited by the time learners spent in copying down the questions prior to actually thinking about the answers. For example, the foundation phase mathematics curriculum calls for the learners to be able to draw the hands on a clock face to show a given time. This is a very short task if the clock face is provided but becomes a long task if the learner must firstly draw the clock face as shown in Fig. 11.2. Similarly, the short task of reading temperatures off a map becomes a long task when the map needs to be hand drawn first.

The provision of DBE sponsored Rainbow workbooks has likely facilitated the increase in quantity we have seen in written work as learners no longer had to copy out the questions before answering. This has reduced the inequality between schools as previously well-resourced schools often had access to copying facilities for worksheets removing the necessity of copying questions into exercise books.

Our analysis of learner books from 2009 to 2011 in schools involved in a nationwide whole school development project showed increasing evidence of written work. On average, the yearly number of written Mathematics exercises evident in the Grade 6 learner books increased from 44 to 138. While the 44 indicates only one exercise every few days, the average of 138 in 2011 is close to an exercise each day (the project researchers worked on there being approximately 160 working days in the school year). In a subsequent project in which Grade 6 learner writing was analysed in 2015, an evaluation of learner books in eight primary schools revealed an average of 170 exercises in Grade 6 Mathematics learner books.

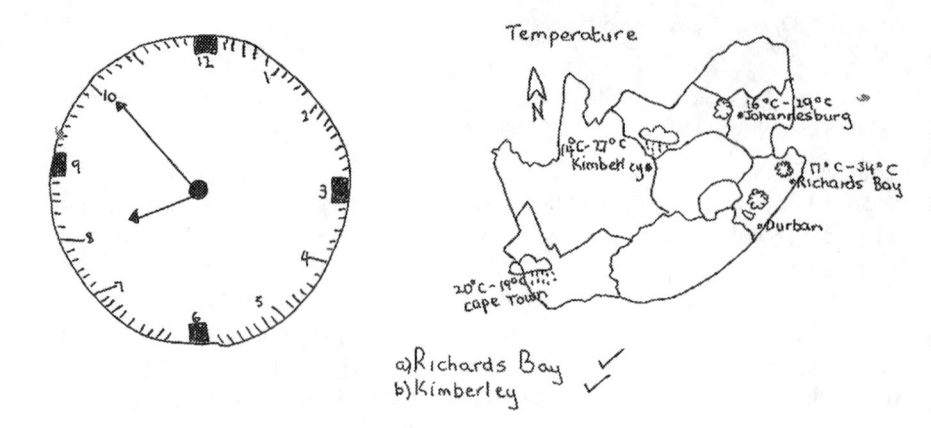

Fig. 11.2 Examples of time consuming learners work for little mathematical gain. (**a**) Hand drawn clock face in learner book. (**b**) Hand copied map used only to read temperatures at various towns

Table 11.1 Average quantity of work done in eight primary schools in Natural Science and Technology

	Number of exercises			
Subject and Phase	2014	2015	2016	DBE norm
Intermediate Phase NS &Tech	19	35	28	105 (3 per week)
Senior Phase Natural Science	18	33	37	105 (3 per week)
Senior Phase Technology	9	9	13	35 (1 per week)

This does indicate that the amount of work is continuing to increase across schools. However, this amount continues to be less than the expected departmental norm of five classwork and two homework exercises per week in grade 6 (if we consider 35 working weeks in a primary school year; $35 \times 7 = 245$ exercises per year).

A 2017 comparison of the number of exercises done in township project schools with the exercises done by learners from a well-resourced fee paying suburban school showed that the quantity of work in all Foundation Phase grades was very similar across schools, with for example, the better resourced school learner in fact having done fewer Grade 3 mathematics exercises than local township schools (164 as compared to an average of 196). Given the disparity in achievement between the schools, this points to the notion that the quantity of written mathematics exercises considered on their own may not be a source of inequality of opportunity to learn. Adding to this notion is the fact that most of the 2015 project schools involved in our analysis achieved the departmental minimum of five pieces of written work per week in Grade 2 and 3 Mathematics, (based on a school year with 35 working weeks requiring 175 exercises for the year), however the achievement of the learners was still very poor in basic numeracy.

A consistent finding over the years has been the paucity of written work, apart from transcribed notes, in Natural Science and Technology. Data from a recent intervention project is provided in Table 11.1. Despite some improvement in the project schools, the low quantity of exercises (about one a week versus department norm of three) is cause for concern since these represent missed chances for individual learners to engage with the content and to make sense of the ideas.

It should be taken into account that the *quantity* of written work in the learner books is only part of the evidence of opportunity to learn. Comparisons are relative indicators as they are not straightforward given, for example, that the time to complete individual exercises varies. In addition, when looking at opportunity to learn it must be taken into account that learners do engage in other meaningful activities such as group discussions that do not leave a writing record or extended project work which is not recorded in this analysis.

11.4.2   Curriculum Coverage and Quality of Work

Curriculum coverage is often uneven over the year and deviates from the CAPS curriculum time allocation to topic areas. The cognitive demand of the written work is low due to neglect of more demanding questions and topic areas in mathematics, and a lack of extended personal writing tasks in the languages.

The learner book analysis instruments were designed to allow researchers to obtain data to both quantify the work done and get an indication of the spread of the work across the curriculum topics. To do this the instruments were designed so that the exercises completed for each CAPS curriculum topic per term could be recorded. The English FAL instruments were slightly different as they were designed to capture a count of exercises under the headings of language structures and grammar, writing, comprehension, and other. Each of these was further divided into categories of half a page or less, and more than half a page of writing since extended writing is a key feature of the curriculum. Once the use of departmental workbooks was well established after 2012, the analysis instruments were modified to include a count of the worksheets completed, or partially completed in the workbooks. For example, in the case of mathematics, the worksheets were classified according to the content area covered for both exercise and workbooks. An extract of the Grade 6 instrument is shown below. The numbers refer to specific worksheets in the DBE Rainbow books (Table 11.2).

Table 11.2   Extract from Grade 6 instrument for workbook analysis

1. Number and Operations

Gr 6 CAPS 1.1 and 1.2 Counting with whole numbers *Count objects (to 100 and by grouping) Count forwards and backwards (multiples as well)*				Exercises in classwork books on this topic (*tally*)					
DBE Rainbow Workbook - Worksheet number	1	2	23	24	25a	25b	27	28	33
DBE Rainbow Workbook – Worksheet number	51	55	56	98	99	100	101	103	104
Total exercises on this topic in Rainbow workbooks and classwork books									

Using the total counts of exercises under each learning outcome, it is possible to calculate the relative proportion of time spent on each, and to compare that with the departmental guidelines. For example, in the Intermediate phase the suggested proportions for Mathematics are; Number and Operations 50%; Patterns, functions and algebra 10%; Shape and Space 15%; Measurement 15%; and Data Handing 10%. Most commonly, the simplest number work is over emphasized. For example, in Foundation Phase Mathematics there is a topic area related to representing and naming numbers. This is very basic knowledge supposedly established in Grade R. In the ex-Model C school in 2017 a Grade 1 learner did 18 exercises on this topic, whereas at the township schools an average of 45 exercises were done on this topic in Grade 1. While the isiZulu number names are long and arguably more difficult to learn, this over emphasis and repetition of low cognitive demand work at the expense of other work is still an area of inequality across schools.

Possibly linked to pressure to complete more written work, it has been noted by the researchers that the written work completed by learners, as evidenced in the analysis of the learner books, is often below the current grade level, or represents the most basic and cognitively undemanding level of the current grade work. The worksheets in the DBE Rainbow books are typically structured to show some progression with the final question being higher order and intended to engage the learner in some thinking. Such questions are very often not completed, seemingly not required by the teacher or ignored by the learner, and consequently a learning opportunity is missed. The lowest demand would be copying work from the chalkboard. From the evidence in the books, we suggest that this is often the case – most of the work in the learner books is marked correct showing no wrong paths in efforts to work problems out, and in instances it is clear that the correct answer could not have been obtained from the working shown in the learner book (perhaps incorrectly transcribed from the chalk board). See for example, Fig. 11.3 where the misalignment of the numerals, and absence of 'borrowing and carrying' annotation are clear indications that the learner did not independently work out the correct answer.

In Mathematics, Grade 7 is the start of the Senior Phase and the foundational work for algebra begins in this grade. The mathematics education researcher noted that teachers were leaving out topics that they are known to perceive as difficult despite having access to the workbooks, text books at the school, and online textbooks that they could use to learn the content that they might be unsure of. Topics hardly done or receiving minimal attention included algebraic equations,

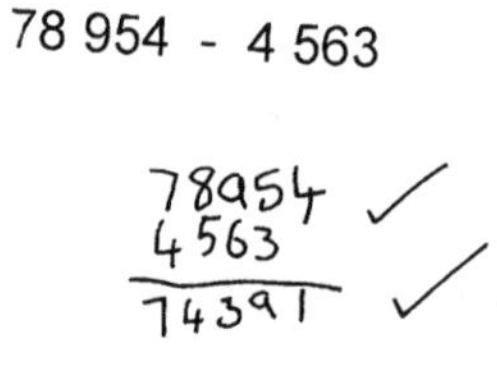

Fig. 11.3 Example of learner transcribed work, not individually worked out

78 954 - 4 563

$$
\begin{array}{r}
78954 \\
4563 \\
\hline
74391
\end{array}
$$

interpretation of global graphs and ratio, and rate and finances, all of which are foundational to further high school mathematics. This means that learners from these primary schools will enter high school unprepared for Grade 8 Mathematics and are likely to fall ever further behind. When the analysis of writing in English FAL is considered, we have noted a plethora of "fill in the gaps" exercises which require less effort and skill than writing an extended response to a question. Where the DBE Rainbow workbooks are fully utilized, leaners have the opportunity to do a variety of writing and comprehension tasks at the appropriate level. Anecdotally, teachers have commented that the work in these books is too demanding for their learners. Typically, we have found that more written work is done in the first part of the year, and it tails off towards the end of the year. This impacts on subjects like Natural Science where complete topic areas are dealt with sequentially. Teachers are in the habit of completing topics before starting the next even when well over the curriculum time allocation. This leads to uneven curriculum coverage with the early topics completed and later topics rushed or incomplete e.g. a biology section in the first term (Life and Living) getting more attention than the section of work designated for the fourth term (Planet Earth and Beyond).

11.4.3   Marking and Feedback to Learners

Marking of learners' work is typically perfunctory with little careful marking of individual items and minimal meaningful task related feedback given to learners.

Ing et al. (2015) showed that student participation is linked to achievement. Given large classes in the primary school, there is often little opportunity for learners to participate. This makes teacher personal task-based feedback to learners even more important in the learning process. The nature of the feedback the learners receive and accept is important. In the analysis of learner writing, we distinguish between a teacher checking that work has been attempted (often by large overall tick across the page), and careful item by item marking intended to notice errors and misconceptions. The latter is typically accompanied by personalized written teacher feedback directly related to the task. Another form of feedback evident in books is the placing of stars and stickers for good work which may have a motivational purpose, but they give little task information except confirmation of correctness. The value of personalised written feedback has been highlighted by Hattie (2008) who regards it as a very effective intervention. Hattie argues that disconfirmation can lead to greater change. This assumes that there are errors or gaps in the work, or possibilities that have been overlooked which in turn implies that the tasks are set at an "appropriate, challenging level of difficulty, and enable successive refinement by allowing for repetition, given room to make and correct errors, and providing informative feedback to the learning" (Van Gog et al. 2005, p. 75). The previously mentioned findings of the low cognitive demand of tasks and more transcribed work

Table 11.3 Extract from instruments for workbook analysis

Marking

Tick appropriate block (according to your considered opinion after going through the books)

	10	8	6	4	0
1. Quantity	**All** work marked	**Most** work marked	About half the work marked	**Very little** work marked	**No** work marked
2. Quality	All individual items carefully and correctly marked.	Most individual items marked.	Some individual items marked and some overall ticks.	Overall ticks used as check that work was done.	Extremely careless and glaring marking errors
3. Written feedback	Errors indicated to learners, with helpful comments	Regular thoughtful comments on aspects of work	Appropriate general comments of "Good" or "Try harder type	Occasional general comments	No written feedback at all

from the chalk board than individual work, suggest that the space for this meaningful learning feedback is minimal.

The analysis instruments for mathematics and languages allowed for the extent of marking of each worksheet in the workbook to be assessed as not marked, marked, or marked with feedback provided to the learners (see Table 11.3). For all subjects, the researchers were asked to use their professional judgement to score the marking and feedback given by a teacher. In this way, considerable differences both between and within schools was noted. Typically, most of the work has been marked but usually just overall ticks and little or no personalized written feedback. Perfunctory and careless marking as evidenced in Fig. 11.4 must leave the learners very bewildered and demotivated. Opportunities to learn have been missed.

Over the many years of learner book analysis in a variety of interventions, we have seen little improvement in the quality of marking beyond minimum compliance with school norms. In fact, we have observed teachers frantically marking and signing learner books as we arrive for collection after learners have departed at year end. An evaluation researcher, a senior academic who has analysed the Grade 7 mathematics books for five consecutive years noted "I am very concerned at a lack of constructive feedback given to learners which I must confess is virtually non-existent and evidently misunderstood by teachers in all the schools in the project".

11.4.4   Teacher Effects and HOD Monitoring

The teacher in the classroom and the HOD responsible for curriculum management can have a profound effect on the quantity and quality of learners' written work, and hence their opportunity to learn.

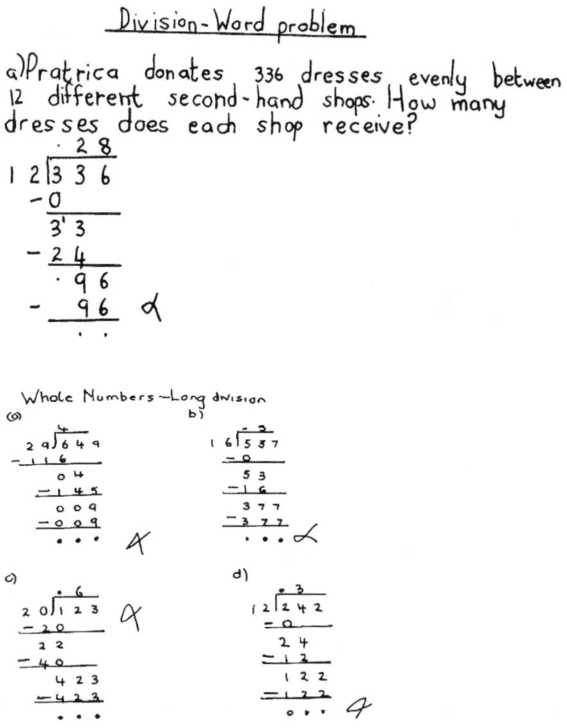

Fig. 11.4 Incorrect and
unhelpful marking. (**a**)
Correct work marked wrong.
(**b**) Succession of incorrect
attempts with no teacher
formative feedback

Division-Word problem

a) Pratrica donates 336 dresses evenly between 12 different second-hand shops. How many dresses does each shop receive?

$$
\begin{array}{r}
.28 \\
12\overline{\smash{)}336} \\
-0 \\
\hline
33 \\
-24 \\
\hline
.96 \\
-96 \quad \alpha \\
\hline
..
\end{array}
$$

Whole Numbers — Long division

a)
$$
\begin{array}{r}
24\overline{\smash{)}649} \\
-116 \\
\hline
04 \\
-145 \\
\hline
009 \\
-009 \\
\hline
... \quad \alpha
\end{array}
$$

b)
$$
\begin{array}{r}
2 \\
16\overline{\smash{)}587} \\
-0 \\
\hline
53 \\
-16 \\
\hline
377 \\
-377 \\
\hline
... \quad \alpha
\end{array}
$$

c)
$$
\begin{array}{r}
.6 \\
20\overline{\smash{)}123} \\
-20 \\
\hline
22 \\
-40 \\
\hline
423 \\
-423 \\
\hline
...
\end{array} \quad \alpha
$$

d)
$$
\begin{array}{r}
.3 \\
12\overline{\smash{)}242} \\
-0 \\
\hline
24 \\
-12 \\
\hline
122 \\
-122 \\
\hline
0.. \quad \alpha
\end{array}
$$

The teacher effect is most pronounced in the Foundation phase where learners have the same teacher for all their subjects. This is a source of inequality within a school. For example, at one township school with three Grade 1 classes, the composite scores for Mathematics, isiZulu HL and English FAL learner books, differed widely with the weakest teacher scoring just 62% of the score of the best teacher on the measure of learner books. The situation where it is simply bad luck to get a weak teacher who provides few opportunities to learn is untenable. This represents a failure of the HOD to monitor the teachers' work, or more likely a failure to assert authority and call the teacher to task. The effect of an efficient HOD is very clearly seen in Fig. 11.5. This graphic was designed to see changes in the relative ranking of eight primary schools in their foundation phase learner writing scores over the four-year duration of a project. School A had been performing very poorly over all grades for three years. In 2016 a new HOD was appointed for the Foundation Phase and she set about getting her phase in order with subsequent remarkable improvement in the learner book scores. In the other two phases, the dismal relative performance of this school in learner book scores continued.

Learners can be badly let down by extended absences of teachers. In one case, we were told without any apparent concern, that no learner books were available for one of the Grade 1 classes since their teacher had been on extended sick leave. This situation is unlikely to occur in schools where the implicit didactical contract

2013	2014	2015	2016
School C	School H	School F	School D
School D	School G	School C	School A
School E	School D	School H	School F
School F	School E	School G	School G
School G	School F	School D	School H
School H	School C	School E	School C
School A	School A	School B	School B
School B	School B	School A	School E

Fig. 11.5 Relative ranking of schools by composite Foundation Phase Learner Book scores 2013–2016

would cause parents to be expectant of more from the school. It is also noticeable that some of the HODs are relatively young teachers whose promotion appointments seem unjustified as they have little or no experience in the subject or phase they are appointed to oversee. These HODs lack the confidence or authority of competence and seem unwilling or unable to take teachers to task for poor curriculum coverage or monitoring of learners progress.

11.5 Why Does This Situation Exist?

It is very difficult to try and describe a normal primary school classroom given the diversity of school contexts in South Africa. However, if it is accepted that we have seen some deviations from the norm, it is useful for our discussion to describe what a typical township primary learner would experience as far as writing is concerned. The focus is on writing because learner writing is our only visible indicator and permanent record (Taylor 2014) of the individual learner's opportunities to learn other than year long classroom observation.

Current analysis indicates that over a full year, the total amount of work set by the teacher requiring an individual written response is close to the quantity norms set by the department. While this appears a positive improvement over previous studies, it must be seen in the light of a deeper analysis. Firstly, there is an imbalance with the learner spending more time with some topics than others. This is especially noticed in the difference between topics in first term and the fourth term. For example, a lot of notes and exercises would be done on Life and Living topics in Natural Science but very little done on Earth and Beyond topics in the fourth term. Secondly, the writing tasks are characterized by being low level with most being copying of notes and responding to questions with lower order cognitive demand e.g. one word answers. For example, the more demanding problems and topic areas in mathematics are neglected and replaced by many repetitions of simple exercises, and there is a lack of extended personal writing tasks in the languages. Thirdly, feedback to help with learning is minimal. Where exercises are done, they are mostly marked correct either by the learner or by the teacher. That the majority are correct creates a suspicion that correct teacher answers have been copied off the chalk board or are the result of being worked in a group. There is very little task specific feedback by the teacher other than ticks and crosses with a minimum of comments similar to 'well done' appearing. Fourthly, although there is evidence that the exercise books have been seen by the HOD (evidenced by a school stamp and signature) there does not appear to be any monitoring other than superficial compliance with covering curriculum topics and certainly no accountability or consequences of any form as confirmed through interviews. The overall picture described is very similar to that obtained by Hoadley (2012) and the NSES data, showing very little progress toward effective teaching and learning over the last seven years.

11.5.1 Ineffective Opportunities to Learn

From the perspective of 'opportunities to learn' a number of issues arise. When the learners in the primary schools we have worked in are given diagnostic tests which focus on foundational knowledge, we find that learners by Grade 3 are already missing many key aspects of foundational knowledge required to succeed in Grade 4. The same can be said throughout the primary grades except it gets worse as we analyse results in the higher grades. The deficit appears to be additive. This leads to the conclusion that the opportunities to learn as evidenced in the learners' writing and provided by these primary teachers are simply not effective. We suggest three reasons for this. Firstly, learners in the different grades have deficits in their foundational knowledge required to learn within their current grade, yet there is no evidence within learner writing of teachers providing differentiated learning opportunities or effective remedial writing tasks. Teachers continue to maintain the imbalance of excessive teacher talk vs learners actively making sense through personal writing tasks. Secondly, the focus appears to be on practice with multiple simple or easy tasks with little opportunity to move to tasks requiring some higher order thinking. The expectations appear low, perhaps because teachers are aiming the opportunities to learn at the average learner. This issue has been well documented in the NSES study (Taylor 2011). Thirdly, for learning with understanding to occur there needs to be some form of feedback and metacognitive reflection on the tasks. Given that examination of exercise books shows nearly everything marked correct, what feedback is required? It would appear that there is a classroom culture of prioritizing the transcribing of correct answers over learners trying to do it themselves. Where learners make errors which are highlighted by the teacher, particularly in the marked tests and examinations, personalised feedback is missing and so the learning process is incomplete.

11.5.2 The Teacher Effect

The question arises as to why this situation prevails despite very similar negative descriptions emanating from the educational research literature over the last ten years e.g. NSES report (Taylor 2011), and the many attempts by projects and the department, through in-service workshops, to focus on curriculum coverage and management. In trying to understand what is going on we use the idea of the didactical contract. What we consider to be the prevailing didactical contract in the majority of these township school classrooms can be used to explain much of what we have found in learners writing. At present learners are accepting of their passive roles within the teaching and learning environment. They accept the teacher spending the majority of the class time talking to them, they accept that their work will not have teacher personalized feedback, they accept teacher absences from class, etc. Neither they or their parents seem to have the agency to demand more of the teachers.

However, learners are also complicit in that they accept and encourage the very slow pace of instruction by doing minimal homework, and their reluctance to take on the challenge of work that exceeds the low cognitive demands of the work they are used to. Teachers know that there will be virtually no consequences to learners failing or missing sections of work or not providing feedback. In turn some of the teachers become passive and accept very poor working conditions for themselves and their learners. For example, recently during observation of a Grade R class, evaluation researchers observed up to ten children placed at a small table surrounded by six chairs in order to practice their writing. This meant that some children were kneeling on the floor and jostling to find room on the table to place their paper. The teachers involved seemed to be unfazed by this and apparently had no plans to arrange teaching time and space differently. Most significantly, this teaching and learning culture negotiated by the participants appears to be accepted by the management of the school. Superficial compliance is monitored but there are no mechanisms of accountability, something we have confirmed in numerous interviews. It appears that the position of HOD is taken more as a personal promotion with little effort being made to monitor and call colleagues to account. This results in much "paper compliance" but little accountability on the part of teachers.

11.5.3 Teacher Role Models and Experiences

It is in our view mistaken to claim that the task of good teaching in the township primary schools is simply beyond the ability of the current teaching cohort. The teachers have all succeeded at school and the majority at their tertiary studies, many of them at post graduate level. They have shown that they are themselves good learners. In addition, most have extensive experience of working in difficult conditions with large diverse classes. The vast majority of teachers are thus likely to be capable of sound effective teaching but it is not certain that all are motivated to make the extra effort to utilize all their knowledge and experience or that they have a vision of what could be more effective. The majority of the teachers have been immersed in the same type of teaching and learning environment, having attended township schools. The majority continue to teach in the same way they were taught and conform to the prevailing teaching and learning environment of the majority of their colleagues in these township schools. Unfortunately, the evidence from numerous local and international tests over the recent past shows that this environment does not provide learners with sufficient opportunities to learn resulting in very poor achievement. We suggest the problem is not with the quality of teachers but with their motivation to change and their lack of models of a different environment.

11.6 How Can Change Be Initiated?

We know that if the current situation prevails in township primary schools learners will continue to show low achievement. This will result in further poor achievement in secondary school or at worse complete alienation toward learning and schooling. Poor results will prevent access to further education and job opportunities which provide a path out of poverty. Given the need of the South African economy for educated people we cannot afford this scenario indefinitely. So where to start? It is our contention that changing this inequality of learning opportunity is largely vested in the teacher. This is supported by research findings such as Hanushek and Woessmann (2007) who looked at a number of studies and found that the single most important factor that influences the quality of teaching and learning is the teacher. In particular, there is research that shows minority and poor students are shortchanged when it comes to access to high quality teaching (Peske and Haycock 2006). Adding evidence to the effects of teacher quality, Goldhaber and Anthony (2007) found that teacher quality had the strongest effects on learners from lower socioeconomic statuses. It is not unreasonable to infer that we are finding inequality in opportunity to learn because the quality of teaching is unequal.

While other factors play a role in determining the didactical contract, we assert that the teacher is central. The published curriculum is the same for all learners while the experienced curriculum is not. Recognising this, the department of education has provided workbooks in the foundation and intermediate phases which appear to have helped in minimising the gap by spelling out exactly what policy envisages. At the level of the foundation phase resources are also not necessarily a major factor in constraining the contract. Taylor (2011) found weak evidence that school resources such as pupil-teacher ratios and school facilities are associated with student achievement. (However, we have seen that overcrowding prevents normal teaching and learning from taking place.) While reducing teacher learner ratios, often brought up as a constraining factor by teachers, might be desired, this does not impact significantly on learner achievement (Taylor 2011). However, our interviews and surveys of teachers in the process of evaluating primary school intervention projects has revealed that many teachers ascribe poor learner achievement to disinterested or absent parents. The most frequent factor impeding learner achievement was given as the lack of family support which manifests in poor learner motivation, failure to complete homework tasks, unwarranted missing of school including the sanctioning of non-attendance at school after exams. It seems that teachers do not regard parents as holding up their end of the didactical contract. Despite all these contributing factors, research points to the quality of the teaching as the main factor associated with learner achievement.

As a first step in bringing about change, teachers need more models of how things could be, and what excellence looks like. This is difficult in circumstances where their own schooling was impoverished, their current teaching conditions are difficult, and they are surrounded by colleagues who teach in very similar ways. Nevertheless, we would argue that expectations could be raised and alternative didactical contracts be envisaged if teachers had opportunities to spend time with colleagues identified as exemplary teachers who could function as role models or mentors. There is evidence that aspirations to higher standards of work can be fostered by interactions with teachers (teachers observing teachers) in different environments using professional development strategies such as *learning studies* resulting in cross pollination of teaching models (Israel 2018). In addition, participation in teacher clusters and learning communities (Jita and Mokhele 2014) that include teachers from diverse environments would also provide teachers with a wider vision of possibilities for change.

However, it is our view that the primary focus of change should be on making the didactical contract explicit to all participants with the teacher taking centre stage. Currently the didactical contract negotiated by participants is implicit and varies from classroom to classroom. It is our firm belief that this contract needs to be explicit and perhaps reduced to a physical contract so all participants can take responsibility and accountability for their role in the teaching and learning. We consider accountability as the single most important component of the revised contracts. For example, teachers must be expected to provide opportunities to learn that involve personal practice on higher cognitive demand tasks with feedback. Learners must expect to be given more difficult tasks and required to write longer paragraphs etc. The learner written products arising from these tasks, lying at the centre of the instructional core, must be open to examination by all such that parents, guardians and management can hold teachers and learners accountable. Expectations of effective teaching and learning have to be raised and the current complacency replaced by active accountable participation.

References

Brousseau, G., Sarrazy, B., & Novotná, J. (2014). Didactic contract in mathematics education. In S. Lerman (Ed.), *Encyclopedia of mathematics education* (pp. 153–159). Dordrecht: Springer Netherlands.

City, E. A., Elmore, R. F., Fiarman, S. E., & Teitel, L. (2009). *Instructional rounds in education: A network approach to improving teaching and learning*. Cambridge, MA: Harvard Educational Press.

Dechaismartin, T. (2013). Writing matters: The neglect of writing in South African schools. In N. Taylor, S. Van der Berg, & T. Mabogoane (Eds.), *Creating effective schools: Report of South African's National Effectiveness Study*. Cape Town: Pearson.

Department of Basic Education. (2014). Circular S5 of 2014. Utilisation of Grade R- 9 workbooks for the academic year 2014. Pretoria.

Doyle, W., & Carter, K. (1984). Academic tasks in classrooms. *Curriculum Inquiry, 14*(2), 129–49.

Gates, M. F. (2010). *Education reform, one classroom at a time*. The Washington Post, Friday, Feb 19. Available at http://www.washingtonpost.com/wp-dyn/content/article/2010/02/18/AR2010021802919.html. Accessed 20 Oct 2017.

Goldhaber, D., & Anthony, E. (2007). Can teacher quality be effectively assessed? National Board Certification as a signal of effective teaching. *The Review of Economics and Statistics, 89*(1), 134–150. https://doi.org/10.1162/rest.89.1.134

Hanushek, E. A., & Woessmann, L. (2007). *The role of education quality for economic growth*. SSRN Scholarly Paper ID 960379. Rochester: Social Science Research Network.

Hattie, J. (2008). *Visible learning: A synthesis of over 800 meta-analyses relating to achievement* (1st ed.). London: Routledge.

Hoadley, U. (2012). What do we know about teaching and learning in South African primary schools? *Education as Change, 16*(2), 187–202. https://doi.org/10.1080/16823206.2012.745725

Hoadley, U., & Galant, J. (2016). An analysis of the grade 3 department of Basic Education workbooks as curriculum tools. *South African Journal of Childhood Education, 6*(1), 1–12. https://doi.org/10.4102/sajce.v6i1.400

Hobden, P. (1998). The role of routine problem tasks in science teaching. *International Handbook of Science Education, 1*, 219–231.

Ing, M., Webb, N. M., Franke, M. L., Turrou, A. C., Wong, J., Shin, N., & Fernandez, C. H. (2015). Student participation in elementary mathematics classrooms: The missing link between teacher practices and student achievement? *Educational Studies in Mathematics, 90*(3), 341–356. https://doi.org/10.1007/s10649-015-9625-z

Israel, M. (2018). Teachers observing teachers: A professional development tool for every school. http://www.educationworld.com/a_admin/admin/admin297.shtml

Jita, L. C., & Mokhele, M. L. (2014). When teacher clusters work: Selected experiences of South African teachers with the cluster approach to professional development. *South African Journal of Education, 34*(2), 01–15.

Kilpatrick, J., Swafford, J., & Findell, B. (2001). *Adding it up: Helping children learn mathematics*. Washington, DC: National Academies Press.

Langer, J. A., & Applebee, A. N. (1987). *How writing shapes thinking: A study of teaching and learning*. NCTE Research Report No. 22. National Council of Teachers of English, Urbana.

Peske, H. G., & Haycock, K. (2006). *Teaching inequality: How poor and minority students are shortchanged on teacher quality: A report and recommendations by the Education Trust*. Washington, DC: Education Trust.

Schubauer-Leoni, M. L., & Grossen, M. (1993). Negotiating the meaning of questions in didactic and experimental contracts. *European Journal of Psychology of Education, 8*(4), 451–471. https://doi.org/10.1007/BF03172700

Stols, G. (2013). An investigation into the opportunity to learn that is available to Grade 12 mathematics learners. *South African Journal of Education, 33*(1), 1–18.

Taylor, N. (2011). *The National School Effectiveness Study (NSES): Summary for the synthesis report*. Johannesburg: JET Education Services.

Taylor, N. (2014). *NEEDU National Report 2013: Teaching and learning in rural primary schools*. Pretoria: Government Printer.

Taylor, N., & Reddi, B. (2012). Writing and learning mathematics. In N. Taylor, S. Van der Berg, & T. Mabogoane (Eds.), *Creating effective schools: Report of South African's National Effectiveness Study*. Cape Town: Pearson.

Van Gog, T., Ericsson, K. A., Rikers, R. M. J. P., & Paas, F. (2005). Instructional design for advanced learners: Establishing connections between the theoretical frameworks of cognitive load and deliberate practice. *Educational Technology Research and Development, 53*(3), 73–81. https://doi.org/10.1007/BF02504799

Chapter 12
Gender Inequalities in South African Schools: New Complexities

Tia Linda Zuze and Unathi Beku

12.1 Introduction

Gender issues in education usually refer to tracking the equality of girls' education as compared to boys. There are many valid reasons for this gender perspective. More than half of children who are not in school around the world are girls (Aikman and Unterhalter 2007; UNESCO 2015). Therefore, global reform efforts have rightly focused on how to increase and equalise the participation of girls so that they get their fair share of the education pie (Aikman and Unterhalter 2006). Without exception, international development goals aimed at eradicating poverty make specific mention of improving the quality of girls' education (United Nations 2015). This is not only because the educational pursuits of girls are marginalised in many societies but also because investing in educating women benefits economic development, health and the general welfare of children in a country (Hanushek 2008; Patrinos 2008).

The terminology that is used to discuss education and gender is important and it is useful to clarify some of the language at the beginning of this chapter. How these terms are understood will influence our discussion and what conclusions we draw. Gender equality means equal rights, responsibilities, power and treatment of boys and girls in education. What distinguishes the term gender equality from other definitions is that gender equality includes the crucial dimension of human rights

T. L. Zuze (✉)
Research on Socioeconomic Policy, Department of Economics, University of Stellenbosch, Matieland, South Africa
e-mail: tlzuze@gmail.com

U. Beku
School of Built Environment and Development Studies, University of KwaZulu Natal, Durban, South Africa
e-mail: unathi.beku@gmail.com

© Springer Nature Switzerland AG 2019
N. Spaull, J. D. Jansen (eds.), *South African Schooling: The Enigma of Inequality*, Policy Implications of Research in Education 10,
https://doi.org/10.1007/978-3-030-18811-5_12

(UNESCO 2016). It is also the term that is most preferred when gender is mentioned in international agreements. Gender equity refers to practices that promote the fair treatment of boys and girls in their education and gender parity implies that there are an equal number of girls and boys in schools. Gender equality can be viewed as the ultimate goal while gender parity and equity are practised in order to achieve the desired goal of equality.

South African educational policies address gender in different ways. In 1996, a Gender Equity Task Team was established in the national Department of Education. Its role was to provide guidance on setting up a permanent Gender Equity Unit at the department (Wolpe 2005). In addition, a National Gender Co-ordinating Committee was created to monitor gender mainstreaming at the provincial level (Pandor 2005). The South African Commission for Gender Equality views gender equality as activities that promote fair treatment for both men and women in different spheres of life. Emphasis, however, is placed on compensating women for the historical disadvantages that they have faced (Commission for Gender Equality 2007).

12.2 A New Perspective on Gender and South African Education

The historical record about gender and racial discrimination is clear. And yet what is also apparent from emerging research is that gender differences in education are far more complex and nuanced than in the past. Future gender education dialogues need to create space for these changes. These shifts raise the important question of how gender and education should be framed based on evidence from recent studies. In this chapter, we take the view that a relevant discussion about gender and education in South Africa should firstly, work on the assumption that girls and boys may have different educational needs that should be addressed, secondly that an equitable education system for girls and boys is both possible and desirable and thirdly, the focus should rest on what boys and girls need to complete a good quality of education (Unterhalter 2006).

Some progress has been made in achieving access to education for girls and boys, particularly in the early grades. In the 2015 school year, 49% of learners enrolled in primary school were female (UNESCO 2017). Addressing gender equality in educational outcomes is far less straightforward than dealing with access issues. It involves looking at the academic performance of girls and boys. It also requires considering teacher-pupil relations, the content of learning materials, the scope of the curriculum, the availability of gender-sensitive resources and the way boys and girls relate to each other at school. Gender inequality in education reflects gender inequality in society. As such, schools, teaching, curriculum, classroom interaction and support systems outside of school can favour one group over the other. A good example is the gender composition of the school workforce. While women are well represented among teachers, most school principals are men (Wills 2015).

While it is certainly worthwhile discussing the many valuable qualitative contributions to gender research in South African education,[1] the chapter relies on quantitative data drawn from nationally representative studies. In addition, given the overall theme of this book, the data are drawn from studies that focus on basic education.[2] There are important interrelationships between gender, race, poverty and location that we reference in our discussion of South African education. We pay particular attention to how gender differences in high-poverty schools compare to the scenario in wealthier schooling environments. Although gender gaps in academic achievement are perhaps the most important and obvious outcomes to explore, the chapter will also reflect on other areas of schooling where gender gaps have been uncovered. In addition to reviewing the results of South Africa's participation in international and national assessments, the discussion will include a comparison of how boys and girls progress through school, whether or not South African boys and girls have different levels of confidence about their studies, what risks they each face in terms of their safety while at school and to what extent their academic outlooks differ.

What is the ultimate goal of gender-targeted educational interventions? If girls achieve similar results to boys, should the focus suddenly shift to an emerging 'boy crisis' in education at the expense of girls? There is a danger in swinging the pendulum too swiftly. Progress, however impressive, can be eroded very quickly. Even in countries where girls outperform boys at school, they continue to face discrimination in the workplace and to be underrepresented in political leadership (Francis and Skelton 2005; Jacobsen 2007; Mason et al. 2013; Wolf 2013). At the same time, if boys are disappearing from the education system in large numbers, then this warrants serious attention. Our aim is to understand trends and to identify gender gaps more systematically but with an intent that improvements in educational quality should be beneficial to both boys and girls. The chapter will conclude by suggesting how gender equitable approaches to schooling can address shifting gender patterns in the South African learning environment.

12.3 International Trends

South Africa has participated in numerous regional and international assessments since the late 1990s. These studies cover different subject areas (mathematics, science and reading literacy) and grades (ranging from Grade 4 to 9). Gender differences in average national test scores are shown in Table 12.5 for the SACMEQ,[3]

---

[1] A very useful, though dated, example is Chisholm and September's review of gender equity in South African education between 1994 and 2004 (Chisholm and September 2005).

[2] See Van Broekhuizen and Spaull (2017) for a contemporary discussion of gender differences in higher education.

[3] Southern and Eastern Africa Consortium for Monitoring Educational Quality.

TIMSS[4] and PIRLS[5] studies. Gender differences aside, South African performance remained very low compared to other countries on the continent and beyond. All of these tests are standardised to an international centre-point of 500 and a standard deviation of 100. Only average national reading scores for girls in SACMEQ 2000 and 2007 exceeded the international mid-point. South African girls scored higher than boys in 15 of the 19 studies listed in the appendix. Crucially, in all of the studies where there was a statistically significant difference in performance based on gender, girls were at an advantage over boys. Also worth highlighting is that these studies span a period of 16 years and it would appear that the differences have persisted over time.

There is no single reason why girls are better readers than boys. Explanations range from the biological and behavioural (Bray et al. 1997; Ready et al. 2005; Warrington and Younger 2000) to societal and cultural factors (Smyth 2007; Sommers 2001). More recent contributions to this debate centre on whether or not the contemporary schooling environment is suited to teaching boys and whether reading materials and approaches to teaching reading appeal to boys (Tatum 2000; Younger and Warrington 1996). Results of a randomised control trial of learners in the North West Province showed that a structured learning programme when combined with on-site coaching seemed to be narrowing the gender gap in reading by helping boys to catch up (DBE 2017).

The widest gaps in South African studies certainly appeared to be in reading and these gaps emerged early in primary school. The difference in reading performance between girls and boys for the SACMEQ 2000 and 2007 studies was 20% of the standard deviation which, according to one estimate, puts boys five months behind girls in terms of their reading skills (Gustafsson 2015). The gender gap favouring girls in the 2016 PIRLS study was a staggering 52 points, or more than one half of a standard deviation. Girls performed better than boys across all languages tested. Internationally, this gender gap was the second widest among all countries that participated in PIRLS (Howie et al. 2017).

International assessments also provide an opportunity to compare the skills acquired by boys and girls in different subjects. For example, analysis of the SACMEQ 2007 reading results for South Africa showed that there was a higher concentration of boys at lower skills levels. Just over half of boys were reading at the pre-reading and basic reading level. However, more than 60% of Grade 6 girls could read from the pre-reading up to the reading for meaning stage (Zuze and Reddy 2014). There were also more girls reading at the most advanced levels. By way of a more recent example, Table 12.1 shows the percentage of boys and girls who achieved scores that were below the TIMSS 400 minimum benchmark in 2015, a score that represents a basic knowledge of mathematics and science. Again, there was a higher percentage of boys among the lowest achievers but the gap was widest

---

[4]Trends in Mathematics and Science Study.

[5]Progress in International Reading Literacy Study.

Table 12.1 Percentage of learners below the TIMSS 400 minimum benchmark, 2015

	Girls	Boys
Grade 5 (mathematics)	58.4	64.1
Grade 9 (mathematics)	64.2	67.2
Grade 9 (science)	66.0	69.4

Source: Mullis et al. (2016) – own calculations

for Grade 5 mathematics where 64% of boys scored below 400 compared with 58% of girls.

A similar result was seen in the 2016 PIRLS (literacy) results where 84% of Grade 4 boys did not reach the lowest benchmark category compared to 72% of girls (Howie et al. 2017).

12.4   Gender, School Type and School Location

There are also vast differences in the conditions of South African schools. One way in which these differences are identified for government schools is by the poverty index of schools (quintile ranking 1 to 5). Quintiles 1 and 2 were declared 'no-fee' schools in 2007, and in 2010 quintile 3 schools were added to the 'no-fee' category. Quintiles 4 and 5 schools are known as 'fee-paying' government schools because they have the discretion to charge school fees. In addition to state-controlled government schools are independently run schools. Though increasing in number, less than 5% of learners attend independent schools (DBE 2016a). There are important differences in school choice that are related to quintile rankings. Learners from wealthier homes have access to a wider selection of schools close to their homes compared to learners from poor households. These schools tend to be in higher quintiles, with better infrastructure and fewer resource shortages (Branson and Zuze 2012).

In Fig. 12.1 we compare gender differences in mathematics and science outcomes based on the category of school.[6] At the Grade 5 level, girls outperformed boys in mathematics in each school category. In fact, the biggest gender gap based on type of school was the 20 point difference favouring Grade 5 girls in no-fee schools. At the Grade 9 level, girls in public schools (both no-fee and fee-paying) achieved slightly higher average scores for both mathematics and science but in independent schools, boys achieved slightly better average results.

Cultural practices in rural areas tend to be more traditional than in urban settings. Remote rural communities that are steeped in poverty can be more restrictive for girls' education than thriving urban centres (Zuze 2017). This is because of some

---

[6]The difference in average score for male and female learners is presented (male minus female) so that values to the left shows instances where girls achieved better results than boys and values to the right are where boys performed better.

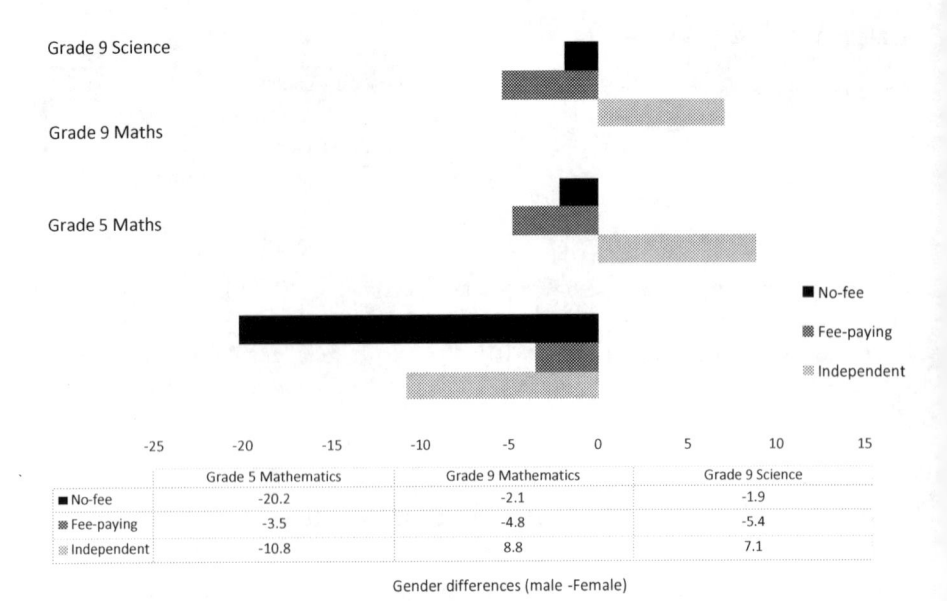

	Grade 5 Mathematics	Grade 9 Mathematics	Grade 9 Science
■ No-fee	-20.2	-2.1	-1.9
▒ Fee-paying	-3.5	-4.8	-5.4
▒ Independent	-10.8	8.8	7.1

Gender differences (male -Female)

Fig. 12.1 Gender differences in mathematics and science by school type, TIMSS 2015. (Source: Mullis et al. (2016) – own calculations)

of the time-consuming domestic responsibilities that are expected of girls such as walking long distances to collect water and firewood, cooking, cleaning and caring for younger siblings (Aikman and Unterhalter 2007). There are occasions where the constraints in rural areas apply to boys as well. For example, in pastoral communities, boys are responsible for herding animals and this can impact negatively on their ability to attend school regularly (Lefoka 2007). In Table 12.6, gender differences in average achievement are compared based on the location of the school. Mathematics and science are two subjects where boys have historically achieved better results than girls. Average test scores in rural areas were lower than in any other location for both boys and girls. Interestingly, boys attending rural schools did not achieve better results relative to girls. The achievement gap in Grade 5 mathematics in remote rural schools favoured girls and was the widest gender gap based on school location.

12.5 Gender and School Safety

School safety is a good example of where new dynamics of gender inequality in education are becoming clear. Studies have shown that boys are at greater risk of being victims of bullying, particularly when physical forms of bullying are considered and that girls are at greater risk of sexual violence in schools (Prinsloo 2006; UNESCO 2016). New threats such as cyber bullying and homophobic bullying are spreading rapidly across South African schools (Anton-Erxleben et al. 2016). Bullying is

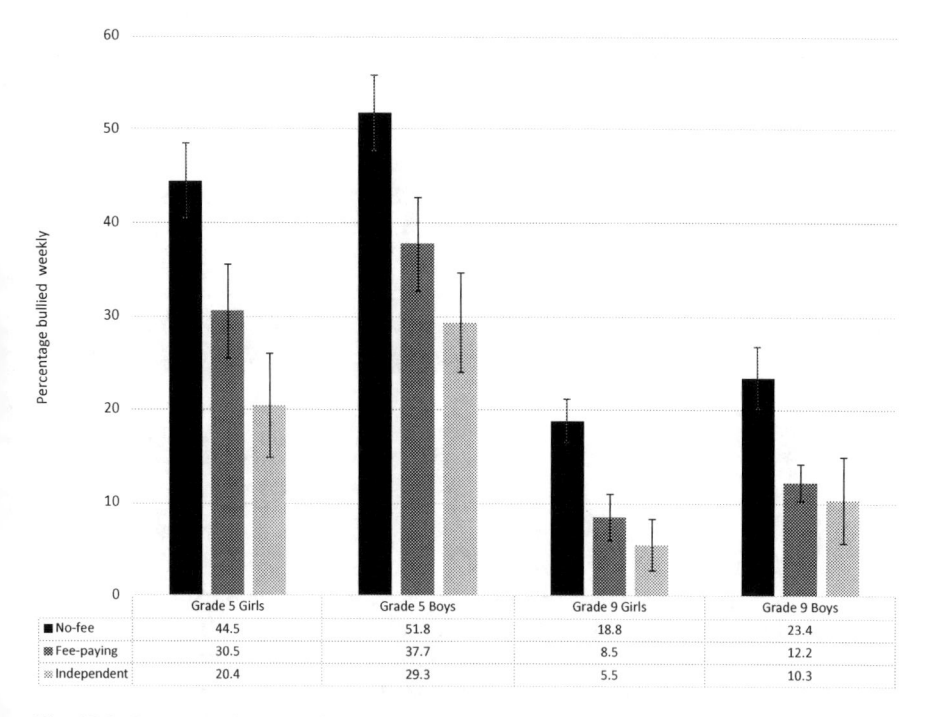

Fig. 12.2 Percentage learners who are bullied on a weekly basis by gender and school type, 2015 (95% confidence intervals are shown above each graph.). (Source: Mullis et al. (2016) – own calculations)

negatively associated with learning outcomes in various contexts including South Africa (Anton-Erxleben et al. 2016). There is also clearly a relationship between social status and bullying. Irrespective of the schooling environment (no-fee, fee-paying or independent), the most socioeconomically disadvantaged learners at a school are more likely to be bullied, even after taking into consideration other background factors like age, gender and academic achievement (Zuze et al. 2016). This implies that the most vulnerable learners are those from the poorest households relative to their peers. This finding raises questions about how status categories from outside of school are recycled within schools, consistently exposing the most disadvantaged children to the greatest risk of abuse (Zuze et al. 2016).

TIMSS collected information on how frequently students experienced physical and verbal forms of bullying.[7] In Fig. 12.2, the percentage of boys and girls in each school category who were victims of bullying on a weekly basis is shown. In general, learners in public schools, particularly those in no-fee schools experienced

---

[7]Learners were asked nine questions on the frequency and type of bullying that they experienced. These questions covered direct and indirect forms of bullying. Direct forms of bullying include both physical and verbal forms.

bullying more frequently. Boys in public schools were at the greatest risk of being bullied. Half of Grade 5 boys and nearly one-quarter of Grade 9 boys attending no-fee schools were bullied on a weekly basis. However, the complexity of discussing gender in the education system is highlighted here.

Although girls in no-fee schools were bullied less frequently than boys in the same category of school, they were at a much greater risk of being bullied than girls in fee-paying and independent schools. Moreover, it is well known that statistics on sexual violence are underreported (Paterson 2017). Although both boys and girls are at risk of sexual abuse, girls face the added risk of abuse both from male pupils and from teachers. Were accurate statistics on this dimension of school violence available,[8] it is quite possible that the gender gap on bullying would be narrower.

12.6   Gender Differences in Educational Attainment

Gender patterns in educational attainment are different at the primary and secondary schooling levels. In this section we consider how boys and girls progress through school as well as explanations for dropping out. Primary school participation has remained high over the last two decades for South African boys and girls. However, there are fewer boys than girls who are in the correct grade for their age. One of the reasons for boys being older is higher repetition rates among boys in the early grades (Fleisch and Shindler 2009). South African boys and girls continue to progress through school at different paces in secondary school. Analysis of the National Income Dynamics Study (NIDS) confirms that repetition is higher at secondary school, especially for boys. Only 30% of boys who were in Grade 9 in 2008 had progressed to Grade 11 two years later (Branson et al. 2014). Results of the South African Youth Panel Study also show that girls have smoother transitions through secondary school (Isdale et al. 2016). The SACMEQ data also revealed that grade repetition rates are higher among boys than girls. In 2000, 50% of Grade 6 boys had repeated at least one grade compared to 36% of girls. In 2007, repetition rates were 35% and 22% for boys and girls respectively. So although repetition rates for boys reduced from one half to one third, female repetition rates also declined leaving the gender gap in repetition unchanged (Zuze and Reddy 2014).

Table 12.2 summarises age differences for girls and boys in Grades 5 and 9 based on TIMSS 2015. Learner age is based on responses at the time of the TIMSS study in August 2015. On average, boys were older than girls in both grades. Moreover, the age gap was evident in different types of schooling environments (no-fee, fee-paying and independent) but it was widest between boys and girls in poorly resourced no-fee schools. Average achievement for girls and boys based on their age is similar. In 2015, there were no statistically significant gender differences in TIMSS achievement for age-appropriate learners although older girls achieved lower average test scores than older boys (Zuze 2017).

---

[8]The IEA studies ask learners whether they were forced to do something they did not want to do but do not explicitly address the question of sexual violence.

Table 12.2 Average age of girls and boys, TIMSS 2015

Grade 9	Girls	SE	Boys	SE
No fee	15.6	(0.04)	16.2	(0.05)
Fee-paying	15.2	(0.05)	15.5	(0.06)
Independent	15.1	(0.05)	15.4	(0.06)
Grade 5	Girls		Boys	
No fee	11.3	(0.04)	11.7	(0.04)
Fee-paying	11.3	(0.03)	11.5	(0.03)
Independent	11.3	(0.07)	11.4	(0.05)

Source: Mullis et al. (2016) – own calculations

Analysis of the General Household Survey (GHS) provides an additional perspective about how boys and girls progress through secondary school. Whereas 92% of girls complete Grade 9, only 87% of boys are able to do so. By Grade 12, the GHS puts attainment for girls at 54% and for boys at only 50% (Gustafsson 2015). It appears that although attainment has generally improved between 2003 and 2013, attainment for girls has improved more rapidly, which has resulted in a wider gender attainment gap in recent years. Gender differences are evident for all races and favour girls. Table 12.3 below summarise Gustafsson's recent findings on gender differences in attainment for different race groups (Gustafsson 2015, p.5). The only exception to the pro-female attainment gap was for Coloured learners in 2003, where male attainment was higher. Although attainment gaps favouring girls were prevalent, the gaps were narrower for White and Indian learners and wider for Black African and Coloured learners. Attainment gaps for White and Indian learners only surfaced at Grades 11 and 12.

Attainment might be greater for girls but explanations for why girls and boys drop out of school are not necessarily the same. One of the most common reasons why girls drop out of school is because of pregnancy (Gustafsson 2015). Analysis of the second wave of NIDS showed that 24% of girls who dropped out cited pregnancy or having a baby as the main reason for not completing school (Branson et al. 2014). For boys, financial constraints or looking for work were the main reason for leaving school (Branson et al. 2014). Both boys and girls mentioned that academic difficulties as a reason for dropping out (Gustafsson 2011). Because the causes of dropout accumulate over many years, it is difficult to pin-point a single cause at the time of dropping out. Responses likely reflect events closest to the point of dropping out. Certainly the effect of poor quality of education and families grappling on a daily basis with how to meet their children's basic needs play a role.

12.7 Gender Differences in the National Senior Certificate (NSC)

Drop out patterns will alter the pool of boys and girls who remain in school. If boys who drop out are weaker learners, then an academically stronger group of boys remains in the schooling system. This select group are then compared to a more

Table 12.3 Gender and race differences in attainment, GHS 2003 and 2013

	Grade	2003 % attained female	2003 Male minus female statistic	2013 % attained female	2013 Male minus female statistic	Magnitude of gap
Black African	9	82	−4	92	−6	20.8
	10	74	−7	85	−7	25.6
	11	63	−6	71	−7	24.6
	12	46	0	50	−3	10.7
Coloured	9	79	8	93	−1	500
	10	66	8	91	−7	2.7
	11	58	3	77	−13	4.6
	12	53	1	65	−8	2.9
Indian	9	100	0	100	0	0
	10	100	0	100	0	0
	11	99	−2	100	−1	100
	12	96	−11	97	−5	400
White	9	100	0	100	0	0
	10	99	1	100	0	100
	11	95	−2	99	−4	1
	12	91	−1	98	−4	1.1
Overall	9	82	−3	92	−5	20.1
	10	75	−5	86	−6	26.9
	11	65	−4	73	−7	32.3
	12	50	1	54	−4	15.9

Source: Gustafsson (2015, p. 5)

academically mixed group of girls. National examinations would then incorrectly conclude that girls are underperforming. Results of the National Senior Certificate (NSC) bear this out. Lower pass marks among girls can partly be explained by lower drop out among weaker female learners, while the reality is that weaker males do not attempt the exam (Perry 2003). In 2016, 55% of candidates who were enrolled for the NSC were female. Of the candidates who wrote the exam, 74% of male candidates achieved NSC passes compared to 71% of female candidates (DBE 2016b). Girls are under-represented in STEM-related degree programmes and efforts to develop a more gender-balanced STEM pool are ongoing. In Table 12.4, NSC results in mathematics and physical science are compared for males and females. These subject areas have been the focus of attention in gender discussions because lack of progress is thought to severely limit female career choices later in life (Zuze 2008, 2017). Although the evidence from standardised assessments like TIMSS and SACMEQ earlier in the chapter revealed little difference based on gender, the picture changes based on the NSC results. The percentage of male candidates who achieve 30% or above has been consistently higher and the gender gap for mathematics is over 10% points.

Table 12.4 NSC Results in Mathematics and Physical Science by gender, 2012 to 2016

Percentage of candidates who achieved 30% and above

	Mathematics			Physical science		
Year	Female	Male	(Male-Female)	Female	Male	(Male-Female)
2012	49.2	59.7	10.5	58.9	64.0	5.1
2013	54.3	64.9	10.6	65.7	69.3	3.6
2014	48.6	59.3	10.7	59.1	64.2	5.1
2015	44.2	54.9	10.7	56.4	61.1	4.7
2016	46.4	57.0	10.6	59.6	64.7	5.1

Source: DBE (2016b)

Claims about why boys are at times advantaged in technical subjects can be quite controversial but countries that have equalised enrolment in technical subjects for men and women have a few qualities in common. Women are active participants in the labour force, gender parity exists in school enrolment, women possess a share of jobs in research and the level of female participation in parliaments is high (Else-Quest et al. 2010; Kane and Mertz 2012; Marks 2008). Most South African public schools are co-educational and this is understandable from a logistics and funding perspective. However, co-educational learning environments can also perpetuate the prevailing gender roles in society. For this reason, international research reveals that girls seem to achieve better results in all subjects (including maths and science) and have higher academic aspirations in a classroom environment that is predominantly female (Hart 2016). Single-sex educational environments, in certain subjects, are thought to be beneficial for both boys and girls. They provide an opportunity for both boys and girls in certain communities to explore their interests and fulfil their potential without the added strain of society's expectations (Gurian et al. 2009).

12.8 Confidence in Mathematics

Girls and boys sometimes have different attitudes about mathematics and science (Frenzel et al. 2007; Mallow 1994). These differences, in turn, influence achievement patterns as well as their outlook. Results from a cross-national study of the Organisation for Economic Cooperation and Development (OECD) countries revealed that girls living in industrialised countries had higher levels of anxiety and lower levels of confidence in their mathematics ability. This included girls who performed equally well to boys in these subjects (OECD 2013; Schleicher 2008).

Responses to questions about confidence in mathematics are shown in Fig. 12.3 for girls and boys in 2015. Learners were either very confident, confident or not confident in mathematics. Only the results for learners who stated that they were not confident are shown in the graph. In Grade 5, although there was a higher percentage of learners in public schools who were not confident in mathematics,

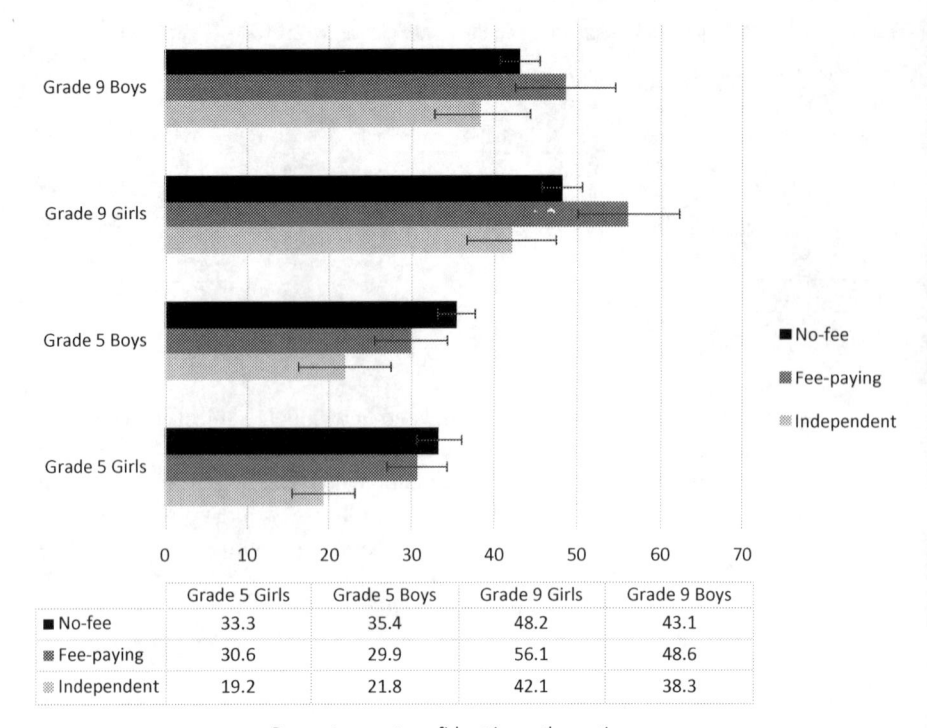

	Grade 5 Girls	Grade 5 Boys	Grade 9 Girls	Grade 9 Boys
■ No-fee	33.3	35.4	48.2	43.1
▨ Fee-paying	30.6	29.9	56.1	48.6
▨ Independent	19.2	21.8	42.1	38.3

Percentage not confident in mathematics

Fig. 12.3 Confidence in studies by gender and school type, 2015 (95% confidence intervals are shown above each graph.). (Source: Mullis et al. (2016) – own calculations)

the gender differences within each school category was small. The gap widened in secondary school as girls' confidence appeared to decline. In the Grade 9 study, the percentage of girls who were not confident in maths was much higher than the percentage of boys. The gap was wider in public schools, meaning that Grade 9 girls in public school environments had the least confidence in mathematics. The gender gap among learners who were not confident was 6% points in no-fee schools, 8% points in fee-paying schools and 4% points in independent schools.

12.9 Summary and Conclusions

This chapter sought to understand what gender differences existed in South African educational achievement, attainment, school climate and confidence using two decades of nationally representative assessment data. Because most of the datasets referenced in this chapter had a cross sectional design, the studies were conducted at a specific point in time and our ability to draw causal inferences is limited. The results do, however, yield insights into overall trends and provide some direction for future research. Nationally, girls achieved better average results than boys across subject areas, grade levels and across time. The gender gap favouring girls was widest for reading assessments. Gender differences based on the type of school that learners attended were discussed and revealed that the widest gaps were in government schools and rural settings, with boys typically disadvantaged. Grade 9 boys in independent schools performed slightly better than girls on average.

Boys were more likely to be bullied in every type of school but boys and girls in public schools were at a greater risk of being bullied than boys and girls in independent schools. Reliable data on sexual violence is not available in the national educational surveys referenced here. Because girls tend to be the victims of sexual assault more frequently than boys and were this information available, it could alter the picture about gender and school violence.

The section on attainment showed that boys tended to be older than girls and dropped out in greater numbers in secondary schools. Attainment was lower for boys than for girls in every racial group. Boys achieved better results in the NSC but because of higher dropout among boys, an academically stronger group of boys tended to be compared to a more academically mixed group of girls. Gender differences in mathematics and science were not statistically significant at the secondary level and girls significantly outperformed boys in Grade 5 TIMSS. And yet girls were less confident about their mathematics ability and secondary school girls in public schools were particularly unconfident of their mathematical skills. This seems to suggest that other factors either at school or in the external environment are undermining how girls view their potential in technical subjects. Internationally, girls continue to have lower levels of confidence in mathematics, even when they perform equally well to boys. This problem persists in advanced economies and is still not fully understood although social conditioning and low expectations of girls in these subjects certainly play a role.

12.9.1 The Way Forward

Successful policies and practices to achieve gender equality in education, like the problems that they seek to address, are far from straight forward. The complexity of gender issues in education does not mean that solutions cannot be found but a stronger gender relevance needs to be promoted. There are two important conclusions that should be embedded in a future public discourse on gender and education. The first is that the challenges that boys and girls face throughout their schooling career are very different. Policy makers need to understand what is behind these challenges and track progress periodically. The second is that there are a number of boys and girls who are at serious risk of disappearing from the education system if gender targeted interventions are not carefully considered. Practically, this means understanding what they spend their time doing in their lives outside of school and integrating these experiences into school-based research. Low performing boys are perhaps the most vulnerable but girls face their own set of challenges, such as low self-expectations in technical subjects. Perhaps the key take-away from this chapter is that girls and boys may face different difficulties in their education that need to be considered carefully. The schooling environment and society as a whole can either support or detract from their ability to flourish in their education.

Appendix

Table 12.5 Gender differences in international assessments

| Year | Study | Subject | Grade | Average achievement (Standard errors) | | | | Gender differences | |
				Girls	SE	Boys	SE	Girls scored higher	Boys scored higher
2000	SACMEQ	Mathematics	6	490	(7.95)	482	(6.71)	8	
2000	SACMEQ	Reading	6	505	(10.13)	478	(7.91)	27	
2007	SACMEQ	Mathematics	6	498	(3.90)	491	(4.10)	7	
2007	SACMEQ	Reading	6	506	(4.80)	484	(4.70)	22	
2006	PIRLS	Reading	5	319	(6.30)	283	(5.50)	36	
2011	PIRLS	Reading	5	434	(7.72)	408	(8.70)	26	
2016	PIRLS	Reading	5	421	(6.0)	391	(6.5)	30	
2006	PIRLS	Reading	4	271	(5.0)	235	(5.0)	36	
2011	PIRLS	Reading	4	475	(3.9)	446	(4.2)	29	
2016	PIRLS	Reading	4	347	(4.00)	295	(5.10)	52	
1999	TIMSS	Mathematics	9	267	(7.50)	283	(7.40)		16
1999	TIMSS	Science	9	234	(9.40)	253	(7.80)		19
2003	TIMSS	Mathematics	9	262	(6.20)	264	(6.40)		2
2003	TIMSS	Science	9	242	(7.30)	244	(7.80)		2
2011	TIMSS	Mathematics	9	354	(3.00)	350	(3.00)	4	
2011	TIMSS	Science	9	335	(4.20)	328	(4.40)	7	
2015	TIMSS	Mathematics	9	376	(5.30)	369	(4.60)	7	
2015	TIMSS	Science	9	362	(6.70)	353	(5.50)	9	
2015	TIMSS	Mathematics	5	384	(3.80)	368	(4.40)	16	

Source: Mullis et al. (2016, 2017) and Ross et al. (2004)

Table 12.6 Gender differences in mathematics and science by school location, TIMSS 2015

		Urban		Suburban		Medium city		Small town		Remote rural	
Grade 5	Mathematics	Mean	SE	Mean	SE	Mean	SE	Mean	SE	Mean	SE
	Girls	415.14	12.25	437.54	12.01	446.38	17.54	383.94	7.66	338.28	4.78
	Boys	404.98	14.18	428.60	12.20	432.24	12.75	358.66	8.28	319.36	5.81
Grade 9	Mathematics	Mean	SE	Mean	SE	Mean	SE	Mean	SE	Mean	SE
	Girls	396.13	12.44	430.58	17.40	411.01	19.83	366.51	10.24	338.11	5.58
	Boys	396.08	10.45	424.53	17.50	404.58	19.83	358.80	6.88	335.78	6.49
Grade 9	Science	Mean	SE	Mean	SE	Mean	SE	Mean	SE	Mean	SE
	Girls	392.4	14.21	431.10	21.18	411.52	22.79	349.97	11.50	310.61	7.25
	Boys	389.79	12.37	423.15	20.22	406.50	24.76	341.26	8.32	309.44	8.30

Source: Mullis et al. (2016) – own calculations

References

Aikman, S., & Unterhalter, E. (2006). Introduction. In S. Aikman & E. Unterhalter (Eds.), *Beyond access: Transforming policy and practice for gender equality in education.* Oxford: Oxfam.

Aikman, S., & Unterhalter, E. (2007). *Practising gender equality in education.* Oxford: Oxfam GB.

Anton-Erxleben, K., Kibriya, S., & Zhang, Y. (2016). *Bullying as the main driver of low performance in schools: Evidence from Botswana, Ghana, and South Africa.* MPRA Paper, No 75555.

Branson, N., & Zuze, T. L. (2012). Education, the great equaliser: Improving access to quality education. *South African Child Gauge, 2012*, 69–74.

Branson, N., Hofmeyr, C., & Lam, D. (2014). Progress through school and the determinants of school dropout in South Africa. *Development Southern Africa, 31*(1), 106–126.

Bray, R., Gardner, C., & Parsons, N. (1997). *Can boys do better?* Secondary Heads Association, Leicester

Chisholm, L., & September, J. (2005). *Gender equity in South African education 1994–2004: Perspectives from research, government and unions: Conference proceedings.* Pretoria: HSRC Press.

Commission for Gender Equality. (2007). *Gender in the curriculum.* The Commission for Gender Equality, Johannesburg.

DBE. (2016a). *Education Statistics in South Africa 2014.* Department of Basic Education, Pretoria.

DBE. (2016b). *National Senior Certificate Examination Report 2016.* Department of Basic Education, Pretoria.

DBE. (2017). *Summary Report. Results of Year 2 Impact Evaluation.* The Early Grade Reading Study, Department of Basic Education, Pretoria.

Else-Quest, N. M., Hyde, J. S., & Linn, M. C. (2010). Cross-national patterns of gender differences in mathematics: A meta-analysis. *Psychological Bulletin, 136*(1), 103.

Fleisch, B., & Shindler, J. (2009). Gender repetition: School access, transitions and equity in the 'Birth-to-Twenty' cohort panel study in urban South Africa. *Comparative Education, 45*(2), 265–279.

Francis, B., & Skelton, C. (2005). *Reassessing gender and achievement: Questioning contemporary key debates.* London: Routledge.

Frenzel, A. C., Pekrun, R., & Goetz, T. (2007). Girls and mathematics-A "hopeless" issue? A control-value approach to gender differences in emotions towards mathematics. *European Journal of Psychology of Education, 22*(4), 497.

Gurian, M., Stevens, K., & Daniels, P. (2009). Single-sex classrooms are succeeding. *Educational Horizons, 87*(4), 234–245.

Gustafsson, M. (2011). *The when and how of leaving school: The policy implications of new evidence on secondary schooling in South Africa.* Stellenbosch Economic Working Papers, 09/11.

Gustafsson, M. (2015). *The relative under-performance of males in the schooling system.* Department of Basic Education, Pretoria.

Hanushek, E. (2008). Schooling, gender equity, and economic outcomes. In M. Embon & L. Fort (Eds.), *Girls' education in the 21st century, gender equality, empowerment, and economic growth.* Washington, DC: World Bank.

Hart, L. C. (2016). When "separate" may be better: Exploring single-sex learning as a remedy for social anxieties in female middle school students. *Middle School Journal, 47*(2), 32–40.

Howie, S., Combrinck, C., Roux, K., Tshele, M., Mokoena, G., & McLeod Palane, N. (2017). *PIRLS Literacy 2016: South African Highlights Report.* Centre for Evaluation and Assessment, Faculty of Education, University of Pretoria, Pretoria.

Isdale, K., Reddy, V., Winnaar, L., & Zuze, T. L. (2016). *Smooth, staggered or stopped? Educational transitions in the South African Youth Panel Study.* Pretoria: HSRC Press.

Jacobsen, J. (2007). *The economics of gender.* Oxford: Blackwell Publishing.

Kane, J. M., & Mertz, J. E. (2012). Debunking myths about gender and mathematics performance. *Notices of the AMS, 59*(1), 10–21.

Lefoka, P. J. (2007). Out of school missing boys–a study from Lesotho. Commonwealth Education Partnerships Available at: http://www.ungei.org/resources/6031.htm

Mallow, J. V. (1994). Gender-related science anxiety: A first binational study. *Journal of Science Education and Technology, 3*(4), 227–238.

Marks, G. N. (2008). Accounting for the gender gaps in student performance in reading and mathematics: Evidence from 31 countries. *Oxford Review of Education, 34*(1), 89–109.

Mason, M. A., Wolfinger, N. H., & Goulden, M. (2013). *Do babies matter?: Gender and family in the Ivory Tower.* London/New Brunswick: Rutgers University Press.

Mullis, I. V., Martin, M. O., Foy, P., & Hooper, M. (2016). *TIMSS 2015 international results in mathematics.* Retrieved from Boston College, TIMSS & PIRLS International Study Center. http://timssandpirlsbcedu/timss2015/international-results

Mullis, I. V., Martin, M. O., Foy, P., & Hooper, M. (2017). *PIRLS 2016 international results in reading.* Chestnut Hill, MA: TIMSS & PIRLS International Study Center, Boston College.

OECD (2013) *PISA 2012 results: Ready to learn: Students' engagement, drive and self-beliefs (volume III): Preliminary version.* Paris: OECD.

Pandor, N. (2005). *Keynote address: The hidden face of gender inequality in South African education.* Gender Equity in South African Education 1994–2004: Perspectives from Research, Government and Unions.

Paterson, K. (2017). Chapter 18: Sexual violence in schools. In F. Veriava (Ed.), *Basic education rights handbook*, Section 27, Johannesburg.

Patrinos, H. (2008). Returns to education: The gender perspective. Girls' Education in the 21st Century: Gender Equality, Empowerment and Economic Growth (pp. 53–661). Washington, DC: The World Bank.

Perry, H. (2003). Female performance in the senior certificate examination: Excellence hiding behind the averages. *Edusource Data News, 39*, 14–25.

Prinsloo, S. (2006). Sexual harassment and violence in South African schools. *South African Journal of Education, 26*(2), 305–318.

Ready, D. D., LoGerfo, L. F., Burkam, D. T., & Lee, V. E. (2005). Explaining girls' advantage in kindergarten literacy learning: Do classroom behaviors make a difference? *The Elementary School Journal, 106*(1), 21–38.

Ross, K., Saito, M., Dolata, S., Ikeda, M., & Zuze, L. (2004). *Data archive for the SACMEQ I and SACMEQ II projects.* Paris: IIEP-UNESCO.

Schleicher, A. (2008). *Student learning outcomes in mathematics from a gender perspective: What does the International PISA Assessment tell us?* (p. 41). Girls' Education in the 21st Century.

Smyth, E. (2007). Cross-national patterns in educational attainment and achievement. In *International studies in educational inequality, theory and policy: Educational inequality: Persistence and change* (Vol 1). Dordrecht: Springer.

Sommers, C. H. (2001). *The war against boys: How misguided feminism is harming our young men*. New York: Simon & Schuster.

Tatum, A. W. (2000). Breaking down barriers that disenfranchise African American adolescent readers in low-level tracks. *Journal of Adolescent & Adult Literacy, 44*(1), 52–64.

UNESCO. (2015). *Gender and EFA 2000–2015. Achievements and challenges*. Paris: UNESCO.

UNESCO. (2016). *Global education monitoring report*. Gender Review Creating Sustainable Futures for All, UNESCO, Paris.

UNESCO. (2017). *Global education monitoring report 2017/18*. Accountability in Education: Meeting our Commitments UNESCO, Paris.

United Nations. (2015). *The millennium development goals report 2015*. United Nations, New York.

Unterhalter, E. (2006). Fragemented frameworks? Researching women, gender, education, and development. In S. Aikman & E. Unterhalter (Eds.), *Beyond access: Transforming policy and practice for gender equality in education*. Oxford: Oxfam.

Van Broekhuizen, H., & Spaull, N. (2017). *The 'Martha Effect': The compounding female advantage in South African higher education*. Stellenbosch Economic Working Papers, WP14/2017.

Warrington, M., & Younger, M. (2000). The other side of the gender gap. *Gender and Education, 12*(4), 493–508.

Wills, G. (2015). *A profile of the labour market for school principals in South Africa: Evidence to inform policy*. Stellenbosch Economic Working Papers, WP12/2015.

Wolf, A. (2013). *The XX factor: How working women are creating a new society*. London: Profile Books.

Wolpe, A. (2005). Reflections on the gender equity task team. In L. Chisholm & J. September (Eds.), *Gender Equity in South African Education 1994–2004: Perspectives from Research, Government and Unions: Conference Proceedings*. Pretoria: HSRC Press.

Younger, M., & Warrington, M. (1996). Differential achievement of girls and boys at GCSE: Some observations from the perspective of one school. *British Journal of Sociology of Education, 17*(3), 299–313.

Zuze, T., Reddy, V., Juan, A., Hannan, S., Visser, M., & Winnaar, L. (2016). *Safe and sound? Violence and South African Education*. HSRC Policy Brief, 06, Pretoria.

Zuze, T. L. (2008). *Equity and effectiveness in East African primary schools*. Ph.D. thesis, University of Cape Town.

Zuze, T. L. (2017). A riddle explained: Gender disparities in East African education. *African Review of Economics and Finance, 7*(2), 29–59.

Zuze, T. L., & Reddy, V. (2014). School resources and the gender reading literacy gap in South African schools. *International Journal of Educational Development, 36*, 100–107.

Chapter 13
Teacher Development and Inequality in Schools: Do We Now Have a Theory of Change?

Yael Shalem and Francine De Clercq

13.1 Introduction

Until 2009, most teacher development (henceforth TD) in South Africa was targeted at the improvement of a few discrete aspects of teacher practice to comply with a new curriculum framework and thus, meaningful learning opportunities were few and far between. Around 2009, the new model of change targeting teachers from poorly performing primary schools relied on a combination of standardized lesson plans, learners' material and training or coaching within a complex framework of accountability and support. This model foregrounds curriculum coverage and tight regulation of a set of teaching practices (some of which are completely new) in specific subjects – language and mathematics.

Our aim in this chapter is to critically examine what begins to be agreed upon and what remains in dispute, in the international and national literature, about this new model of teacher change. The chapter is a sequel to a publication titled *Do we have a theory of change? Calling change models to account* (Shalem 2003). In that journal article, Shalem argues that bureaucratic/managerial forms of interventions do not make teachers unlearn what the change agents want them to change.[1]

The distribution of inequalities in South Africa clearly reflects economic and social patterns of inequalities, whereby poorly-resourced schools are also the ones with the less able teachers (Van der Berg et al. 2011; Motala & Carel in this volume)

---

[1] Model' refers to any teacher development programme which has been tried in South Africa and is included in the review.

Y. Shalem (✉) · F. De Clercq
School of Education, University of the Witwatersrand, Parktown, South Africa
e-mail: Yael.shalem@wits.ac.za; Francine.DeClercq@wits.ac.za

© Springer Nature Switzerland AG 2019
N. Spaull, J. D. Jansen (eds.), *South African Schooling: The Enigma of Inequality*, Policy Implications of Research in Education 10,
https://doi.org/10.1007/978-3-030-18811-5_13

whose pedagogy tends to inhibit learning (Hoadley 2018). Most teachers in South Africa experience inequalities in terms of their access to:

- resources
- learners who are cognitively well-prepared for schooling, are physically healthy and whose homes function as a second site of acquisition;
- meaningful learning opportunities in the past and in the present and a reservoir of cognitive resources at the level of the school; and
- functional school management that mediates the bureaucratic demands on teacher time (Shalem and Hoadley 2009).

What this suggests is that access to meaningful learning opportunities by teachers of poorly performing schools and functional management can be seen as a fundamental equality distribution imperative. The challenge is to understand why, since 1994, TD for teachers' improved practice has been a cause of serious concern, because, until very recently, research reveals a poor teacher take-up of any TD programme, let alone an improvement of their teaching quality and learners' performance (NEEDU 2013). To investigate this enigma, we borrow Elmore's idea of 'reciprocal accountability' (Elmore 2005) which he defines as: for every unit of change performance that is required, an equivalent unit of support and capacity building is expected to be invested.

The idea of meaningful learning opportunities (Cohen and Ball 1999) consists of developing ways of working with teachers first, on what they might find too hard or foreign to what they already know about a curriculum topic, and second, on how learners learn a specific topic or what raison d'être is hidden behind the failure of particular learners to grasp an aspect of the topic. For them, 'opportunities to learn' improve when they are focused and specific, when they are linked to the curriculum, and when the 'professional argot' of the programme is properly reflected upon. Cohen and Ball also argue that the more subject specific the program is, the more it includes examples of adaptation processes (direct modelling, video materials) and the more it gives teachers opportunities to work under supervision with their learners, the more effective it is (see also Fullan et al. 2015).

Research on TD (Bertram 2011; Charalambous and Hill 2012; Cohen and Ball 1999; Darling-Hammond 1995; Hiebert and Morris 2012; Morris and Hiebert 2011) suggests that improvement of teacher learning opportunities requires an appropriate pedagogy of instruction with a clear learning focus. In South Africa, the TD challenge is specific – for historical reasons of poor schooling and racially segregated and unequal training system, the majority of teachers, more so in poor socio-economic provinces, display poor professional knowledge. Based on his examination of various analyses of large systemic evaluations (SACMEQ), Nick Taylor (chapter in this volume) strongly demonstrates the lack of disciplinary knowledge (in English and Mathematics) amongst primary school years.

Our descriptive historical analysis unpacks different TD models which have been tried in South Africa since the early 1990s, bearing in mind the gaps in teacher knowledge evidenced in research. Our conclusion is that the idea of improving the performance of the most disadvantaged teachers by scripting a new practice and putting emphasis on a mix of teacher accountability and support are understandable in the light of the general agreement that TD in South Africa has for a long time failed to make a meaningful difference to teachers' practice especially in poorly performing schools. We argue, however, that by examining the idea of meaningful learning opportunity from the perspective of teacher knowledge and reciprocal accountability a more nuanced view of teachers' practice emerges, which has implications for evaluating the learning opportunities foregrounded by the theory of change which underpins the prevailing TD model. We argue that it is important to distinguish between two clusters of teaching routines: ways of organizing one's teaching over time; and pedagogical means of helping learners to understand the meanings, rules, and procedures of the subject matter. The former cluster is knowledge of sequencing and pacing of the content required to be covered and which can be covered by lesson plans. The latter is a far more specialized knowledge, about enabling learners to learn. This knowledge does not develop by following a protocol that tells the teacher what to say and do, but from a deep understanding of the telos of the practice the teacher is intending to teach i.e. the rules and procedures that have developed over time in the history of the practice (of teaching reading, for example). And so, the question for us is: to what extent the tool of teacher development which takes the form of following a lesson plan (with supportive coaches and learning materials) relies, in fact, on an already quite developed resource, which is teacher knowledge.

13.2 Teacher Development in South African Education

Since 1994, there have been major frustrations expressed by different sectors of the South African school system at the lack of meaningful learning opportunities for disadvantaged teachers both to counter the apartheid legacy of poor in-service training provisions and to assist with the implementation of the post-1994 complex, ambitious and ever-changing curriculum policies.

The first post-1994 curriculum and assessment policies (the 1998 Curriculum 2005 and the 2002 Revised National Curriculum Statement) underspecified subject content matter, pacing and progression. They required of teachers to select and provide their own content knowledge, as well as design and implement their own learning programmes and lesson plans to meet pre-specified learners' outcomes. For most of the disadvantaged teachers who, during the apartheid era, were treated as workers compelled to follow prescribed syllabi, this represented an insurmountable expectation (Jansen and Christie 1999). Research studies at the time (Taylor and Vinjevold 1999) showed evidently that most disadvantaged teachers had weak subject knowledge and were equipped with a very narrow repertoire of pedagogical approaches. They did not have the confidence required to develop their own learning programmes.

The challenges were enormous. The scholarship in teacher education (Barasa and Mattson 1998; Jansen and Christie 1999) grew fast to investigate, *inter alia*, the meaning of 'teachers as facilitators' and 'life long learners', the weaknesses of an under-specified curriculum, the importance of school context and the idea of how to teach for better learner performance. One of the most important TD challenges was to identify different teachers' needs and mobilize the human and financial resources to provide differentiated, appropriate and sustainable TD activities. So, what were the post-1994 TD strategies and policies?

As from 1998, most TD programmes focused on transmitting an outcomes-based curriculum philosophy, the underlying values and the educational rationale. It consisted of broad orientation workshops about the meaning of the curriculum, its new terms and directives, followed by subject-specific workshops for a particular learning area and phase (De Clercq and Shalem 2014). Unfortunately, teacher subject matter knowledge and preferred ways of teaching it as well as curriculum sequencing and pacing (henceforth teacher knowledge) were backgrounded (De Clercq and Shalem 2014).

Provincial departments adopted what has been found in research as the problematic 'cascade approach' (Bett 2016). In the case of Gauteng, for example, most training took the form of district-organized workshops. The workshops were poorly contextualized, of short duration and without any demonstration, modelling or follow-up at school level (De Clercq and Shalem 2014).

Many teachers and principals complained that the material was laborious to read, too generic and unhelpful. Teachers came out of training workshops feeling

> unsupported, overburdened with paperwork and frustrated by the 'one-size-fits-all' curriculum training approach with hardly any guidance on curriculum content, lesson planning and assessment. (De Clercq and Shalem 2014, p.133)

In addition, there was district-based and cluster-based training which consisted of voluntary courses. These courses were of short duration and were held outside school hours at district venues. They were facilitated by district officials or outside professionals of uneven expertise and with different quality hand-outs. They were not conceptualized as part of a continuum of learning with follow-up or more advanced courses. The take-up by teachers and the alignment between the courses' aims, design and delivery were not monitored. Tertiary institutions were asked to offer longer formalized upgrading diplomas, including the then Advanced Certificate in Education (ACE), to ensure poorly qualified secondary school teachers could get a M+4 (or Matric+4 years' training) teacher qualification. Tertiary institutions were expected to offer an academic focus in line with the demands of the National Qualification Framework (NQF) Level 6 qualification programme. But, in the growing climate of curriculum compliance, most teachers were looking for practical competences to teach the National Curriculum Statement (Council on Higher Education 2010). Such tensions created a difficult balancing act for tertiary institutions to find an equilibrium between systematic teaching of academic concepts and guiding teachers on their school-focused group activities and individual assignments (Steinberg and Slonimsky 2004). The Council on Higher Education (2010) report argued that many of the ACEs were of different quality: most ACEs were 'locked into the school curriculum', privileged practical knowledge, under-emphasized subject matter knowledge and did not attain NQF level 6 learning outcomes.

At the time of this despair about teacher knowledge, poor school management and poor learner performance, a new angle on TD was advocated by Taylor (2002) with his push for accountability. Below, we describe some of the features of Taylor's view because the current preferred model of change, which we discuss later, contains similar key features, with important suggestions for changes and improvements in TD.

Taylor (2002) argues that teacher support should be conditioned upon the establishment of demand measures (or accountability measures) from teachers. He offers a 'convergence' view of change, according to which demand measures must come first. These will monitor the day-to-day performance of teachers (at school and at the instructional classroom level) and, through a combination of incentives and sanctions, will motivate teachers to apply what they learn in TD courses. The accountability measures will also "give direction to support measures like teacher appraisal, provision of learning material and systematic training" (p. 14). Taylor claims that the results of systemic assessment will provide information on "knowledge needs" (p. 10) and that performance management systems, or "micro-technologies" (p. 11), will be used to monitor the coverage of the intended curriculum and the quality of teaching.

In his notion of "micro-technologies", Taylor (2002) includes "line management responsibilities of district managers and school principals"; "systematic curriculum management subsystem through which the delivery of the curriculum is planned and monitored throughout the school"; and "school inspections" (p. 16).

Critical of the often-impoverished TD programmes, Taylor calls for the systematization of TD. He argues that primary school teachers need to receive "structured reading and numeracy INSET programs" and senior phase teachers "programs which systematically take them through the content of their specialised subject areas" (2002, p.15). Taylor asks universities to supplement TD by an approach "which places centre stage the quality of the knowledge transactions which occur between teacher and pupil, including the subject knowledge of teachers and their pedagogical content knowledge" (p. 15). He draws an important distinction between "institutional vision and culture", which he defines as soft issues (p. 5) and "deep knowledge structures embodied in instructional knowledge", which he defines as core. At the beginning, this view was interpreted as a process of change that has to begin with the work of a strong agent located outside of the school – the hands of managerial/bureaucratic authorities that closely monitor teachers' work (see for example Education Action Zones (EAZ) in Fleisch 2001).

TD changes started to occur at departmental level. The 2007 National Policy Framework for Teacher Education and Development (NPFTED) Act was introduced to provide coherence, direction and focus for a new teacher education system. It made the DoE responsible for teacher education planning, funding and monitoring and for partnering with universities, NGOs, unions and other approved providers. The Continuing Professional Teacher Development (CPTD) system was formalized and expected teachers to continuously update and strengthen their professional knowledge by accumulating 150 professional development points every three years (Department of Education (DoE) 2007). The South African Council for Educators (SACE) was supposed to manage and coordinate this new system and accredit the various TD providers.

In addition, the 2009 Teacher Summit resolved that the NPFTED had to be operationalised through a coherent strategic TD plan that would specify the type of funding and respective responsibilities of all stakeholders expected to contribute. In 2011, the Integrated Strategic Planning Framework for Teacher Education and Development (ISPFTED) was passed, committing the Department of Basic Education (DBE) and Department of Higher Education and Training (DHET) to put aside large funds for the establishment of national and provincial teacher development institutes, district teacher development centres and the establishment of Professional Learning Communities (PLCs) (DHET and DBE 2011, p.14). Although interesting, the ISPFTED seems to have encountered considerable implementation problems in different provinces and districts, mainly because of the lack of funds, quality TD developers and urgency among provincial departments and districts (Mahomed 2017).

Most importantly, radical changes were introduced on the curriculum side. Given the strong criticisms of Outcomes-Based Education from practitioners and academic researchers alike, Ms Angie Motshekga was the first Minister of Education to show the political will to commission a new review of the curriculum. In line with the relative success of the 2008 Foundations for Learning Campaign which, inter alia, provided Foundation Phase (FP) teachers with standardized lesson plans, the 2009 Ministerial Commission of Enquiry Report (Department of Basic Education and Department of Higher Education and Training 2009) recommended greater specifications on the curriculum content, sequencing and pacing for each grade and subject. Subsequently, the Curriculum and Assessment Policy Statement (CAPS) was introduced in three phases (2012–2014).

This specified national curriculum brought about new possibilities and new kinds of learning opportunities for teachers. For the first time the demand for TD, focused on "deep knowledge structures embodied in instructional knowledge" (Taylor 2002), began to be addressed and especially through large-scale school-based systemic change programmes.

The most innovative and longest sustained programme was the Gauteng Primary Language and Mathematics Strategy (GPLMS), a four-year large-scale literacy and numeracy strategy (2010–2013). The GPLMS targeted around 1000 underperforming primary schools (65% of the Gauteng Department of Education (GDE) primary schools) that scored below the provincial average in assessment. Known for its 'triple cocktail' form of intervention (Fleisch 2016), the GPLMS focused on what has become a very popular term, the instructional core, which broadly refers to the pedagogical interactions between teachers and learners about specific content, organized systematically within sets of curriculum materials (City et al. 2009). The triple cocktail includes Scripted Lesson Plans (SLPs), sophisticated learning resources, just-in-time training and on-site coaches.

In a much tighter way than anything before in South Africa, each lesson plan specified the topics and objectives, work to be completed by the end of the calendar week, teaching methodology to be followed, teaching activities with the specific pacing and resources needed for each lesson and learner assessment. The GPLMS leadership argued then that:

> bureaucratic controls of highly specified standardized teaching routines, expert-designed learning and teaching resources and on-going support and monitoring by coaches are the best way to ensure that more school learners are exposed to the intended curriculum and its expected sequence, pacing and coverage. (De Clercq and Shalem 2014, p.137)

The SLPs were designed as "a practical mechanism to provide knowledge resources to teachers in a direct manner" (NEEDU 2013, p.62). The GPLMS developers hoped that, by embedding detailed core teaching routines sequentially into a full lesson plan, teachers would be enabled to "improve time on task and establish new daily and weekly routines" (Fleisch and Schöer 2014, p.3). These SLPs represented an attempt to fuse support and demand, but with more weight on teachers practicing the new pedagogical regime than on developing teacher knowledge.

Similar large-scale programmes are now commissioned by the DBE (for example, the Early Grade Reading Study (EGRS) in the North-West and Mpumalanga Provinces) and involve, with the support from funding agencies, randomized controlled trials (RCTs) to evaluate which of the GPLMS components are the most effective. The results so far indicate that the SLPs and their key teaching practices mediated by on-site coaching are the most effective component of the strategy in terms of improved learners' results (Fleisch 2016; Fleisch and Dixon 2017). Another large-scale systemic change programme was developed by the Programme to Improve Learning Outcomes (PILO) in two education districts of KwaZulu-Natal (KZN) in 2014. This programme – known on the ground as the Jika iMfundo improvement campaign – aims to transform and improve the organizational culture, practices and leadership of schools and districts (De Clercq et al. 2018). The programme targets the collegial practices and experiences of staff within schools and districts. District advisors are trained by outside specialists, and then train schools' heads of department (HODs) who, in turn, are expected to work directly with teachers (similar to a cascade model of training). It developed and supplied mandatory curriculum planners and trackers that teachers of 1000 primary and secondary schools from these two districts have to follow to improve their curriculum coverage with the help, monitoring and support of their HODs. The FP teachers are also provided with SLPs for isiZulu and mathematics. Differently to the GPLMS, PILO puts a greater emphasis on the organizational capacity of school and district leadership personnel than on teachers to establish 'professional accountability'.

To understand fully the principles of improvement, which underpin these large-scale school-based systemic change programmes, we take a step back and, in the next section, review the relationship between demand and support, or what we call the theory of change that informs these programmes.

13.3   View of Change: Accountability and Support

Teacher support and improvement in South Africa and internationally has increasingly been seen through the lens of 'accountability'.

In the past 30 years, the literature on theories of change has debated how to calibrate, balance and align the two main change tools of support and accountability (Darling-Hammond 2004; Elmore 2005; McLaughlin 1987). The challenge is to establish the most effective combination and sequencing of support and accountability measures, by aligning the foci and forms of the TD programme to the needs of the targeted teachers, and to the way its impact is monitored.

Broadly, support for schools and teachers ranges from better curriculum material resources, means of improving schools' professional culture, improved working conditions and programmes to enhance teacher knowledge. A combination of these is provided within a framework of accountability. School accountability is the process of evaluating school performance on the basis of different performance measures, the learner performance measures being the most popular.

A complication arises, however, because there are different dominant forms of school accountability, each with slightly different scopes and goals.

'Bureaucratic accountability' – accounting to the line of authority – refers to following the policies, rules and procedures; it tends to emphasise day-to-day monitoring and compliance. 'Professional accountability' – accounting to the profession over the specialized knowledge and standards of practice of the profession – involves examining the appropriateness of professional judgements; it tends to emphasise discretion and personal judgement. Lastly, 'performance-based accountability' refers to accounting for results to the superior line of authority or to the public; in the case of successful performing schools, compliance is minimized, but in the case of poorly performing schools, prescriptiveness is enhanced. O'Day (2004) argues that the best accountability impact comes from a combination of bureaucratic and professional modes of regulation. The relation between accountability and support revolves also around the distinction in the literature between internal and external accountability. This distinction encapsulates the three forms of accountability mentioned above. 'External accountability' is about making schools or other educational institutions account to the department and the public for their performance, often measured in terms of learners' results. It encapsulates bureaucratic and performance-based measures of accountability. Important to our argument, however, is that, according to Elmore (2005), external accountability depends on the degree to which a school can achieve 'internal accountability'. By this, Elmore refers to "coherence in the organization around norms, values, expectations, and processes for getting the work done..." (Elmore 2006, p.7). According to Hargreaves and Shirley (in Fullan et al. 2015, p.4) internal (or professional) accountability is achieved when different educational agents at different levels of authority "willingly take on personal, professional and collective responsibility for continuous improvement and success for all students." The challenge in this view is that programmes which target schools with poor organizational capacity need to also develop 'reciprocal accountability' which Elmore (2005, p.297) defines as:

an explicit contractual agreement between system-level and school-level people that every unit of increased performance that the system demands carries with it an equal and reciprocal obligation on the part of the system to provide access to an additional unit of individual or organizational capacity, in the form of additional knowledge and skill.

In terms of our main concern in this chapter, this suggests that large-scale school-based systemic change programmes differ in terms of their focus (for example Taylor's distinction between "institutional vision and culture" and "deep knowledge structures embodied in instructional knowledge"), types of support, types of the accompanying accountability, and the relation between accountability and support. Tensions can emerge because different mixes foreground different kinds of scopes and goals.

For example, in the case of PILO, our research (De Clercq et al. 2018) shows that the curriculum planners and trackers help HODs to change the form in which they monitor teachers' work. The programme enables them to regulate teachers' work in a reciprocal manner. In that sense, PILO is slowly building professional collegial set of practices (signalling a shift to a mix between bureaucratic and professional accountability). But there are consequences to PILO's model of change – placing curriculum coverage at the centre of its institutional vision seems to have resulted in HODs and teachers focusing on the monitoring (accountability) of curriculum coverage and general reciprocity and much less on substantive improvements in teacher practice (let alone teacher knowledge).

The discussion so far allows us to offer a periodisation of TD in South Africa by focusing briefly on the relationship between accountability and support.

13.4   Periodisation of Teacher Development in South Africa

Pre-1994: Repressive bureaucratic regime In the apartheid era, teachers' work and status were shaped by racially segregated education departments known for their top down bureaucratic approach. In addition, the black (and in particular the coloured and African) departments adopted rather authoritarian and repressive structures to control their teachers. From the late 1970s onwards, as mass struggles against apartheid grew and spread to black schools, this teacher control intensified and became more oppressive even if it was resisted in many urban black schools where inspectors were no longer allowed to visit. Real meaningful pre- and in-service education for most black teachers was not on the agenda and contributed, inter alia, to severe inequality in the distribution of TD. By the late 1980s, there were only a few NGOs funded by foreign agencies that provided developmental support to usually urban black schools and their teachers (e.g. the Thousand Schools Project).

Post 1994: Accountability first Around the late 1990s, given the continuing poor culture of teaching and learning existing in many black schools, the national and provincial education departments started to assert their bureaucratic authority to stabilize, among other things, the school system. The Department of National Education (DNE) introduced unilaterally the 2000 Whole School Evaluation Policy which mandated a school self-evaluation exercise which was verified by provincial teams of school supervisors. Scholars argued then that, without restoring bureaucratic authority and accountability in many black schools, support would go to waste (Fleisch 2001; Taylor 2002). The dominant slogan was therefore accountability first.

2003–2009: Support first The Integrated Quality Management System (IQMS) policy was introduced in 2003. The unions had been complaining about the lack of departmental capacity to support appropriately teachers and agreed to sign the IQMS Education and Labour Relations Council policy agreement as long as no appraisal would be made without prior support. The IQMS concept of teacher development for performance appraisal appears to establish the sequence of support first and then accountability, supposedly introducing a form of reciprocal accountability within schools and between district officials and teachers. But, the focus of support was vague; in fact, the IQMS appraisal criteria did not even mention teachers' subject matter knowledge and little emphasis was given to teachers' pedagogical content knowledge. Worst of all, the IQMS became perceived by teachers mainly as a means to gaining the bonus attached to the performance appraisal rather than as a developmental exercise (Bisschoff and Mathye 2009).

Although support was foregrounded in public rhetoric and policy, the form of support provided, as we mentioned earlier, was fragmented, generic and ad hoc and it did not have much positive impact on teacher knowledge and performance. It could therefore be argued that, during this period, the form and focus of TD programmes did not redress much the knowledge gaps within the teacher labour-force.

2010 to now: Scripted lesson plans, coaching and professional regulation of teachers' learning A new trend has developed in South African education with the introduction of large-scale school-based systemic change programmes targeted at teachers from poorly performing schools (such as GPLMS, EGRS and PILO). As mentioned earlier, these programmes provide standardized lesson plans, teachers' and learners' material as well as teacher training or coaching to regulate a set of teaching practices and cover the curriculum within a framework of accountability and support. With research increasingly showing that the GPLMS and EGRS versions can lead to some improvement in learner performance (Fleisch and Schöer 2014; Fleisch 2016), these programmes appear to hold promise in reducing somewhat the inequalities in TD and in turn in learners' performance.

On the basis of our brief analysis of the trajectory of TD models in South African schools, we now turn to the identification of the aspects of an emerging theory of change, framed within a theory of teacher learning, which begin to be agreed upon and those which, we believe, are still in dispute.

13.5 Do We Now Have a New Theory of Change?

Arguably, the following five claims sum up what begins to be agreed upon in the international and national literature on TD and change. First, accountability for better results is more likely to work if it is framed within some form of 'reciprocal accountability' in terms of providing appropriate and differentiated teacher support.

Second, it is increasingly recognised that there are advantages in focusing TD on "deep knowledge structures embodied in instructional knowledge" (Taylor 2002, p.5). The term mostly used today is 'the instructional core' (Fleisch and Schöer 2014). In defining the knowledge involved in the instructional core, Elmore asserts that teachers need to know

> the ways in which to sequence, pace and assess the content they teach, the tasks which are appropriate for the content being taught, typical misunderstandings exhibited by learners of that content, and how to scaffold learners' learning up to the complexity of the task. (In City et al. (2009), p.29)

Third, TD programmes, which are subject-specific, classroom-anchored, systemic, sustained over time and with a focus on the instructional core are more promising than ad hoc workshops which are generic in focus: "Direct, sustained, classroom-anchored training is the only means for beginning to disrupt the grammar of schooling" (Jansen 2002, p.4).

Fourth, meaningful learning opportunities for teachers are essential all the way through the process of change (Shalem 2003). But, as has been argued in the last two decades, these are labour intensive, expensive (Elmore and Burney 1997), and require time (Hargreaves 2002).

Fifth, interventions which target poorly performing schools cannot succeed without substantial investment in appropriate reciprocal accountability (De Clercq 2008; Elmore 2005).

These five claims are likely to lead to some reduction in the disparities in teacher and learner performance in South Africa, although we want to argue that they will not necessarily reduce gaps in teacher knowledge (see below). But, what is not yet agreed upon in the international and national literature on TD and change?

First, there is a disagreement about the issue of scale. While advocates of RCTs (Hutchison and Styles 2010) argue that a well-designed sophisticated RCT can assist with generalizability, qualitative researchers, such as Fullan, argue that going to scale is not obvious:

> The pilots are not typically replicable for one or more of the following reasons: the first users are more motivated; there are not enough resources; solutions in each new situation are not exactly the same; the program loses momentum as key sponsors move on, or new ideas come along. (Fullan 2016, p.549)

Second, what is the kind of professional learning which supports teachers in the process of acquiring 'deep knowledge structures embodied in instructional knowledge' or 'the instructional core?' Elmore (2016, p.532) asks for a shift of mindset. Instead of "basing new learning designs on received ideas that are feasible. . . in existing institutions," he says we need to be basing "learning designs on the theory and science of how humans learn." On this view, how teachers learn is a key element of the answer to the question: which model of change works better?

Research about teacher learning is divided. Guskey (1986) argues that, it is teachers' behaviours and practices rather than their cognitive beliefs that need to be changed first, as learning by doing will eventually change teachers' beliefs. This means engaging teachers in their context, with activities and teaching material which are required for their practice (Bertram 2011).

A different view, which valorizes the practical application of teacher knowledge and experimentation, is held by Winch (2010) who argues that teachers need to know facts and concepts central to the subject matter they teach as well as the conceptual structure and the way ideas have been developed by experts who researched that specific subject matter. Understanding the conceptual structure of the subject matter refers to the depth of knowledge teachers are expected to have about what they teach. This, which is referred to as the discipline knowledge or propositional knowledge, is very different to the situated mode of learning advocated by Guskey (see also Shalem 2018; Shalem et al. 2016) and requires a very different TD programme.[2]

Third, can the learning of the instructional core be mandated from above or is it necessary to establish first: some form of professional accountability, buy-in from stakeholders (including teachers' unions) and engagement of teachers to reflect on their practice and how to improve it? The GPLMS (and EGRS interventions) and PILO propose two radically different responses to this question. The GPLMS limits its intervention to changing teachers' practice without engaging the school culture and the school accountability system, something that may undermine the sustainability of the change process (De Clercq et al. 2018). PILO, in contrast, does not appear to target sufficiently deeply the change in teachers' practice and knowledge. It seems to believe that professional accountability will eventually generate appropriate internal support to sustain a change and improvement in teachers' practice and knowledge (Ibid). Thus, one could argue that the GPLMS and PILO conceptualize SLPs and curriculum planners and trackers as the main tools of support and accountability even though they understand the key change mechanisms rather differently.

Fourth, do prescriptive lesson plans result in teachers' deskilling and the constraining of teacher professional autonomy? Some scholars argue that SLPs render teachers simple transmitters (Beatty 2011; Bryk 2009; Janks 2014; Msibi and Mchunu 2013). Our research (Shalem et al. 2018) shows that following lesson plans does not translate into sheer compliance. We found that the SLPs were leaving room for teachers to be creative, by, for example, combining two different lessons and finding other ways not prescribed by the lesson plan to reinforce learning.

---

[2]In this regard, "Wits Maths Connect Secondary Project", a small-scale teacher development project, is a relevant example. In this programme teachers undergo professional development courses (in Transition Maths) which explicitly aim to improve teachers' mathematical knowledge (75% of the course content) and teaching expertise (25% of the course content), and ultimately improve learner performance (Pournara et al. 2015, p. 3).

We concur with the main findings reported by some proponents of SLPs (Hiebert 2017; Hiebert and Morris 2012) that, by providing guidelines about the curriculum knowledge to teach, by complementing the national curriculum with the sequence and pace of what is taught, and by providing a new repertoire of teaching routines, SLPs that are mediated and monitored by coaches guide teachers' learning of what is important in the curriculum (Fleisch 2016). We also agree that, by following pre-annotated teaching routines, teachers could learn the routines in the context of "the surrounding feature of the lesson" rather than as a technique in isolation. Eventually, by testing the routines in their own context, teachers would learn to generalise; they will "induce that the routine is a more general skill that might play a useful role in lessons not yet taught" (Hiebert and Morris 2012, p.96).

However, the SLPs currently used in South Africa do not fully spell out the aims and key concepts of the lessons, the rules that need to be foregrounded and the pedagogical reasoning behind a teaching activity. They do not clarify how teachers could respond to learners who take them beyond the protocol of the prescribed lesson plan. In that sense, the SLPs do not act sufficiently as 'an authority' (a-la R.S. Peters) on key educational preferences embedded in them and this has negative consequences for learners' learning. Two examples of our research are worth nothing here:

- Teachers reinforced incorrect rules. A teacher told the class that in English you use "a" when referring to "countable" nouns and "the" when referring to "uncountable" nouns. When learners wrote "the" in front of pineapples and "a" in front of juice, the teacher accepted these answers with praise ("you were really listening"). Only at a later point did she realise the answers were incorrect within the framework she had created. Her response was to emphatically repeat the (incorrect) rule: "If you can count the item, you use 'a'; if you cannot count it, you use 'the'".

- Teachers did not seem to understand phonics as a mnemonic tool, which assists with decoding words or non-words and to read new words in future. They assigned a sound to a letter and retained this sound, regardless of whether it was the sound represented in the word. For these teachers, phonics functioned as a second alphabet rather than as a sound system. They mentioned that phonics "is a way to learn how to sound out and then spell these sounds and new words" and "this is how learners learn to read and write".

What these examples tell us is that for teachers to gain the full benefit of the systematic organisation of subject content knowledge in curriculum material such as SLPs, they need to have prior knowledge of the conceptual relations between parts and the whole of the content inscribed in the new prescribed practices they are expected to teach. We argue that the reduction in the inequalities in South African teacher development requires us to confront and resolve conceptually and empirically these four points of disagreements.

13.6 Potential of Scripted Lesson Plans for South African Schools

The question we want to end with is: what learning opportunities does the following of a lesson plan offer to teachers? Can SLPs, mediated by coaches, address the gap in teacher knowledge?

This is an important question in view of research in South Africa that consistently shows that gaps in teacher knowledge have a major influence on the teaching and learning in underperforming schools (Hoadley 2012; Taylor and Taylor 2013; Centre for Development and Enterprise 2014; Taylor N in this book). We suggest that, in thinking about this, it is important to distinguish between two clusters of teaching routines which together form 'the instructional core": (1) ways of organising one's teaching over time and (2) pedagogical means of helping learners to understand the meanings, rules and procedures of the subject matter.

The first cluster is knowledge of sequencing and pacing the content required to be covered, using a coherent lesson structure, establishing routines of work, selecting learning material for teaching and designing learning and assessment activities that are focussed on how to order and structure one's teaching. This cluster can be pre-specified for teachers through a standardized curriculum and with more detail through textbooks and lesson plans. The second cluster is a far more specialised knowledge about the manner in which a teacher enables learners to learn. We argue that this cluster requires formal learning and an expanded form of curriculum material. Organising systematic learning, scaffolding the complexity of subject for learners, making explicit the formal properties of a topic matter and knowing and working with learners' misunderstandings cannot be made explicit by lesson plans; it depends on teachers' knowledge of the content they are teaching as school subject specialists. This is demonstrated unequivocally in a study on teacher knowledge and lesson enactment (Charalambous and Hill 2012).

For a teacher to organise systematic learning (Morrow 2007), the conceptual relations between ideas in the lesson need to be understood. Overarching concepts regulate existing forms of understanding and transform them into new possible forms; they represent ideas and transcend their meaning in time and space. In Young and Muller's (2013) terms, they provide 'powerful knowledge'. If the knowledge the teacher transmits is insufficiently developed, it loses its regulatory function (Shalem and Slonimsky 2010). It remains common-sense. Powerful knowledge does not develop by following a book which tells the teacher what to do but from a deep understanding of bodies of knowledge and how they are delineated within the practice the teacher is intending to teach (see Morrow's piloting example in Shalem and Slonimsky 2010, p.21)

Recognising the two different clusters of knowledge of the instructional core is important. It foregrounds the reliance of teachers' 'know how' on powerful knowledge, which professionals use to make decisions in situations, and which, at any point in time, could in principle be justified by reference to a chain of reasoning that goes beyond the specific context. This means that, if it is accepted that because "the possession of relevant systematically organized knowledge is not a by-product of the action, but a prerequisite" (Winch 2010, p.104), one would expect that a TD programme will foreground mastery of central concepts within the subject.

Our research raises questions as to whether the new trend towards large-scale, school-based systemic change programmes targeted at the most disadvantaged teachers can contribute to redress the inequality distribution of meaningful learning opportunities for teachers. We want to argue that it can but in a somewhat limited manner. We suggest a possible irony: teachers who understand the conceptual structure and the way ideas have been developed in their subject area of specialisation, all things being equal, are likely to benefit from having SLPs, mediated and monitored by coaches, more than those whose knowledge is weak. Teachers whose knowledge is weak would struggle to access the rules that underlie the steps and activities prescribed by the lesson or to unravel the conceptual point of the lesson. They will struggle to control the occurrences which arise in practice and which are hard to predict but which need to be controlled.

This brings us to our last point. The large-scale model of TD emerging for the most disadvantaged teachers in the last decade or so points to the value of expanded lesson plans offered together with systematic, high quality in-service training to improve teacher knowledge. The lesson plans could be used as referral points for such knowledge training. Variants of such combination of support which also focus on the knowledge structures embodied in instructional knowledge are likely to assist in reducing the inequalities in teacher development.

The literature on SLPs draws a distinction between two different types: 'Scripted Instruction', known also as Direct Instruction (DI), and 'Educative Curriculum Material' (ECM). A lesson plan designed as DI contains statements which include examples, prompts and correct and incorrect inferences built for teachers in a logical sequence; these statements allow for only one correct answer from the learners. By scripting in detail what teachers (and learners) say and do, proponents of DI (Engelmann 2005) do not intend to teach teacher knowledge but to minimise ambiguous communication on the part of teachers. ECM refers to scripted lessons which are produced by teachers, an important point to acknowledge. It is envisioned that a case-by-case lesson plan design process, which culminates in archived instructional products (artefacts), will be available for public use and revision (Morris and Hiebert 2011, p.9). These types of SLPs include steps, activities and teaching routines to be followed, as well as the underlying reasons and rationale for the lesson's content and pedagogy, the explanation of the ideas underlying the tasks and the background information of key concepts (Davis and Krajcik 2005; Remillard 2005). Most importantly, rather than merely guiding what the teachers need to do, ECMs aim to "speak to teachers about the ideas underlying the tasks" (Davis and Krajcik 2005, p.5).

But, here is the crux: the success of developing ECMs relies on knowledgeable and confident teachers who understand the concepts which underlie the routines and activities of annotated lessons, know how to experiment with lesson plans, and can advise on what needs to change as well as affect the actual changes to such plans.

13.7 Conclusion

Given the poor impact of most previous TD activities on improving teaching and learning, which continued to widen the TD equality distribution, it appears as if, since 2010, engineering a regime of preferred teaching practices and scripting it to teachers has begun to achieve some legitimacy in improving learner performance in some disadvantaged schools. It is also true, we would argue, that South Africa has gone a long way in developing a better understanding of meaningful learning opportunities for the most disadvantaged teachers and in balancing these with internal accountability.

Educational and material resources, research insights and large-scale investments have enabled a good start in the development of teachers from poorly performing schools. We have better knowledge of the teaching focus and the organisational structure of TD. Some independent research indicating better learners' results in poorly performing schools is undertaken to test what components of these system-wide interventions work best (Fleisch 2016). In that sense, some reduction in the gaps in teacher and learner performance is likely to occur.

What is still missing is a robust debate backed by research on how to reduce gaps in teacher knowledge through appropriate and differentiated TD. Such research should examine what counts as quality lesson plans, how to expand and deepen teacher knowledge of at least the complex subject matter covered by the SLPs (such as phonics or graded group reading, for example), how teachers should use lesson plans, and how they should gradually grow their independence from them. Given the centrality of scripting in this model of change, until we develop a deeper knowledge of these questions about SLPs, we would not have sufficient understanding of the desired equation in the emerging theory of change in South Africa: for every unit of change performance required, an equivalent unit of appropriate support and capacity building is to be provided. With this new understanding, we will be able to answer with real confidence the equality distribution question, of providing teachers, particularly of poor performing schools, with access to meaningful learning opportunities.

References

Barasa, F., & Mattson, E. (1998). The roles, regulation, and professional development of educators in South Africa: A critical analysis of four policy documents. *Journal of Education, 23*(1), 41–72.

Beatty, B. (2011). The dilemma of scripted instruction: Comparing teacher autonomy, fidelity, and resistance in the froebelian kindergarten, montessori, direct instruction, and success for all. *Teachers College Record, 113*(3), 395–430.

Bertram, C. (2011). What does research say about teacher learning and teacher knowledge? Implications for professional development in South Africa. *Journal of Education, 52*, 5–26.

Bett, H. K. (2016). The cascade model of teachers' continuing professional development in Kenya: A time for change? *Cogent Education, 3*(1), 1139439. https://doi.org/10.1080/2331186X.2016.1139439

Bisschoff, T., & Mathye, A. (2009). The advocacy of an appraisal system for teachers: A case study. *South African Journal of Education, 29*(3), 393–404.

Bryk, A. S. (2009). Support a science of performance improvement. *Phi Delta Kappan, 90*(8), 597–600.

Centre for Development and Enterprise. (2014). *What does research tell us about teachers, teaching and learner performance in mathematics.* Johannesburg: Centre for Development and Enterprise.

Charalambous, C. Y., & Hill, H. C. (2012). Teacher knowledge, curriculum materials, and quality of instruction: Unpacking a complex relationship. *Journal of Curriculum Studies, 44*(4), 443–466. https://doi.org/10.1080/00220272.2011.650215

City, E. A., Elmore, R. F., Fiarman, S. E., & Teitel, L. (2009). Instructional rounds in education: A network approach to improving teaching and learning. Boston: Havard Education Press.

Cohen, D. K., & Ball, D. L. (1999). *Instruction, capacity, and improvement.* CPRE Research Report Series RR-43.

Council on Higher Education. (2010). *Report on the national review of academic and professional programmes in education.* Pretoria CHE.

Darling-Hammond, L. (1995). Changing conceptions of teaching and teacher development. *Teacher Education Quarterly, 22*, 9–26.

Darling-Hammond, L. (2004). Inequality and the right to learn: Access to qualified teachers in California's public schools. *Teachers College Record, 106*(10), 1936–1966.

Davis, E. A., & Krajcik, J. S. (2005). Designing educative curriculum materials to promote teacher learning. *Educational Researcher, 34*(3), 3–14.

De Clercq, F. (2008). Teacher quality, appraisal and development: The flaws in the IQMS. *Perspectives in Education, 26*(1), 7–18.

De Clercq, F., & Shalem, Y. (2014). Teacher knowledge and employer-driven professional development: A critical analysis of the Gauteng Department of Education programmes. *Southern African Review of Education with Education with Production, 20*(1), 129–147.

De Clercq, F., Shalem, Y., & Nkambule, T. (2018). Teachers' and HODs' accountability on curriculum coverage: Pilo's contribution to the theory of change. In P. Christie & M. Monyokolo (Eds.), *Learning about sustainable change in education: Jika iMfundo 2013–2017.* Johannesburg: SAIDE.

Department of Basic Education. (2009). *Report of the task team for the review of the implementation of the national curriculum statement.* Statement by Minister of Basic Education on Curriculum Review Final Report Pretoria: Government Printers.

Department of Basic Education and Department of Higher Education and Training. (2011). *Integrated strategic planning framework for teacher education and development in South Africa: 2011–2025.* Pretoria.

Department of Education (DoE). (2007). *The national policy framework for teacher education and development in South Africa.* Government Gazette No. 29832, 26 April. Pretoria: DoE.

Elmore, R. (2005). Agency, reciprocity, and accountability in democratic education. In S. Fuhrman & M. Lazerson (Eds.), *The institutions of American democracy: The public schools* (pp. 277–301). Oxford: Oxford University Press.

Elmore, R. (2006). *Leadership as the practice of improvement, international conference on school leadership for systemic improvement, OECD activity on improving school leadership.* Prepared for the International Conference on Perspectives on Leadership for Systemic Improvement, sponsored by the Organization for Economic Cooperation and Development (OECD), July 6, London.

Elmore, R. F. (2016). "Getting to scale…" it seemed like a good idea at the time. *Journal of Educational Change, 17*(4), 529–537. https://doi.org/10.1007/s10833-016-9290-8

Elmore, R. F., & Burney, D. (1997). *Investing in teacher learning: Staff development and instructional improvement in Community School District# 2, New York City.* New York: National Commission on Teaching and America's Future and the Consortium for Policy Research in Education.

Engelmann, S. (2005). *Improving reading rate of low performers*. Retrieved from www.zigsite. com/PDFs/readingratefinal.pdf.

Fleisch, B. (2001). *Draft research report on the education action zones*. GDE. Commissioned by the Joint Education Trust, Braamfontein.

Fleisch, B. (2016). System-wide improvement at the instructional core: Changing reading teaching in South Africa. *Journal of Educational Change, 17*(4), 437–451.

Fleisch, B., & Dixon, K. (2017). *Identifying generative mechanisms from qualitative study of the early grade reading study in South Africa*. Paper Presented at the UKFIET Conference, Oxford, 4–7 Sept 2017.

Fleisch, B., & Schöer, V. (2014). Large-scale instructional reform in the global South: Insights from the mid-point evaluation of the Gauteng primary language and mathematics strategy. *South African Journal of Education, 34*(3), 1–12.

Fullan, M. (2016). The elusive nature of whole system improvement in education. *Journal of Educational Change, 17*(4), 539–544. https://doi.org/10.1007/s10833-016-9289-1

Fullan, M., Rincón-Gallardo, S., & Hargreaves, A. (2015). Professional capital as accountability. *Education Policy Analysis Archives, 23*(15). Retrieved from http://dx.doi.org/10.14507/epaa. v23.1998

Guskey, T. R. (1986). Staff development and the process of teacher change. *Educational Researcher, 15*(5), 5–12.

Hargreaves, A. (2002). Sustainability of educational change: The role of social geographies. *Journal of Educational Change, 3*(3–4), 189–214.

Hiebert, J. (2017). *The unfortunate reputation of scripted instruction*. Teachers College Record.

Hiebert, J., & Morris, A. K. (2012). Teaching, rather than teachers, as a path toward improving classroom instruction. *Journal of Teacher Education, 63*(2), 92–102. https://doi.org/10.1177/0022487111428328

Hoadley, U. (2012). What do we know about teaching and learning in South African primary schools? *Education as Change, 16*(2), 187–202. https://doi.org/10.1080/16823206.2012. 745725

Hoadley, U. (2018). *Pedagogy in poverty: Lessons from twenty years of curriculum reform in South Africa*. Abingdon/New York: Routledge.

Hutchison, D., & Styles, B. (2010). *A guide to running randomised controlled trials for educational researchers*. Slough: NFER.

Janks, H. (2014). Globalisation, diversity, and education: A South African perspective. *The Educational Forum, 78*(1), 8–25.

Jansen, J. (2002). On the relationship between accountability and support. Paper presented to the National Consultation on School Development. Department of Education, 29 Jan 2002.

Jansen, J. D., & Christie, P. (1999). *Changing curriculum: Studies on outcomes-based education in South Africa*. Johannesburg: Heinemann.

Mahomed, H. (2017). Progress and challenges with the implementation of the ISPFTED in South Africa 2011–2025. Challenges-implementation-integrated-strategic-planning-framework-teacher-education-development-South-Africa-2011–2025-ISPFTED. Retrieved from http://www.bridge.org.za/knowledgehub/progress

McLaughlin, M. W. (1987). Learning from experience: Lessons from policy implementation. *Educational Evaluation and Policy Analysis, 9*(2), 171–178.

Morris, A. K., & Hiebert, J. (2011). Creating shared instructional products: An alternative approach to improving teaching. *Educational Researcher, 40*(1), 5–14. https://doi.org/10.3102/0013189X10393501

Morrow, W. (2007). *Learning to teach in South Africa*. Cape Town: HSRC.

Msibi, T., & Mchunu, S. (2013). The knot of curriculum and teacher professionalism in post-apartheid South Africa. *Education as Change, 17*(1), 19–35. https://doi.org/10.1080/16823206. 2013.773924

NEEDU. (2013). *National report 2012: The state of literacy teaching and learning in the foundation phase*. Pretoria: National Education Evaluation and Development Unit.

O'Day, J. (2004). Complexity, accountability and school improvement. In S. Furhman & R. Elmore (Eds.), *Redesigning accountability systems for education*. New York: Teachers College Press.

Pournara, C., Hodgen, J., Adler, J., & Pillay, V. (2015). Can improving teachers' knowledge of mathematics lead to gains in learners' attainment in mathematics? *South African Journal of Education, 35*(3), 1–10. https://doi.org/10.15700/saje.v35n3a1083

Remillard, J. T. (2005). Examining key concepts in research on teachers' use of mathematics curricula. *Review of Educational Research, 75*(2), 211–246.

Shalem, Y. (2003). Do we have a theory of change? Calling change models to account. *Perspectives in Education: Assessment of Change in Education: Special Issue, 21*(1), 29–49.

Shalem, Y. (2018). Scripted lesson plans – What is visible and invisible in visible pedagogy? In B. Barrett, U. Hoadley, & J. Morgan (Eds.), *Knowledge, curriculum and equity: Social realist perspectives*. London: Routledge.

Shalem, Y., & Hoadley, U. (2009). The dual economy of schooling and teacher morale in South Africa. *International Studies in Sociology of Education, 19*(2), 119–134.

Shalem, Y., & Slonimsky, L. (2010). The concept of teaching. In Y. Shalem & S. Pendelbury (Eds.), *Retrieving teaching: Critical issues in curriculum, pedagogy and learning*. Cape Town: Juta and Company Ltd.

Shalem, Y., Steinberg, C., Koornhof, H., & De Clercq, F. (2016). The what and how in scripted lesson plans: The case of the Gauteng primary language and mathematics strategy. *Journal of Education, 66*, 1–24.

Shalem, Y., De Clercq, F., Steinberg, C., & Koornhof, H. (2018). Teacher autonomy in times of standardised lesson plans: The case of a primary school language and mathematics intervention in South Africa. *Journal of Educational Change, 19*(2), 205–222.

Steinberg, C., & Slonimsky, L. (2004). Pedagogical responsiveness to learning. Students confronting an unfamiliar text-based reality. In H. Griesel (Ed.), *Curriculum responsiveness: Case studies in higher education*. Pretoria: South African Universities Vice- Chancellors Association.

Taylor, N. (2002). Accountability and support: Improving public schooling in South Africa: A systemic framework. Paper presented to the National Consultation on School Development Department of Education, 29 Jan 2002.

Taylor, N., & Taylor, S. (2013). Teacher knowledge and professional habitus. In N. Taylor, S. Van Der Berg, & T. Mabogoane (Eds.), *Creating effective schools*. Cape Town: Pearson.

Taylor, N., & Vinjevold, P. (1999). *Getting learning right: Report of the President's Education Initiative Research Project*. Joint Education Trust.

Van der Berg, S., Burger, C., Burger, R., & de Vos, M., du Rand, G., Gustafsson, M., Moses, E., Shepherd, D. L., Spaull, N., Taylor, S., van Broekhuizen, H., & van Fintel, D. (2011). *Low quality education as a poverty trap*. Stellenbosch: University of Stellenbosch, Department of Economics. Research report for the PSPPD project for Presidency.

Winch, C. (2010). *Dimensions of expertise: A conceptual exploration of vocational knowledge*. New York: Continuum International Pub. Group.

Young, M., & Muller, J. (2013). On the powers of powerful knowledge. *Review of Education, 1*(3), 229–250. https://doi.org/10.1002/rev3.3017

Chapter 14
Inequalities in Teacher Knowledge in South Africa

Nick Taylor

14.1 Knowledge and Teaching

Teaching is a complex occupation which requires teachers to understand and operationalize knowledge of a number of different types. These include knowledge of the subject(s) they are responsible for (disciplinary knowledge), theoretical and research findings concerning the nature of the subject and methods of teaching it (pedagogical content knowledge or subject knowledge for teaching), understanding how the different curricular topics and subjects fit together and how they relate to each other at successive Grade levels (curriculum knowledge) (Shulman 1986). In addition they need to blend these knowledge components into a coherent sequence of classroom activities over a sustained period in order to convey the subject to learners (pedagogical competence) (Taylor 2014).

This chapter commences with the argument that disciplinary knowledge, while it may be insufficient on its own to support excellent teaching, is the foundation on which all other types of knowledge needed for effective pedagogy rest. We then proceed to describe the weak disciplinary knowledge resources held by the majority of South African teachers, the sources of this deficient knowledge base and, most important from the perspective of the current chapter, the inequitable distribution of disciplinary knowledge. The chapter ends with a set of recommendations for addressing the inequitable and generally inadequate distribution of disciplinary knowledge among teachers, the central school-level factor contributing to the inequitable distribution of learning outcomes produced by the country's schools.

N. Taylor (✉)
JET Education Services, Parktown, Johannesburg, South Africa
e-mail: ntaylor@jet.org.za

© Springer Nature Switzerland AG 2019
N. Spaull, J. D. Jansen (eds.), *South African Schooling: The Enigma of Inequality*, Policy Implications of Research in Education 10,
https://doi.org/10.1007/978-3-030-18811-5_14

14.2   The Centrality of Disciplinary Knowledge

Significant progress has been made in delineating the features of the second of the knowledge components listed above, pedagogical content knowledge (PCK), in the field of mathematics education. Particularly illuminating in this regard are the examples of what is called mathematical knowledge for teaching (MKT) provided by Heather Hill and her colleagues (Hill et al. 2008). Figure 14.1 shows one such item designed to measure teachers' MKT.

According to Hill et al. (2008), to respond to this situation teachers must draw on mathematical knowledge, including making sense of the steps shown in each example, then gauging whether the steps might make sense and work for all whole numbers. Taylor and Taylor (2013) argue that a complete answer to the question posed in Fig. 14.1 depends on an understanding that the three algorithms shown are based on three variations of the distributive law, respectively derived from different ways of decomposing 35 and 25. Only by invoking the mathematical principles underlying the notion of place value and the operations of addition and multiplication can a fully satisfactory explanation for the equivalence of options A-C be constructed. It follows from this discussion that MKT (at least in this particular example) depends on understanding the concepts of the discipline of mathematics (decomposition, distribution and generalization), and the forms of representation of mathematical entities and operations. These entities, transformations and representations constitute the disciplinary spine of the school mathematics curriculum, and without disciplinary proficiency no student can offer a complete explanation for the answer to the question posed in Fig. 14.1.

In the field of English education the debate concerning the relationship between PCK and disciplinary knowledge has not received the same degree of academic attention, perhaps because the dependence of the latter on the former is self-evident. For example, a PCK item to assess any teacher's proficiency in teaching English First Additional Language (EFAL) in the Intermediate Phase (Grades 4–6) might look like Fig. 14.2.

Fig. 14.1 Item designed to measure MKT. (Source: Constructed from Hill et al. 2004, p. 28)

```
1. Which of these three methods will
   work for multiplying ANY two whole
   numbers? Explain why.

A.     35        B.    35        C.     35
      x 25             x 25             x 25
       125             175              25
     +750             +700             100
      875              875             150
                                      +600
                                       875
```

The following is a passage from Nelson Mandela's *Long Walk to Freedom*
Passage quoted here
1. Construct a comprehension exercise for a Grade 4-6 EFAL class exercise.
2. Items in the exercise should cover all four PIRLS Benchmarks (or levels of Bloom's taxonomy): literal comprehension, making straightforward inferences, providing text-based support for inferences, and analysing cross-textural features.
3. Total marks for the exercise should be 20.
4. Marks should be accorded as follows: Literal understanding: 4 Straightforward inference: 6 Provide support from the text for answers: 6 Analysis: place text in its historical or geographical framework: 4
5. Construct a short marking memorandum for this exercise to share with other Grade 4-6 teachers of EFAL.

Fig. 14.2 Item to assess teachers' PCK for EFAL

The ability of any teacher to provide a test and memo which meet these specifications will depend, in the first instance, on the extent to which she herself is mistress of the four categories of cognitive tasks listed in Part 4 of the exercise which, according to the Progress in Reading Literacy (PIRLS) test frameworks (Mullis and Martin 2015), comprise reading literacy at the Grade 4 level (see Table 14.3 for details). While PCK remains a fledgling field of study in all disciplines, the examples shown in Figs. 14.1 and 14.2 illustrate the point that strong disciplinary knowledge is a prerequisite for developing proficiency in pedagogical content knowledge, which is about strategies required to bring learners to an understanding of the concepts and procedures comprising the discipline.

14.3 What Is the State of Disciplinary Knowledge of South African Teachers?

Descriptions of the generally poor state of disciplinary knowledge held by many primary school teachers in South Africa has featured in the research literature for some time. Thus, after reviewing the 35 classroom focused research projects commissioned by the President's Education Initiative (PEI) in 1998, Taylor and Vinjevold (1999, p.147) commented as follows:

> One of the most consistent findings of a number of PEI projects pointed to teachers' low levels of conceptual knowledge, their poor grasp of their subjects and the range of errors made in the content and concepts presented in their lessons.

Research of the kind undertaken by the PEI has, on its own, been criticised for its unrepresentative nature. However, more than a dozen years and many more studies of this type later (see for example Schollar 2004; Ensor et al. 2009), Hoadley commented on the convergence of findings of these small-scale research initiatives in identifying the features of classroom practice which appear to affect student learning: low levels of cognitive demand of the material presented; the predominance of concrete over abstract meanings; the dominance of oral discourse accompanied by a lack of opportunities for reading and writing; slow pacing;

collectivised (as opposed to individualised) learning, characterised by repetitive, whole-class chorusing; a lack of explicit feedback by teachers to learner knowledge displays; and poor command of English (the medium of instruction) by learners and teachers alike (Hoadley 2012, p. 197).

The conclusions of these descriptive studies regarding teacher disciplinary knowledge were unambiguously confirmed by the results of teacher tests conducted during the third iteration of the Southern African Consortium for Monitoring Educational Quality (SACMEQ) in 2007.

14.3.1 Mathematics

The mathematics tests written by SACMEQ teachers in 2007 consisted of 42 multiple choice items. Sixteen of the items were taken from the Third International Mathematics and Science Study (TIMSS) administered to Grade 8 learners in more than 40 countries in 1995. Results on the common test items enabled comparisons to be made between the mathematics knowledge of SACMEQ teachers and that of Grade 8 students in TIMSS countries. Making this comparison, Spaull (2012) found that the average Grade 6 mathematics teacher in South Africa, Lesotho and Mozambique has the same level of mathematics knowledge on these 16 items as the average Grade 8 student in the Netherlands, Switzerland and Canada, but knows considerably less than the average Grade 8 student in Hong Kong, Korea or Singapore.

Venkat and Spaull (2015) classified the 42 items in the SACMEQ mathematics test into Grade-level bands according to specifications in the South African curriculum: 9 could be matched to the Grade 4 or 5 curriculum statements, 19 to Grade 6 or 7, and 14 to Grade 8 or 9. Of course, such small numbers of items in each Grade band are insufficient to provide a psychometrically defensible picture of teacher knowledge at the respective levels. But they do give a broad indication of how teachers are performing in relation to the school curriculum. Using the benchmark of 60% or higher to indicate mastery of the items in any of these bands, Venkat and Spaull (2015) found that 79% of South African Grade 6 mathematics teachers were classified as having content knowledge levels below Grade 6, the level at which they are teaching. In detail they concluded that:

- 17% of Grade 6 students in South Africa were taught by maths teachers who had content knowledge below a Grade 4 or 5 level,
- 62% were taught by teachers with a Grade 4 or 5 level of content knowledge,
- 5% were taught by teachers with a Grade 6 or 7 level of content knowledge, and
- 16% were taught by teachers with at least a Grade 8 or 9 level of content knowledge.

Even in schools serving the most affluent 20% of the population (Q5) the performance of South African Grade 6 mathematics teachers gives great cause for concern. The Conference Board of the Mathematical Sciences (2012) recommends that, in order to be adequately equipped to teach mathematics, teachers should exhibit mastery at some Grade levels beyond the level at which they are teaching. Only 45% of South African Q5 teachers tested scored at least 60% on the Grade 8/9 items in the test, and are thus adequately equipped to teach Grade 6, according to this yardstick. Only 5% exhibit mastery at the Grade 6/7 level, with 45% of teachers in South Africa's wealthiest schools at Grade 4/5 level and 5% below Grade 4/5. In other words, even in schools serving the wealthiest communities, the majority of South African Grade 6 teachers are inadequately prepared to convey mathematics subject matter to their classes.

In order to understand the precise nature of these knowledge shortcomings, Taylor and Taylor (2013) classified the 42 items in the SACMEQ mathematics test for teachers into five strands: arithmetic operations; fractions, ratio and proportion; algebraic logic; rate of change; and space and shape. Item 6 (Fig. 14.3) is an example of the first of these, arithmetic operations, a good grasp of which at the Grade 6 level is essential for any further progress in the discipline.

The question requires a simple application of the '*BODMAS*'[1] rule, which dictates the order in which to perform operations in a problem requiring more than one operation. Just over half (54%) of the South African teachers who wrote the test were able to apply the rule correctly. The first distractor for this multiple choice item is obtained by ignoring the rule and performing the operations from left to right, a procedure followed by 37% of teachers, clearly indicating a good proportion of teachers are ignorant of the application of this fundamental arithmetic property.

The mathematics test contains 10 items involving fractions, ratio and proportion, a solid understanding of which underlies much of the mathematics at high school level and beyond, including algebra, graphs, calculus, trigonometry, probability and statistics and the geometry of similarity (Fig. 14.6). South African teachers did not fare well at all on these items: on only 4 of the 10 questions falling into this strand did at least 70% of teachers select the right responses. Only 40% were able to answer item 35 correctly, a question which draws on the definition of a simple 3-part ratio involving single-digit whole numbers.

The strand of mathematical activity commonly referred to as space and shape is concerned with spatial perception and the measurement of various entities,

6. $10 \times 2 + (6-4) \div 2 =$

Fig. 14.3 Example of item requiring knowledge of arithmetic operations

---

[1]BODMAS is a mnemonic for remembering: Brackets, Of, Division, Multiplication, Addition, Subtraction.

including angles, areas and volumes. At high school level this strand evolves into investigations in deductive logic, transformation geometry (the manipulation of shapes) and trigonometry. Item 27 (Fig. 14.4) provides an example of this type of problem.

In contrast to an average of 44% of teachers from the 12 SACMEQ countries who got the correct answer (option C), only 31% of South African teachers were successful. Nearly half of the South African teachers (45%) chose option B, which is the area of each of the 5 smaller squares in the diagram, the identification of which is a prerequisite step to calculating the final answer.

Overall, the performance of South African teachers mirrored that of their other SACMEQ counterparts, in scoring best on problems involving arithmetic operations and worst on those requiring rate of change logic (Table 14.1). However, on every category, South African teachers performed below the SACMEQ average.

The state of disciplinary knowledge in mathematics of high school teachers in South Africa has received far less attention than that of teachers in primary schools. However, there are indications that teachers in high schools are also very poorly prepared. Thus, the responses of a sample of 253 Grade 12 teachers to items taken from the National Senior Certificate examination paper were analysed by Bansilal (2015), who found that teacher scores were located close to the means exhibited by Grade 12 learners. Furthermore, the levels of almost one-third of the teachers were below that of all the Level 3 (complex procedures) and Level 4 (problem solving) items in the test.

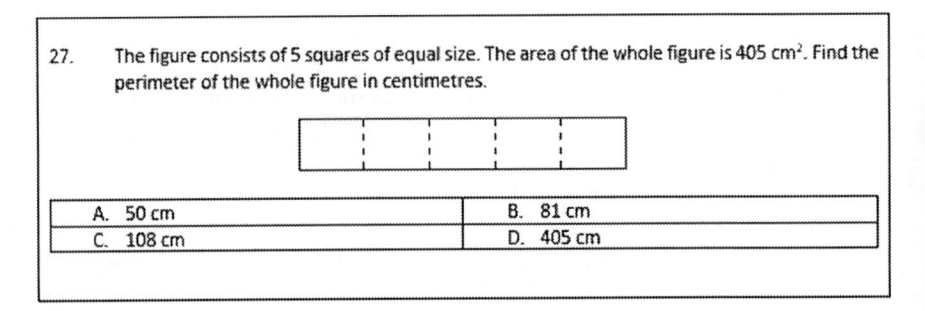

27. The figure consists of 5 squares of equal size. The area of the whole figure is 405 cm². Find the perimeter of the whole figure in centimetres.

| A. 50 cm | B. 81 cm |
| C. 108 cm | D. 405 cm |

Fig. 14.4 Example of a space and shape problem

Table 14.1 Teacher percentage scores on the SACMEQ maths test

		Arithmetic operations	Fractions, ratio and proportion	Algebraic logic	Rate of change	Space and shape	Total
No. of items		8	10	9	7	8	42
Mean score (%)	SACMEQ	69.55	57.65	48.75	44.47	66.33	57.47
	SA	67.15	49.68	46.51	42.30	56.44	52.39

14.3.2 English Reading Comprehension

While the poor performance of South African primary teachers in mathematics gives great cause for concern, their rudimentary English literacy skills are of even greater importance. This is because English is the language of teaching and learning from Grade 4 in around 90% of schools and a poor grasp of English poses a severe limitation on learners' ability to master any of their subjects to any degree of cognitive complexity. And if teachers themselves do not have a relatively sophisticated grasp of the language they are unable to improve the linguistic competence of their learners or to convey complex ideas in class (Taylor 2016).

As in the case of mathematics, the SACMEQ English reading comprehension tests provide detailed insights into the English language competency of Grade 6 teachers. The test consists of comprehension exercises on 11 separate texts, ranging in difficulty from those containing only very simple vocabulary and syntax, to relatively dense technical descriptions and Grade-appropriate discursive passages. A variety of text types are included in the test: literary writing, expository descriptions, philosophical speculation, a school timetable, a job advertisement, and a collection of 3 posters on health matters. Taylor and Taylor (2013) classified the 52 multiple choice items into the four processes of comprehension which structure PIRLS (Table 14.2).

On the question of disciplinary knowledge the mean scores obtained by South African Grade 6 teachers according to the PIRLS categories are given in Table 14.3. While no direct parallel can be drawn between the PIRLS and SACMEQ tests, the general impression given by these scores is that around 75% of teachers attained the

Table 14.2 PIRLS International Benchmarks and associated reading comprehension skills

International benchmark	Reading skills
Advanced	**Advanced readers**. Learners are able to integrate information across relatively challenging texts and can provide full text-based support in their answers. Learners are able to make interpretations and can demonstrate that they understand the function of organizational features in texts
High	**Competent readers**. Learners exhibit the ability to retrieve significant details embedded across the text, to provide text-based support for inferences, and to recognise main ideas, some textual features and elements and are able to begin to integrate ideas and information across texts
Intermediate	**Some reading proficiency**. With regards to reading stories, learners are able to understand the plot at a literal level and to make some inferences and connections across texts
Low	**Basic reading skills**. Learners able to recognise, locate and reproduce information that is explicitly stated in texts, and make straightforward inferences

Source: Constructed from Mullis and Martin (2015)

Table 14.3 Teacher percentage scores on the SACMEQ English comprehension test

		Retrieve	Infer	Interpret	Evaluate	Total
No. of items		31	9	8	4	52
Mean score	SACMEQ	74%	55%	37%	36%	62%
	SA	75%	55%	37%	40%	63%

How to Read The Age of a Tree

If you can find a tree which has been cut down, you will see many rings on the base of the trunk. By learning to read these rings, you can find out about the tree's life.

The number of rings tells you how old the tree is. Each year, new wood is formed on the outside of the tree. This new wood is light in colour when the tree is growing in the spring and summer, and dark in winter when the tree is not growing much. So, if you count the rings of dark-or-light-coloured wood, you can often find out how old the tree is.

....

15. When the wood of a tree is mostly light in colour, this means that the tree ...

A. grew quickly	B. grew slowly
C. only grew in winter	D. only grew in summer

Fig. 14.5 Extract from the text '*How to Read the Age of a Tree*'

Low International Benchmark, around 55% attained the Intermediate Benchmark (which 82% of all Grade 4 children who participate in PIRLS achieve), and numbers fall off rapidly when items demand the exercise of higher cognitive functions.

Many teachers did poorly when faced with items involving inferential reasoning. Item 15 is based on the opening 8 lines shown in Fig. 14.5 of a 32 line informational (non-fiction) passage.

58% of South African teachers selected the correct response (option A), compared with 67% of all SACMEQ teachers who wrote the test, while 40% of SA teachers chose distractor D, compared with 28% of the whole sample. In the latest round of PIRLS testing, 78% of South African Grade 4 learners could not attain the Low International Benchmark in reading comprehension in their home language, compared with only 4% on average across the 50 countries participating (Mullis et al. 2017). Clearly there is a problem in most South African primary schools regarding reading instruction. Effective reading pedagogy involves not only being a good reader (disciplinary knowledge) on the part of the teacher, but also understanding how children learn to read and the various techniques available to promote learning (PCK).

The PIRLS results indicate that the majority of South African teachers lack the most basic PCK required to teach their learners to decode words – to know which words are denoted by particular configurations of symbols on the page. Consequently, 78% of Grade 4 learners cannot ascend the cognitive ladder of either comprehending or conveying in textual form successively more complex thought processes (Table 14.2). These children are excluded from participating in the lowest levels of the knowledge economy, let alone accessing the much talked-about Twenty-First century skills.

14.3.3 What Is the Relationship Between Teacher and Learner Disciplinary Knowledge?

A number of authors have used regression techniques to investigate the relationship between teacher and learner scores on the SACMEQ tests. Spaull (2011) found that teacher knowledge was statistically significantly related to learner achievement, with a stronger relationship in reading comprehension than in mathematics. However, the magnitudes of the estimated effect sizes were rather small: a change in the teacher reading score of 100 points was associated with a change in the learner reading score of only about 7 points. Shepherd (2015) concluded that the association between teacher knowledge and learner performance in the case of mathematics in South Africa was strongest in Q5 schools. Altinok (2013) concluded that pupils with high socio-economic level tend to be taught by teachers who score more highly in reading in Namibia, South Africa and Zanzibar. These inequalities are particularly acute in South Africa where the difference is higher than 90 points between pupils from poor homes and their more affluent peers.

Taylor and Taylor (2013) divided teachers in the SACMEQ dataset into four quartiles of mathematics content knowledge and showed that the impact of improved teacher knowledge is greater at higher levels of teacher knowledge. The magnitude of increasing teacher knowledge by one standard deviation from a score of 4 to 5 is associated with about 13 points in learner performance. They concluded that truly sound teacher knowledge is linked to better student performance while teachers with some gaps in their knowledge do not produce significantly better student achievement than teachers with large gaps.

One of the most informative aspects of the SACMEQ data is that 15 items in the 42 item teacher test for mathematics and 21 items in the 52 question teacher English comprehension test also occur in the respective learner tests. This design feature allows direct comparison between teacher and learner performance on the same tasks. Taylor and Taylor (2013) examined teacher and learner scores on each of these common items. They distinguished three patterns: high teacher/high learner scores (HH), high teacher/low learner scores (HL), and low teacher/low learner scores (LL). The relative frequencies of these patterns is given in Table 14.4, and a feasible explanation is suggested for each pattern.

While conclusive proof remains elusive, all the evidence presented in this section is compatible with the hypothesis that, in order to be effective, a teacher needs to have a deep understanding of the principles of the subject discipline, and that different degrees of a relatively shallow understanding have no marked effect on learner performance. In the words of Liping (Ma 1999) effective teaching requires

Table 14.4 Relationship between teacher and learner scores on common SACMEQ items

Pattern	Frequency maths (%)	Frequency language (%)	Feasible explanation
H/H	2/15 (12%)	11/21 (52%)	In both subjects these were the easiest items: straightforward calculations in maths, and retrieval of information explicitly stated in the relevant language text
H/L	5/15 (33%)	7/21 (33%)	Mismatch between teacher and learner scores could be due to poor pedagogy, insufficient disciplinary knowledge of teachers, or because the question is posed in language beyond the reading level of the children
L/L	8/15 (51)	2/21 (9%)	Teachers can't teach what they themselves don't know

teachers to have a *broad, deep and thorough* understanding of the fundamental concepts of mathematics, as exhibited in an awareness of connections between concepts and of progressions of key ideas, allowing for flexible movements between representations and related ideas. It goes without saying that high levels of language proficiency are prerequisite tools for achieving the level of understanding in mathematics benchmarked by Ma.

14.4 What Are Teacher Educators Doing to Ensure Strong Teacher Disciplinary Knowledge?

14.4.1 What Is Needed?

The task faced by teacher educators responsible for in-service education (or continuing professioinal development, CPD) is very different to those working in the initial teacher education (ITE) sector. All CPD must take account of the generally very low levels of disciplinary knowledge held by the teachers they work with, and high variation in knowledge across the population. In mathematics, the SACMEQ scores show that many Grade 6 teachers sit at the lower end of the evolution of concepts through the primary school curriculum (Fig. 14.6), in that they do not have a firm grasp of the 4 fundamental operations, while the large majority have, at best, a shaky understanding of fractions, ratio and proportion.

While learning does not follow the same pathways for different learners, is often not a linear process, and all concepts held by a learner undergo continuous change, what Fig. 14.6 signals is that in a discipline such as mathematics, a sound understanding of any concept is not possible without a good grasp of those that precede it. The same principle applies in the field of language and literacy. Here, while the majority of Grade 6 teachers exhibit reading comprehension skills which

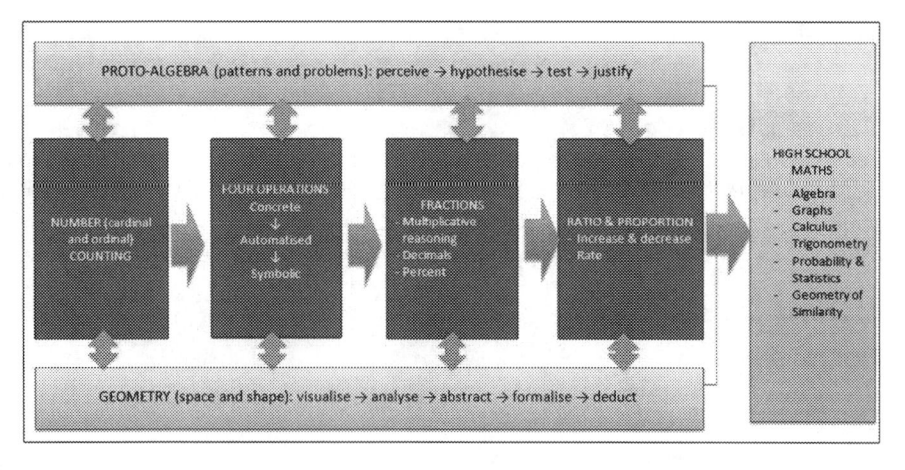

Fig. 14.6 The evolution of mathematical concepts in the primary school

meet the PIRLS Low International Benchmark (Table 14.2), many do not, and most struggle with tasks involving the higher cognitive processes mapped by PIRLS (Table 14.4).

14.4.2 Continuing Professional Development

In both language and mathematics, the lower conceptual functions are where CPD initiatives must begin if they are to address the knowledge needs of teachers working in the middle years of primary schooling. Development opportunities for educators at all levels of the system (teachers, school leaders, district, provincial and national level curriculum leaders) are provided by government, which budgets in excess of R1bn annually to this task (NEEDU 2017). Donor-funded NGO-driven professional development programmes have been prominent in South Africa for at least the past three decades. While the scale of the sector has declined somewhat since the heyday of international donor aid to the country in the 1990s and 2000s, CPD activity supported by both international and local corporate agencies remains robust. Following a survey of 99 Corporate Social Investment (CSI) managers and 171 Non-profit Organisations, Trialogue (2015) concluded that in 2014 total CSI expenditure by companies in South Africa was estimated at R8.2 billion. The authors estimated that more than half of these funds go to supporting education initiatives, which means that the CSI contribution to CPD is at least of the same order of magnitude as government spends on this item.

In conclusion to its 2013/14 Annual Report on Training and Work Skills Plans (DBE 2015), DBE notes that it is not possible to discern from the data, with any degree of certainty, whether and to what extent provincial education departments are addressing the challenges of low educator capacity. This point signals a telling gap in the training terrain: although very significant sums are spent annually on CPD, involving thousands of educators and person hours, little is known about the quality of this activity and the extent to which it is meeting its objectives.

Encouragingly, a body of policy-applicable work in the fields of early literacy and mathematics is beginning to emerge, particularly in the literacy field (Schollar and Roberts 2006; Piper 2009; Fleisch and Schöer 2012; Fleisch et al. 2016; Taylor et al. 2017). If the considerable expenditure in this field, from public and private sources alike, is to have increased purchase in improving the knowledge resources and pedagogical expertise of teachers, then CPD programmes need to adopt a rigorous research-focussed approach to measuring their impact and to understanding the mechanisms which effect learning.

14.4.3 Initial Teacher Education

Addressing the knowledge backlogs of hundreds of thousands of teachers currently in the system will remain an urgent task for years to come. But until we ensure that new teachers are sufficiently knowledgeable, skilled and prepared to face the realities of working in South African schools the problem will extend into perpetuity. In this regard, a damning research report published by the Council on Higher Education in 2010 (CHE 2010) revealed that the state of the initial teacher education (ITE) sector is far from healthy. These conclusions were confirmed by the Initial Teacher Education Research Project (ITERP) (Deacon 2016a). One component of ITERP examined the extent to which the ITE programmes in English and mathematics offered by five universities are adequately preparing Intermediate Phase teachers to teach in South African schools (Bowie 2014; Reed 2014). Another component examined the disciplinary and pedagogical content knowledge in these subjects of a sample of newly qualified teachers (NQTs) from the 5 universities. The universities were selected so as to include the main institutional types (historically advantaged/disadvantaged, urban/rural, contact/distance) offering ITE. Collectively, in 2012 these five case study universities graduated 7 437 (54.3%) of the country's total of 13 708 new teachers (DHET 2013, p.4).

14.4.3.1 The State of Knowledge of Newly Qualified Teachers (NQTs)

The English and mathematics knowledge of a sample of 30 teachers who had graduated with BEd degrees from the 5 case study institutions 18 months previously was tested during a week-end CPD workshop in July 2015 (Deacon 2016b). Given the very small sample size no generalised conclusions can be drawn from these results. Nevertheless, they do give cause for concern regarding the state of knowledge which these universities, including some of the most prestigious in the country, are prepared to accept from their BEd graduates.

Proficiency in Mathematics

The ITERP mathematics test includes items from a spread of topics (whole numbers, fractions, decimals, percentages, patterns, understanding of variables, and beginning notions of the function idea) from the curricula for Grades 4–7, across various levels off cognitive demand (Bowie 2015). Generally speaking, the test aimed to assess the extent to which NQTs were able not only to do the Mathematics in which Grade 4–7 learners can be expected to be competent, but also to understand how to teach it and to have a sense of how it connects more broadly to further mathematics. The results are shown in Table 14.5.

Taken as a whole, the 30 NQTs achieved an average of 56% on the Mathematics test, including 59% for subject knowledge and 44% for PCK. One third (10) of all the participants obtained less than 50%, while the highest individual mark was 82% (shared by two NQTs) and the lowest was 12%.

The 12 NQTs in the group who had specialised in mathematics during their degrees achieved 66% on average, while the 18 non-specialists achieved 49%. Both specialists and non-specialists did considerably better on subject knowledge than on PCK.

Teachers' responses to the following decimal problem provided an interesting insight:

A learner in your class calculates that $2, 6 + 3, 7 = 5, 13$ and that $4, 5 + 12, 6 = 16, 11$. (a) Please explain what the learner was doing incorrectly. (b) Provide a diagram, model or explanation to convince the learner why her approach was incorrect.

The majority of NQTs (22, or 73%) answered (a) correctly. However, in response to part (b) the NQTs managed an average of only 18%, i.e. only one obtained full marks, and nine others obtained 1 mark each. This is an indication of how few of these teachers both understood the mathematical principles involved and could explain why they work. This is what is referred to as 'insufficient disciplinary knowledge' in Table 14.4.

Proficiency in English

Given the text-based nature of the current CAPS curricula for English as home language and as first additional language, the ITERP English test was based on several short texts, including an extract from an autobiography, a poem, a cartoon

Table 14.5 Scores of 30 newly qualified teachers on ITERP mathematics test

Topic	Mean percent correct
Number (whole number and rational numbers)	60%
Patterns and algebra	52%
Geometry and measurement	44%

Source: Deacon (2016b)

Table 14.6 Scores of 30 newly qualified teachers on the ITERP English test

	No of NQTs	Disciplinary knowledge	PCK	TOTAL
English specialists	16	67.8	69.5	68.5
Non-English specialists	14	62.3	63.3	63.5
All NQTs	30	65.2	67.5	66.2

Source: Deacon (2016b)

strip, a review of a book written for primary school learners, a table reporting a survey, and a passage of prose together with a captioned photograph extracted from a children's book (Reed 2015b). Items were constructed to assess both disciplinary and pedagogical content knowledge. NQTs' overall and subject and pedagogical knowledge and skills in English are shown in Table 14.6, which distinguishes between NQTs who took English as a specialist subject during their BEd and those who did not.

More than half (16) of the testees, of whom 8 had specialised in English, could not identify the main idea in a paragraph drawn from Nelson Mandela's Long Walk to Freedom. Almost half (14) could not rewrite a sentence in the passive voice; and 12 could not explain a poem's title, with the same number unable to write a suitable heading or title for an extract they were asked to read.

Finally, the 30 NQTs were given the short writing task of describing a parent or family member in 4–6 sentences, guided by a rubric which specified the length and mark allocation of four components: Paragraph format, Content, Descriptive language, and Grammar. Seven NQTs scored 80% (i.e. 8/10) or more for their paragraphs, while 15 achieved 60% or less, and nearly a third (9) scored 50% or less. The relatively poor writing skills reflected in these results elicited the following comment from the examiner:" . . . the pedestrian nature of many of the responses (limited vocabulary and little creativity in sentence construction) is some cause for concern" (Reed 2015a, p. 4).

Discussion

Intermediate Phase teachers are expected by government policy and often required by schools to teach mathematics, regardless of whether they have specialised in the subject. Thus, of the 12 NQTs tested by ITERP who had specialised as mathematics teachers, only 8 were teaching the subject, the other 4 being deployed to teach other subjects in their schools. And of the 18 teachers in the sample who were teaching mathematics, more than half (10) had not specialised in the subject. Under these circumstances the 56% average achieved by all 30 NQTs on the ITERP mathematics test, the 49% achieved by the 18 NQTs who did not specialise in the subject, and even the 66% obtained by the 12 mathematics specialists ought to disappoint the universities that trained them and disconcert the schools currently using or planning to use them to teach mathematics (Deacon 2016b).

Similar questions arise in relation to the English test, on which the overall results of 66% for all NQTs, 69% for the English specialists, and 64% for those who did not specialise in English, are mediocre at best. It is not acceptable for newly minted teachers armed with a degree to know, on average, barely two-thirds of what their learners can be expected to know of the subject; and this is even less acceptable when English is also the primary language of learning and teaching in the country.

14.4.3.2 The Nature of the Programmes Offered by the Case Study Institutions

An important component of the ITERP study described the ITE programmes offered by the five institutions attended by the 30 NQTs whose knowledge was analysed above. This analysis found that the extent, complexity and foci of the English subject and pedagogical knowledge being taught to IP teachers specialising in English varied widely across these universities (Reed 2014; Taylor 2014, 2016; Deacon 2016a). These divergences were even more acute in relation to the preparation of those not specialising in English who were given very few opportunities to develop their English language and literacy skills. For instance, English modules for specialist English teachers constituted between 15% and 31% of the BEd degree, while those for non-specialists took up between 5% and 8% of the degree.

None of the five universities was found to be adequately teaching prospective Intermediate Phase teachers how to teach reading and writing, not just in English but in any language, and this was compounded by the absence of a focus on children's literature in most ITE curricula.

A greater degree of convergence across the case study institutions was manifest in the Intermediate Phase mathematics subject knowledge modules for mathematics specialists, which focused on both IP- and SP-level Mathematics and both common and specialised subject content knowledge and covered the full spectrum of cognitive demand. One university, however, focused exclusively on common subject content knowledge mainly at FET and university levels and generally at a lower level of cognitive demand, raising questions about how this institution's IP Mathematics specialists would become familiar with the routine IP level Mathematics that they would be presumed qualified to teach in schools (Bowie 2014).

Overall, all mathematics modules for mathematics specialists made up between 13% and 25% of the degree, and those for nonspecialists comprised between 3% and 13%. As we have seen above, 10 of the 30 NQTs tested by ITERP were teaching mathematics without having specialised in it, and it is apparent that their university education was not preparing them adequately for this task.

Regarding the teaching practice component of the BEd degree, there appeared to be no common standard as to the length of teaching practice, with the total amount of time being reported by institutions varying significantly, from 10 to 35 weeks across the five ITERP case study institutions (Rusznyak and Bertram 2013; Rusznyak 2015; Deacon 2016b). Furthermore, the quality of this time spent on teaching practice is questionable. For instance, there appears to be insufficient variation in school placements; in some cases students may simply not be getting enough practice, or no quality practice, or may not be fully exposed to the everyday requirements of being a teacher; and the quantity and quality of supervision – and sometimes the complete lack of supervision due to the literal physical absence of a supervisor – is cause for concern.

In summary, in terms of both mathematics and English (and probably other school subjects as well), serious questions need to start being asked of universities and their ITE programmes as to their student selection practices, their teaching and development of coursework modules, and the manner in which and by whom students are mentored and supervised on teaching practice.

14.5   Inequalities in Teacher Knowledge

In their analysis of the SACMEQ teachers scores in mathematics, Venkat and Spaull (2015) agree with Altinok (2013) that South African Grade 6 teachers with relatively high levels of mathematical disciplinary knowledge are highly inequitably distributed and concentrated in Q5 (the wealthiest) schools. Of the 12 SACMEQ countries in which teachers were tested, South Africa is the only country where the difference in teacher knowledge between the top and bottom quintiles is statistically significant. In all other countries the upper-bound estimate of Q1 overlaps with the lower-bound estimate of Q5 indicating that the differences between these two groups are not statistically significantly different from one another.

Much of this inequality reflects the pernicious persistence of skewed resource distribution under apartheid and continued widespread poverty. The majority of Q5 schools are situated in suburban areas where, under apartheid, they served an exclusively white clientele. While the profile of learners in most of these schools now more accurately reflects the country's racial demographics, by and large, they continue to serve the more privileged classes. At the same time, schools situated in townships and rural areas continue to serve the poorest two-thirds of the population, which are almost exclusively of black African descent.

The most distressing aspect of these inequalities is their reproductive nature. Thus, graduates from the country's poorest schools situated far from the metropoles, constitute the bottom-most fraction of these who manage to obtain an NSC certificate at the end of Grade 12. These students tend to attend the country's least prestigious universities, where they constitute the bottommost fraction of matriculants who enter university, receive generally poor teacher educations, and are recycled as qualified teachers back into the same schools they attended. While there is insufficient data currently to prove the case conclusively, results from the ITERP tests indicate that these students receive a generally poorer tertiary education than their peers in the cities: in this way teacher education completes the vicious cycle of poor schooling and its association with poverty and race.

The evidence for this association is suggested from the pilot of the ITERP tests described in the previous section. For example, the English test was piloted in the

5 case study institutions, with 183 students participating from the poorest, most rural, historically disadvantaged campus serving the poorest students, together with 33 students spread across the other 4 universities (3 urban, 1 distance), all in their final year of BEd study. The test scores from such small numbers of self-selected students cannot be used for anything but posing hypothesising. However, the much lower performance of the rural students was striking. The examiner characterised their English proficiency as follows:

> Some of the fourth year BEd students tested were not functionally literate. They were unable to write a descriptive paragraph of the kind expected of IP learners [Grade 4–7], appeared to have very little visual literacy, were unable to formulate questions with correct question structures and frequently seemed not to understand what the questions or tasks asked of them. (Reed 2015c, p. 2)

14.6 Conclusion: What Is to Be Done?

The South African school system, of which ITE is an integral part, faces the twin tasks of raising quality across the board, while ensuring that the bottom end rises faster than the top. This is a systemic task, requiring coordination between the 24 universities offering ITE, and support from the Department of Higher Education and Training, the Department of Basic Education, the South African Council for Educators, the Council for Higher Education, and the nine provincial departments.

Without very significantly improving teacher disciplinary knowledge and pedagogic proficiency, all other efforts are likely to come up against low ceiling effects. And the responsibility for building these competencies must rest primarily with university-based teacher educators, who face no small task, caught between matriculants with the lowest literacy and maths skills of their cohort (Prince 2018), on one hand, and schools unable to provide adequate teaching practice, on the other. But pre-service teacher education does seem to provide the optimal point at which to break South Africa's vicious cycle of school mediocrity.

What does it mean to improve teacher disciplinary knowledge? Without inferential reasoning there can be no interpretation of text, and hence little engagement with political, social and scientific analysis. And without proportional reasoning there can be no mathematics, only mechanical responses of set algorithms to standard problems. Consider the conceptual pathways in reading comprehension (Table 14.2) and mathematics (Fig. 14.6) required to be followed by primary school learners. The data outlined above show that teachers currently being produced by the universities sit at their lower ends (straightforward inferences and number operations), while their older peers are lower still.

If ITE is to move students coming out of schools with weak language and number skills towards the upper reaches of the disciplinary fields, it will be best to start with those who are furthest along the conceptual pathways, and improving the quality of teacher education must start with selecting the most academically able and highly motivated students into ITE programmes.

Once selected, is it too much to ask that, over a four year BEd programme for primary teachers, students should graduate with a sound knowledge of English literacy (up to the High-Advanced levels of PIRLS), good conversational proficiency in one other official language, mathematical proficiency (up to a flexible understanding of proportional reasoning) and, most important of all, the ability to teach reading and writing effectively?

References

Altinok, N. (2013). *The impact of teacher knowledge on student achievement in 14 sub-saharan African countries*. Background paper prepared for the Education for All Global Monitoring Report 2013/4 Paris:UNESCO Downloaded on 27 Dec 2017 from http://unesdoc.unesco.org/images/0022/002258/225832e.pdf

Bansilal, S. (2015). A Rasch analysis of a Grade 12 test written by mathematics teachers. *South African Journal of Science, 111*(5–6), 1–9. http://dx.doi.org/10.17159/sajs.2015/20140098

Bowie, L. (2014). *Report on mathematics courses for intermediate phase student teachers at five universities*. Johannesburg: JET Education Services.

Bowie, L. (2015). *Report on performance in ITERP maths test*. Johannesburg: JET Education Services.

CHE. (2010). *Report on the National Review of Academic and Professional Programmes in Education*. HE Monitor No 11. Pretoria: Council on Higher Education.

Conference Board of the Mathematical Sciences. (2012). *The mathematical education of teachers II*. Providence, RI/Washington, DC: American Mathematical Society and Mathematical Association of America.

DBE. (2015). *2013/14 Annual Report on Training Interventions and 2014/15 Work Skills Plan*. Unpublished. Pretoria: Department of Basic Education.

Deacon, R. (2016a). *The initial teacher education research project: Final report*. Johannesburg: JET Education Services.

Deacon, R. (2016b). *The initial teacher education research project: Newly qualified intermediate phase teachers in South Africa: Final report on the ITERP NQT symposium, July 2015*. Johannesburg: JET Education Services.

DHET. (2013). *Trends in teacher education 2012: Teacher education enrolment and graduation patterns at public universities in South Africa*. Pretoria: Department of Higher Education and Training.

Ensor, P., Hoadley, U., Jacklin, H., Kuhne, C., Schmitt, E., Lombard, A., & Van den Heuvel-Panhuizen, M. (2009). Specialising pedagogic text and time in foundation phase numeracy classrooms. *Journal of Education, 47*(2009), 5–30.

Fleisch, B., & Schöer, V. (2012). Large-scale instructional reform in the Global South: Insights from the mid-point evaluation of the Gauteng primary language and mathematics strategy. *South African Journal of Education, 34*(3), 1–12.

Fleisch, B., Schöer, V., Roberts, G., & Thornton, A. (2016). System-wide improvement of Early-Grade mathematics: New evidence from the Gauteng primary language and mathematics. *International Journal of Educational Development, 49*, 157–174.

Hill, H. C., Schilling, S. G., & Ball, D. L. (2004). Developing measures of teachers' mathematics knowledge for teaching. *The Elementary School Journal, 105*(1), 11–30.

Hill, H. C., Blunk, M. L., Charalambous, C. Y., Lewis, J. M., Phelps, G. C., Sleep, L., & Ball, D. L. (2008). Mathematical knowledge for teaching and the mathematical quality of instruction: An exploratory study. *Cognition and Instruction, 26*(4), 430–511.

Hoadley, U. (2012). *What do we know about teaching and learning in South African primary schools? Education as Change, 16*(2), 187–202.

Ma, L. (1999). *Knowing and teaching elementary mathematics: Teacher's understanding of fundamental mathematics in China and the United States*. Mahwah: Lawrence Erlbaum Associates.

Mullis, I. V., & Martin, M. O. (2015). *PIRLS 2016 assessment framework* (2nd ed.). Retrieved on 18 Feb 2018 from http://timssandpirls.bc.edu/pirls2016/framework.html

Mullis, I. V., Martin, M. O., Foy, P., & Hooper, M. (2017). *PIRLS 2016: International results in online informational reading*. International Association for the Evaluation of Educational Achievement(IEA). See also http://timssandpirls.bc.edu/pirls2016/international-results/

NEEDU. (2017). *Prepared for the twenty-first century? The quality of high school education in South Africa*. Pretoria: National Education Evaluation and Development Unit.

Piper, B. (2009). *Integrated education program impact study of SMRS using early grade reading assessment in three provinces in South Africa*. Research Triangle Park: Research Triangle International.

Prince, R. (2018). *The National benchmark tests. Presentation to PrimTEd seminar 17 Apr 2018*. Cape Town: CETAP, University of Cape Town.

Reed, Y. (2014). *Initial teacher education research project: Report on English courses for intermediate phase student teachers at five universities*. Johannesburg: JET Education Services.

Reed, Y. (2015a). *Analysis of the responses of final year B Ed students and newly qualified teachers from five universities to an assessment of aspects of 'English-for-teaching' (subject and pedagogic knowledge and skills)*. Johannesburg: JET Educational Services.

Reed, Y. (2015b). *Initial teacher education research project. Intermediate/Senior phase teacher test: English*. Johannesburg: JET Educational Services.

Reed, Y. (2015c). *Report to the initial teacher education research project reference group on the English test (pilot version)*. Johannesburg: JET Educational Services.

Rusznyak, L. (2015). *A comparative analysis of five South African BEd programmes: Education theory and general teaching principles*. Johannesburg: JET Educational Services.

Rusznyak, L., & Bertram, C. (2013). *An analysis of teaching practice assessment instruments: A cross-institutional case study of five universities in South Africa*. Johannesburg: JET Educational Services.

Schollar, E. (2004). *Empirical investigation into the outcomes of mathematics education in South African primary schools*. Report of the Primary Schools Project Pretoria: Government Printers.

Schollar, E., & Roberts, J. (2006). *Meta-evaluation of 34 evaluations of projects funded by ZF*. Unpublished. Johannesburg: Zenex Foundation.

Shepherd, D. (2015). *Learn to teach, teach to learn: A within-pupil across subject approach to estimating the impact of teacher subject knowledge on South African Grade 6 performance*. Stellenbosch: Stellenbosch University working paper: 01/15. Stellenbosch: University of Stellenbosch.

Shulman, L. (1986). Those who understand: Knowledge growth in teaching. *Educational Researcher, 15*(2), 4–14.

Spaull, N. (2011). *A preliminary analysis of SACMEQ III South Africa*. Stellenbosch: Stellenbosch University working paper: 11/11.

Spaull, N. (2012). *Content knowledge of Grade 6 mathematics teachers in 12 African countries: Composition, levels and comparisons*. Unpublished.

Taylor, N. (2014). Knowledge and teacher professionalism: The case of mathematics teaching. In M. Young & J. Muller (Eds.), *Knowledge, expertise and the professions*. London: Routledge.

Taylor, N. (2016). Thinking, language and learning in initial teacher education. *Perspectives in Education, 34*(1), 10–26.

Taylor, N., & Taylor, S. (2013). Teacher knowledge and professional habitus. In N. Taylor, S. van der Berg, & T. Mabogoane (Eds.), *Creating effective schools: Report of South Africa's National School effectiveness study* (pp. 204–233). Cape Town: Pearson.

Taylor, N., & Vinjevold, P. (1999). *Getting learning right: Report of the President's Education Initiative Research Project*. Johannesburg: JET.

Taylor, S., Cilliers, J., Prinsloo, C., & Reddy, V. (2017). *The early grade reading study: Impact evaluation after two years of interventions*. Technical Report Unpublished.

Trialogue. (2015). *CSI growth slows in 2014*. Downloaded from http://trialogue.co.za/csi-growth-slows-in-2014/ 28 Apr 2015.

Venkat, H., & Spaull, N. (2015). What do we know about primary teachers' mathematical content knowledge in South Africa? An analysis of SACMEQ 2007. *International Journal of Educational Development, 41*, 121–130.

Chapter 15
Race, Class and Inequality in Education: Black Parents in White-Dominant Schools After Apartheid

Tshepiso Matentjie

15.1 Introduction

In this chapter I report on research[1] which explores how black middle-class parents in white-dominant schools utilise their agency in pursuit of quality education for their children in the post-apartheid era. Drawing on clinical interviews with 19 black parents residing in Roodepoort, six were fathers while 13 were mothers. The research offers a micro-scale study of how such parents seek to overcome inequality of education provision by enrolling in white dominant schools.

The evidence suggests that black parents choose predominantly white public and private schools in order to optimise the educational opportunities of their children and to secure their future (see Kunene et al. 2015, p. 131; as well as Nkomo et al. 2004). As citizens in a post-apartheid democracy, black parents now have freedom of choice (Fitz et al. 2003, p. 14–15) which means that they seek a better education for their children (Sefara 2002, p. 17); they expect these schools to offer quality education that will secure the future of their children in a decent vocation (Singh et al. 2004, p.30); and they choose these schools because they have better facilities than predominantly Black township schools (Kumalo 1998, p.15).

Martin (2004, p.135) defines agency as "the capability of individual human beings to make choices and act on these choices in ways that make a difference

---

[1]This research emanates from my PhD study titled: The educational motivations and strategies of black middle-class parents in predominantly white schools in post-apartheid South Africa, University of the Free State, 2017.

T. Matentjie (✉)
Matentjie Consulting Services Pty Ltd, Strubensvalley, South Africa
e-mail: tmatent@mweb.co.za

N. Spaull, J. D. Jansen (eds.), *South African Schooling: The Enigma of Inequality*, Policy Implications of Research in Education 10,
https://doi.org/10.1007/978-3-030-18811-5_15

in their lives". According to Bandura (2006; p. 164) to be an agent is to influence intentionally one's functioning and life circumstances. This view recognises people as co-constructors of their own reality. Using parental agency to explore the psychological processes involved in parental decision-making, this study reveals intimate stories of the strategies that black parents employ to breach inequality at the school level, as well as the costs and consequences of such attempts. Here I draw parallels with the work of Vincent (2001) and Auerbach (2002) who studied parental agency within minoritised groups to explore how these parents employ certain interventions and strategies to advocate for their children who face racial barriers in educational settings.

15.2 What We Know from Prior Research

In South Africa, there is a formidable body of research about the problems of racial integration in white schools after apartheid (Naidoo 1996; Vally and Dalamba 1999; Jansen 1998; Pillay 2004; Carrim and Soudien 1999; Goduka 1998; Sekete et al. 2001; Meier 2005); school admission policies and how they served to facilitate or stifle racial integration (Beckmann and Karvelas 2006); the role of principal leadership in facilitating integration (Phatlane and others 2007); and the role of teachers in the process of racial integration (Dornbrack 2007; Meier and Hartell 2009). Others studied the patterns and trends of integration (Soudien et al. 2004; Chisholm and Sujee 2006) and the role of parents in the governance of integrating schools (Mncube 2009).

Yet despite this burgeoning literature on racial integration, there is no South African research on the ways in which black middle-class parents exercised their agency within predominantly white schools. There is, however, a small but influential literature on the agential roles of Black middle-class parents in white schools, albeit in countries where Blacks are demographic minorities (Chapman and Bhopal 2013; Vincent et al. 2012; Cousins and Mickelson 2011; Irwin and Elley 2011; Harris and Khanna 2010).

However, research from other countries on the educational strategies of Black middle-class parents focuses on the issues largely from a sociological perspective rather than from a psycho-social perspective. As a result, while the individual differences in the parenting values (Irwin and Elley 2011), strategies (Vincent et al. 2012) and voices (Vincent and Martin 2002) within the middle-class black parents are acknowledged, the differences are in fact not explained beyond their social meanings.

We know little about what creates the variation in the levels of personal agency used to advocate for their children when critical racial incidents occur in predominantly white schools even when Black middle-class parents have the material and cultural capital to 'fight' for equality in the interests of their children (Gillborn et al. 2012). And while we do know that Black people do not form a homogenous group in terms of cultural and ethnic differences (Harris and Khanna

2010) we do not know how these multiple forms of social identity influence how parental agency is exercised.

15.3 Research Approach

This study offers a 'close-up reality' (Cohen et al. 2011, p. 290) and 'thick description' (Geertz (1973) in Cohen et al. (2011); p. 290) of the parents' lived experiences of, thoughts about, and feelings for a situation (ibid). I was more interested in the parent's perspectives and personal experiences as individuals and as black persons. A qualitative research approach allowed one to do what DeCuir-Gunby and Schutz called for in studying race-imaged constructs (2014, p. 248).

The parents in my study were drawn from public and private schools in the Roodepoort area. Only quintile 5 public schools were targeted, which comprises of former Model C schools who admit black learners, however, they mostly service wealthy communities and admit white learners from within the neighbourhood as well as those from outside the neighbourhood who are bussed in. All the parents were married except for two who are single mothers. Only one school is a private remedial school, the rest are mainstream schools. According to Hofmeyer and Lee (2002, p. 79) public and private schools differ in terms of funding, the former is funded by the state whereas all schools that are not funded primarily by the state are grouped under independent schools. The schools also differ according to the curriculum; public schools offer the national core curriculum, independent schools offer the national core curriculum, however, the well-resourced independent schools offer a 'widely-enriched curriculum', and others such as the Montessori and Waldoff schools offer a different curriculum (ibid). Interviewing parents from each type of school offered a unique opportunity to conduct a comparative analysis of the level of influence these parents enjoy and whether their advocacy efforts are equally fruitful on either side of the fence when compared to each other as well as when compared to their white counterparts.

Through clinical interviews, the behavioural, emotional and cognitive processes used by black middle-class parents as they endeavour to advocate for their children were explored. The chief goal of clinical interviewing is to ascertain the nature and extent of an individual's knowledge about a particular domain by identifying relevant conceptions he/she holds and the perceived relationships among those conceptions (Posner and Gertzhog 1982). Applying it to research, diSessa (2007, p. 525) explains that clinical interviewing involves the interviewer proposing usually problematic situations or issues for the respondent to think about. The respondent is encouraged to engage these as best as they can. The issue could be a problem to solve, something to explain, or merely something to think about. In the study I focused on critical racial incidents to explore how the parents handled problem situations as well as learn about the strategies that they used to advocate for their children. An interview schedule with semi-structured questions was completed in advance of face-to-face interviews which lasted up to 90 min.

The study aligns itself with the tenets of Critical Race Theory as it places importance on understanding how the motivation and strategies of black middle-class parents were informed by identities of race, ethnicity and social class in their interaction with white school authorities. The qualitative research design also allowed an exploration of how the parents managed their interactions with white school officials and how they drew on or activated their racial, class, and cultural resources to advocate for their children inside predominantly white schools.

In line with CRT, my study is based on the premise that Black middle-class parents, are not simply 'acted upon' by the system, but that they actively influence, resist, remonstrate and withdraw at various points in their endeavour to represent their cause. Vincent (2001, p. 349) defines Parental Agency as the actions and responses undertaken by the parents in response to their concerns. In this way I also draw on Parental Agency to study how the parents understand themselves as actors or agents in addressing inequality in the educational lives of their children. In order to do this, I aimed to answer the following questions:

1. What assumptions and expectations underpin the choices and engagement of Black middle-class parents within predominantly White schools?
2. What educational strategies do Black middle-class parents employ in their advocacy for their children when engaging with predominantly White schools?
3. How does the intersection of race, ethnicity and social class impact Black middle-class parents' sense of personal agency?

15.4   Key Findings

In this chapter I report only on the strategies that the parents employ to advocate for their children particularly when they encounter inequality and discrimination within the schools.

15.4.1   They Invoke and Project Their Personal Status

The parents from my study invoke their personal status in order to be heard. However, unlike existing research on status utilisation, what my research found is that for these parents, their use of personal status is actually influenced by the public image of how the Black middle-class is perceived in South Africa. They feel a need to emphasise the fact that their class resources were attained through hard work and educational achievement rather than from tenders and government intervention. There is also a pressing need by the parents to set themselves apart from the public image of conspicuous consumption associated with the Black middle-class. As Barbara puts it:

It makes you feel like you always have to prove a point to them ukuthi [that] you know what? You are not talking to a fool; you are talking to someone who is highly educated. . . . I think white people kind of view you like you are just one of those black parents who've made money. I don't know how through tenders; I don't know what they think about us but I think they don't have a very high opinion of us. They would look at us say you might have the money but you probably don't have the intellect.

Kedibone uses assertiveness to advocate for her child. Her advocacy efforts were triggered by ill-treatment of her child and other black children, and because of diligently raising her concerns with the schools, she was then put in a committee at the school:

> After school the school had an after care. The lady who was running it was a white person. I would pick up when they would give them food. She would give the white kids first and one day when I asked that, is it just my eyes? All the white kids are in the front and all the black kids are at the back. "Oooh no, we just call them and they come". It's amazing that for some odd reason all the white kids are in front and the black kids are at the back. Even the way she would talk to them. She would talk on loudspeaker with black kids and talk normal with white kids. . . I went to the school principal and I said its either they get rid of this woman or address her.

Kedibone uses her personal status to challenge the subtle ways in which race and white children are privileged and treated better than black children. By bringing the school management's attention to the manner in which the aftercare teacher chooses to speak normally to white kids, yet she uses a loudspeaker when addressing the black learners, how roles are allocated for the school concert according to race, she is highlighting the pervasiveness of racism within the school. Kedibone is exposing how the white teachers' every day, taken for granted practices, utterances and ways of engaging with black children ubiquitously perpetuates racial inequality in spite of claiming that "it's not a race thing". She is exposing how racial micro-aggressions (Rollock 2012) are articulated and performed within the school. This raises the question of whether her appointment to the committee was actually in acknowledgement of her critical but valuable inputs to the school or whether it was in fact to shut her up. Nonetheless, Kedibone was able to use her personal status to raise her concerns to the extent that her capabilities were recognised, leading to her appointment to the committee.

> Another incident was in class, where you know when you have school concerts. The white kids would be given the main characters if it's your choral verse. The black ones would participate if it's a dance thing. Those that need more intellect would be white, bo majiva jiva [the ones who dance] would be black. . . I went to the principal and said: "the kids didn't get the opportunity to choose, you chose for them and you are saying black kids are good in this and white kids are good with the intellect". . . I guess the school figured that I am too into it. They put me in whatever committee. With time they changed and as more black kids came into the school.

The parents used their personal status to find 'out of the box' ways of engaging with the school, outside of the traditional ways typically planned out by the school. For instance Lesedi, works in Marketing and Sales, she explains how she donates pet food to the school as her way of setting herself apart from other Black parents:

> For foundation phase they have a drive where they are looking after animal shelters. So because I'm in that space, I give. There are products that we can give at work, so I give them...I must be known that I am present; I am present in this school. I am there. We are there, they must know I exist.

Lesedi uses her work resources to benefit the school, thus engaging with the school differently to how traditionally Black parents would be perceived. The parents also used their personal status to achieve collective advocacy, further highlighting the impact of being racial minorities in a predominantly white school. In addition, this, highlights the values of Ubuntu that underpin cooperation and a sense of community crucial to African society. Kedibone explains how she advocated for another child whose mother is a domestic worker who receives financial aid from the school to educate her child at the school:

> The child's mother is a domestic worker ...the mother tried to talk to the teacher and the teacher didn't have time. The reason was they were given homework and they were told to go on the internet. So I said let's meet here tomorrow and go to the teacher. When we got to the teacher, she went in first and I could see the teacher's annoyance in her face. When I got in, her facial expressions changed. I told her I'm actually with her and you can see the confusion in her face. Quickly I could pick on the confusion her face...

The principle of Ubuntu "*Motho ke motho ka batho*" is the driving force behind the collective advocacy stated by Kedibone. In her comment, she is using her personal status to benefit another, less privileged parents' child. This challenges the public perception of the Black middle-class as self-centred, and self-absorbed. This way of getting involved in education, is not typically mentioned or encouraged by teachers during parent-teacher meetings, in fact, it would often be considered by the school as interference. However, it is an educational strategy that is essential in establishing the sense of community that Black parents in particular because of their culture, and the isolation of being racial minorities in predominantly White schools, would deem as vital.

15.4.2 They Make Strategic Use of 'Null Actions'

Null actions refers to strategies that seem passive but in fact involve closely monitoring the situation even though no overt action is undertaken by the parents because the situation might not call for direct response (Schnee and Bose 2010, p. 101). In my study, null actions indicate that the parents are more discerning rather than passive in their tactical responses. They are actively and constantly evaluating the situation to determine if it is necessary to act or not. Furthermore, they are able to adjust their strategy should the situation change or require for them to be more hands-on. Dr Molly explains that she is not doing 'anything' with the Cambridge school where her daughter is currently attending because her daughter is thriving. However, she mentions that she was more actively involved in the previous school when she perceived racial segregation:

> Mmm hmm, you know what I really don't have anything to say about my engagement with the school that made me uncomfortable. I am usually a very vocal mom, cause I tell you the school that she used to go to prior down the road from the Cambridge school. I had a lot of those encounters where I felt like the black kids would be put in one class and then the white kids would be in one. Just to blend in, they would put one Indian child, so that I was very vocal about. But with the Cambridge school I haven't had any of that.

For Dr Molly, when all is well, she does nothing, however, when things are not going well, she "has encounters". Dr Molly on the one hand employs null actions with the school, only as far as all is well; she is actually surveiling the situation, because when she was 'uncomfortable' with the school she confronted them. Lesedi is another parent who initially used null-actions; she was 'hands-off' when her daughter was thriving academically, but she changed her strategy to be more active with her son's teacher because her son required more support:

> You see for me my daughter has always been comfortable, she's been a go getter. She takes charge of her life. She's been an athletics champ all her life, she's very proud and delivers good results. My son on the other hand, ... it was very critical that he gets a solid structure because he needed to focus... so for me I had to engage with the teachers... every second week I phone the teacher, I make an appointment when I drop the kids off and I go and see them just to see how far we are with my son. ... But I engage with the teachers with him in particular a lot.

The saying in Sepedi "O sere go nwa metse wa nyela didiba", means 'one ought not to defecate in a stream you have just drank from, lest you need to drink from it later', captures the value of leveraging on null actions by Lesedi. She explains how she leveraged on her null actions with her daughter's teacher, to request for the same teacher to teach her son:

> So the specific teacher for my son what I found is she taught my daughter and I actually asked for her in particular because I could see, very strict, but I could see the results from my daughter. So I was hoping to see the same for my son.

Lesedi reveals that her use of null actions was because the teacher who taught her daughter, challenged her daughter to excel. The reference to the teacher being 'very strict' and that 'she could see the results from her daughter' explains why she employed null actions with the daughter's teacher. Her comment suggests that she established a working relationship with the teacher even though she was not as actively involved in the teacher as she would be in subsequent years when advocating for her son. Her use of null actions during her daughter's term was strategic, through the teacher, they empowered her to build a relationship with the school, that later enabled her to make requests that benefit her son. Typically, it is unusual for a parent to request a specific teacher to teach their child as children are often allocated teachers and classes without recommendations or requests from the parents. Furthermore, it is uncommon for Black parents to make such requests.

Null actions are also used to avoid 'rocking the boat'. In her explanation about why they did not pressure the Cambridge school to include isiZulu as a subject or employ black teachers in their staff, Barbara reported:

> Exactly then you go there and be like how come we don't have Zulu? and why don't we have black teachers teaching here? So you are becoming political about the thing. It might just be taken the wrong way.

Barbara explains that she makes a conscious effort to avoid altercations and causing tensions:

> I think it happens because we don't want to rock the boat from fear that if I do this what's going to happen. I know parents who when something happens to their child they get very angry and they would say if this doesn't change there is going to be hell to pay! Their child might struggle a little bit somewhere but you might find another teacher sucking up to them because they know that parent yho!

Barbara reports that she chooses to avoid 'rocking the boat' for fear of what might happen even though she is aware that there are parents who stand up for their children and get positive outcomes, however, that still does not motivate her to speak out. In essence, Barbara's use of null actions is out of fear and insecurity. At first, the apparent fear and insecurity is confusing, however, it highlights the fact that where Barbara is not sure about the likely outcome, or she believes that her child is not personally afflicted by the situation, then she chooses null actions. She chooses null actions even if precedence has been created by other parents who have gotten positive outcomes by being more active.

Yoliswa's choice of null actions comes from a sense of powerlessness as a black parent who constitutes a racial minority in the school:

> ...I just want my child to do her best and push her. Like I said, I feel even if I can it's not in me; I don't want to be involved. Because even if I get involved I know there's nothing that can be done because of my race. Like you said, it's a predominantly white school...Parents cried about Zulu and Afrikaans they asked if our black kids can do Zulu and their white kids do Afrikaans. What they did, I think they cut Zulu and the kids did Afrikaans something like that? It's something that was raised by white people then it was done. They just removed Zulu ...It's their school we are putting our kids there so what can we do? You have to follow suit, we can fight a bit just for them to be aware that this is what we want, but they won't do anything about it. Except if you take your child out.

Yoliswa is aware that she voluntarily enrolled her child at the school and there is very little that she can do to advocate for her child against racial inequality. Her class consciousness does not translate to the level of feeling equal to White parents and White teachers, to fight for Zulu to be offered at the school. Thus far I have discussed the use of null actions as a strategy particularly in terms of parent-adult or parent-school engagement. Below I focus more specifically on how the perception or reality of harm can lead some parents to avoid engaging with the school or the teacher, because of fear of a backlash, while others engage confrontationally with the school after being triggered. Parental agency manifests differently because of the goal the parent hopes to achieve, informed by their personal characteristics, personal histories and memory of apartheid.

15.4.3   They Choose Child-Directed Strategies

In addressing inequality in how academic support is offered to Black children, I found that all the parents took personal responsibility to help their child at home in order for them to succeed academically.[2] Some conceded that they do not engage with the school at all, instead they chose to focus on the child and help the child thrive. It seems from the perspective of the school, these parents might appear uninvolved or disengaged, however, the results indicate that from the home front, or behind the scenes, they are actually very actively involved. Mxolisi illustrates:

> Yes, of course both kids went to a math enrichment programme when they were four and the reason why I sent them to it was obviously from previous experience from people that went to school with me. They only discovered in standard nine that now they are struggling with maths and that they need extra classes. So my belief is that maths is like a language the earlier you learn the language the more proficient you become

It is important to mention that Mxolisi enrolled his children in the enrichment programmes not because they have a learning difficulty or are underperforming in school. Instead he enrolled them to give them extra stimulation and strengthen their foundational knowledge in Math, as well as to prevent any difficulties that might arise in subsequent grades. His eldest daughter was enrolled in the Math enrichment programme from the age of four to give her a solid foundation in Math and English prior to grade R. Like other parents, Motshidisi gives numerous examples of enrolling his children in various programmes to get extra tuition in Math and English, enrolling them in dance, swimming, golf and modelling classes. In addition, together with his wife, they help their grade 4 daughter with homework, they attend parent-teacher meetings to learn about her progress and they communicate with the teacher via the school diary. The following insert from Motshidisi is illustrative:

> Normally the school would say that our daughter needs to do extra lessons with another teacher at the school...but we have gone further on to look for external providers that provide extra lessons on the respective subjects. That's the intervention we have done. At home as well and partly that's the reason we decided that I should stay at home...We realised that it didn't help for you to come home at about 8pm and try get her to concentrate on some exercise.

Motshidisi's daughter is in high school; she is 15 years old and in grade 9. Motshidisi and Mxolisi demonstrate how agency is directed at enabling the child to succeed academically 'behind the scenes'. Most of their work is directed towards the child and is being done away from the school, beyond the school gates. Therefore, redirecting energies towards the home front involved helping the children with homework in order to provide academic support and help the children develop a

---

[2]The parents in my study did not simply drop off their children at the school gate and drive off to work or gym in their fancy cars as it was alleged in the media that they "cede their responsibility towards their children once they are dropped off at the school gates" (source: The Times (2012) time 00:21).

positive self-identity. This was done as a preventative measure, as was the case of Mxolisi, in order to strengthen the child's foundational knowledge. Other parents used the same strategy for remedial purposes, as in the case of Motshidisi, because the child had learning difficulties and was under-performing. Others used the same strategy to close the gap created by work commitments and time constraints associated with being working parents, as in the case of Barbara.

15.4.4 They Draw on Gendered Strategies of Response

Gendered strategies are evoked strategically and differently by mothers and fathers, and the parents in my study used a more feminine or womanly approach to make the point that they choose to be more diplomatic in their strategy use rather than confrontational like their husbands would be. It is almost as though the parents play 'good cop bad cop' with the teachers where the husband is the trump card that is called upon only when the situation gets out of control i.e. beyond the mother's control. However there is also an awareness that the father's approach would escalate the situation and alienate the teachers, likely resulting in the victimisation of the child, rather than resolving the situation amicably. Lorry makes this point well in advancing her own child's interests:

> Being a woman for starters, I'm always of the opinion that as a woman if you are in leadership, you do not have to necessarily act like a man. You don't have to change your personality to fit a man. You can always get results in leadership as a woman by just being tactical and strategic in terms of your approach.

As a woman, Lorry seems to make a conscious decision not to be like her husband in the strategies that she employs:

> Ummm because me and my husband are very competitive that is one thing about us. We do debate a lot of things. We are very robust about certain things that are happening around us. Especially politics, we talk about politics a lot and talk about the economy, things that are happening around us. He can be very chauvinistic and I show that woman aspect. He wants to be at the top so I allow him to think that he is up there. Whereas strategically I am doing things.

It is common practice during Lobola negotiations, where the wives' family are paid a dowry by the groom's family, that the elders will sternly warn the wife that "Monna ke hlogo ya lelapa" meaning that the man is the head of the family. This is emphasised especially where the wife is educated, as educated women are often viewed as controlling, challenging and difficult as wives. What Lorry alludes to here, exposes the cultural ways in which women are viewed as subservient to the husband, and that if you are going to challenge your husband, you had better do it in subtle ways, away from the public eye. Lorry is using her role as a mother to subtly challenge not only her husband and his way of doing things, but also, she challenges her culture. Behind the scenes she uses the strategy of: "You be the head, I'll be the neck" to activate her power as a woman within the marriage; it is this power that she draws upon in the strategies that she employs when dealing with white school officials:

> What will happen is his daughter is his princess. So she will start complaining the teacher said this and this. My husband will say, "I am going there now, you know this woman I need to give her a piece of my mind". I will say you don't do that and how you deal with people like her. Let's rather assess the situation and see how bad the situation is. Because you go there and you start shouting, what will happen? At the end of the day your child will mistreated. You need to go there knowing that whatever you will say at the end of the day no one will vent at our child.

There's two Sepedi sayings that "Mmagongwana o swara thipa ka bogaleng" translated that "a mother holds the knife at its edge" and that "Mosadi o dula mollo ka marago" translated that "a woman sits on top of the burning fire with her bottom", that capture the values behind employing gendered-strategies. It is seen as the woman's role in African culture to diffuse the situation and think about the long-term implications of one's behaviour and its impact on the child. Lorry elaborates:

> The first time around when she [the teacher] said stuff about the books, he [the husband] wanted to go and I said no. Let's let it go we will see if something else happens; then when this thing happened with his brother passing, he was so angry and mad. He said I am going there now and I said we're not going there now, we are going to make a proper appointment. . . , I may come across as being polite but what comes out of my mouth leaves something. . . So you don't necessarily be robust in terms of your negotiation. You can be very polite but very strategic in how you will achieve those goals. . .

Sandy makes a similar point, when comparing her strategy use to that of her husband's:

> Ummm hmmm my husband is how I describe him. He is in sales so he is a very, he has this strong personality and character. So that in itself is the way he, not to say he has an attitude but he is very black conscious. Yah, that also affects the way he interacts with other people. Based on what happens ko mosebetsing [at work]. "I am not going to let a white person push me around so to speak". So already o kena [he comes] with that attitude.

According to Sandy, she views her husband as drawing upon his experience of apartheid and his 'black consciousness' to influence how he engages with white colleagues at work as well as at their child's school. This does not in any way suggest that Sandy has never suffered from prejudice and discrimination in her life, far from it, in fact during the interview she recounted her experience of vicious racial attacks by white children at her high school. Nonetheless, she chooses to handle her child's teachers with humility:

> Like we went for a parents' evening, . . . It's almost like he [the husband] doesn't give them the time of day. And sometimes I come in with my personality and I accommodate people and be nice sometimes. With him, he is not willing to accommodate, so he wants you to do things straight. With me ha ke kopana le di teachers [when I meet with teachers] I try to be nice and make small talk. With him, he is there to see mosebetsi ya ngwana [the child's school work] and let's get on with it.

As Sandy elaborates, it became evident that her choice of being accommodating and gentle is strategic, she does not want to alienate the teacher, and she does not want her child to adopt a negative attitude towards her teacher, and so she leads by example. In African culture, all adults are your parents and you treat every adult with respect as though they are your real parents. The Sepedi saying "Kgaka sena mabala, mabala a kgakaneng": means that "the true character of a parent is seen in the behaviour of the child":

> Like I said I try to be accommodating. Like you said he is like business, let's get on with it, with business. Yena self he is kinda like a hard person. So when it comes to white people it's even worse...Then my son is now going to think that something is wrong with white people. Ko-classeng [in class] I think he is the only black kid!...So now I am thinking when he [her son] goes back to school otlo tla [he will come] with that thing that there is something wrong with white people...

There is a responsibility carried by the mothers in my study, that how they choose to engage with other people, particularly white school officials, is a reflection of their character, that they are actually leading by example. So even as they use gendered strategies, they are very discerning in choosing which strategy to use, when and where, resulting in a myriad of choices manifesting in multiple ways of advocating for their children.

15.5 Discussion

The findings revealed a myriad of strategies which parents draw upon in order to deal with inequality. Child directed strategies are employed to close the learning gaps and provide support to the child at home, going beyond what white schools offer black children. Gendered strategies are deployed to navigate the sensitive cultural nuances that belie the power differentials between men and women, as well as the cultural roles designated towards wives and husbands within the family, which should be balanced against supporting or undermining the father while protecting the child from possible victimisation.

I learnt that the strategies parents employed to activate their agency was context-dependent. Depending on the situation, the parents could access their inner activist or inner "taker"[3] and thus react in ways consistent with that inner sense of self, depending on their assessment of whether that strategy was adequate and consistent with their goal or not. In short, complex patterns of inequality/equality or inclusion/exclusion are not simply a result of school actions on black parents and their children; it is also a consequence of the active decisions made, or not made, by Black parents within white-dominant schools. For instance, the advocacy efforts of these parents were narrowly directed towards helping the child at home so that they could perform optimally in school. However in employing child-directed strategies, the parents also opted not to engage the school in terms of how the school can adopt

---

[3] Here I am borrowing from what Babalwa, one of the parents in my study suggested that Black parents are takers, referring to incidents where black parents seem to cooperate without question or dissent to what the school officials demand, even to their own detriment.

the language policy to be representative of its racial demographics. The parents also did not press the school further on how it can remove whatever barriers that may hinder the child's progress, or that the school should go the extra mile to advance the success of their children. Furthermore, the child-directed strategies, for some of the parents, actually served as a visor, hiding the fact that they feel disempowered, as in the case of Yoliswa, to challenge racial inequalities.

The black parents worked behind the scenes because, in spite of being able to afford the same quality education as their white counterparts, they believed that black children did not receive the same support and attention as their white counterparts from teachers and the school. The parents acknowledged that white teachers were not necessarily as supportive and nurturing towards black children in terms of challenging them and expecting them to excel academically. Furthermore, despite their class resources, black children remained at a disadvantage in terms of readiness and stimulation in their foundational learning, largely because they were not learning in their mother tongue. The perspective of agency as redirecting energy inward involves working from behind the scenes, in the privacy of the home. In fact, for some of these parents, they admit that the burden to change the system does not sit on their shoulders; they simply shrug it off and choose to ignore it. Strategy choice is strongly informed by the intentions and likely outcomes of strategy use; in fact, this is how agency is activated. Therefore, in order to level the playing field, the black parents used their class and financial resources, to access better schools as well as invest in extra tuition. How this field is levelled is adapted depending on the child, the context, the school and the matter at hand.

The everyday racism and inequality persist in spite of political advancements in South African society, in general, and policy reforms within the education sector, specifically. The parents in my study were not always aware or fully utilising these resources for the benefit of their children. For instance, policies such as the White Paper 6 on Inclusive Education intended to empower all children to access learning support within the school, such as amanuenses, concessions and accommodation were unknown to some of the parents in my study. The fact that all the parents, except for Lesedi, were not aware that they could request teachers to offer individual support to their children, was very surprising.

In a way I learnt that despite their education and class resources, the black middle-class parents were not optimally utilising their class resources, some like Yoliswa, felt powerless as they are in the minority. This raises a point that perhaps there is an under-estimation of what racial integration would require at all levels of education. It is evident that even within middle-class schools and the private education sector there is a gap between policy and practice, and that racial inequalities persist in spite of advancement in equity and redress policies. In addition, it is also evident that the racial inequalities persist because perhaps as black middle-class parents there is a psychological block that creates a dissociation between the reality of being middle class and the class consciousness that would manifest in mobilising the assets and cultural capital acquired in concrete ways.

Disparities along gender lines were reflected in how mothers, who perceived the fathers as militant and confrontational as a result of their black consciousness beliefs, tended to censor the fathers and choose more gentle and accommodating strategies when engaging with white school officials. During the apartheid era, such militant and confrontational strategies would have been encouraged, and even applauded. This indicates the effect that time has had on how Personal Agency is activated and how the applicability of certain strategies over others has evolved historically.

The use of null actions and the mother's adoption of less confrontational strategies when dealing with white officials is intended to prevent possible backlash and victimisation of the child. While making sense of the circumstances under which certain strategies are chosen over others, I realised that the key point of departure is "the perception of harm", and that what constitutes harm is very personal. In raising the question of "harm", I was delving deeper into the parents' experience of trauma induced by racism and racial discrimination. I learnt that the parents' perception of racial trauma creates the context as well as the circumstances under which agency is activated, and thus the deployment of strategies. Harm in this sense constitutes reprisal, or an act of retaliation or retribution that may be triggered by the parents as they advocate for their children when engaging with white school officials. The mere threat of retribution levelled against the child is just as powerful as the very act of retribution inflicted, overtly or covertly, directly or indirectly on the child.

Carter (2007, p. 14) has written extensively on racism and its impact on mental health. He argues that a major contributing factor to racism and its impact on mental health is a failure to clearly understand the emotional, psychological and, to some extent, the physical effects of racism on its targets. Carter(ibid) further argues that what is less clear is what specific aspects of racism are related to emotional and psychological harm given a person's unique way of responding and coping with such experiences. One wonders, if the strategies deployed were actually in response to racial trauma and race-based stress, why call them educational strategies? Are they actually about education or are they about dealing with trauma? Given the South African Constitution, and its stance against racism and discrimination, if we acknowledge that these strategies are about dealing with racial trauma and race-based stress will that in any way compel our society in general and predominantly white schools in particular to abolish these practices or face the full might of the law?

Will the acknowledgement of trauma and stress in any way demand a more compassionate approach from the white school officials when dealing with black learners and parents? Are teachers and teacher training institutions reflecting this in their training programmes and should job specifications require these attributes as part of the job requirements for teaching? To what extent do educational psychologists employed by the schools actually expand their repertoire of interventions to include how teachers can minimise triggering racial trauma and race-based stress, and to what extent do parent guidance sessions address the parents' experiences of racial trauma and race-based stress induced by white school officials? I acknowledge that these questions lie beyond the scope of my study; however, they suggest a need for a closer investigation. Further research employing the strategies suggested by

DeCuir-Gunby and Schutz (2014, p. 248) drawing on Critical Psychology as its theoretical framework can help answer these question. Such an exploration will take further the initiative shown in this study to traverse disciplines between educational psychology and sociology.

CRT and PA fall short of explaining how actions taken by parents to cope with race-based stress and trauma actually influence strategy choice and strategy use when engaging with school officials. Future research could investigate this further. This study stopped short of including the experiences and perspective of parents who are black foreign nationals residing in South Africa who also constitute a demographic minority; other studies could expand on this in future. In addition, the following could also be considered for further research: a comparison of black and white middle-class parents' strategies used in addressing the educational concerns of their children with the school authorities; a larger national study, beyond Roodepoort, on the strategies deployed by black middle-class parents in the context of racial incidents affecting their children; a study of black parents who leave these white-dominant schools, exploring why they leave and where they take their children; finally, further research could focus on the children themselves and how they experience their racial minority status in mainly white schools despite being a majority population in the country as a whole.

References

Auerbach, S. (2002). "Why do they give the good classes to some and not to others?" Latino parent narratives of struggle in a college access program. *Teachers College Record, 104*(7), 1369–1392.

Bandura, A. (2006). Toward a psychology of human agency. *Perspectives on Psychological Science, 1*(2), 164–180.

Beckmann, J., & Karvelas, N. (2006). Stifling transformation through the manipulation of enrolment: A case study of two public high schools in Gauteng Province. *Africa Education Review, 3*(1–2), 13–29.

Carrim, N., & Soudien, C. (1999). A critical antiracism in South Africa. In S. May (Ed.), *Critical multiculturalism: Rethinking multicultural and antiracist education* (pp. 153–171). London: Falmer Press.

Carter, R. T. (2007). Racism and psychological and emotional injury: Recognizing and assessing race-based traumatic stress. *The Counseling Psychologist, 35*(1), 13–105.

Chapman, T. K., & Bhopal, K. K. (2013). Countering common-sense understandings of 'good parenting': Women of color advocating for their children. *Race Ethnicity and Education, 16*(4), 562–586.

Chisholm, L., & Sujee, M. (2006). Tracking racial segregation in South African schools. *Journal of Education, 40*, 141–159.

Cohen, L., Manion, L., & Morrison, K. (2011). *Research methods in education* (7th ed.). London: Routledge Falmer.

Cousins, L., & Mickelson, R. A. (2011). Making success in education: What black parents believe about participation in their children's education. *Current Issues in Education, 14*(3), 1–17.

DeCuir-Gunby, J. T., & Schutz, P. A. (2014). Researching race within educational psychology contexts. *Educational Psychologist, 49*(4), 244–260.

diSessa, A. A. (2007). An interactional analysis of clinical interviewing. *Cognition and Instruction, 25*(4), 523–565.

Dornbrack, J. (2007). Reflecting on difference: An intervention at a public high school in post-apartheid South Africa. *Journal of Education, 41*(1), 97–111.

Fitz, J., Gorard, S., & Taylor, C. (2003). *Schools, markets and choice policies*. London: Routledge Falmer.

Geertz, C. (1973). The interpretation of cultures. In L. Cohen, L. Manion, & K. Morrison (Eds.), *Research methods in education* (7th ed.). London: Routledge Falmer.

Gillborn, D., Rollock, N., Vincent, C., & Ball, S. J. (2012). 'You got a pass, so what more do you want?' Race, class and gender intersections in the educational experiences of the Black middle class. *Race Ethnicity and Education, 15*(1), 121–139.

Goduka, I. (1998). Linguistic and cultural diversity implications for learning, educating and curricular transformation. *South African Journal of Higher Education, 12*(1), 34–43.

Harris, C. A., & Khanna, N. (2010). Black is, Black ain't: Biracials, middle-class Blacks, and the social construction of Blackness. *Sociological Spectrum, 30*(6), 639–670.

Hofmeyer, J., & Lee, S. (2002). Demand for private education in South Africa: Schooling and higher education: The private higher education landscape: Developing conceptual and empirical analysis. *Perspectives in Education, 20*(1), 77–85.

Irwin, S., & Elley, S. (2011). Concerted cultivation? Parenting values, education and class diversity. *Sociology, 45*(3), 480–495.

Jansen, J. (1998). Why education policies fall. *Indicator South Africa, 15*, 56–58.

Kumalo, M. (1998). *Let's fix up these emptying schools*. City Press, 15 Nov 1998.

Kunene, B., Mubila, M., & Akinkugbe, O. (2015). Education. In M. Ncube & C. Lufumpa (Eds.), *The emerging middle class in Africa*. South Africa: Routledge.

Martin, J. (2004). Self-regulated learning, social cognitive theory, and agency. *Educational Psychologist, 39*(2), 135–145.

Meier, C. (2005). Addressing problems in integrated schools: Student teachers\'perceptions regarding viable solutions for learners\'academic problems. *South African Journal of Education, 25*(3), 170–177.

Meier, C., & Hartell, C. (2009). Handling cultural diversity in education in South Africa. *SA-eDUC Journal, 6*(2), 180–192.

Mncube, V. (2009). The perceptions of parents of their role in the democratic governance of schools in South Africa: Are they on board? *South African Journal of Education, 29*(1), 83–103.

Naidoo, J. (1996). Racial integration of public schools in South Africa: A study of practices, attitudes and trends. EPU Research Paper. ERIC

Nkomo, M. O., McKinney, C., & Chisholm, L. (2004). *Reflections on school integration: Colloquium proceedings*. Cape Town: HSRC Press.

Phatlane, R. S., others. (2007). *Experiences of diversity in a South African public school*. Ph.D. thesis, University of Pretoria.

Pillay, J. (2004). Experiences of learners from informal settlements. *South African Journal of Education, 24*(1), 5–9.

Posner, G., & Gertzhog, W. (1982). The clinical interview and the measurement of conceptual change. *Science Education, 66*(2), 195–209.

Rollock, N. (2012). Unspoken rules of engagement: Navigating racial microaggressions in the academic terrain. *International Journal of Qualitative Studies in Education, 25*(5), 517–532.

Schnee, E., & Bose, E. (2010). Parents" Don't" Do Nothing: Reconceptualizing parental null actions as agency. *School Community Journal, 20*(2), 91–114.

Sefara, M. (2002). *Black teachers favour formerly white schools*. Sowetan, 14 Feb 2002.

Sekete, P., Shilubane, M., & Moila, B. (2001). *Deracialisation & migration of learners in South African schools*. Pretoria: HSRC.

Singh, P., Mbokodi, S., & Msila, V. (2004). Black parental involvement in education. *South African Journal of Education, 24*(4), 301–307.

Soudien, C., Carrim, N., & Sayed, Y. (2004). School inclusion and exclusion in South Africa: Some theoretical and methodological considerations. In M. Nkomo, C. McKinney, & L. Chisholm (Eds.), *Reflections on school integration: Colloquium proceedings*. Cape Town: HSRC Press.

The Times. (2012). Editorial. The Editor, dated 31/01/2012.

Vally, S., & Dalamba, Y. (1999). *Racism, racial integration and desegregation in South African Public Secondary Schools*. A report on a study by the South African Human Rights Commission. Pretoria: Government Printers.

Vincent, C. (2001). Social class and parental agency. *Journal of Educational Policy, 16*, 347–364.

Vincent, C., & Martin, J. (2002). Class, culture and agency: Researching parental voice. *Discourse: Studies in the Cultural Politics of Education, 23*(1), 108–127.

Vincent, C., Rollock, N., Ball, S., & Gillborn, D. (2012). Being strategic, being watchful, being determined: Black middle-class parents and schooling. *British Journal of Sociology of Education, 33*(3), 337–354.

Chapter 16
School Leadership and Management: Identifying Linkages with Learning and Structural Inequalities

Gabrielle Wills

16.1 Introduction

It is rare to engage in a conversation about improving education in South Africa without the topics of leadership, management or school principals emerging as key elements in creating effective schools. Amongst the various education reforms ushered in under the new post-apartheid order were significant changes to how schools were to be led, managed and governed (Fleisch and Christie 2004). This spurred the burgeoning development of studies on these topics. Bush and Glover (2016) in their systematic review of local literature on school leadership and management (henceforth SLM), reference over 60 articles, theses, reports or books published in the past decade alone. These referenced studies, however, are mostly qualitative, employing small-scale case study approaches (1–20 schools). While individually their foci may be limited, they are collectively very informative; generating thick contextual descriptions and exposing important SLM narratives in a complex interplay with socio-political factors. However, within previous stock-takings of the local SLM literature (Bush et al. 2006; Bush and Glover 2016; Hoadley and Ward 2009) scant attention is given to existing quantitative research. This may be due to these reviews being tackled with the lens of informing the development of SLM training material, namely the Advanced Certificates in Education, and the more recent Advanced Diploma in Education (in School Leadership and Management); with quantitative research somewhat disconnected from these development processes. Another possible reason is that quantitative research, often linked to school effectiveness and improvement literature, is criticised for being a-theoretical in its approach.

G. Wills (✉)
Research on Socio-Economic Policy (Resep), Department of Economics, Stellenbosch University, Stellenbosch, South Africa
e-mail: gabriellewills@gmail.com

© Springer Nature Switzerland AG 2019
N. Spaull, J. D. Jansen (eds.), *South African Schooling: The Enigma of Inequality*, Policy Implications of Research in Education 10,
https://doi.org/10.1007/978-3-030-18811-5_16

This chapter draws together insights from over two decades of quantitative research, largely positioned within the discipline of education economics, that collectively describe features of SLM in South Africa, as well as its relationship with learning outcomes.[1] Two overarching research questions inform the review of this evidence. First, what do we know about the linkages between SLM competencies, practices or processes and learning, especially in the historically disadvantaged system of schools? In a context where redistributing state resources has been limited in its ability to close the learning gap between poorer and wealthier schools, is SLM a potential lever for raising learning outcomes in poorer parts of the schooling system? The chapter reviews what it is that we have learnt from available studies, classifying them into three waves or phases of research development and associated methodological rigour. In the first phase, studies shifted our attention beyond input resources to efficiency dimensions, and the possibility that management may matter. Then indicators to proxy for SLM were incorporated into models of learning in South Africa, not withstanding the fact that the quantitative literature on these linkages (and in developing countries more broadly) is in an emergent phase with little to no 'causal' evidence yet available. Nevertheless, complementary existing analyses using different datasets do confirm clear associations between various indicators of SLM and levels of learning (phase two) or learning gains (phase three). The discussion also suggests that we are on the crest of a fourth wave of new *causal* empirical evidence.

An interesting presumption of much of the SLM research is that leadership and management is in fact present in schools. 'Leadership adjectives' such as instructional leadership are discussed, with calls to raise the competence of principals, direct changed behaviour or provide more support to school leaders, without addressing the first reality that school management positions may not be filled. The second research question asks what we know about the presence of management in South African schools and whether this differs systematically across poorer and wealthier schools. Drawing on previous work about the structure and dynamics of school principalship (Wills 2015, 2016a) and Gustafsson's (2016b, 2017) analyses of educator personnel and the filling of Head of Department (HoD) posts,[2] the discussion explores the extent to which management posts are filled, who is filling these posts and disparities in this regard. Emphasis is given here to how national policy and its implementation with respect to provincial administration strongly influence post-provisioning[3] patterns at the level of school management team (or promotion) posts. As one feature of the broader 'national context' that shapes leadership in schools (Fleisch and Christie 2004), addressing administrative effectiveness is currently a critical tool in a larger improvement basket for ensuring that schools are well led and managed and reducing related inequalities. This has

---

[1] This work was supported by the Economic and Social Research Council [grant ES/N01023X/1].

[2] Gustafsson's unpublished reports were obtained via personal communication.

[3] Post-provisioning is a process that determines the number of teachers allocated to each public school. It ensures that an adequate teacher-to-learner ratio exists in classrooms.

been overlooked as the local SLM literature has been dominated by a training lens (Hoadley and Ward 2009, p. 4).

16.2   Method

The inclusion criterion for papers considered in Bush and Glover's (2016, p. 212) systematic literature review was that they be centrally focused on leadership or management in the South African schools' context. Such a criterion would limit potential quantitative studies for consideration to less than a handful. Rather the chapter identifies empirical studies that either directly or indirectly bring evidence to bear on this topic through applying econometric or descriptive analyses to schooling data in South Africa. No constraints are placed here on datasets considered which may vary in reach from population-wide administrative data and nationally representative data on schooling to smaller data sources that are less generalisable but provide much larger samples sizes than case study approaches. While the chapter largely reviews previous studies, primary analyses are also conducted on national payroll data[4] to describe recent patterns in School Management Team post-provisioning and updating statistics from earlier studies with more recent data.

The chapter highlights findings that are applicable to poorer schooling contexts and exposes critical inequalities in relation to SLM. As a qualification, these findings are best interpreted in relation to more in-depth descriptions in the qualitative literature on SLM, but combining the two literatures would lend itself to a much larger discussion than is possible here. Throughout this chapter management and leadership are referred to interchangeably. These are distinct concepts as Hoadley et al. (2009, p. 6) explain where *leadership can be exercised throughout the school, by different people at different levels, while management, in contrast, is a structural position, which carries with it specific roles and responsibilities.* However, the related quantitative literature in South Africa is still too thin to treat these separately. Governance, which is briefly touched on, is treated distinctly in relation to the work of school governing bodies in establishing policies and engaging in their oversight functions.

16.3   SLM and its Linkages with Learning

16.3.1   A Brief Look at the International Evidence

Significant international contributions in the economics literature have confirmed that management and/or leadership matters for improved learning outcomes. In the United States, principals are identified as second only to teachers in terms of their

---

[4]Permission to access educator payroll data (Persal) was obtained via the Department of Basic Education's official data request processes.

importance for learning (Branch et al. 2012; Coelli and Green 2012; Grissom et al. 2015). Access to a higher quality principal can raise student outcomes by about two to seven months of learning in a year. Lower quality principals can lower student outcomes by the same amount (Branch et al. 2013).

While principal quality studies attach educational value to leadership, they generally provide little specificity as to what practices and behaviours distinguish better quality managers and leaders from lower quality ones. A few studies are somewhat clearer on the bundles of management and leadership support being targeted for changed behaviour. Fryer's (2017) evaluation of a principal training programme in Texas, USA, involving lesson-planning, data-driven instruction, teacher observation and coaching yields significant increases in student achievement in all subjects a year after the programme, with sustained gains into a second year if schools did not experience principal turnover. These learning gains are particularly impressive given the low per-pupil cost of the intervention. In the developing country context of Brazil, a management programme targeting data-driven performance monitoring, target-setting, and incentive schemes was shown to have significant positive causal impacts on 8th graders' mathematics scores, especially for lower performing students but with less success in raising language scores (Tavares 2015).

Although not necessarily showing causal relationships, studies connected to the larger World Management Survey show that indices of target-setting, monitoring, planning and leading teacher management vary significantly across and within countries. These indices are also strongly associated with student outcomes in developed and developing countries including Uganda, Brazil and India (Bloom et al. 2015; Crawfurd 2017). The cross-national study by Bloom et al. (2015, p. 648) also highlights the extent to which institutional environments shape the way schools are managed. In the second part of this chapter, it becomes clear that the institutional environment, reflected in policy and appointment processes, strongly shapes the structure of management in South African schools.

The aforementioned studies could be criticised as being too grounded in new public management approaches with less appreciation for the complexities of guiding a learning organisation or broader issues of instructional leadership. Yet methodologically they are more successful at identifying convincing linkages with learning than studies in the education discipline which typically find smaller indirect effects of leadership on learning (Hallinger and Heck 1996; Robinson et al. 2008).

16.3.2   South African Evidence

In South Africa, no causal research yet exists on the influence of SLM on learning outcomes. Nevertheless, two decades of quantitative research on education has suggested how SLM shapes learning outcomes. The development of local empirical work fits into three waves of phases with new research producing an emergent fourth wave.

Phase 1: Large unexplained differences in school performance shift our attention to efficiency dimensions of schooling, including SLM

Following an intense period of equalising education resources across schools in the early to mid-1990s, studies noted a large remaining residual or unexplained component in modelling student performance, despite controlling for a variety of resource inputs (Case and Deaton 1999). The elegantly titled work of Crouch and Mabogoane (1998), *When the Residuals Matter More than the Coefficients*, brought to the fore the importance of shifting the discourse from one of increased input resources to how they are used more effectively, and particularly in the historically disadvantaged system of schools. They argued that over 30% of the matric performance differential across schools could not be accounted for in their models (Crouch and Mabogoane 1998, 2001). They posited that school quality, and particularly management, accounted for this unexplained component, noting that *South Africa has done much too little on this score so far, and what little it is doing seems half-formed* (Crouch and Mabogoane 2001, p. 65). These research developments were vital in driving home the message that it not necessarily the presence of school resources that matters for learning outcomes, but rather the ability of schools to convert these resources into outcomes (Van der Berg 2008; Van der Berg and Louw 2006).

School efficiency may explain a portion of performance variation within the historically disadvantaged system of schools. For example, Kotze (2017) in more recent years confirms significant learning gains of attending a better quality school within this part of the system (represented by no-fee schools). But relative to the gap in learning that needs to be closed across historically advantaged and disadvantaged parts of the system, these efficiency gains are still small (Shepherd 2016; Von Fintel and Van der Berg 2017). In Shepherd's decomposition of literacy gaps between learners in African language and English/Afrikaans language schools, she identifies that 60% of the gap is largely attributable to home background factors, followed by school resources (explaining 14–35% of the gap) and then school efficiency (explaining only 16%). This is a reminder of the limits of schooling processes, including SLM to address learning inequalities. Nevertheless, if even partial gaps can be closed this is worth our attention. In this vein, research focus has shifted to the residuals.

Phase 2: Studies incorporate indicators of SLM into education production function analyses

Assisted by the increased availability of school-based surveys, researchers began exploring how student and school level indicators as described in school effectiveness frameworks relate to learning levels (distinct from learning gains over time) using production function analyses. Where available, potential indicators of SLM processes and practices were added into production function models in the hope of catching these underlying constructs.

Hoadley et al. (2009, p. 375) classified SLM indicators that appeared to be associated with learning outcomes into 5 dimensions: protecting and extending learning time which includes managing teacher absenteeism (Gustafsson 2007; Van der Berg and Louw 2006), monitoring and support for planning and delivery in relation to curriculum coverage (Taylor and Prinsloo 2005), the procurement and management of books and stationary (Spaull 2013; Van der Berg 2008), and the quality assurance of tests and the monitoring of results. These findings strongly supported calls for the increased management of time-on-task, opportunity to learn and monitoring curriculum coverage (Taylor and Prinsloo 2005). Another factor positively related to learning improvements was simply the amount of time given by principals to their management function (Gustafsson 2007; Shepherd 2011, p. 24). While study results were often complementary, they must be interpreted with extreme caution due to substantial biases that were unaccounted for in production function analyses. What may appear to be significant relationships may simply be driven by some unobserved feature of the school. For example, higher levels of time-on-task or curriculum coverage observed in better performing schools or classrooms may not necessarily be due to managers. It could *just happen* through teachers working interdependently and being driven by a strong sense of personal agency and ability to teach (Lee and Dimmock 1999). Furthermore, the explanatory power of SLM indicators was small in comparison to how much student background explained variation in performance across schools – a finding that is unaltered in more recent research. SLM may be necessary for more effective schools but cannot address inequalities in learning that are positioned in home background inequalities.

What is often not recognised enough is how many SLM indicators that one would assume to matter for learning were insignificant and excluded from general models (Gustafsson 2005; Van Staden and Howie 2014). As Gustafsson (2005, p. 20) reflects, this does not necessarily indicate that these management factors are not important but is more about the *tenuousness* of their measurement, particularly a strong reliance on unreliable principal self-reports of management practices and behaviours. There may also not be enough variation in management practices and/or learning to identify significant linkages, particularly in historically disadvantaged schools (Zuze and Juan 2018).

Phase 3: The use of gain scores, value-added models, or fixed effects models produce more reliable relationships

More recent research on SLM has become increasingly sensitive to the biases that accompany production function models. Studies began to rely on gain scores, value-added models, or other fixed effects approaches to produce more reliable results on links between indicators of SLM and learning. These studies do not provide causal relationships in the strictest sense but they more effectively consider that cumulative educational processes and student background factors may be underlying the apparent linkages.

Taylor (2011) makes an important contribution with the use of panel data from the National School Effectiveness Study (NSES) – a representative study in eight of nine provinces tracking literacy and numeracy performance of a grade 3 cohort over 3 grades. His findings confirmed earlier conclusions about the positive links with learning of protecting time through improved teacher punctuality, increasing opportunity to learn as reflected in the frequency of written tasks, monitoring through classroom visits, and simply having a principal present at school. Despite initial concerns that these linkages would only be found in wealthier school contexts, he shows that these results hold for previously disadvantaged schools. Two other studies confirm the presence of books in schools and effective management of these resources as linked with higher learning in poorer school contexts (Kotze 2017; Shepherd 2016). A student's achievement is also shown to be higher when taught by a teacher that reports meeting monthly with the principal to get advice on their teaching (Wills 2016a, p. 135).

Lam et al.'s (2011) exposition of schooling as a *lottery* with grade attainment very loosely tied to valid assessment of the ability of learners, also implied how monitoring of assessment practices is critical to improved functionality in historically disadvantaged schools (see also Van der Berg and Shepherd 2015). However, it is not clear that heads of department (HoDs) and principals are necessarily more equipped than the teachers they oversee to judge if learner ability is adequately assessed. As expressed by Stein and Nelson (2003), they may lack necessary *leadership content knowledge* to provide effective instructional leadership. However, the capacity of managers to raise the quality of instruction in a school is intricately tied not only to their own knowledge resources but of those they oversee. As Stein and Nelson (2003, p. 446) reflect '[W]ithout knowledge that connects subject matter, learning and teaching to acts of leadership, leadership floats disconnected from the very processes it is designed to govern'. This is illustrated in Carnoy et al. (2015)'s cross-regional study. Using grade 6 value-added mathematics scores, their results emphasise again how opportunity to learn (OTL), as measured through mathematics topics covered in exercise books, is key to higher student achievement in schools in the North-West province. But they find that OTL is strongly mediated through the capacity of teachers to deliver the curriculum as measured through content knowledge test scores. Without equipped teachers this implies that there are limits to the extent to which monitoring of OTL by HoDs or principals can influence how much work is accomplished in class.

In this third phase of research, Wills (2016b) also shows how stable leadership is necessary for learning, particularly in poorer no-fee schools. Matric performance is negatively impacted by principal leadership transitions in no-fee schools. By contrast in wealthier schools, leadership transitions appear to have no impact on learning. Higher levels of contestation surrounding principal appointments in more challenging school contexts could possibly explain these differential impacts (Department of Basic Education 2016b). It may also be more difficult to embed institutional functionality beyond a few critical leaders in more challenging school contexts. Despite the promise of appointing good leaders for school turnaround (Leithwood et al. 2004), or training programmes to equip better leaders in these contexts, the fidelity of these interventions may be diminished if organisational improvements and leadership *magic* are tied to one or two individuals who leave the school (Fryer 2017).

In addition to SLM, governance also emerges as an enabler for learning. Compared with other studies, Hoadley et al. (2009) find less stable links between SLM indicators and two-year gains in matric performance across 142 schools in the Eastern Cape and Western Cape. However, they show that the willingness of a School Governing Body (SGB) to engage in school matters emerges as significant as well as parents' value and support of education in the school. Kotze (2017) also finds that no-fee primary schools with functioning SGBs have higher learner performance. Closely tied to governance, financial management of school budgets and their appropriate allocation to learning resources may also be important. But financial management has received little attention in the wider SLM literature in South Africa (Bush and Glover 2016). This is concerning in a context of increasing complaints from the public on corruption in schools and the mismanagement of funds by school managers (Corruption Watch 2015).

Finally, this phase of research also begins to highlight the value of administrative functionality. Evidence of good assessment record keeping, the presence of timetables, having an academic improvement plan and a clear knowledge about school budget allocations are found to be significantly associated with learning gains or residual performance in no-fee schools (Kotze 2017; Taylor 2011). District accountability functions such as observing teachers or ensuring EMIS-related data is captured effectively in schools are also associated with higher performance (Kotze 2017). These administrative indicators may merely proxy for wider elements of functionality but collectively suggest that effective administration is important. This discussion does not intend to undermine a thread of qualitative research that beleaguers the overt conceptualisation of management roles as being administrative rather than instructional (Bush 2013; Chisholm et al. 2005) or criticism of management by *compliance* that has a form of functionality but lacks substance to shift learning. It just affirms that administrative competence in addition to instructional leadership is necessary for a learning environment (Grissom and Loeb 2011; Loveless 2016).

Towards causal linkages using fuller measures of the SLM construct

With increasing numbers of local studies using quasi-experimental methods supported by large-scale administrative data (Branson et al. 2015; Gustafsson and Taylor 2016; Taylor and Von Fintel 2016), the emergence of randomised control trial (RCT) interventions in South African education research and a growing appreciation for the nuances of measuring SLM, studies are on the crest of a fourth wave of SLM research. In this phase, studies move towards causal evidence with SLM measured as a fuller construct rather than proxied by a few indicators.

A relevant study, with a casual interpretation, establishes the importance of effective administration and management at higher tiers of the system for effective learning. Gustafsson and Taylor's (2016) study exploiting unusual provincial boundary line changes reveals considerable increases in matric mathematics performance when schools are placed under more functional provincial administrations. What is now needed is to understand better how administrative capacity at the school, district and provincial level may reinforce each other to augment the development of functional learning environments. As Lassibille (2016) shows in the context of Madagascar, programmes to streamline the work process of school managers are much more likely to positively shape practice and behaviour when reinforced through the concurrent development of district oversight.

What is critically missing to date from the local literature is evidence on whether capacity development and training programmes can raise the quality of management in South African schools. Monitoring and evaluation of South Africa's Advanced Certificate in Education in School Leadership and Management (ACESLM) was a missed opportunity in this regard. Without a clear experimental design, it was not possible to draw conclusions on the effectiveness of the ACESLM programme (Bush et al. 2009).

Despite the absence of clear evidence on how to improve the quality of leaders and managers in South African schools, the next section highlights that there are potential improvement opportunities in merely addressing inequalities in the presence of management and leadership in schools. Here provinces are key nodes in the larger education institutional environment for affecting change. This closely connects to Gustafsson and Taylor's (2016) research that provincial functionality matters for learning.

16.4 Improving and Equalizing the Presence of Managers in Schools

16.4.1 Policy vs. Practice

South African legislation implicitly describes SLM as a shared function, distributing these roles to a principal and set of middle-managers (deputy principals and heads of department) which comprise a School Management Team (SMT). The number and type of SMT members allocated to schools are guided by post-provisioning norms (Department of Basic Education 2016a). School enrollment weighs in most strongly in determining how many educators are allocated to the school. The application of SMT post-provisioning ratios to the number of allocated educators in turn determines how many and which types of SMT posts a school *should* have (Deloitte 2013; Sephton 2017).[5] Simply put, and shown in Table 16.1, a larger school is entitled to more managers. These management roles are also more likely to be specialised, attached to a specific phase level or subject. The converse is that smaller schools (which are typically poorer schools on average) will have less of a management presence. With fewer SMT post entitlements for smaller schools, this may be misperceived as the non-filling of posts. While national formulas in the Personnel Administrative Measures (PAM) document stipulate criteria for the allocation of post establishments including SMT posts (Department of Basic Education 2016a), provinces often deviate notably from the 'intent and spirit' of these norms (Deloitte 2013).

---

[5]In addition to enrolment numbers, the number of learners with special educational needs at the school, the number of grades each school caters for and the subjects offered by a school inform educator post-provisioning allocations.

Table 16.1 An application of post-provisioning ratios

Post-level	Ratio per 1000 educators		Post-level distributions in a school							
	Policy (PAM)	Actual practice (lower & upper bound)	10 educators		20 educators		30 educators		40 educators	
			R	E	R	E	R	E	R	E
Teacher, senior teacher, master teacher	697.2	799.5–803.2	7.0	8	13.9	15	20.9	22	27.9	29
Departmental head (HoD)	182.2	111.9–129.4	1.8	1	3.6	3	5.5	5	7.3	7
Deputy Principal	84.5	29.9–34.6	0.8	0	1.7	1	2.5	2	3.4	3
Principal	34.2	57.9–63.4	0.3	1	0.7	1	1.0	1	1.4	1

Notes: R = ratio calculated numbers, E = expected numbers after rounding down SMT numbers as per the Personnel Administrative Measures (PAM) 2016 guidelines, assigning the non-integers to post-level 1 positions and ensuring each school has a school principal. The actual practice post-provisioning ratios are calculated for educators in Persal, November 2016, linked to ordinary public schools in the 4th quarter 2016 masterlist. The lower and upper bounds are calculated using samples that differ in terms of the inclusion of educators by permanency of position and number of job-titles

In practice, actual national post-provisioning ratios are substantially less favourable to management posts compared with those envisaged in the PAM as shown in Table 16.1. SMT posts are considerably more expensive than teacher posts and there is a strong temptation for provinces to 'save' by not filling SMT vacancies or just appointing individuals in an 'acting' role at little additional cost. In recent years, in particular, the number of SMT members that schools of a given size *should* have has been compromised through a combination of increased budgetary pressures, weak planning by provinces, a wave of retirements and pre-retirement exits of managers which has left vacancies that are not being filled (Gustafsson 2016a; Wills 2015). This situation is also aggravated by temporary hiring freezes imposed on provinces. The total number of school-based managers had declined nationally by 6% between 2012 and 2015 – in absolute terms over 5000 fewer managers in schools (Gustafsson 2016a). This is juxtaposed against a situation of rising learner enrollments. What is particularly concerning are declines in middle management. There has been a national decline of 7% in schools-based HoDs (in absolute terms 3400 fewer of these middle-managers) between 2012 and 2016 (Gustafsson 2017).

The decline in SMT positions poses a threat to school functionality, sustained learning and realising national plans to harness the potential of school leadership as a lever for educational improvements (National Planning Commission 2011, p. 40). Taylor's (2011) analyses suggest that the presence of a principal at school for example is linked to higher learning. The converse is likely to be equally true. The decline in HoDs – a critical *middle* management position that is typically more connected to the day-to-day practices of teachers than that of principals – is a key area to monitor. HoDs play a crucial accountability and monitoring function in managing teacher's curriculum coverage (Naidoo and Petersen 2016) – the very dimension of SLM that is identified as being most connected to learning in schools. Not appointing HoDs may be a cost-saving measure in the short-run; however, this not only leaves a management and instructional leadership vacuum in schools but may compromise teacher effort (and general levels of satisfaction) as it undermines the promotion and related incentive system (Deloitte 2013, p. 61). The prospect of an HoD promotion is a key node in the teacher incentive system where HoD salaries are on average 35% higher than that of a teacher. *When a teacher becomes an HoD, the average pay increase experienced is 20%* (Gustafsson 2017, p. 2).

What is clear is that improvements can be made in dealing with management declines as some provinces have evidently managed SMT post-provisioning better than others over similar periods. For example Gustafsson (2017, 2016a) shows that some provinces and districts have experienced increases in HoD appointments while other provinces, typically with larger concentrations of the most marginalized children, have experienced very large declines. In Limpopo – the province with typically the lowest levels of learner achievement – appointments of all HoDs in the province had *virtually halted* between 2014 and 2016.

As the nation faces increased fiscal demands in a low growth environment there is an increased likelihood that the non-filling of SMT posts will continue and possibly worsen unless the filling of these posts is prioritised. Provinces must streamline processes related to post-provisioning, including getting clearer on budgeting requirements with concurrent planning and up-to-date EMIS data to inform human resourcing in schools.

16.4.2 Inequalities in SMT Post-provisioning

16.4.2.1 Widening Inequalities in the Presence of Management Across Schools

In general, the current patterns of SMT declines has the potential to widen existing inequalities in the presence of management across poorer and wealthier schooling contexts. Payroll data (Persal) for 2016 was used to explore SMT resourcing patterns across schools. Although payroll is not well suited to exploring resourcing patterns at the school level due to poor quality data linkages between educators in payroll and the schools in which they work, it remains instructive for these purposes.[6] After accounting for learner enrollment, urban status, distance from a metropolitan area, phase level and province, quintile 5 schools consistently have statistically significantly more government paid SMT members than quintile 1 schools and in almost all estimations schools classified in quintiles 2–4 have statistically significantly more SMT numbers than quintile 1 schools. Relative to Gauteng province, schools in all other provinces have fewer government paid SMT members with the starkest contrast between Gauteng and Limpopo province. These results are robust to limiting 2016 payroll data to samples of schools with better data quality in terms of educator and school linkages.

Wealthier schools may be able to buffer shortfalls in the provincial allocation of managers, charging school fees to pay for additional management or administrative support staff to execute some functions. Poorer schools, however, do not have this luxury and typically bear the greatest burden of idiosyncratic provincial post-provisioning practices. This situation is aggravated when schools are administratively weak, submitting inaccurate EMIS data that informs educator establishments, unaware of post-provisioning calculations to know what their educator and SMT allocations should be; or to effectively lobby for these staff entitlements from provinces (Sephton 2017).

Bureaucratic inefficiency in SMT post-provisioning has most affected the poorest provinces, perpetuating inequalities in the provision of schooling. However, there are various other structural inequalities evident in school management and leadership in the public sector resulting from apartheid legacies of power and privilege, cultural norms, and the current patterns of educator movement across schools. The following discussion highlights these inequalities.

---

[6]As payments are made to teachers into their bank accounts, the efficacy of Payroll data is unaffected by the availability of accurate data on the schools in which teachers work.

16.4.2.2   The Unequal Distribution of Principals in Terms of Credentials Across Poorer and Wealthier Schools

A defining feature of principalship in South Africa is the unequal distribution of principals across schools with respect to experience and qualifications. Poorer no-fee charging schools are significantly less likely to have well-qualified principals than wealthier schools. For example, Wills (2015) identified that in 2012 38% of quintile 5 schools (fee-charging schools) had well-qualified principals with roughly a post-graduate degree[7] compared to 14% of the poorest no-fee charging quintile 1 schools. This pattern is partly an inertial legacy of historically imposed policies that matched teachers and principals to schools along racial lines while systematically limiting educational opportunities for black teachers who are also over-represented in poorer schools. But post-provisioning in post-apartheid South Africa is currently perpetuating these inequalities. Between 2008 and 2012 access to principal promotion posts in poorer schools was possible with lower qualifications and fewer years of experience even after controlling for compositional differences across schools (Wills 2015). For example, principal positions can on average be reached three years earlier in the poorest (quintile 1) schools compared with positions in quintile 4 and 5 schools. Wealthier schools are also increasingly appointing more qualified principals over time compared with poorer schools. Although principal quality extends beyond credentials, these observable inequalities are likely to point to much larger quality differentials in principalship across poorer and wealthier parts of the schooling system with potential implications for widening inequalities in learning.

More rigorous appointment processes and oversight of principal appointments in poorer schools could go some way to addressing these concerns. The Volmink report, a commission of enquiry into irregularities of promotion post appointments, makes some good recommendations in this regard. However current suggestions and a draft bill to completely dismantle the power of School Governing Bodies to make selections of promotion post candidates is a highly contested development. While this is seen as an approach to prevent corruption and nepotistic appointments, it assumes that district and provincial officials are better positioned than parents in schools to determine the suitability of SMT candidates (Department of Basic Education 2016b). But direct and indirect incentives may also be necessary to attract a higher quality pool of potential principal candidates to harder to staff schools. Current incentives, for example higher pay for those principals positioned in larger schools (Department of Basic Education 2016a) (which are more likely to be in urban and wealthier areas), stands in direct contrast to intents for more equity in the system (Wills 2016a). The lower pay for principal posts in smaller schools coupled with the likelihood of receiving less management support with fewer SMT members, presents a double disincentive to apply for posts in smaller schools.

---

[7] Signalled by a Relative Educational Qualifications Value (REQV) of 16 or 17.

Notwithstanding, attracting a better pool of candidates to rural areas and lower performing schools is not as simple as just introducing incentives. An incentive system of this kind assumes the geographical movement of individuals from different communities to targeted schools which is not common practice (Gustafsson 2016b; Wills 2016a, p. 35). For example, less than 3% of principals who moved within the system between 2008 and 2012 took up a post in another province. Moreover, over half of newly appointed principals (55%) are promoted from within the same school (Wills 2016a, p. 35). Histories of contested management in schools has also shown us that the effectiveness of principals is closely tied to communities' perceptions of their authenticity and legitimacy (Fleisch and Christie 2004). Without these, their influence over a school environment is curtailed. What begs further consideration is whether authenticity and legitimacy is compromised if leaders are culturally and politically disconnected from the communities they serve?

16.4.2.3   The Unequal Appointment of Men Over Woman

Men dominate school leadership positions in South Africa. In 2016, despite the majority of teachers being women (74%), women only held 63% of HoD posts. Gustafsson (2017) identifies that women are less likely to be appointed as an HoD in every province even after controlling for their age, race, experience, gender of the principal, union affiliation and indicators of quality as represented in Integrated Quality Management System (IQMS) scores.[8] As the gender bias in the promotion of female teachers emerges at the lowest tier of the SMT hierarchy, a reduced pool of females with HoD credentials coupled with additional gender discrimination results in even less equality in deputy and principal appointments. In 2016 women held only 44% of deputy principal posts and a mere 36% of school principal posts as reflected in Fig. 16.1. Furthermore, there has also been little progress in the gender transformation of school leadership positions. For example, the percentage of principals who were women only improved by 2% points from 34% in 2004 to 36% in 2012 (Wills 2016a).

The observed gender leadership gap is larger in South African primary schools than the average for SACMEQ countries, but it is not a unique issue to South Africa (Hungi 2011; OECD 2014). From a policy perspective, however, the solutions to address these gaps are not immediately clear. Affirmative action policy, which applies directly to promotion appointments in education, should give preference to women over men in selection processes. However, Moorosi (2010, pp. 548,555) appropriately comments that "the law does not address the stereotypes and subtle practices of discrimination suffered by women in the work place and at home, and that gendered cultural factors impact substantially on the implementation of the anti-discriminatory mandate of the law". Policies to promote the growth of a pool of female principal candidates are clearly needed, not just in improving the

---

[8]IQMS is a low-stakes educator evaluation system applied in all public schools.

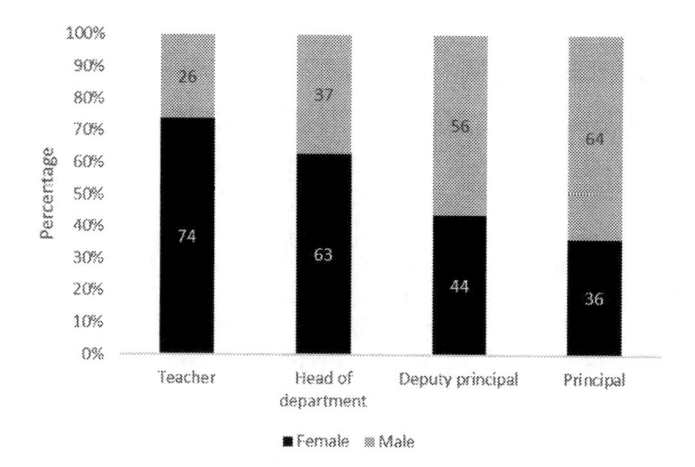

Fig. 16.1 Gender division by post-level, 2016. Source: National payroll (Persal), November 2016. Own calculations

implementation of appointment processes and existing affirmative action policy which favours their hire. Policies should target the preparation of female teachers for leadership through organised networking and formalised mentorship programmes and targeted career development coaching. The gender disparity in school leadership positions in South Africa may also be attributed to the possibility that fewer female teachers apply for leadership positions in schools rather than merely reflecting the unequal appointment of men over women.

16.5   Discussion

This chapter set out to identify what available quantitative evidence reveals about the linkages between school leadership and management (SLM) and learning outcomes, particularly in historically disadvantaged schools. Three phases of research developments have successively brought more reliable evidence in this regard, particularly emphasising the educational value of managing time-on-task and curriculum coverage. However more recent evidence suggests that these management practices may be mediated through teacher capacity where future research should give more attention to the interactions between the quality of SLM and teacher effectiveness.

Current linkages that have been identified in South Africa are typically informed through mere associations rather than causal evidence. It is also necessary to highlight that very often indicators of SLM are not significantly associated with learning outcomes, particularly in historically disadvantaged schools. Even where significant associations are identified, indicators of SLM have certainly not accounted for the extent of large remaining unexplained differences in school performance which Crouch and Mabogoane (1998) initially attributed to management. It may be that other efficiency aspects such as teacher quality account for a larger proportion of this residual than management. It is also possible that the SLM construct has not been adequately measured or that enough variation in SLM quality has been identifiable across schools to detect stronger linkages.

It is also important to qualify that despite the likely importance of school efficiencies (including SLM) in explaining performance variation within the historically disadvantaged system of schools, efficiency gains are unlikely to compensate for inequalities in learning that are largely attributable to home background (Shepherd 2016). SLM may be a necessary but certainly not a sufficient condition for levelling inequalities in learning. Nevertheless, if improved SLM can shift learning and reduce inequalities in the provision of effective schooling to some degree, and international evidence suggests that it does, then it is still worthy of our attention.

To this end, furthering our understanding of the extent to which SLM may matter for learning will require rigorous evaluation of leadership intervention or management capacity development programmes. But even in the absence of interventions or experiments there is much value to be realised from using existing large-scale administrative data (such as payroll data) in contributing to our understanding of SLM relationships (Wills 2016a). In future work, it is also necessary to address a key shortcoming of existing measurement approaches that rely on indicators of SLM to proxy for broader constructs. The contribution of SLM to learning is likely to remain in the residuals when taking this approach. Only those indicators or dimensions that are measured have a chance to emerge as important for learning, and in turn will shape policy debates. Other aspects of leadership, such as creating cultures of care, inner cohesion, and high expectations are regularly identified as setting apart more resilient schools from dysfunctional counterparts in case studies but are seldom quantified in surveys (Fleisch and Christie 2004; Jansen and Blank 2014). Clear theoretical frameworks should inform the SLM measurement process to capture broader SLM constructs (Taylor et al. 2013); and it is the development of these frameworks that provides the critical interface between the depth of qualitative research on SLM in South Africa and calls for more empirical work.

Although there is no convincing evidence to date in South Africa on how to raise the quality of management in schools, analyses of distributional patterns and trends in school management team (SMT) post-provisioning reflect key areas that could be targeted to at least improve the quantity of SLM in schools and related inequalities. The discussion highlighted the national declines in the numbers of school-based managers with attention drawn to declines in middle-managers (HoDs) who are typically responsible for monitoring time-on-task and curriculum coverage – the SLM indicators most associated with learning improvements (Gustafsson 2017). These trends are likely to be aggravating existing inequalities in SMT post-provisioning across schools.

The discussion also highlighted structural inequalities in the presence of management across schools, some of which are augmented through current post-provisioning processes. Current appointment outcomes perpetuate structural inequalities in the experience and qualifications of principals across poorer and wealthier schools. In levelling these differences, improved planning, budgeting, post-provisioning, appointment processes and their implementation at the level of provinces should receive priority attention. The varying capacity of provinces to staff schools with managers is a sure sign that improvements can be made to current post-provisioning patterns if some provinces evidently manage this process better than others. Large gender inequalities in SMT post-provisioning in favour of men also point to inefficiencies in appointment processes. Improved equity in SMT selection may have implications for school functionality and learning outcomes if there exists a pool of high quality female leaders that have been overlooked for appointment.

Quantitative research on SLM in South Africa has arguably provided more specificity in describing the structure and features of school management resourcing across schools than identifying its linkages with learning. Nevertheless international evidence on the value of quality leaders and managers for raising learning (Branch et al. 2013; Fryer 2017) supports calls for the capacity development of incumbent SMTs. New research developments should rigorously consider whether training programmes can raise SMT quality and how this impacts on learning. But ensuring SMT members are allocated to schools and selecting the best people for these jobs at the outset are obvious steps to improve and level differences in the school leadership and management landscape.

References

Bloom, N., Lemos, R., Sadun, R., & Reenen, J. V. (2015). Does management matter in schools? *The Economic Journal, 125*(584), 647–674. https://doi.org/10.1111/ecoj.12267

Branch, G. F., Hanushek, E. A., & Rivkin, S. G. (2012). *Estimating the effect of leaders on public sector productivity: The case of school principals.* Working Paper 17803, National Bureau of Economic Research. https://doi.org/10.3386/w17803

Branch, G. F., Hanushek, E. A., & Rivkin, S. G. (2013). School leaders matter; measuring the impact of effective principals. *Education Next, 13*(1), 62–69.

Branson, N., Hofmeyr, C., & Lam, D. (2015). The impact of the no-fee school policy on enrolment and school performance: Evidence from NIDS Waves 1–3, Commissioned by the presidency, SALDRU, Cape Town, Working Paper Number 197, 29.

Bush, T. (2013). Instructional leadership and leadership for learning: Global and South African perspectives. *Education as Change, 17*(sup1), S5–S20. https://doi.org/10.1080/16823206.2014.865986

Bush, T., & Glover, D. (2016). School leadership and management in South Africa: Findings from a systematic literature review. *International Journal of Educational Management, 30*(2), 211–231.

Bush, T., Glover, D., Bischoff, T., Moloi, K., Heystek, J., & Joubert, R. (2006). *School leadership, management and governance in South Africa: A systematic literature review.* Johannesburg: Matthew Goniwe School of Leadership and Governance.

Bush, T., Duku, N., Glover, D., Kiggundu, E., Kola, S., Msila, V., & Moorosi, P. (2009). *External evaluation research report of the advanced certificate in education: School leadership and management.* Pretoria: DBE.

Carnoy, M., Ngware, M., & Oketch, M. (2015). The role of classroom resources and national educational context in student learning gains: Comparing Botswana, Kenya, and South Africa. *Comparative Education Review, 59*(2), 199–233.

Case, A., & Deaton, A. (1999). School inputs and educational outcomes in South Africa. *The Quarterly Journal of Economics, 114*(3), 1047–1084.

Chisholm, L., Hoadley, U., Kivulu, M., Brookes, H., Prinsloo, C., & Kgobe, A. (2005). Educator workload in South Africa. Report prepared for the Education Labour Council. Pretoria.

Coelli, M., & Green, D. A. (2012). Leadership effects: School principals and student outcomes. *Economics of Education Review, 31*(1), 92–109.

Corruption Watch. (2015). *A loss of principle: A report on corruption in schools.* Johannesburg: Corruption Watch.

Crawfurd, L. (2017). School management and public–private partnerships in Uganda. *Journal of African Economies, 26*(5), 539–560.

Crouch, L., & Mabogoane, T. (1998). When the residuals matter more than the coefficients: An educational perspective. *Journal for Studies in Economic and Econometrics, 22*, 1–14.

Crouch, L., & Mabogoane, T. (2001). No magic bullets, just tracer bullets: The role of learning resources, social advantage, and education management in improving the performance of South African schools. *Social Dynamics, 27*(1), 60–78.

Deloitte. (2013). *National implementation of post provisioning: National report.* Unpublished report for the Department of Basic Education.

Department of Basic Education. (2016a). *Personnel Administrative Measures (PAM)* Government Gazette No. 39684, 12 Feb 2016. Pretoria.

Department of Basic Education. (2016b). *Report of the ministerial task team appointed by Minister Angie Motshekga to investigate allegations into the selling of posts of educators by members of teachers unions and departmental officials in provincial education departments.* Pretoria.

Fleisch, B., & Christie, P. (2004). Structural change, leadership and school effectiveness/improvement: Perspectives from South Africa. *Discourse: Studies in the Cultural Politics of Education, 25*(1), 95–112.

Fryer, R. G. (2017). Management and student achievement: Evidence from a randomized field experiment (No. 23437). NBER Working Paper Series, Cambridge, MA.

Grissom, J. A., & Loeb, S. (2011). Triangulating principal effectiveness: How perspectives of parents, teachers, and assistant principals identify the central importance of managerial skills. *American Educational Research Journal, 48*(5), 1091–1123.

Grissom, J. A., Kalogrides, D., & Loeb, S. (2015). Using student test scores to measure principal performance. *Educational Evaluation and Policy Analysis, 37*(1), 3–28.

Gustafsson, M. (2005). *The relationships between schooling inputs and outputs in South Africa: Methodologies and policy recommendations based on the 2000 SACMEQ dataset.* Ph.D. thesis, Stellenbosch University, Stellenbosch.

Gustafsson, M. (2007). Using the hierarchical linear model to understand school production in South Africa. *South African Journal of Economics, 75*(1), 84–98.

Gustafsson, M. (2016a). *Personnel spending pressures. Hiring and promotion cuts with enrolment growth.* Unpublished report. No. 03/16, Stellenbosch Economic Working Papers, Stellenbosch.

Gustafsson, M. (2016b). *Teacher supply and the quality of schooling in South Africa: Patterns over space and time.* (No 05/16), Stellenbosch Economic Working Papers Stellenbosch.

Gustafsson, M. (2017). *Who becomes an HOD?* Unpublished report. Technical report. Pretoria: DBE.

Gustafsson, M., & Taylor, S. (2016). *Treating schools to a new administration: Evidence from South Africa of the impact of better practices in the system-level administration of schools.* No. 05/16, Stellenbosch Economic Working Papers, Stellenbosch.

Hallinger, P., & Heck, R. H. (1996). The principal's role in school effectiveness: An assessment of methodological progress, 1980–1995. In *International handbook of educational leadership and administration* (pp. 723–783). Dordrecht: Springer.

Hoadley, U., & Ward, C. (2009). *Managing to learn: Instructional leadership in South African secondary schools.* Pretoria: HRSC Press.

Hoadley, U., Christie, P., & Ward, C. L. (2009). Managing to learn: Instructional leadership in South African secondary schools. *School Leadership and Management, 29*(4), 373–389.

Hungi, N. (2011). *Characteristics of school heads and their schools (No. 3)*. SACMEQ Working Paper. SACMEQ, Gaborone 3:1–38.

Jansen, J. D., & Blank, M. (2014). *How to fix South Africa's schools: Lessons from schools that work* (1st ed.). Johannesburg: Bookstorm.

Kotze, J. (2017). *Social gradients, early childhood education and schools performing above the demographic expectation: Empirical insights into educational issues*. Stellenbosch University.

Lam, D., Ardington, C., & Leibbrandt, M. (2011). Schooling as a lottery: Racial differences in school advancement in urban South Africa. *Journal of Development Economics, 95*(2), 121–136.

Lassibille, G. (2016). Improving the management style of school principals: Results from a randomized trial. *Education Economics, 24*(2), 121–141. https://doi.org/10.1080/09645292.2014.985288

Lee, J. C. K., & Dimmock, C. (1999). Curriculum leadership and management in secondary schools: A Hong Kong case study. *School Leadership & Management, 19*(4), 455–481. https://doi.org/10.1080/13632439968970

Leithwood, K., Seashore, K., Anderson, S., & Wahlstrom, K. (2004). Review of research: How leadership influences student learning, learning from leadership project. https://doi.org/101007/978-90-481-2660-6

Loveless, T. (2016). Principals as instructional leaders: An international perspective, 2016 Brown Center Report on American Education. Houston.

Moorosi, P. (2010). South African female principals' career paths: Understanding the gender gap in secondary school management. *Educational Management Administration & Leadership, 38*(5), 547–562. https://doi.org/10.1177/1741143210373741

Naidoo, P., & Petersen, N. (2016). Towards a leadership programme for primary school principals as instructional leaders. *South African Journal of Childhood Education, 5*(3), 1–8. https://doi.org/10.4102/sajce.v5i3.371

National Planning Commission. (2011). *Our future – Make it work. National Development Plan 2030*. Executive Summary. Government Printers, Pretoria.

OECD. (2014). *TALIS 2013 results: An international perspective on teaching and learning*. OECD Publishing. https://doi.org/doi:10.1787/9789264196261-en

Robinson, V. M. J., Lloyd, C. A., & Rowe, K. J. (2008). The impact of leadership on student outcomes: An analysis of the differential effects of leadership types. *Educational Administration Quarterly, 44*(5), 635–674. https://doi.org/10.1177/0013161X08321509

Sephton, S. (2017). Post provisioning. In F. Veriava, A. Thom, & T. Hodgson (Eds.), *Basic education rights handbook – education rights in South Africa* (pp. 246–263). Section27: Johannesburg.

Shepherd, D. L. (2011). *Constraints to school effectiveness: What prevents poor schools from delivering results*. No 05/11 Stellenbosch Economic Working Papers, Stellenbosch.

Shepherd, D. L. (2016). *The open door of learning–Access restricted: School effectiveness and efficiency across the South African education system*. Stellenbosch University, Stellenbosch.

Spaull, N. (2013). Poverty & privilege: Primary school inequality in South Africa. *International Journal of Educational Development, 33*(5), 436–447. https://doi.org/10.1016/j.ijedudev.2012.09.009

Stein, M. K., & Nelson, B. S. (2003). Leadership content knowledge. *Educational Evaluation and Policy Analysis, 25*(4), 423–448.

Tavares, P. A. (2015) The impact of school management practices on educational performance: Evidence from public schools in São Paulo. *Economics of Education Review, 48*, 1–15. https://doi.org/10.1016/j.econedurev.2015.05.002

Taylor, S. (2011). *Uncovering indicators of effective school management in South Africa using the National School Effectiveness Study*. No. 10/11, Stellenbosch Economic Working Papers, Stellenbosch.

Taylor, N., & Prinsloo, C. (2005). *The quality learning project: Lessons for high school improvement in South Africa*. Johannesburg: Joint Education Trust.

Taylor, S., & Von Fintel, M. (2016). Estimating the impact of language of instruction in South African primary schools: A fixed effects approach. *Economics of Education Review, 50*, 75–89. https://doi.org/10.1016/j.econedurev.2016.01.003

Taylor, N., Gamble, J., Spies, M., & Garisch, C. (2013). School leadership and management. In N. Taylor, S. Van der Berg, & T. Mabogoane (Eds.), *Creating effective schools*. Cape Town: Pearson Education.

Van der Berg, S. (2008). How effective are poor schools? Poverty and educational outcomes in South Africa. *Studies in Educational Evaluation, 34*(3), 145–154. https://doi.org/10.1016/j.stueduc.2008.07.005

Van der Berg, S., & Louw, M. (2006). Unravelling the mystery: Understanding South African schooling outcomes in regional context. In *Conference for the study of African economics* (pp. 1–32). Citeseer: Oxford University.

Van der Berg, S., & Shepherd, D. L. (2015). Continuous assessment and matriculation examination marks – An empirical examination. *South African Journal of Childhood Education, 5*(2), 78–94.

Van Staden, S., & Howie, S. (2014). Reflections on Creemers' comprehensive model of educational effectiveness for reading literacy: South African evidence from PIRLS 2006. *Perspectives in Education, 32*(3), 172–192.

Von Fintel, M., & Van der Berg, S. (2017). What a difference a good school makes! Persistence in academic performance and the impact of school quality. No 07/2017 Stellenbosch Economic Working Papers, Stellenbosch.

Wills, G. (2015). Informing principal policy reforms in South Africa through data-based evidence. *South African Journal of Childhood Education, 5*(2), 95–122.

Wills, G. (2016a). *An economic perspective on school leadership and teachers' unions in South Africa*. Thesis, Stellenbosch University.

Wills, G. (2016b). Principal leadership changes and their consequences for school performance in South Africa. *International Journal of Educational Development, 51*, 108–124. https://doi.org/10.1016/j.ijedudev.2016.08.005

Zuze, T., & Juan, A. (2018). School leadership and local learning contexts in South Africa. *Educational Management Administration and Leadership*. https://doi.org/10.1177/1741143218814006

Chapter 17
How Can Learning Inequalities be Reduced? Lessons Learnt from Experimental Research in South Africa

Stephen Taylor

17.1 Introduction: Why Experimental Research Has a Crucial Role to Play

Unacceptably wide inequalities persist in South Africa's education outcomes. Meanwhile the basic education sector faces an environment of increasingly tight budget pressures. Therefore, more than ever, public and Corporate Social Investment (CSI) spending must be directed to those programs and policies that we know actually impact on the most important education outcomes. And if we are to know what works, then experimental research will have a valuable role to play in figuring out South Africa's education policy questions.

17.1.1 What Is Experimental Research?

Experimental research includes both actual field experiments, such as Randomised Control Trials (RCTs), and quasi-experimental research designs where circumstances provide occasion to interpret the correlation between having received a particular policy or program and the outcome of interest as if an experiment had been set up. In experimental research, one can legitimately interpret an observed correlation between receiving a program, policy or resource and an educational outcome of interest as an accurate reflection of the *causal* relationship.

Identifying the causal effect of a policy or resource – school libraries for instance – on educational outcomes is of primary relevance for policy-making, but

S. Taylor (✉)
Department of Basic Education, Pretoria, South Africa
e-mail: stephentaylor17@gmail.com

© Springer Nature Switzerland AG 2019
N. Spaull, J. D. Jansen (eds.), *South African Schooling: The Enigma of Inequality*, Policy Implications of Research in Education 10,
https://doi.org/10.1007/978-3-030-18811-5_17

is often a technically challenging task. We can easily observe that average reading achievement in schools with libraries is considerably higher than it is in schools without libraries. But it is also no doubt true that schools with swimming pools achieve better reading outcomes than schools without swimming pools. This is because schools with swimming pools and libraries are very different in a multitude of ways from schools without these facilities. Determining the impact of building more libraries would ideally require being able to observe the same schools with and without libraries at the same time – something which is of course impossible. A second-best solution is to identify a group of comparable schools which one can argue are similar in all relevant respects aside from having a library. This can most easily be achieved by setting up an experiment.

When schools or learners are randomly assigned to an intervention, as in experimental research, there are no reasons to expect any systematic differences between intervention and comparison groups, and as the sample size increases the statistical likelihood of chance differences arising diminishes (Imbens and Wooldridge 2009, p.19). Therefore, if significant differences *do* occur after the intervention one can confidently attribute those differences to the impact of the intervention, and the intervention alone.

As this chapter's review of experimental studies will indicate, evaluations using a rigorous experimental method typically reveal relatively small effect sizes (if they are even greater than zero). Effect sizes, even of 'effective' programs, are usually small relative to all the other factors affecting learning outcomes – factors which confound estimates in the absence of an experimental design. For example, if one compares maths performance between children who attend extra maths lessons and children who do not (as one could using TIMSS data), it will not be clear what to make of whatever difference is observed. Those who attend extra lessons may do so precisely because they are struggling and therefore need to attend. On the other hand, those who attend extra lessons may do so because their parents care about their education and can afford to pay for extra lessons, meaning that these children would do better in mathematics even aside from the extra lessons. All of these confounding factors (prior ability, parent involvement, socio-economic status, and others) would no doubt have a much larger impact than the extra lessons themselves. Therefore, one cannot interpret the correlation between taking extra lessons and observed maths performance as any sort of approximation of the impact of those lessons.

17.1.2 Limitations of Experimental Methods and How to Mitigate These

Merely knowing the size of an intervention's impact is of course only part of the relevant story. Questions about why an intervention worked or did not work, where it worked better, as well as what mechanisms were driving the change are also interesting and important. RCTs are sometimes criticised for not addressing such questions. However, an RCT does not preclude other quantitative and qualitative methods that allow one to explore these questions, as was done in the Early Grade Reading Study which is discussed below.

However, merely knowing the impact of an intervention is better than knowing nothing at all. If it is possible to measure impact without the additional funding necessary to answer the "why", "where" and "how" questions, it is still valuable to know whether the program 'worked' (i.e. its estimated impact). A discussion of the impact evaluation of the Grade R program will show how this knowledge of program impact size, influences the interpretation of other information about the successes and challenges experienced in program implementation. In this respect, quantitative and qualitative results interpret each other. For example, if a quantitative impact evaluation shows that a program has zero impact, one will not get carried away by positive features of the program, and one will understand the problematic features of the program implementation as being prohibitive of impact.

While experimental research clearly has the advantage of strong internal validity when measuring causal impact, RCTs are sometimes criticised on the grounds of external validity – if it worked in one place or time will it necessarily work in another place and time? Of course these concerns apply to any research methodology when implemented in a particular place and time, and so we should not throw the baby out with the bathwater when it comes to RCTs. Rather, there are a number of things that can be done to maximise the relevance of experimental results to other settings. For example, mixed methods research can investigate why and under what conditions an intervention was most successful, thus informing the likely impact in other settings that conform to those conditions to a greater or lesser extent. Also, interventions should have a clear theory of change where specific mechanisms are activated, so that the results have relevance to other types of interventions using similar mechanisms. For this reason, evaluating the impact of a package of all sorts of intervention components has less relevance to other contexts and programs.

Another type of external validity concern relates to the artificial experimental conditions that may exist during an RCT. Children in both intervention and control schools may be subjected to testing or other measurement, which could itself impact on the outcomes. Similarly, when research subjects know they are part of the experiment this can create confounding motivational effects. Ideally, research participants would be blind to which group they are in, and in fact would not even know that they are part of an experiment. Therefore, perhaps the very best methods are the quasi-experimental methods, where an experiment was not planned but fortuitously did occur (and participation in the program was definitely caused by something unrelated to the outcome of interest). For example, Gustafsson and Taylor (2018) use provincial boundary changes that occurred in 2006 to measure the impact of alternative provincial administrations on school performance – this paper is discussed below.

One can further circumvent the potential bias created by artificial experimental conditions if the outcome of interest can be measured using administrative data that already exists, so that there is no chance of research participants reacting to being observed. If we were to speak of a "gold standard" for measuring causal impact, then, it would not be an RCT but a valid natural experiment where suitable administrative data can be used as the outcome measure.

In reality, such natural experiments rarely arise, while administrative data is often incomplete and unreliable, if available at all. Therefore, RCTs will certainly have a role to play in evaluating the impact of new programs. More should also be done to use available administrative data, especially National Senior Certificate data as an outcome for measuring the impact of secondary school interventions. Between 2012 and 2014 there were also the Annual National Assessments (ANA) in South Africa, which provided a learning outcome measure for the population of primary schools. Despite its limitations, ANA offered some valuable possibilities for evaluating policies and programs, as Sect. 17.3 will illustrate.

17.1.3 Addressing Educational Inequality Means Finding Out How to Improve Learning Outcomes for Poor Children

Quantitative research on South Africa's education system over the past 10 or 15 years has done a reasonable job at describing the perpetuation of social and economic inequality by educational inequalities. Labour market inequalities reflect the inequalities in the school system (Van der Berg et al. 2011), where educational outcomes continue to reflect historical patterns of exclusion and privilege (Spaull 2013), and where early learning outcomes are strongly predictive of matric outcomes (Taylor et al. 2015), which are in turn strongly predictive of higher education access and success (Van Broekhuizen et al. 2016). In fact, Van Broekhuizen et al. (2016) find that university access and completion is not biased against black youths or those from poorer schools after accounting for their matric performance. In other words, although there are large racial gaps in accessing and completing university, such gaps do not exist between youths of different race groups with similar matric marks. Therefore, inequalities in South Africa's educational *outcomes* are mainly attributable to earlier inequalities in early childhood development and foundational learning in school.

In South Africa virtually all children enter and complete primary school. We do, however, observe substantial dropout rates in grades 10 to 12, and whilst this may be triggered by specific factors like family responsibilities, the root cause of dropout is weak learning foundations (Department of Basic Education 2017). Therefore, educational inequality cannot be much reduced by improving access to schooling, but only by improving learning for those in school.

This all means that the root inequality is a learning inequality and therefore the challenge of reducing inequality amounts to a challenge to improve the quality of learning and teaching in the less well functioning parts of the school system. Whilst it may be possible to come up with ways to redistribute public resources in an even more pro-poor manner than is currently done, for example through lowering pupil-teacher ratios in poorer schools, this will only be effective to the extent that it leads to improved learning outcomes in these schools. Such policies may have negative implications for more affluent schools and this could be justified if the result is better learning outcomes in poor schools. Merely harming learning and teaching in well-performing schools as a way to reduce inequality seems perverse, and in any case might not be possible to accomplish without also harming schools serving poorer communities in the long run since the well-functioning section of the school system supplies the economy with people of all race groups possessing the scarce skills required for economic growth, which in turn creates jobs and funds the government's pro-poor spending on education, health and social grants. However one looks at it, the way to deal with educational inequality is to improve learning and teaching in schools serving poor children.

It also makes sense to begin addressing learning inequalities in the early grades since the evidence is clear that early grade literacy and numeracy proficiency is strongly predictive of later educational outcomes and hence labour market success (Taylor et al. 2015; Van Broekhuizen et al. 2016; Branson et al. 2012). It is not an exaggeration to assert that meaningful and sustainable social and economic transformation in South Africa is not possible without a dramatic improvement in the teaching and learning of basic literacy and numeracy in the early grades at schools serving mainly poor children.

However, we still know very little about how to reduce these educational inequalities. What types of policies and programs (and their underlying behavioural mechanisms) actually generate improved learning outcomes in poor schools? Merely describing the characteristics of poorly functioning schools, and perhaps contrasting this with well-functioning schools, only takes one so far. Rather, we require experimental and quasi-experimental evidence about the types of policies and programs that lead to improved learning outcomes – and this chapter reviews the emerging literature using such methods.

17.2 Review of Experimental Studies

The availability of nationally representative data on learning achievement through TIMSS, PIRLS and SACMEQ has led to a much better understanding of the level and distribution of learning outcomes in South Africa. These datasets have also been used to conduct so-called "education production function" analysis, where correlates of achievement are explored (Gustafsson 2007; Van der Berg 2008; Taylor and Yu 2009; Taylor 2011; Spaull 2013). More recently, a growing number of studies have emerged, which aim to measure the causal effects of specific programs, resources or policies.

In 2009 Benjamin Piper reported on an RCT measuring the impact of the Systematic Method for Reading Success (SMRS). The program involved a set of 45 detailed lesson plans to be implemented over a 6-month period during the first half of grade 1. Some additional reading materials were also provided. It is not clear from the report how much training teachers received on the learning program or whether this learning program was aligned to the official curriculum. The SMRS was implemented in 10 intervention schools in each of the North West, Limpopo and Mpumalanga provinces. For evaluation purposes, five control schools in each province were also assessed, yielding a total of 30 intervention and 15 control schools. Despite the fact that on average, only 21 out of the 45 lessons were implemented, the evaluation found extraordinarily large gains in reading outcomes in intervention schools relative to control schools, of about 0.8 standard deviations (Piper 2009). The small sample size combined with the fact that such large effects were observed after such a short intervention raises some doubt about the reliability of the results. Nevertheless, this study does at least point to potentially large benefits that can be accrued through systematic teaching of reading in grade 1. Although this study was considered in the design of the DBE's Early Grade Reading Study (implemented from 2015) one might well question why there was no follow-up on these promising results.

Another literacy RCT conducted in 2014, also using lesson plans as well as additional materials and on-site coaching, showed a negligible impact (Fleisch et al. 2017). This "Reading Catch Up Program" (RCUP), which supported grade 4 learners with English as an additional language, had been reported to be highly effective in Gauteng as part of the Gauteng Primary Literacy and Mathematics Strategy (GPLMS) (Hellman 2012). However, there were two main limitations to the Hellman evaluation: it was not conducted by independent evaluators and it used a pre- and post-test to estimate impact but with no control group. Gains between pre- and post-testing were substantial – but it is impossible to know what children would have gained over the same period in the absence of the intervention.

In order to test the promising results of the RCUP program with more rigor and in a different setting, Fleisch et al. (2017) conducted an RCT in Pinetown, KwaZulu-Natal, during 2014. Although the intervention group experienced test score gains between pre- and post-testing, the control group improved by a similar amount, meaning that overall the causal impact of the program was negligible. Only those with relatively strong pre-test scores benefited from the program. This type of result is sometimes referred to as the "Matthew Effect" where those initially doing well tend to benefit most from additional support. It is likely that this program was unsuccessful because most learners did not have a good enough foundation in English from the Foundation Phase, and because it was too short – only a ten week program. These lessons informed the design of the Early Grade Reading Study.

The Early Grade Reading Study (EGRS) has been led by the Department of Basic Education, in collaboration with Wits University and the Human Sciences Research Council (HSRC). Three interventions were implemented, each aimed at improving home language literacy in grades 1 to 3. These were evaluated using an RCT in which over 4500 children across 230 schools in the North West Province were tracked over time from grade 1 in 2015 into and through grade 2 in 2016.

One EGRS intervention conducted meetings with parents to equip them with ways to support their child's reading development. Unfortunately, this intervention had a negligible effect on reading outcomes after two years. The main obstacle was ensuring that parents who were not sufficiently involved in their child's education actually attended these meetings – only about 30% of parents attended at least three sessions per year. Of course parent involvement is crucial in a child's reading development, but this intervention found it very difficult to shift parent involvement.

A second EGRS intervention provided teachers with daily lesson plans aligned to the curriculum as well as additional African language reading materials. Teachers in this intervention received training using the traditional model of centralized workshops (two-day workshops at the start of the year and in the middle of the year). Lesson observations indicated that this intervention began to shift teacher practice in more superficial ways – more reading materials were actually used during lessons and teachers attempted to implement new instructional methods. However, the quality of implementation was weak, and ultimately learner reading improved only marginally – the impact on Setswana literacy test scores after two years was 0.12 standard deviations, which represented an extra 19% of a year of learning.

A third intervention provided the exact same set of lesson plans and materials, but instead of centralized training, teachers received in-classroom support from specialist reading coaches once a month. This intervention was about 40% more expensive than the centralised training model (R557 per learner per year compared to R397), but had about twice the impact on learner reading. Compared to the control group, between 10% and 20% more children surpassed specific reading fluency benchmarks at the end of Grade 2 as a result of the coaching intervention. Not only did home language reading improve but so did English achievement. This finding is in line with other research suggesting that learning to read in one's home language facilitates better acquisition of a second language.

The coaching intervention helped boys catch up some of the way to girls. One of the alarming results of the PIRLS 2016 study is that South African boys in Grade 4 are a full grade level behind girls. This is consistent with the data from the EGRS, in which large gender gaps were apparent at the start of Grade 1 and persisted thereafter. However, in those schools that received the coaching intervention the gender gap was smaller than in comparison schools. Machin and McNally (2005, p.363) note evidence from the United Kingdom that boys benefit from highly structured methods of teaching and are more likely than girls to "respond negatively to poor teaching through disengagement and indifference or through disruptive behaviour". The focus in the lesson plans on opportunities for individualised attention and on structured classroom activities like group-guided reading may have helped boys especially.

None of the EGRS interventions, however, had a significant impact on reading outcomes in the intervention schools located in deep rural areas. Based on monitoring data collected by the EGRS service provider, the most likely barrier to impact in rural areas seems to have been lost teaching time and coaching contact time due to a combination of teacher absenteeism and disruptions to schooling caused by weather conditions, memorial services, protest action and extra-mural activities such as sports and choir competitions.

Taken together, the EGRS illustrates how hard it is to shift reading outcomes at scale, but also points to at least one intervention model that has demonstrated success. The implicit theory of change behind conventional teacher in-service training is that teachers will increase their knowledge and will then go back to their classrooms and change their practice. This may be naïve. Lesson plans provide a prompt to enact those methods which the training focussed on, and on-site coaching provides a further encouragement to ensure that enactment is happening, as well as to reflect on the quality thereof and to re-implement in an improved way. Furthermore, the EGRS results build on the positive findings of the Piper (2009) study where a structured learning program with daily lesson plans appeared to be highly effective.

At the time of writing the DBE is in the process of establishing an improvement plan to respond to the findings of the EGRS. It remains to be seen how this study will influence policy and programs in the sector on a wider scale.

Another RCT tested the impact of a parent involvement program, this time administered across 41 schools in the Eastern Cape (Bouguen et al. 2015). This program used teachers to facilitate meetings with parents of grade 4 and 5 children. The program consisted of three sessions aimed at encouraging parents to work more closely with schools and teachers and providing guidance about how to support their children with homework, test preparation and overall educational support (Bouguen et al. 2015, p.6). As in the case of the EGRS, parent attendance at the organised meetings was low, and although there was some evidence of changed behaviour amongst those parents who did attend, there was no discernible impact on any pupil outcomes.

An RCT reported on by Böhmer (2014) found strong positive effects of an after-school mathematics program using Khan Academy videos amongst grade 8 students in Cape Town. The study was conducted on a relatively small scale (only nine schools) and was highly resource-intensive in that each class was assigned their own coach who was a university student. This limits the scope for scaling such a program, especially outside urban centres. Secondly, it is not clear what the underlying change mechanism driving the results was. On the face of it, the Khan Academy program represents a technological innovation. However, receiving regular additional learning time with supervision from a coach represents a substantial intervention that may well have had a positive impact if a different set of materials was used. Moreover, there was a parent involvement component to the intervention. Nevertheless, this experiment points to the potential value of after-school interventions that extend learning time to improve mathematics outcomes in early secondary school.

A final RCT to report on is that evaluating the impact of the DBE's "Mind The Gap" study guides on matric performance (Taylor and Watson 2015). This intervention (and the evaluation thereof) was quite different from a project like the EGRS, in that it was less intensive and at the end of the school program (grade 12). Another difference is that the evaluation costs were minimal since National Senior Certificate (NSC) data could be analysed. During 2012, "Mind The Gap" study guides were provided to grade 12 students for the subjects of Accounting, Geography, Economics and Life Sciences. Books were not distributed throughout the country, and this allowed an experiment to be set up in Mpumalanga where no distribution had taken place.

A positive impact of about two percentage points was observed on Geography and Life Sciences results, and since scores were concentrated around the 30% and 40% pass thresholds, a simulation predicted that full scale distribution of the geography and life sciences study guides would have improved the overall matric pass rate by about 1 percentage point. Although the impact was smallish, the low cost of providing a study guide (R41.82) made this a relatively cost-effective intervention (Taylor and Watson 2015, p.22). Although this study does not hold the key to transforming educational outcomes in South Africa, it does illustrate how administrative data can be used at no cost to measure program impact. Since the DBE was only planning on distributing a limited number of study guides in 2012, choosing to randomly allocate them in one area not already covered by the intervention allowed for causal evaluation of their impact. The fact that the Geography and Life Sciences study guides had an impact but the Accounting and Economics guides did not, also illustrates that the effectiveness of an intervention model may depend on the content of the materials or the subject itself, and should caution researchers against generic interpretations of RCT results, such as "study guides work".

17.3 Review of Quasi-experimental Studies

The "Learning for Living" intervention administered by READ Educational Trust in the early 2000s appears to have followed a similar recipe to that of the GPLMS and EGRS instructional support interventions. Almost 1000 Foundation Phase classrooms across South Africa received additional home language reading materials, monthly coaching visits and a structured teaching cycle aligned to the curriculum, not entirely different to daily lesson plans.

Sailors et al. (2010) report on an impact evaluation of the "Learning for Living" project, in which intervention schools were matched to similar control schools on the basis of demographic characteristics. The report does not provide any further detail on how intervention schools were selected, how exactly the matching was done, or how well balanced the two groups of schools were on observable characteristics. The learner testing conducted after program implementation indicated noticeably better performance amongst intervention schools compared to control schools. Like the evaluation of the Systematic Method for Reading Success (Piper 2009), this project therefore points to a promising (though, due to methodological limitations, not proven) intervention model that was not properly followed up in terms of wider implementation.

Another quasi-experimental study using matching to identify control schools was the evaluation of the Dinaledi program (Blum et al. 2010). This program, which was administered by the Department of Education since 2008 through a conditional grant, provided more than 500 secondary schools with additional Mathematics and Science resources such as books, calculators and science laboratory equipment, as well as additional teachers and teacher in-service training. By comparing NSC data between intervention and matched control schools, the Dinaledi program was found to have had a significant and positive impact on the number of physical science and mathematics passes achieved by schools. The standard methodological limitations of the matching method apply (i.e. non-random selection of schools into the program) plus one further possible concern: it is possible that becoming a Dinaledi school may have attracted more and "better" learners to affected schools, thus having a negative impact on other nearby schools. This possibility was not investigated in the impact evaluation.

The Dinaledi program is no longer running in its original form, but the impact evaluation is somewhat instructive for how to reduce one important dimension of inequality. The 500 or so Dinaledi schools accounted for a relatively large proportion of high-level black African mathematics and physical science matric passes, partly because these schools were typically relatively large schools (Gustafsson and Taylor 2012). Mathematics and Physical Science interventions in targeted secondary schools with high enrolments does offer a way to substantially increase the numbers of black African candidates achieving strong results in Mathematics and Science thus facilitating entrance into key university courses where they are still underrepresented.

Two studies used Annual National Assessments (ANA) data for the full population of primary schools to evaluate program or policy impact. Firstly, Van der Berg et al. (2013) conducted an impact evaluation of the introduction of the Grade R program (Grade R is the year before Grade 1). Measuring impact is complicated by the fact that one cannot simply compare learning outcomes in schools with Grade R to outcomes in schools without the program since there may be systematic differences between these two groups of schools. In order to more plausibly identify impact, therefore, the study exploited the fact that between 2006 and 2011 many schools were introducing and expanding their Grade R program. Therefore, within a school there would have been cross-grade variation in the proportions of learners who attended grade R. Using ANA data from 2012 for grades 1 to 6, and a "school fixed effects" statistical method (where a control group is always identified from within the same school), it was possible to estimate the impact of grade R attendance on subsequent literacy and numeracy outcomes. The evaluation produced sobering results: Grade R only led to significant benefits in relatively wealthier schools (Quintiles 4 and 5) in more affluent provinces, but had a negligible effect in the poorest contexts.

The significance of the Grade R evaluation is twofold. Firstly, it illustrates the value of population-level performance data for the purpose of measuring impact of programs or policies. The fact that data for all schools existed and that there were outcomes for different grades was crucial for the methodology. Secondly, it is another instance of the so-called "Matthew Effect" where a program intended to be pro-poor had a larger impact in more affluent and more functional schools. Perhaps it makes sense that an additional year of schooling would have more impact when implemented within a well-functioning school, but observing actual quantitative estimates of test score gains provides a reality check on how easily the inequalities in the school system *can* be reduced.

A similar "school fixed effects" methodology was applied by Taylor and Von Fintel (2016) to measure the impact of mother tongue versus English as the language of instruction in the Foundation Phase. One cannot simply compare schools using mother tongue in the Foundation Phase with schools using English since these two groups of schools tend to differ socio-economically. Between 2007 and 2011 some schools made changes in their language of instruction policy with the effect that it is possible to compare learners in different grades within the same school who received different language policy regimes. The 2012 ANA data was used as the outcome measure. As in the Grade R evaluation, having data for more than one grade per school was critical to this method.

Taylor and Von Fintel (2016) found that, on average, learners who were taught in their mother tongue during grades 1 to 3 did better in grades 4 to 6 in the English ANA tests than children in the same schools who had been taught in English from Grade 1. This finding confirms theoretical predictions from linguistic research that a strong foundation in one's home language enables better second language acquisition. This study illustrates the value of quasi-experimental research methods using adminstrative data, even if those data are not perfect, as in the case of the ANA. The results also point to the importance of strengthening home language instruction (including materials provision) in the Foundation Phase for the sake of better subsequent learning outcomes in other subjects. The inequalities that exist in the quality and quantity of reading materials across the languages must be reduced as part of the battle against overall educational inequality.

Fleisch and Schöer (2014) also applied a quasi-experimental method to ANA data in order to measure the effect of the GPLMS program. They employ a Regression Disconuity Design (RDD), which exploits the fact that an arbitrary cutoff (a school average score of 40% on a prior systemic assessment) was used to assign schools to the GPLMS program. Whilst all schools below the cutoff (and hence allocated to GPLMS) cannot be compared to all schools above the cutoff, it is plausible to assume that those schools who achieved just below the cutoff are comparable to those who scored just above the cutoff – this is the rationale behind the RDD approach. Fleisch and Schöer (2014) find a strong positive effect of GPLMS on those schools who just made it into the program. Aside from a few methodological concerns around a possible test instrument effect discussed by the authors, the main limitation of the RDD method is that the result only applies to schools in the vacinity of the cutoff. Therefore, one has to assume that the program would have had a similar effect on schools with lower initial performance. Nevertheless, this study provided preliminary support for the mix of lesson plans, additional materials and on-site coaching.

Gustafsson and Taylor (2018) use a quasi-experimental method as well as administrative outcomes data from the NSC examinations over the years to measure the effect of the quality of provincial government administration. Nearly all experimental research measures the effect of specific inputs or policies, and is limited in its ability to measure the effect of system-level factors such as overall governance. Although there is some work describing education systems that have improved or deteriorated over time (for example, Bruns et al. 2012), those studies cannot easily isolate the effect of the administration from other changing characteristics within a country, such as economic growth or other time-specific trends. In short, schools are not randomly assigned to governments.

Gustafsson and Taylor (2018) exploit a natural experiment created by changes in provincial boundaries that occurred in South Africa in 2005. This meant that about 150 secondary schools experienced a change in their provincial education department. It was found that 'moving' into a better performing province was associated with large student performance improvements, equal in magnitude to around a year's worth of progress in a fast improving country. Gustafsson and Taylor (2018) discuss several factors which might have accounted for the better governance, and these have implications for how system-level reforms could reduce educational inequality. Overall per student funding is not significantly different across provinces, and is actually slightly pro-poor, so this was not a significant explanatory variable in itself, although the discretionary use of funds may have differed somewhat across provinces. What did seem to matter was more efficient use of non-personnel funds by the authorities, with a special focus on educational materials, the brokering of pacts between stakeholders, including teacher unions, schools and communities, and better monitoring and support to schools from officials.

17.4   Key Lessons from Experimental Studies

In considering these experimental and quasi-experimental studies as a body of research, a number of key lessons emerge.

Firstly, we observe that when program impact is measured with a high degree of methodological rigour, effect sizes are perhaps disappointingly small. Back-of-the-envelope calculations would suggest that the most successful EGRS intervention using on-site coaching can be expected to close about one-fifth of the reading gap between non-fee schools and quintile 5 schools. Indeed there is no magic bullet to close the gap between South Africa's well performing and poorly performing sections of the school system.

Secondly, we see that change takes time. The experience of the Reading Catch Up Program (RCUP), which was implemented over only 11 weeks, as compared with the EGRS which was implemented over two years and used a similar intervention design, suggests that it takes at least a year or two for an intervention aimed at large scale change in classroom practice to gain traction.

Thirdly, it is often the initially better performing or more advantaged children that benefit more from particular programs or policies. This sort of result was observed in the RCUP evaluation, the Grade R impact evaluation, the EGRS and the "Mind The Gap" study guide evaluation.

While it is unfortunate that many interventions do not benefit those most in need of support, it is not entirely unexpected. It stands to reason, for example, that in a well-functioning primary school adding an additional preschool year will be beneficial for those who attend. As technological innovations increasingly form part of the way education happens, it is again likely that more affluent children will benefit most. But this should not prevent us from investigating ways to leverage technology for educational improvement. Perhaps a practical recommendation is that policies and programs should be designed with the least well-functioning schools and contexts in mind, but at the same time capitalize on improving outcomes in a tier of schools that are "change-ready" even if this may technically increase inequality.

Importantly, many of the evaluations discussed above excluded the most affluent schools from the interventions. The EGRS, RCUP and "Mind the Gap" studies, for example, all restricted the experiments to lower quintile schools. In the case of EGRS, therefore, the "urban township" schools that saw large gains relative to the "deep rural" schools should not be regarded as the most affluent schools in the country. For purposes of equity it could be argued that special interventions and overall policy design should always be targeting improved learning in relatively poor schools. Following Rawlsian principles of justice, the key question to ask is whether the least well-off in society benefit, and if the more affluent also happen to benefit then so be it.

It is also important to consider that the needs of the South African economy dictate that it is not only essential to improve outcomes in the least well-functioning schools for the sake of poverty reduction, but also to fill certain skills shortages for the sake of economic growth and to do so through more black graduates. Given that even within quintile 5 schools black candidates account for more NSC passes than any other race group (own calculations using NSC 2017 data), it is by no means clear that we should reject interventions that improve outcomes in this group of schools on the basis that they increase inequality. Overall, the focus should be on finding implementable interventions that do benefit the weakest and most vulnerable learners, and on implementing these, even if the strongest learners end up benefiting more.

Fourth and last, based on the results of existing experimental research, the most convincing evidence about early grade interventions that work in South Africa's non-fee paying schools points to structured pedagogic programs aligned to the curriculum and supported by regular on-site coaching. The next phase in this area of research will explore how such programs can be taken to a greater level of scale, how more cost-effective means of implementation can be developed, and to what extent this basic model can also deliver positive outcomes in English as a First Additional Language and in Mathematics which together with home language literacy form the key learning areas in the Foundation Phase.

17.5 Conclusion

No matter how one approaches the subject of inequality, the current levels of educational inequality are unacceptable. Unfortunately, we cannot choose from a menu of alternative equilibria or alternative distributions of educational outcomes – we can only choose amongst alternative means (policies or programs) by which we hope to get there. Experimental and quasi-experimental methods allow for a robust measurement of the impact of specific policies and programs, thereby telling us what is likely to improve outcomes and how quickly that improvement is likely to occur.

Experimental research indicates that there are no known programs or policies that can be expected to dramatically reduce inequalities through improving learning outcomes. Even comprehensive system-level change, through for instance a new and better administration, takes time to bring about improvement. Despite this sobering outcome of a review of experimental studies, such a review is also instructive about how to improve things, even if it will be slow.

The available evidence is supportive of sustained classroom-level pedagogical support to teachers involving additional learning materials and regular follow-up visits. We have not yet conducted rigorous evaluations of attempts to improve teacher content knowledge or to improve the functionality of schools as organisations. Dramatic changes in the political economy of South Africa and of the educational landscape may well result in more substantial positive or negative shifts in inequality and learning outcomes, but this is beyond the scope of experimental research or of education policy design.

Experimental research will continue to provide scarce information about the cost-effectiveness of alternative policy options. This tool should be used (where appropriate) to find out how to improve learning outcomes in poor communities and the least well-functioning schools. If education faculties devoted time and resources to training their post-graduate students on quantitative research methods this would increase the pool of people doing experimental and quasi-experimental research. This would also contribute to an increased awareness of the limitations of other methods for measuring the impact of policies and programs. Better administrative data will enable more quasi-experimental studies, and could reduce the cost of experimental pilot evaluations. Where experimental studies point to successful programs or program features these should be incorporated into policy as far as possible.

References

Blum, J., Krishnan, N., & Legovini, A. (2010). *Expanding opportunities for South African youth through math and science: The impact of Dinaledi programme*. Washington, DC: World Bank.

Böhmer, B. (2014). *Testing numeric*: Evidence from a randomized controlled trial of a computer based mathematics intervention in Cape Town high schools. Masters Dissertation, University of Cape Town.

Bouguen, A., Gumede, K., & Gurgand, M. (2015). *Parent's participation, involvement and impact on student achievement: Evidence from a randomized evaluation in South Africa*. https://halshs-01241957

Branson, N., Garlick, J., Lam, D., & Leibbrandt, M. (2012). Education and inequality: The South African case. In *A Southern Africa Labour and Development Research Unit Working Paper Number 75*. Cape Town: SALDRU, University of Cape Town.

Bruns, B., Evans, D., & Luque, J. (2012). *Achieving world class education in Brazil: The next agenda*. Washington, DC: World Bank.

Department of Basic Education. (2017). GHS 2015: Focus on schooling 2015. https://wwweducationgovza/Portals/0/Documents/Reports/2015%20GHS%20Reportpdf?ver=2017-07-03-102540-673

Fleisch, B., & Schöer, V. (2014). Large-scale instructional reform in the Global South: Insights from the mid-point evaluation of the Gauteng primary language and mathematics strategy. *South African Journal of Education, 34*(3), 1–12.

Fleisch, B., Taylor, S., Schöer, V., & Mabogoane, T. (2017). Failing to catch up in reading in the middle years: The findings of the impact evaluation of the reading catch-up programme in South Africa. *International Journal of Educational Development, 53*, 36–47.

Gustafsson, M. (2007). Using the hierarchical linear model to understand school production in South Africa. *South African Journal of Economics, 75*(1), 84–98.

Gustafsson, M., & Taylor, S. (2012). The state of mathematics, science and technology in our schools. Internal DBE memo.

Gustafsson, M., & Taylor, S. (2018). Treating schools to a new administration: Evidence of the impact of better practices in the system-level administration of schools. *Journal of African Economies*. https://doi-org.ez.sun.ac.za/10.1093/jae/ejy005

Hellman, L. (2012). *GPLMS intersen catch-up programme: Analysis of results*. Unpublished report produced for the Gauteng Department of Education.

Imbens, G. W., & Wooldridge, J. M. (2009). Recent developments in the econometrics of program evaluation. *Journal of Economic Literature, 47*(1), 5–86.

Machin, S., & McNally, S. (2005). Gender and student achievement in English schools. *Oxford Review of Economic Policy, 21*(3), 357–372.

Piper, B. (2009). Integrated education program: Impact study of SMRS using early grade reading assessment in three provinces in South Africa. RTI International, Research Triangle Park, NC Retrieved from https://www.eddataglobal.org/courses/survey/resources/Handout_3_FINAL_RSA_SMRS_EGRA_Impact_Study.pdf

Sailors, M., Hoffman, J. V., Pearson, P. D., Beretvas, S. N., & Matthee, B. (2010). The effects of first-and second-language instruction in Rural South African Schools. *Bilingual Research Journal, 33*(1), 21–41.

Spaull, N. (2013). Poverty & privilege: Primary school inequality in South Africa. *International Journal of Educational Development, 33*(5), 436–447.

Taylor, S. (2011). *Uncovering indicators of effective school management in South Africa using the national school effectiveness study*. Stellenbosch: Stellenbosch Economic Working Papers. 10(11).

Taylor, S., & Von Fintel, M. (2016). Estimating the impact of language of instruction in South African primary schools: A fixed effects approach. *Economics of Education Review, 50*, 75–89.

Taylor, S., & Watson, P. (2015). The impact of study guides on "matric" performance: Evidence from a randomised experiment. Stellenbosch: Stellenbosch Economic Working Papers 13(15)

Taylor, S., & Yu, D. (2009). *The importance of socio-economic status in determining educational achievement in South Africa*. Stellenbosch: Stellenbosch Economic Working Papers.

Taylor, S., Van der Berg, S., Reddy, V., & Janse van Rensburg, D. (2015). The evolution of educational inequalities through secondary school: Evidence from a South African panel study. *Development Southern Africa, 32*(4), 425–442.

Van Broekhuizen, H., Van der Berg, S., & Hofmeyr, H. (2016). *Higher education access and outcomes for the 2008 national matric cohort*. Stellenbosch Economic Working Papers, 16/16

Van der Berg, S. (2008). How effective are poor schools? Poverty and educational outcomes in South Africa. *Studies in Educational Evaluation, 34*(3), 145–154.

Van der Berg, S., Burger, C., Burger, R., de Vos, M., Du Rand, G., Gustafsson, M., Moses, E., Shepherd, D., Spaull, N., & Taylor, S. (2011). Low quality education as a poverty trap. Stellenbosch Economic Working Papers: 25/11

Van der Berg, S., Girdwood, E., Shepherd, D., Van Wyk, C., Kruger, J., Viljoen, J., Ezeobi, O., & Ntaka, P. (2013). *The impact of the introduction of grade R on learning outcomes*. University of Stellenbosch: RESEP.

Chapter 18
Taking Change to Scale: Lessons from the Jika iMfundo Campaign for Overcoming Inequalities in Schools

Mary Metcalfe and Alistair Witten

18.1 Introduction

This chapter reflects on learning from a large-scale system improvement intervention, the Jika iMfundo campaign, which was conducted from 2015–2017 in the Pinetown and King Cetshwayo districts in KwaZulu-Natal.[1] The intervention was funded by the National Education Collaboration Trust, led by the provincial Department of Education and other key stakeholders, and supported by the Programme to Improve Learning Outcomes (PILO). The project is distinguished from many other interventions by the ambitious design requirement of testing a methodology simple enough in construction to be implemented across the system within existing resources, legislative frameworks and administrative structures, but – because of the urgency of need for change – designed to have a significant and a sustainable positive impact on learning across the system. The unit of scale for the pilot was all 1,200 public primary and secondary public schools in the 2 districts.

The campaign focused on building management routines at the institutional levels of school and district to support the improvement of curriculum coverage. The

---

[1] Jika iMfundo has been extended to a further 4 districts from 2018. PILO is also working in the Gauteng and Free State provinces and some of the learnings reflected on in this chapter have been sharpened by experiences in those provinces.

M. Metcalfe (✉)
University of Johannesburg, Soweto, South Africa
e-mail: metcalfe.mary11@gmail.com

A. Witten
The Bertha Centre for Social Innovation and Entreprenuership, Graduate School of Business, University of Cape Town, Cape Town, South Africa
e-mail: amw056@mail.harvard.edu

© Springer Nature Switzerland AG 2019
N. Spaull, J. D. Jansen (eds.), *South African Schooling: The Enigma of Inequality*, Policy Implications of Research in Education 10,
https://doi.org/10.1007/978-3-030-18811-5_18

assumption, yet to be verified, was that if curriculum coverage improves (defined as more learners learning more, and more at the appropriate depth), learning outcomes will improve. The framing of management routines explicitly focused on supporting teachers as an entry point into the 'instructional core' of teaching – the only place where learning can improve (Elmore 2006, 2010). These practices aimed to institutionalize professional agency in problem-identification and problem-solving conversations within schools (between teachers and between teachers and the SMT) as well as between the school and district officials in which evidence about learning was used as the basis for professional conversations and professional judgements related to curriculum coverage decisions.

18.2   Background and Context

Working in schools across the two districts underscored the importance of the socio-political and economic contexts and the influence of these on processes of implementation. The King Cetshwayo and Pinetown districts mirror the many faces of urban and rural poverty. 80% of King Cetshwayo is classified rural and a large section of the District fell under the administration of the KwaZulu Bantustan prior to 1994. The annual household income of 50% of the population is less that R19 600 per year, and less than R38 200 for 80% of the population, with many pensioner-headed households (King Cetshwayo District Municipality 2017, p. 31). The Pinetown district is half of the eThekwini Metropolitan District. Here, urban wealth and poverty exist side by side, with large informal settlements both in the urban centres, and in the peri-urban peripheries. The education contexts, especially that of the Pinetown district, reflect high levels of social and educational inequality, with the well-established and better-resourced schools contributing to the relatively higher education performance of Pinetown.

18.3   Inequality, Opportunity to Learn, and Curriculum Coverage

There is an urgent need to improve education outcomes in South Africa. Although significant public and private investments have been made in education, learning outcomes remain poor. South Africa was placed last out of all 50 countries participating in PIRLS 2016 (Howie et al. 2017, p. 2). Retention is poor – as many as 50% of learners who enter school, leave with no credentials (Department of Basic Education 2017, p. 24). Poor communities are the most affected, slow progress in achieving impact perpetuates pervasive inequality, and the attendant risk to society poses a threat to the future of the democratic state. PILO was established in 2013 as a response to the continuing crisis in education. Its mission is to develop and test a model for systemic improvement that can impact positively on learning outcomes on scale, especially for the poor, and to share learning with the system and the sector.

Inequitable education outcomes in South Africa are a function of social and economic inequalities. The seminal 1966 Coleman study in the United States, *Equality of Educational Opportunity*, found that poverty influences learner academic outcomes and school performance, with achievement being closely tied to family background. It concluded that "it is for the most disadvantaged children that improvements in school quality will make the most difference in achievement" (Coleman et al. 1966, p. 22). The imperatives of both social justice and the efficient management of resources require that what happens in schools and how they are resourced and managed must be transformed to mediate greater success for the learners and students for whom it matters most.

One of the underpinnings of PILO's focus relates to Schmidt et al. (2011)'s association of education equality in the US with 'opportunities to learn'. He argues that content coverage (and the quality of coverage) is the central element in providing opportunities to learn, and notes that "Without equality in content coverage, there can be no equality in opportunity related that content" (Schmidt et al. 2011, p. 2).

Schmidt further notes that "whether a student is even exposed to a topic depends on where he or she lives" (2010, p. 13), and that "socioeconomic status and opportunity to learn are both independently related to achievement" (2010, p. 16). He concludes by arguing that:

> . . . with focused, rigorous, coherent, and common content-coverage frameworks, the United States could minimize the impact of socio economic status on content coverage. . . (Schmidt et al. 2011, p. 16).

A number of studies on the quality of schooling in South Africa concur that poverty remains the most powerful determinant of school improvement and educational opportunity in the country (Van der Berg 2001; Van der Berg and Burger 2003; Gustafsson 2005). PILO's focus on improving content coverage sought to demonstrate that this could be an achievable and significant variable within the zone of possibility of system improvement despite the effects of poverty and social inequality on learning outcomes.

In South Africa, the Annual National Assessments can be seen as a proxy for curriculum coverage, understood as mastery of the official curriculum. These results show a close correlation between coverage as performance and socio-economic quintiles. In Table 18.1 below, quintile one includes the poorest households, and quintile five the most affluent. The achievement gap in mathematics at Grade 1 is 13%. By Grade 6 this has increased to 22% (Department of Basic Education 2014, p. 89).

Inadequate curriculum coverage has consistently been identified as among the key reasons for poor learning outcomes, especially in schools serving poor communities in South Africa (Taylor and Moyane 2005; Oosthuizen and Bhorat 2006; Hoadley 2010; NEEDU 2013). Management and leadership at school and district levels is important, especially in creating the enabling conditions that increase

Table 18.1 Average % mark in mathematics by grade and poverty quintile, annual national assessment 2014

	Gr1	Gr2	Gr3	Gr4	Gr5	Gr6	Gr7
Quintile 1	6.51	5.92	5.25	3.28	3.21	3.81	1.01
Quintile 2	6.66	6.02	5.29	3.43	3.34	3.96	0.87
Quintile 3	6.74	6.04	5.39	3.56	3.45	4.04	0.82
Quintile 4	7.12	6.35	5.8	4.04	4.12	4.61	0.92
Quintile 5	7.84	7.14	6.89	5.29	5.5	6.03	2.16

Source: DBE, 2014

opportunities to learn. Wills (2018) notes that the quality of management and leadership is crucial to improving learning outcomes. Hoadley's (2010) meta-review of the SA literature has shown that among the key management variables related to curriculum coverage in schools and improved learner academic performance are regulation of time; monitoring and support for planning and delivery in relation to curriculum coverage; and quality assurance of tests and the monitoring of results.

The design of the Jika Imfundo campaign thus focused on the centrality of curriculum coverage in providing opportunities to learn as a key variable in mitigating the effects of poverty and social inequality on learner well-being and academic performance. Curriculum coverage and its location in the core work of schools was regarded as an important starting point for change and improvement in the system. The design focused on educational leadership and management as a key enabler of teacher practices structuring coverage and therefore of opportunity to learn. The focus on both Principals and HoD as managers of the implementation of the curriculum is critical. Hoadley et al. (2009) found that only 17% of principals identified overseeing curriculum and instruction as their main task. The role of leaders at the school and district levels in strengthening the connections between their work and the core functions of teaching and learning in schools thus became crucial in a design focused on creating opportunities to learn.[2]

18.4 The PILO Change Methodology

The Jika iMfundo trial-at-scale provided an opportunity to test PILO's core methodology for change and deepen the understanding of its application in relation to systemic challenges. This required a methodology and design that fulfilled a number of conditions. Firstly, the change has to be consistent with government policy priorities and assist in making the policy intentions of government routine in the work of officials and schools. All of the design elements of Jika iMfundo reinforced components of key government policy documents and provided the tools

---

[2]For a detailed account of the interventions at school level (for teachers, department heads and lead teachers, principals and deputy principals) see (Metcalfe 2018). For a detailed account of the interventions with circuit managers at district level see McLennan (2018).

for translating these into effective practice. In this sense, the work of PILO can be described as assisting with the execution of policy. This breaks with the current practice of 'magical thinking' – the assumption that changes will take place in schools on the basis of policy dictum without evidence of a plausible link of causation involving on-scale activities of support.

Secondly, change requires that responsibility for implementing the change must be located where the responsibility will remain for sustaining the programme. Jika iMfundo was a campaign owned by the Districts and the schools and was constructed to achieve the adoption of new behaviours and practices as part of the professional repertoire of educators and district officials. Policy intentions and instructions do not change behaviour. These are filtered through what educators and officials already understand and believe, what they are convinced will work in their context, and what they think is possible. A core principle informing the PILO approach to embedding new behaviours was a positive appreciation of how educators and officials exercise agency in making daily decisions about their work. Compliance alone is an inadequate vehicle for meaningful and enduring change, and passive compliance is inimical to professional agency and a sense of responsibility.

The third design principle focuses on building systems-wide capacity for change. As Levin (2012) notes, personal agency and moral purpose are not enough for effective change. These have to be accompanied by the knowledge, skills, and dispositions required to enable the change. The campaign built confidence in the use of tools within the school and between schools and districts to make the routine practices of educators and officials complementary and mutually reinforcing.

Fourth, a broad alliance of key stakeholders is necessary to ignite and sustain change, especially in education. Influence (to make decisions and drive change) is distributed across the school, district, and provincial levels of the system. The more different centres of influence maintain alignment to shared purpose and urgency, the greater the possibility of success. A broad alliance committed to change helps stabilise the system and maintain momentum through inevitable setbacks and disruptions. Teacher unions formed an important part of the coalition for change in the campaign, and regular reporting and consultation meetings were convened at provincial, regional and branch levels. These meetings were invaluable as an opportunity to co-design, and as a source of monitoring information that guided implementation. Jika iMfundo was a campaign to be joined by all role players. The by-line 'what I do matters' represented the appeal to moral purpose and recognition of the agency and impact of all the stakeholders.

The fifth principle of the programme's design focused on monitoring and tracking as integral to the change process within the school and the districts. School management teams were supported to regularly track teachers' curriculum coverage reports so that they could respond timeously and offer appropriate support. These improvements were designed to be visible to the educators and officials so that they could track, validate, and celebrate success. The change programme of Jika iMfundo used the progress made in tracking as a motivator to 'stay the course' and 'accelerate the pace'.

Sixth, PILO's approach to change is rooted in the two important conceptions of internal and reciprocal accountability (Elmore 2000, 2005, 2010). Internal accountability relates to the clarity of roles, expectations, practices and processes around how work is carried out within the organization or the team. It focuses on creating a coherent system that enables and supports teaching and learning in the school. Reciprocal accountability emphasises the importance of providing requisite support to enable change and improve practice. Well-functioning institutions have strong internal and reciprocal accountability systems. Elmore (2010) argues that schools are unlikely to be able to respond to external accountability without effective practices of internal accountability. This view is supported by City et al. (2010), who note that schools with "chronically weak institutional cultures...have no capacity to mount a coherent response to external pressure, because they have no common instructional culture to start with" (p. 37). Jika iMfundo sought to establish a common instructional culture of curriculum management with routines of tracking, reflecting, reporting, monitoring and collaborative problem-solving.

Seventh, the primary site of teacher professional development in South Africa is inevitably the school. Teachers do not have regular opportunities to participate in professional development opportunities provided by the employer, teacher unions, or by professional associations. Elmore (2008) notes that schools are ideal sites for professional development as, "teachers learn in settings in which they actually work, through observing and being observed by colleagues confronting similar problems of practice" (p. 73). City et al. (2010) support this view and note that professional development must be relevant and, "deliberately connected to tangible and immediate problems of practice to be effective" (p. 75).

Professional development at the level of the school challenges the notion of teaching as a 'private practice' – where the work of teachers is conducted in individual classrooms that are isolated from the rest of the school and the broader community (Lortie 1977). Talbert and McLaughlin (1994) argue that "privacy norms characteristic of the profession undermine capacity for teacher learning and sustained professional commitment"(p. 124). The campaign and its interventions promoted schools as sites for professional learning by creating the organizational arrangements and routines that promote collaboration and the de-privatization of professional practice. The core design of the programme was to enable schools to build practices that enabled functioning as a professional learning community, with internal accountability systems and practices characterized by a culture of professional, supportive, evidence-based conversations.

Eighth, in order for the change to be sustainable, it must have systemic support. If attempts are made to change any element of the system without systemic reinforcement, it is likely to fail. Peurach and Peurach (2011) has argued this:

> ...The logic of systemic reform held that ambitious outcomes would not be realised with piecemeal, uncoordinated reforms. Rather, the problems to be solved were understood to be many and interdependent...(Peurach and Peurach 2011, p. 6).

The Jika iMfundo campaign was designed to be coherent and mutually reinforcing across the structures and practices of the different levels of the system. The implications of this for PILO meant a high degree of coordination across the school, district, and provincial levels that was underpinned by collaboration and co-design to promote ownership and garner support of the district officials, who implemented the campaign under their line-authority.

The ninth design principle is that the intervention had to be scrupulously costed to be replicable at scale within the resource constraints of government. In the case of Jika iMfundo, the proposed interventions that were proposed initially had to be re-appraised and rigorously remodelled so that they were implementable within the resource constraints of the districts and schools. This affected the 'dosage' of the intervention, which is relatively light compared to initiatives working on a smaller scale. Given the lesson that many excellent 'pilot' interventions cannot be taken to scale because of resource constraints, PILO committed from the outset that its work would be cost-effective, scalable, and replicable.

Lastly, to effect change across a system is ambitious, so there must be a relentless focus on the scope of change consistent with the key elements of design. PILO focused on a few key elements of change and pursued these in a purposeful and consistent manner. For Jika iMfundo, the simple story was, "we are improving learning outcomes by improving curriculum coverage". This compelling narrative bound the role players at different levels of the system around a common purpose, and a shared programme of action. An unwavering focus also served to counter the 'change fatigue' brought about by previous 'quick fix' solutions that had been introduced into the system.

It is hoped that the documenting of lessons of change in Jika iMfundo will serve to inform change management practices for other interventions in South African education. For the Jika iMfundo intervention, the chosen object of change was management support for improved curriculum coverage.

18.5 Curriculum Coverage as the Object of Change

Curriculum coverage was chosen as the key object of change because it is more amenable to high-impact and short-term systemic improvement than some of the more powerful but difficult-to-change system capabilities such as teacher content or pedagogical knowledge content. Curriculum coverage was selected as the entry point because of its potency in increasing opportunities to learn; its focus on addressing curriculum coverage challenges and deficits; and its unifying role in mobilising different stakeholders. Curriculum coverage is a multi-dimensional phenomenon. Each dimension was central to the different component of the campaign.

Firstly, curriculum coverage provides a lens for exploring the dynamics of the instructional core. Elmore (2004) argues that improvement occurs in the core by influencing what teachers do in their daily teaching practice. He notes that the influence of SMT members in improving classroom instruction is determined by how leadership practices influence the knowledge and skill of teachers, the level of work in they do in their classrooms, and the engagement of learners in the learning tasks. The focus on curriculum coverage – with particular emphasis on evidence of learning and its supportive management by the SMT – gives the SMT a direct 'line-of-sight' into the instructional core. Curriculum coverage provides a vehicle for the SMT and the teachers it supports to establish routine practices of monitoring, identifying and solving problems of coverage through professional conversations. Where reflection and learning form part of these conversations, there is a greater likelihood that teaching practice will improve. The Jika iMfundo campaign invested heavily in guiding the SMT to supervise practice in a supportive manner so that teachers were open to sharing their challenges and exploring effective ways to deal with these.

Secondly, curriculum coverage provides the disparate components of the system with a common 'message' of what needs to change. Teachers, SMT members and District officials all understand the fundamental necessity of improving curriculum coverage and their respective roles in achieving this. The goal of these collective efforts is an improvement in learning. This was maintained as the core moral and professional focus and motivation throughout the implementation of the project.

Some variables in education are hard to change. Social and economic factors erode learning potential, material constraints hamper education delivery, poor teacher knowledge undermines the delivery of the intended curriculum – but more effective planning and monitoring of curriculum coverage is an achievable goal that lies within the zone of improved capability of schools. Improving curriculum coverage is a professional action that allows school management teams and district officials to exercise agency despite working in challenging circumstances.

Thirdly, curriculum coverage is quantifiable, despite the pitfalls of quantification. It can allow systems level diagnosis and can inform the development of appropriate responses to address these. The pilot created dashboards reflecting coverage relative to learner performance that can be used for reflection, for monitoring and support, and for reporting to the levels at school or district where action can be taken. Hargreaves et al. (2013) have argued that accountability contributes to improvement when there is "collaborative involvement in data collection and analysis, collective responsibility for improvement, and a consensus that the indicators and metrics involved . . . are accurate, meaningful, fair, broad and balanced". This is as true within the school as it is within the broader education system.

Lastly, curriculum coverage is an acknowledged problem and a key policy goal of the Department of Basic Education's Action Plan 2019: Goal 18 – Ensure that learners *cover all the topics and skills* areas that they should cover within their current school year. The DBE's Macro Indicator report indicated that:

> Poor learning outcomes can be traced to differential 'input indicators' or characteristics of school and teacher practices. The report showed, in particular, that incomplete coverage of the curriculum and inadequate teacher subject knowledge are examples of the problematic 'inputs' to educational quality (Department of Basic education 2015, p. 63)

The design of the Jika iMfundo intervention responded to this by developing, testing and improving tools for effective monitoring of curriculum coverage at the school and district levels. The focus on monitoring moved away from a 'tick box approach' – compliance reporting within stipulated timeframes and schedules without substantive engagement with the practices required to improve teaching and learning in the classrooms.

18.6 Lessons Learned: Assumptions Challenged and Insights Deepened

The pilot was a learning journey. We underestimated the depth of the dysfunction between teachers' experiences of the rigidity of the demands of the curriculum policy, and the structural inability of the system to support teachers and school managers. When curriculum coverage was chosen as the object of change, we did not anticipate the extent to which it would touch at the heart of teacher frustration with rigid policy implementation that is context-blind and fails to acknowledge the realities on the ground.

18.6.1 Curriculum Coverage: Tick-Box Thinking and Professional Realities

We have learned that a compliance regime underestimates the primacy of the role of the teacher in exercising professional judgment in interpreting curriculum policy injunctions relative to her context and the overwhelmingly difficult conditions under which these judgments are made. Using Schmidt and Prawat (2006), it could be argued that curriculum governance is weak because of the poor coherence and credibility of the prescribed curriculum experienced by teachers.

The South African Curriculum is prescriptive, ambitious and driven by coverage reporting that prioritises pace over depth of learning. Learning backlogs are cumulative, with teachers constantly reporting that learners have failed to master concepts foundational to learning in subsequent years. This intersects with progression policies which limit the number of times a learner can be held back and repeat a year. Many classes are in fact multigrade – the ANA results for KZN in 2014 indicated that in Grade 4, only 40% of learners in Maths and 43% in EFAL mastered the required content, and these figures remain more or less constant from Grades 4–6. However, nationally less than 10% of learners repeat Grades 4 to 6 (Department of Basic Education 2016, p. 14) suggesting that 50% who had not mastered the content were 'progressed'. Teachers report that they are faced with a widely divergent performance range within each class and must teach a curriculum which depends on a prior knowledge and skill base for its successful delivery, but which is absent.

Teachers need to constantly make professional judgments in the interface between four key variables of curriculum implementation: pace, inclusion, conceptual depth and topic progression relative to time. They find these judgements hard to make, and generally feel locked into a treadmill of sacrificing quality of learning for pace – but still lag behind. The making of these judgements is typically an isolated professional activity with rare opportunities for collaboration. The teachers receive inadequate support and are disempowered from sharing and seeking guidance by the belief that they are not permitted to change the sequence and timing of the guidance given by CAPS. Curriculum coverage problems are, from the classroom up, under-reported and undetected, and are concealed by the imperative to report compliance.

A question that unlocks the agency of teachers and subject advisers is, 'What percentage of children should be performing at what level in order to proceed to the next topic?'. The emancipatory power of this question is the realisation that there is no correct answer. The response is context-specific and lies within the professional judgment of the teacher who must discern the optimum balance between firstly, the pressures of meeting externally imposed coverage targets; secondly, professional commitment to the success of all learners; thirdly, the level of difficulty of the material; and lastly judging content pace relative to the annual requirements. In a compliance-driven reporting system, teachers tend to compromise cognitive level and conceptual depth of the topic that needs to be covered. The emancipation of professional judgement, articulated and tested with peers at school level, requires a movement away from a compliance mind-set to the concept of *professional interaction* with CAPS rather than *compliance* with CAPS. This was a discomfiting thought for many educators. The compliance imperative results in reporting on what is required in the system rather than on the reality of what is happening in the classroom.

In terms of the analysis offered by Schmidt and Prawat (2006), the experience of schools is that curriculum coherence and credibility are weak. Teachers report being unable to "devote a fairly consistent amount of time to each of the topics" (p. 650) prescribed, and generally report that the allocated times are insufficient. For Schmidt, curriculum coherence does not require homogeneity of time allocation, but that teachers would, on average, find that topics can be taught at a grade level in a similar time frame. The experience of teachers in the programme confirms that where "students have not mastered the important initial elements of the topic, teachers will spend more time on a topic than expected" (Schmidt and Prawat 2006, p. 646). This is perceived by teachers to be a consequence of learner progression policy. Schmidt and Prawat (2006) have shown that greater curriculum coherence at classroom level leads to increased achievement (p. 650). Where time prescriptions for coverage do not match the realities of the classroom, it follows that learning – and therefore learner achievement – will be negatively affected. Without curriculum coherence the prescribed curriculum cannot 'inspire action and belief on the part of teachers', and thus does not enjoy credibility amongst teachers – which for Schmidt and Prawat (2006), is "the minimum for effective curriculum governance" (p. 657).

Current departmental curriculum coverage monitoring practices nationally and in provinces use a one-dimensional and impoverished operational definition of coverage which prioritises pace by checking activity completion ('tick-box') by the teacher rather than of quality of learning. This danger has been identified by both the DBE, and in the Auditor General's 2018 Performance Audit on Curriculum Coverage

> There is a real risk that must be managed, namely the risk that monitoring leads to a 'tick box approach' to the curriculum, where teachers seem to comply with timeframes, but there is too much compromising in terms of depth and actual learning. In this regard, it has become increasingly clear that there is not enough good guidance offered to teachers on how to deal with a multitude of abilities within the same class. Decisions on when to move from one topic to the next in the curriculum when some learners are still clearly struggling with the previous topic are extremely difficult decisions for teachers. Support and guidance for teachers here is crucial. (Department of Basic education 2015, p. 43)

Our experiences have also shown us that while the DBE's Action Plan to 2019 shows an understanding of the pace-inclusion-quality nexus, compliance-driven reporting exerts a downward pressure to 'keep-up' with the pace of the Annual Teaching Plan. In administratively strong systems, this is more extreme. The Auditor General of South Africa's Educational Performance Monitoring Unit (Rambau 2018) has identified the risk that department heads at school level complete monitoring templates only for compliance purposes, and there are no standardised planning and reporting processes for curriculum coverage in the system. This is precisely the challenge identified in Action Plan 2019, "to move from systemic research to practical tools that can be used by all districts and school principals to monitor curriculum coverage" (Department of Basic education 2015, p. 43).

The Jika iMfundo experience has led to a conceptualisation of coverage problems as falling broadly within two categories: curriculum coverage problems that are related to pedagogy, and those that are related to management. Coverage problems related to pedagogy require the collaboration of professional knowledge communities sharing the same phase and subject specific pedagogical preoccupations. These problems are usually complex; solutions have to be developed and tested, and professional mastery of content and coverage is a career-long pursuit. Coverage problems related to management are more amenable to easy identification and immediate institutional responses. They are moreover a necessary (but not sufficient) condition for creating the institutional practices required for sustained collaborative attention to problems of pedagogy. These management practices require structured and supportive interaction with the teacher reflections to make visible the basis of professional judgments regarding curriculum pace relative to the range of learning needs, the cognitive depth required, and the overall coherence of the conceptual design of the subject for the year. School management teams need to access these judgments in order to offer appropriate support. While the activity of tracking and reporting of curriculum coverage makes the slow pace of teaching relative to the prescribed pace visible within schools, it is easier to render invisible to a manager that teaching and assessment have been pitched to lower levels of conceptual demand to facilitate pacing requirements. For school managers to provide guidance and support to teachers in navigating the complexity of curriculum coverage reporting, they require greater understanding of the architecture of the national curriculum and assessment policy, and the tools to manage this. Curriculum management training and tools in the pilot had to be deepened and extended to enable managers to monitor coverage relative to learner performance at the appropriate conceptual level.

18.6.2   Structural Impediments to Support for Teachers

We under-estimated how poorly resourced and ill-defined support for teachers' work is within the school, and to the school. We understand more deeply the structural constraints that inhibit the internal capacity of the system to provide support to teachers.

At school level, department heads have little time for supervision because of the unrealistic supervisory span of control relative to time. The workloads of educators are regulated by the 'PAM' – The Personnel Administration Measures shown in Table 18.2 below.

The difference in teaching allocation between a teacher and an HoD is minuscule. Table shows that the difference could be as little as 2%, and at most 7% of their working time. In this 2–7%, they have a wide, and unrealistic, range of additional responsibilities to fulfil.

Department heads typically supervise between 5 and 10 teachers. Finding time for effective supervision is a challenge, particularly for Foundation Phase Heads who would inevitably be teaching for 100% of the school teaching time. Department Heads in the intermediate, senior and further phases carry the additional burden of supervising subjects that they are not teaching, and in which they may not be confident. These factors compromise the ability to supervise meaningfully and reinforce compliance monitoring and reporting.

Our reality is that the primary locus of teacher support and development is by default the school community. Teachers need institutional resourcing and processes that enable school leaders to have professional, supportive conversations about curriculum coverage, teaching and learning with teachers. Current resource allocations are unworkable for department heads to do their work effectively and develop the routines that enable meaningful support within schools.

If department heads have little time to provide support to teachers, the availability of subject advisers to provide meaningful support to teachers presents a far worse crisis. In the two districts the number of advisers varied with resignations, retirements, and the slow pace of filling vacant posts. In the 'snapshot' of advisers relative to schools in Table 18.3 below, the average school load for advisers in Pinetown was 151 schools per adviser, and in King Cetshwayo the average load was 190 schools per adviser.

The work of subject advisor as currently structured and resourced, is under-conceptualised and poorly understood in the education system. Their 'performance

Table 18.2 Teacher and HD allocation

	Teacher (Post level 1)	HoD (Post level 2)
Primary school	85–92	85–90
Secondary school	85–90	85

Terms and conditions of employment of educators determined in terms of section 4 of The Employment of Educators Act 1998, p. 6. (Published in 1999 and last amended in 2003)

Table 18.3 Snapshot of Subject Advisors (SA) actual numbers relative to schools Pinetown and King Cetshwayo, 2015

Band	Phase	Subjects	Pinetown			Pinetown		
			Subject advisers	Schools	Ratio advisers to schools	Subject advisers	Schools	Ratio advisers to schools
GET	Foundation phase	Foundation phase	4	383	96	5	470	94
	Intermediate phase	English FAL	4	556	139	3	696	232
	Senior phase	Maths	3	556	185	1	696	696
		Natural science	2	556	278	3	696	232
FET	FET phase	English FAL	1	173	173	1	226	226
		Maths	1	173	173	2	226	113
		Physical science	2	173	87	2	226	113

area responsibilities' require them to play a key role in supporting teachers by providing professional support and advice, by ensuring that teachers received a regular flow of curriculum information, by monitoring curriculum management and ensuring curriculum compliance. But the probability of adviser 'school visits' providing substantive support to all teachers is miniscule. The number of teachers that an adviser is responsible for varies but would typically be a minimum of 3 teachers per school, usually more. The discrepancy between the requirements of the adviser role and the impossible scale of their responsibilities are so wholly inadequate that the official model is not fit for purpose.

Our greatest asset to system improvement in education is the responsiveness, even hunger, of teachers, school managers, and their unions, to solutions that they believe will assist them. Any initiative to improve learning in South African schools will depend on deepening the exercise of teachers' professional judgment in the instructional core. For teachers to adopt and improve any new practice, routines of support are needed within schools. For these routines to be possible, school leaders need support to institutionalise practices supportive of reflection on learning and improvement of teaching at the core. For new practices to be introduced to schools, sufficient resources for meaningful teacher support must be provided. Without addressing these capacity blockages at scale for all schools, any possibility for system improvement is hobbled.

18.7 Conclusion

The Jika iMfundo campaign is a change-at-scale approach to improving learner outcomes by increasing curriculum coverage. It aims to achieve its goals by operating within existing policy mandates and institutional structures within the Department of Education to develop systems-wide practices and relationships that strengthen teaching and enhance learning in schools. This chapter frames curriculum coverage within the broader goal of increasing opportunities to learn, and points to it as one of the ways of addressing the social and educational inequalities in South African society over the longer term.

Christie (2018) in her review of the findings in a volume of research on Jika iMfundo emphasized the need to strengthen curriculum management at school level.

> What is perhaps most striking about the findings … is the extent of the existing problems of curriculum management in schools such as these. Teachers in these schools reported being clear for the first time about the benefits of structured planning to cover the curriculum and HoDs reported being clear for the first time what their role entailed. The extent to which these basic requirements of curriculum management were not in place speaks to minimal organisational capacity in these schools and signals the absolute necessity of structured support if they are to prepare their students to meet the content and assessment requirements of a nationally standardised curriculum (p. 8).

Building teachers' professional judgement in applying policy frameworks to their classroom practice is fundamental to achieving improvements in learning outcomes.

Establishing structures and systems at school level (and supported by districts) to make professional reflection and collaboration around student learning a routine in the school is an essential element in addressing the challenges to curriculum coverage. Systemic blockages that may inhibit the development of professional judgement and agency include: policy frameworks that are communicated through the system as inviolable rules that cannot be adapted to contextual realities (rather than being regarded as frameworks to guide professional judgement); compliance thinking that restricts the exercise of collaborative professional judgment; the limited capacity of the system (at school and district levels) to support the professional development of teachers; and notions of accountability that favour compliance reporting rather than reciprocal accountability that responds to contextual challenges.

Most importantly, our growing understanding of achieving change in the education system can be applied to other 'objects of change'. For policy intentions to 'land' and be received on the uneven and unequal contours of contextual realities so that we accelerate the reduction of gross educational inequality, our understanding of what drives and institutionalizes change must be deepened.

References

Christie, P. (2018). Chapter 1: Introduction. In M. Monyokolo (Ed.), *Learning about sustainable change in education in South Africa: The Jika imfundo campaign* (pp. 2013–2017). Johannesburg: SAIDE.

City, E. A., Elmore, R. F., Fiarman, S. E., & Teitel, L. (2010). Instructional rounds in education: A network approach to improving teaching and learning. *Teacher Librarian; Bowie, 37*(3), 69–70.

Coleman, J. S., Campbell, B., Hobson, C., McPartland, J., Mood, A., Winefeld, F., & York, R. (1966). *Equality of educational opportunity report*. U.S. Washington DC: Government Printing Office.

Department of Basic Education. (2014). *Report on the annual national assessment of 2014 grades 1 to 6 & 9*. Pretoria: Department of Basic Education.

Department of Basic Education. (2015). *Action plan 2019 towards the realisation of schooling 2030: Taking forward South Africa's national development plan 2030*. Pretoria: Department of Basic Education.

Department of Basic Education. (2016). *Personnel administrative measures (PAM)*. Technical Report Government Gazette No. 39684. Pretoria: Department of Basic Education.

Department of Basic Education. (2017). *Report on implementation evaluation of CAPS*. Summary Report. Technical report, Pretoria: Department of Basic Education.

Elmore, R. F. (2000). *Building a new structure for school leadership*. Washington, DC: Albert Shanker Institute.

Elmore, R. F. (2004). *School reform from the inside out: Policy, practice, and performance*. Cambridge: Harvard Education Press.

Elmore, R. F. (2005). Accountable leadership. *The Educational Forum, 69*(2), 134–142. https://doi.org/10.1080/00131720508984677

Elmore, R. (2006). Leadership as the practice of improvement. In *Paper Prepared for the International Conference on Perspectives on Leadership for Systemic Improvement*. Paris: OECD.

Elmore, R. (2008). *Improving the instructional core*. Graduate School of Education, Harvard University.

Elmore, R. (2010). Leading the instructional core. *Conversation, 11*(3), 1–12.

Gustafsson, M. (2005). *The relationships between schooling inputs and outputs in South Africa: Methodologies and policy recommendations based on the 2000 SACMEQ dataset*. Ph.D. Thesis, Stellenbosch University, Stellenbosch.

Hargreaves, A., Braun, H., & Gebhardt, K. (2013). *Data-driven improvement and accountability*. Boulder: National Education Policy Centre.

Hoadley, U. (2010). *What do we know about teaching and learning in primary schools in South Africa? A review of the classroom-based research literature*. University of Stellenbosch: Department of Economics.

Hoadley, U., Christie, P., & Ward, C. L. (2009). Managing to learn: Instructional leadership in South African secondary schools. *School Leadership and Management, 29*(4), 373–389.

Howie, S., Van Staden, S., Tshele, M., Dowse, C., & Zimmerman, L. (2017). *Progress in international reading literacy study 2016. South African children's reading literacy achievement*. Summary Report. Pretoria: Centre for Evaluation and Assessment.

King Cetshwayo District Municipality. (2017). King Cetshwayo district municipality integrated development plan (2017/18-2021/22). http://www.uthungulu.org.za/images/IDP/201718.%20DRAFT%20IDP%20Sections%20A-%20B.pdf. Accessed 3 Feb 2018.

Levin, B. (2012). System-wide improvement in education. *Education Policy Series, 13*, 1–38.

Lortie, D. C. (1977). *Schoolteacher: A sociological study*. Chicago: University of Chicago Press.

Mc Lennan, A. (2018). *District support for Curriculum Management Change in Schools*. Presentation made at learning about sustainable change in education in South Africa colloquium.

Metcalfe, M. (2018). Jika iMfundo 2015–2017: Why, what and key learnings. In Christie, P. & Monyokolo, M. (Eds.), *Learning about sustainable change in education in South Africa: the Jika iMfundo campaign 2015–2017*. Johannesburg: Saide.

NEEDU. (2013). *NEEDU national report 2012: The state of literacy teaching and learning in the foundation phase. National education and evaluation development unit*. Technical report, Pretoria: Department of Basic Education.

Oosthuizen, M., & Bhorat, H. (2006). Educational outcomes in South Africa: A production function approach. Canada: Secretariat for institutional support for economic research in Africa Working Paper No. 2006/05.

Peurach, D., & Peurach, D. J. (2011). *Seeing complexity in public education: Problems, possibilities, and success for all*. New York: Oxford University Press.

Rambau, T. (2018). *Enabling accountability and oversight for effective monitoring of school curriculum coverage*. Presentation made at learning about sustainable change in education in South Africa colloquium. https://www.dropbox.com/preview/Colloquium%20presentations/1.%20Takalani%20Rambau%20PILO%20Colloquim%20on%20Curriculum%20Coverage%207-8%20June%202018.%20pptx.pdf?role=work

Schmidt, W. H., & Prawat, R. S. (2006). Curriculum coherence and national control of education: Issue or non-issue? *Journal of Curriculum Studies, 38*(6), 641–658. https://doi.org/10.1080/00220270600682804

Schmidt, W. H., Cogan, L. S., & McKnight, C. C. (2011). Equality of educational opportunity: Myth or reality in U.S. schooling? *American Educator, 34*(4), 12–19.

Talbert, J. E., & McLaughlin, M. W. (1994). Teacher professionalism in local school contexts. *American Journal of Education, 102*(2), 123–153. https://doi.org/10.1086/444062

Taylor, N., & Moyane, J. (2005). Khanyisa education support programme: Baseline study part 1: Communities, schools and classrooms. Johannesburg: JET Education Services.

Van der Berg, S. (2001). Resource shifts in South African schools after the political transition. *Development Southern Africa, 18*(4), 405–421.

Van der Berg, S., & Burger, R. (2003). Education and socio-economic differentials: A study of school performance in the Western Cape. *South African Journal of Economics, 71*(3), 496–522.

Wills, G. (2018). *A quantitative perspective on School Leadership and Management in South Africa*. Presentation made at learning about sustainable change in education in South Africa colloquium.

Chapter 19
Inequality in Education: What is to Be Done?

Jonathan D. Jansen

19.1 Introduction

In any of South Africa's nine provinces you could within 30 min or less drive from one of the most affluent schools in the world to one of the poorest and most dysfunctional schools anywhere. The one set of schools would boast rolling green sports fields and state-of-the-art computer laboratories and the other would be fitted with pit latrines into which, from time to time, a child falls and even drowns.[1] This is the most visible face of inequality in the nation's schools but what is less obvious are the many other ways in which education institutions remain unequal more than two decades since the end of legal apartheid. While *face inequality* draws dramatic attention to the inequalities of school infrastructure (buildings, sports grounds, libraries and laboratories) much of the research attention has focused on differences in learning outcomes between well-resourced and poor schools.

The purpose of this final chapter is to offer a critical synthesis of this rich body of research on those many ways in which schools remain unequal despite small and large-scale interventions to shift the needle in the quest for equality (the sameness of treatment) and equity (the distinction of treatment through, for example, the redistribution of resources from the privileged to the poor). This review of the research presented in the book seeks not only to be critical and synthetic but also

---

[1] The two cases of pit-latrine drownings that received considerable media attention was that of five-year old Lumka Mketwa in Bizana (Eastern Cape) in 2018 and of five-year old Micheal Komape in Polokwane (Limpopo) in 2014.

J. D. Jansen (✉)
Faculty of Education, Stellenbosch University, Cape Town, South Africa
e-mail: jonathanjansen@sun.ac.za

© Springer Nature Switzerland AG 2019
N. Spaull, J. D. Jansen (eds.), *South African Schooling: The Enigma of Inequality*, Policy Implications of Research in Education 10,
https://doi.org/10.1007/978-3-030-18811-5_19

generative in that the very process of making sense of existing knowledge asks whether there is new knowledge that can be developed from what we now know about inequality in education.[2]

19.2 Face Inequality

The continued co-existence of vastly unequal school infrastructures in South Africa is itself an enigma. That these most visible forms of inequality are not challenged or disrupted speaks to a social narrative of aspiration rather than disdain. The aspirant black middle class wants access to former white schools because of their association with quality education. It is the very contrast—desegregated white schools that work and segregated black schools that often do not—which pushes black parents towards the more impressive institutions. This is what the research of Tshepiso Matentjie (2019) in this book so powerfully demonstrates; the quest as well as the costs of black middle class aspirations for access to the well-established and privileged schools.

But the settled images of face inequality unbuttons some difficult political and policy dilemmas in this redress society (Barnes 2006).[3] Those emphatic images of contrasting wealth and poverty in school infrastructure betray a set of compromises made on the eve of South Africa's transition from apartheid to democracy (Bell 2016). There would be no radical redistribution of material resources from white schools to black schools; in fact as the research by Motala and Carel (2019) demonstrate, government's allocations in resources were incremental and lacked what the education finance literature calls *adequacy* to redress the massive inequalities in what is often described as two school systems. Nor would there be any redistribution of school personnel—teachers, principals and other administrators—despite the inherited differences in qualifications and competence between staff in white schools compared to those in black schools. What this means, in effect, is that the structural racism that created these inequalities in society were not being addressed even at the school level (see Noguera 2017) and it is a concern that only the chapter by Matentjie (2019) in this volume even begins to address racism as a factor in inequality.

The decision not to radically redistribute resources from white, privileged schools to black, disadvantaged schools only partly explains these continuing inequalities; it is also the fact the political transition allowed for private funding (read, parent

---

[2]It is my view that a major shortcoming in edited books is the lack of a conceptual framing chapter at the beginning (impressing intellectual focus and coherence on the multi-authored contributions) and a generative knowledge chapter at the end (offering new knowledge on the central topic—in this case, inequality in education—that is garnered from the separate author chapters). This is what our book hopes to do differently as a contribution to research on educational inequality.

[3]It is worth remembering that *redress* as an instrument to resolve inequality was a founding rationale for educational change in South Africa.

contributions) to supplement declining public funds in the privileged school market (Motala and Carel 2019, in this book). What this meant, in practice, is that the inequality gap remained unresolved, and even widened, between the poorest and the wealthiest schools.

19.3 Schools as Settled Arrangements

The ugliness of face inequality in the school sector hardly stirs reaction, let alone revolt, in this otherwise "protest nation" (Duncan 2016). Where students rebel it is more often against inequality on campuses whether in terms of the exclusionary costs of higher education (the so-called #FeesMustFall movement) or the alienating cultures of former white universities (the so-called #RhodesMustFall moment) as witnessed since 2015 (Jansen 2017). When communities revolt it is typically in response to what is known as "service delivery protests" because of the lack of housing or sanitation or the timely payment of social grants (Twala 2014).

Where schools are implicated in protests, it is far more likely to be led by teacher unions in regard to salaries and conditions of service (Pattillo 2012).[4] There has not been since the advent of democracy in 1994 the kind of spontaneous protests against the poor quality of education except in one instance. The NGO *Equal Education* often leads protests (i.e. Hendricks and Washinyira 2016 and Groundup 2017)[5] and brings legal challenges against the poor standards of infrastructure in the provinces. Yet outside of such organized protests by one organization, students, parents and teachers seldom take to the streets to engage in mass protests against the unequal quality of education across the country's 27,000 schools. It is as if communities have come not only to accept these settled arrangements but to seek participation within the advantaged schools. Why there is such social acquiescence in the face of rampant *educational* inequalities requires depth research in the sociology and politics of education not covered in the contributions to this book. One reason might be the assumption that inequality only exists because of limitations of resources.

19.4 If Only There Was More Money

There is a long established discourse in South African education and society about "the lack of" things that are needed to correct problems such as quality education. If

---

[4] It is most unusual to cite a pre-doctoral study thesis as evidence in a research book but this is one of the most exceptional qualitative studies yet done on teacher unions in South Africa by a young student.

[5] Sample of reports on Equal Education's activism from Cape Town in the Western Cape to King Williams Town in the Eastern Cape.

only there were more textbooks or better teachers then education would improve. To address this problem the answer given was typically more money. But as research has consistently shown during the early transition from democracy (Crouch and Mabogoane 1998; Fiske and Ladd 2004) and more recently (Motala and Carel 2019), South Africa has made significant shifts in education spending as evident in global indicators—percentage of GDP (about 7%) and proportion of national expenditure (around 20%)—or in direct, corrective funding measures such as the Equity Share Formula (the education component) and the School Fee Exemption Policy. And yet, as one study after another has demonstrated, despite these relatively strong investments in education South Africa still appears last or second last when compared with other nations in international tests of achievement (Reddy et al. 2019). The problem is, as studies in this book has shown, the incapacity of the system to translate resources into results (Crouch and Mabogoane 1998).

This claim should not, however, be used to discount the massive amounts of additional funding needed to achieve face equality given the vast and visible disparities in infrastructure. These simple facts—such as the fact that 4557 out of 23,495 schools still have pit latrines as toilets and 45 have no toilets at all—imply serious capital expenditure demanded of the national government.[6] And this is where the collection of research contributions in this book pivots far too easily from the infrastructural argument for equity to more narrow pedagogical arguments for equality. Face inequality is not simply a question of an embarrassing optics in politics but a concern about social justice in how a country provides education to the poorest of the poor.

And yet even if there was some awakening of the political conscience within government to accelerate attention to equity of infrastructure that in itself would not translate into equal learning outcomes. This is where the argument has merit—the system is inefficient given the failure to translate resources available into results required. With about 80% of government expenditure on basic education going towards teacher salaries, it would make sense to regard this important human resource as key to turning around the unequal outcomes in the public school system. But how unequal are those outcomes to begin with?

19.5 What We Know About Learning Outcomes in Schools: A Note on Measurement

The chapter contributions in this book reveal an interesting trend in the trajectory of South African educational research over time. For a long time schools research came largely in the form of small-scale qualitative investigations such as case study research or critical policy studies. Three developments changed that: South Africa's participation in international achievement studies (principally TIMSS, SACMEQ

---

[6]Data drawn from the National Education Infrastructure Management System (Neims) of 2017.

and PIRLS),[7] the timely establishment of quantitative education research units in the Human Sciences Research Council (The Education, Science and Skills Development Research Programme) and at the University of Stellenbosch (Research in Socio-Economic Policy or RESEP) and the capacity for such research created within the government's Department of Education. The blend of textured qualitative research and rigorous quantitative research that resulted has extended but also strengthened the range of studies available on educational inequality.

It has to be said, in passing, that the quest for ever more refined studies of intervention impact deserves a word of caution. The notion of moving from bland statistical summary studies to quasi-experimental research to randomized control trials (RCTs) in an attempt to "really, really know" the effects of intervention X on learning outcomes Y is not beyond criticism. What such admirable studies do achieve is to give us a summary sense of "what works" but they cannot explain how, why and under what conditions the specified treatment delivers the narrowing outcome—the overstatement of findings is not uncommon in such studies. We are not dealing here with the clinical trial of drugs on patients but with very complex organisations in which cause-effect relationships are notoriously difficult to pin down. As Nelson et al. (2018) and his colleagues point out in their feature article; *Can measures change the world?*—"the social and institutional context of measurement ... has been relegated to the periphery of measurement theory and practice" and this may "limit the potential impact of the measures" themselves. And Samoff (2018) makes the same point that "by design, quasi-experimental approaches ignore context and complexity" and that with few exceptions "the experimental model is misplaced for education, where the effort to hold things constant is a problem not a solution."

19.6 So What Do We Know?

We know that there have been improvements in "the education system's underlying performance" (Van der Berg and Gustaffson 2019). What we also know is that those improvements are from a very low base, that the comparative scores still places South Africa at or near the bottom of achievement tables, and that whatever progress made seems to have stalled in subsequent achievement studies. In fact, the more recent 2016 PIRLS data provided a sobering counterpoint these optimistic accounts of "system improvements" when it was reported that almost 8 out of 10 South African children in Grade 4 cannot read for understanding (Howie et al. 2017).

Regardless of claims about aggregate achievements in the national frame, we know that inequality in schools still remains a major blight on the post-apartheid

---

[7]Trends in International Mathematics and Science Study (TIMSS), The Southern and Eastern Africa Consoritum for Monitoring Educational Quality (SACMEQ) and The Progress in International Reading Literacy (PIRLS).

education system. So much so that researchers in this book speak regularly about "a two-tiered bi-modal schooling system" (Spaull and Pretorius 2019) with high performing schools (about 20%) at one end of the achievement distribution and low performing schools at the other end (about 80%). This classification however might oversimplify a more complex distribution in that a large number of schools are located at neither of the extremes and occupy a stable middle group of institutions. These are schools with moderate functionality and reasonable achievement scores but certainly not located at either end of a bi-modal distribution. As Van der Berg and Gustaffson (2019) point out, there is also "inequality within the bottom 80% of the system, the historically disadvantaged part of the system."

Still, the research reported here makes it clear that who you are (race), where you come from (urban/rural), what your parents earn (class) and which school you attend strongly determines the educational outcomes and the life chances of a student. Put plainly, a black child born to poor parents in a deep rural area while attending a dysfunctional school on average has little to no chance of escaping a life of poverty despite the education received. Over and over again the data reported in this book shows that education policy since 1994 has not reversed unequal outcomes. For students of inequality this finding is perhaps not surprising since the first major study on the subject found that "schools bring little influence to bear on a child's achievement" and that *the inequalities imposed on children by their home, neighborhood and peer environment are carried along to become the inequalities with which they confront adult life at the end of school.* (Coleman 1966).

What is also clear from the South African data is that long before children come to school their futures are already being determined even during prenatal development (Ashley-Cooper et al. 2019—in this book). That said, we know more about the specific operations of inequality. For example, the education levels of the mother is a good indicator of children's futures (Reddy et al. 2019). The quality of the preschool determines subsequent academic success. The home environment is telling—books and the internet—of both educational and life chances. All of this before a child even reaches Grade 1.

The worse news, however, is evidence that suggests that even though poor children coming from such impoverished social backgrounds start with a clear academic disadvantage relative to their privileged peers, that achievement gap is likely to remain over subsequent years of schooling (Spaull and Pretorius 2019). Here the South African research finds confirmatory evidence from studies elsewhere. For example, a recent report in the USA found that:

> the bulk of inequality in reading and math scores is already present at the start of kindergarten, and changes very little over the next three years. This result implicates early childhood as the primary source of inequality in reading and math. (Von Hippel et al. 2017)

Which begs the question; what happened to the liberal view of education as an instrument for overcoming inequality in school and society?

It turns out the reproduction theorists such as Bowles and Gintis—the famed authors of *Schooling in Capitalist America (1976)*—might have been right all along: schools tend to reproduce the social order rather than reduce the inequalities within society (Bowles and Gintis 2011). In this regard there are two striking examples in this book about the inner workings of education in South Africa. One is the finding by Spaull and Pretorius (2019) in their study on reading literacy in the early grades: "Those [children] who do not learn to match the sounds of language with the symbols of text remain in catch-up mode for the rest of their lives." And another observation that poor students from dysfunctional schools attend weak universities to become inadequately trained teachers in the same class of schools from which they barely graduated. In fact, shows this research, "some of the fourth-year BEd students were not functionally literate"[8] (Taylor 2019) and that "the most distressing aspect of these inequalities is their reproductive nature."

This does not mean that *individuals* might not escape the poverty trap through a unique combination of favourable circumstances or even that the occasional school surrounded by rural disadvantage might not excel in its academic endeavours (Jansen and Blank 2014; Hoadley 2012). We now know that these exceptional cases of individuals or schools do not and cannot represent the majority. We also know that the lessons from "effective schools" in ecologies of disadvantage cannot simply be transplanted into other contexts. That is because each school has unique social, cultural and political characteristics that makes some effective but the majority less so.

And yet it is true that schools (if not systems) do change as a result of external intervention and in the process alter the learning and the lives of children. This is what several studies report in this book and the findings are remarkably consistent. We now know that the kinds of interventions that work in dysfunctional schools bring to the change project three important elements—scripted lessons, quality materials and in-classroom coaching. The refinement of measurement methodologies in some of these studies demonstrate—such as the research of Fleisch (2018)—what can happen when his "triple cocktail" is applied to the change project.

There are however critical shortcomings underpinning the new evangel for school reform. Such highly scripted lessons with strict instructions on what to teach, when and how on a tight timetable have one serious consequence—it changes our understanding of who the teacher is and what we understand by teaching. In this new image of teaching the teacher is no longer the autonomous professional with the capacity for independent decision-making with regards to knowledge, pedagogy and assessment but a compliant instrument that dutifully delivers on the prescriptions of a government-sanctioned curriculum regardless of context. This in other literatures is called the deskilling of teachers and while scripted lessons "may improve examination results for some students [it] cannot resolve South Africa's education crisis, reduce inequality, or promote social justice" (Samoff 2018).

---

[8]In South Africa there are two main pathways towards achieving a university-based teacher qualification. One is through a four-year professional Bachelor of Education (BEd degree) offered in a Faculty or School of Education. Another path is through a Postgraduate Certificate in Education (PGCE) which is a single year of pre-service teacher education after a first degree was attained with school subjects (e.g. Mathematics III in a BSc degree) in another Faculty (e.g. Science).

Nor is this the critically conscious teacher of progressive education who is able to discern truth from fiction and empower learners with the democratic competences to act on the world. This narrowly scripted, socially anemic teacher is what's left of a once elevated notion of teachers as professionals let alone activists within their classrooms (Jansen 2001; Cappy 2016).

How education change thinking in South Africa got to this point is understandable—decades of frustration at not being able to significantly improve cognitive outcomes among the majority of children has led to a narrowing down of the curriculum under considerable pressure for greater content coverage and improved learning achievements. The tight timelines and an overloaded curriculum are supposed to enforce greater accountability among teachers. The very language of reform, inconceivable in the heady days of progressive pedagogy, is now reduced to bloodstream metaphors like "dosage" (how much of an injection of the reform intervention is needed to ensure gains in learning outcomes?) and "cocktails" (what potent mix of drinks can be swallowed to produce desired effects?). And yet the inequalities of inputs, processes and outputs remain as the contributions in this volume attest. Again, what is to be done?

19.7   Coverage or Competence?

The research in this book is unequivocal about the fact that the school system remains highly unequal in terms of learning attainments by race, class and gender. In this respect the South African data is to some extent exceptional—girls do better than boys in the school system. Indeed, "in all the studies where there was a statistically significant difference in performance based on gender, girls were at an advantage over boys" (Zuze and Beku 2019). Girls do better in reading and boy's progress through the system slower than girls. There is much speculation but little solid evidence that explains these differences in gender outcomes. Gender differences notwithstanding, the strongest and most enduring inequality association is between race and educational achievement (Van der Berg and Gustaffson 2019).

When it comes to acting on research knowledge, however, there is a flailing to the left and right among contending change initiatives about what needs to be done. One of the key contrasting actions recommended is between coverage and knowledge.

The coverage advocates see a direct link between curriculum coverage and improved learning outcomes. The *Programme to Improve Learning Outcomes* (PILO) accordingly seeks to improve management capacity at all levels of education so that "the policy intentions of government [is made] routine in the work of officials and schools" (Metcalfe and Witten 2019). We know that in a national school system that operates at such high levels of dysfunctionality, almost any intervention at the lower end of that system will yield positive learning results. But there is no evidence that curriculum coverage in itself produces sustainable, systemic and scaled-up learning effects across a school system. Nor would it be easy given the state of the bottom schools, as one of PILO's own reviewers rightly observed: "a certain pre-existing level of functionality may be necessary for curriculum coverage to be achieved" (Pam Christie, cited in Metcalfe and Witten 2019).

The knowledge advocates, on the other hand, locate the problem not in curriculum coverage but in teacher competences; not in capacity at upper levels of the system (province, district and even school) but in "what happens inside the classroom" (Muller and Hoadley 2019). From this vantage point the research points to marked inequalities—disciplinary knowledge (mathematics, in this case) is "highly inequitably distributed" between those teachers in the privileged or quintile 5 schools and those in poorest or quintile 1 schools (Taylor 2019). Subject matter knowledge (knowing enough mathematics, for example) correlates with pedagogical content knowledge (knowing how to teach mathematics efficaciously) and here too there are inequalities of performance inside classrooms.

In Hoadley's (2017) qualitative accounts of what happens inside South African classrooms she found deeply embedded classroom practices marked by a "communalizing pedagogy" in dysfunctional schools and "individualized pedagogies" in established schools. In the latter schools the students encounter teachers with specialized knowledge and considerable autonomy that enables individual learning, active exchange and in-class participation. In the former schools there are rituals and routines marked by memorization, chorusing, as well as rote and repetitive learning. Furthermore, in poor schools "the encounter with knowledge is primarily an oral rather than a textual one" (Muller and Hoadley 2019).

Is teacher development the answer to bridging the gap between competence and coverage of the curriculum? South Africa has come a long way from experiments with the centre-based, cascade model of teacher training to the in-classroom, coaching model of teacher support (Shalem and De Clercq 2019). The evidence in this book certainly points to the benefits of coaching over centralized training (Taylor 2019) which perhaps unintentionally resolves another problem—inspection. Given the intense emotional reaction to inspection systems among teacher unions— deemed judgmental, top-down and reminiscent of the old apartheid system of teacher evaluation—coaching implies mentorship, support and peer review inside the classroom. But individual coaching of teachers in their classrooms is an expensive model even though the developmental benefits are more likely to be sustained over time.

The important observation to be made here is that the school system needs to develop competent teachers (knowledge, teaching) to make curriculum coverage effective in terms of learning outcomes (Shalem et al. 2016). The evidence however shows that when insecure and ill-prepared teachers are placed under the pressure of coverage, there is an inevitable drift towards *curriculum mimicry*—meaning the pretence of compliance where teachers appear to be conforming to coverage requirements without actually doing so in practice.

Hobden and Hobden (2019) are not alone in observing "paper compliance" and found "teachers frantically marking and signing learner books as we arrive for collection." So too the PILO (forthcoming) researchers found evidence of "a culture of assumed bureaucratic compliance" [which] often leads to the exercise of "ticking off boxes" rather than allowing for substantive engagement with the work of change and improvement (Metcalfe and Witten 2019).

This is a danger in all education systems where the political pressure for coverage and compliance comes up against the realities of teacher incapacity in the face of difficult conditions for teaching and learning such as overcrowded classrooms. And it is in the disadvantaged segment of the school system where such superficial compliance is more likely to occur with the result that the inequality dilemmas remain unresolved. The routines of compliance behaviours in the face of external pressure points, however, to something deeper in the malaise of public schooling in South Africa—that of school cultures and how they impact on learning.

The shift from a fixation on measured outcomes (the economics of education chapters in this book) to research on "opportunities to learn" (OTL) is an important one since we have little evidence as to the processes that produce those results. It is in fact the case that "we know far too little about inequality of opportunity, relative to what we know about inequality of outcomes" (Carter and Reardon 2014).

The assumption among OTL researchers is that if we understand the distribution of opportunities within school and classroom processes, it is possible that the outcomes that result from inequalities could be altered. OTL holds that "learning is to some degree a function of time and effort" and that *engaged learning time* is consequential in terms of the quality of learning outcomes (Schuh Moore et al. 2012). Time—or rather how instructional time is used—is one of the "invisible inequalities" that continue to separate privileged schools from poor schools in terms of learning outcomes.

There are however several concerns that should accompany discussions about time as a critical variable in the inequality stakes. In the first place the availability of time in and of itself does not guarantee learning. It is what is done with that time; in other words, constructive learning time at the very least has to mean the active organization by a competent teacher of structured learning opportunities that draws out students into meaningful engagement with the teacher and the texts (broadly defined) made available in the classroom. Such a conception of time and teaching means that coverage is not enough especially when a crowded curriculum and/or a less capable teacher or a crumbling infrastructure constrain learning.

Furthermore, what is seldom addressed in such time-on-task research are the cultures of *schools* as "(dis)organisation" in which such opportunities to learn are embedded (Christie 1998). That is, OTL's do not float free from organizational cultures that enable or disable productive learning cultures. In such cultures the inequalities are stark—schools that use time efficiently to translate available resources into optimal results compared to schools where time is lost to absentee teachers, union strike actions or the lethargy of the educators on the school premises (Jansen and Blank 2014; Hoadley 2012). In other words, simply placing competent teachers with adequate materials in a classroom does not itself translate into productive learning environments when the school culture and climate are not conducive to achieving positive learning outcomes for all children. The contributions to this book by economists and sociologists of education would no doubt be strengthened by future research on school cultures by anthropologists of education.

19.8 Why Inequalities Persist

Simply conducting and restating through more and more refined research what is already known—that the school system in post-1994 South Africa remains highly unequal in outcomes—is not enough. The fixation with such a perspective could leave the impression that inequality is simply an economic reality or even "a sociological necessity" (Reardon 2011). More commonly, such a perspective on inequality assumes that the problem lies within the system (lazy teachers, inattentive learners) rather than within the social and political arrangements that sustains the status quo (Oaks et al. 2006).

Yet educational inequality is neither inevitable nor immutable. It is of course a consequence of the burden of a divided past but also the result of choices made in the present.

The important analytical question therefore is this—"what are the precise mechanisms that sustain the inequalities in South African schools?" Understanding the mechanics of inequality can lead to informed action that changes the settled arrangements of two school systems.

The first and by far the most important inequality-preserving factor is *politics*. The decision to retain whites and the middle classes within the public school system is admirable from a humane point of view but also least disruptive from a political standpoint. The political conditions at home and the threat of global repercussions abroad were real considerations contemplated by the negotiating parties in matters of economy and society. But leaving such arrangements in place has not changed the educational outcomes and social forecasts for the majority. Such decisions in fact kept redistributive questions off the table except in the smallest, ineffectual ways as we saw with education finance. The political frame that governed decisions in the transition from apartheid to democracy can and should be revisited.

But a major contributor to the politics of education and the problem of inequality remains, without question, the role of the largest teacher union—an ally of the ruling party—the South African Democratic Teachers Union (SADTU). In this respect the evidence is clear that privileged schools are hardly affected by prolonged strike action whereas in the lower two-thirds of schools "the magnitude of the effect is roughly equivalent to a quarter of a year's lost learning" (Wills 2014). This disruptive effect of the majority teacher union on teaching and learning has been identified as one of the "binding economic constraints in South African education" (Van der Berg et al. 2016). It is however not only strike action that constrains education in the poorest schools but also criminal activity on the part of the union through the corruption of educator appointments. As a Ministerial Task Team investigation found,

> the Department is effectively in control of one-third of South Africa's provinces… where authority is weak, inefficient and dilatory, teacher unions move into available spaces and determine policies, priorities and appointments achieving undue influence over matters which should primarily be the responsibility of the department [thereby] defeat[ing] the achievement of quality education (Department of Education 2016, p. 18)

What this means is that strike action and corruption together contribute to the growing inequalities between privileged schools with predictable timetables and poor schools which are disproportionately affected by chronic instabilities in the sector.

The second and related factor is policy. It was the policy decision to not set a ceiling on private funding—by which I essentially mean parent contributions—for tuition. Under these arrangements white and middle class parents in quasi-private public schools could pay exorbitant fees that ensured more qualified teachers and therefore smaller classes, more subject specialisations as well as an extended and enriched curriculum. To understand the ways in which inequality is sustained in this instance the research reported in this book by Motala and Carel (2019) found that in the Western Cape province, 20% of schools charge fees of R1000 or less; 55% charge R7040 or less; and 10% charge more than R35,794 per annum.

All of this happens at the same time as the poorer provinces under severe budget constraints continue to assign teachers to much larger classrooms (60 and more students are not uncommon). Then there is the policy, mentioned earlier, not to redistribute new and existing teachers to schools where highly qualified and experienced teachers are most needed.

The third factor is *planning*. The government did not have in place from the beginnings of democratic rule a systematic plan that ensured the timely delivery of adequate infrastructure or delivery of textbooks or the allocation of teachers in the poorest areas of the country. When such plans did emerge—such as the Regulations relating to Minimum Norms and Standards for School Infrastructure—they were not implemented even under legal challenge from civic organisations (Equal Education 2016).

Budgets were not prioritized for these purposes. Monitoring was inadequate as corrupt service providers defrauded the state. And the capacity for usage and security of brand new equipment such as computers were simply not installed. For the first decades of post-apartheid education, the glamour of policymaking took precedence over the routines of solid planning.

In their groundbreaking research report, *Planning to Fail*, Equal Education found "the absence of a capable state" in poor provinces like the Eastern Cape where 31% of all schools without water supply, 31% of schools without electricity and 91% of schools without sanitation facilities (Equal Education 2016). The reasons for this incapacity had to do with inherited dysfunction from the old apartheid administrations (including the ethnic homelands), the political interference by the main teachers union, and endemic corruption at all levels of the provincial government (Equal Education 2016). The political and administrative capacity to plan for a more equal education is strikingly lacking within the poorer provinces in particular.

The fourth factor sustaining inequalities is *programming* and here I refer in particular to curriculum change as an instance of new programmatic reforms within schools. Our research has shown that when complex curricula are introduced into schools those institutions with available teacher capacity are able to translate those new ideas into advantage for their students while weaker schools fall further behind because of an incapacity to make sense of new programmes to the benefit of their charges (Jansen and Christie 1999). Take the simple example of project work as a requirement of the new wave of curriculum reform in the early post-apartheid period; children with additional resources from the home (the internet, parent education, financial resources) had a clear advantage over those from informal settlements. Small wonder that the research reported in this book found that "test scores reflect the knowledge mastered from all sources, not only from the school" (Muller and Hoadley 2019).

19.9 Conclusion

Almost 100 years ago the progressive educator George Counts wrote a pamphlet bearing the provocative title, *Dare the schools built a new social order?* Counts recognized then, as is the case now, that the roots of inequality lay beyond the school in an unequal society. Short of a social revolution that upturns a capitalist economy and overthrows the class-based system of inequality, school systems will continue to for the most part reflect and reproduce rather than challenge at its roots an unequal society. The question raised in these research chapters is rather *how much* schools can make a difference in the lives of individuals, communities and even a country.

The policy options available to a democratic government are invariably tempered by the political economy in which it functions. It is unlikely therefore that there will be a radical redistribution of *private* resources from privileged former white public and independent schools to the majority black schools in South Africa. There has already been an equalization of *public* resources which is less controversial and some measure of redress built into imperfect policy instruments such as "no-fee schools." What can be done is a much more effective and efficient deployment of existing resources preceded by a massive, once-off infrastructural grant that once and for all eliminates the inadequate infrastructure and facilities of schools. This will have to be managed and implemented with great diligence and smart politics to ensure that no corruption of this capital facility is tolerated in provinces like the Eastern Cape. Such a concerted action will do much to create greater face equality in South African education.

The most important political decision that can and should be taken is that the relationship between government and the majority union has to be redefined. This will take considerable political skill and determination by the leadership in government to strike a new deal with two critical commitments—that schools will be run by the government and teacher concerns are the domain of the unions. In this respect no school—which happens to be the poorer schools—will sacrifice its academic calendar for the sake of teacher union concerns. That agreement must be sacrosanct for the unstable school calendar and the loss of instructional time in poor schools is a major reason for sustained inequalities.

There is a case from the evidence available for an urgent national intervention in the teaching resources available to disadvantaged schools. The incremental, small-

368 J. D. Jansen

scale efforts to change schools on a regional or local basis will take years before any sustained change becomes evident. Then it is not even clear whether system-wide effects will be achieved. The focal point should be the most expensive resource in the budget and the most direct target for change in classrooms and schools—teachers. Given the research reviewed, the change effort should focus on teachers (competence, capacity and commitment).

In this regard the specific focus of teacher competence should be less on behaviours and more on the subject matter knowledge and the pedagogical content knowledge (how to teach) which, the research in this book illustrates, is the bridge between curriculum coverage and learner outcomes. The interventions that build teacher competence should, however, include all three dimensions of change that impact on teacher identities in South Africa—the practical, the professional and the political.

The narrow, specific focus on the *practical knowledge* needed to competently cover the scripted curriculum is important as a starting point in the development and support of disadvantaged teachers. That basic competence should consciously migrate towards *professional knowledge* where the teacher is empowered to make choices about the selection of knowledge, materials and forms of assessment judged to be appropriate in a particular classroom context. And both forms of competence should enable *political knowledge* such that the teacher is capable of teaching critical concepts of democracy, equality and justice across the curriculum. How do teachers best acquire these competences?

An important policy instrument available to government is teacher deployment in the weakest schools. In this regard government should make a significant investment in the in-classroom mentoring (coaching) of teachers through a model of peer review and support; this is an area in which private resources can and should be mobilized to supplement governmental resources to make a targeted difference in teaching and learning at the classroom interface. There are various sources for the recruitment of these teacher mentors—recently retired teachers *with a track-record of achievement* in the subject or phase of schooling (this cannot be a simple employment strategy for teachers out of work; that would defeat the purpose of such an expensive intervention) and an appeal to the privileged schools to release at least two teachers per school for work alongside their peers in disadvantaged schools. The winning over of teacher union support for such a drive is something that should be resolved at the level of government leadership.

The evidence suggests that such interventions should happen in the foundation years of primary schooling. This is where inequality is received—from unequal preschool or early childhood opportunities—and where inequality is sustained if not widened between the children of the privileged and the children of the poor. Near universal enrolments in primary schooling has been achieved; quality education offered equally, has not. And the research reviewed shows clearly that whatever equalization of funding or enrolments has been achieved this is 'washed out' by the unequal access to quality education (Lam et al. 2011, p. 135) and the limiting access to higher education (Branson et al. 2012, pp 1, 12). In other words, it makes sense to build the South African education system on its foundations—early primary education.

None of these interventions will be as effective over the long term without a policy determination to offer quality pre-school education to all South African children. This is where the inequality already pre-determined by the socio-economic status of the home is bedded down. The increase in pre-school or Grade R enrolments is not in itself an achievement. The research shows that it is the unequal quality of these early interventions that produce unequal outcomes that remain so over the course of the 12 years of education. A policy commitment to invest in quality early childhood education combined with building the foundations of early primary education will move the needle on key concerns such as reading literacy and basic numeracy.

That the South African school system struggles with the legacy of apartheid is clear. That there are policy choices and fiscal capacity within government to alter that legacy are equally evident. That there is also the moral clarity and political commitment to act on the knowledge available to reduce inequality in school and society remains to be seen.

References

Ashley-Cooper, M., van Nieker, L., & Atmore, E. (2019). Early childhood development in South Africa: Inequality and opportunity. In *South African schooling: The enigma of inequality*.

Barnes, T. (2006). Changing discourses and meanings of redress in South African higher education, 1994–2001. *Journal of Asian and African Studies, 41*(1–2), 149–170. https://doi.org/10.1177/0021909606061751

Bell, D. (2016). The conflict for compromise: An analysis of South Africa's post-Apartheid transition period. *International Journal of Advanced Research, 4*(7), 2285–2290. https://doi.org/10.21474/ijar01/1123

Bowles, S., & Gintis, H. (2011). Schooling in capitalist America: Educational reform and the contradictions of economic life. Haymarket Books.

Branson, N., Garlick, J., Lam, D., & Leibbrandt, M. (2012). *Education and inequality: The South African case*. Southern African Labour and Development Unit (SALDRU), University of Cape Town (Working Paper Series 75).

Cappy, C. L. (2016). Shifting the future? Teachers as agents of social change in South African secondary schools. *Education as Change, 20*(3), 119–140. https://doi.org/10.17159/1947-9417/2016/1314

Carter, P. L., & Reardon, S. F. (2014). *Inequality matters. William T Grant Foundation Paper*. New York: William T Grant Foundation.

Christie, P. (1998). Schools as (dis) Organisations: The 'breakdown of the culture of learning and teaching' in south African schools. *Cambridge Journal of Education, 28*(3).

Coleman, J. S. (1966). Equality of Educational Opportunity, Washington DC, US Government Printing Office, p 325. Quoted in Douglas B Downey and Dennis J Condron (2016) Fifty years since the Coleman report: Rethinking the relationship between schools and inequality. *Sociology of Education, 89*(3), 207–220.

Crouch, L., & Mabogoane, T. (1998). When the residuals matter more than the coefficients: An educational perspective. *Journal for Studies in Economic and Econometrics, 22*, 1–14.

Department of Education. (2016). Report of the Ministerial Task Team appointed by Minster Angie Motshekga to investigate allegations into the selling of posts of educators by members of teachers unions and department officials in provincial education departments. Pretoria.

Duncan, J. (2016). *Protest Nation: The right to protest in South Africa.* Pietermaritzburg: University of KwaZulu-Natal Press.

Equal Education. (2016). *Planning to fail: A report on equal education's Eastern Cape school visits, Nov 2016.* https://equaleducation.org.za/wp-content/uploads/2016/07/PLANNING-TO-FAIL-SUMMARY-OF-FINDINGS.pdf

Fiske, E. B., & Ladd, H. F. (2004). *Elusive equity: Education reform in post-apartheid South Africa.* Washington DC: Brookings Institution Press.

Fleisch, B. (2018). *Education triple Cocktail: System-wide education reform in South Africa.* Cape Town: University of Cape Town Press.

Groundup. (2017). Failure in eastern cape education, 28 April.

Hendricks, A., & Washinyira, T. (2016). High school students protest over safety and sanitation. Groundup, 21 Oct 2016 https://www.groundup.org.za/article/high-school-students-protest-over-safety-and-sanitation/

Hoadley, U. (2012). What do we know about teaching and learning in South African primary schools? *Education as Change, 16*(2), 187–202. https://doi.org/10.1080/16823206.2012.745725

Hoadley, U. (2017). *Pedagogy in poverty: Lessons from twenty years of curriculum reform in South Africa.* New York: Routledge.

Hobden, P., & Hobden, S. (2019). The quality, quantity and focus of individual learner written work contributing to inequality in primary schools. In *South African schooling: The enigma of inequality.*

Howie, S., Van Staden, S., Tshele, M., Dowse, C., & Zimmerman, L. (2017). Progress in International Reading Literacy Study 2016. South African Children's Reading Literacy Achievement. Summary Report. Centre for Evaluation and Assessment, Pretoria.

Jansen, J. (2017). *As by fire: The end of the South African University* (1st ed.). Cape Town: NB Publishers.

Jansen, J. D. (2001). Image-ining teachers: Policy images and teacher identity in South African classrooms. *South African Journal of Education, 21*(4), 242–246.

Jansen, J. D., & Blank, M. (2014). *How to fix South Africa's schools: Lessons from schools that work* (1st ed.). Johannesburg: Bookstorm.

Jansen, J. D., & Christie, P. (1999). *Changing curriculum: Studies on outcomes-based education in South Africa.* Cape Town/Johannesburg: Juta and Company Ltd.

Lam, D., Ardington, C., & Leibbrandt, M. (2011). Schooling as a lottery: Racial differences in school advancement in urban South Africa. *Journal of Development Economics, 95*(2), 121–136.

Matentjie, T. (2019). Race, class and inequality in education: Black parents in white-dominant schools after apartheid. In *South African schooling: The enigma of inequality.*

Metcalfe, M., & Witten, A. (2019). Taking change to scale: Lessons from the Jika iMfundo campaign in KZN. In *South African schooling: The enigma of inequality.*

Motala, S., & Carel, D. (2019). Educational funding and equity in South African schools. In N. Spaull & J. Jansen (Eds.), *South African schooling: The enigma of inequality.* New York: Springer Nature. https://doi.org/10.1007/978-3-030-18811-5_1

Muller, J., & Hoadley, U. (2019). Curriculum reform and learner performance: An obstinate paradox. In *South African schooling: The enigma of inequality.*

Nelson, C., Chandra, A., & Miller, C. (2018). Can measures change the world? *Stanford Social Innovation Review, 16*, 1.

Noguera, P. (2017). Introduction to "racial inequality and education: Patterns and prospects for the future". *Educational Forum, 81*(2), 129–135.

Oaks, J., et al. (2006). *Learning power. Waynflete lectures delivered at College of St. Mary Magdalen, Oxford, 1961.* New York: Teachers College Press.

Pattillo, K. (2012). *Quiet corruption: Teachers unions and leadership in South African township schools*. Ph.D. thesis, Weslyan University, Middletown, Connecticut.

Reardon, S. F. (2011). The widening academic achievement gap between the rich and the poor: New evidence and possible explanations. In R. Murnane & G. Duncan (Eds.), *Whither opportunity? Rising inequality and the uncertain life chances of low-income children* (pp. 91–116). New York: SAGE Foundation Press.

Reddy, V., Juan, A., Isdale, K., & Fongwa, S. (2019). Mathematics achievement and achievement gaps: TIMSS 1995 to 2015. In *South African schooling: The enigma of inequality*.

Samoff, J. (2018). Critical commentary on earlier draft of this chapter.

Schuh Moore, A., DeStefano, J., & Adelman, E. (2012). Opportunity to learn: A high impact strategy for improving educational outcomes in developing countries. Working Paper. USAID, EQUIP2.

Shalem, Y., & De Clercq, F. (2019). Teacher development and inequality in schools: Do we now have a theory of change? In N. Spaull & J. Jansen (Eds.), *South African schooling: The enigma of inequality*. New York: Springer Nature. https://doi.org/10.1007/978-3-030-18811-5_1

Shalem, Y., Steinberg, C., Koornhof, H., & De Clercq, F. (2016). The what and how in scripted lesson plans: The case of the Gauteng primary language and mathematics strategy. *Journal of Education, 66*, 13–36.

Spaull, N., & Pretorius, E. (2019). Still falling at the first hurdle: Examining early grade Reading in South Africa. In N. Spaull & J. Jansen (Eds.), *South African schooling: The enigma of inequality*. New York: Springer Nature. https://doi.org/10.1007/978-3-030-18811-5_1

Twala, C. (2014). The causes and socio-political impact of the service delivery protests to the South African citizenry: A real public discourse. *Journal of Social Sciences, 39*(2), 159–167. https://doi.org/10.1080/09718923.2014.11893279

Taylor, N. (2019). Teacher knowledge in South Africa. In *South African schooling: The enigma of inequality*. In N. Spaull & J. Jansen (Eds.), South African schooling: The enigma of inequality. New York: Springer Nature. https://doi.org/10.1007/978-3-030-18811-5_1

Taylor, S. (2019). How can learning inequalities be reduced? Lessons learnt from experimental research in South Africa. In N. Spaull & J. Jansen (Eds.), *South African schooling: The enigma of inequality*. New York: Springer Nature. https://doi.org/10.1007/978-3-030-18811-5_1

Van der Berg, S., Spaull, N., Wills, G., Gustafsson, M., & Kotzé, J. (2016). Identifying binding constraints in education. Stellenbosch: Research on Socio-economic Policy. Available from: http://resep.sun.ac.za. Accessed May 2016.

Van der Berg, S., & Gustafsson, M. (2019). Educational outcomes in post-apartheid South Africa: Signs of Progress despite great inequality. In N. Spaull & J. Jansen (Eds.), *South African schooling: The enigma of inequality*. New York: Springer Nature. https://doi.org/10.1007/978-3-030-18811-5_1

Von Hippel, P., Workman, J., & Downey, D. B. (2017). *Inequality in reading and math skills comes mainly from early childhood: A replication, and partial correction, of 'Are Schools the Great Equalizer?'* SSRN Scholarly Paper ID 3036094, Social Science Research Network, Rochester.

Wills, G. (2014). *The effects of teacher strike activity on student learning in South African primary schools*. Technical Report 01/2014, Stellenbosch University, Department of Economics.

Witten, A., & Makole, K. (forthcoming). *Mapping the pathways of systemic change in education in South Africa: A case study of the Programme to improve learning outcomes (PILO)*.

Zuze, T. L., & Beku, U. (2019). Gender inequalities in south African schools: New complexities. In *South African schooling: The enigma of inequality*.

Index

A

'Absolute Returns for Kids' (ARK) schools, 113
Action Plan 2019, 347
Adler, J., 190–193, 195–197, 200
Adler's theorization of resources
  basic resources, 190
  cultural resources, 190–191
  human resources, 191
  material resources, 190
  teacher-pupil ratios and class sizes, 190
Advanced Certificate in Education (ACE), 246
Advanced Certificate in Education in School Leadership and Management (ACESLM), 309
African National Congress (ANU), 10, 51–52
African Teachers' Association of South Africa's (ATASA), 130
Afrikaner Great Trek, 128
Alexander, N., 139–144
Allais, S., 117
Altinok, N., 271, 278
American Core Knowledge curriculum, 113
Anglophone Africa, 140
Annual National Assessments (ANA), 43, 60–61, 324, 330, 331, 339
Anthony, E., 221
Apartheid, 129–130
Applebee, A.N., 205
Artificial experimental conditions, 323
Ashley-Cooper, M., 87–103
Askew, M., 198
Atmore, E., 87–103
Auditor General's 2018 Performance Audit on Curriculum Coverage, 346
Auerbach, S., 284
Australian Council for Educational Research (ACER), 55

B

Ball, S.J., 70
Bandura, A., 284
Beku, U., 225–239
Bernstein, B., 115–117
Bertram, C., 121
Bidirectionality, language and literacy, 149–150
Biersteker, L., 98, 99
Bilingualism, 136
Black parents
  behavioural, emotional and cognitive processes, 285
  child-directed strategies, 291–292, 294, 295
  close-up reality, 285
  Critical Psychology, 297
  Critical Race Theory, 286
  cultural and ethnic differences, 284
  disparities, 295
  gendered strategies, 292–294
  interview schedule, 285
  micro-scale study, 283
  null actions, 288–290
  Parental Agency, 286
  Personal Agency, 296
  personal status, 286–288

© Springer Nature Switzerland AG 2019
N. Spaull, J. D. Jansen (eds.), *South African Schooling: The Enigma of Inequality*, Policy Implications of Research in Education 10,
https://doi.org/10.1007/978-3-030-18811-5

Black parents (*cont.*)
  post-apartheid democracy, 283
  principal leadership, 284
  psychological processes, 284
  qualitative research design, 285, 286
  racial integration, 284, 295
  racism and inequality, 295, 296
  school admission policies, 284
  trauma and stress, 296, 297
Bloom, N., 304
BODMAS rule, 267
Böhmer, B., 328
Bruns, B., 28
Bush, T., 301, 302

C
CAPS, *see* Curriculum and Assessment Policy
      Statement
Carel, C., 356, 366
Carel, D., 67–83
Carnoy, M., 28, 194, 307
Carter, K., 207
Carter, R.T., 296
Casale, D., 140
Centralised training model, 327
Centre for Development and Enterprise (CDE),
      61
Child-directed strategies, 291–292, 294, 295
Child support grant (CSG), 100
Christie, P., 350
City, E.A., 342
Cognitive horizons, 121, 123
Colclough, C., 7, 83
Colonial era classification, 142
Colonialization, 128–129
Communalising pedagogy, 120–121
Communication skills, 89, 117
Competence, 115–116
Confederation of South African Trade Unions
      (COSATU), 10
Confluence of maladies, 192
Constitutional Court, 8, 130, 137
Consumer Price Index (CPI), 17
Continuing professional development (CPD),
      273–274
Continuing Professional Teacher Development
      (CPTD) system, 247–248
Corporate Social Investment (CSI), 273, 321
Council of Education Ministers (CEM), 135
Council on Higher Education, 201
Coverage problems, 347
Critical Race Theory, 286
Crouch, L., 7, 14, 37, 83

Cunha, F., 171
Curriculum 2005 (C2005), 118–120
Curriculum and Assessment Policy Statement
      (CAPS), 54, 63, 113, 119, 198–200,
      248, 346
Curriculum coverage
  acknowledged problem, 344
  design of, 340
  disparate components, 344
  gender differences, 362
  instructional core, 343–344
  OTL, 364
  paper compliance, 363–364
  PILO, 362–363
  poor learning outcomes, 339
  professional realities, 345–347
  quantification, 344
  research knowledge, 362
  tick box approach, 345–347
  time-on-task research, 364
Curriculum reform
  C2005, 118–120
  CAPS, 119, 120
  colonial imposition, 110
  competence, 115–116
  curriculum paradox
    autonomous performance model, 122,
        123
    'dysfunctional' form, 122, 123
    performance-based curriculum model,
        121
  in developed countries, 113–114
  in developing countries, 111–112
  Dewey's system, 115
  didaktik/bildung, 110
  Further Education and Training band,
        118–120
  General Education and Training band of
        schooling, 117–120
  pedagogy problem
    CAPS, 121
    communalising pedagogy, 120–121
    GET and FET levels, 120–122
  performance-based curriculum, 116–117
  Subject Assessment Guidelines, 119
  traditional and progressive model, 109
  traditional curriculum, 114–115

D
Dawes, A., 89
DBE's Early Grade Reading Study, 326
DBE's Macro Indicator report, 344
DBE Rainbow books, 213–214

Deacon, R., 275, 276
De Clercq, F., 10, 243–258
Decoding, 158, 159, 161
DeCuir-Gunby, J.T., 297
Democratic Alliance (DA), 52
Democratic South Africa, 130–131
Department of Bantu Education, 130
Department of Basic Education (DBE), 30–31, 53–54, 95–97
Department of Higher Education and Training (DHET), 248
Department of Planning, Monitoring and Evaluation (DPME), 56–57
Department of Social Development (DSD), 98, 99, 102
Dewey's system, 115
Dinaledi program, 329, 330
Direct Instruction (DI), 257
Disciplinary knowledge
  centrality of, 264–265
  central school-level factor, 263
  CPD, 273–274
  evolution of mathematical concepts, 272, 273
  inequalities, 278–279
  in-service education, 272
  ITE
    case study institutions, 277–278
    ITERP, 274
    Newly Qualified Teachers, 274–277
  PEI, 265
  SACMEQ teachers
    english reading comprehension, 269–271
    mathematics tests, 266–268
    teacher and learner scores, 271–272
diSessa, A.A., 285
Donor-funded NGO-driven professional development programmes, 273
Doyle, W., 207
DSD, see Department of Social Development
Dutch language, 128

E
Early childhood development (ECD)
  child outcomes
    income level, 89
    socio-economic background, 89
  early learning group programme
    attendance in, 93, 94
    ECD centre programmes, 97–99
    enrolment in, 92, 93

General Household Survey data for, 93, 94
  population group, 95
  Grade R programmes, 95–97
  inequality, 87–88
  overcoming inequality, 99–101
  reducing inequality, 101–103
  role, 87
Early Grade Reading Assessment (EGRA), 54, 159
Early Grade Reading Study (EGRS), 15, 54, 138, 162, 249, 326–328
ECD centre programmes, 97–99
Economic domination of English, 139–141
Economic Policy Research Institute (EPRI), 98, 99
Education Action Zones (EAZ), 247
Educational inequality
  international assessments
    cognitive performance, 37
    Gini coefficient, 37
    household and urbanisation, 36–37
    intermediate benchmark, 39, 41
    matric improvement, 36
    PIRLS, 31–34
    SACMEQ, 30–33, 37–39, 41
    social gradient, 42
    TIMSS, 27–30, 32, 37–40
    under-performing schools, 41–42
    UN's Sustainable Development Goals, 37
  matric performance, mathematics, 34–36
  progress in educational attainment
    Grade R and university enrolment, 26
    percentage of young adults, 26–28
    years of education completed, race gaps, 26–27
Education Labour Relations Council (ELRC), 17
Educative Curriculum Material (ECM), 257
e-education, 57
Elite schooling, 2, 6, 50, 110, 117, 122
Elmore, R.F., 250, 251, 253, 342, 343
English First Additional Language (EFAL), 210, 264, 265
Ensor, P., 112
Equality of Educational Opportunity, 339
Equitable Share Formula (ESF), 71–72, 358
Equity
  accountability problems, 9–10
  educational inequality, 3, 12–14, 20–21
  Elusive Equity, 2
  explanation, justification and analysis, 2

Equity (*cont.*)
  informal mechanisms of exclusion, 8–9
  Mathematics distinctions, 1–2
  per-learner funding, 17–18
  personnel distribution
    PPN, 75
    user fees, 76–77
    wealthier public schools, 76
  policy proposals
    adequacy, 81
    cultural capital, 83
    fee exemption policy, 81
    fiscal resource inputs, 81
    non-personnel funding, 82
    personnel funding, 82
    pro poor funding framework, 81
    recommendations, 83
    revised policy, 83
    shifting funding, 82
    social and political implications, 82
    wealth flight, 83
  political economy, 14
  post-apartheid period, trends in,
    10–12
  poverty and privilege, 2–3
  problems of capacity, 10
  racial and spatial apartheid, 3
  school funding norms
    ESF, 71–72
    personnel expenditure, 72–73
    private funds, 79–81
    wealthier schools, 73–75
  schooling education finance (*see* Schooling
    education finance)
  structural features, 3–4
  targeted resources
    benefit incidence analyses, 15
    fee-charging private schools, 16
    fee-charging public schools, 16
    Funza Lushaka, 14–15
    poorer learners, 16–17
    pro-poor allocation, 15–16
  two-tiered education system
    black middle-class, 7
    democratic transition, 5–6
    elite-performance, 6
    Grade 4 learners percentage, 5
    high-performance category, 6–7
    long-term benefits, 4
    low-quality no-fee schools, 4
    moderate-performance, 6
    post-apartheid periods, 5
    pre-apartheid periods, 5
    within-race inequality, 6
  in Western Cape
    non-personnel expenditure, 77–78
    overview of school fees, 77–78
    personnel expenditure, 77–78
    private fees, 77–78
  White schools, teachers and students, 7–8
Equivalent years of schooling (EYOS), 31
ESF, *see* Equitable Share Formula
Eurocentric nationalist movement, 141
Evans, D, 31
Experimental research
  centralised training model, 327
  coaching intervention, 327
  definition, 321
  education production function, 325
  EGRS, 326–328, 332
  Geography and Life Sciences results, 329
  Khan Academy program, 328
  learning outcomes, poor children, 324–325
  limitations, 322–324
  "Mind The Gap" study, 328, 333
  on-site coaching, 333
  parent involvement program, 328
  policy/resource, 321–322
  quasi-experimental methods, 323
    Dinaledi program, 329–330
    GPLMS program, 331
    Grade R program, 330
    "Learning for Living" intervention, 329
    school fixed effects, 331
    system-level factors, 331, 332
  RCUP program, 326, 332, 333
  SMRS, 325–326
EYOS, *see* Equivalent years of schooling

F
Face inequality, 356–357
Feeder-zones, 8
Fee-paying schools, 173–179, 181
Fiske, E.B., 2
Fitz, J., 113
Fixed effects models, *see* Value-added models
Fleisch, B., 326, 331
Fongwa, S., 169–185
Foundation Phase Bachelor of Education
    program, 161
Foundation Phase mathematics teaching, 195
Foundation Phase (FP) teachers, 248
Foundations for Learning policy, 196–198
Fraser, N., 67
Fryer, R.G., 304
Further Education and Training (FET) band,
    118–120

G

Galant, J., 199, 200, 206, 209
Gauteng Primary Language and Mathematics
    Strategy (GPLMS), 248–249, 326,
    331
GDP, *see* Gross Domestic Product
Gender differences
    challenges, 237
    confidence in mathematics, 235–236
    educational attainment
        causes of dropout, 233
        GHS, 233
        primary school participation, 232
        and race differences, 233–234
        secondary school, 232–233
        TIMSS, 232–233
    international trends, 227–229, 238
    NSC, 233–235
    perspectives, 226–227
    school location, 230, 239
    school safety, 230–232
    school type, 229–230
    targeted interventions, 237
Gender equality, 225–226
General Education and Training (GET) band of
    schooling, 117–120
General Household Survey (GHS), 233
Genootskap van Regte Afrikaners, 129
Geography and Life Sciences study, 329
Gewirtz, S., 67
Glover, D., 301, 302
Goldhaber, D., 221
GPLMS, *see* Gauteng Primary Language and
    Mathematics Strategy
Grade 6 Mathematics learner books, 211
Grade R program, 95–97, 323, 330
Gross Domestic Product (GDP), 70
Group Areas Act, 8
Guskey, T.R., 254
Gustafsson, M., 6, 8, 11, 25–43, 47–65, 95, 96,
    302, 306, 309, 311, 314, 323, 332,
    362

H

Hall, K., 93
Hanushek, E.A., 221
Hargreaves, A., 344
Harries, P., 141
Hattie, J., 215
Hellman evaluation, 326
Hendricks, S., 98
Heugh, K., 141
Heystedt, D., 154

Hill, H.C., 264
Hoadley, U., 109–123, 133, 161, 162, 193,
    195, 196, 199, 200, 206, 209, 219,
    303, 305, 308, 340
Hobden, P., 205–222
Hobden, S., 205–222
Hofmeyer, J., 285
Howie, S., 154
Human Sciences Research Council, 359
Hypothesis of double jeopardy, 70

I

Incentive system, 314
Information and communication technologies
    (ICTs), 57
Ing, M., 215
Initial teacher education (ITE)
    case study institutions, 277–278
    ITERP, 274
    Newly Qualified Teachers, 274–277
Initial Teacher Education Research Project
    (ITERP) study, 161, 195, 274
'Innovation and Enterprise' programme, 112
Integrated Quality Management System
    (IQMS), 57–58, 252, 314
Integrated Strategic Planning Framework for
    Teacher Education and Development
    (ISPFTED), 248
Intermediate international benchmark, 39, 41
Internal accountability, 342
Isdale, K., 169–185
Item response theory (IRT) scores, 31

J

Jansen, J.D., 101, 355–369
Jika iMfundo campaign
    curriculum coverage
        acknowledged problem, 344
        design of, 340
        disparate components, 344
        instructional core, 343–344
        poor learning outcomes, 339
        quantification, 344
        tick box approach, 344–345
    inequality, 338–339
    opportunities to learn, 339
    PILO, 337
        broad alliance, 341
        change consistent, 343
        government policy documents, 340–341
        internal and reciprocal accountability,
            342

Jika iMfundo campaign (*cont.*)
    monitoring and tracking, 341
    resource constraints, 343
    responsibility, 341
    systemic support, 342–343
    systems-wide capacity, 341
    teacher professional development, 342
    socio-political and economic contexts, 338
    support for teachers, 348–350
Jita, L., 191, 193
Jones, L., 117
Juan, A., 169–185

K
Kazima, M., 121
Khan Academy program, 328
Kilpatrick, J., 207
'Knowledge-based' curriculum, 113
'Knowledge is Power Programme' (KIPPS)
    schools, 113, 114
Kotzé, J., 26, 199, 305, 308

L
Ladd, H.F., 2
Lam, D., 307
Langer, J.A., 205
Language Compensation policy, 136
Language of Learning and Teaching (LOLT),
    131, 133, 134, 136, 137, 178
Language policy
    apartheid, 129–130
    colonialization of South Africa, 128–129
    democratic South Africa, 130–131
    economic domination of English, 139–141
    in education policy
        CAPS, 138
        CEM members, 135
        Constitutional Court, 137
        curriculum limitations, 138–139
        curriculum policy, 137
        home language, 135, 137
        Language Compensation policy, 136
        NCS, 138
        NEPA of 1996, 135
        1997 Norms and Standards for
            Language Policy in Public Schools,
            135
        NSC, 136
        official languages for governance, 134
        PANSALB, 134
        pronouncement of policies, 136
        SASA, 135

        SGBs, 135, 136
        Southern Bantu language families, 135
literacy
    definition, 131
    in English language, 133, 134
    first language spoken and province, 132
    home language, 133–134
    LOLT, 131, 133
    LTSMs, 133
    NSES and SE for, 131, 133
    multilingual policy development
        African language formalization, 141
        history and language structures, 142
        language unification, 142
        prioritization, 143
        religious sectarianism, 141
        shared language, 142
    union of South Africa, 129
Lanzi, D., 171
Lassibille, G., 308
LCPM, *see* Letter-sounds read correctly per
        minute
Learner writing
    best learners, 209
    cognitive demand of tasks, 206
    constructive feedback, 206
    curriculum coverage and quality of work,
        213–215
    definition, 205
    didactical contract, 207, 221, 222
    English FAL instrument, 210
    evaluation studies, 206
    formal summative assessments, 205
    foundational curriculum topics, 206
    Foundation and Intermediate phases, 210
    HOD monitoring, 216–218
    ineffective opportunities, 219
    learner book analysis, 210
    marking and feedback, 215–217
    NEEDU report, 209
    NSES study, 209
    NS&Tech instruments, 210
    OTL, 207–209
    practice tool, 206
    productive cognitive demand, 206
    pupil-teacher ratios, 221
    quantity of work, 211–213
    reproductive cognitive demand, 206
    school development project, 206
    school facilities, 221
    teacher effect, 216–218, 220
    teacher quality, 221
    teacher role models and experiences,
        220–221

teaching and learning environment, 208
"Learning for Living" project, 329
Learning outcomes, schools, 358–359
Learning-to-read process, 157
Lee, S., 285
Letter-sound knowledge, 158
Letter-sounds read correctly per minute
       (LCPM), 159, 160
Levin, B., 341
Learning and teaching support materials
       (LTSM), 133
'loi Jospin' reforms, 114
LOLT, see Language of Learning and Teaching
Luque, J., 31

M
Mabogoane, T., 14, 26, 305
Machin, S., 327
Martin, J., 283
Matentjie, T., 283–297, 356
Mathematical knowledge for teaching (MKT),
       264
Mathematical skills
   home resources, 171
   importance, 169
   inequalities in home
      fee-paying and no-fee schools, 177–178
      maternal education, 178
      parental occupation, 178
   inequalities in schools
      average class mathematics achievement,
         183, 184
      school climate, 182, 183
      school resources, 181, 182
      TIMSS *Home Resources for Learning
         Index,* 182, 183
   low and unequal achievement, 184–185
   low income countries, 170
   opportunity inequality, 170–171
   schools, 172–173
   TIMSS, from 1995 to 2015
      achievement gaps, 174
      achievement score, 173, 174
      competency level, 175
      fee-paying and no-fee schools, 175, 176
      post-secondary education, 177
   varied early educational environments,
         179–181
Mathews, C., 200
Matthew Effect, 326, 330
McLaughlin, M.W., 342
McNally, S., 327
Mesthrie, R., 141, 142

Metcalfe, M., 337–351
"Mind The Gap" study, 328, 333
Ministerial Task Team, 365
Minister of Basic Education, 55
MKT, *see* Mathematical knowledge for
       teaching
Mohohlwane, N.L., 127–144
Monolingualism, 141
Moore, R., 117
Moorosi, P., 314
Moses, E., 14
Motala, S., 67–83, 356, 366
Muller, J., 109–123, 256
Mullis, I.V.S., 32, 154, 229, 238, 269
Multilingualism approach, 135, 136, 140, 143,
       144, 190, 193
Murray, S., 137
Murugan, A., 172

N
Naspers, 129
'NATED' curriculum, 118, 119
National Curriculum Statement (NCS), 119
National Curriculum Statement Grades R-12,
       138
National Education and Training Forum, 118
National Education Policy Act (NEPA) of
       1996, 135
National Income Dynamics Study (NIDS),
       140, 232–233
National Integrated Early Childhood
       Development Policy, 100, 101
National Party, 129
National Policy Framework for Teacher
       Education and Development
       (NPFTED) Act, 247
National Qualification Framework (NQF), 119,
       246
National School Effectiveness Study (NSES),
       131–133, 153, 157, 194, 209, 219,
       220, 306
National Senior Certificate (NSC), 136,
       233–235, 324
Nattrass, N., 6
Natural Science and Technology (NS&Tech)
       instruments, 210
Nelson, B.S., 276, 307
Nelson, C., 359
New Labour, 113
Newly qualified teachers (NQTs)
   on ITERP english test, 275–276
   on ITERP mathematics test, 275
Nguni language, 142

Nhlapo, J.M., 142–144
'No Excuses' schools, 113, 114
No-fee schools, 155, 156, 173, 175–179, 181–184, 305–308
Non-generic performance-based curriculum, 120
1997 Norms and Standards for Language Policy in Public Schools, 135
Norms and Standards for School Funding (NSSF), 69

O
O'Day, J., 250
OECD's PISA test, 112
Opportunity to learn (OTL), 207–209, 307, 364
Oral language comprehension, 158
Organisation for Economic Cooperation and Development (OECD) countries, 235
Outcomes-based curriculum systems, 117
Outcomes based education (OBE), 54
Outlier child hypothesis, 156

P
Pan South African Language Board (PANSALB), 134
Parental Agency, 286
Pedagogical content knowledge, 264
Performance-based curriculum, 116–117
Personnel Administrative Measures (PAM), 309, 310, 348
Peurach, D., 342
Peurach, D.J., 342
Phonemic awareness, 158
Piper, B., 328
PIRLS Low International Benchmark, 154
Planning, 366
Politics, 365
Population-level performance data, 330
Posel, D., 140
Post provisioning norms (PPN), 75
Prawat, R.S., 345, 346
President's Education Initiative (PEI), 265
Pretorius, E., 11, 147–165
Primary Teacher Education (PrimTEd), 202
Production function analyses, 305–306
Professional knowledge, 347
Professional Learning Communities (PLCs), 248
Professional realities, 345–347
Program for International Student Assessment (PISA), 28, 112

Programme to Improve Learning Outcomes (PILO), 249, 337, 362–363
broad alliance, 341
change consistent, 343
government policy documents, 340–341
internal and reciprocal accountability, 342
monitoring and tracking, 341
resource constraints, 343
responsibility, 341
systemic support, 342–343
systems-wide capacity, 341
teacher professional development, 342
Programming, 366–367
Progress in International Reading Literacy Study (PIRLS), 148, 359
gender differences, 227–229
Grade 9 mathematics, 53
improvements, 34
matric co-hort of 2005, 32–34
overview of, 11–12, 18
standard deviation, 31–32
test frameworks, 265, 269, 270
Protest nation, 357

Q
Quasi-experimental methods, 323
Dinaledi program, 329–330
GPLMS program, 331
Grade R program, 330
"Learning for Living" intervention, 329
school fixed effects, 331
system-level factors, 331, 332
Quintiles, 73–75

R
Rajoo, L., 172
Randomized controlled trials (RCTs), 249, 253, 322–323, 326, 328–329, 359
Rawl, J., 67
Reading
acquiring oral language, 151
bidirectionality of language and literacy, 149–150
classroom and school libraries availability, 162
conflate language of instruction, 157
curriculum advisor, 164
decoding, 158, 159, 161
definition, 148
environmental input, 151–152
goal in primary school, 152
inadequate nutrition and early childhood stimulation, 165

in-service teachers, 164
instruction quality, 157
ITERP, 161
learning-to-read process, 157
letter-sounds and oral reading fluency, 159, 160
managing and mediating books, 162–163
oral language comprehension, 158
orthography, 148
PIRLS 2006 to 2016
  at basic level, grade 4, 155
  PIRLS Low International Benchmark, 154
  reading outcomes in grade 4 scores, 153, 154
  stark inequalities, 154–155
  wealthiest vs. poorest schools, 155, 156
systematic phonics/balanced approach, 151
twenty-first century, 148
whole language approach, 151
Reading Catch Up Program (RCUP), 326, 332, 333
Reading fluency, 158
Reciprocal accountability, 342
Reddy, V., 32, 169–185
Regression Disconuity Design (RDD), 331
Relative Educational Qualifications Value (REQV)
  average educators, 73–74
  school principals, 73–75
  unequal distribution of principals, 313
Republic of South Africa (RSA), 91, 100, 104
Review Committee's report, 120
Revised National Curriculum Statement, 193
Right to Education Act, 16
Roberts, N., 198
Rollout of national workbooks, 199–201
Ross, K., 238
Rubio-Codin, M., 89

S
SACE, see South African Council for Educators
SACMEQ, see Southern and Eastern African Consortium for Monitoring Educational Quality
SADTU, see South African Democratic Teachers Union
Sahn, D.E., 37
Sailors, M., 329
Samoff, J., 359
SASA, see South African Schools Act
Sayed, Y., 67, 101

Schmidt, W.H., 339, 345, 346
Schoenfeld, A.H., 202
Schöer, V., 331
School Fee Exemption Policy, 358
School fixed effects, 331
School Governing Body (SGBs), 9
  Afrikaans-medium schools, 8
  average number of educators, 79–80
  learner-educator ratios, 79–81
  LOLT, 137
  no-fee primary schools, 308
  practitioners and administrative support staff, 79–80
  SASA, 69, 135
  unequal performance outcomes, 70
  wealthier schools, 73
Schooling education finance
  resource redistribution
    exemption policy, 69
    GDP, 70
    no fee policy, 69
    provincial and national programmes, 69
    provincial departments, 70–71
    in public schools, 70
    SASA, 69
    social equity and education equity, 70
  right to education, 68
Schooling sector 2007–2017
  black schools, 48
  charter schools, 61–62
  curriculum reform, 53–54
  e-education, 57
  evidence-based policy discourse, 64
  Grade 9 qualification, 56
  national assessments and school principal accountability, 60–61
  national planning systems, 62
  national workbooks, 54–55
  policy impact, 49
    Centre for Development and Enterprise, 52
    Democratic Alliance, 52
    Early Grade Reading Assessment, 51
    'inspectorate' of schools, 51
    pedagogic support, 51
    policy positions and consensus, 52
    poor schooling, 51
    qualifications, 50
    resourcing and accountability, 50–51
    right to offer schooling, 50
    SADTU, 51–52
    teacher incentives, 52–53
    teacher shortages, 51

Schooling sector 2007–2017 (*cont.*)
  rules governing teachers
    financial incentives, 58–59
    Funza Lushaka bursary scheme, 60
    IQMS, 57–58
    non-financial, 58
    performance-linked differentiation, 58
    pupil-teacher ratio, 58
    remote and 'difficult' schools, 59
    schools-based head of department, 59
    teacher pay, 58
    teacher policy space, 59
  SACMEQ, 48–49
  schools-based 'reception year,' 56–57
  system-wide governance, 49
School leadership and management (SLM)
  leadership adjectives, 302
  method, 303
  planning and leading teacher management, 304
  policy *vs.* practice
    day-to-day practices of teachers, 311
    post-provisioning ratios, 310, 311
    SMT, 309, 311–312
  post-provisioning inequalities
    unequal appointment of men over woman, 314–315
    unequal distribution of principals, 313–314
    widening inequalities, 312
  principal quality studies, 304
  quantitative research, 301
  South African evidence
    gain scores, 306–309
    production function analyses, 305–306
    school efficiency, 305
    value-added models, 306–309
  target-setting and monitoring, 304
School Management Team (SMT), 309, 311–312
Schools-based 'reception year' (Grade R), 56–57
Schutz, P.A., 297
Scripted Lesson Plans (SLPs), 248, 249, 256–257
Seekings, J., 6
Service delivery protests, 357
Setati, M., 190
Setswana literacy test scores, 327
SGBs, *see* School Governing Bodies
Shalem, Y., 10, 161, 196, 243–258
Shepherd, D., 271
Shepherd's decomposition, 305
Shriewer, J., 110

Sign Language, 134
Simkins, C., 26
Skill begets skill, 171, 185
SMRS, *see* Systematic Method for Reading Success
SMT, *see* School Management Team
Snapshot of Subject Advisors (SA), 348, 349
SNAP Survey data, 79
Socio-economic status (SES), 38–39, 99, 131, 133, 175
Sotho language, 142
South African Council for Educators (SACE), 248
South African Democratic Teachers Union (SADTU), 9–10, 51–52
South African Early Childhood Review 2017, 88
South African Schools Act (SASA), 69, 135, 136
Southern and Eastern African Consortium for Monitoring Educational Quality (SACMEQ), 358, 359
  access to textbooks, 192
  english reading comprehension, 152, 155, 269–271
  gender differences, 227–229
  Grade 12 examinations, 48–49
  Grade 4 learners, 31
  Grade 6 mathematics
    assumptions, 32–33
    DBE's final report, 30–31
    distributions, 41
    grade-on-grade learning gains, 31
    standard deviations, 31
  Grade 8 mathematics, 37–38
  mathematics tests, 266–268
  overview of, 11–12
  socio-economic status, 38–39, 194
  teacher and learner scores, 271–272
Southern Bantu language families, 135
SPARK schools, 113
Spaull, N., 1–19, 133, 135, 142, 147–165, 199, 227, 271, 278
Statistics South Africa (StatsSA), 37, 92, 93, 96
Stein, M.K., 307
Stein, N., 8
Stewart, F., 172
Studies of Foundation Phase mathematics teaching, 192
Subject Assessment Guidelines, 119
Sustainable Development Goal, 37, 101
Systematic Method for Reading Success (SMRS), 325–326, 329

T
Talbert, J.E., 342
Tatto, M.T., 201, 202
Taylor, N., 10, 26, 133, 136, 147, 194, 202, 209, 221, 247, 263–280
Taylor, S., 263, 271, 306, 308, 309, 311, 321–334
Teacher development (TD)
  challenges, 245–246
  classroom-anchored training, 253
  cognitive beliefs, 254
  departmental level, 247–248
  district-based and cluster-based training, 246–247
  examples, 255
  institutional vision and culture, 247
  instructional core, 253–254
  knowledge needs, 247
  large-scale programmes, 248–249, 254
  learning opportunities, 244
  lesson plans, 254
  micro-technologies, 247
  Outcomes-Based Education, 248
  periodisation of, 251–252
  post-1994 curriculum and assessment policies, 245
  primary school teachers, 247
  process of change, 253
  provincial departments, 246
  RCT, 253
  reciprocal accountability, 244–245, 253
  senior phase teachers, 247
  SLPs, 256–257
  subject matter, conceptual structure of, 254
  subject-specific workshops, 246
  support and accountability, 250–251
  Taylor's view, 247
  Teacher Summit, 248
  teaching routines, 255
Teachers' mathematical knowledge and classroom practices
  Adler's theorization of resources
    basic resources, 190
    cultural resources, 190–191
    human resources, 191
    material resources, 190
    teacher-pupil ratios and class sizes, 190
  CAPS, 196, 198–199
  Council on Higher Education, 201
  Foundations for Learning policy, 196–198
  ITERP study, 201
  pedagogical content knowledge and classroom practices, 201
  PrimTEd, 202
  resource terrain
    cultural resources, 192–194
    human resources, 194–196
    material resources, 192
  rollout of national workbooks, 199–201
  university-based Advanced Certificate in Education, 201
'Teach Less, Learn More' programme, 112
Theil, T., 37–39
Third International Mathematics and Science Study (TIMSS), 266
Tick box approach, 345–347
Trends in International Mathematics and Science Study (TIMSS), 358, 359
  gender differences, 227–229, 233
  Grade 8, 37–40
  Grade 9, 27–30, 32, 53
  overview of, 11–12
Tshivenda language, 142
Twenty first century skills, 117
"Two-tiered bi-modal schooling system," 360

U
Umalusi Council, 136
UNESCO 'Education for All' World Declaration, 111
Union, South Africa, 129
United Nations Children's Fund (UNICEF), 70, 98, 99, 111, 192
University-based Advanced Certificate in Education, 201

V
Value-added models
  ACESLM programme, 309
  administrative functionality, 308
  casual interpretation, 308
  leadership content knowledge, 307
  matric performance, 307–308
  NSES, 306
  OTL, 307
  quasi-experimental methods, 308
  SGBs, 308
  student's achievement, 307
Van Broekhuizen, H., 227, 324
Van der Berg, S., 6, 10, 11, 14, 25–43, 67, 73, 95–97, 330, 331, 360
van Niekerk, L.-J., 87–103
Venkat, H., 189–202, 278
Vincent, C., 284, 286
Vinjevold, P., 265
Vocabulary development, 159

Von Fintel, M., 133, 331
Vorster, C., 136

W
Weber, E., 67
Western Cape Education Department (WCED),
      77
Willms, J.D., 43, 70
Wills, G., 301–317, 340
Winch, C., 254
Witten, A., 337–351
Woessmann, L., 221
Word reading, 158
Words read correctly per minute (WCPM), 159
Workbooks programme, 54–55

'Working in a team,' skills, 117
World Management Survey, 304

X
xiTsonga language, 135, 142, 160

Y
Younger, S.D., 37
Yuan, F., 31

Z
'Zero tolerance' approach, 113
Zuze, T.L., 172, 225–239